AMERICA ON FILM

SECOND EDITION   Harry M. Benshoff and Sean Griffin

AMERICA ON FILM

REPRESENTING RACE, CLASS, GENDER, AND SEXUALITY AT THE MOVIES

WILEY-BLACKWELL

A John Wiley & Sons, Ltd., Publication

Library of Congress Cataloging-in-Publication Data

Benshoff, Harry M.
America on film : representing race, class, gender, and sexuality at the movies / Harry M. Benshoff and Sean Griffin. – 2nd ed.
    p. cm.
  Includes bibliographical references and index.
  ISBN 978-1-4051-7055-0 (pbk. : alk. paper)
  1. Minorities in motion pictures.   2. Motion pictures–United States–History.
I. Griffin, Sean.   II. Title.
  PN1995.9.M56B46 2009
  305.5′6–dc22

                                                                2008021455

A catalogue record for this book is available from the British Library.

Set in 10.5/13pt Minion by Graphicraft Limited, Hong Kong
Printed in Singapore by C.O.S. Printers Pte Ltd

012   2016

CONTENTS

Part IV Gender and American Film   211
Introduction to Part IV: What is Gender?

10 Women in Classical Hollywood Filmmaking 217

11 Exploring the Visual Parameters of Women in Film 238

12 Masculinity in Classical Hollywood Filmmaking 257

ACKNOWLEDGMENTS

The origins of this book can be traced back to a class we both taught at Antelope Valley Community College in Lancaster, California, when we were PhD students at the University of Southern California's School of Cinema-Television. We "inherited" the class from Jaime Bihlmeyer when he took another position. Jaime had created his own set of readings for the course, because, as we quickly discovered, there were very few published texts available that covered "diversity in American film" with the historical and theoretical consistency that we desired. Thus, our colleagues and students at Antelope Valley College are the first people we wish to thank.

Sean Griffin then taught revised versions of this class at California State University at Long Beach, the University of California at Santa Cruz, and Florida Atlantic University, while Harry Benshoff developed individual courses in African American film and lesbian, gay, and queer media. Our colleagues and students throughout those years contributed to this project in myriad ways, and we especially want to thank Shelley Stamp and Michael Cowan at UCSC.

It was while we were living and working in Santa Cruz that Jayne Fargnoli, our soon-to-be editor at Blackwell, asked us what kind of textbooks were needed in film and media studies. We both immediately told her there was a need for a text like *America on Film*, and a few months later Jayne asked us if we wanted to write the book ourselves. Her support and feedback have been immeasurable, as have those of her assistant, Margot Morse. Our project manager and copy-editor, Fiona Sewell, was also extremely helpful in the final stages of the project, as was the books production manager, Lisa Eaton.

We would like to thank our current colleagues, students, and support staff at the University of North Texas and at Southern Methodist University. Harry Benshoff's research and teaching assistants at UNT have contributed to the project in different ways. We'd also like to thank our anonymous readers and especially Alexander Doty, Peter Lehman, David Lugowski, Jacqueline Foertsch, and Travis Sutton, all of whom read various chapters and offered constructive feedback. We also wish to thank those readers who wrote or spoke to us after the first edition was published. Their feedback (and occasional corrections!) continues to matter to us. Much of the new material in the second edition came directly from their suggestions on how to make the book even better.

This book is dedicated to our families and friends, the people who have taught us and instilled in us the values of diversity, understanding, education, and love – in both our professional and personal lives. Such acts of sharing can lead to greater understanding and compassion across families, across communities, and across the world. We hope this book encourages people to examine and understand the biases and shaping discourses of contemporary American culture, so that the future may not just promise but also deliver the goal of equality for all Americans, regardless of race, class, gender, sexuality, or ability.

The authors and publisher wish to acknowledge the copyright material used in this book:

pp. 18–19: *The Lion King*, copyright © 1993, The Walt Disney Co.

p. 18: top, left. Photo: Umberto Adaggi

p. 18: top, right. Photo: Michael Ansell

p. 27: *Indiana Jones and the Temple of Doom*, copyright © 1984, Paramount

p. 31: "Automatic Vaudeville (1904–05)," courtesy of the Museum of the City of New York, The Byron Collection

p. 32: The Comet Theatre, courtesy of the Quigley Photographic Archive, Georgetown University Library

p. 33: The Majestic Theatre, courtesy of the Quigley Photographic Archive, Georgetown University Library

p. 35: MGM Studios, unidentified publicity photo, authors' personal collection

p. 38: John Garfield, unidentified publicity photo, authors' personal collection

p. 41: *Rocky*, copyright © 1976, United Artists

p. 42: Cinemark Marquee, authors' private collection

p. 59: *Going My Way*, copyright © 1944, Paramount

p. 60: *The Quiet Man*, copyright © 1952, Republic

p. 63: *Little Caesar*, copyright © 1930, Warner Bros.

p. 64: *The Godfather*, copyright © 1972, Paramount

p. 68: *The Jazz Singer*, copyright © 1927, Warner Bros.

p. 74: *Crash*, dir. Paul Haggis, copyright © 2004, Lions Gate Films

p. 75: *Funny Girl*, copyright © 1968, Columbia

p. 80: *The Birth of a Nation*, copyright © 1915, Griffith

p. 83: Stepin Fetchit, unidentified publicity photo, authors' personal collection

p. 84: *The Little Colonel*, copyright © 1935, 20th Century-Fox

p. 86: *Pinky*, copyright © 1949, 20th Century-Fox

p. 87: Dorothy Dandridge, unidentified publicity photo, authors' personal collection

p. 88: Sidney Poitier, unidentified publicity photo, authors' personal collection

p. 93: *Get On the Bus*, dir. Spike Lee, copyright © 1996, Columbia/Tri-Star. Photo: Lester Sloan

p. 96: *Hustle & Flow*, dir. Craig Brewer, copyright © 2005, MTV Films/Paramount Classics

p. 98: *Bamboozled*, dir. Spike Lee, copyright © 2000, New Line Cinema. Photo: David Lee/New Line

p. 109: *The Lone Ranger*, copyright © 1949–1957, ABC-TV

p. 112: *Cheyenne Autumn*, copyright © 1964, Warner Bros. Photo: Kobal Collection

p. 114: *Billy Jack*, copyright © 1971, Warner Bros.

p. 116: *Last of the Mohicans*, copyright © 1992, 20th Century-Fox. Photos: Frank Connor

p. 119: *Smoke Signals*, dir. Chris Eyre, copyright © 1998, Miramax. Photo: Jill Sabella

p. 120: *The Education of Little Tree*, dir. Richard Friedenberg, copyright © 1997, Paramount. Photo: Jan Thijs

p. 127: Warner Oland as Charlie Chan, unidentified publicity photo, authors' personal collection

p. 128: *The Mask of Fu Manchu*, copyright © 1932, MGM/Universal

p. 129: Anna May Wong, unidentified publicity photo, authors' personal collection

p. 130: Keye Luke, unidentified publicity photo, authors' personal collection

p. 135: Russell Wong, unidentified publicity photo, authors' personal collection

p. 137: Ang Lee directing *Sense and Sensibility*, copyright © 1995, Columbia

p. 139: *Mississippi Masala*, dir, Mira Nair, copyright © 1991, The Samuel Goldwyn Company

p. 141: *Eat a Bowl of Tea*, copyright © 1990, Columbia

p. 146: Ramon Novarro, unidentified publicity photo, authors' personal collection

p. 148: Dolores Del Rio, unidentified publicity photo, authors' personal collection

p. 151: *Sombra Verde* (a.k.a. *Untouched*), copyright © 1954, Calderon Productions

p. 158: *From Dusk Till Dawn*, dir. Robert Rodriguez, copyright © 1996, Dimension

p. 161: *My Family/Mi Familia*, dir. Gregory Nava, copyright © 1995, New Line. Photo: Rico Torres

p. 162: *Spanglish*, dir. James L. Brooks, copyright © 2004, Columbia Pictures

p. 176: Harold Lloyd, unidentified publicity photo, authors' personal collection

p. 177: *The Gold Rush*, copyright © 1925, United Artists

p. 183: *It Happened One Night*, copyright © 1934, Columbia

p. 185: *The Grapes of Wrath*, copyright © 1940, 20th Century-Fox

p. 194: *Easy Rider*, copyright © 1969, Columbia

p. 195: *Five Easy Pieces*, copyright © 1970, BBS/Columbia

p. 197: *The Honeymooners,* copyright © 1952–1957, CBS-TV

p. 201: *Norma Rae*, copyright © 1979, 20th Century-Fox

p. 203: *Titanic*, dir. James Cameron, copyright © 1997, 20th Century-Fox and Paramount

p. 205: *Bulworth*, dir. Warren Beatty, copyright © 1998, 20th Century-Fox. Photos: Sidney Baldwin

p. 219: Mary Pickford, unidentified publicity photo, authors' personal collection

p. 221: Theda Bara, unidentified publicity photo, authors' personal collection

p. 223: Clara Bow, unidentified publicity photo, authors' personal collection

p. 226: Dorothy Arzner, unidentified publicity photo, authors' personal collection

p. 228: Mae West, unidentified publicity photo, authors' personal collection

p. 229: *Imitation of Life*, copyright © 1934, Universal

pp. 235–6: *All that Heaven Allows*, copyright © 1955, Universal

p. 241: *How to Marry a Millionaire*, copyright © 1953, 20th Century-Fox

p. 247: Betty Grable, unidentified publicity photo, authors' personal collection

p. 249: *Footlight Parade*, copyright © 1933, Warner Bros.

p. 250: *Gilda*, copyright © 1946, Columbia

p. 252: *Gold Diggers of 1933*, copyright © 1933, Warner Bros.

p. 261: John Wayne, unidentified publicity photo, authors' personal collection

p. 263: *The Son of the Sheik*, copyright © 1922, Paramount

p. 265: *Public Enemy*, copyright © 1931, Warner Bros.

p. 267: *I Was a Male War Bride*, copyright © 1949, 20th Century-Fox

p. 268: *Sands of Iwo Jima*, copyright © 1949, Republic

p. 270: *Double Indemnity*, copyright © 1944, Paramount

p. 271: *T-Men*, copyright © 1947, Eagle-Lion

p. 273: *Dead Reckoning*, copyright © 1947, Columbia

p. 275: James Dean, unidentified publicity photo, authors' personal collection

p. 276: Rock Hudson from *Send Me No Flowers*, copyright © 1964, Universal

p. 282: *The Sting*, copyright © 1973, Universal

p. 286: *Roseanne*, copyright © 1988–97, Carsey-Werner Company/ABC-TV

p. 288: *Rambo*, copyright © 1985, Tri-Star

p. 290: *Halloween*, copyright © 1978, Falcon/Anchor Bay Entertainment

p. 291: Penny Marshall, unidentified publicity photo, authors' personal collection

p. 292: *Lost in Translation*, dir. Sophia Coppola, copyright © 2003, Focus Features/Universal

p. 295: Martha Coolidge directing *Real Genius*, copyright © 1985, Tri-Star

p. 297: *The Ballad of Little Jo*, copyright © 1993, JoCo/Fine Line. Photo: Bill Foley

p. 299: *Thelma and Louise*, copyright © 1991, MGM-Pathé

p. 300: *Lara Croft: Tomb Raider*, dir. Simon West, copyright © 2001, Paramount

p. 313: William Haines, unidentified publicity photo, authors' personal collection

p. 315: *Morocco*, copyright © 1930, Paramount

p. 318: *Showboat*, copyright © 1936, Universal

p. 319: *The Philadelphia Story*, copyright © 1940, MGM

p. 323: *Tea and Sympathy*, copyright © 1956, MGM

p. 327: *The Maltese Falcon*, copyright © 1941, Warner Bros.

p. 332: *The Killing of Sister George*, copyright © 1968, Palomar Pictures/Cinerama Releasing

p. 333: *Boys in the Band*, copyright © 1970, Leo/Cinema Center

p. 335: *Making Love*, copyright © 1982, 20th Century-Fox. Photo: Wynn Hammer

p. 341: *Will & Grace*, copyright © 1998–2006, NBC-TV

p. 344: Gus Van Sant directing *To Die For*, copyright © 1995, Columbia. Photo: Kerry Hayes

p. 345: *The Incredibly True Adventure of Two Girls in Love*, dir. Maria Maggenti, copyright © 1995, Smash Pictures/Fine Line. Photo: Alyson Levy/Fine Line

p. 346: *Love! Valour! Compassion!*, dir. Joe Mantello, copyright © 1997, Fine Line. Photo: Attila Dory

p. 350: *Boys Don't Cry*, dir. Kimberly Pierce, copyright © 2000, Killer Films/Fox Searchlight. Photo: Bill Matlock

p. 351: *Far From Heaven*, dir. Todd Haynes, copyright © 2002, Focus Features/Universal

p. 365: *Son of Frankenstein*, copyright © 1939, Universal

p. 367: *The Wizard of Oz*, copyright © 1939, MGM

p. 368: *Willow*, dir. Ron Howard, copyright © 1988, MGM

p. 373: *The Miracle Worker*, copyright © 1962, United Artists/MGM

p. 378: *Children of a Lesser God*, dir. Randa Haines, copyright © 1986, Paramount

p. 380: *The Station Agent*, dir. Thomas McCarthy, copyright © 2003, Miramax

p. 382: *Sound and Fury*, dir. Josh Aronson, copyright © 2000, Aronsonfilm/Artistic License

p. 383: *Murderball*, dirs. Henry Alex Rubin and Dana Adam Shapiro, copyright © 2005, MTV Films/Paramount

p. 387: *Queen Christina*, copyright © 1933, MGM

p. 389: *The Old Maid*, copyright © 1939, Warner Bros.

p. 390: Carmen Miranda, unidentified publicity photo, authors' personal collection

p. 392: *A Patch of Blue*, copyright © 1965, MGM

p. 394: *Erin Brockovich*, dir. Steven Soderbergh, copyright © 2000, Jersey Films/Columbia TriStar

p. 396: *8 Mile*, dir. Curtis Hanson, copyright © 2002, Imagine Entertainment/Universal

p. 398: *Better Luck Tomorrow*, dir. Justin Lin, copyright © 2002, MTV Films/Paramount

p. 400: *Saving Face*, dir. Alice Wu, copyright © 2004, Sony Pictures Classics

p. 402: *Crash*, dir. Paul Haggis, copyright © 2004, Lions Gate Films

p. 404: *The Prize Winner of Defiance, Ohio*, dir. Jane Anderson, copyright © 2005, Dreamworks SKG

p. 406: *Brokeback Mountain*, dir. Ang Lee, copyright © 2005, Focus Features/Universal

p. 408: *Quinceañera*, dir. Richard Glatzer and Wash Westmoreland, copyright © 2006, Sony Pictures Classics

The publisher apologizes for any errors or omissions in the above list and would be grateful if notified of any corrections that should be incorporated in future reprints or editions of this book.

HOW TO USE THIS BOOK

America on Film is a textbook designed to introduce undergraduate students to issues of diversity within American film. It is the first synthetic and historical text of its kind, and provides a comprehensive overview of the industrial, socio-cultural, and aesthetic factors that have shaped and continue to shape cinematic representations of race, class, gender, sexuality, and physical ability. The book aims to chronicle the cinematic history of various cultural groups, stimulate discussion of human difference, examine forces and institutions of bias, and ultimately provoke thought about the relationship between film and American national culture.

This textbook can be used in a variety of classroom settings and at a variety of educational levels. Primarily, it is suited for a class on media culture and diversity issues, although we have also used it as a supplemental text in basic "Introduction to Film Studies" and "American Film History" classes. The book could also be used for courses in twentieth-century American history, cultural and American studies, and courses devoted to specific topics surrounding race, class, gender, sexuality, and/or ability. In addition, courses in the sociology and/or psychology of human difference may also find the book useful.

The text was written with first and second year undergraduate students in mind, but would also be appropriate for advanced high school or college-prep students. The book can also be used in higher-level undergraduate or graduate student seminars, although such classes would ideally use *America on Film* in conjunction with more advanced materials and/or other primary readings. Because of its user-friendly style and general accessibility – everyone loves movies! – it may also be possible to use the text within certain types of corporate or social seminars designed to stimulate discussion of human diversity.

America on Film is divided into six parts. The first outlines the basic terms and issues of cultural theory and cinematic representation. Each of the following parts is devoted to a specific aspect of race, class, gender, sexuality, and ability, and each begins with a helpful "What is . . . ?" introductory essay. Part II examines the cultural construction of whiteness as well as the complex historical lineages of African

American, Native American, Asian American, and Latino representations. Part III explores issues of American capitalism and examines the cinematic representation of class struggle before and after the Great Depression. Part IV explores the changing images of both femininity and masculinity within American film, and includes a chapter on how Hollywood film form itself has been critiqued as having a male bias. Part V explores how various forms of sexuality have (or have not) been figured on American movie screens. Part VI analyzes various ideas about physical ability, and how what is termed disability has been represented across American film history. The final chapter, comprised exclusively of individual "case studies" (in-depth film analyses), emphasizes the multiple and complex links between all of these various forms of identity markers.

The book is comprised of a total of 17 chapters. While this number exceeds the typical number of weeks in a semester-long course of study, the text has been designed to adapt to those parameters. Generally, each week of any given semester can be devoted to a single chapter of *America on Film* and a representative film screening, either shown in class or assigned as homework. (Many of the films suggested within the text for further screening are easily available from video stores and other commercial media outlets.) Depending on the preferences of the instructor, additional readings and/or screenings can be used in conjunction with *America on Film*. Chapters may also be assigned on a more concentrated basis or even used "out of order," although we have provided a logical and easy-to-follow structure for the issues discussed.

Each chapter of *America on Film* is organized within a broad historical framework, with specific theoretical concepts – including film genre, auteur theory, cultural studies, Orientalism, the "male gaze," feminism, queer theory, etc. – integrated throughout. Each chapter features a concise and accessible overview of the topic at hand, a discussion of representative films, figures, and movements, a case study of a single film, and key terms highlighted in bold. Each chapter concludes with questions for discussion and a short bibliography and filmography. *America on Film* also contains a glossary of key terms, a comprehensive index, and over 130 photos and diagrams illustrating key points and figures.

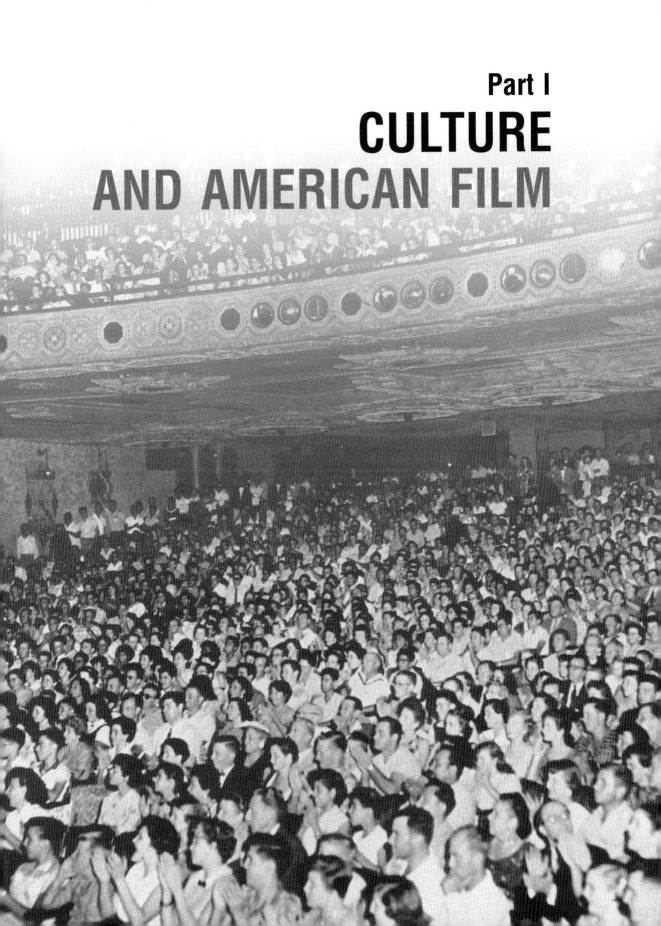

Part I
CULTURE
AND AMERICAN FILM

Chapter 1

INTRODUCTION TO THE STUDY OF FILM FORM AND REPRESENTATION

The purpose of this book is to analyze how American films have represented race, class, gender, sexuality, and ability throughout the twentieth century and into the early twenty-first. It is a basic principle of this work that by studying American film history, we can gain keen insights into the ways that different groups of American people have been treated (and continue to be treated). Images of people on film actively contribute to the ways in which people are understood and experienced in the "real world." Furthermore, there are multiple and varied connections between film and "real life," and we need to have agreed-upon ways of discussing those connections and their ramifications. Therefore, before examining in detail how specific groups of people have been represented within American cinema, we need to understand some preliminary concepts: how film works to represent people and things, how and why social groupings are and have been formed, and how individuals interact with the larger socio-cultural structures of the United States of America. This chapter introduces some basic ideas about film form, American history, and cultural studies.

Film Form

Film form refers to the constitutive elements that make a film uniquely a "film" and not a painting or a short story. All works of art might be said to have both form and content. **Content** is *what* a work is about, while **form** is *how* that content is expressed. Form and content are inextricably combined, and it is an old adage of art theory that "form follows content," which means that the content of a work of art should dictate the form in which it should be expressed. For example, many different poems might have the same content – say, for example, a rose – but the content of a rose can be expressed in various forms in an infinite number of ways: in a sonnet, a ballad, an epic, a haiku, a limerick, and so forth. Each of these formal structures will create a different "take" on the content. For example, a limerick tends to be humorous or flippant, while a sonnet tends to be more serious and romantic. Likewise, different films with similar content can be serious, frivolous, artistic, intellectual, comedic, or frightening. Therefore, understanding how cinema communicates or creates meaning requires more than paying attention to what is specifically going on in the story (the film's content); it also requires paying attention to how various artistic choices (the film's form) affect the way the story is understood by the viewer.

Many entire books have been written analyzing the various formal elements of film but, for the purposes of this basic introduction, they can be broken into five main aspects: **literary design**, **visual design**, **cinematography**, **editing**, and **sound design**. The first aspect of film form, **literary design**, refers to the elements of a film that come from the script and story ideas. The literary design includes the story, the setting, the action, the characters, the characters' names, the dialog, the film's title, and any deeper subtexts or thematic meanings. Film is capable of many literary devices: metaphor, irony, satire, allegory, and so forth. Some films are black comedies and must be understood according to that form. Other films are dramas to be taken seriously while still others try to make us laugh by being deliberately juvenile. Yet other films try to shock or provoke us with new and unexpected ideas. Analyzing a movie's literary design is a good place to start when analyzing a film, but one should not ignore the four other axes of film form and how they contribute to a film's meaning.

Another broad aspect of film form has been labeled **mise-en-scène**, a French term for what goes into each individual **shot** (or uninterrupted run of film). Aspects of mise-en-scène include our second and third formal axes: the **visual design** of what's being filmed (the choice of sets, costumes, makeup, lighting, color, and actors' performance and arrangement before the camera) and the **cinematographic design** – that is, how the camera records the visual elements that have been dictated by the literary design. The cinematographic design includes things like the choice of framing, lenses, camera angle, camera movement, what is in focus and what is not. Each of these choices of mise-en-scène can affect the viewer's feelings toward the story and its characters. A room that is brightly lit may seem comfortable or even festive; that same room with heavy shadows may seem threatening or scary. If everyone in a crowd scene is wearing various shades of gray and black, the viewer will tend to see them as just a crowd; if one person is wearing red, the viewer will tend to focus on that one person. Similarly, a camera shooting up from the floor at a character will create a different feeling than a camera aimed at eye-level. In yet another example, if only one couple on a dance floor are kept in focus, the viewer will pay attention to them; if the whole ballroom is kept in focus, the viewer may choose to look in a number of directions.

The fourth axis of film form is called **montage** or **editing**, and refers to how all the individual shots the camera records are put together in order to create meaning or tell a story. Most movies are made up of hundreds and hundreds of shots which are edited together to make a full-length feature film. Many choices get made at the editing stage. Not only do filmmakers usually have multiple takes of the same scene to choose from, they also choose which shots to place together with other shots. It may seem obvious to an audience, since the editing would seem to need to follow the story (A follows B follows C), but an editor may choose to break up a shot of a group of people talking with individual close-ups of people in the group. Such a choice affects audience understanding by forcing the viewer to pay attention to just one person instead of the entire group. Audience identification with specific characters can be encouraged or discouraged in this manner. Montage also involves choosing the length of each shot. Usually, longer shot lengths are used to create quiet or contemplative moments, while action sequences or chases often are put together with short, quick shots.

The fifth and final formal axis of cinema is **sound design**. Although cinema audiences are usually referred to as viewers or spectators, audiences both watch and listen to films, and the same types of artistic choices that are made with the visual images are also made with the soundtrack. The dialog of some of the characters on the screen is easy to hear, while the dialog of others is inaudible (thus directing the audience member to pay attention to the conversation that the filmmakers want them to pay attention to). Most films have a musical score that the audience can hear but which the characters cannot. Choosing what type of music to play under a scene will greatly affect viewer comprehension – that is why the music is there in the first place – by directing the viewer toward the preferred understanding of the images. Playing a luscious ballad during a scene between a woman and her fiancé helps create a romantic sense, but playing ominous music during the same scene may make the viewer think the man is out to hurt the woman (or vice versa).

Although this only begins to introduce the subject of film form, these few examples do point out how cinema's basic aesthetic qualities help to create meaning. Discussing how various types of people are represented in American cinema, then, requires more than analyzing only the stories and the characters. For example, let's imagine a film about both a white man and a Native American man. The story alternates between the two characters, showing their daily activities: getting up, eating, interacting with their family and friends, working, and then going to sleep. There would seem to be nothing necessarily biased or prejudiced according to this description of the film's content. Yet, in this hypothetical film, all the scenes with the white man are brightly lit, with the camera placed at eye-level; the shots are of medium length, and calm, pleasant music is used for underscoring. In contrast, all the scenes of the Native American man are composed with dark shadows, with the camera constantly tilted at weird angles; the shots are quick and choppy, and dark, brooding music is used for underscoring. Such choices obviously slant how a viewer is supposed to react to these two characters. The content of the film may have seemed neutral, but when the other axes of film form are analyzed, one realizes that the white man was presented in a favorable (or neutral) light, while the Native American man was made to seem shifty or dangerous.

The above example is an imaginary one, but throughout this book actual films will be analyzed in detail in terms of both content and form, in order to examine how various American identities are represented in American films. As the next chapters will discuss in detail, the Hollywood studio system developed certain traditions in its formal choices that would vastly affect how race, class, gender, sexuality, and ability were and are treated in mainstream narrative films. But before turning to specifics, we must also examine the social and political nature of American society itself, as well as the theoretical tools that have been developed to explore the relationship between film and "real life."

American Ideologies: Discrimination and Resistance

The Constitution of the United States of America famously begins with these three words: "We the People." Their importance highlights one of the founding principles of the nation: that the power of government is embodied not in the will of a dictator, nor in that of a religious leader or a monarch, but in the collective will of individual citizens. In conceptualizing "the power of the people," the newly formed United States based its national identity on the principle of equality or, as Thomas Jefferson wrote in the Declaration of Independence, that "all men are created equal." Yet, as admirable as these sentiments were (and are), the United States of the late 1700s saw some individuals as "more equal" than others. Jefferson's very words underline the fact that women were excluded from this equality – women were not allowed to vote or hold office, and they were severely hampered in opportunities to pursue careers outside the home. People of African descent were also regularly denied the vote, and the writers of the Constitution itself acknowledged (and thus implicitly endorsed) an institutional system of slavery against blacks and others. The Constitution did at least acknowledge the presence of African Americans in the country (although they were valued by the government as only three-fifths of a person). Native Americans were denied even this dubious honor and were considered aliens. Even being a male of European descent did not necessarily guarantee inclusion in the great experiment of American democracy, for many statesmen at the time argued that only landowners (that is, those of a certain economic standing) should have the right to vote or hold office.

Over the years, Americans have come to understand that the Constitution is a living document, one that can be and has been changed to encompass a wider meaning of equality. In America today, there is a general belief that each and every individual is unique, and should have equal access to the American Dream of "life, liberty, and the pursuit of happiness." Not everyone will necessarily reach the same levels of happiness and success, but most Americans believe that the results of that quest should be based on individual effort and merit rather than preferential treatment (or, conversely, exclusionary tactics). The United States professes that these opportunities are "inalienable rights." However, just as in the late 1700s, barriers, conflicts, biases, and misunderstandings continue to hamper these ideals. While most American citizens philosophically understand and endorse these principles of equality, many of those same people also recognize that equality has not been totally achieved in the everyday life of the nation.

Why is there such a disparity between the avowed principles of equality and many citizens' actual lived experience? First, while ostensibly acknowledging that each person is unique, most of us also recognize that individuals are often grouped together by some shared trait. This grouping comes in many forms: by racial or ethnic heritage, by gender, by income level, by academic level, by sexual orientation, by geographic region, by age, by physical ability, and so forth. Almost invariably, such categorization of various identity types becomes a type of "shorthand" for describing people – a working-class Latino, a black deaf senior citizen, a Southern middle-class gay man. Quite often, this shorthand is accompanied by assumed traits that people belonging to a certain category supposedly have in common: that women are more emotional than rational, that gay men lisp, that African Americans are good dancers. When such oversimplified and overgeneralized assumptions become standardized – in speech, in movies, on TV – they become **stereotypes**. Stereotypes are often said to contain a "kernel of truth," in that *some* women are more emotional than rational, *some* gay men do lisp, and *some* African Americans do excel at dance. The problems begin when people make unsupported leaps in logic and assume that everyone of a certain group is "naturally inclined" to exhibit these traits, thus reducing complex human diversity to simple-minded and judgmental assumptions.

In their oversimplification, stereotypes inevitably create erroneous perceptions about individuals. Stereotypes become even more problematic when they are used to favor certain groups over others, which unfortunately occurs quite commonly. While ostensibly living in a "free and equal" society, most Americans are aware that certain groups still have more opportunities and protection than others. In almost all of the categories listed above, there is one group that tends to have more access to "life, liberty, and the pursuit of happiness" than the others. Within race, those considered **white** or of Anglo-Saxon descent still seem to have more privilege and opportunity than do those of other races. Within gender, women are still working to achieve equity with men, while within sexual orientation, heterosexuality is more accepted and privileged than other orientations. And since notions of success and happiness are intricately tied to income level in contemporary US culture, one can see that working-class people hold less power than middle-class people (and that middle-class people in turn hold less power than do people of the upper classes). One need merely glance at the demographic makeup of Congress or the board-rooms of most major American corporations to see that wealthy heterosexual white men dominate these positions of power. American films over the past century also disproportionately focus on stories of strong and stalwart heterosexual white men finding happiness and success.

In everyday conversation, less privileged groups are frequently referred to as **minority groups**. Such a term positions these groups as marginal to the dominant group that holds greater power. The term also implies that the disempowered groups are smaller numerically than the dominant group – an implication that may not necessarily be true. Census statistics often indicate that there are slightly more women living in the United States than men, yet men hold far more social power and privilege than do women. Current population projections are forecasting that, in many states, white citizens will be outnumbered by other racial or ethnic groups some time in the near future. Hence, the term "minority group" more often refers to types of people with less social power than to any group's actual size.

One common method of keeping minority communities on the margins of power has been to pit their struggles for equality against one another, while the dominant group continues to lead. Another method has been to exclude members of minority groups from being considered "American" in the first place. The creation of a sense of national identity consistently involves social negotiations of who gets included and who gets excluded. Identity in general becomes more fixed when it is able to define *what it is not*: someone who is white is *not* black; a man is *not* a woman; a heterosexual is *not* a homosexual. America gains a greater sense of itself through such juxtapositions: it is not a British colony, it is not the various nations of Native Americans, and it is not the other countries that make up the American continents (which can also lay claim to the name "America"). Consequently, if certain population groups can be considered "alienable," then it becomes easier to feel that they are not entitled to those "inalienable rights" that "We the People of the United States of America" have supposedly been granted.

While women, homosexuals, the differently abled, and people of non-white heritage have made tremendous gains in social power during the last few decades, white heterosexual men still dominate the corridors of power in America. Many people feel that this is "how things ought to be," that this is simply the "natural order of things." In theoretical terms, considering white heterosexual males obviously or essentially better (stronger, more intelligent, etc.) is called an ideological assumption. **Ideology** is a term that refers to a system of beliefs that groups of people share and believe are inherently true and acceptable. Most ideological beliefs are rarely questioned by those who hold them; the beliefs are naturalized because of their constant and unquestioned usage. They are, to use a word made famous in the Declaration of Independence, "self-evident." No one needs to explain these ideas, because supposedly everyone knows them.

When an ideology is functioning optimally within a society or civilization, individuals are often incapable of recognizing that these ideas are socially constructed opinions and not objective truths. We call these assumptions **dominant ideologies**, because they tend to structure in pervasive ways how a culture thinks about itself and others, who and what it upholds as worthy, meaningful, true, and valuable. The United States was founded on and still adheres to the dominant ideology of **white patriarchal capitalism**. This does not mean that wealthy white men gather together in some sort of conspiracy to oppress everyone else in the nation, although such groups have been formed throughout American history in order consolidate and control power. Rather, white patriarchal capitalism is an ideology that permeates the ways most Americans think about themselves and the world around them. It also permeates most American films.

White patriarchal capitalism entails several distinct aspects. The first – **white** – refers to the ideology that people of Western and Northern European descent are somehow better than are people whose ancestry is traced to other parts of the world. **Patriarchal** (its root words mean "rule by the father") refers to a culture predicated on the belief that men are the most important members of society, and thus entitled to greater opportunity and access to power. As part of American patriarchy, sexuality is only condoned within heterosexual marriage, a situation that considers all other sexualities taboo and reinforces women's role as the child-bearing and child-raising property of men. The third term – **capitalism** – is also a complex one, which multiple volumes over many years have attempted to dissect and define, both as an economic system and as a set of interlocking ideologies.

For the working purposes of this introduction, capitalism as an ideology can be defined as the belief that success and worth are measured by one's material wealth. This fundamental aspect of capitalism has been so ingrained in the social imagination that visions of the American Dream almost always invoke financial success: a big house, big car, yacht, closets full of clothes, etc. Capitalism (both as an economic system and as an ideology) works to naturalize the concept of an **open market economy**, that the competition of various businesses and industries in the marketplace should be unhindered by governmental intrusion. (The US film industry, a strong example of capitalist enterprise, has spent much of its history trying to prevent governmental oversight.) One of the ideological strategies for promoting capitalism within the United States has been in labeling this system a "free" market, thus equating unchecked capitalism with the philosophies of democracy. Capitalism often stands in opposition to the ideology and practice of **communism**, an economic system wherein the government controls all wealth and industry in order to redistribute that income to the population in an equitable fashion. (The history of the twentieth century showed that human greed usually turns the best communist intentions into crude dictatorships.) **Socialism**, an economic and ideological system mediating capitalism and communism, seeks to structure a society's economic system around governmental regulation of industries and the equitable sharing of wealth for certain basic necessities, while still maintaining democratic values and a free market for most consumer goods. Since the United States was founded under capitalism, American culture has largely demonized socialism and communism as evil and unnatural, even though many US government programs can be considered socialist in both intent and practice.

The ideology of white patriarchal capitalism works not only to naturalize the idea that wealthy white men deserve greater social privilege, but to protect those privileges by naturalizing various beliefs that degrade other groups – thus making it seem obvious that those groups should not be afforded the same privileges. Some argue that capitalism can help minority groups gain power. If a group is able to move up the economic ladder through capitalist means, then that group can claim for itself as much power, access, and opportunity as do the most privileged Americans. As persuasive as this argument is (as can be seen by its widespread use), capitalism has often worked against various minority groups throughout US history. The wealthy have used their position to consolidate and insure their power, often at the expense of the rest of the population. Since this wealthy group has almost exclusively been comprised of white men, the dissemination of racist and sexist stereotypes has helped keep people of color and women from moving ahead economically. To use an early example, arguing that individuals of African descent were barely human allowed slavery to continue to thrive as an economic arrangement that benefited whites.

Today, racist, sexist, and homophobic attitudes work to create in corporate culture a **glass ceiling**, a metaphoric term that describes how everyone but white hetero-sexual males tends to be excluded from the highest executive levels of American industries.

In this way, one can see how the impact of social difference (race, gender, sexual-ity, physical ability) can have an impact upon one's economic class status. In fact, the social differences that this book attempts to discuss – race, gender, class, sexuality, and ability – cannot be readily separated out as discrete categories. For example, people of color are men and women, rich and poor, straight and gay. Being a black female means dealing with both patriarchal assumptions about male superiority and lingering ideas of white supremacy. Being a lesbian of color might mean one is triply oppressed – potentially discriminated against on three separate levels of social difference. Encountering real-world prejudice on account of those differences, non-white, non-male, and non-heterosexual people, as well as those considered dis-abled, may have trouble finding good jobs and subsequent economic success.

Most ideologies, being belief systems, are only relatively coherent, and may some-times contain overlaps, contradictions, and/or gaps. The dominant ideology of any given culture is never stable and rigid. Instead, dominant ideologies and ruling assumptions are constantly in flux, a state of things referred to by cultural theorists as **hegemony** – the ongoing struggle to maintain the consent of the people to a sys-tem that governs them (and which may or may not oppress them in some ways). Hegemony is thus a complex theory that attempts to account for the confusing and often contradictory ways in which modern Western societies change and evolve. Whereas "ideology" is often used in ahistorical ways – as an unchanging or stable set of beliefs – hegemony refers to the way that social control must be won over and over again within different eras and within different cultures. For example, we should not speak of patriarchal ideology as a monolithic concept that means the same thing in different eras and in different situations. Rather, the hegemonic struggle of patriarchy to maintain power is a fluid and dynamic thing that allows for its ongoing maintenance *but also the possibility of its alteration*. For example, specific early twentieth-century patriarchal *ideologies* were challenged and changed when women won the right to vote in 1920, but that did not destroy the *hegemony* of American patriarchy.

Thus, the dominant ideology of a culture is always open to change and revision via the ebb and flow of **hegemonic negotiation**, the processes whereby various social groups exert pressure on the dominant hegemony. In another example, over the last fifty years, American civil rights groups have worked to expose and overturn the entrenched system of prejudice that has oppressed their communities for genera-tions. Often, these fights include attempts to instill pride and self-worth in the minor-ity groups that have been traditionally disparaged. In the process, the ideological biases of racial superiority are being challenged, but the basic assumption that indi-viduals can be grouped according to their race is not. While these efforts attempt to disrupt one level of assumptions, a more basic ideological belief is kept intact. In this case the dominant hegemonic concept of racial difference as a valuable social marker remains untouched, even as the individual ideologies of white supremacy are challenged. (More recent cultural theorists have begun to challenge the very notion of such categorizations, a topic explored more fully in future chapters.)

Ideological struggle is therefore an ongoing political process that surrounds us constantly, bombarding individuals at every moment with messages about how the world should and could function. Such struggles can be both obvious and subtle. One obvious way of disseminating and maintaining social control is through oppressive and violent means, through institutions such as armies, wars, police forces, terrorism, and torture – institutions known as **repressive state apparatuses (RSAs)**. Violent, repressive discrimination is part of American history, as evidenced by terrorist groups such as the Ku Klux Klan, political assassinations, police brutality, and the continued presence of hate crimes. More subtly, the state can also enforce ideological assumptions through legal discrimination. For example, the so-called **Jim Crow Laws** of the American South during the first half of the twentieth century legally inscribed African Americans as second-class citizens. Current examples would be the lack of federal laws that prohibit discrimination based on gender or perceived sexual orientation. Such legal discrimination tacitly helps maintain occupational discrimination. What these few examples also show is that discrimination and bias are systemic problems as well as individualized ones. Just as a single person can be a bigot, those same biases can be incorporated into the very structures of our "free" nation: this is known as **institutionalized discrimination**.

While institutionalized discrimination and other oppressive measures overtly attempt to impose certain ideologies upon a society, there are still more subtle means of doing so that often do not even feel or look like social control. Winning over the "hearts and minds" of a society with what are called **ideological state apparatuses (ISAs)** usually proves more effective than more oppressive measures, since the population acquiesces to those in power frequently without even being aware that it is doing so. ISAs include various non-violent social formations such as schools, the family, the church, and the media institutions – including film and television – that shape and represent our culture in certain ways. They spread ideology not through intimidation and oppression, but by example and education. In schools, students learn skills such as reading and math, but they are also taught to believe certain things about America, and how to be productive, law-abiding citizens. The enormously popular *Dick and Jane* books taught many American youngsters not only how to read, but also how boys and girls were supposed to behave (and most importantly, that boys and girls behave differently). Institutionalized religion is also an ideological state apparatus, in which theological beliefs help sustain ideological imperatives. Many Christian denominations during the country's first century used the Bible to justify slavery and segregation of the races. Some faiths still demonize homosexuality and argue that women should subjugate themselves to men. Others regard children born with differing physical abilties as signs of sin or evil. Even the structure of the family itself is an ISA, in which sons and daughters are taught ideological concepts by their parents. In the United States, families have traditionally been idealized as patriarchal, with the father as the leader. Parental prejudices (about the lower classes, about homosexuals, about the disabled, about other races or ethnicities) can also be passed down to their offspring, help-ing maintain those beliefs.

As these examples of ISAs show, ideology functions most smoothly when it is so embedded in everyday life that more overt oppressive measures become unneces-sary. In fact, the use of oppression usually indicates that large sections of a society are beginning to diverge from the dominant ideology. At their most successful, ISAs act as reinforcements for individuals who have already been inculcated into dominant ideology. Such individuals are said to have **internalized ideology**, or to have adopted socially constructed ideological assumptions into their own senses of self. Such internalizing can have significant effects on people, especially members of minority groups. No matter what social group one might identify with, we all are constantly bombarded by images, ideas, and ideologies of straight white male superiority and centrality, and these constructs are consciously and unconsciously internalized by everyone. For straight white men, those images can reinforce feel-ings of superiority. For everyone else, those images and ideas can produce mild to severe self-hatred or create a psychological state in which individuals limit their own potential. In effect, we might allow the dominant ideology to tell us what we are or are not capable of – that women are not good at math, that African Americans can only excel at sports, that people from the lower classes must remain uneducated, that someone in a wheelchair cannot be an elected official, or that being homosexual is a shameful thing. Possibly the least noticeable but potentially most damaging, this type of **internalized discrimination** is sometimes termed **ego-destructive**, because it actively works against an individual's sense of psychological well-being. Such ego-destructive ideologies may be especially harmful because they are often fostered by those groups and individuals who allegedly love and nurture us: rejection from families and religions is still a common occurrence for people who are perceived as different from the "norm."

The strength and tenacity of such internalized ideologies within an efficiently working hegemonic system allow people to consider their society open and free, since it appears that no one is forcing anyone else to live a certain way, or keeping them from reaching their highest possible levels of achievement. Yet the subtlety of ideological state apparatuses and the subconscious impact of ego-destructive discrimination severely undercut and problematize the avowed principles of liberty and equality upon which the United States was founded. Hallowed as these prin-ciples are, the functioning of white patriarchal capitalism as our nation's dominant ideology militates against social equality in a variety of ways.

Culture and Cultural Studies

While the school, the church, and the family serve as classic examples of ideolog-ical state apparatuses, potentially the most pervasive of ISAs (at least in the past century) is the mass media – newspapers, magazines, television, radio, film, and now the Internet and the World Wide Web. Many theorists feel that in today's electronic world, the media has more influence on cultural ideas and ideologies than do schools, religions, and families combined. The bulk of this book will examine historically how one branch of this mass media, the American cinema, has worked to exemplify and reinforce (and more rarely challenge) the hegemonic domination of white patriarchal capitalism.

One of the first arguments used to resist focusing on American cinema as a conveyer of ideological messages is that Hollywood movies are merely "entertainment." Consequently, as the argument goes, academics are reading too much into these things. What do ideas like ideology and hegemony have to do with mindless escapism? To answer such questions, one has to recognize that cinema (and all other mass media) are important parts of American culture. **Culture** refers to the characteristic features of a civilization or state, or the behavior typical of a group or class. Culture is thus deeply connected to ideology: one might say it is the "real-world" manifestation of ideology, since characteristic features, social behaviors, and cultural products all convey ideology.

Historically, European culture judged itself to be superior to all other cultures on the globe. "True" culture was thought to be synonymous with Western notions of **high art** – classical music, "serious" literature and theater, etc. – and other cultures were judged to be deficient by those standards. Today we try to discuss different cultures without making such value judgments; we also understand that any given group's culture is more than just its most "respectable" and officially "important" art works. Culture also encompasses the modes of everyday life: how one behaves in a social situation, the type of clothes one wears, the slang one uses when talking to friends, etc. This definition of culture includes the so-called **low art** of popular music, comic books, paperback novels, movies, and television – forms of culture that interact with far more people than do those found only in museums or opera houses. Even language itself shapes and is shaped by culture, and thus conveys ideological meanings. For example, the Euro-American cultural tradition that associates "white" with goodness and "black" with evil cannot help but influence how we think about race, which we often define in the same terms.

Within any given society, there are multiple cultures that differ in varying degrees from one another. In the United States, one can find a variety of cultures: hip-hop, Chicano, Mennonite, conservative Christian, and yuppie, just to name a few. These cultures co-exist and may overlap (for example, a Chicano yuppie), but cultural groupings rarely exist in equal balance with one another. Rather, the culture of the ruling or most powerful group in a society tends to be the dominant culture, expressing its values and beliefs through ideologies and other cultural forms. The group with the most control has the greater means to produce and disseminate their preferred cultural attitudes throughout the rest of the society – *their* music, *their* literature, *their* standards of behavior become the norm for the rest of the society. For example, Native Americans have historically had less opportunity than Anglo Americans to get the funding or training necessary to make films or television programs. Consequently, the white man's version of "how the West was won" has been filmed and televised literally thousands of times, while Native Americans have had very little chance to present their viewpoint of that era on film or video.

The culture of any marginalized or minority group is often labeled a **subculture**. Subcultures can have their effect on the dominant culture by contributing to the active hegemonic negotiation of dominant ideology, but usually this only happens to the extent that a subculture's concerns can be adapted to the needs of the dominant ruling interests. For example, hip-hop and rap music styles have crossed over into mainstream popular music – but in an altered (and some might say watered-down) version. This is broadly called **commodification** (turning something into a product for sale) and more specifically **incorporation** (the stripping of an ideology or cultural artifact's more "dangerous" or critical meanings so that the watered-down artifact can be sold to mainstream culture). Another good example of this process is the recent history of earrings worn on men. Some men in the 1970s started to wear earrings as a "coming out" gesture – to announce to the world that they belonged to the emerging gay male subculture. As an act of coming out, the gesture was political and meant to challenge a dominant culture that ignored or suppressed the existence of gay men. In the 2000s, however, many, many men wear earrings – not because they want the world to know that they are gay, but because earrings for men have become a commodity that can be bought and sold as part of a depoliticized fashion trend. The gay political meaning of men wearing earrings has been stripped from the act – it was commodified and incorporated within the dominant culture.

In recent decades, scholars in various disciplines (sociology, political science, literature, communications, history, media studies) have begun to study and theorize concepts and issues surrounding culture and ideology. This interdisciplinary research has coalesced under the term **cultural studies**. As its theorists come from such different backgrounds, cultural studies as a field of academic inquiry has consistently focused on multiple aspects of how culture works (and needs to be analyzed), but one of the basic foundations for this new discipline has been that every **cultural artifact** – book, movie, music video, song, billboard, joke, slang term, earring, etc. – is an expression of the culture that produces it. Every cultural artifact is thus a **text** that conveys information, carrying the ideological messages of both its authors and the culture that produced it. As a result, many cultural studies scholars are interested in how media texts express a view of the world, how these expressions create ideological effects, and how the users of such texts make meaning from them. This area, sometimes called **image studies**, looks at the processes of **representation** – the systems we use to communicate and understand our world – language, art, speech, and more recently TV, movies, and newer forms of media. These are **representational systems** that show us reconstructed (or **mediated**) versions of life, not "real life" itself. Most US citizens have never been to China, but probably know something about it from reading books or newspapers, or seeing images of it on television or at the movies. Since all media texts reflect in some way the ideological biases of the culture from which they emanate, the images of China shown in Hollywood movies or on American television will be different from the mediated images of China made in some other area of the world (and different from China's *own* images of itself).

There are two stages of making meaning within any given text: **encoding** and **decoding**. **Encoding** encompasses the actual production of the text. A common method of analyzing encoding in film studies has been termed **auteur studies**. French for "author," the auteur concept understands film or films as the imaginative work of a single specific artist, usually the director. By examining a number of films made by the same auteur, one can supposedly find common stylistic choices (ways of using the camera, editing, etc.) as well as common themes. Auteur studies became popular during the 1960s, and even now journalists will refer to "the latest Quentin Tarantino film" or "a typical Steven Spielberg picture." The auteur theory argues that it is important to know *who* made a film, because aspects of a filmmaker's personality and social position will affect the meanings encoded within it. Historically, straight white men in Hollywood made most American films; it has only been in recent decades that women, people of color, and/or homosexuals have had greater opportunities to make films.

Thus, during the encoding stage, the maker(s) of a film place meaning, including ideological meaning, into the text. Sometimes this involves specific, overt editorializing: a character gives a speech about a certain issue, or the entire story attempts to teach a moral lesson. However, the encoding of ideological meaning need not be so obvious; it might be done casually, and even unconsciously. Certain choices in creating mood or emotion, or in fostering audience sympathy (or antipathy), will also carry ideological weight. (Recall our earlier discussion of the hypothetical film about a white man and a Native American man.) To many, the process of encoding may initially sound like it applies solely to the production of **propaganda**, in which ideas, opinions, or allegations are presented as incontestable facts in order to sway public opinion toward or away from some cause or point. Texts that are labeled propaganda are usually encoded with overt ideological messages – cultural artifacts like advertisements, public service announcements, and political speeches. Hollywood movies are rarely labeled propaganda, yet they always encode certain ideologies. In other words, while all propaganda conveys ideological messages, not all texts are or should be labeled propaganda.

Students sometimes want to ask about a film text, "Did the author really mean it that way?" Such a question assumes that filmic analysis is "reading too much into things" unless one can find definite evidence of a filmmaker's intent. The response to this criticism is that *all* texts encode ideological meanings and messages, but those messages are not always *consciously* embedded in the text by its producer(s). Usually, filmmakers simply want to make a good film, tell an entertaining story, and sell tickets. Yet what is considered good or entertaining is itself going to differ according to cultural and ideological standards. Furthermore, the makers of cultural texts

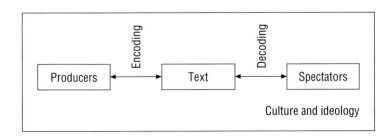

A cultural studies model of encoding and decoding. Producers, texts, and spectators all exist within larger spheres of culture and ideology.

are not somehow removed from or above the society in which they live. They are just as much shaped by the dominant ideology as anyone else – and this can have an unconscious effect on what they put into their work. A white heterosexual middle-class Protestant male is going to have had a certain experience of life that will translate in some fashion into the films he writes or directs, even if he is not aware of it. Similarly, a non-white or female or homosexual or disabled filmmaker is going to have had a different life experience that will result in him or her making a different type of film (consciously or unconsciously). Also, a film from the 1950s is recognizably different from a film from the 1970s, not only because of the changes in cars and fashions, but also because of the changes in the ideological assumptions about social issues (such as race, class, gender, sexuality, and ability).

The other stage of making meaning, **decoding**, involves the reception of a text. Once a text is produced, it is distributed to others (to be read, listened to, watched, worn, etc.). Those who use the produced text (that is, the audience) then decode the text's meanings on the basis of their own conscious and unconscious cultural, ideological positioning(s). In other words, producers, texts, and receivers make up a system of communication or meaning production, and that system exists within the larger social spheres of culture and ideology. Like encoding, decoding can be overt or subliminal. At certain times, an audience member will consciously recognize she or he is being "preached to." If an ideological position becomes too strong or apparent, people may easily reject it as propaganda (especially if the ideology being espoused challenges their own). Yet, at other times, the messages may be decoded below one's consciousness. An imbalance that favors men instead of women as the main characters of Hollywood films might be decoded by audiences (without ever stopping to really think about it) as meaning that men are more important (or do more important things) than women.

When producers and readers share aspects of the same culture, texts are more easily decoded or understood. (If you doubt that, try reading a newspaper written in a language you do not understand!) However, not every reader is going to take (or make) identical meanings from the same text. Depending upon their own cultural positioning, different people may decode texts in different ways – sometimes minutely different, sometimes greatly so. Readings that decode a text in accordance with how it was encoded are said to be **dominant readings**. On the other side of the spectrum are **oppositional readings**, which actively question the ideological assumptions encoded in a text. Most readings lie somewhere in between these two extremes. **Negotiated readings** resist some aspects of what has been encoded, but accept others. Frequently, members of minority groups have social standpoints that differ from those encoded in mainstream texts, and sometimes this allows such individuals to perform readings that are more regularly negotiated or oppositional.

In most cases, Hollywood filmmakers don't want moviegoers to question the politics of their films. Hollywood promotes its films not as political tracts but as mindless escapism, and an audience member who accepts that tenet will rarely be alert to the cultural and ideological assumptions that the films encode and promote. (One should remember that ideology is often most effective when it goes unnoticed.) The fact that Hollywood films are generally understood as mere entertainment (without political significance) is itself an ideological assumption, one that denies the importance of image studies and therefore represents white patriarchal capitalist film practice as neutral, natural, and inevitable.

Yet the act of performing a negotiated or oppositional reading is not in and of itself a radical denunciation of dominant cinema. (After all, even the oppositional spectator has signaled his or her "approval" of the text by purchasing a ticket to the film.) While such readings may criticize and critique certain ideological notions, they are nonetheless created within the same basic hegemonic framework as are dominant readings. They cannot completely negate the ideological messages found in the text, only resist them. Still, oppositional and negotiated readings can have an effect on the hegemonic negotiation of dominant ideologies through-out time. When a certain oppositional reading strategy grows within a culture to the point that future similar texts are no longer accepted by consumers, then certain ideological assumptions must be altered, and future texts may exhibit those changes. As we shall see throughout this book, the overtly racist and sexist images that were found in many films from previous decades are – in many cases – no longer considered acceptable in the twenty-first century. Nonetheless, white patriarchal capitalism maintains its hegemonic dominance, in both American film and culture-at-large.

Case Study: *The Lion King* (1994)

Issues of culture and ideology can be illustrated by examining a text that many people would probably consider totally apolitical and meaningless except as mere entertainment – the Walt Disney Company's animated feature *The Lion King* (1994). One of the biggest box office successes in motion picture history, *The Lion King* embodies what most people refer to as escapist family entertainment. Since the film was about animals – and cartoon animals at that – the film might seem to have little to say about human relations or ideologies. Yet, since cultural artifacts always reflect in some way the conditions of their production and reception, it is not surprising that *The Lion King* has interesting things to convey about late twentieth-century American culture and its dominant ideology – white patriarchal capitalism. These messages reflect the place and time in which the film was made: the songs are typical 1990s soft rock music, some of the jokes refer to current events, and the storyline evokes concepts popularized in the 1990s by New Age spirituality. Using ideas and concepts that were familiar and reassuring to many Americans probably helped strengthen the film's popularity.

According to our cultural studies model, the **cultural artifact** *The Lion King* is the **text** under consideration, its **producer** is the Walt Disney Company (the animators, performers, and other employees involved in making the film), and the **readers** are all the people who have seen the film since its release in 1994. The Disney filmmakers **encoded** meaning into the cartoon, and every viewer, whether preschooler or senior citizen, works to understand the text by **decoding** it. The film was arguably as popular as it was because it playfully and joyfully encoded dominant hegemonic ideas about white patriarchal capitalism into its form and content: the film's story is a coming-of-age tale in which Simba, a young male lion, learns that his proper place in the world is to be the leader of those around him. Readers who enjoyed the film were probably performing **dominant readings** of the text, as they cheered on the young lion's rise to the throne, defeating his adversaries amid song and dance and colorful spectacle.

Yet, while the film was a huge box office hit, there emerged a small but vocal opposition to *The Lion King*, criticizing it on a number of levels. These critics of the

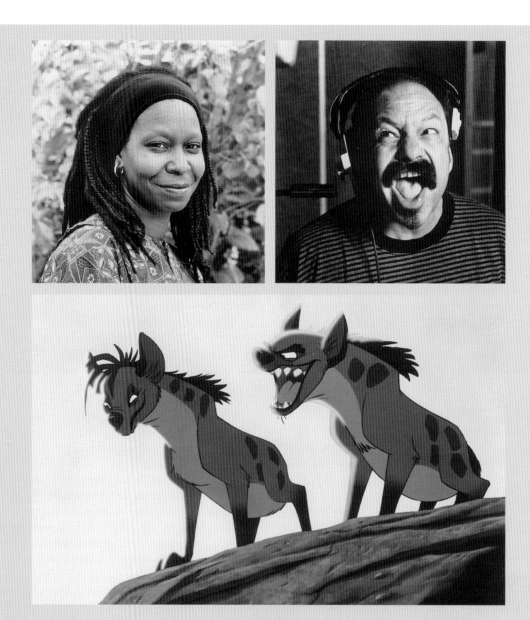

Scar's moronic and evil sidekicks are voiced by actors of color, Whoopi Goldberg and Cheech Marin.
The Lion King, copyright © 1993, The Walt Disney Co. Top left, photo: Umberto Adaggi; top right, photo:
Michael Ansell

film performed **oppositional** and/or **negotiated readings**. For example, some readers were annoyed that the film focused on patriarchal privilege by dramatizing how a son inherits the right to rule over the land from his father. The film literally "nature"-alizes this ideology by making it seem as if this is how real-life animals behave, when in fact female lions play active roles in the social structure of actual prides, a detail the film minimizes (and which, by extension, minimizes the importance of females in human society). The female lions in the film are minor "love interest" characters, and females of other species are almost non-existent. One might also note that the film's very title is suggestive of male authority and supremacy – lions and kings are longstanding symbols of patriarchy.

Uncle Scar preens with an arched eyebrow (a stereotypical signifier of male homosexuality) as he plots against Simba, the "true" and "rightful" ruler of the jungle, in Walt Disney's *The Lion King* (1994).
The Lion King, copyright © 1993, The Walt Disney Co.

Other oppositional or negotiated readings noted that the first Disney animated feature to be set in Africa had erased all evidence of *human* African culture, and employed white musicians to write supposedly "African" music. (This is a good example of the dominant culture industry **commodifying** and **incorporating** African style while ignoring the politics of race and nation.) Furthermore, Simba and his love interest are both voiced by white actors. Disney did hire a few African American actors as character voices (including the assassinated patriarch), but some viewers felt that these characters came close to replicating derogatory racial stereotypes. For example, although the baboon character Rafiki (voiced by African American actor Robert Guillaume) holds a place of respect in the film as the community's mystic/religious leader, he frequently acts foolish and half-crazed, a variation on old stereotypes used to depict African Americans. Furthermore, two of the villain's dim-witted henchmen were also voiced by people of color (Whoopi Goldberg and Richard "Cheech" Marin), linking their minority status to both stupidity and anti-social actions.

Villainy in the film is also linked to stereotypical traits of male homosexuality. The villainous lion Scar is voiced by Jeremy Irons with a British lisp and an arch cynicism; the Disney animators drew him as weak, limp-wristed, and with a feminine swish in his walk. Other characters refer to him as "weird," and, in his attempt to usurp the throne for himself, he disdains the concept of the heterosexual family. Scar's murder of Simba's father and his attempt to depose the "rightful" heir to the throne posit him as a threat to the "natural order" itself (a fact made literal when Scar's rule results in the environmental desolation of the savanna). It is only with the restoration of Simba to the throne that the land comes back to life, in a dissolve that makes the change seem miraculously immediate. Perhaps most disturbingly, the film connects Scar's implied homosexuality with one of the twentieth century's most heinous evils: his musical solo, complete with goose-stepping minions, is suggestive of a Nazi rally.

Immediately, the question of which reading is "correct" gets raised. Are all these people who were bothered by *The Lion King*, those who performed oppositional readings, getting antagonistic over nothing? Or do they know what is *really* going on in the film, while everybody else (performing dominant readings) is just not "getting it"? A cultural studies theorist would answer that there are no right or wrong readings, but rather different interpretive strategies. There is no single definitive reading of any text. If a reader decodes a certain understanding of *The Lion King*, and can point to specific examples from the film to support his or her reading, then that reading is valid. And in order to make a persuasive defense of one's reading of a film (instead of just saying "I liked it – I don't know why"), one needs to work at finding supporting textual evidence – the specific ways the text uses **film form** to encode meaning. (Note how the oppositional reading just presented pointed out story elements, the actors involved, how the characters were drawn, the use of music, and even aspects of editing.) This process of analysis need not destroy one's pleasure in the text. Learning to analyze film form and ideology can enrich and deepen one's experience of any given text, and one can become a more literate, and aware, media consumer.

This book hopes to provide its readers with the tools and encouragement to become active decoders – to help students develop the skills needed to examine media texts for their social, cultural, and ideological assumptions. Throughout this book, specific films will be decoded from divergent spectator positions, pointing out how the context of social and cultural history can and does influ-

ence different reading protocols. Furthermore, one will see that judging textual images as merely "positive" or "negative" vastly oversimplifies the many complex ways that cultural texts can be and are understood in relation to the "real world." This textbook itself is part of American culture, and thus meshes in its own way with the dominant and resistant ideologies within which it was forged. Its ultimate aim is not to raise its readers somehow out of ideology (an impossible task), but to make its readers aware of the ideological assumptions that constantly circulate through American culture, and especially through its films.

Questions for Discussion

1   What labels do you apply to your own identity? What labels do other people apply to you? Ultimately, who has the right to name or label you?
2   Can you think of other cultural artifacts (like rap music or earrings on men) that have been developed in a specific subculture and then **incorporated** into dominant culture? How was the artifact changed when it went mainstream?

3   What is your own ideological positioning? What are some of the ideologies you may have internalized? Do any of them clash with your own self-identity?

Further Reading

Althusser, Louis. *Lenin and Philosophy and Other Essays.* New York: Monthly Review Press, 1971.

Bordwell, David and Kristin Thompson. *Film Art: An Introduction.* New York: McGraw Hill, 2001.

Gray, Ann and Jim McGuigan. *Studying Culture: An Introductory Reader.* New York: Oxford University Press, 1997.

Hall, Stuart, Dorothy Hobson, Andrew Lowe, and Paul Willis, eds. *Culture, Media, Language.* London: Unwin Hyman, 1980.

Hebdige, Dick. *Subculture: The Meaning of Style.* London: Methuen, 1979.

Morley, David and Kuan-Hsing Chen, eds. *Stuart Hall: Critical Dialogues in Cultural Studies.* New York: Routledge, 1996.

Turner, Graeme. *British Cultural Studies: An Introduction.* New York: Routledge, 1996.

Williams, Raymond. *Marxism and Literature.* Oxford: Oxford University Press, 1977.

Williams, Raymond. *Problems in Materialism and Culture.* London: NLB, 1980.

Chapter 2

THE STRUCTURE AND HISTORY OF HOLLYWOOD FILMMAKING

This chapter examines what Hollywood film is and how it developed. Hollywood film can be identified by a specific set of formal and stylistic structures as well as by a set of historical, industrial, and economic determinants. These underlying structures affect how Hollywood films represent America, and how they conceive of issues of race, class, gender, sexuality, and ability. Because Hollywood film is so prevalent in American culture (and world culture), many people think that the way Hollywood makes movies is the only way to do so – that there are no other possible methods for making films. However, there are many types of movies and many different ways to make them. As we shall see throughout this book, these other, non-Hollywood movies often present different **representations** of race, class, gender, sexuality, and ability than do Hollywood films. Both Hollywood and non-Hollywood films have evolved since the beginning of the twentieth century, in conjunction with the broader social, political, and cultural events of American history. This chapter broadly addresses those concerns, and will lay the basis for future chapters' more detailed analyses of how these issues relate to specific cinematic representations of race, class, gender, sexuality, and ability.

Hollywood vs. Independent Film

Hollywood film refers to movies made and released by a handful of filmmaking companies located in and around Hollywood, California. The names of most of these companies – Universal, MGM, 20th Century-Fox, Paramount, Warner Brothers, etc. – have been recognized as cinematic brand names around the world since the 1920s. These companies have produced and distributed tens of thousands of films, films that have found long-term success at the box office, and often make it seem (especially in other countries) that Hollywood film *is* American film. Hollywood's global predominance obscures its historical development, and in effect works to naturalize the structure and style of its films. This is itself another example of ideology working to erase the socially constructed nature of a specific cultural institution: Hollywood gains strength and power by making its form and practice seem to be basic common sense. This tends to hide the fact that Hollywood form and practice developed over time in response to specific socio-political factors, and it also works to erase awareness that there are *other* ways of making (and understanding) film as a cultural artifact.

Hollywood films so dominate American theaters (and video-store shelves and cable programming schedules) that US citizens have relatively little access to other types of films – films often made by minority filmmakers that tell stories and express viewpoints and that are ignored or underexplored in Hollywood movies. These non-Hollywood films are sometimes broadly referred to as **independent films**. For example, **avant-garde** or **experimental films** explore the multiple formal possibilities of cinema (not just storytelling), and they are often tied to specific movements in the other arts, such as Surrealism. **Documentaries** are films that use actual events as their raw material – they are usually made without actors or fictional stories, and attempt to convey these events as realistically as possible. Americans classify films made outside the United States as **foreign films**. They can be fictional films that look more or less like Hollywood films, or they can be avant-garde or documentary films. Finally, the term "independent film" also describes fictional feature films that are made in America, but outside the usual Hollywood channels. Broadly speaking, independent, foreign, avant-garde, and documentary films tend to represent a broader spectrum of humanity than do Hollywood films.

Sometimes, to audiences weaned solely on Hollywood films, these types of films can seem weird, boring, or badly made. If avant-garde films (for example) were trying to play by the rules of Hollywood film, such judgments might have merit, but these films have consciously decided to use other rules. These types of films make formal choices (in mise-en-scène, montage, sound, and narrative design) that often differ vastly from those used in Hollywood films. Most of these films are also produced in different ways than are Hollywood films – they can be funded and filmed by a collective, for example, or by one individual working on his or her own project over a number of years. Unlike Hollywood filmmaking, sometimes these types of films are even made without the intention of turning a profit. Avant-garde and experimental films usually only play at museums, or in film classes at universities. Documentaries might play on television or at film festivals, or occasionally be screened at independent or **art-house theaters**, theaters usually located in urban areas that specialize in off-beat, non-Hollywood film fare. A well-stocked video store or an Internet DVD service are other places one might find these films.

Experimental films, documentaries, and independent fictional films are an important part of American film history and culture, even though they are quite frequently a lesser-known part. As might be expected, these types of films often differ from Hollywood films in the ways that they depict issues of race, class, gender, sexuality, and ability (as well as a host of other topics that are often considered taboo by Hollywood filmmakers). However, while one may in practice contrast fictional Hollywood film with fictional independent film, the distinction between these two terms is not always so clear cut. Frequently there are similarities and connections between independent films and Hollywood. Sometimes successful independent filmmakers go on to sign deals with the major Hollywood companies, and many Hollywood employees dabble in independent filmmaking. A popular independent film such as Quentin Tarantino's *Reservoir Dogs* (1991) may seem somewhat different from most Hollywood films, but it is much closer to a Hollywood film (in both subject matter and style) than most experimental films.

For the purposes of this book, Hollywood and independent film practice might best be understood as the end points of a continuum of American fictional film production, and not as an either/or binary. One of the best ways to distinguish between independent and Hollywood films is to see *where* the film is playing. If it is playing on 3,000 screens in America at once, at every multiplex across the nation, it is probably a Hollywood film. If it is playing at one theater in selected large cities, it is probably an independent film. Because Hollywood films reach far wider audiences than do most independent films (much less avant-garde films or documentaries), it might be said that they have a greater ideological impact on American culture (and arguably, the world). And although Hollywood film is not as popular a medium as it once was (having been surpassed by television and even now competing with video games and the World Wide Web), Hollywood film remains a very powerful global influence. Indeed, most of the stylistic choices developed by the Hollywood studios during the first half of the twentieth century have strongly influenced the "rules" of how TV shows and computer games make meaning. As we hope to show, many of Hollywood's representational traditions have also carried over from its classical period to the present. The rest of this chapter examines how the style, business, and history of Hollywood have structured and continue to structure cinematic meaning, specifically the various meanings of race, class, gender, sexuality, and ability.

The Style of Hollywood Cinema

Over the first few decades of the twentieth century, Hollywood filmmakers developed a set of formal and stylistic conventions that came to be known as the **classical Hollywood style**. (Recall that film **form** refers to specific cinematic elements such as mise-en-scène and editing; the term **style** refers to a specific way in which those formal elements are arranged.) Classical Hollywood style is not rigid and absolute – slight variations can be found in countless Hollywood films – but this way of cinematically telling stories is basically the same today as it was in the 1930s. And because Hollywood's business practices have dominated both American and global cinema, classical Hollywood style is often considered the standard or "correct" way to make fictional films.

The main objective of classical Hollywood style is to "spoon feed" story information to the spectator, thus keeping everything clearly understood by the audience. Hollywood filmmakers believe that that if some plot point or stylistic maneuver is too different or challenging, the audience will become disoriented, dislike the movie, tell their friends not to see it, or even demand their money back. Classical Hollywood style is sometimes referred to as the **invisible style**, because it does not call attention to itself as even being a style. It permits the viewer to stay emotionally enmeshed in a film's story and characters, instead of being distracted by obvious formal devices (or thinking too much about the ideological meanings of the text). Indeed, when classical Hollywood style is working at its best, audiences are barely aware that any formal choices are being made at all: most untrained spectators don't consciously notice the lighting of the sets or the edits between shots. Obscuring the formal decisions not only keeps the viewer centered rather unthinkingly on following the story, but also limits the viewer's choice in what she or he is meant to find important. Say, for example, a film shows a white business tycoon praising American capitalism while his black butler brings him a mint julep. A viewer might be interested in learning the butler's reaction to the tycoon's statement. However, if the camera does not keep the butler in focus, or never cuts to show the butler's reaction, then it becomes impossible to see what his reaction might be. In helping to keep things understandable, Hollywood's invisible style subtly eliminates complexity, and in this example, implicitly makes the white tycoon more important than his butler.

All of the formal aspects of cinema under the classical Hollywood style work to keep the story clear and characters simple and understandable. Lighting, color, camera position, and other aspects of mise-en-scène consistently help the audience remain engaged with the story. The most important details are the ones most prominently lit, kept in focus, and framed in close-up shots. Hollywood films also employ various rules of **continuity editing**, a system of editing in which each shot follows easily and logically from the one before. If a person looks over at something, the next shot is of that something; if a person walks out of a room through a door, the next shot is of that same person coming through the door into a new room. Sound design in Hollywood films also keeps audiences aware of the story's key points, often by making the main characters' dialog louder than the noise of the crowd around them. And the Hollywood film score is there to tell an audience exactly how they are supposed to feel about any given scene.

Style is thus subordinated to story in classical Hollywood style. The way Hollywood films structure their stories is referred to as (**classical**) **Hollywood narrative form**. Hollywood stories usually have a **linear narrative** – they have a beginning, middle, and an end, and story events follow one another chronologically. (Flashbacks are an exception to this format, but they are always clearly marked – often with a shimmering dissolve – so as not to confuse the viewer.) Hollywood narrative form usually centers on a singular character or **protagonist**, commonly referred to as the hero. Sometimes the protagonist might be a family or a small group of people. The narrative is driven by carefully and clearly laying out the goals and desires of the protagonist – the desire to get home in *The Wizard of Oz* (1939) or to kill the shark in *Jaws* (1975). Obstacles to this desire are created, usually by a villainous force or person, called the **antagonist** (the wicked witch, the shark). Hollywood narrative also usually pairs the protagonist with a **love interest**, who either accompanies the main character in reaching the goal, or functions *as* the protagonist's goal.

The differences between heroes and villains in Hollywood film are obvious and simplified. Sometimes, as in old-fashioned Westerns, the good guys even wear white hats while the villains wear black. Even when dealing with complex social issues, Hollywood usually reduces them to matters of personal character: in Hollywood films there are rarely corrupt institutions, merely corrupt people. In seeking to make conflicts as basic and uncomplicated as possible, the antagonist is often "pure evil" and not the bearer of his or her own legitimate world view. Protagonists and antagonists are not the only ones simplified in a Hollywood film, as other roles are also represented by quickly understood stock characters such as the love interest, the best friend, or the comic relief. Such "instant characterization" often draws upon pre-existing social and cultural **stereotypes**. Some may seem benign, like villains wearing black. Others, like repeatedly casting Asians as mysterious mobsters, or Hispanics as gang members, can have vast effects on how those identified as Asian or Hispanic are treated outside the movie house.

In the linear design of Hollywood narrative form, each complication in the attempt to reach the protagonist's goal leads to yet another complication. These twists and turns escalate toward the **climax**, the most intense point of conflict, wherein the antagonist is defeated by the protagonist. In the final moments of the film, all the complications are resolved, and all questions that had been posed during the film are answered. This is known as **closure**. Hollywood's use of the **happy ending**, a specific form of closure, ties up all of the story's loose ends and frequently includes the protagonist and the love interest uniting as a romantic/sexual couple. Even when the couple is not together at the end of the film (as in *Titanic* [1997]), the narrative is designed to make that separation acceptable to the audience. In *Titanic*, the ending may be sad, but the mystery of the diamond necklace has been resolved, and the film suggests that Jack and Rose will reunite in heaven. Closure is a potent narrative tool in managing ideological conflict, because closure makes it seem as if all problems have been solved. Any actual ideological issues or social strife that may have been raised by a film are allegedly resolved by narrative closure, and thus there is no longer any need for spectators to think about them. Closure in Hollywood film tends to reaffirm the status quo of American society.

Since the ideological status quo of American society is **white patriarchal capitalism**, it should come as no surprise that most Hollywood films (throughout its history and still today) encode white patriarchal capitalism as central and desirable via both Hollywood narrative form and the invisible style. First, the protagonist of most Hollywood films is constructed as a straight white male seeking wealth or power. He emerges victorious at the end of the film, proving his inherent superiority over those who challenged him. In consistently drawing audience attention to and celebrating his acts, the invisible style reinforces his "natural" abilities while not allowing the audience to think about the often far-fetched qualities of those heroics. Since the white male commands the most narrative attention, the (usually white) female love interest is relegated to a minor or supporting part. Whereas the male is defined by his actions, job, and/or principles, the heroine is defined chiefly by her beauty and/or sex appeal. Their romance affirms patriarchal heterosexuality as well as the desirability of same-race coupling. If homosexuals, people of color, or disabled people appear in the film at all, they might be associated with the villains or relegated to smaller supporting parts, in effect supporting the dominance of the white male hero and his female love interest.

Imagine any of the "Indiana Jones" movies as typical of this formula. Our hero or protagonist, Professor Jones, is a straight white man of charm, wit, intelligence, and social standing. He is opposed by evil male super-criminals or antagonists who are out to destroy or dominate the world. Frequently the villain is from another country or is non-white: in *Indiana Jones and the Temple of Doom* (1984), Professor Jones must first battle double-crossing Asian gangsters and then face off against a corrupt cult of Indians who enslave children and practice human sacrifice. Good and evil are thus reduced to simplified and racialized stereotypes: white male hero versus villains of color. In this particular film, Professor Jones is accompanied on his adventures by a small Asian boy who idolizes him, and a dizzy blonde heroine whose screaming distress is meant to be a running gag throughout the film. The film proceeds in a linear manner through a series of exciting twists and turns (action-filled set pieces) until the climax, when Jones saves the woman and the child, destroys the Indian temple, and restores harmony to the land. The closure of the film sets up a symbolic nuclear family, with white man as heroic patriarch, woman as helpmate and romantic/sexual object, and the Third World quite literally represented as a child under their protection. Among the film's basic ideological messages are that straight white men can do anything, that women are hysterical nuisances, and that non-white people are either evil or childlike.

But haven't Hollywood representations of women and minorities changed over the years? Haven't the formulas been adapted to be less sexist and racist? Yes and no. There are now Hollywood films made in which the hero is not white, not male, or (more recently) not heterosexual. And Hollywood has always made a type of film that features female protagonists, the so-called **woman's film** (discussed more fully in later chapters), but these stories usually emphasize the female character's desire for a man, and thus reinforce patriarchy in their own way. It is true that black and Hispanic actors in Hollywood have made gains in the last few decades and now regularly play the hero part in many movies every year. Occasionally there will even be a female action hero as well. But even then, these are hegemonic negotiations within the dominant white patriarchal ideology and not inversions of it: most African American protagonists are still male, and most female protagonists are still white. The very few homosexual protagonists in recent Hollywood film are usually male *and* white. On the rare occasions when a Hollywood film centers on a deaf, blind, or otherwise differently abled protagonist, he or she is usually white (and invariably played by an actor without said disability). While the real world is comprised of people of all different races, genders, classes, sexualities, and physical abilities, the world depicted in Hollywood film usually posits straight white men as central and heroic, and everyone else as peripheral (or even non-existent).

The drive for simplicity and obviousness in the classical Hollywood style has other implications for Hollywood narrative form. Not only are Hollywood storylines

In *Indiana Jones and the Temple of Doom* (1984), the white male hero protects both his white love interest and Third World children from the villainy of an evil Asian cult. In this still, he is figured as a symbolic father of all the other characters.
Indiana Jones and the Temple of Doom, copyright © 1984, Paramount

excessively linear, using simplified stock characters engaged in clear-cut struggles ending in closure, but Hollywood often consciously reuses popular (that is, already understood) storylines and characters. The proliferation of remakes and sequels guarantees that most audiences are already familiar with many main characters and basic narrative situations. The *Nightmare on Elm Street* films, for example, rely on audience knowledge not only of the previous films in the series, but also of the specific formal elements that go into making a scary movie. Many Hollywood films are thus identifiable by their **genre**, a term that this book uses to refer to a specific type of fictional Hollywood film such as the horror film, the Western, the war movie, the musical, or the gangster film. As will be explored in future chapters, racial and ethnic markers are activated within genres in unique and interesting ways. For example, Italian Americans (and more recently African Americans) have been closely tied to the gangster film, while the representation of Native Americans in Hollywood film is almost exclusively tied to the Western.

A genre can be identified by its surface structure or **iconography** – what the genre looks and sounds like. (The iconography of the **horror film** might include monsters and mad scientists, blood and gore, dark woods at night, screams, and so forth.) Genres can also be defined by their deeper ideological concerns, sometimes referred to as their **thematic myth.** Genres are popular with audiences when these thematic myths in some way relate to current social concerns, and as such, genres function as a sort of feedback loop between filmgoers and filmmakers. Certain genres make money and flourish when their specific thematic myth correlates to something the public is interested in or wants (or needs) to see dramatized. Other genres "die" when their thematic myths are no longer thought valid within the ever-changing spheres of history and culture. For example, the musical was once a staple of Hollywood filmmaking, but it grew generally unpopular after the 1960s. Today, the public rarely accepts the genre's convention of characters spontaneously breaking into song and dance, and our cynical age sees their usual, simple thematic messages of love and harmony as outmoded.

Thus, the popularity (or unpopularity) of certain genres can tell the film historian interesting things about the culture that produced them. Genre films reflect social concerns, but only rarely do they challenge the underlying ideological biases of Hollywood narrative form itself. (Most genre films, being Hollywood films, still feature straight white male protagonists, while women and people of color are relegated to peripheral roles.) Rather, popular Hollywood genres often attempt to shore up the dominant ideology by repeating over and over again certain types of stories that seem to resolve social tensions. For example, the horror film's emphasis on the threat posed to "normality" by the monstrous reinforces social ideas about what is considered normal. Not surprisingly, in classical Hollywood horror films, "normality" is conventionally represented by middle-to-upper-class, white, heterosexual couples and patriarchal institutions. Monsters and villains, on the other hand, are often coded as non-white, non-patriarchal, and/or non-capitalist. In many cases, they even have physical "abnormalities" that are meant to symbolize or enhance their deviance.

The Business of Hollywood

By examining the structure of Hollywood filmmaking, and exploring when and why certain films were popular with American audiences, one can gain insight into the changing ideological currents of twentieth- and early twenty-first-century America. Yet one must also take into consideration the specific economic and industrial conditions that determine how Hollywood produces its films. Indeed, Hollywood must be understood not just as a set of formal and stylistic structures, but also as an industry that produces certain types of fictional films *for profit*. As such, Hollywood is an excellent example of capitalism at work. Hollywood companies make and sell films that they think people want to see (that is, films that in some way reflect the dominant ideology), and Hollywood's business practices use every tool at their disposal to lessen competition, increase buyer demand, and reduce the cost of production. Though Hollywood films are sometimes discussed as "art" by critics and some filmmakers, a Hollywood film's merit is chiefly judged by its box office revenues. Even when awards are given for artistic achievement, these too are drawn into a film's economic evaluation – winning a Best Picture Oscar will boost a film's profits.

Since the earliest days of cinema, film as an industry has been divided into three main components: **production, distribution,** and **exhibition. Production** involves the actual making of a film: the financing, writing, shooting, editing, etc. **Distribution** refers to the shipping of copies (or prints) of the finished film to various theaters. The theaters where the film is actually projected to audiences make up the third arm, or **exhibition.** More recently, cable television sales, video-cassette and DVD rentals, etc. also comprise film exhibition. Hollywood producers have always been highly dependent upon the distribution and exhibition arms of the business: no matter how many films you make, or how high-quality they are, if no one ships them or shows them, then they cannot make any money. Hollywood companies have thus consistently worked to maintain close ties with distribution networks and theaters. One method of doing this is called **vertical integration**, in which one parent company oversees the business of all three branches. This was the strategy adopted by the major studios in the first half of the twentieth century, and it helped to ensure that American theaters were almost exclusively dominated by Hollywood film during that period.

Another strategy that helped Hollywood come to dominate the US film industry was the creation of an **oligopoly**, a state of business affairs in which a few companies control an entire industry. (An oligopoly is thus very similar to a **monopoly**, wherein *one* company controls an entire industry.) In an oligopoly, several large companies agree to work together, keeping potential competitors weak or driving them out of business altogether. In the case of film in America, the Hollywood oligopolies worked throughout the twentieth century, and continue to work, to keep foreign and independent American films marginalized. This has had a specific effect on minority filmmakers. Excluded from the Hollywood studios, independent films made by non-white, non-patriarchal, and/or non-capitalist people often had trouble being distributed and exhibited. Furthermore, Hollywood's control of production, distribution, and exhibition has not been limited to the United States alone. Motion pictures have been one of America's leading exports for almost a century, and Hollywood maximizes its profits by distributing its films globally. Since Hollywood films usually make back their cost during domestic release, most of the money earned from foreign exhibition is pure profit. Consequently, Hollywood films can offer foreign theater owners their films at a discount – a price calculatedly lower than the cost of films made locally in their native country. This makes it very difficult for other countries to support their own film industries.

As such, the Hollywood system is an example not just of industrial capitalism but also of **cultural imperialism**, the promotion and imposition of ideals and ideologies throughout the world via cultural means. **Imperialism** means one country dominating another through force and economic control, but in cultural imperialism, one nation doesn't conquer another with force, but rather overwhelms it with cultural products and the ideologies contained within them. People around the world are inundated with American ways of viewing life when they go to the movies, and often they have little or no access to films made by people of their own nationality. Furthermore, since Hollywood films dominate the world, Hollywood *style* tends to define film practice for all filmmakers around the world, since Hollywood style is what most people are accustomed to seeing and understanding. Many filmmakers in other countries, having grown up themselves watching Hollywood films, make pictures that duplicate the Hollywood style, again reinforcing its dominance.

As the following history hopes to show, various restructurings of Hollywood's business practices have affected the ability of other types of films (and their different representations of race, class, gender, sexuality, and ability) to get made and to find audiences. Yet, although new technologies and legal decisions have occasionally challenged and disrupted the business strategies of the Hollywood oligopoly, its dominance has not changed very much in 80 years or so. Most of the major companies that founded the Hollywood industry are still around: Paramount, Warner Brothers, 20th Century-Fox, Universal, Columbia. If anything, these companies have grown stronger and more diversified. The main purpose of Hollywood's business practices – to keep profits high and inhibit competition by maintaining centralized control over the industry – has been upheld. Hollywood film, with its formulas and genres that uphold white patriarchal capitalism, affects not just people in America, but people around the globe.

The History of Hollywood: The Movies Begin

The United States did not always dominate the international film industry, and a number of people around the globe could arguably take credit for inventing motion pictures at the end of the nineteenth century. In America, **Thomas Edison**'s company first demonstrated moving images in 1894 through a mechanical peep-hole device, the **kinetoscope**. In France, the **Lumière Brothers** first projected their moving pictures upon a screen in 1895, giving birth to cinema as a shared social phenomenon for paying audiences. The Lumières' method of exhibition soon became the standard worldwide, and French filmmakers often led the way in cinema's early years. French film companies such as Pathé became the first to accomplish vertical integration, long before the Hollywood studios even existed.

The first movies were short travelogs, documentaries, and "trick" films shown at traveling tent shows and vaudeville theaters. As the novelty of seeing photographs brought to life faded, filmmakers moved to telling fictional stories, first in one-reel shorts (which lasted about 5–10 minutes) and then in two-reel and four-reel short features. Films grew so popular that a wave of **nickelodeons**, small store-front theaters devoted solely to showing films, opened their doors across the United States. During this period, American filmmakers began refining the methods of storytelling, methods that eventually became Hollywood's invisible style. Since films were silent during this period, filmmakers had to learn how to emphasize key nar-

Arcades filled with Thomas Edison's Kinetoscopes, such as this one in New York City, were a popular early space for exhibiting motion pictures. Courtesy of the Museum of the City of New York, The Byron Collection

rative points without the use of sound. Often this involved exaggerated gestures by the actors, but filmmakers also learned how to communicate through the choice of camera placement, lighting, focus, and editing. Simultaneously, audiences learned and accepted what these choices meant. By the 1910s, fictional films that told melodramatic or sensationalistic stories over the course of one of more hours were becoming the norm.

In the United States, Hollywood was incorporated as a town in 1911 and, for a number of reasons, quickly became the center for the nation's film production. Southern California provided almost year-round sunny weather (needed to illuminate early cinematography). The diversity of terrain in and around Los Angeles (beaches, mountains, forests, and deserts) allowed many different locations for filming. In the 1910s, Los Angeles was still a relatively small town and film companies could buy land cheaply to build their mammoth studios. Growing unionization in all US industries had not made a significant impact in Los Angeles yet, and the availability of cheap labor also drew filmmakers to Hollywood. These pioneering filmmakers were also seeking an escape from Thomas Edison's east-coast patent lawyers, who wanted them to pay royalties.

When American film was still a small cottage industry, individuals from various minority groups had more opportunity to move into the business. While a consortium of **WASP** (White Anglo-Saxon Protestant) males and their lawyers were trying to control the American film industry, women and some racial/ethnic minorities were able to carve out a niche. Many pioneering Hollywood film businesses

The Comet Theatre in New York City was a typical nickelodeon; note the price of admission and the various short films advertised.
Courtesy of the Quigley Photographic Archive, Georgetown University Library

were started by recent European Jewish immigrants such as Samuel Goldwyn, Adolph Zukor, and Carl Laemmle. However, as film in America became a bigger and bigger business, more controlled by companies rather than individuals, the opportunities for minorities behind the camera dwindled. Laemmle, Zukor, and others of Jewish descent were able to maintain their power, but people of color were rarely permitted any creative control behind the scenes in Hollywood. Increasingly, the producing and directing of motion pictures was regarded as man's work, and women were pushed aside. American women did not even have the right to vote prior to 1920, and non-white people were rarely permitted into white social spheres or business concerns during these decades.

During the 1910s, cinema was commonly regarded in the United States as entertainment for immigrants and the working class. Some middle-to-upper-class white Americans felt that cinema was potentially a disturbing social institution that

This interior shot of the Majestic Theatre shows the size and opulence of a typical movie palace. Courtesy of the Quigley Photographic Archive, Georgetown University Library

promoted "dangerous" ideas to the lower classes, and thus many local and state censorship boards began to monitor the content of films. (In 1915, the Supreme Court ruled that cinema was not an art form protected as free speech, but simply a business and therefore open to regulation.) The film industry thus felt pressure to become more "respectable," a euphemism for affirming the social ideals of the era's white patriarchy. The industry also wanted to capture the more lucrative middle-class audience. One of the ways it did this was by replacing nickelodeons with opulent theaters known as **movie palaces**. It was not unusual for movie palaces to have marble foyers, crystal chandeliers, and curtained boxes. Able to seat thousands of patrons at once, the palaces helped elevate the cultural status of film to something closer to that of live theater.

During the 1910s and 1920s, studios also developed the concept of the **movie star** (an actor or actress the public recognizes and likes), realizing that a star's fans would pay to see any of the star's films. Stars are thus used to sell films, giving them a kind of brand-name appeal. Often stars were (and still are) associated with a specific type of role or a stereotypical **persona.** **Charlie Chaplin**'s beloved "Little Tramp" character was a poor but optimistic everyman figure, while **Lillian Gish** and **Mary Pickford** usually played helpless ingénues, dependent upon swashbuckling heroes like Douglas Fairbanks to save them. In this way, the Hollywood star system (in conjunction with the form of Hollywood narrative itself) endorsed middle-class American values of strong active men and passive women, heterosexual romance, and the centrality of **whiteness.** At its most basic level, the star system is a caste system, creating a class of individuals who supposedly shine brighter than the rest of us, and, as the word "star" suggests, glitter in the night sky *above* us. Indeed, the terms "movie god," "movie goddess," and "Hollywood royalty" have been part of the Hollywood publicity machine for many years. The star system thus elevates some human beings above others, and constructs specific ideals of beauty, appropriate gender behavior, skin color, class, sexuality, and so forth.

The Classical Hollywood Cinema

By the 1920s (sometimes known as the Golden Age of Silent Cinema), Hollywood had streamlined its production, distribution, and exhibition practices, and was regularly exhibiting its opulent entertainments in lush movie palaces attended by middle- and upper-class patrons. In 1927, sound was added to the silent movie, and by the 1930s, Hollywood had entered what many historians now call its classical phase. During this period of **classical Hollywood cinema** (roughly the 1930s to the 1950s), Hollywood developed a standardized product that employed classical Hollywood narrative form and the invisible style. Film production occurred mostly under the oligopolistic control of eight Hollywood companies. The so-called **Big 5** or the **major studios** (Warner Brothers, Metro-Goldwyn-Mayer [MGM], 20th Century-Fox, RKO, and Paramount) were each vertically integrated, while the **Little 3** or **minor studios** (Columbia, Universal, and United Artists) did not own their own theaters and had fewer assets with which to produce the lush expensive movies for which the Big 5 were famous. At the bottom of the economic ladder in Hollywood were the **Poverty Row studios** (such as Monogram, Mascot, and Producers Releasing Corporation), studios that made cheap genre films and serials that were often used by exhibitors to fill out the second half of a double feature.

Most of these Hollywood companies were centralized around their own production facilities, referred to as **movie studios.** A Hollywood movie studio housed any number of large sound stages, on which sets could be built and torn down as needed, so that multiple films could be shot simultaneously. Most studios included a number of permanent (or standing) sets, such as a Western town, an urban street, a European village, a jungle, etc., that could be used repeatedly in different films. The studios also had large lists of actors, directors, camera operators, editors, screenwriters, musicians, costumers, set designers, and makeup artists under contract.

During Hollywood's classical era, the studios (such as Metro-Goldwyn-Mayer) were huge industrial complexes that filled several city blocks.
Unidentified publicity photo, authors' personal collection

Studios also employed janitors, bookkeepers, electricians, carpenters, and security guards. The major Hollywood studios even had commissaries, hospitals, and their own fire departments. Without exception, white men held most of the creative and executive positions at the studios, while people of color and women – if they were hired at all – were usually relegated to manual labor or assistant-type jobs.

The **studio system** of motion picture production increasingly forced workers to specialize in certain areas. While early filmmakers did multiple tasks (wrote the scripts, directed the actors, worked the camera, and edited the film), classical Hollywood movie studios divided these jobs into various departments. This kept any individual, other than the (straight, white, male) heads of the studios themselves, from having too much control over the films being made, and it streamlined the filmmaking process. Much like Henry Ford's assembly-line production of automobiles, studio employees figuratively stood at certain places on a filmmaking conveyor belt, contributing their own small area of expertise to the product as it rolled smoothly down the line toward completion. During its classical period, the Hollywood industry produced about 500 films a year, or about a film per week per studio. (Today's Hollywood output is considerably less, usually under 200 films per year.)

Some American movies were made independently of these companies during the classical period, but it was difficult to get these films distributed or exhibited without making a deal with one of the major Hollywood studios. Smaller independent filmmaking companies that produced Hollywood-type films (examples of which would include the Walt Disney Company and the Samuel Goldwyn Company) often distributed their work through one of the Big 5 or Little 3. Other independent filmmakers produced work that the Hollywood majors had little interest in distributing. For example, independently produced films starring African Americans or all-Yiddish casts were produced during Hollywood's classical period, but these films never reached wide audiences outside of specific ethnic movie houses. For many years these films were ignored or dismissed by film historians, but in the last 30 years or so, film scholars have begun to study them in more detail. One thing that is immediately apparent about many of these independent films is that they allowed people of color to be in control behind the camera, representing issues of race, class, gender, sexuality, and ability in different ways than did Hollywood.

The studio system was established to minimize costs and reduce possible financial liabilities – and the risk of financial ruin ran high during the **Great Depression** (1929 until the start of World War II). Hollywood maintained profitability in the first few years after the stock market collapsed through audience interest in the new sound technology. But by 1932, all of the major studios had begun to feel the effects of the country's economic despair. Ticket sales began to dwindle, and by 1933 every studio (except powerhouse MGM) had run into debt. Some studios even went into receivership or declared bankruptcy. Employee rosters were reduced, and those that remained faced slashed salaries. Most of those let go occupied the lowest rungs on the studio ladder – positions largely held by women and people of color – and most of these studio employees had no unions to bargain for them.

One of the methods Hollywood used to woo potential customers back into the theaters was to emphasize lurid stories that promised increased violence and sexual titillation, even in the face of local and state censorship campaigns. The studios worked to forestall any federal censorship by asserting that the industry could police itself. In the 1920s, Hollywood moguls appointed former postmaster general **Will Hays** to head an in-house association to oversee the content of Hollywood films. In 1930, the studios officially adopted the Hollywood **Production Code**, written by a Jesuit priest and a Catholic layman, as a list of what could and could not be depicted in Hollywood movies. Not only were overtly political themes and acts of graphic violence to be censored, but issues of sex and sexuality in the movies were strictly monitored. For example, the Code outlawed the depiction or discussion of homosexuality and forbade **miscegenation** – the romantic or sexual coupling of people from different races. (The Production Code is a good example of how discrimination can become institutionalized, embedded within a corporate or bureaucratic structure.) Yet, as it existed in the first years of the Depression, the Production Code had no way to enforce its rules, and studios willfully disregarded its pronouncements when box office returns slid. Gangster films, horror films, and stories of "fallen women" proliferated, providing not only large doses of sex and violence, but also a cynical, pessimistic view of America and, to some degree, a critique of capitalist ideology.

In 1933, coinciding with Roosevelt's inauguration and a general turn toward optimism in US society, the Catholic Church and other groups renewed their protests against Hollywood films. Facing boycotts and more urgent calls for federal censorship, the Production Code was revised in 1934 to include a **Seal of Approval** that would be given only to those films deemed acceptable. Hollywood companies agreed only to show films in their theaters that had the Seal of Approval attached (or face a large fine), and thus the industry became self-censoring. This was also a new way of denying exhibition to other types of films, further consolidating Hollywood's oligopoly. As a result, Hollywood films became a dependable source of escapist fantasy through the rest of the Depression and into World War II. While some films of the 1930s did acknowledge contemporary issues of poverty and unemployment, more regularly Depression-era Hollywood films showcased the lifestyles of the rich and beautiful (as in the Fred Astaire and Ginger Rogers musicals). Anything too political (such as race relations, class division, or women's rights) was not allowed to be discussed in a Hollywood film. Most women were depicted as asexual wives and mothers, people of color were consistently marginalized as stereotypical servants, and homosexuals officially disappeared from the movies altogether.

World War II and Postwar Film

World War II substantially upended the day-to-day life of almost every American citizen. Many men entered military service, while women contributed to the war effort by entering the home front workforce. Although unemployment was practically non-existent, Americans could spend their paychecks on very little due to war rationing. The movies benefited as a result, and Hollywood studios made considerable sums during the war years. Hollywood continued to provide escapism, but also made films supporting the war effort (despite the Production Code's prohibitions on political themes). The **war movie** as a genre reached its classical apex during these years, thematically promoting American unity in the face of our enemies' aggressions. Often these films showed members of different ethnic groups or racial backgrounds overcoming their differences and learning to work together as a unit. On the other hand, Hollywood war films often featured grotesque stereotypes of Japanese enemies.

When World War II ended, many American citizens continued to fight for social causes. Groups began campaigning more vocally for African American civil rights, and some homosexuals began to organize as well. Hollywood made a number of films in the late 1940s that addressed various social issues. These **social problem films** explored topics previously considered taboo or financially risky, and a few of them even dared to examine racism, anti-Semitism, and the plight of disabled war veterans. In addition to the social problem films, audiences watched stories of frustration and corruption told in a number of dark mysteries and thrillers.

John Garfield was a popular Hollywood actor whose career was destroyed by the Red Scare; he suffered a heart attack and died in 1952. Unidentified publicity photo, authors' personal collection

Termed **film noir** by French film critics, these films questioned the ideals of American capitalism that citizens had just been fighting to preserve. Film noir also expressed the social and personal tensions between men and women in the postwar period, tensions that had been created by women's wartime independence versus the postwar patriarchy's need to make them once again subservient to men.

Turning back the calendar on women's roles after the war exemplified a general reactionary trend in American society as the 1940s ended. Following World War II, America found itself in a **Cold War** of espionage with the Soviet Union, and began to fight communism abroad in actions both open and covert. The resultant **Red Scare**, a term that refers to the hysteria about possible communist infiltration that swept America at this time, caused immense changes to American film practice in the postwar years. The congressional committee known as **HUAC** (the **House Un-American Activities Committee**) investigated allegations of communist infiltration in various American industries and institutions. In 1947, HUAC came to Hollywood, and charged that leftist and communist filmmakers were instilling anti-American messages into their films. The owners of the Hollywood companies quickly closed ranks and offered up sacrificial victims to the committee. The **Hollywood Ten**, as these people became known, refused to answer the committee's questions, and most of them served time in prison. Soon, studios were making employees sign loyalty oaths, and **blacklists** (rosters of people who were to be considered unemployable because of their political beliefs) were circulated throughout the industry. Careers were ruined and in many cases lives were destroyed. Other people under investigation recanted their former political beliefs and were readmitted to the industry.

In retrospect, the people targeted by HUAC during these years were disproportionately Jewish, homosexual, non-white, or people struggling to organize the working classes – in other words, people who were legitimately critiquing the elitism of the white patriarchal capitalist ruling class. The heads of the studios used the Red Scare to weaken the power of labor unions in Hollywood, since unionizing seemed dangerously close to communism in those trying times. (A number of other industries also used this gambit against unions.) This type of communist "red baiting" came to an unofficial end around 1954 when Senator Joseph McCarthy (one of the leading alarmists who had used the Red Scare for his own political gain) was discredited and censured by Congress, after he alleged that the US Army itself was infiltrated by communists. Yet the blacklists that had been created in Hollywood and many other industries lingered well into the 1960s.

Partly in response to the Red Scare, mainstream American culture throughout the 1950s stressed conformity to white patriarchal capitalist ideals, under the assumption that even discussing cultural difference or social inequity would be misconstrued as un-American. Hollywood filmmakers deliberately avoided making films that might be understood as in any way critical of American foreign or domestic policy. Social problem films and film noir dried up as filmmakers became afraid that such movies could get them fired and/or blacklisted. Musicals, melodramas, lush historical romances, and Biblical epics became the mainstay of 1950s Hollywood film production, as these genres were felt to be safe and apolitical. The 1950s is often spoken about nostalgically as a time when people migrated to crime-free suburbs to raise perfect nuclear families. Yet underneath that facade lay ugly reminders of social inequity that many people choose to forget. Many of those perfect neighborhoods were zoned to keep out blacks and/or Jews, women often chafed under the restrictions placed on them, and gay and lesbian people could be arrested and fired from their jobs for merely meeting in a bar.

The Red Scare was not the only problem facing the Hollywood studios after the war. Postwar migration to the suburbs took customers away from urban areas where film theaters were located, and many preferred to stay home with their new television sets rather than drive to the movies. By 1960, about 90 percent of all American homes had TV. In an attempt to hold onto its audience, Hollywood responded with expansive technologies that TV did not have – widescreen formats, stereo sound, and color, as well as novelty techniques such as 3-D. Even more dire, the Supreme Court declared in 1948 that the Hollywood industry *had* formed an illegal and oligopolistic business trust. The **Paramount Consent Decrees** (as the rulings became known) forced the Hollywood studios to dismantle their vertical integration throughout the 1950s. Hollywood companies chose to sell off their exhibition outlets as a way of complying with this decision. However, without guaranteed theaters to show their films, and with the loss of filmgoers to TV, the Hollywood studios were again forced to cut back production and whittle down their employee rosters. Many stars, directors, and writers became independent agents, no longer tied to one particular studio. This development, along with theaters that were now free to book non-studio-produced films, encouraged more independent filmmaking, even as the political climate of the 1950s did not exactly encourage independent thinking.

While Hollywood filmmakers aimed for a broad appeal that would offend no one, some independent filmmakers slowly ventured into less-traveled territories. Rather than trying to sell films to everyone, many independent filmmakers aimed at smaller, specialized sections of the audience – teenagers, intellectuals, the socially concerned. Independent filmmakers learned that their films might alienate some customers, but would draw in others eager to see something more complex than the usual Hollywood fare. The Supreme Court had reversed itself in 1952 and declared that film was indeed an art form guaranteed protection under the First Amendment, and thus independent filmmakers began to deal with topics considered taboo by the Production Code, such as miscegenation or homosexuality. Yet most independent films during this period (and the Hollywood studio films that sought to imitate them) raised these topics only to uphold traditional beliefs.

More forthright explorations of mid-century social issues were to be found in other art forms and movements. Poets and artists who comprised the **Beat**

movement criticized American class consciousness and sexual hypocrisy. The **civil rights movement**, fighting for equal rights for African Americans, burgeoned throughout the 1950s and eventually became more vocal, militant, and successful. By the 1960s, Native Americans, Hispanics, women, and homosexuals were also protesting for their civil rights. Many of these movements were closely linked to protests against American military involvement in Vietnam, and all of these movements were connected by a larger youth movement that openly challenged the conformity of the 1950s. The term **counterculture** is often used to describe this broad patchwork coalition of leftists, liberals, and libertarians who wanted to increase freedom for all members of society and bring an end to what they felt was an unjust war. "Sex, drugs, and rock and roll" became a mantra of this new social force. Since the personal was equated with the more broadly political, it was felt that social freedoms could be increased by expanding personal freedoms and vice versa.

Hollywood had a difficult time dealing with the social changes of the 1960s. Many younger Americans, people of color, and women began to reject the stereotypes and simplistic formulas of Hollywood films, and turned instead to independent, foreign, and avant-garde films (both as audiences and as filmmakers). As a result, by the end of the decade, several of the Hollywood majors were again on the verge of bankruptcy. As part of these financial shake-ups, most of the major studios were being bought out by larger non-filmic corporations such as Gulf and Western (absorbing Paramount) and Kinney (absorbing Warner Brothers). These new corporate managers were desperate to make Hollywood profitable once again, and they began to experiment with different sorts of movies and film styles in an attempt to address the counterculture's concerns. Slowly, a few women and African American men began gaining a small degree of power in Hollywood. The studios began targeting specific sections of the population, most notably in what came to be known as **blaxploitation films** – cheaply made genre pictures that featured African American protagonists. However, still being Hollywood films, most of them failed to address in any significant way the deeper political issues of 1960s America.

"New" Hollywood and the Blockbuster Mentality

During this same period (the late 1960s and early 1970s), in yet another effort to tap into the interests of younger audiences, studios began to hire a new generation of filmmakers who had learned their craft in the growing number of film departments in American universities. Mostly white, male, and heterosexual, these so-called **Film School Brats** (including George Lucas, Steven Spielberg, Martin Scorsese, and Francis Ford Coppola) reinvigorated the Hollywood industry throughout the 1970s and 1980s. Having studied film as an art, this new generation made films that reflected their knowledge of Hollywood (and global) film history. The Film School Brats revamped traditional genre formulas that had worked during Hollywood's classical period, spicing them up with liberal doses of sex and violence, now that the Production Code had been replaced by the **Ratings System** in the late 1960s. (The ratings system restricted audiences rather than filmmakers.) Genre films that criticized or deconstructed American myths, which had been briefly popular with the counterculture, were now supplanted by genre films that reinscribed traditional form and ideology in a nostalgic fashion. In most of these films, women were once again cast as princesses, people of color appeared as villains or helpers, and conventionally strong white men remained the central heroes. This type of film, sometimes called the **nostalgic Hollywood blockbuster**, still drives the Hollywood industry today. *Indiana Jones and the Temple of Doom*, discussed earlier in this chapter, is an excellent example of a nostalgic Hollywood blockbuster, and that particular franchise (with all of its outdated ideologies about race and gender) continues to thrive: *Indiana Jones and the Kingdom of the Crystal Skull* (2008) is its most recent incarnation.

Today, most of these Hollywood blockbusters are shrewdly calculated remakes and recyclings of what has worked (that is, made money) in the past. They are designed according to marketplace research, and work not to raise questions or explore social issues but to maintain the ideological status quo. They are usually **pre-sold** (they have name recognition from a previous incarnation as TV show, novel, comic book, etc.), and are considered **high concept** (they have a story that can be reduced to simple phrases and tag-lines). Today's blockbusters are sold via **saturation advertising** and **saturation booking**, which means that the country is blanketed with ads for a film for weeks before it opens in thousands of theaters at once. The concept of **synergy** also drives current Hollywood production, wherein the film acts as an advertisement for other related products (and vice versa) – CDs of music, movie novelizations, behind-the-scenes mini-features, magazine specials, comic books, websites,

Rocky (1976) is a good example of the nostalgic Hollywood blockbuster, a type of film that uses classical Hollywood formulas to reinscribe traditional concepts of race, class, gender, and sexuality.
Rocky, copyright © 1976, United Artists

fast food franchises, posters, toys, games, action figures, theme park rides, clothes, and other assorted collectibles. All of this media saturation convinces filmgoers of these films' alleged importance. Independent films, which tend to offer the viewpoints of various marginalized groups, are frequently lost in the media flurry surrounding the more formulaic Hollywood output, films that still tend to center on white patriarchal capitalist ideals.

This situation is the result of the increasingly occurring merger of media companies into **corporate conglomerates**, large multinational businesses that control multiple aspects of the entertainment industry. Today, the same seven or eight giant media corporations that make Hollywood movies (including Disney, Time-Warner-AOL, News Corp.-20th Century-Fox, Viacom-Paramount, Sony-Tristar-Columbia, NBC-Universal) also make and distribute the world's books, CDs, newspapers, magazines, and TV shows. They are the same global corporations that own theme parks, sports teams, TV channels, cable TV distributors, video and DVD

Most contemporary Hollywood films are screened at multiplex theatres, such as this one, the Cinemark 17 in Dallas, Texas.
Authors' private collection

rental companies, and many of the chains of movie theaters. This is a new type of corporate oligopoly, since these global conglomerates control almost all of the world's mass media. It is thus increasingly difficult for truly independent filmmakers to have their work screened within mainstream cinematic outlets, which are for the most part controlled by these multimedia corporate conglomerates.

Independent filmmaking *did* flourish briefly in the 1980s and 1990s, because of the developing technologies of home video and cable TV, which desperately needed scores of films to fill program schedules and video-store shelves. A large number of the independent films of this period dealt with race, class, gender, sexuality, and ability in new and important ways. Some of this was a result of the *newest* generation of film-school graduates, a group that now included women and people of color, partly because of affirmative action legislation. A number of openly lesbian and gay filmmakers also found opportunities in independent filmmaking at this time. The success of some of these filmmakers has led Hollywood conglomerates to hire and promote more women, people of color, open homosexuals, and disabled people, and to make a few films not focused on white heterosexual males and their adventures. By the mid-1990s, however, many of the smaller independent film distributors were either driven out of business or absorbed by the major Hollywood corporations. For example, in the 1990s, Miramax was absorbed by Disney, and New Line Cinema became a part of the Time-Warner corporation, which was itself acquired by the Internet company America On Line in 2001. Today it is not unusual for the major Hollywood corporations to release "independent" films made or distributed by their own "boutique" subsidiaries, such as Focus Features (owned by Universal) or Fox Searchlight (a division of 20th Century-Fox), further blurring the line between what is considered an independent or a Hollywood film.

The merger of Time-Warner with AOL highlights the growth of even newer methods of distributing motion pictures as downloads to computers, cell phones, and iPods. Many in the industry are worried about a rise in media piracy from illegal DVD copies or file sharing – particularly as their product is handled outside the United States, where copyright laws (and their enforcement) are not always the same. In addition to numerous lawsuits and raids, public relations campaigns in the early years of the new millennium have tried to convince consumers that media piracy takes jobs and money away from the average film worker (the stunt driver, the carpenter, the electrician). Yet the money coming from these new modes of delivery goes almost exclusively to the producers and company executives. The Writers Guild strike of 2007–8 was largely about trying to get a more equitable share of this new revenue. (The Directors and Actors Guilds have also had to bargain hard with the studios over this issue.)

In corporate Hollywood today, billions of dollars are at stake and, while the industry may be on the cutting edge of technology, Hollywood films rarely seek to make radical *aesthetic* innovations or challenge pre-existing ideas. They adhere to decades-old formulas and genres that for the most part uphold the centrality of white patriarchal capitalism. Hollywood narrative form and the invisible style remain similar to what they were during the classical years. Although Hollywood's distribution and exhibition venues have changed a great deal, the basic economic goals of the Hollywood industry are still in place: to maintain tight control on the market in order to minimize risk and maximize profit. Hollywood's corporate dominance keeps smaller, independent films – those more regularly made by minority group filmmakers and/or containing subcultural themes and issues – marginalized.

Questions for Discussion

1 What types of movies do you prefer to watch? Are there art-house or independent theaters close to you, or many miles away? What types of films does your local video store stock? Are you ever bothered by the lack of diversity in local video stores or multiplex theaters?

2 Pick a few current Hollywood releases and see if they fit into the structure of classical Hollywood narrative form. How are concepts of race, class, gender, sexuality, and ability positioned by your chosen films?

3 Can you name some examples of synergy (cross-marketing) associated with recent nostalgic Hollywood blockbusters?

Further Reading

Balio, Tino, ed. *The American Film Industry*. Madison: University of Wisconsin Press, 1985.

Bordwell, David, Janet Staiger, and Kristin Thompson. *The Classical Hollywood Cinema*. New York: Columbia University Press, 1985.

Grainge, Paul. *Brand Hollywood: Selling Entertainment in a Global Media Age*. London and New York: Routledge, 2008.

Kramer, Peter. *The New Hollywood: From* Bonnie and Clyde *to* Star Wars. London and New York: Wallflower Press, 2005.

Lewis, Jon, ed. *The New American Cinema*. Durham: Duke University Press, 1998.

Neale, Steve and Murray Smith. *Contemporary Hollywood Cinema*. New York: Routledge, 1998.

Structure and History of Hollywood

Ray, Robert. *A Certain Tendency of the Hollywood Cinema, 1930–1980*. Princeton: Princeton University Press, 1985.

Schatz, Thomas. *The Genius of the System*. New York: Henry Holt, 1996.

Sklar, Robert. *Movie-Made America*. New York: Vintage Books, 1994.

Wasko, Janet. *Hollywood in the Information Age*. Austin: University of Texas Press, 1995.

Wood, Robin. *Hollywood from Vietnam to Reagan*. New York: Columbia University Press, 1986.

Wyatt, Justin. *High Concept: Movies and Marketing in Hollywood*. Austin: University of Texas Press, 1994.

Further Screening

Mr. Smith Goes to Washington (1939)
Since You Went Away (1943)
Meet Me in St. Louis (1944)
The Ten Commandments (1956)
Indiana Jones and the Temple of Doom (1984)

Independence Day (1996)
Pleasantville (1998)
Gladiator (2000)
Lord of the Rings (2001–3)
Indiana Jones and the Kingdom of the Crystal Skull (2008)

RACE AND ETHNICITY
AND AMERICAN FILM

INTRODUCTION TO PART II:

What is Race?

This part of the book examines how different racial and/or ethnic groups have been **represented** in American film. Although most Americans probably would say they have a fairly good understanding of race, American ideas about race often vary a great deal. Sometimes it is confused with ethnicity, or nationality, or religion, or some other marker of cultural difference. What one person regards as a "racial" issue may be regarded as something else by another. What this means from the outset is that ideas about race are heavily dependent upon social, ideological, and historical concepts. Although historically race has been thought to be a stable category based upon biological evidence, today we approach race as a set of social and cultural understandings about human difference – understandings that are malleable and ever-changing. As with all labels, the terms we use to discuss race tend to reduce the complex nature of human beings and their differences into separate and often simple-minded categories. Sadly, the historical cost of dividing human beings into such broadly labeled racial groups has been enormous. Wars, genocide, slavery, bigotry, and prejudice have all resulted from understanding people not as individualized human beings, but rather as members of a racially designated grouping.

For generations of Western culture, textbooks defined **race** as a division of humankind based upon a set of identifiable traits that are transmitted generationally, that is, through sexual reproduction. Scholars and scientists of earlier eras spent considerable time and energy examining people of the world according to their external features: hair texture, head shape, nose and lip size, and most notably skin color. These studies were done to classify people into one of three main racial groupings: **Caucasoid**, or the "white race" (people descended from European heritage); **Negroid**, or the "black race" (people descended from African heritage); and **Mongoloid**, or the "yellow race" (people with Asian and/or Native American roots). Although people of previous centuries felt that skin color was a significant marker of human difference, today we recognize that even though human beings come in all shapes, sizes, and colors, all of us are basically the same on the cellular and genetic level. For example, no human beings are actually white, black, or yellow in coloration. No one on earth is the color of this page or the ink printed upon it. Instead, all human beings are different shades of the same human skin pigment, **melanin**. Furthermore, modern thought acknowledges that each of these three main racial labels (Caucasoid, Negroid, and Mongoloid) encompasses a large variety of individuals, groups, and cultures. There is also considerable mixing and overlap between these three simple racial categories.

Allegedly "scientific" theories of race have now been debunked as culturally constructed ideological arguments meant to uphold the supremacy of one group over another. Historically, it has always been easier to discriminate or even enslave one group of people when another group can justify "scientifically" that groups of people are either inferior or superior. Another way of putting this is that skin color in itself does not make someone better or lesser than someone else: it is the cultural and ideological meaning of skin color that allows for such classifications to be made. Scientific discourse, though, is not the only manner in which ideological messages about race are dispersed. Consequently, even as modern science has given up the idea that race is an important biological distinction to make, it remains a powerful socio-cultural concept embedded in many **ideological state apparatuses**, including the media. To the present day, most people still consider human beings according to certain racial criteria.

Complicating matters further is the concept of **ethnicity**, which is a term similar to race but often used in less specific ways. Unlike most classical definitions of race (based on "scientific" data), definitions of ethnicity usually acknowledge a social dimension to its meaning. Ethnicity is thus understood as a social grouping based upon shared culture and custom. For example, while Native Americans as a whole have been historically thought of as part of the Mongoloid race, the various Native American tribes that flourished hundreds of years ago might be thought of as **ethnic groups** within the race, bound together by shared cultural customs. Race and ethnicity are also sometimes confused with **nationality** – the grouping of people based upon geographical and/or political boundaries. Obviously, cultural experiences and customs (ethnicities) often overlap with and themselves help define nationality, although in today's world most nations are themselves comprised of people from a multitude of racial and ethnic groups.

As with race, ethnicity and nationality are classificatory systems that reduce the vast complexity of human experience to single, simplified terms. Too often people think of race, ethnicity, or nationality as absolute categories and fail to understand the great differences that exist within any given grouping. Conversely, consistently grouping people according to their race, ethnicity, or nationality overlooks or undervalues the similarities and commonalties that exist between all human beings. Around the globe throughout history, many wars have been fought and lives have been lost over questions of nationality, race, and ethnicity. Even today, people continue to be rounded up and imprisoned because of their perceived membership in one of these categories. Within American culture, there is a long history of white people and white institutions discriminating against various racial and ethnic groups. Such discrimination stems from **racism**, the belief that human beings can be meaningfully categorized into racial groups and designated as superior or inferior on the basis of those characteristics. Similarly, **ethnocentrism** means regarding one's own ethnic group as better than another, while **nationalism** or **jingoism** means believing that one's national grouping is superior to all others. Although racial discrimination in America was officially outlawed by the Civil Rights Amendment of 1964, politicians, public figures, and media producers still invoke racist and ethnocentric concepts in order to win votes, sway opinions, or "merely" entertain.

As this introduction implies, many people today argue that race and ethnicity (and even nationality) are outmoded concepts that only foster inequity and violence. Some cultural theorists have suggested that these concepts should be done away with altogether, reasoning that the only way to move beyond them is to stop speaking of them. While there is strength in this position, such an argument has also been used to downplay or ignore America's racist past, and deny its racist present. Simply because race and ethnicity are increasingly recognized as social concepts, it does not follow that they no longer have tremendous power to shape the actual lives of Americans today. We cannot simply pretend that race and racial concepts have suddenly disappeared from American society. Despite certain assertions to the contrary, America is still a nation that is deeply divided by race, which suggests the ongoing importance of race to discussions of culture and politics. Many academic theorists as well as everyday citizens feel that it is absolutely necessary to examine the history of race and racial oppression, in order to better understand how America (and the rest of the world) deals with race and racism today.

The following chapters explore how Hollywood film has represented America's changing concepts of race and ethnicity in complex and sometimes contradictory ways. By focusing on the issues these chapters do, it may seem as though they are attempting to divide Americans into separate groups rather than unite us as one. However, it is not the goal of this part (or the book as a whole) to divide people, but rather to explore the histories of how and why such divisions have been created in the past, and how they continue to be exploited. Chapter 3 introduces the topic of **whiteness** and further examines some of the critical concepts raised in this introduction. Chapters 4 through 7 serve as an introduction to the history and issues involved in representing African Americans, Native Americans, Asian Americans, and Hispanics on our nation's movie screens. In most cases, Hollywood has contributed to simplified notions of race and ethnicity via the use of **stereotypes**. In other films, Hollywood has rewritten our racist and ethnocentric past in order to downplay our role in national tragedies such as slavery or the so-called **Indian Wars**. In yet other instances, a few Hollywood films have challenged racist and ethnocentric assumptions, and have helped bring about social change. The rise of American independent filmmaking in the last few decades has also tended to make American movie screens more sensitive to racial and ethnic issues. However, while there have been considerable gains for racial and ethnic minorities in Hollywood over the years, both Hollywood narrative form and the industry itself continue to marginalize non-white people in many ways.

Chapter 3

THE CONCEPT OF WHITENESS AND AMERICAN FILM

It may seem odd to begin an exploration of the **representations** of racial and ethnic minorities with a chapter on the images of white people in American cinema. However, to fully understand how certain people and communities are considered to be racial minorities, it is also necessary to examine how the empowered majority group conceives of and represents itself. Doing so places white communities under a microscope, and reveals that the concept of **whiteness** (the characteristics that identify an individual or a group as belong to the Caucasian race) is not as stable as is commonly supposed. Under **white patriarchal capitalism**, ideas about **race** and **ethnicity** are constructed and circulated in ways that tend to keep white privilege and power in place. Yet surveying representations of whiteness in American film raises fundamental questions about the very nature of race and/or ethnicity. Although it may surprise generations of the twenty-first century, some people who are now commonly considered to be white were *not* considered so in the past. The most common designation of whiteness in the United States is the term **WASP**, which stands for White Anglo-Saxon Protestant. People of non-Anglo-Saxon European ancestry have historically had to negotiate their relation to whiteness. If American culture had different ideas about who was considered white at different times over the past centuries, then claims about race and ethnicity as absolute markers of identity become highly problematic.

This chapter explores the differing socio-historical and cinematic constructions of whiteness throughout the history of American film. It examines the representations of several (but not all) of the communities that were not originally welcomed into American society as white, but which have been more recently assumed to belong to this racial category. The following discussion examines how these groups were represented with certain **stereotypes**, how these communities developed strategies for acceptance by white society, and how cinema functioned as part of this cultural negotiation. We also discuss a population group, Arab Americans, that many currently consider unable to blend into white society, even though a number of Arab American individuals have done so. But first, the chapter begins with a discussion of how film works within dominant hegemonic culture to subtly – and almost invisibly – speak about the centrality of whiteness.

Seeing White

One of the hardest aspects of discussing how white people are represented in American cinema (and in Western culture-at-large) is the effort it takes for individuals even to see that racial/ethnic issues are involved with white characters or stories. By and large, the average moviegoer thinks about issues of race only when seeing a movie about a racial or ethnic minority group. For example, most romantic comedies find humor in how male and female characters each try to hold the upper hand in a relationship. Yet *Two Can Play That Game* (2001), starring two African American actors (Morris Chestnut and Vivica A. Fox), is often regarded as a "black" film, whereas *You've Got Mail* (1998), starring two white actors (Tom Hanks and Meg Ryan), is usually regarded as simply a romantic comedy, and not as a "white" film. Similarly, audiences, critics, and filmmakers considered *Spawn* (1997) to be a film about an African American superhero, whereas *Batman* (1991) was simply a film about a superhero – period. These points underscore the Hollywood assumption that all viewers, whatever their racial identification, should be able to identify with white characters, but that the reverse is seldom true. Even today many white viewers choose not to see films starring non-white actors or films set in minority ethnic environments, allegedly because they feel they cannot identify with the characters. Because of that fact, Hollywood tends to spend more money on white stars in white movies, and far less money on non-white actors in overtly racial or ethnic properties.

The very structure of **classical Hollywood narrative form** encourages all spectators, regardless of their actual color, to identify with white protagonists. This may result in highly conflicted viewing positions, as when Native American spectators are encouraged by Hollywood Westerns to root for white cowboys battling evil Indians. This situation was especially prevalent in previous decades, when non-white actors were rarely permitted to play leading roles in Hollywood films, and when racialized stereotypes in movies were more obvious and prevalent. However, in an acknowledgement of our population's diversity, over the last several decades an ever-increasing number of non-white characters have been appearing in Hollywood movies. More and more films each year now feature non-white leads, and even more regularly, non-white actors in supporting roles. Sometimes this practice is referred to as **tokenism** – the placing of a non-white character into a film in order to deflate any potential charge of racism. **Token** characters can often be found in small supporting roles that are peripheral to the white leads and their stories. For example, in war movies featuring mixed-race battalions, minor black and Hispanic characters frequently get killed off as the film progresses, leaving a white hero to save the day. This phenomenon has become so prevalent that some audience members consider it a racist cliché. For many others, however, the phenomenon goes unnoticed, and the dominance of whiteness remains unquestioned.

Film scholar Richard Dyer's work on how cinema represents whiteness ties this unthinking (or unremarked-upon) white centrism to larger ideological issues of race. As pointed out in chapter 1, a society's dominant ideology functions optimally when individuals are so imbued with its concepts that they do not realize that a **social construct** has been formed or is being reinforced. The relative cultural invisibility of whiteness within the United States serves as a perfect example of this idea: the white power base maintains its dominant position precisely by being consistently overlooked, or at least unexamined in most mainstream texts. Unless whiteness is somehow pointed out or *over*emphasized, its dominance is taken for granted. A rare Hollywood film such as *Pleasantville* (1998) calls attention to whiteness, even down to its black-and-white visual design, in which characters are literally devoid of color. (The film is a satire of 1950s nostalgia as represented by that era's all-white television sitcoms.) More regularly, however, Hollywood films that are just as white as 1950s television – from *E.T. The Extra-Terrestrial* (1982) to *Stepmom* (1998) – fail to point out their whiteness and therefore work to naturalize it as a universal state of representation.

When it goes unmentioned, whiteness is positioned as a default category, the center or the assumed norm on which everything else is based. Under this conception, white is then often defined more through what it is *not* than what it *is*. If whiteness must remain relatively invisible, then it can only be recognized when placed in comparison to something (or someone) that is considered *not* white. For example, in the romantic comedy *You've Got Mail*, Joe (Tom Hanks) interacts with Kevin, an African American co-worker (David Chappelle). The presence of a token African American character allegedly negates any potential accusation of Hollywood racism, but his presence may also make viewers aware of racial difference – that Joe is white because he is *not* black. Some of Kevin's lines also point out Joe's whiteness. Up until that point, however, viewers have not been encouraged to see anything racial about Joe. The subtle ideas about whiteness that are present in the film may go unnoticed by most viewers, or if they are noted during Kevin's scene, they may be forgotten the moment he is no longer on screen.

Kevin's friendly put-downs of Joe also reveal that whiteness is most often invisible to people who consider themselves to be white. However, many non-white individuals are often painfully aware of the dominance of whiteness, precisely because they are repeatedly excluded from its privileges. Sometimes racialized stereotypes get inverted to characterize whiteness. Thus, if people of color are stereotyped as physical and passionate, whiteness is sometimes satirized as bland and sterile, represented by processed white bread, mayonnaise, and elevator music. The stereotypes that white people lack rhythm, can't dance, or can't play basketball (as the title of the film *White Men Can't Jump* [1992] would have it) are simply reversals of racist stereotypes that assert that people of color are "naturally" more in touch with their physicality than are white people. Many of these stereotypes seem to invoke (and probably evolved from) the racist beliefs of earlier eras. One such belief was the assumption that white people were a more evolved type of human being – and thus suited for mental and intellectual tasks – while non-white people were thought of as being more basely physical and even animalistic.

This process of defining one group against another is sometimes referred to as **Othering**. More specifically, Othering refers to the way a dominant culture ascribes an undesirable trait (one shared by all humans) onto *one specific group of people*. Psychologically, Othering depends on the defense mechanism of **displacement**, in which a person or group sees something about itself that it doesn't like, and instead of accepting that fault or shortcoming, projects it onto another person or group. For example, white culture (with its Puritan and Protestant taboos against sex) has repeatedly constructed and exploited stereotypes of non-white people as being overly sexualized. Throughout US history, fear and hysteria about "rampant and animalistic" non-white sexualities (as opposed to "regulated and healthy" white sexualities) have been used to justify both institutional and individual violence against non-white people. Other character traits common to all human groups – such as laziness, greed, or criminality – are regularly denied as white traits and projected by dominant white culture onto racial or ethnic Others. In this way, and simultaneously, whiteness represents itself as moral and good, while non-white groups are frequently characterized as immoral or inferior.

The process of Othering reveals more about white frames of mind than about the various minority cultures being represented. This was often embodied within classical Hollywood filmmaking, when racial or ethnic minority characters were played by white actors. This common practice allowed white producers to construct images of non-white people according to how they (the white producers) thought non-white people acted and spoke. How non-white **Others** helped to define whiteness can also be seen in the silent and classical Hollywood practice of using minority-group performers to play a variety of racial or ethnic characters. For example, African Americans and Latinos were often hired to play Native American characters, and Hispanic, Italian, and Jewish actors played everything from Eskimos to Swedes. Such casting practices again reinforce the notion that people are either white or non-white, and Hollywood did not take much care to distinguish among non-white peoples, often treating them as interchangeable Others.

In socially constructing this concept of whiteness, Western culture had to define who got to be considered white. Many attempts were made over the past centuries to "measure" a person's whiteness. In the United States, laws were passed defining who was and who was not to be considered white. People claimed that "one drop of blood" from a non-white lineage excluded an individual from being "truly" white. Marriages were carefully arranged to keep a family lineage "pure," and laws prohibiting interracial marriage were common in most states. If there were non-white relationships within a family tree, they would frequently be hidden or denied. Throughout much of American history, **lynching** – the illegal mob torture and murder of a suspected individual – was a white community crime commonly spurred by fears over interracial sex. All these measures to "protect" whiteness indicate a serious cultural anxiety about the permeable borders between white and non-white races. In reality, the sexual commingling of different racial and ethnic groups was common in the United States almost from the moment European settlers landed on the continent. On the Western frontier, white men often took up relations with Native American women. In the Eastern United States, many white slave owners regularly forced sex upon their female slaves. Even President Thomas Jefferson fathered children by his slave, Sally Hemings. Needless to say, these incidents have rarely been represented in Hollywood cinema.

Struggles over the definition of whiteness were especially pronounced during the 1800s and the early 1900s, when film was in its infancy. The idea of the **American melting pot** arose during this period. The metaphor expressed the way various immigrant cultures and traditions were to be forged or melted together into an overall sense of American identity. Obviously, the American melting pot most readily accepted those groups that could successfully blend into or **assimilate** into the ideals and assumptions of white patriarchal capitalism. Assimilation was (and is) easier for some groups than for others, and the reason for that was (and is) based on longstanding notions about racial difference. European immigrants, although from different national and ethnic cultures, were more readily assimilated into mainstream white American culture than were people of African, Asian, or Native American backgrounds. Partly this was because European immigrants had a certain amount of cultural, racial, and religious overlap with white America; people from other areas of the globe were (and still are) more likely to be considered as racially and culturally Other. Nonetheless, even European immigrants had to struggle for acceptance in the United States, and a history of those struggles can be found in that era's cinematic record.

Assimilation remains a contested issue to this day. While many people (of all racial, ethnic, and national backgrounds) support the idea that Americans should strive to assimilate into the dominant (white) way of life, others find that proposition disturbing. Some people feel that racial and ethnic cultures should be celebrated and not phased out of existence, arguing that one of the basic strengths of America is its very diversity of cultures, and – hopefully – cinematic representations. Another controversial issue related to assimilation is the phenomenon of **passing**, wherein some people of color deny their racial or ethnic backgrounds in order to be accepted as white. People who pass are sometimes accused of "selling out" their racial or ethnic heritages. However, people who can pass often choose to do so precisely because whites are still afforded more privilege and power in our national culture, and those who pass often want to share in those opportunities. It is this social reality that led many European immigrants to work toward assimilation and acceptance as being white. That process can be seen occurring in American films made throughout the twentieth century, especially in regard to changing representations of Irish, Italian, and Jewish Americans. In film and culture-at-large, the shift to whiteness occurred for these groups of people when they were no longer regarded as separate *races*, but rather as ethnicities or nationalities that could then be assimilated into the American concept of whiteness.

Bleaching the Green: The Irish in American Cinema

Irish people first came to the "New World" long before the United States declared its independence from Great Britain. These first Irish Americans were predominantly middle-class Protestants, and therefore somewhat similar to settlers from Great Britain, the majority of whom were also middle-class and Protestant. However, the cultural makeup of Irish immigrants changed dramatically during the 1800s. The great potato famine of the 1840s drove hundreds of thousands of Irish citizens – mainly of poor Catholic background – across the Atlantic ocean to the United States. Facing their first significant wave of immigration, many Americans reacted with fear and hostility. Conveniently forgetting their own recent resettlement from Europe, a number of American citizens rallied around the new cause of **Nativism**: that "America should be for Americans" and not for foreigners. Laws were passed in various states restricting immigration, denying voting rights, and prohibiting Irish American citizens from holding elective office. Speeches, newspaper editorials, and political cartoons often described Irish Americans as barely human: they were represented as small, hairy, apelike creatures with a propensity for violence, drunkenness, and unchecked sexual impulses.

Similar descriptions were used for African Americans during these years, and comparisons were often made between the two groups. Irish Americans were commonly called "white niggers" while African Americans were sometimes referred to as "smoked Irish." Such shared discrimination at times tied the two communities together. Some people saw that the groups had a shared struggle and linked the institutional slavery of African Americans to the "wage slavery" of Irish immigrants, many of whom worked as servants in white households. Yet, more often than not, Irish American communities responded to such comparisons by distancing themselves from African Americans, in some cases through violent race riots. By strenuously denying similarities to African Americans, Irish Americans strove to be regarded as white and not black. Similarly, conceptions of Irish whiteness were dramatized on stage via the conventions of **blackface**, a popular theatrical tradition of the 1800s that featured white performers darkening their faces with makeup in order to perform broad, comedic stereotypes of African Americans. Blackface was one way that popular culture distinguished between white and non-white behaviors and identities. By leading the blackface trend, Irish American performers did acknowledge on some level how many people conflated the two groups. These performers thus positioned themselves as *white* people who needed to "black up" to play the parts, defining themselves against a racial Other of blackness. In so doing, Irish American performers promoted their own whiteness, in effect saying "you may consider us lesser, but at least we are not black."

Representations of Irish Americans in early American cinema drew upon already-established stereotypes and misconceptions developed in other media such as literature, newspaper cartooning, and the theater. Alternatively referred to as "Paddy," the "Boy-o," or the "**Mick**," early films typically showed Irish Americans as small, fiery-tempered, heavy-drinking, working-class men. Irish American women also appeared in many early films, typically as ill-bred, unintelligent house servants, often named Bridget. *The Finish of Bridget McKeen* (1901) serves as a good example of these early cinematic representations: Bridget is a stout, slovenly scullery maid who tries to light an oven, and in her frustration stokes it with kerosene. When she lights a match, an explosion results, and the film dissolves to its supposedly uproarious punch line: a shot of Bridget's gravestone. Yet these derogatory images of Irish Americans were short-lived, for by the advent of early cinema, public perceptions about Irish Americans were shifting. Irish Americans had been assimilating into American whiteness for half a century, and by the early 1900s, new waves of immigrants from other countries began to inundate the United States. Many of these immigrants originated from Southern and Eastern Europe, and many Americans regarded these new immigrants as darker or more swarthy (that is, less white) than immigrants from Northern and Western Europe. The Irish suddenly seemed more white in comparison.

Irish Americans began to be positioned as exemplars of immigrant assimilation, a group upon whom other immigrants should attempt to model themselves. Increasingly, the Irish were regarded as an ethnicity and a **nationality**, whereas they had previously been considered a race. As a consequence, Irish Americans (and their cinematic representations) moved up the scale of whiteness. Images of drunken, boisterous Micks still occurred throughout the 1920s – on stage in the long-running *Abie's Irish Rose*, and on film in *The Callahans and the Murphys* (1927). However, the predominant image of the Irish American in 1920s film shifted to that of the **Colleen**. Replacing the slovenly, stupid Bridget, Colleen was a spunky, bright-eyed young woman who was quickly welcomed into American life; films about Colleen characters often ended in her marriage to a wealthy white man. Films such as *Come On Over* (1922), *Little Annie Rooney* (1925), and *Irene* (1926, based on the stage musical) center on young Irish American women, who, under the direction of white masculinity, successfully blend into the country's melting pot. Often these films dramatized assimilation as an issue of generational difference: in them, parents who embodied the old Mick and Bridget stereotypes were shown to be less capable of assimilation than were their more Americanized offspring.

A number of the actresses who played these Colleen roles (such as Colleen Moore, Mary Pickford, and Nancy Carroll) were themselves of Irish heritage. Just as the stage had been one of the arenas in which Irish Americans "became" white, so did the Hollywood film industry help Irish Americans assimilate into whiteness. Unlike many other ethnic groups during the first half of the twentieth century, most Irish Americans actors did not feel the need to Anglicize their names – George O'Brien, Sally O'Neil, Maureen O'Sullivan, and Mickey Rooney (to name just a few) became stars under their own names. Irish American men also found work behind the camera as directors: Mickey Neilan, Raoul Walsh, and John Ford were all well-established directors by the end of the silent film era. Furthermore, one of the first Irish American millionaires, Joseph P. Kennedy, became himself a film executive, producing films for Gloria Swanson in the late 1920s and helping found the RKO Radio studio in 1928.

In the 1930s, a few gangster films would acknowledge Irish Americans in organized crime. Based on real-life criminals "Machine Gun" Kelly and "Baby Face"

Nelson, these thugs portrayed by actor **James Cagney** might have presaged an anti-Irish backlash. Yet films centered on Irish American hoodlums were invariably balanced by those that portrayed Irish Americans as law-abiding citizens. For example, Cagney's gangster character in *Public Enemy* (1931) has a policeman brother, and his character in *Angels With Dirty Faces* (1938) has a priest for a best friend. Cagney's career itself dramatized Irish American assimilation into whiteness: his roles evolved from rebel outsiders to all-American heroes. By 1940, he was starring in *The Fighting 69th*, a film about a famed Irish American regiment that fought in World War I. Two years later, Cagney won an Oscar for playing the flag-waving Irish American showman George M. Cohan in *Yankee Doodle Dandy* (1942).

Irish Americans in film (and in real life) worked hard to assimilate through overt indications of patriotism and loyalty. Irish Americans came to dominate urban police forces and fire departments, and many joined the armed forces. Overt displays of Irish American patriotism were made in the movies as well. **John Ford** became known for directing films that glorified the United States – primarily his legendary Westerns, but also a number of overtly patriotic war films during World War II. In both types of films, Irish American characters consistently appeared as true-blue Americans. Picturing Irish Americans as ultra-nationalists often went hand in hand with seeing them as pious and moral, specifically by linking them to Catholicism. By the 1940s, the most common image of Irish Americans in Hollywood films was either as policeman or as priest. Films such as *Boys Town* (1938), *Angels With Dirty Faces*, the Oscar-winning *Going My Way* (1944), its sequel *The Bells of St. Mary's* (1945), and *Fighting Father Dunne* (1948) showed Irish American priests kindly dispensing wisdom and morality to future generations. This image of Irish Americans as upholders of American moral rectitude extended to the industry itself. The Hollywood **Production Code** was written in 1930 by two Irish Americans, Martin Quigley and Jesuit Fr. Daniel Lord. When the Catholic Church organized the **Legion of Decency** to protest against violent and sexually licentious Hollywood films, Irish American priests led the way. And when the Production Code Administration responded in 1934 by instituting the **Seal of Approval** provision that enforced the Code, Irish American Joseph Breen helmed the organization (and did so for the next 20 years). Picturing Irish Americans as moral guardians possibly reached its apex with the short-lived popularity of Senator Joseph McCarthy, a politician who exploited the **Red Scare** by pursuing potential communist agents in the United States.

When McCarthy's popularity diminished in the mid-1950s, the Production Code Administration's power was also beginning to wane. While one might suppose this to signal a loss of Irish American influence on Hollywood film, the 1950s also seemed to signal the end of Irish American struggles for inclusion. By the end of World War II, the Irish American population had largely been assimilated. Evidence of this was plain on American movie screens: actors of Irish heritage regularly played a variety of roles instead of being typecast as only Irish characters. For example, in the 1940s, Gene Kelly had often played overtly Irish American characters, but by the 1950s, his characters were considered simply American. He was, after all, *An American in Paris* (1951), not an *Irish American* in Paris. A few years later, Bing Crosby and Grace Kelly, both of Irish descent, starred as the epitome of

Going My Way (1944) told the story of two generations of Irish American priests – the older (Barry Fitzgerald) portrayed in broad fashion, and the younger (Bing Crosby) as almost thoroughly assimilated.
Going My Way, copyright © 1944, Paramount

upper-class white culture in *High Society* (1956). Even in a film *about* Ireland and Irish immigration, one can find successful assimilation dramatized. For example, in John Ford's Oscar-winning *The Quiet Man* (1952), John Wayne plays an Irish American so thoroughly assimilated to American whiteness that he has difficulty coping with the culture and people of Ireland itself. The election of President John F. Kennedy in 1960 might be said to symbolize the pinnacle of Irish American assimilation, although there were still many Americans who were outspokenly prejudiced against his Irish heritage, as well as his Catholicism.

Many Irish Americans today still strongly hold onto their ethnic heritage and identity, as can be seen across the country every St Patrick's Day. Being white and being Irish are no longer incompatible, though, as the common phrase "everyone's Irish on St Patrick's Day" attests. Irish Americans today can choose to proclaim their

John Ford's *The Quiet Man* (1952) showed John Wayne's Irish American attempting to assimilate when he moves to Ireland (and win the heart of Maureen O'Hara's local lass).
The Quiet Man, copyright © 1952, Republic

ethnicity or to blend into an undifferentiated whiteness. This status is evident in the way Irish Americans have been shown in Hollywood films since the 1960s. Explicitly ethnic Irish Americans surface only sporadically – often in nostalgic period films like *The Sting* (1973), *Miller's Crossing* (1991), or *The Road to Perdition* (2002). *Gangs of New York* (2002) is one of the few films that acknowledges what Irish Americans endured in the struggle for acceptance into whiteness during the 1800s. The social and political problems faced by Ireland itself have been the subject of several Irish, British, and American films, including *The Crying Game* (1992), *In the Name of the Father* (1993), *Michael Collins* (1996), and *Angela's Ashes* (1999). However, many more Irish American characters appear in Hollywood films in ways that are indistinguishable from any other white characters. When audiences watched *Saving Private Ryan* (1998), most probably did not even consciously think about the title character being Irish American. He was simply a white American soldier.

Looking for Respect: Italians in American Cinema

During the early 1800s, Italian people emigrated to America in relatively small numbers. However, many Italians (along with Poles, Slavs, Russians, Greeks, and other people from Southern and Eastern Europe) were part of a great surge in immigration that occurred in America during the final years of the nineteenth century.

According to some sources, by 1900, 75 percent of the population of major urban areas (including New York City, Chicago, and Boston) were made up of immigrants. This influx of people produced a new round of **xenophobia**, the irrational fear and/or hatred of foreigners, among many Americans. Much as Irish immigrants had been compared to and equated with African Americans a few decades earlier, so too were Italian immigrants thought by some to be "black." Conventional representations of Italian Americans in newspapers and early films depicted them as having darker skin tones, thick curly hair, and little to no education. Consequently, while Irish Americans were slowly coming to be regarded as white during the silent film era, Italian Americans were just beginning their own struggle for assimilation. Furthermore, Italian Americans themselves were sometimes prejudiced against other Italian Americans. Until the late 1800s, Italy was not a unified nation but a collection of separate principalities – thus many Italian immigrants had a stronger regional than national identity. Not all people from mainland Italy liked being compared to those from Sicily (and vice versa), although the popular media of the day often used the same stereotypes to represent people from both regions.

One of the earliest of those stereotypical representations (in newspapers, theater, and film) was that of an assimilationist small businessman. Sometimes named Luigi, or Carmine, or Guido, this Italian American stereotype was a simple-minded, working-class man who spoke in broken English and who often wore a bushy moustache. He was always smiling and gracious, and he worked as a street vendor, cranked a street organ, or ran a small café in order to support his large family. This stereotype continued to be a recognizable stock character throughout decades of Hollywood film. He appears as a friendly restaurateur, small business owner, or fruit-stand manager in countless small roles in countless Hollywood films. The type was so prevalent that one of the Marx Brothers (who were of Russian and Jewish heritage) became famous for his Italian American persona "Chico." The type was also popular on radio (and later television) programs such as *Life with Luigi* (CBS-TV, 1952–3). To this day, the name "Guido" is sometimes used to describe a young, none-too-bright Italian American working-class man, as in the film *Kiss Me Guido* (1997). The stereotype is also invoked by the video-game (and film) characters, the *Super Mario Brothers* (1993).

While the Luigi or Guido figure was somewhat simple-minded, he was at least non-threatening, and seemed to indicate that Italian Americans could eventually be assimilated into American whiteness via their hard work and capitalist ethics. However, there was another more ominous Italian American stereotype present in the public consciousness during the first decades of the twentieth century: that of the socialist radical or **anarchist**. An anarchist is someone who believes in toppling all forms of social control and/or government, often through violent means. The Italian American anarchist type (sometimes he was also depicted as coming from neighboring Southern or Eastern European countries) actively battled *against* white America rather than trying to assimilate into it. In films of the era, this dark-skinned antagonist was defeated by heroic white men.

By the 1920s, yet another image of Italian American men could be found on the nation's movie screens: the **Latin Lover**, a handsome and exotic, sexually alluring leading man. The most famous Latin Lover of the decade was **Rudolph Valentino**, an actor who had been born in Italy and who appeared in films such as *The Four Horsemen of the Apocalypse* (1921) and *The Sheik* (1921). While the ascendancy of Valentino and the Latin Lover type may be seen as a step toward acceptance and assimilation, the appeal of the Latin Lover lies precisely in his Otherness. He is bold, aggressive, and potentially violent in his sexual passions – quite unlike respectable white men. Furthermore, as will be discussed in chapter 7, the Latin Lover type also included men from Hispanic cultures – a fact that again suggests how the dominant culture groups together different racial/ethnic Others as a means of opposing (and therefore defining) whiteness. The Latin Lover image was also used in more forthrightly derogative ways, as when he was represented as a gigolo trying to sleep his way into wealth and white society.

By the early 1930s, the image of the Italian American man looking for success and respect via disreputable means took a more ominous turn on the nation's movie screens. Italian Americans became the ruthless lead characters of the **gangster film**. Partly, this linkage of Italian Americans and mobsters was drawn from real life. Stories of Italian American ghettoes being controlled by almost feudal family gangs (the so-called **Mafia**, a concept originally derived from Sicilian culture) had begun to proliferate in the American popular press in the earliest years of the century. During the Prohibition era (1919–33), various criminal organizations thrived by distributing illegal alcohol. While people of numerous backgrounds were part of these organized crimes, many people focused on the Italian names being reported in the nation's newspapers: Al Capone, Frank Nitti, Johnny Torrio, etc. Thus, when Hollywood began its cycle of gangster films in the early 1930s, Italian Americans were prominently featured. *Little Caesar* (1930), a film that many regard as the first film of this genre, focuses on the rise and fall of Italian American gangster Rico Bandello (played by Jewish actor Edward G. Robinson). *Little Caesar* was followed by *Scarface* (1932), which focuses on the corrupt, ultra-violent, and vaguely incestuous Tony Camonte (played by another Jewish actor, Paul Muni). Throughout the 1930s and continuing for decades, the most conspicuous representation of Italian Americans on Hollywood movie screens would be as mobsters.

Other stereotypical and more fully developed Italian American characters began to emerge during and after World War II. As the United States fought a war against Germany, Italy, and Japan, Italian Americans increasingly promoted their patriotism and loyalty to America. As a consequence, they were often featured in Hollywood's wartime propaganda movies. In the many **war movies** made during these years, such as *Sahara* (1943), *The Purple Heart* (1944), *Back to Bataan* (1945), and *The Story of G.I. Joe* (1945), Italian American characters were included; they fought with courage and dedication alongside American soldiers of a variety of other ethnicities. In the postwar years, Italian American musical performers such as Frank Sinatra, Dean Martin, and Mario Lanza became increasingly popular, both on radio and in Hollywood films.

Postwar filmmaking in Italy also had an affect on Hollywood images of Italian Americans. The popularity and critical regard of the film movement known as **Italian Neorealism** spurred greater attempts at cinematic realism in a number of countries;

Edward G. Robinson played Italian American mobster Rico Bandello in one of the most famous classical Hollywood gangster movies, *Little Caesar* (1930). *Little Caesar*, copyright © 1930, Warner Bros.

the movement regularly represented Italians as poor and/or working-class people. Consequently, 1950s American film also saw an increase in down-to-earth, working-class Italian American characters. Part of this "earthiness" expressed itself via sensuality. Italian actresses such as Sophia Loren, Gina Lollobrigida, and Anna Magnani became internationally famous during these years, partly because of their uninhibited sexuality. Like that of the 1920s Latin Lover, the sexual appeal these women exuded for American audiences was partly due to their Otherness. (The fact that many of their films were made overseas – far away from the Hollywood Production Code – also contributed to their reputation as sexually unbridled.) Earthy, working-class representations of Italian Americans became so popular that they swept the Oscars in 1955, when a film about a lonely Italian American butcher (*Marty*) won Best Picture and Best Actor (Ernest Borgnine), and Anna Magnani won a Best Actress award for her first American film, *The Rose Tattoo*.

During the 1960s and 1970s, a new generation of Italian American actors and directors became prominent in the Hollywood film industry. Actors such as Al Pacino, Robert DeNiro, Talia Shire, Sylvester Stallone, and John Travolta rose to prominence, while directors like Francis Ford Coppola, Martin Scorsese, and Michael Cimino were also highly successful. While such success might possibly signal an erasure of Italian ethnicity into a general sense of whiteness, this was not the case. Recall that during the 1960s, dominant American culture was coming under severe criticism from various sectors of the **counterculture**. As part of those critiques, whiteness was being taken off its pedestal and racial and ethnic identities were being celebrated as more authentic and meaningful. White suburban lifestyles (on display, for example, in comedies such as *Please Don't Eat the Daisies* [1960] or *The Thrill Of It All* [1963]) were increasingly seen as bland and mind-numbing. As a consequence, ethnicity was suddenly "in," and starched symbols of whiteness (such as Doris Day and John Wayne) were supplanted by actors who did not hide their ethnic heritage.

Yet what types of stories and characters did these new Italian American filmmakers create? To a great extent, they replicated old-style Hollywood formulas in **nostalgic Hollywood blockbusters.** One of the first and most important of these films was Francis Ford Coppola's *The Godfather* (1972), a period gangster film about Italian American mobsters. While the film was protested against by many Italian American media watchdog groups who objected to the revival of the gangster stereotype, it became one of the most successful films of all time, spawning two sequels (1974 and 1990). Many of Martin Scorsese's films also centered on Italian American gangs and gangsters. Although he has made all sorts of films, including a personal documentary about his parents and their ethnic heritage (*Italianamerican* [1974]), it is Scorsese's violent gangster films that most moviegoers recall: *Mean Streets* (1973), *Goodfellas* (1990), and *Casino* (1995). Still other films from this era (reworking another earlier stereotype) focus on Italian American working-class men who struggle to

Even in the New Hollywood, filmmakers still associated Italian American culture and tradition with the mobster stereotype, particularly in the enormously successful *The Godfather* (1972).
The Godfather, copyright © 1972, Paramount

achieve the American Dream. *Rocky* (1976) and *Saturday Night Fever* (1977) both position their Italian American protagonists not just as characters representative of Italian American concerns, but also as larger symbols of American spirit and determination. Similarly, Coppola had envisioned the Corleone family in *The Godfather* to be a symbol of America – but not in the patriotic style of *Rocky*. Rather, Coppola used his *Godfather* films (especially *Part II* [1974]) to indict and critique white patriarchal capitalism.

Many of these types of images of Italian Americans remain in contemporary Hollywood film. While characters of Irish descent often appear without any mention of their heritage, Italian American characters are still frequently depicted as earthy, working-class types (as in *Moonstruck* [1988]), or mobsters (as in *The Untouchables* [1988] or the cable TV series *The Sopranos* [1999–2007]). While across culture-at-large Italian Americans have become for the most part regarded as white, many Italian Americans still choose to maintain a pronounced ethnicity, actively celebrating the culture and traditions of their heritage. Consequently, representing Italian Americans as a distinct ethnicity remains a common practice in American film.

A Special Case: Jews and Hollywood

Jews in America and in American cinema have faced (and still do face) a different set of circumstances than either Irish Americans or Italian Americans in their negotiation of whiteness. For example, being Jewish frequently encompasses religion as well as ethnicity. Also, Jewish immigrants came to America from a wide variety of countries and thus claim a wide range of national heritages. Unlike most Irish and Italian people, who left their native lands for America as a matter of choice, many Jews were forced out of European nations via state-sanctioned acts of murder and terrorism (such as the pogroms of Tsarist Russia or the Nazi-induced Holocaust). Furthermore, while most of the US population now regards citizens of European Jewish background to be white, a small but highly vocal group of white supremacist Americans still regard Jews as a "race" that are out to destroy white Aryan purity through intermarriage. (Their use of the term "race," rather than "ethnicity," is further meant to exclude Jews from their definition of whiteness.) The roots of such **anti-Semitism,** or hatred of Jews, are complex and can be traced back thousands of years. Even in contemporary America, people of Jewish heritage are still regularly targeted by hate crimes and hate speech. Conversely, most European immigrants from Christian belief systems have been more readily assimilated into the ideals of American whiteness.

Anti-Semitism was an even stronger force in the United States during the first half of the twentieth century. One can see this in films made during the earliest days of cinema, before the advent of Hollywood. Short films made by white Protestant men (such as those who worked for Thomas Edison) sometimes featured grotesque stereotypes of Jews as hunchbacked, hook-nosed, and greedy cheats. Such subhuman depictions, found in films like *Levitsky's Insurance Policy* (1903) and *Cohen's Advertising Scheme* (1904), presented an image of Jews as money-grubbing and untrustworthy. Jewish immigrants of the era responded in different manners to anti-Semitic attitudes and representations. As with other ethnic groups, some Jews drew in closer to each other in urban ghettoes, where they fiercely clung to their traditions. Examples of this philosophy can be found in a number of **Yiddish-language films** made during the 1920s and 1930s. These films were small-budget, independent films made by and for the Jewish community and were rarely shown outside urban neighborhood theaters. On the other hand, many Jewish immigrants struggled to assimilate into the culture of white Christian America. (Interestingly, the term "American melting pot" itself was coined by a Jewish immigrant playwright, Israel Zangwill.) Also, just as Irish American theatrical performers had done, a number of Jewish American performers began donning blackface on stage, an act that emphasized that Jews were indeed white people who had to "black up" in order to play African Americans.

Intriguingly, many of the most popular Jewish stage entertainers of the period used blackface in complex ways. While attempting to differentiate (white) Jews from (black) African Americans, Jewish entertainers also used blackface to indicate shared oppression and outsider status. For example, under the guise of blackface, Jewish entertainers sometimes felt safe to tell critical jokes about the white power structure. Jewish entertainers also blurred boundaries between racial and ethnic categories – they may have been performing in blackface, but they sprinkled their dialog with Yiddish slang. Such tomfoolery, practiced by major stars such as **Al Jolson** and **Eddie Cantor**, tended to expose the artificiality of racial and ethnic categories by jumbling them all together. When Eddie Cantor made a film version of his hit stage musical *Whoopee!* (1930), he bounced from one racial/ethnic type to another: Jewish in one scene, then in blackface, and then Native American. The film's story revolves around Cantor's friends, who are forbidden to marry because the man is Native American and the woman is white. This conflict is resolved when it is discovered that the male was only raised by Native Americans and is "actually" white. The resolution of the plot, as well as Cantor's parody of racial stereotypes, demonstrate the highly subjective and constantly fluctuating nature of racial and ethnic identities.

By the time that Al Jolson and Eddie Cantor moved from stage to film, circumstances for Jews in the American film industry had changed immensely. During the 1920s, Jews came to dominate Hollywood. Initially, a number of Jewish immigrants had opened and run nickelodeons in the urban ghettoes of large Eastern cities. From those beginnings, these same men built film production companies, moved to the West Coast, and wrested control of the industry away from Eastern entrepreneurs like Thomas Edison. Most of the heads of the major studios during the classical Hollywood era were Jewish: Carl Laemmle (Universal), Adolph Zukor (Paramount), Louis B. Mayer (MGM), Harry Cohn (Columbia), and the Warner Brothers. With Jewish men as the leaders of the film industry, many other people of Jewish heritage went into the business as directors, writers, actors, and technicians. Consequently, American Jews have had a greater say in how their images were being fashioned in American cinema than any other racial or ethnic minority.

This is not to say that mainstream Hollywood movies became non-stop celebrations of Jewish culture. On the contrary, Jewish filmmakers had to negotiate their images (both as industry leaders and in film texts) within a larger white society. Classical Hollywood films therefore emphasized a vision of America as largely white and Christian, in order to appeal to white mainstream audiences and avoid the wrath of potential anti-Semites. For example, there are numerous fondly remembered classical Hollywood Christmas films (*A Christmas Carol* [1938], *It's A Wonderful Life* [1946], *Miracle On 34th Street* [1947]) but, until *8 Crazy Nights* (2002), there were no comparable Hollywood Hanukkah films. In fact, overtly Jewish characters rarely appeared in 1930s Hollywood films, and Jewish executives often went out of their way to efface their (and their employees') Jewish heritage. Jewish actors were encouraged to change their names to "whiter-sounding" ones: Emanuel Goldenberg, Julius Garfinkle, Betty Perske, Danielovitch Demsky, David Kaminsky, and Bernard Schwartz became, respectively, Edward G. Robinson, John Garfield, Lauren Bacall, Kirk Douglas, Danny Kaye, and Tony Curtis. These efforts were a conscious strategy to deal with recurrent worries about anti-Semitism. Repeatedly, Christian protest and reform groups asserted that Jews in Hollywood were destroying the moral fiber of the country. Jews in Hollywood were constantly on the defensive, ready for the shadow of prejudice to emerge and attempt to destroy their industry. It is no wonder that producer David O. Selznick (most famous for producing *Gone With the Wind* [1939]) told an interviewer at one point, "I'm American and not a Jew."

Possibly the one studio to show some commitment to upholding its Jewish heritage was Warner Brothers. Consistently hiring more Jewish actors than did other studios, Warner Brothers also made films about Jewish characters on a somewhat regular basis. The studio won a Best Picture Oscar for *The Life of Emile Zola* (1937), a film that focused on the notorious "Dreyfus affair," a major French military trial that pivoted on anti-Semitism. Warner Brothers was also the first studio to repudiate Nazi Germany in its films, several years before the United States entered World War II, most memorably in *Confessions of a Nazi Spy* (1939). Executives at the other studios refrained from making films critical of Nazi Germany so that they could maintain their European film distribution deals. While these decisions were thus partly fueled by capitalist desires, Jewish industry heads were also worried that taking a forthright stand against Hitler could reawaken anti-Semitic sentiment against Hollywood. In fact, that is exactly what happened in the wake of films like *Confessions of a Nazi Spy*. Special US Senate committee hearings were held, accusing Hollywood of trying to push the United States into World War II. The transcripts of these hearings are filled with ugly anti-Semitic rhetoric, a good example of how pervasive (and acceptable) such feelings were during this era.

After the war, as American citizens learned the extent of the Holocaust, re-evaluations of American anti-Semitism began to occur. Yet many Jewish Hollywood moguls feared tackling the subject. It took the one non-Jewish studio head (Darryl F. Zanuck at 20th Century-Fox) to make the first **social problem film** about American anti-Semitism. *Gentleman's Agreement* (1947) starred Gregory Peck as a gentile reporter going undercover as a Jew in order to expose prejudice. The film was a critical and commercial success, and won a Best Picture Oscar. That same

Case Study: *The Jazz Singer* (1927)

The Jazz Singer stands as one of the most important movies in American film history because it is considered to be the first Hollywood studio motion picture feature with synchronized sound. Produced by Warner Brothers in 1927, this silent film with sound sequences revolutionized the industry; it also deals with issues of race and ethnicity in very interesting ways. The story of *The Jazz Singer* focuses on the problems faced by Jewish immigrants in the first few decades of the twentieth century, and dramatizes the process of ethnic assimilation into whiteness. The film also points out historical connections between Jewish immigrants and African Americans (primarily via the blackface tradition), and even obliquely comments on the connections between Jews and Irish Americans.

As a way to foreground the use of sound, *The Jazz Singer* is fundamentally about two different types of music: liturgical sacred music and modern American popular song (under the catch-all term "jazz"). Jakie Rabinowitz (Al Jolson) has been trained by his father to follow in his profession: all the men in the Rabinowitz family have been cantors, men who lead a synagogue's congregation in sung prayer. Jakie, however, as a second-generation American Jew exposed to the American melting pot's wealth of new rhythms and melodies, prefers to sing jazz. His father becomes angry that his son is seemingly forsaking the music of his Jewish heritage for American jazz. (In one inventive sequence, while Jakie is singing "Blue Skies,"

his father comes in and shouts "Stop!"; just at that point, the film switches from a sound sequence back into a silent film.) Forced to choose between the two types of music and the cultures they represent, Jakie runs away from home and tries his luck singing on stage. Jakie's interest in leaving behind his heritage in favor of American popular music indicates his aptitude for assimilation. As part of that trend, Jakie Rabinowitz changes his name to Jack Robin – in effect erasing his Jewish identity (his minority-ethnic-sounding name) for a more nondescript

Al Jolson in blackface as Jake Rabinowitz/Jack Robin in his most famous role, *The Jazz Singer* (1927).
The Jazz Singer, copyright © 1927, Warner Bros.

year, a film about an anti-Semitic murder, *Crossfire* (1947), was released. Sadly, many of the people involved in making it were soon targets of suspicion and hatred themselves. Director Edward Dmytryk and actor Sam Levene (along with many other Jewish people in the film industry) were accused of being communist agents by **HUAC**, the **House Un-American Activities Committee**. The ensuing Red Scare threw studio executives into a panic. These allegations of communist influence in Hollywood were again tinged with (and, some have argued, fueled by) the anti-Semitism of prominent politicians and social commentators. The results of this postwar paranoia did put a disproportionate amount of Jews in Hollywood out of work. Fear of being considered un-American also curtailed the production of social problem films. Images of Jews in Hollywood films did not disappear in the wake of the Red Scare, but they were now rarely shown as part of present-day America. Rather, Hollywood films of the 1950s tended to represent Jews as oppressed minorities in Biblical epics white-sounding name, just as many other Jewish actors in show business were being encouraged to do.

Intriguingly, the person who guides Jack to stardom is fellow stage performer Mary Dale. Mary actively attempts to usher Jack into the inner circle of assimilated whiteness, by helping him move up the ladder of theatrical success. The character of Mary Dale is enacted by "real-life" Irish American actress May McAvoy, who played the Colleen type in many 1920s movies. While she kept her Irish-sounding name, McAvoy was accepted as white, and in playing this role, she embodies a successful example of Irish American assimilation. Most audiences today would probably not even think of her character as Irish. Mary Dale/May McAvoy literally personifies the whiteness that Jack is moving toward. During the one moment in the film in which we see May perform on stage, she is wearing a fluffy white tutu and a peroxide wig that makes her hair appear to be gleaming white, literally a vision of whiteness.

On the other hand, Jack's big chance on Broadway is tied to his performing in blackface, simultaneously emphasizing his difference from African Americans *and* the similarities in their marginal racial/ethnic status. Star Al Jolson was himself renowned for his blackface act. Yet the film does not introduce blackface until a key point in the story. Jack is just about to perform his final dress rehearsal before opening night on Broadway when he finds out that his father is dying and wants his son to take his place as cantor. The film draws out the emotional tug-of-war going on in Jack as he grapples with the lure of stardom/assimilation and his love of and sense of

obligation to his Jewish upbringing. It is at this moment, as Jack is suffering through this turmoil, that he puts on blackface. The sadness and sense of difference he feels become linked to his transformation into an African American stereotype. In one shot, Jack/Jakie looks sadly in the mirror at himself in blackface, and his reflection dissolves to a vision of his father as cantor. The superimposition of the two images further strengthens the sense of Jewish blackface performance as somehow expressive of an outsider status.

The film resolves these tensions when Jakie decides to sing for his father instead of appearing on opening night – yet by the next season Jack Robin has nonetheless become a star on Broadway. The film does not bother to explain how this came to be, even though Mary and the show's producer had told Jack that he would be finished in show business if he opted for his father instead of the play. Yet, in typical Hollywood "happy-ending" style, Jack has been able to hold onto his Jewish heritage and *still* assimilate. A more consistent motif of the film that expresses the same idea is, again, tied to sound. Many people tell Jack that, unlike the average jazz singer, he sings "with a tear in his voice," a description of his singing that associates his uniqueness directly with his training as a Jewish cantor. Jack is a better singer *because* of his ethnic heritage, even as he must assimilate to some degree in order to find acceptance. Produced by American Jews in Hollywood, *The Jazz Singer* endorses Jewish assimilation into whiteness, but not by necessarily denying Jewish identity in the process.

such as *The Ten Commandments* (1956) and *Ben-Hur* (1959). These films addressed social prejudice, but from a safe historical distance and within the framework of mainstream Christianity.

Contemporary Jewish American characters returned to American films during the 1960s. Just as the countercultural critique of whiteness resulted in a new generation of Italian American film actors, so too did a number of Jewish American performers become stars at this time: Barbra Streisand, Elliot Gould, Dustin Hoffman, Woody Allen. However, unlike their counterparts of earlier generations, these actors did not have to efface their Jewish identity by changing their names, revamping their looks, or playing only Christian characters. Today, Jewish Americans remain a strong presence in the film industry, and most of them no longer fear the possibility of anti-Semitic backlashes. While many Jewish filmmakers still focus on stories and issues central to white Christian America, there is ever-greater room for films about the Jewish American experience or films that center on issues of historical importance, such as *Schindler's List* (1993) or *Focus* (2001). Some contemporary films, like *Keeping Up With the Steins* (2006), use gentle humor to celebrate the peccadilloes of Jewish American culture and/or American ethnicities in general. Similarly, the romantic comedy *Keeping the Faith* (2000) starred Ben Stiller as a rabbi, Edward Norton as an Irish American priest, and Jenna Elfman as the woman torn between them. The film acknowledges many of our contemporary culture's ethnic and religious differences with humor and sensitivity.

While such developments seem to indicate that Jewish Americans have largely been accepted as white, anti-Semitism continues to be kept alive within various white supremacist groups and fundamentalist Christian communities. The survival of demonic Jewish stereotypes was made vividly clear with the release (and enormous box office success) of *The Passion of the Christ* (2004). This harrowing retelling of Jesus Christ's torture and crucifixion, directed by Mel Gibson, acknowledges that both Romans and Jews were involved in his death, yet presents his Jewish persecutors as the more twisted and grotesque figures. Jewish communities were aghast and protested the film across the country. And although Gibson denied any anti-Semitic intentions in his film, he was caught making anti-Semitic comments during an arrest for drunk driving in 2006. (He later issued a public apology.) Such films and incidents highlight the fact that assimilation into whiteness is a process that is always ongoing, as well as that fear and/or hatred of the Other remains a powerful force in many Americans' lives.

Veiled and Reviled: Arabs on Film in America

Like all of the cultural groups discussed throughout this book, the five million people of Arab descent living in America today are a highly diverse group of people. They can trace their national heritages to over 20 nations that stretch across Northern Africa (such as Morocco, Libya, Egypt) and onto the Arabian Peninsula (including Lebanon, Syria, Yemen, Saudi Arabia, and Iraq). The Arab world overlaps with the Middle East, which also includes Israel, Turkey, and Iran. Often what seems to define the idea of the Middle East in Western thinking is the Arabic language and/or the Muslim religion, although there are many different languages spoken and religions practiced throughout the entire region. In fact, there are more African American Muslims in the United States than Arab American Muslims, and most Lebanese Americans identify themselves as Christians.

Much of the current strife in the Middle East is a continuation of centuries-long struggles between religions, tribes, and nations. During the Middle Ages, Christian Europeans waged war against Muslims (and others) in an attempt to claim and colonize the Holy Lands. These so-called **Crusades** eventually gave way to more modern forms of **colonialism**, wherein various European powers controlled the region, extracting material wealth and strategic advantages. The situation was exacerbated by the creation of the Jewish state of Israel by the United Nations in 1948. Israel was created by dividing the former British territory of Palestine; Palestine was mostly inhabited by Arabs, and they vehemently rejected the partitioning. Wars and armed conflict between Israel, Palestine, and Palestine's Arab supporters immediately resulted and continue to this day. In yet other parts of the Middle East, corruption and greed for the area's wealth and strategic location allowed for the rise of brutal dictators (Muammar Qaddafi of Libya, Saddam Hussein of Iraq), and most recently anti-Western religious extremists such as the Taliban, Hezbollah, and Al Qaeda. Much of the Middle East continues to be an unstable region filled with violent struggle, fueled by highly diverse and opposing nations, religions, cultures, and ideologies. As such, Americans of Middle Eastern descent are themselves a highly diverse group of individuals.

Intriguingly, one of the most significant things about Arab Americans onscreen in America is their relative scarcity: Hollywood has much more regularly depicted images of *Middle Eastern Arabs* while nearly ignoring the presence of *Arab Americans*. In classical Hollywood cinema, Middle Eastern Arabs could sometimes be found interacting with British or French protagonists (as soldiers, explorers, archaeologists, or tourists), images that reflected the history of European colonialism in the region. In films such as *Beau Geste* (1926 and 1939) and *The Four Feathers* (1915, 1929, 1939, and 2002), European armies battle scores of Arab tribesmen, and the films somehow make it seem as though the Arabs rather than the colonizing nations are the villainous invaders. Sultans are shown sending their armies to lay siege to the white soldiers' fortresses, scimitars blazing and ululations rending the air to make them seem strange and terrifying. Some critics have referred to these films as "Easterns," because their narrative tropes seem almost identical to those of the Hollywood Western, replacing **bloodthirsty** Indian **savages** with bloodthirsty Arab ones.

In other films, Arabs were sexualized figures who either enticed or otherwise served the lusts of white lead characters. Intriguingly, a number of Hollywood films show Europeans "going native" – being personally transformed by participating in Arabic culture – one aspect of **Orientalist** desire. As discussed more fully in chapter 6, Orientalism is the term used to describe the ways in which the West has imagined the East (including the Middle East) as an exciting, primitive, and sensual landscape, the alleged opposite and repressed Other of white Western civilization. Thus, in the incredibly popular silent film *The Sheik*, "Latin Lover" Rudolph Valentino plays the titular Sheik Ahmed, who forcefully and lustfully kidnaps a chaste British heiress named Diana. She is simultaneously terrified and thrilled, but their romance cannot become acceptable until it is discovered that Ahmed is actually of European lineage. Decades later, the epic *Lawrence of Arabia* (1962) dramatized how English soldier T. E. Lawrence (Peter O'Toole) was attracted to and eventually adopted into Arab tribes as they fought for independence from their colonizers. Similar to the sexual and racial overtones of *The Sheik*, there are subtle indications that Lawrence's fascination with Arab culture is linked to both homosexual and sadomasochistic desires on his part.

Probably the most pervasive image of sexualized Arabs in Hollywood films is that of the belly dancer or harem girl. Again a function of Orientalism, the Hollywood harem is presented as an exotic *Arabian Nights* fantasy wherein anything (sexual) is possible. From the early silent film *A Prisoner in the Harem* (1913) to the Bob Hope–Bing Crosby musical comedy *The Road to Morocco* (1942) to Elvis Presley in *Harum Scarum* (1966), harems have been a constant source of fascination for white audiences, reducing Arab women to little more than dark-skinned and sensual objects. Arab culture as a site of mysterious unbridled sexuality is even at the heart of the classical Hollywood horror film *The Mummy* (1932), as well as its countless sequels, remakes, and updates (even into the twenty-first century). In *The Mummy*, Im-Ho-Tep (played by British actor Boris Karloff) is a monstrous living-dead Egyptian prince who lusts after a Western woman who may or may not be the reincarnation of his lost love.

As noted above, rarely have Arabs been shown becoming part of the fabric of either European or American communities. There has been an attitude among many that people of Arab heritage cannot assimilate into Western society (as in the adage "East is East and West is West, and never the twain shall meet"). Just as Irish and Italian Catholic Americans were once considered unable to assimilate because they supposedly held a stronger allegiance to the pope than to the president, so too do many today assume that Arab Americans pledge allegiance to the Muslim faith and not the United States. One of the few assimilated Middle Easterners to appear in Hollywood film is the Persian peddler Ali Hakim (Eddie Albert) in *Oklahoma!* (1955). Yet Ali Hakim is more an all-purpose exotic character used for comic effect than a genuine expression of emigration and/or assimilation. An inflammatory representation of an unassimilated Arab American character from the same era can be found in Herschell Gordon Lewis's cult gore film *Blood Feast* (1963). In it, Egyptian caterer Fuad Ramses brutally murders a string of women in order to prepare a cannibalistic feast in honor of an Egyptian deity. This linkage of sex, violence, and (non-Christian) religion continues to mark more contemporary stereotypes of Arabs and Arab Americans.

By the late 1960s, as the United States became more involved in the Middle East due to both the need for oil and support of the new nation of Israel, the old image of the sultan was reconfigured into that of the modern-day oil mogul. A small number of films included subplots about wealthy Arabs being sent to America for schooling. Although this younger generation were often pictured as enjoying American culture, their presence was more often played for comic "culture clash" shtick. For example, in *John Goldfarb, Please Come Home* (1965), the "Crown Prince of Fawzia" (Patrick Adiarte) tells his father King Fawz (British actor Peter Ustinov) that he has been expelled from Notre Dame because he is Arab and not Irish. Many Arab Americans have taken offense at the almost comic-book stereotypes in this film. Yet it is also possible to read this little-known comedy, written by Arab American screenwriter William Peter Blatty (who would later go on to write the novel and Oscar-winning screenplay of *The Exorcist* [1973]), as a parody of Arab stereotypes – as well as American foreign policy. The king creates his own football team with his guards, coached by a bumbling American pilot named John Goldfarb (Richard Crenna), and uses his connections with the US State Department to force Notre Dame to play them. Although a few Arab Americans of the era protested the film, it was the University of Notre Dame that was most upset. They sued (unsuccessfully) its studio, 20th Century-Fox, at least in part because the Arab team wins the football match!

The growing economic power of Arab nations (and resentment of them in some Americans) was exacerbated in the 1970s as OPEC (Organization of Petroleum Exporting Countries) instituted a petroleum embargo, resulting in gas shortages and higher prices. Also, by the 1970s, a number of radical groups working for the liberation of Palestine or for other Arab or Muslim causes made headlines with bombings, kidnappings, and airplane hijackings, culminating in the 1979 kidnapping of 52 American hostages in Iran, who were held for more than a year. These various developments led to the rise of what has become today the most prevalent image of Arabs: the **Muslim terrorist**. Ever since the 1970s, Arab terrorists have become an easy cliché in action films like *The Delta Force* (1986), *Executive Decision* (1996), *G.I. Jane* (1997), and *Rules of Engagement* (2000). While often these films show white American heroes battling Arabs in foreign lands, Arab terrorists have also been shown "infiltrating" (as opposed to assimilating) into US society in order to bring it down. *Black Sunday* (1977), for example, shows a Palestinian terrorist plotting to hijack the Goodyear Blimp and hold the Super Bowl hostage. Other Arab terrorists in the US factor into films as diverse as *Back to the Future* (1985), *True Lies* (1994), and *The Siege* (1998). *The Siege* is a curious film. While it presents Arab Americans as terrorists, it also includes an Arab American FBI agent. Furthermore, the film eerily presages the aftermath of the 9/11 attacks by dramatizing both a growth of racism against Arab Americans as well as America's willingness to rescind personal liberties guaranteed under the Constitution.

Another film that seemed almost designed to inflame prejudices against Middle Easterners and people of Middle Eastern descent was *Not Without My Daughter* (1991). Based on a true story, the film is about an all-American (that is, white) woman played by Sally Field who marries an Iranian American man and begins a family. He convinces her to make a visit to his homeland, which turns into a permanent stay. In an extreme example of the supposed inability to assimilate, the husband "reverts" to Islamic fundamentalism, much to the shock and fear of his wife. He is willing to let her go, but not his daughter, whom he regards as Iranian and not American. The rest of the film entails the wife's attempt to escape the country with her daughter. The film and its relevance to Middle Eastern cultures remain hotly debated on fan-based websites: some maintain it is an accurate depiction of how women are treated in some Middle Eastern nations, while others see it as negative stereotyping at its worst.

During the 1990s, growing groups of American citizens such as the **ADC** (the **American-Arab Anti-Discrimination Committee**) began to protest these types of media stereotypes. They picketed films like *The Siege* and *Rules of Engagement*, handing out leaflets challenging the films' portrayal of Muslim and Arab cultures. An even more vociferous action was waged against the use of stereotypes in Disney's *Aladdin* (1992). Disney eventually agreed to rewrite some offensive song lyrics, but not to eliminate or alter other scenes – and the studio has continued to use

Arab stereotypes for comic effect in live-action pictures such as *Father of the Bride II* (1995) and *Kazaam* (1996). Such protests against media stereotyping have continued into the twenty-first century, but the events of September 11, 2001, seemed to give terrifying credence to the "accuracy" of the terrorist stereotype. Of course, most Muslim and/or Arab Americans have nothing to do with terrorism, yet they have been subjected to increased surveillance, random hate crimes, and continued stereotyping and profiling. Many Americans seemingly make no distinction between Arabs, Arab Americans, and Muslim terrorists. The United States itself was content to invade Iraq in alleged retaliation for the September 11 attacks, despite the fact that Iraq had few-to-no connections with the international terrorists who caused them.

Occasional independent or Hollywood films (such as *Party Girl* [1995], *Sorry, Haters* [2005], *Crash* [2004], or *American Dreamz* [2006]) may try to individuate Arab Americans, even as the Arab American characters often still fall back into stereotypes. Still, the image of the Arab terrorist continues to be prevalent in American films and television shows. Most recently, and perhaps most egregiously, the "historical" action film *300* (2006) cast white British actors as heroic Spartans battling hordes of (literally) monstrous, dark-skinned, and sexually perverse Persians. The film seemed almost designed to exploit and capitalize on current anti-Arab and anti-Muslim feelings in American culture; its grotesque stereotyping encourages audiences to hate and fear its Persian characters while simultaneously inflaming and justifying white masculine violence. However, the film did not go unchallenged by media scholars and even the Iranian government itself.

Against this complex socio-political backdrop, it is perhaps no surprise that Arab and/or Arab American actors in Hollywood have not had an easy time finding challenging or complex characters to play. One of the first actors of openly Arab descent to make a name for himself was **Omar Sharif**, who was an Egyptian film

Shaun Toub as a Persian shopkeeper in *Crash* (2004), one of the few Hollywood films of recent years to include even one American character of Middle Eastern descent. *Crash*, dir. Paul Haggis, copyright © 2004, Lions Gate Films

Egyptian-born Omar Sharif, seen here as Jewish entrepreneur Nicky Arnstein opposite Barbra Streisand as Jewish comedienne Fanny Brice in *Funny Girl*. Who is white and who is not? *Funny Girl*, copyright © 1968, Columbia

star before his performance in *Lawrence of Arabia* earned him an Oscar nomination and catapulted him to international fame. After his lead role as *Dr Zhivago* (1965), he played leading men in several Hollywood films including *Funny Girl* (1968) and *Funny Lady* (1975). Today he works mostly in Europe. American actors of Lebanese heritage such as Danny Thomas, Jamie Farr, and Casey Kasem have worked more regularly in television and radio. Thomas was the star of the popular sitcom *Make Room for Daddy* (1953–65), Farr played the cross-dressing Corporal Klinger in the TV show *M*A*S*H* (1972–83), and Kasem has had a decades-long career as a successful radio host and voice-over artist, performing the voice of Shaggy in the long-running *Scooby-Doo* cartoons.

Other actors of Arab descent include F. Murray Abraham (who won an Oscar for his role as Salieri in *Amadeus* [1984]), Shohreh Aghdashloo (who garnered an Oscar nomination for her role as an Iranian immigrant in *House of Sand and Fog* [2003]), Alexander Siddig (Dr Bashir on *Star Trek: Deep Space Nine* [1993–9]), and Tony Shaloub (*Monk* [2001–]). It should be noted, though, that many actors of Middle Eastern heritage are still regularly cast as terrorists or sheiks; if they want to work, they are sometimes compelled to accept those roles. Also, many still feel compelled to alter or change their Arabic-sounding names in order to work in the business. For example, F. Murray Abraham's birth name is Fahrid Murray Abraham; the actor's official stage name potentially hides his Middle Eastern heritage.

Conclusion: Whiteness and American Film Today

Whiteness is still the unspoken ideal in American movies. Yet, as our society continues to become more diverse, so too do our movie screens. During the 1990s, multiculturalism was increasingly endorsed and/or celebrated in America, culminating in the Federal Census Bureau allowing people to check off more than one racial category for the first time in 2000. Possibly in response, many people who regarded themselves as white in the 1990s began reconnecting to their ethnic heritages, taking pride in their Irish, Italian, or other roots. Thus, these individuals could consider themselves *both* white and part of the nation's diversity. Also, a number of white-identified youth (predominantly male) increasingly adopted the trappings of African American urban culture (its music, its fashion, its slang) in an effort to distance themselves from whiteness. (Songs like "Pretty Fly for a White Guy" and the film *Malibu's Most Wanted* [2003] satirize this trend.)

Furthermore, actors, like all Americans, are coming from increasingly diverse backgrounds, including mixed-race and mixed-nation families. F. Murray Abraham, mentioned above, was born in Pennsylvania to parents of Italian and Syrian descent. Salma Hayek's heritage is Lebanese and Mexican. Jessica Alba's father is from Mexico, while her mother is of French and Danish descent. Rashida Jones, who plays Karen Filippelli in the hit comedy *The Office* (2005–), is the daughter of African American musician Quincy Jones and white actress Peggy Lipton. Other contemporary actors with mixed-ethnic backgrounds include Dwayne "The Rock" Johnson, Jennifer Beals, and Vin Diesel. For a brief moment, Vin Diesel seemed poised to become the next big Hollywood action star, allegedly appealing to black and white audiences simultaneously. Before his Hollywood successes, however, Diesel wrote and directed a short film about media stereotypes. *Multi-Facial* (1999) follows Diesel's character as he auditions for roles as an Italian American, a Latino, and a black rapper. His shifting personas in front of the casting directors (as well as his fellow actors) suggest that race and/or ethnicity is merely a matter of performance, a certain attention to and replication of behavioral traits and speech patterns. As a calling card, the film propelled Diesel into his Hollywood career, but it also chides the film industry (and especially casting directors) for perpetuating racial and ethnic stereotypes.

The growth in the number of performers who seem to transcend racial or ethnic categories may seem like a positive development in American film and television. Yet it should be recognized that industry interest in such individuals is often more due to economic interests than social or political ones. If some people regard, for example, Dwayne "The Rock" Johnson as white, and others as a person of color, then he potentially draws in multiple audiences. Furthermore, the public perception of such stars taps into the historically complex issues and opinions over passing and assimilation within white communities *and* communities of color. Still, the growing awareness and acceptance of multi-ethnic identities further complicates what many usually assume as the unproblematic nature of whiteness.

Questions for Discussion

1   Think about your own national, ethnic, or racial heritage. To what extent does it shape your personal identity? Share your thoughts with your classmates. Are people of color more aware of these issues than are many whites? If so, why?

2   What are the pros and cons of assimilation? What should America's "national identity" be? How does film help to construct that national identity?

3   Religion is a powerful **ideological state apparatus**. How does religion intersect with questions of race and nation? What role does religion play in the process of assimilation (or resistance to assimilation)? Are some cultural groups more defined by their religion than by their race or nation?

Further Reading

Bernardi, Daniel, ed. *The Birth of Whiteness: Race and the Emergence of U.S. Cinema*. New Brunswick, NJ: Rutgers University Press, 1996.

Bernardi, Daniel, ed. *Classic Hollywood, Classic Whiteness*. Minneapolis: University of Minnesota Press, 2001.

Bernstein, Matthew, and Gaylyn Studlar. *Visions of the East: Orientalism in Film*. New Brunswick, NJ: Rutgers University Press, 1997.

Dyer, Richard. *White*. New York: Routledge, 1997.

Foster, Gwendolyn Audrey. *Performing Whiteness: Postmodern Re/Constructions in Cinema*. Albany, NY: State University of New York Press, 2003.

Freidman, Lester D., ed. *Unspeakable Images: Ethnicity and the American Cinema*. Chicago: University of Illinois Press, 1991.

Gubar, Susan. *RaceChanges: White Skin, Black Face in American Culture*. New York: Oxford University Press, 1997.

Hill, Mike, ed. *Whiteness: A Critical Reader*. New York: New York University Press, 1997.

Lester, Paul Martin and Susan Dente Ross, eds. *Images That Injure: Pictorial Stereotypes in the Media*. 2nd edition. Westport, CT: Praeger, 2003.

Lipsitz, George. *The Possessive Investment in Whiteness: How White People Profit from Identity Politics*. Philadelphia: Temple University Press, 2001.

Miller, Randall, ed. *The Kaleidoscopic Lens: How Hollywood Views Ethnic Groups*. Englewood, NJ: Jerome S. Ozer, 1980.

Negra, Diane. *Off-White Hollywood: American Culture and Ethnic Female Stardom*. New York: Routledge, 2001.

Negra, Diane, ed. *The Irish in Us: Irishness, Performativity, and Popular Culture*. Durham, NC: Duke University Press, 2006.

Rogin, Michael. *Blackface, White Noise: Jewish Immigrants in the Hollywood Melting Pot*. Los Angeles: University of California Press, 1996.

Semmerling, Tim Jon. *"Evil" Arabs in American Popular Film: Orientalist Fear*. Austin: University of Texas Press, 2006.

Sheehan, Jack G. *Reel Bad Arabs: How Hollywood Vilifies a People*. New York: Olive Branch Press, 2001.

Further Screening

Going My Way (1944)
Gentleman's Agreement (1947)
The Quiet Man (1952)
Marty (1955)
Annie Hall (1976)
Moonstruck (1988)
You've Got Mail (1996)

Pleasantville (1998)
The Siege (1998)
Multi-Facial (1999)
Focus (2001)
Gangs of New York (2002)
House of Sand and Fog (2003)

Chapter 4

AFRICAN AMERICANS AND AMERICAN FILM

The cinematic **representations** of African Americans analyzed in this chapter provide specific historical examples of this book's central tenets. By studying the history of these images, one can see that there have been significant changes in the ways that African Americans have been depicted on screen. Those varying images are in many ways reflective of the changing social climate of America over the past century, and those images have, in turn, contributed to the ways in which all Americans understand the meaning of "African American-ness." While contemporary Hollywood images of African Americans may still leave something to be desired, they are recognizably different from the images presented during the early days of cinema. Opportunities for African Americans within the film industry are also measurably different than they were during previous eras. However, since American cinema for the most part functions under the dominant ideology of **white patriarchal capitalism**, it should not be surprising to discover that most popular film helps maintain dominant cultural attitudes toward African Americans (and issues of race in general). For example, something that has not changed significantly throughout the past century is that there still is a concept of this group, African Americans, as markedly not white, unlike several of the cultural groups surveyed in the last chapter.

African Americans in Early Film

Stereotyped images of African Americans appear in some of the earliest films ever made, including Thomas Edison's *The Watermelon Contest* (1896) and *Sambo and Aunt Jemima* (1897). Many of these exaggerated and derogatory images were borrowed from pre-existing cultural artifacts (books, music, and theater) popular in the so-called **antebellum** (or pre-Civil War) South, where African people (among others) had been routinely treated as chattels and bred as slave labor for over 400 years. Popular cultural images which depicted slaves as less than human greatly aided in their subjugation, for if African Americans could be thought of as beasts in the field, slavery could be justified as a moral economic endeavor. One of the most popular antebellum theatrical entertainments was the **minstrel show**, a type of musical comedy variety show that featured white actors impersonating blacks (or, as discussed in the previous chapter, European immigrants striving to be accepted as white). This tradition of **blackface** continued into the theatrical and cinematic traditions of the twentieth century. Although recent research has revealed many cultural complexities within the blackface tradition, the practice was still dependent upon broad and mostly demeaning stereotypes, being in effect the white man's misguided perception of what black lives were actually like.

Film historian Donald Bogle has identified five stereotypes of African Americans that repeatedly appear in **classical Hollywood cinema**; several of these are directly traceable to the nineteenth-century minstrel show. The ineffectual and lazy **Coon** stereotype was a foolish, jive-talking simpleton who would do anything to avoid work. The **Uncle Tom** character was a black house slave who faithfully served his white master. Uncle Tom's female counterpart was the **Mammy**, an overweight black woman who took care of the white master's children, without concern for her own. The Coon, Uncle Tom, and Mammy figures all represented black people as childlike, asexual, and happily docile. They were images that directly supported the supposed beneficence of slavery. Once slavery was ended however, the stereotypes turned even more disturbing. The **Tragic Mulatto** was a woman born of a mixed-race marriage or sexual union. She invariably died at the end of her story, punishment for her "sin" of being of mixed race (and for being sexual herself). The **Black Buck** was a brutal, animalistic, and hypermasculine African American man who threatened the white establishment because of his alleged sexual prowess. Both the Tragic Mulatto and the Black Buck stereotypes suggest a psycho-sexual dimension to social prejudice, centered as they are on fears of **miscegenation**, the sexual or romantic mixing of races. The Black Buck stereotype seems to be a reflection of white men's fears about black male power, and especially the fear that black men might brutalize and rape white women in retribution against white slave owners, who had done the same to black women for centuries.

These five stereotypes were prevalent throughout the first decades of film history, perhaps most vividly on view in D. W. Griffith's infamous film, *The Birth of a Nation* (1915). Griffith's film was based upon a novel by Thomas Dixon entitled *The Clansman*; both book and film celebrate the birth of the Ku Klux Klan, a white supremacist group that was responsible throughout much of the late nineteenth and twentieth centuries for waging terrorist attacks on African American people. Griffith's three-hour film was also a breakthrough in epic, emotionally manipulative moviemaking. It uses Hollywood form and style to whip up audience sympathy – and prejudice. *The Birth of a Nation* was so effective at inciting hatred for blacks that it was used for decades as a recruiting tool by the Klan. Certain scenes also employed what Griffith termed "historical reconstructions" of actual events, a stylistic move that allowed the entire film to be perceived by some as documentary truth and not manipulative Hollywood fiction. Even President Woodrow Wilson, mistaking fiction for actuality, allegedly said it was "like writing

In *The Birth of a Nation* (1915), a mulatto rabble rouser played by a white actor in dark makeup (right) plays on the sympathies of white liberal politicians; his evil plans include "equal marriage" between the white and black races. *The Birth of a Nation*, copyright © 1915, Griffith

history with lightning" – surely a powerful metaphor for the ideological effects of cinema.

Throughout *The Birth of a Nation*, African Americans are depicted as lazy, ignorant, vicious, and rapacious. The few "good Negroes" in the film are those who faithfully serve their white masters: a Mammy and an Uncle Tom figure. The primary villain of the story is a mulatto rabble rouser named Silas Lynch who lusts after white women, a plot point designed to inflame social taboos against inter-racial relationships. Similarly, in another plot strand, Gus, a Black Buck figure, chases a young white woman through the woods until she throws herself over a cliff in order to preserve her "honor." As was common for the era, both Silas Lynch and Gus were played by white actors in blackface – African Americans were only used as extras in the background scenes. Furthermore, while the story focuses on two noble white families (the Northern Stonemans and the Southern Camerons), black people are more regularly shown as members of unruly mobs, apparently without families. During the film's climax, for example, when black mobs take over the streets, Griffith repeatedly cuts away to **tableau** shots of good white families endangered by the menace. Erasing images of African American families works further to estrange the black characters from audiences, making them less sympathetic and more animalistic. (Accusing minority groups of having no sense of "family," in order to justify prejudice against them, continues to this day.)

In 1915, the year *The Birth of a Nation* was released, African Americans lived under severe social restrictions brought about by prejudice. In the South, the so-called **Jim Crow Laws** defined in detail ways that black people were to be afforded unequal treatment, while in the North prejudicial treatment was less legally inscribed but still a fact of everyday life. One aspect of this institutionalized racism was the segregation of community facilities: separate white and black public restrooms, drinking fountains, etc. This included seating in movie houses: except for theaters in African American neighborhoods, blacks were required to sit in balconies or attend separate screenings, segregated from white patrons. Various African Americans did what they could to combat the racism of the era. The **NAACP** (**National Association for the Advancement of Colored People**) had been founded in 1908 out of a pre-existing group called the Niagara Movement. The NAACP and other groups battled racism in all sectors of American life. They organized protests against *The Birth of a Nation*, but as often happens with the marketing of Hollywood films, such protests actually made the film more successful, as audiences flocked to see the source of the controversy.

A few black filmmakers decided the best way to counter the racist images in *The Birth of a Nation* was to make another film that would show African Americans in a more favorable light. From 1916 to 1918, African American filmmakers struggled to produce *The Birth of a Race* (1918), but because of white patriarchal capitalist control of the industry, the film emerged as a very muddled epic about the current world war. *The Birth of a Race* was a commercial failure, but it did foreshadow the rise of **race movies**, independently produced black-cast films which were distributed to black movie theaters from the late 1910s to the 1950s. (The rise of the race movie coincided with – but was separate from – the **Harlem Renaissance**, a flowering of black art, music, literature, and culture that occurred in the urban north during the 1920s and 1930s.) Compared to Hollywood films, race movies were frequently cheaply made and technically inferior; African Americans were not allowed to enter trade unions to learn skills such as editing or cinematography. Nonetheless, many small filmmaking companies, including Reol, the Lincoln Motion Picture Company, the Ebony Film Corporation, and the Colored Players Corporation, made films that presented more complex images of African Americans and their concerns than did Hollywood.

The most famous filmmaker to come out the race movie industry was **Oscar Micheaux**. Micheaux wrote, produced, and directed 30 films, many adapted from his own novels. His Micheaux Book and Film Company produced his first movie, *The Homesteader*, in 1918. In films such as *Within Our Gates* (1919) and *Body and Soul* (1925), Micheaux tackled the issues of lynching, light-skinned African Americans **passing** for white, and corruption within black churches. Other Micheaux films were simply mysteries or melodramas, but even they were significant because they presented a range of black characters, from middle-class professionals to illiterate Southern sharecroppers.

In the late 1920s, Micheaux and his colleagues had a difficult time making the costly transition to sound film production that the Hollywood majors were undertaking. Many of the black-owned and black-operated filmmaking companies of the silent period were therefore taken over by white entrepreneurs. These new white backers shifted their productions away from potentially controversial material toward more escapist fare. Thus, throughout the 1930s and 1940s, these white producers of race movies copied popular Hollywood genres, and produced black Westerns, black gangster films, and black musicals. Most of them lacked any of the critical commentary on race that could be found in earlier black-produced race movies. One potential exception to this trend was the work of **Spencer Williams**, a prolific actor, writer, and director of race movies. He directed at least nine films during the 1940s, and his *Blood of Jesus* (1941) is often said to have been the most popular race movie of all time. His films bear his trademark self-deprecating humor and an interest in Christian morality as it was expressed within African American communities of the era.

Adapting film genres for African American concerns, as race movies frequently did, raises several important issues about the structure and form of Hollywood cinema. On the one hand, it was probably pleasurable for many black audiences to see black cowboys and black gangsters on the screen. African American actors were now playing the same types of roles that white actors were playing within Hollywood movies. Yet embedded within film **genres** are codes and conventions that carry **ideological** significance in and of themselves. For example, in the simplified Hollywood Western formula, the good guy often wears a white hat and rides a white horse while the villain wears black. This color code is present in our language and culture as well: white signifies purity, grace, and heavenly goodness while black is usually associated with night, dirt, and evil. In the making of black-cast Westerns, these codes were rarely challenged (and perhaps they were not even consciously recognized by 1930s audiences and filmmakers). Yet in following that particular genre formula, black-cast Westerns continued to inscribe darkness as villainous, even as the films themselves championed black heroes. The issue also extended to casting: frequently, lighter-skinned blacks played heroes and heroines while darker-skinned actors were chosen for the villains. Thus, even as race movies showcased more diverse and heroic black characters, at the same time they potentially reinscribed certain racist tropes common to Hollywood film practice.

Blacks in Classical Hollywood Cinema

Hollywood in the 1930s and 1940s, as a conservative business with its eye on making money and not offending the status quo, did little to challenge the racist ideologies of the era. The stereotypes of African Americans that *The Birth of a Nation* had capitalized upon became Hollywood's usual way of representing African Americans until the end of World War II. If anything, the range of African American images presented in Hollywood films grew smaller after the enforcement of the **Production Code** in 1934. The Tragic Mulatto was used less and less because her very presence invoked the idea of miscegenation, a topic the Code had expressly forbidden. The hypersexual implications of the Black Buck stereotype were also taboo to classical Hollywood filmmakers, although one can find traces of the stereotype in the "wild natives" of countless "Tarzan" movies, or in the zombies and henchmen of numerous **horror films**. Consequently, the few representations of African Americans in classical Hollywood films were pre-dominantly unthreatening and almost childish. The comedic Coon stereotype remained prevalent, exemplified by the work of character actors such as Stepin Fetchit, Willie Best, and Mantan Moreland. The Uncle Tom stereotype was reworked for modern-day stories as the servile doorman, butler, or shoeshine "boy" that populated the background of many classical Hollywood films. The Mammy was also the helpmate or servant to white women and children in countless films.

Thus, throughout the 1930s and 1940s, African Americans appeared most often in stereotyped supporting roles, and almost never in leading ones. African American actors who wanted to work in Hollywood film found themselves forced into playing these often demeaning roles. Nevertheless, many African American actors were able to turn their bit parts into memorable characters. Hattie McDaniel, Clarence Muse, Louise Beavers, and Rex Ingram were among those actors often able to create characters with dignity and self-respect, even when the film's stories set them up as comedic stereotypes. For example, Hattie McDaniel won an Oscar for her role as Mammy in *Gone With the Wind* (1939), a historic first which seemed to foreshadow the increasing liberalism of 1940s Hollywood. Yet it must be remembered that even winning an Oscar did not mean that Hattie McDaniel could suddenly be cast in

Stepin Fetchit was a character actor from the 1930s whose "Coon" roles made him briefly famous.
Unidentified publicity photo, authors' personal collection

roles played by Bette Davis or Joan Crawford. Because of institutionalized racism and the cultural codes of glamor and beauty, Hattie McDaniel was typecast for most of her career as a maid. And while Hollywood may have appeared liberal and progressive in awarding her the Oscar, it should also be remembered that she lived in an area of Los Angeles known as "Black Beverly Hills," because African Americans – no matter how famous or rich – were unwelcome in Beverly Hills itself.

One of the reasons Hollywood kept African American actors in smaller supporting roles was so that prejudiced audiences would not have to watch an entire movie about a Negro, or worse yet, see a black character who was smart, strong, and independent. Sometimes a Hollywood film would feature a black musical performer in a nightclub attended by the white hero and heroine. These musical performances were often shot and edited in such a way that if the number was found to be offensive to white audiences, it could simply be cut from the print by theater managers. This often happened to Lena Horne, the first black musical star to be placed under contract at MGM. Furthermore, the Production Code mandate against miscegenation even went so far as to prohibit interracial dance couples. Bill "Bojangles" Robinson, whom the famous (white) dancer Fred Astaire considered to be the greatest dancer of the era, rarely had the chance to let his talent shine on screen. He could not be shown dancing with a white woman, and studios were loath to cast him in a leading role with an African American love interest.

Bill "Bojangles" Robinson, seen here as a butler in the Shirley Temple film *The Little Colonel* (1935), was considered one of the greatest dancers of his era.
The Little Colonel, copyright © 1935, 20th Century-Fox

Thus, Bill Robinson spent his years in Hollywood enacting mostly character parts, playing servants and butlers and dancing up and down staircases with Shirley Temple. It was assumed that this adult–child dance couple was "safe" and inoffensive in that it did not suggest a romantic relationship between the two.

During the classical period, Hollywood did produce a handful of all black-cast films, mostly musicals with religious overtones that the studios frequently sold as prestige pictures, and with which they could advertise their commitment to art and liberal ideals. These films include *Hallelujah* (1929), *Hearts in Dixie* (1929), *The Green Pastures* (1936), *Cabin in the Sky* (1943), *Stormy Weather* (1943), *Carmen Jones* (1954), and *Porgy and Bess* (1959). Despite the fact that these films were allegedly about black culture and (some of them) feature black musical idioms, all of these films were produced, written, and directed by white men. Because of this, the films present a romanticized and somewhat paternalistic vision of black culture, and they are also filled with stereotypes now commonly viewed as derogatory. Interestingly, Christianity was invoked in many of these films in order to make a plea for social tolerance, much as the **civil rights movement** of the 1950s would be galvanized by Christianity. Yet it should also not be forgotten that many white supremacist groups invoked (and continue to invoke) Christianity to uphold their beliefs regarding the superiority of white people.

World War II and the Postwar Social Problem Film

During the 1940s, the United States experienced a tentative surge of liberalism. As World War II was fought against avowedly racist Axis nations, many people in the United States felt the need to examine racism within our own country. Also, since much of the nation's workforce had become part of the armed forces, home-front industries began hiring both women and racial minorities. (However, such war-induced integration caused riots and retaliatory violence in many places.) African Americans were encouraged by both Hollywood and the federal government to get involved in the war effort, most famously through a government-produced documentary entitled *The Negro Soldier* (1943). This film was made for two main reasons: to explain to American blacks why they should fight, and to help eradicate racism in the ranks. The film was so popular that it crossed over into mainstream distribution, and it remains a powerful example of the US government using film as a means of educating the population about social issues. Even so, the armed forces would not be integrated until after the war, when President Truman issued an executive order for them to be so. President Truman also ordered a special report on US race relations, and a civil rights plank became part of the Democratic party platform during those years. Many Southern Democrat politicians, including Strom Thurmond, left their party over this issue, and eventually found careers within the Republican party. (Strom Thurmond was the US Senator from South Carolina for many decades; in 2002, when Senate Majority Leader Trent Lott implicitly praised Thurmond's racist past, Lott was forced to resign his leadership post.)

The NAACP and other concerned groups petitioned Hollywood throughout the 1940s to make more diverse, less stereotypical representations of African Americans, yet films such as Walt Disney's *Song of the South* (1946) still depicted blacks as happy, docile servants. The spate of **social problem films** that were made in the late 1940s, though, began to tackle the issue of racism in America (in addition to such social issues as returning war veterans, alcoholism, and mental illness). Perhaps unsurprisingly, two of the first films to deal specifically with discrimination against African Americans were independent films. (Recall that the Paramount Consent Decrees [1948] had given more impetus to independent film production in America.) *Home of the Brave* (1949) and *Lost Boundaries* (1949) both addressed racism against black Americans in bold ways (for their era) and, when they made money, the Hollywood majors jumped on the bandwagon, producing films such as *Pinky* (20th Century-Fox, 1949), *Intruder in the Dust* (MGM, 1949), and *No Way Out* (20th Century-Fox, 1950).

The narrative formula of most of these films is to deal with racial issues not from a black point of view, but from a white one. For example, *Intruder in the Dust* focuses on a white boy and his father more than on the black man around whom the story actually revolves. In the somewhat later social problem film *Black Like Me* (1963), white actor James Whitmore literally dons blackface to experience at first hand what racism feel like. Even when the lead characters were African American, white actors sometimes played the parts. For example, in *Lost Boundaries*, a film about

Pinky (1949) was a postwar social problem film that explored contemporary race relations. Here, Jeanne Crane, as a light-skinned African American, is comforted by her granny (Ethel Waters).
Pinky, copyright © 1949, 20th Century-Fox

light-skinned black characters passing for white, the roles were played by white actors. In *Pinky*, a light-skinned black woman is played by white actress Jeanne Crain. (This move also helped the studio get past the Code's miscegenation taboo, allowing Pinky to kiss her white fiancé.) Hollywood obviously felt that this formula – dealing with racism from a white perspective – was necessary to draw in white audiences. Even to this day, many Hollywood social problem films about race feature a white star as the lead character; Hollywood has rarely made a film about racism from an African American perspective. Furthermore, it should be reiterated that these films were all produced, written, and directed by white men.

The production of social problem films waned in the early 1950s, partly because of the **Red Scare** and the witch-hunting tactics of Senator Joe McCarthy. Hollywood stopped making movies that suggested in any way that America was less than perfect. While discussions of racial discrimination receded from movie screens, they became louder in the "real" world. Led by men such as Martin Luther King, African Americans organized for equality throughout the 1950s, demonstrating at boycotts, sit-ins, and marches to draw attention to racism. A major victory for racial equality occurred in the Supreme Court in 1954 when the **Brown v. Board of Education** decision formally outlawed the "separate but equal" Jim Crow Laws that existed throughout the Southern United States. As the 1950s became the 1960s, more and more Americans of all colors and persuasions joined the struggle for civil rights. Northern university students organized in the early 1960s to help the cause, and the country slowly began to become more aware of the terrible effects of American racism. Yet opposition to those movements also became more pronounced, and terrorist crimes against the black community continued to be perpetrated. Institutionally, white racists in positions of power in both state and federal governments repeatedly sought to halt the advance of the civil rights movement.

Hollywood played it very safe during this era, and films about race or featuring African American stories were few and far between. Ethel Waters played memorable and dignified roles in *Member of the Wedding* (1952) and *The Sound and the Fury* (1959), while Dorothy Dandridge was promoted – cautiously – as Hollywood's first African American leading lady. But like many black actresses before her, Dandridge was trapped within the old Hollywood formulas and stereotypes. Even as the Production Code began to weaken and interracial relationships began to be addressed, Dandridge was forced to play jungle goddesses and an array of Tragic Mulattoes who died for their "sin" of miscegenation. Enduring the institutionalized racism of Hollywood may have been too much for Dandridge, and most likely contributed to her death from an overdose of pills in 1965. By far the most successful black actor of the era was **Sidney Poitier**, who starred in films like *The Defiant Ones* (1958), *A Raisin in the Sun* (1961), *A Patch of Blue* (1965), and *Guess Who's Coming to Dinner* (1967). Poitier was considered by many to be a positive role model throughout his career, usually playing educated and articulate characters with great nobility and humanity. He also became the first African American actor to win an Oscar for best lead performance (for *Lilies of the Field* [1963]). Poitier's dignified persona perfectly fit the "passive resistance" strategy of the African American civil rights movement of the 1950s and early 1960s. His characters were non-confrontational black men with whom white viewers could sympathize, while black viewers could appreciate that his characters were markedly different from past stereotypes.

Dorothy Dandridge was one of Hollywood's first African American leading ladies; she was nominated for a Best Actress Oscar for her role in *Carmen Jones* (1954).
Unidentified publicity photo, authors' personal collection

Successful 1960s leading man Sidney Poitier often portrayed educated and polite African American characters, in films like *Guess Who's Coming to Dinner* (1967).
Unidentified publicity photo, authors' personal collection

The Rise and Fall of Blaxploitation Filmmaking

By the mid-1960s, the civil rights movement had become more militant. After years of cautious optimism about the struggle for equal rights, a younger generation of activists grew tired of the slow pace of progress and began to demand civil rights in more vocal and inflammatory ways. Some suggested that equality for African Americans might have to come through violent means. Leaders such as Malcolm X and various members of the Black Panther Party advocated violence against the system where necessary, as such violence was in effect only self-defense. Physical attacks on African Americans were also becoming more violent: Malcolm X was assassinated in 1965, and Martin Luther King in 1968. Racial violence in America reached unprecedented levels, and riots broke out in many major American cities. Many black leaders saw the need for African Americans to close ranks and develop a strong group identity if they were going to challenge the power of institutionalized white supremacy. African culture was rediscovered by many black Americans, and popular slogans of the era such as "Black Power," "Black Pride," and "Black is Beautiful" reveal the forceful charge of this new Black Nationalist movement.

For many filmgoers in this younger, angrier generation, the go-slow, carefully integrationist Hollywood films of Sidney Poitier were an anachronism, and the work of previous African American character actors such as Stepin Fetchit, Hattie McDaniel, and Mantan Moreland were an outright embarrassment. There was clearly a demand for a new type of African American image on screen, and he appeared in a film with the memorable title *Sweet Sweetback's Baaadasss Song* (1971). This film was independently made by African American filmmaker Melvin Van Peebles, and it followed the adventures of Sweet Sweetback, a streetwise hustler, sexual stud, and "justified" white cop killer who escapes to Mexico with the aid of the black and Hispanic communities. The film was a tremendous hit in the independent urban black theaters where it was shown, and it seemed to reflect the new defiant attitude of late 1960s civil rights activists. Huey Newton, leader of the Black Panthers, called it "the first revolutionary Black film."

Hollywood saw the profits *Sweet Sweetback* was making and began to produce its own gritty films about urban black protagonists. These films collectively became known as **blaxploitation films**. Some of the most famous are *Shaft* (1971), *Superfly* (1972), *Blacula* (1972), *The Mack* (1973), and *Willie Dynamite* (1974). Hollywood's blaxploitation films were firmly rooted in traditional genre formulas – gangster, crime thriller, horror movie – and their black leading figures were violent, flashy, and charismatic. Many of the films represented images of black pride and black power, and they frequently exposed the horrors of ghetto living and institutionalized white racism. Blaxploitation filmmaking also provided new and greater opportunities for African American artists in Hollywood. While the majority of these films were still written and directed by white men, many black actors, writers, musicians, and directors did find work making these pictures. Indeed, the music they featured – still-familiar compositions by musicians such as Isaac Hayes and Curtis Mayfield – helped change the very sound of Hollywood films.

Blaxploitation films were not, however, without multiple controversies. As the term "blaxploitation" implies, these films exploited African American audiences in that they took money out of African American communities to fill white Hollywood's bank accounts. These movies were also **exploitation films** – cheaply made and sensationalistic movies that draw audiences by promising gratuitous amounts of sex and violence. Many middle-class blacks began to decry what they saw as negative images in these films. When *Superfly*, a gangster film about a sleek drug dealer, became a huge hit (and black youths started dressing and acting like the lead character), many concerned Americans of all races questioned Hollywood's motives. What kind of a role model for impressionable inner-city youth is a sexy, super-cool cocaine dealer? The short-lived Committee Against Blaxploitation was formed in Hollywood by members of the NAACP and other civil rights groups. Yet when opposition was felt from African American filmmakers who were finding much-needed work within these films, the Committee soon disbanded.

The more usual charge of Hollywood sexism was also leveled against these films. In most of them, the black lead character is a smooth ladies' man, a sort of black James Bond figure who beds women of all races as he fights against "The Man." Some critics charged that this violent blaxploitation hero was simply another version of the old Black Buck stereotype, and that there was no space in the films for complex female characters. Blaxploitation filmmakers responded by placing women in the lead role, and in films like *Cleopatra Jones* (1973), *Coffy* (1973), *Foxy Brown* (1974), and *Friday Foster* (1975), black women "kicked whitey's butt" just as black men had. Yet many people were unhappy with this development as well, especially black spokesmen who felt that the black man had to be raised up before (and often at the expense of) the black woman. To those critics, films with strong females and weaker males were another slap at black manhood, and by extension, the black community. Because of these controversies and the limited nature of the films' generic formulas, blaxploitation filmmaking soon ran out of steam.

Yet not all films produced within this era were cheaply made and sensationalistic. There was a handful of more serious and complex films dealing with African American concerns, including *Lady Sings the Blues* (1972), *Sounder* (1972), *Buck and the Preacher* (1972), *Cooley High* (1975), and *Mahogany* (1975). Throughout the 1970s, movie audiences began to see and recognize serious black actors such as Cicely Tyson, Ossie Davis, James Earl Jones, Paul Winfield, Diana Ross, and Billy Dee Williams. Still, age-old Hollywood formulas persisted, most notably in the movie adaptation of the popular black stage musical *The Wiz* (1978). Sidney Lumet, a white filmmaker who had never before made a musical, was hired to direct this high-budget, black-cast project. Despite the star power of Michael Jackson, Diana Ross, Richard Pryor, and Lena Horne, it was a box office disappointment. For almost a

Box: Blacks on TV

Television became America's most important communication medium in the 1950s. In the early part of the decade, several shows, including *The Jack Benny Program* (1950–65) and *Beulah* (1950–3), featured African American actors in supporting roles, as menservants and maids. The most famous African American show of the era was *Amos 'n' Andy* (CBS, 1951–3). It had been adapted for television from a popular radio show created by Freeman Gosden and Charles Correll, two white "dialecticians" who gave voice to the antics of the show's titular African American characters. When the show was moved to television, black actors were hired to fill the roles. Alvin Childress played Amos, and Spencer Williams, the prolific race-movie filmmaker, played the role of Andy for the show's brief run. Later generations have condemned *Amos 'n' Andy* as a showcase of negative stereotypes created by white men, but the series was hugely popular among both white and black audiences of the early 1950s, and it arguably demonstrated the basic humanity of black people to a pre-civil-rights-era America. It would be many years after its cancellation before another television show would devote itself to leading African American characters.

During the late 1960s and early 1970s, television became more aware of race and racial issues. TV shows such as *Hogan's Heroes* (1965–71), *The Mod Squad* (1968–73), and *Star Trek* (1966–9) began to integrate black characters into their casts. *I Spy* (1965–8) was a **black and white buddy** show starring Bill Cosby and Robert Culp as international secret agents. In 1968, ABC's *Julia* became the first modern situation comedy starring and centering on an African American woman; despite vehement protest from white racists, the show ran until 1971. But it was the work of white television producer Norman Lear that broke much new ground in shows such as *All in the Family* (1971–9), *Sanford and Son* (1972–7), *Good Times* (1974–9), and *The Jeffersons* (1975–85). Norman Lear's shows dealt with topical issues and afforded a wider range of African American images on TV than ever before. For example, the Jeffersons were an upwardly mobile African American family who had an interracial couple as close friends, while *Good Times* chronicled life in the projects for the Evans family. But by far the most important television event of the 1970s centering on America's understanding of race was the broadcast premiere of *Roots* in 1977. One of US television's first mini-series, *Roots* was based on Alex Haley's best-selling novel about the history of slavery in America. The mini-series ran for twelve hours over eight nights, and its broadcast was truly a national event watched by millions of

decade afterwards, Hollywood mostly avoided producing any film projects it considered "black."

Hollywood in the 1980s and the Arrival of Spike Lee

The 1980s were paradoxical years for representations of African Americans. Black superstars in music and on television (Michael Jackson, Prince, Whitney Houston, Bill Cosby, Arsenio Hall, and Oprah Winfrey) were riding high, but it was still very difficult for African Americans to gain power within the Hollywood film industry.

Americans. The compelling drama put a human face on the tragedy of slavery, and afforded Americans the chance to contemplate that terrible institution in emotional as well as intellectual terms.

In the 1980s, *The Cosby Show*, created by and starring actor and comedian Bill Cosby, became one of the most highly rated shows of the decade; it aired from 1984 to 1992. Centering on a modern, professional African American family with several children, the show dramatized in a gentle, humorous way the basic values of familial love and respect; it was watched by millions of Americans, regardless of race. As black filmmaking began to boom in the 1990s, so too did the production of black television shows. Will Smith, who would soon become a Hollywood movie star, starred in the popular sitcom *The Fresh Prince of Bel-Air* (1990–6). One of the era's most important new sketch shows, *In Living Color* (1990–4), was created by and starred Keenan Ivory Wayans. Although the show was criticized at times for its politically incorrect approach to humor, it helped to launch (or boost) the careers of many talented performers including Jim Carrey, Tommy Davidson, David Alan Grier, and several members of the Wayans family. Importantly, *In Living Color* was a "flagship" show for the just-created Fox TV network. Executives at Fox realized that in creating a new broadcast network (not initially available to all cable subscribers), it would need to target an urban demographic who could receive its over-the-air broadcast signal for free. Thus Fox deliber-ately "green lit" (that is, gave the go-ahead to make) a show with specific African American ("urban") appeal. This same strategy was followed in ensuing years, as the first thing newly formed broadcast networks such as UPN and The WB did was to target African American viewers with a deluge of sitcoms such as *The Parent 'Hood* (1995–9), *Moesha* (1996–2001), *The Parkers* (1999–2004), and *Girlfriends* (2000–).

At the start of the twenty-first century, American television was offering a wide range of African American characters and performers. One of the most powerful and financially successful TV personalities of all time – Oprah Winfrey – continues to be a cultural force with considerable impact: one book recommendation or political endorsement from her can send sales (and votes) sky-rocketing. In 2008, she announced the imminent debut of her OWN cable network. Another cable channel, Black Entertainment Television (BET), narrowcasts to young black audiences, while other subscription channels like Black Starz showcase films of interest to the African American community. Most of today's network dramas and reality shows are integrated to some degree. And although some critics still note the ghettoization of black performers into silly situation comedies – arguing that America still prefers to see blacks as comedic Coons rather than complex dramatic characters – there is more diversity of African American images on television than ever before.

In front of the cameras, comedies and action films continued to integrate themselves. Eddie Murphy, who had been discovered on TV's *Saturday Night Live*, made concert films and buddy action movies. In fact, the **black and white buddy** film formula was one that Hollywood was happy to exploit throughout most of the 1980s and 1990s. In films such as *48 Hours* (1982) and *Lethal Weapon* (1987) – as well as their many sequels and imitators – a black and white duo bicker and argue but eventually come to value one another, all while defeating the bad guys. This formula has been an enormously successful one for Hollywood because the biracial casting of the lead roles makes the film appeal to both white and black audiences. Hollywood producers don't want to finance an expensive "black" film unless they are sure it will also attract white audiences, which usually means the casting of a white star alongside a black one. Nevertheless, a new generation of African American actors, including Morgan Freeman, Danny Glover, Denzel Washington, Larry Fishburne, and Wesley Snipes, became well known through work in these (and other) types of films.

Probably the most important (and controversial) 1980s Hollywood film about the African American experience was *The Color Purple* (1985), directed by Hollywood mogul Steven Spielberg and starring Whoopi Goldberg, Oprah Winfrey, Margaret Avery, and Danny Glover. The film was based on Alice Walker's Pulitzer prize-winning novel about black women struggling for survival in the South during the first decades of the twentieth century. Much of their struggle was against the black men in their lives, who abused them in physical, sexual, and psychological ways. When the film was released, there were predictable complaints about why it had been directed by a white man, but the largest controversy centered on the film's alleged "male bashing." Reiterating the arguments made in earlier decades, some critics and audiences felt the film was demeaning because while it celebrated black women, it also depicted African American men as rapists and abusers. The film did diminish many of the novel's more important points. For example, the novel makes it clearer than does the film that black men abuse black women as part of a "chain of oppression" that stems in the first place from white brutality. The novel also deals centrally with a lesbian relationship between characters Shug and Celie, an important aspect of the book's feminist project that was reduced to several chaste kisses in the movie.

As if in answer to many of these controversies, African American independent filmmaking was jump-started the next year by the premiere of Spike Lee's first feature film, *She's Gotta Have It* (1986). This black and white comedy of manners among contemporary African American men and women became a big hit both in black communities and on the independent film circuit. Spike Lee had learned his craft at the New York University film school, where his 50–minute short film *Joe's Bed-Stuy Barbershop: We Cut Heads* won him considerable praise. After the success of *She's Gotta Have It*, Lee was offered a distribution deal with a major Hollywood studio for his second feature, *School Daze* (1988), a film that explores issues of assimilation and gender at an all-black college. It was his next film however, that affirmed his position as the leading African American filmmaker of his generation. *Do the Right Thing* (1989) explores the racial tensions in a small New York neighborhood during one very hot summer day. Complex and uncompromising, the film (like all of Spike Lee's work) offers no easy solutions to America's racial problems. The film's depiction of a race riot, police brutality, and unabashed sexuality made it one of the most talked-about movies of the year. When it was overlooked for a Best Picture nomination, at least one Oscar presenter took to the podium to call attention to that fact. (The more conventional race drama *Driving Miss Daisy* [1989] won the Best Picture Oscar that year, again reflecting Hollywood's preference for a glossy, soft-pedal approach to controversial subjects.)

Throughout the 1990s, Spike Lee continued to explore issues concerning race and racism in films such as *Mo' Better Blues* (1990), *Jungle Fever* (1991), *Crooklyn* (1994), *Clockers* (1995), *Girl 6* (1996), and *He Got Game* (1998). His epic film on the life

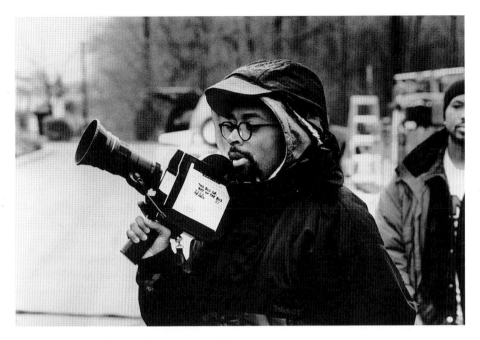

Spike Lee is seen here on the set of *Get On the Bus* (1996), one of his more independent, smaller-budget films that focus on race in America.
Get On the Bus, dir. Spike Lee, copyright © 1996, Columbia/Tri-Star. Photo: Lester Sloan

of *Malcolm X* (1992) is a powerful statement about the slain civil rights leader. Even though the film failed to attract large audiences, it garnered a Best Actor Oscar nomination for Denzel Washington as Malcolm X. More recently, Spike Lee has also made several smaller, more challenging films such as *Get On the Bus* (1996) and *4 Little Girls* (1997), the latter a documentary about a 1963 terrorist bombing at a black Baptist church. In addition to his filmmaking, Spike Lee has also become a recognized and respected public figure, one who rarely shies away from the spotlight and is known for his straightforward statements on race in America. When Warner Brothers threatened to take *Malcolm X* away from him because he had gone over budget, Spike Lee noted loudly in the press that white directors go over budget all the time without the studio threatening to take their films away. Eventually the needed money was raised from various members of the African American community. Spike Lee has also shot television ads for Nike shoes and rigorously markets both himself and his films through merchandising tie-ins, a fact that some leftist critics find troubling. Nonetheless, Spike Lee remains America's pre-eminent African American filmmaker.

Black Independent vs. "Neo-Blaxploitation" Filmmaking

As they did for Spike Lee, university film schools (which had slowly integrated themselves under policies of affirmative action) have helped to train the current generation of African American filmmakers. As early as the 1970s and 1980s, university-trained filmmakers such as Haile Gerima (*Bush Mama* [1976]) and Bill Woodberry (*Bless Their Little Hearts* [1984]) released independent films exploring multiple aspects of the African American experience. Yet, being independent films, they never received much distribution in the United States, and many of them remain difficult to see even today. Facing similar problems is the work of Charles Burnett, who has struggled to make personal and meaningful films throughout his career, including *Killer of Sheep* (1977), *My Brother's Wedding* (1983), and *To Sleep With Anger* (1990). Due to the presence of Danny Glover in the cast, the last of these films received a limited art-house run via the Samuel Goldwyn Company, but it too failed to attract much of an audience, either black or white. In 2007, *Killer of Sheep* was restored and released to art-house theatres and DVD outlets, finally making its grim and moving critique of African American urban poverty accessible to wider audiences.

The failure of black independent filmmaking to cross over and be seen by more audiences is a complex phenomenon. As previously noted, Hollywood's control of distribution and exhibition outlets is designed to crush independent competition. Furthermore, independent theaters are rarely located within or near African American communities. And again, some white moviegoers – even those who attend independent films – still choose not to see what they perceive to be "black movies." Perhaps most importantly, audiences (regardless of race) have learned to expect and desire only Hollywood form and content when they go to the movies. For example, Julie Dash's *Daughters of the Dust* (1991) was a critical hit but never crossed over to a wider audience, most likely because of its baroque narrative structure and the fact that it was about African American women. Kasi Lemmons's *Eve's Bayou* (1997), a film that made many critics' "top ten" lists the year it was released, has also remained somewhat marginalized, perhaps because its protagonist is a young black girl. Similarly, Cheryl Dunye's film *Watermelon Woman* (1995), a fascinating exploration of the issues of representation as they relate to racial and sexual identity, has rarely been seen outside of gay and lesbian film festivals. The video documentaries of Marlon Riggs (*Ethnic Notions* [1987], *Tongues Untied* [1989], *Color Adjustment* [1991], *Black Is . . . Black Ain't . . .* [1993]) are also important explorations of African American identity and the politics of gender and sexuality. Yet various conservative politicians and action groups have actively worked to keep PBS from airing some of these works.

The African American films that find wide audiences are the films that Hollywood itself allows to be produced and distributed. Consequently, these films mostly follow Hollywood formulas and rarely challenge or address the dominant structuring ideologies of white patriarchal capitalism. Nonetheless, in the early 1990s, there was a tremendous surge of African American men writing and directing films in Hollywood. Filmmakers such as Reginald and Warrington Hudlin, John Singleton, Mario Van Peebles, and Allen and Albert Hughes became well known for writing and directing films such as *House Party* (1990), *Boyz N the Hood* (1991), *New Jack City* (1991), and *Menace II Society* (1993). The fact that many of the most successful of these films were genre films (and especially violent gang/gangster films) led some critics to see them as a sort of **neo-blaxploitation** movement for the 1990s.

(Indeed, John Singleton remade *Shaft* in 2000, and has continued to make similar action thrillers in the 2000s.) The controversies these films generated were similar to those of the 1970s: many of them, either deliberately or unwittingly, glorify the figure of the violent gangster. Like the ideological message of much gangsta rap – the musical idiom to which these films are intricately connected – the films promote a black macho criminal-capitalist ethic and are often violently sexist and homophobic. While many urban black filmgoers (as well as white suburban teen males who responded to the films' hypermasculine aesthetics) made these films into box office hits, other more middle-class black audiences were frequently appalled by them.

In the latter half of the 1990s, again as if to appease the critics of these violent macho action films, Hollywood released a series of films marketed at African American women, including *Waiting to Exhale* (1995), *Soul Food* (1997), *How Stella Got Her Groove Back* (1998), *The Best Man* (2000), and *Love and Basketball* (2000). Yet, in adapting the classical Hollywood formula of the **woman's film**, which centers on a woman's suffering as she searches for love, these films also promote patriarchal ideologies. The films of this genre often suggest that the most important thing for black women to do is to find a good black man to marry. Gender roles for African American characters in most Hollywood films remain bound by traditional white patriarchal structuring, and Hollywood still remains wary of depicting successful interracial relationships. Furthermore, black gay and lesbian characters are almost entirely absent from the Hollywood screen, except for the stereotype of the effeminate gay male "snap queen."

New Images for a New Century – Or Not?

For the year 2001, the Academy Awards honored African American actors in an unprecedented way: for the first time in history, both top acting awards went to African American actors. Denzel Washington won for *Training Day*, while Halle Berry won for *Monster's Ball*, becoming the first African American actress to win the Best Actress trophy. While some critics saw these wins as indicating a sea change in Hollywood's attitudes toward African Americans, others reported that Hollywood quickly went back to business as usual. Nonetheless, recent years have seen a huge increase in the number of African American actors honored by the Academy. Don Cheadle was nominated for Best Actor for his role in *Hotel Rwanda* (2004), a chilling look at genocide in Africa. Terrence Howard was nominated for his role as a pimp in *Hustle & Flow* (2005), and Forest Whitaker won the Best Actor trophy for playing Ugandan dictator Idi Amin in *The Last King of Scotland* (2006). Best Actor honors also went to Jamie Foxx as Ray Charles in the biopic *Ray* (2004). Black actors have also scored many Best Supporting Actor nominations and wins. Djimon Hounsou was nominated twice (for *In America* [2003] and *Blood Diamond* [2006]) and Jamie Foxx was nominated for *Collateral* (2004), as was Eddie Murphy for *Dreamgirls* (2006). Morgan Freeman, who had been previously nominated three times, won a Best Supporting Oscar for his role as Clint Eastwood's sidekick in *Million*

Dollar Baby (2004). Although their recognition has not been as prominent, African American actresses have also been nominated and/or won a few Oscars in recent years: Queen Latifah was nominated for a Supporting Actress award for her role in *Chicago* (2002), and newcomer Jennifer Hudson won the award in the same category for her acting and singing in *Dreamgirls*.

Also nominated for two Best Actor Oscars (for *Ali* [2001] and *The Pursuit of Happyness* [2006]), Will Smith has arguably become one of the most famous (and profitable) black actors in Hollywood. Smith's career started in music and television, and since then he has become a bankable leading man, starring in action thrillers (*Bad Boys* [1995], *Bad Boys II* [2002]), comedies (*Hitch* [2005]), and science fiction blockbusters (*Independence Day* [1996], *Men in Black* [1997], *I, Robot* [2004], *I am Legend* [2007], and *Hancock* [2008]). Yet Smith, like several of the actors mentioned above, has also been accused by some critics of taking roles that seem to suggest the stereotypes of years gone by. For example, in *The Legend of Bagger Vance* (2000), Smith plays a **Magical Negro**, a new age version of the old Mammy or Uncle Tom stereotypes, an African American who uses his or her "mystical powers" to help white people in distress. Other versions of the Magical Negro stereotype can be found in *Ghost* (1990), *Kazaam* (1996), *The Green Mile* (1999), *Bruce Almighty* (2003), and *The Bucket List* (2008). Perhaps more disturbing are lingering images of the Black Buck stereotype, used to terrify audiences in films like *Requiem for a Dream* (2000) and *Traffic* (2000). In both of these films, sex with Black Buck figures is used to show the depths of depravity to which white female characters

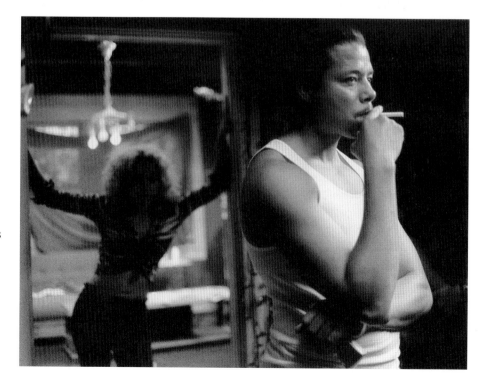

Terrence Howard was nominated for a Best Actor Oscar for *Hustle & Flow* (2005), but does his performance as a pimp recirculate negative stereotypes about African Americans?
Hustle & Flow, dir. Craig Brewer, copyright © 2005, MTV Films/ Paramount Classics

have fallen (because of their drug habits). And although Hollywood's use of the black and white buddy formula (or black and Asian buddy formula) may be abating somewhat, it is still exemplified by films like *Wild Wild West* (1999), the *Men in Black* films (1997, 2002), and the *Rush Hour* films (1998, 2001, 2007).

While most Oscar-nominated films are serious prestige pictures, run-of-the-mill Hollywood movies that feature African American characters, and/or are directed by black filmmakers, are still often dictated the formulas and the expectations of generic neo-blaxploitation filmmaking. For example, the Wayans Brothers – Keenan Ivory, Marlon, Damon, and Shawn (who first came to prominence in the Fox TV show *In Living Color*) – continue to write, direct, produce, and/or star in formulaic comedies such as *White Chicks* (2004), *Little Man* (2006), and the string of *Scary Movie* horror film spoofs (2000, 2001, 2003, 2006, 2008). Rap music stars whose reputations are based on their "gangsta cred" continue to cross over into Hollywood acting roles, as did Curtis "50 Cent" Jackson in films like *Get Rich or Die Tryin'* (2005) and *Home of the Brave* (2006). Another rapper-turned-actor, Snoop Dogg has carved out a small Hollywood career for himself in horror films (*Bones* [2001], *Hood of Horror* [2006]) as well as comedies (*Soul Plane* [2004], *Starsky and Hutch* [2004]). A few rap stars have been more daring in their film careers, choosing films that expand upon their original personas as rap artists. For example, André Benjamin and Big Boi, the duo behind the music group OutKast, produced and starred in a period hip-hop gangster musical called *Idlewilde* (2006). Mos Def has earned good notices in serious dramatic roles (*Monster's Ball*, *The Woodsman* [2004]), and Queen Latifah has carved out a sizable film career for herself, appearing in movies such as *Chicago*, *Beauty Shop* (2005), and *Hairspray* (2007).

A few films featuring African American characters have been successful in mixing comedy, drama, and social commentary. The *Barbershop* films (2002, 2004), for example, were popular with audiences for their humor but also for their sometimes salty and irreverent commentary on contemporary American race relations. The films also celebrate a physical space – the African American owned and run barbershop – where generations have felt the freedom to discuss things openly. Another modest hit of recent years was *Diary of a Mad Black Woman* (2005), a comedy-drama starring Kimberley Elise as Helen, a wealthy black suburbanite with a crumbling marriage. *Diary of a Mad Black Woman* was based on a play by Tyler Perry, and Perry himself appears in the film in three different roles, most notably as Madea, Helen's sassy, gun-toting, straight-talking grandmother. Perry also wrote and directed the follow-up film, *Madea's Family Reunion* (2006), and has aggressively marketed straight-to-DVD versions of his other plays. Despite his cross-dressing to play Madea, Perry's work is infused with a warm Christian sensibility, and although mostly specific to middle-class African American life in and around Atlanta, his work has been popular with African Americans all over the nation. However, other critics have been less celebratory of Perry's work, arguing that his drag act is yet another instance of black actors making fun of heavyset black women, as in Martin Lawrence's *Big Momma's House* films (2000, 2006) or Eddie Murphy's *Norbit* (2007).

Case Study: *Bamboozled* (2000)

Spike Lee wrote and directed *Bamboozled* in response to what he felt was the ongoing racial stereotyping of and institutionalized discrimination against African Americans within the US television industry. The film is a dark satire on race, assimilation, corporate media, and the ways that the dominant hegemonic power structure is able to divide and conquer those it subjugates. *Bamboozled* (the title refers to the state of having been cheated or conned, often through flattery) attempts simultaneously to entertain and educate its audiences about the history of African American representation within popular culture. The film tells the story of Pierre Delacroix (Damon Wayans), an assimilated African American television writer who toils under the complex institutionalized racism of both his network and his white boss (who professes to be "blacker" than Pierre). Hoping to get fired, Delacroix presents to his boss the idea of *Mantan: The New Millennium Minstrel Show*, a show about lazy Coon stereotypes who live in a watermelon patch. To his surprise and ultimate horror, the network actually produces the show and it becomes a controversial hit. At the end of the film, a black activist rap group kidnap and murder the star of the show for his alleged crimes against black people (that is, performing as a racist stereotype). The police arrive and gun down the activist gang (except, quite pointedly, their one white member), and Pierre is shot by his assistant (Jada Pinkett-Smith), who holds him responsible for the spiraling madness the show has created.

From within this framework, Spike Lee develops a thoughtful meditation on the issues of African American representability at the turn of the millennium. The con-cept and history of minstrelsy and blackface are explored within the storyline as two homeless black street performers (Savion Glover and Tommy Davidson) are seduced into

Tommy Davidson (left) and Savion Glover starred as African American street performers coerced to appear in a modern-day minstrel show in Spike Lee's *Bamboozled* (2000). *Bamboozled*, dir. Spike Lee, copyright © 2000, New Line Cinema. Photo: David Lee/New Line

More independently minded black filmmakers continue to struggle to make challenging work. For example, Kasi Lemmons has only made two films since her highly acclaimed *Eve's Bayou*. Her challenging psychological thriller *The Caveman's Valentine* (2001) was mostly ignored by critics and audiences, but *Talk to Me* (2007), starring Don Cheadle as real-life 1960s radio talk-show host Petey Greene, garnered considerable acclaim. Rodney Evans's *Brother to Brother* (2004), a film about a young black gay man discovering the queerness of the Harlem Renaissance, earned good festival buzz but made very little money at the box office. Music video producer Sanaa Hamri made her first feature, *Something New* (2006), a film about an interracial romance. And presiding over all remains Spike Lee, who continues to make mainstream Hollywood action thrillers (*The 25th Hour* [2002], *Inside* starring on the show: they accept the offer because they want to earn a living and perform for wider audiences. They agree to the network producers' demands that they wear blackface and change their names to "Mantan" and "Sleep 'n' Eat," two names that recall actual black character actors from the 1930s and 1940s. The complex character of Pierre Delacroix, whose name literally means "Peter of the Cross," suggests both a betrayal (in this case Pierre's betrayal of his racial heritage) and his eventual martyrdom. Various aspects of **mise-en-scène** also help develop the film's themes. By shooting *Bamboozled* in a variety of media (high definition video, Super 16 mm film, 35mm film, computer animation), Lee implicitly asks his audience to consider issues of film form and how they relate to media power. For example, the expensive computer animation appears as part of the network's title sequence for the *Mantan* show, while the film itself is shot in less expensive media. This is, after all, not the sort of film in which Hollywood would invest much money. In further breaking from smooth Hollywood-type filmmaking, Lee intercuts within the film snippets of footage from earlier films and television shows that both illustrate the history of African American representation and serve as a sort of counterpoint to the actions of Delacroix et al. Lee also creates within the film parodies of contemporary music video advertisements that exhort African Americans to purchase happiness and style by drinking cheap liquor and wearing designer jeans. Most effectively, as the film progresses and Delacroix begins to lose his soul and his sanity, the visual design of the film becomes increasingly cluttered with racist toys and dolls from earlier decades, almost as if the history of racist representation is swallowing up what is left of Pierre's self-image. He too appears in blackface as he dies. The end credits, which also roll over these images, suggest that their effects are lingering even into the new millennium.

Bamboozled is typical of Spike Lee's work in that it raises difficult issues without offering clear-cut answers via the closure of a happy Hollywood ending. This is no simplified polemic that pits good black people against evil whites: indeed, the film's militant black activists, the Mau Maus, are also satirized as ignorant and/or foolish. By extension, the Mau Maus can be understood to represent gangsta rap subcultures and the types of characters and ideologies celebrated in neo-blaxploitation filmmaking, and Lee shows that the violence inherent in those artifacts is tragic, not liberating. *Bamboozled* is instead a sophisticated take on how the institutional power of giant white patriarchal capitalist media corporations exploits both individuals and entire communities of people. Lee explores how some aspects of contemporary African American culture relate to and are indeed created by the racist practices of the media industries. Furthermore, the film addresses how ideas about gender can also be manipulated by those in power in order to divide and conquer. When Delacroix realizes that his assistant is trying to persuade Mantan to stop appearing in blackface, Delacroix smears her with a sexual allegation that Mantan is only too willing to believe. Even Mantan and his streetwise partner are driven apart by the machinations and demands of the TV industry. Ultimately, the character of Pierre Delacroix emerges as the film's most tragic figure, a man whose drive for success and internalized racism lead him to deny his own cultural heritage. *Bamboozled* is a social satire on racial representation that paradoxically underlines both how greatly – and how little – African American stereotypes have changed over the years.

Man [2006]), as well as more politically charged independent films (*She Hate Me* [2004]) and documentaries (*Jim Brown: All American* [2002], *When the Levees Broke: A Requiem in Four Acts* [2006].) His highly acclaimed short *Jesus Children of America*, about a young girl who discovers that she has been HIV positive since birth, was anthologized in *All the Invisible Children* (2005), but the film failed to find theatrical distribution in the United States. Ever true to his own artistic vision, Spike Lee continues to work in whatever cinematic medium he can, reaching different audiences with his entertaining and often educational films.

Looking back from the early twenty-first century, one can see how greatly the cinematic images of African Americans have changed. From crudely stereotyped silent films, through the social problem and blaxploitation eras, today's films exhibit a much larger variety of African American characters and concerns. Behind the camera, black filmmakers have also made great progress: gone are the days of segregated studio lots and "separate but equal" movie houses. However, people who work in the Hollywood industry continue to note the prevalence of a structural racism that makes it difficult for blacks to advance to the highest positions of power. It is often said that there are few-to-no African American film executives in Hollywood who have the power to green light a film. The struggle for equal representation on America's movie screens will continue to parallel the struggle for equal representation in the boardrooms, studio lots, and creative guilds of Hollywood.

Questions for Discussion

1 Some critics argue that the five stereotypes of African Americans found in early cinema (the Coon, the Uncle Tom, the Mammy, the Tragic Mulatto, and the Black Buck) can still be found in contemporary Hollywood films. Can you think of recent examples of these stereotypes? When does a black comedian become a Coon, or a nurturing black woman become a Mammy?

2 Have you ever gone to see a film especially because it was about African American issues or starring black actors? Have

you ever avoided a film – consciously or not – because it was about African American issues or starring black actors? Why or why not?

3 What are the differences between Hollywood films that seem to be aimed at African American men and those apparently aimed at African American women? What do those differences tell us about how Hollywood conceives of gender and sexuality in relation to race?

Further Reading

Bogle, Donald. *Toms, Coons, Mulattoes, Mammies and Bucks.* New York: Continuum, 2001.

Cripps, Thomas. *Slow Fade to Black: The Negro in American Film 1900–1942.* New York: Oxford University Press, 1977.

Diawara, Manthia, ed. *Black American Cinema.* New York: Routledge, 1993.

Donalson, Melvin. *Black Directors in Hollywood.* Austin: University of Texas Press, 2003.

Guerrero, Ed. *Framing Blackness: The African American Image in Film.* Philadelphia: Temple University Press, 1993.

hooks, bell. *Reel to Real: Race, Sex, and Class at the Movies.* New York: Routledge, 1996.

Leab, Daniel J. *From Sambo to Superspade: The Black Experience in Motion Pictures.* Boston: Houghton Mifflin, 1975.

Massood, Paula J. *Black City Cinema: African American Urban Experiences in Film.* Philadelphia: Temple University Press, 2003.

Reid, Mark. *Black Lenses, Black Voices: African American Film Now.* Lanham, MD: Rowman and Littlefield, 2005.

Sims, Yvonne D. W*omen of Blaxploitation: How the Black Action Film Heroine Changed American Culture.* Jefferson, NC: McFarland, 2006.

Smith, Valerie, ed. *Representing Blackness: Issues in Film and Video.* New Brunswick, NJ: Rutgers University Press, 1997.

Stewart, Jacqueline Najuma. *Migrating to the Movies: Cinema and Black Urban Modernity.* Berkeley: University of California Press, 2005.

Watkins, S. Craig. *Representing: Hip Hop Culture and the Production of Black Cinema.* Chicago: University of Chicago Press, 1998.

Weisenfeld, Judith. *Hollywood Be Thy Name: African American Religion in American Film, 1929–1949.* Berkeley: University of California Press, 2007.

Yearwood, Gladstone. *Black Cinema Aesthetics: Issues in Independent Black Filmmaking.* Athens: Ohio University, Center for AfroAmerican Studies, 1982.

Further Screening

The Birth of a Nation (1915)
Cabin in the Sky (1943)
Pinky (1949)
Sweet Sweetback's Baaadasssss Song (1971)
Superfly (1972)
The Color Purple (1985)
Do the Right Thing (1989)

Boyz N the Hood (1991)
Malcolm X (1992)
Waiting to Exhale (1995)
Barbershop (2002)
Dreamgirls (2006)
Talk to Me (2007)

Chapter 5

NATIVE AMERICANS AND AMERICAN FILM

In fostering a national identity for America, the first European settlers were faced with an immediate and concrete dilemma: numerous indigenous people already lived on the land. By most accounts, when Columbus first landed, there were over 500 different groups or nations of people living in the "Americas," many with their own cultures, customs, religions, and languages. In most cases, Europeans considered the native people of North and South America to be less than human. They were "godless heathens" to Europeans who were searching for a new Christian Eden, and thought to be vicious animals by those who wanted the riches of the land for themselves. In creating such impressions of America's first inhabitants, European settlers could justify to themselves the many crimes and cruelties that were launched against Native Americans. Just as white slave owners argued that blacks were more like animals than they were human in order to justify slavery, so did the first settlers of the New World deny the very humanity of Native American people.

Indian was the term most commonly used to describe Native Americans until the 1970s, and it is still used by many people today, even though it drastically reduces and essentializes different groups of people to a single, simplified label. The term is also a historical misnomer. Christopher Columbus had been searching for a water route to India (to further trade between Europe and India) when he accidentally discovered "the New World" instead, and mistook its inhabitants for Indians. Actually, as many people have more recently pointed out, the people living in the Americas knew where they were and didn't need to be "discovered" or named. This incident is an excellent example of what has come to be called **Eurocentrism** – the process of understanding the world and all of its cultures and ideas from a (conquering) white European perspective. The very name "America" is itself a European derivative from the name of Amerigo Vespucci, an Italian explorer who first mapped some of what is today known as South America. After Columbus and Vespucci, subsequent European peoples renamed all the lands of the Western hemisphere and eventually colonized it in order to extract its riches. The indigenous people of the Western hemisphere were often slaughtered when they failed to assimilate to European demands.

As the British colonies became an independent country, the newly formed United States needed to define what it meant to be American. Following the formula of **Othering** described in chapter 3, some defined American identity as "not British," but even more quickly and repeatedly, American national identity was conceived of as "not Indian." Despite their presence long before European settlers arrived, it was not until 1924 that the United States officially granted Native Americans citizenship; until that time they were considered foreigners or aliens. Hence, a sense of "what America stands for" has been strongly tied to images of Native Americans as the **Other** to European Americans.

All sorts of cultural texts – made by and for non-Native audiences – have represented and reinforced notions of what Native Americans were allegedly like. Books, plays, paintings, games, and songs all contributed to white attitudes regarding Native Americans, and cinema would inherit many of those conventions, including basic **stereotypes** and the dramatic narrative of American settlers needing to battle Indians in order to form a great country. As this chapter will show, Native Americans were strongly associated with one of Hollywood's most prolific genres, the Western, which usually replayed that basic narrative over and over. By relegating **representations** of Native Americans almost exclusively to this one genre, American film reinforced stereotypes and ideological assumptions that had been circulating for generations. And although the Western as a film genre is no longer a popular type of film in America, the ideas and ideologies embedded in it have had devastating effects upon the cultural representations and subsequent understanding and treatment of Native Americans.

The American "Indian" Before Film

Soon after Columbus and other explorers returned to Europe, accounts of Native Americans began to proliferate. In published journals, novels, and adventure stories, writers of European descent constructed an image of Native Americans that suited their own needs, disregarding anything that might complicate matters. Two basic stereotypes evolved in this literature (whether fictional or not): the Indian as either a marauding, bloodthirsty savage or a more benign and helpful noble savage. The **bloodthirsty savage** view constructed Native Americans as violent, aggressive, and demonic, bent on destroying innocent white settlers, including women and children. Lurid stories and paintings of Indian raiders kidnapping and raping white women were consistently popular during this period. While Native warriors definitely did attack white settlements on numerous occasions, most Eurocentric narratives softened or denied altogether the European aggression that had caused indigenous people to fight back. In other stories, Native Americans were regarded as **noble savages**, primitive and childlike rather than threatening and violent. According to this stereotype, Native Americans, lacking in European customs, supposedly maintained purer instincts about nature and the world around them. These links to the natural world gave Native Americans a certain majesty or nobility in the Eurocentric imagination, and that "nobility" was further enhanced when Native Americans aided and abetted white settlers. Examples of the noble savage character type include "Indian princesses" such as Pocahontas and Sacajawea, or the title character of James Fenimore Cooper's novel *The Last of the Mohicans*. While the image of the noble savage may seem the opposite of the bloodthirsty savage, both still conceive of Native Americans as barely one step above animals, guided by instinct rather than complex thought, and without their own cultures or civilizations.

The stereotypes of the bloodthirsty and the noble savage were in place long before the American Revolution, and they continued to be used in popular cultural artifacts throughout the nineteenth century, when **Manifest Destiny** became a prevailing political philosophy in the United States. Under the doctrine of Manifest Destiny, many Americans felt that it was their God-given right (and indeed duty) to settle throughout North America, bringing democracy, Christianity, and the American way of life to new lands and new people. Manifest Destiny was thus the ideological platform used to justify US expansionism (or **imperialism**) into the Western territories, as well as into the Pacific Islands, Central America, and the Caribbean. In most places, indigenous people were converted through assimilation into the American, Christian way of life, or, failing that, eradicated through violent means so that whites could settle the land.

Genocide, which means the deliberate destruction of an entire cultural group of people, is a very strong word, but one that in recent years has been applied to official (and not-so-official) US policies toward Native Americans during the nineteenth century. For example, under policies that aimed to relocate Native Americans onto reservations and contain them there, the United States forcibly drove many Indian tribes into desolate arid lands where they starved to death. The US government made outright war upon those Native Americans who would not allow themselves to be relocated. Those conflicts between the US Cavalry and various Native American nations became known as the **Indian Wars**; they lasted roughly from 1850 to 1900. Other violent tactics against Native American people were less obvious, such as delivering small-pox-infected blankets to various tribes under the guise of charity, or hunting the buffalo to near extinction as a means of destroying the Plains Indians, whose means of living depended upon their use of the buffalo. Many other abuses and historical atrocities have been documented, but rarely came to light in white middle-class America until the second half of the twentieth century. History is written by those in power, and it was (and still is) not unusual for American historians to overlook facts and events that would have reflected badly upon America's national image.

Simultaneous with the Indian Wars, depictions of white male heroism and derring-do in the West became wildly popular in the United States and Europe. Before long, the stories had been told and retold so many times that they codified into a relatively coherent **genre**: the **Western**. As was discussed in chapter 2, one of the ways a genre can be identified is by its iconography and its thematic myth. The Western's **iconography** (its sights and sounds) include cowboys, Indians, six-shooters, tumbleweeds, horses, saloons, cattle drives, etc. Its **thematic myth** (the issues and ideas, themes, and meanings upon which it focuses) might be understood to be about bringing civilization to the Western wilderness. Often, this is embodied by a strong individual (almost always a straight white male) standing "tall in the saddle" and using righteous violence (his gun) to protect the expanding American community from those who would harm it. In the Western genre, Native Americans are posited as part of "the wilderness" that must be tamed and thus, many (but not all) Western artifacts represent indigenous people as a threat to the expansion of American civilization. More than most genres, the Western is closely tied to actual issues and events in American history, and has been influential in helping to create a sense of national identity. It is often said that the Western is the "most American" of genres.

Even before the invention of cinema, the iconography and thematic myth of the Western were disseminated through a variety of nineteenth-century media. Woodcuts, sketches, sculptures, and paintings captured the look of the Old West. **Dime novels,** cheaply made books filled with high adventure, told stories of Western heroes conquering the land and proving the superiority of white American masculinity. Often these Western stories were based on actual people, a fact that created an aura of truth around the fantastic exploits (as well as the stereotypes) that they depicted. Buffalo Bill Cody was one such man, immortalized in a series of dime novels. Buffalo Bill (who allegedly earned his name for killing so many buffalo, itself an indirect attack on the Plains Indians) was also instrumental in popularizing another form of Western entertainment, the **Wild West show.** This was a combination circus, rodeo, and vaudeville performance that was performed for Eastern American and European audiences. It featured trick shooters, cattle roping, riding demonstrations, and frequently a fictionalized vignette dramatizing a battle between innocent white settlers and villainous Indians. Buffalo Bill's Wild West show is also notable for briefly headlining the captured Native American leader Sitting Bull, who was put on display for white patrons, exhibited almost as a side-show curiosity.

These art works, novels, plays, and shows presented stereotypical Indians to Eastern audiences, many of whom had never encountered a Native American before. While some of these artifacts attempted to take a scientific tone, describing the "innate" features of the "Red Man" (skin tone, skull shape, musculature) and his "primitive" lifestyle, most of these works overtly demonized Native Americans in order to justify the nation's genocidal policies. For centuries, many white Americans were taught that "the only good Indian is a dead Indian," a catch phrase that could still be heard on the lips of adults as well as children throughout the twentieth century. It was a sentiment that the Hollywood Western did little to alter.

Ethnographic Films and the Rise of the Hollywood Western

The birth of cinema coincides with cultural announcements signaling "the close of the American frontier." By the end of the nineteenth century, the US Cavalry had decisively won the Indian Wars. Many Indian nations had been decimated, relocated, or eradicated altogether. However, the doctrine of Manifest Destiny continued unabated. The Western genre, arguably a justification for Manifest Destiny, continued to be popular in literature, painting, and theater. It took a few years for American film to adapt the Western into cinematic form, since the earliest motion pictures were little more than simply shot, one-take scenes devoid of much narrative action. **Actualities**, as these first films were sometimes called, were short "slices of life" that displayed foreign lands, famous people, or important events. A number of actualities focused on other cultures, and thus a tradition of **ethnographic films** (films that record another culture's way of life) emerged. Native Americans were among the most common subjects for these early ethnographic films, as in the Edison film *Sioux Ghost Dance* (1896). This film ostensibly allowed white viewers to see a sacred tribal ritual, but it is actually a fictionalized account, concocted by white filmmakers to make Native Americans seem more exotic and foreign. Actualities, as the name implies, were generally accepted by the public as non-fiction works, and thus they helped to legitimate and naturalize certain stereotypes of Native Americans, even before the development of the cinematic Western.

Similar problems of authenticity and documentary veracity surrounded ethnographic films for many years. One of the most famous ethnographic films ever made, *Nanook of the North* (1922), also involved the staging of Native American life by a white filmmaker. Director Robert Flaherty did film actual Inuit people – but he requested that they revert to "traditional" Inuit living so he could film them as romanticized primitives, noble savages for 1920s audiences. Flaherty also staged certain scenes, such as the seal hunt, a sequence that was praised for its realism by many critics. Also, as a white filmmaker assuming a white audience, Flaherty used film techniques to "Other" his Eskimo subjects. He inserted subtitles that claim that they are fascinated with how a gramophone works, suggesting that they have never seen such a device before. He also cut back and forth between Inuit people eating and a dog pack snarling hungrily, thus making a formal association between the dogs and the "animalistic" tendencies of these people. Under the claim of scientific veracity, such ethnographic accounts of Native Americans often served up the same stereotypical representations as did fictional films.

The early actualities were soon eclipsed in popularity by narrative films – films that told fictional stories. As storytelling in cinema developed, film genres evolved in fits and starts. Many film historians refer to *The Great Train Robbery* (1903) as the first Western film, and its enormous success ensured imitators. However, the film (which was shot in New Jersey) features no Native Americans, although it does involve a chase on horseback and a climactic gun battle. Arguably, an even earlier film, one from 1894, entitled *Parade of Buffalo Bill's Wild West*, might be considered to be the first Western. Although, as an actuality, the film contained no narrative battle between whites and Indians (needed to express the genre's thematic myth), it did convey the genre's iconography. All of these early films with Western motifs might be thought of as **experimental Westerns** – in that they were trying out various visual and narrative formulas that would soon become codified into the **classical Western**. Many experimental Westerns made use of pre-existing forms such as the Wild West show, simply by filming their novelty acts and fictional vignettes. In fact, many Wild West show performers also found work in the movies. Film production companies such as Bison 101 and Essanay were formed from Wild West show stock companies, complete with Native American actors and a catalogue of dramatic scenarios (gunfights, stagecoach rescues, fort attacks, etc.) that could be enacted before the camera.

The participation of Native Americans in these early films may have had an effect on the types of stories being produced. Films such as *Hiawatha* (1910), *Indian Justice* (1911), and *A Squaw's Love* (1911) focused squarely on Native Americans as people, and not simply as barbaric heathens. Some film historians classify these films as belonging to an **Indian Story** genre, related to but separate from classical Westerns because they don't oppose white heroes to bloodthirsty savages. Some of these early films were even written and directed by Native Americans. **James Young Deer** created films such as *Red Wing's Gratitude* (1909), *White Fawn's Devotion* (1910), *The Red Girl and the Child* (1910), and *A Cheyenne Brave* (1910). His films dealt with relations between Native Americans and whites in a more complex manner than most classic Westerns. *White Fawn's Devotion*, for example, acknowledges "mixed-race" relationships, a topic that other Indian films of this period also explored. Many of them, such as *Ramona* (1910, directed by D. W. Griffith), showed interracial coupling as leading to tragedy, while others, such as *Flaming Arrow* (1913, from Bison 101) did end happily.

As did early ethnographic films, films of the Indian Story genre often misrepresented actual Native American customs to create exotic appeal for white audiences. However, the films' sympathetic attitude marks them as different from the usual Hollywood Western, which increasingly centered on the plights of white settlers forced to battle crazed "Injuns." D. W. Griffith's *Battle at Elderbush Gulch* (1913) is a good example of an early film that looks a lot like the classical Hollywood Western. It depicts a full-scale Indian attack against a white encampment. However, just when things look darkest for the settlers, the US Cavalry comes to the rescue – bugles blowing, horses racing, guns blazing – in a scene that becomes emblematic of the genre during its classical period. (It also recalls the charge of the Ku Klux Klan in another Griffith film, *The Birth of a Nation* [1915], a film that substituted marauding African Americans for marauding Indians.) Within the narrative pattern of the classical Hollywood Western, Native Americans are structured as part of the wild and wooly environment that needs to be subdued, to be brought under the control of a benevolent white patriarchal civilization. Furthermore, unlike in the Indian Story films, Native Americans in the classical Hollywood Western are rarely given basic character motivation. For example, in many classical Hollywood films the real-life Native American leader Geronimo is depicted as a bloodthirsty savage bent on destroying white civilization. Yet the fact that his wife, mother, and children were all killed by white people in unprovoked attacks is a detail that most Hollywood Westerns fail to mention.

By the mid-1910s, the Western film genre had been formed and its popularity eclipsed the Indian Story altogether, often by focusing on charismatic white male cowboy heroes such as William S. Hart. The few possibilities for Native Americans to be writers and directors evaporated, and by the 1920s, James Young Deer could only find work directing films in Great Britain. Native American actors were forced to accept smaller and increasingly stereotyped roles. Hollywood also began to hire more and more white actors to play larger Indian parts, a practice of "redface" makeup that continued well into the 1960s. Thus, for most classical Hollywood filmmakers (and their audiences), the **Hollywood Indian** became a readily identifiable composite stereotype, one that drew traits from a variety of Native American cultures. He carried a bow and arrows, wore a feathered headdress and moccasins, slept in a teepee, and smoked a peace pipe. Not surprisingly, whenever Hollywood Westerns *did* distinguish specific Indian nations, they tended to name and depict tribes that had fought back against white encroachment with fierce determination. In this way, the Sioux and Apache tribes became synonymous in Hollywood films with the bloodthirsty savage stereotype.

The Western genre became so popular during the 1920s and 1930s – some film historians estimate that up to 25 percent of all classical Hollywood films might be considered Westerns – that it developed various subdivisions, or **subgenres**, plus a wide array of Western film stars. There were silent Western epics such as *The Iron Horse* (1924) and *Tumbleweeds* (1925), escapist kiddie-fare like the films of Tom Mix, and even a series of singing cowboy movies starring Gene Autry, Tex Ritter, and Singing Sandy (played by **John Wayne** before he became a major star). The Western was also popular on the radio: *The Lone Ranger* began airing in 1933 and eventually became a long-running television show (ABC-TV, 1949–57, plus an even longer life in syndication). Like the **black and white buddy** formula discussed in the previous chapter, *The Lone Ranger* attempted to draw the white man and the Indian together as a team that fought injustice. Yet **Tonto**, the Native American half of the team, was always clearly subservient to the Lone Ranger (and in fact, Tonto means "crazy" in Spanish). Tonto is a good example of the Indian as noble savage stereotype, playing helpful sidekick to white men and white culture.

By the 1930s, most Westerns were considered unimportant, low-budget films. However, the genre was revitalized in 1939 when **John Ford** directed John Wayne in *Stagecoach*. The high point of the film, an Indian attack on the titular vehicle, provides another good example of how Native Americans were presented in classical Hollywood Westerns. Before they even appear onscreen, the audience is alerted to them by the sound of ominous (and now clichéd) war drums in the background music. Although the sequence begins with a few close-ups of Indians on a high plateau looking down threateningly at the stagecoach, the rest of the sequence gives close-ups only to the white characters (who are, of course, the central characters in the film). In this way, the film positions the spectator to view the attack from the perspective of the white travelers. The white characters' various reactions to the battle are individuated, while the Indians are kept in long shot, figured as one large, frightening mass. And while the Indians are certainly constructed as threatening, white superiority is still maintained. The dozens of Indians aiming directly at the stagecoach manage to kill only one man and wound two others. On the other hand, the whites are sure shots, and at one point John Wayne's character seems to bring down two Indians (and their horses) with one bullet! As in Griffith's *Battle at Elderbush*

In the TV series *The Lone Ranger*, the hero (Clayton Moore) was accompanied by his loyal sidekick Tonto (Jay Silverheels) – an example of the noble savage stereotype.
The Lone Ranger, copyright © 1949–1957, ABC-TV

Gulch, one of the men plans to shoot a female passenger when it seems that all will be lost (to save her the horror of being raped by an Indian), but true to form, the Cavalry rushes in to save the day.

   Stagecoach, perhaps more than any other film, cemented in the public's mind what the classical Hollywood Western was all about – thrilling action sequences among the breathtaking scenery of the Old West in which a white male hero defeated Indians and other bad guys. Director John Ford, who had made silent Westerns in the 1910s, continued to make them into the 1960s; he has been valorized as one of Hollywood's greatest directors. John Wayne, who had toiled in low-budget films for most of the 1930s, was catapulted into stardom by the success of *Stagecoach*; he became a Hollywood icon as the pre-eminent American hero. Whether he was fighting Indians on the plains or battling the Japanese in World War II movies, John Wayne came to represent the spirit of the nation: masculine individuality, strength, and justified violence in the name of God and country. The fact that that violence was frequently exerted against Native American populations was simply part of the Western formula. Ford once noted that in his films he had "killed more Indians than [actual US Cavalry officers] Custer, Beecher, and Chivington put together." A balm for the historical crimes of the nation against indigenous peoples, the classical Hollywood Western was ultimately one of the most racist of American film genres. It was not until the **civil rights movement** of the postwar era that some American filmmakers began to challenge the assumptions and implications of the form.

The Evolving Western

In the post-World War II era, the Hollywood **social problem film** became briefly popular. As part of this trend, a few Westerns were produced that attempted to treat Native Americans with more care and respect. The formation in 1950 of an advocacy group, the National Film Committee of the Association on American Indian Affairs, also helped to foment change in Hollywood by lobbying for better representations. There was also at least one film produced during this era that chronicled the life of a *contemporary* Native American, Olympic and baseball star *Jim Thorpe, All American* (1951). (Note how the very title of the film stresses his assimilation into white national culture.) Yet, as is still true of Hollywood today, historical films about Indians, that is, Westerns, were much more likely to be produced than were films centering on contemporary Native American lives. Nonetheless, the Westerns of the 1950s and 1960s continued to evolve, sometimes in bizarre ways. By the 1970s, a few films even dared to celebrate Native American cultures and indict white racism.

Two of the first social problem Westerns of the immediate postwar era were *Devil's Doorway* (1950) and *Broken Arrow* (1950). In the former, an Indian who has fought for the Union during the Civil War returns home to find prejudice and injustice in his supposedly free home town. In *Broken Arrow*, Jimmy Stewart plays a Civil War veteran who falls in love with an Indian maiden; however, true to another Hollywood formula, their marriage ends in tragedy. (It is interesting to note that *Broken Arrow* was written by then-**blacklisted** Albert Maltz; along with the film's pleas for non-violent racial tolerance one can also discern a subtle critique of mob rule and witch-hunting as it was then occurring in **Red-Scared** Hollywood.) The producers of *Broken Arrow* solicited Native American input for the film's various tribal scenes, and while many allegedly authentic details were still fabricated, the film at least *attempted* to acknowledge and accurately depict Apache culture. However, most of these films still featured white actors playing the lead Indian roles: Burt Lancaster in *Jim Thorpe, All American*, Robert Taylor in *Devil's Doorway*, and Jeff Chandler and Debra Paget in *Broken Arrow*. As in the 1930s, actual Native American actors were relegated to bit parts or were employed as extras. For example, Jay Silverheels, who appears (uncredited) in a small role in *Broken Arrow*, found his greatest success on TV as *The Lone Ranger*'s sidekick, Tonto. Another "Indian extra" of the era was Iron Eyes Cody, perhaps best known for his appearance as a weeping Native American on the famous 1970s "Keep America Beautiful" TV public service announcement. In truth, although Cody lived and worked as a Native American for most of his professional life, his parents were actually Italian immigrants.

During the 1950s and early 1960s, the so-called **adult Western** began to deal in more complex ways with the genre's thematic issues. Whether or not gunfighters make good role models for small boys was a question asked by *Shane* (1953). The Westerns of director Anthony Mann often figured their white heroes as obsessed neurotics, and the inherent racism of the Western hero was questioned in John Ford's *The Searchers* (1956). In it, a character played by John Wayne becomes so pathological in his hatred for Indians that the audience fears he will kill his cousin (Natalie Wood) because she was raised by them. The violent and myth-making capacity of the genre was also explored in Ford's *The Man Who Shot Liberty Valance* (1962). Toward the end of his career, John Ford even attempted to make a pro-Indian movie, or at least a film that depicted the plight of a specific Native tribe forced by the Cavalry to relocate. Titled *Cheyenne Autumn* (1964), the film is a bloated epic that interrupts its tale of resettlement with a grotesque "comic interlude" that attempts to play the genre's violence and brutality for easy laughs. It too failed to cast Native American actors in leading Cheyenne roles, instead drawing on Hispanic actors such as Dolores Del Rio and Gilbert Roland. Furthermore, it should be noted that on most of Ford's Western films, the production staff maintained segregated restrooms for white and non-white performers. Such was the baseline racism of the era.

As the civil rights struggles of the 1960s became more pronounced, the **American Indian Movement (AIM)**, founded by **Russell Means**, added its voice to the growing countercultural call for social justice and equal opportunity for all Americans. Hollywood began to realize that their simple-minded Indian stereotypes were out of date, and for a time in the 1960s, Hollywood Westerns tended to pit white heroes against Mexican bandits instead of bloodthirsty savages. The war in Vietnam was also sensitizing Americans to issues of US imperialism and warfare against non-white people, and many countercultural critics began drawing comparisons between American jingoism and the violent thematics of the cinematic Western. As if to confirm that theory, when John Wayne made his controversial pro-Vietnam-war movie *The Green Berets* (1968), he staged it like a classical Hollywood Western, with marauding non-white Others storming the army camp, a type of warfare that did not occur in Vietnam. (Allegedly Wayne had enlisted the aid of John Ford in making this film, but even that did not fail to correct the many inaccuracies that the film depicts, including most infamously a shot where the sun sets into the East.) As the 1960s wore on, the Western became increasingly apocalyptic, with films like *The Wild Bunch* (1969) killing off its exhausted heroes in a barrage of slow-motion bullets and blood. Western heroes of the 1960s, best embodied by the violent and cynical Clint Eastwood character in the **spaghetti Westerns** (so-called because they were made in Italy or other parts of Europe), no longer upheld American ideals. Now they were violent, greedy, petty criminals who ruthlessly murdered others before they themselves were killed by equally cynical gunfighters.

Latino actors Gilbert Roland and Dolores Del Rio were hired to play Native American characters in John Ford's apologetic Western, *Cheyenne Autumn* (1964). *Cheyenne Autumn,* copyright © 1964, Warner Bros. Photo: Kobal Collection

As the counterculture mocked and disparaged the traditional Western hero as embodied by John Wayne, it also began to embrace aspects of Native American culture. As part of a larger quest to find meaning, value, and spirituality in American life, some members of the counterculture adopted Native clothing and studied Native customs. Environmentalists upheld Native cultures as exemplars of ecological harmony between human beings and nature. While some of this appropriation could be seen as a different version of white interest in exotic Others, American youth's interest in Native American cultures radically challenged the traditional Western's notions of who was "the good guy" and who was "the bad guy." A strong sign of how the image of the Native American came to symbolize countercultural rejections of traditional American society came during the Academy Awards in 1973. Marlon Brando won and then refused his Best Actor Oscar for *The Godfather* (1972), and sent Native American actress Sacheen Littlefeather to the stage to protest Hollywood's (and the nation's) mistreatment of Native American people.

By the early 1970s, a few films, including Arthur Penn's satire *Little Big Man* (1970), attempted to rework the Western genre into a more pro-Indian formula and actually critique white expansionism. *Little Big Man* was also understood as an anti-Vietnam-war film, as its depiction of an Indian massacre appeared to be an allegorical representation of the recent real-life massacre in My Lai, Vietnam. *Little Big Man*'s central character, a white man played by Dustin Hoffman, spends much of the film moving between Native American societies and white frontier towns. Through this character the viewer is invited to compare the two cultures, and the film makes its points fairly explicitly: Native Americans were peaceful, respectful people while whites were cruel, violent, and even insane. *Little Big Man* was also important in that it featured a Native American actor in an important role, and Chief Dan George became the first Native American nominated for an Oscar for Best Supporting Actor. *Little Big Man* attempted to upset and rework the tenets of the classical Hollywood Western, yet the film also upholds usual Hollywood narrative form by focusing these issues through the character of a straight white male.

Also released in 1970, *A Man Called Horse* claimed to be an accurate representation of a historical Native American culture. True yet again to the Hollywood formula, the film starred white actor Richard Harris, as an Englishman captured by a tribe of Sioux Indians. Most of the film is about his experience within the Native culture and how he eventually learns to respect and honor it. However, the film's historical accuracy has been challenged on many accounts, and it too features non-Native actors in lead Indian roles. The film was a success at the box office, but perhaps that was due to its infamous "sun vow" ritual scenes, in which the Englishman is strung up by his pectoral muscles and left to hang in the heat. While the ritual depicted was based on an actual practice (but one followed by the Mandan Indians, not the Sioux), it is more than possible that this gory, sadomasochistic sequence is what attracted audiences to the box office, and not the cultural uplift of learning about Sioux culture. The film was so popular that it spawned two sequels, *Return of a Man Called Horse* (1976) and *Triumphs of a Man Called Horse* (1983).

Also very popular with audiences during this era were the "Billy Jack" films: *Born Losers* (1967), *Billy Jack* (1971), *The Trial of Billy Jack* (1974), and *Billy Jack Goes to Washington* (1977). Somewhat analogous in narrative construction to the blaxploitation films, these films might be thought of as a sort of "Indian-ploitation." In each film, Billy Jack (played by writer-director Tom Laughlin), who is identified in the films as a "half-breed" (half Native American and half white), encounters corruption and prejudice at the core of the American system. Although Billy Jack just wants to find peace and justice, he (like a blaxploitation hero) is usually called upon to battle his oppressors in increasingly violent ways. Cheaply made and sensationalistic, the "Billy Jack" films may have provided a cathartic experience for some Native American moviegoers, even as they reinforced values of violent machismo.

In 1976, iconoclastic film director Robert Altman (who had exposed some of the Western genre's mythic clichés in *McCabe and Mrs. Miller* in 1971), returned to the genre with a highly satiric Western. *Buffalo Bill and the Indians, or Sitting Bull's History*

Tom Laughlin as Billy Jack (1971), a half-Indian karate expert who battled small minds and social prejudices in a series of popular films.
Billy Jack, copyright © 1971, Warner Bros.

Lesson (which was based on Arthur Kopit's play *Indians*) starred Paul Newman as Buffalo Bill and Frank Kaquitts as Sitting Bull. In the film, the mythic Buffalo Bill is debunked as a hammy stage actor who impersonates an American hero in his Wild West show. Bill is revealed to be an alcoholic, a coward, a poor shot, a terrible tracker, and an ignorant racist. When he "acquires" the imprisoned Sitting Bull from a federal prison as a side-show attraction, the differences between the two men and the cultures they represent are highlighted and explored. Eventually Sitting Bull is killed and Bill goes back to playing the Western hero. In many ways the film is a powerful criticism not only of the American Western's thematic myth, but also of a contemporary, media-saturated America that all too often believes that the fantasy images of its fictional entertainments are more real than reality itself. In 1976, the year of the American Bicentennial, the film failed miserably with US audiences who were in no mood to see cherished American icons and beliefs tarnished.

A Kinder, Gentler America?

By the 1980s and 1990s, the sheer number of Hollywood representations of Native Americans had declined a great deal since the classical period, primarily because the Western film genre was no longer very popular. The nation's evolution throughout the 1960s and 1970s had made the Western's thematic myth outmoded, and new attitudes toward Native Americans made it difficult to continue to figure them as the opposition to white progress. This new awareness of and respect for Native American cultures sometimes challenged lingering stereotypes. Toward the end of the twentieth century, sports teams such as the Atlanta Braves and the Washington Redskins came under attack for their use and exploitation of outmoded images, many of which still carry negative connotations for Native Americans.

Yet, if the bloodthirsty savage stereotype was slowly fading away, a reworking of the noble savage stereotype became increasingly prevalent: the Indian as holder of divine, transcendental spirituality. In the 1980s and 1990s, many white Americans embraced what they believed to be a simpler, nobler, "new age" type of spirituality, frequently derived from Native American customs and culture. This new use and function of Native Americans can be seen in films as diverse as *The Doors* (1991), *Natural Born Killers* (1994), and Disney's *Pocahontas* (1995). This softer, gentler version of cultural stereotyping was also prevalent in the few American Westerns of the era. Care was taken during the production of most of these films to consult Native American historians, cultural experts, and advisors. Yet the Hollywood formulas still at work within these films complicated their messages of cultural respect. In many, the Indian experience is still refracted through the eyes of white people, and usually a white male. For example, the film *Windwalker* (1980) took care to employ Native American languages (Cheyenne and Crow), but then placed British actor Trevor Howard in "redface" makeup in the main Indian role.

Probably the most significant representations of Native Americans from this period can be found in *Dances With Wolves* (1990), a revisionist Western that won numerous Oscars including Best Picture. The film is a good example of a **nostalgic Hollywood blockbuster**, attempting to update the Western's formulas for a more politically sensitive era. *Dances With Wolves* also draws on the conventions of the Hollywood social problem film, wherein a white lead character investigates a social problem, here figured as the historical situation of nineteenth-century Native Americans. Kevin Costner, who also directed the film, stars in it as Lt. John Dunbar, a US Cavalry officer who, through a series of adventures, comes to live among the Lakota Indians. Dunbar experiences Lakota culture at first hand, and finds it to be more ecologically sound and spiritually fulfilling than his own. Much like the earlier film *Little Big Man*, in *Dances With Wolves* the brutality and ignorance of the US Cavalry are vividly dramatized, while the Lakota culture is shown to be peaceful and honorable. The complexity and humanity of those characterizations allowed them to move beyond the noble savage stereotype, but the marauding Pawnee Indians still appear as rather one-dimensional, bloodthirsty savages. And a somewhat contrived love interest also exposes the Hollywood formulas at work in the film: Mary McDonald plays another white person living among the Indians, conveniently placed there by the scriptwriter so that Dunbar may have a love interest of his own race. Still, despite its formulaic nature, the film was popular with many Native Americans, especially for its rousing spectacle of a buffalo hunt and its careful reconstruction of Lakota culture.

Dances With Wolves also gave much-needed work to Native American actors who comprised the strong supporting cast, including Oneida Indian Graham Greene (who was nominated for a Best Supporting Actor Oscar), Omaha Indian Rodney Grant, Lakota Indian Floyd Red Crow Westerman, and Cree/Chippewa actress Tantoo Cardinal. Cherokee actor Wes Studi also appeared in *Dances With Wolves*, and he played the title role in *Geronimo: An American Legend* (1993), although

Russell Means, founder of the AIM (American Indian Movement), later became an actor; here he appears in costume and makeup for his role as Chingachgook in *The Last of the Mohicans* (1992).
Last of the Mohicans, copyright © 1992, 20th Century-Fox. Photo: Frank Connor

Eric Schweig, seen here in *The Last of the Mohicans* (1992), has also played more contemporary characters; in *Big Eden* (2000) he played a gay Native American who falls for an artist from New York City.
Last of the Mohicans, copyright © 1992, 20th Century-Fox. Photo: Frank Connor

he received fourth billing after Jason Patric, Robert Duvall, and Gene Hackman. (*Geronimo* was written and directed by John Milius and Walter Hill, two Hollywood filmmakers best known for their action films, but the film did poorly at the box office, perhaps because of its focus on Indians rather than cowboys.) Russell Means, the Oglala/Lakota Sioux activist who was the first national director of the American Indian Movement, has also become an actor in recent years: among other roles, Disney employed him for the voice of Powhatan in *Pocahontas*. These and other Native American actors continue to work in Hollywood, but almost always in supporting roles. Hollywood does not seem to know what to do with them: they are typecast as Indians in an era when Hollywood's version of an Indian movie (that is, the Western) is no longer popular. And Hollywood still shies away from films that feature contemporary Native American characters or issues.

One rare film that attempted to do that, *Thunderheart* (1992), was a mystery-conspiracy-thriller set on a Sioux reservation. In it, Val Kilmer played an FBI agent of Sioux heritage investigating corruption and government abuse. The film was loosely based on the actual story of Leonard Peltier, a Native American activist who was jailed in 1975 for the murder of two FBI agents. *Thunderheart*'s director, Michael Apted, also made a documentary about Leonard Peltier entitled *Incident at Oglala* (1992); the film suggests that Peltier was wrongly convicted. Other more recent documentary films about Native Americans include *Imagining Indians* (1992) and *Navajo Code Talkers* (1996). The former is an exploration of the cinematic representation of Native Americans, while the latter documents the US military's use of Navajo languages as strategic communication codes during World War II. This subject was turned into the Hollywood blockbuster *Windtalkers* (2002), but true to form, that film starred Nicholas Cage as the white male lead and relegated Native Americans to supporting roles.

Along with documentaries, American independent film has been more able than Hollywood to represent more varied images of Native American characters and concerns. For example, one of the first successful films about contemporary Native American culture was Jonathan Wach's independently produced *Powwow Highway* (1989). In it, life upon a Cheyenne reservation is the backdrop for a story that explores personal and social identities, family ties, the role of the warrior, and friendship. Jim Jarmusch's *Dead Man* (1996), an art-house fable, was about a man (Johnny Depp) searching for meaning with the aid of an outcast Indian (Gary Farmer). *The Education of Little Tree* (1997) was a small family drama about an 8-year-old Cherokee boy growing up during the Great Depression, while *Big Eden* (2000) featured Eric Schweig as a contemporary gay Indian living in Idaho. Similarly, *The Business of Fancydancing* (2002), the directorial debut of prolific Native American author Sherman Alexie, centered on a gay poet from Spokane revisiting the Indian reservation of his childhood years. As with the other types of social difference explored within this book, American independent filmmaking is more likely to address the issues and concerns of any given minority group, as well as provide some of the first opportunities for minority-group filmmakers to create images of themselves. Native American filmmakers have just begun to do so.

Case Study: *Smoke Signals* (1998)

Advertised as the "first feature film written, directed, and produced by Native Americans," *Smoke Signals* became an art-house hit after winning several awards at the 1998 Sundance Film Festival. One of few American films to deal with contemporary Native American culture, it was based on Sherman Alexie's book *The Lone Ranger and Tonto Fistfight in Heaven*, and was directed by first-time director Chris Eyre. It follows the adventures of Victor (Adam Beach) and Thomas (Evan Adams), two young friends from the Coeur d'Alene Indian Reservation, as they travel to Arizona to retrieve the ashes of Victor's dead father. Victor and Thomas are a rare screen couple in American cinema – fully developed and complex Native American characters. Victor is tall, athletic, quiet, and full of resentments and repressed emotions. Thomas is shorter and almost effeminate; he wears glasses, pigtails, and a three-piece suit which mark him (at least in Victor's eyes) as slightly eccentric. In one of the film's highlights, the two young men discuss just what a "real" Indian is supposed to look like. For Victor, a real Indian wears long hair and has a stoic expression – he should look like a warrior who has been killing buffalo. Comically deflating that image, Thomas notes that their particular tribe was made up of fishermen, not warriors. In this way, the film raises and gently deconstructs stereotypical ideas about Indians – ideas that have been internalized by some Native Americans themselves.

Thomas, who has been raised by his grandmother, is always telling stories that may or may not be true, and it is these stories that link the film in a direct way to the traditionally oral history of many Native American cultures. The truth or accuracy of these stories is not always the point, one learns, as fictionalized stories are also meaningful and in some ways can be more "true" than "real life" itself. Thus the film uses metaphor and allusion to address the historical conditions of oppression which have faced Native American cultures. For example,

the film begins as baby Thomas's home and family are destroyed by a fire on July 4, 1976. By setting this opening event on the date of the American Bicentennial, the filmmakers subtly link America's founding day with a holocaust that deprives Thomas (and by extension all Native Americans) of their fathers and their cultures. That same struggle (between Native Americans and white invaders) is metaphorically depicted in a basketball game that Joseph and Victor play against two Jesuit priests. In one version of the story, Victor wins the game, overturning the historical reality spoken by the characters elsewhere, that "cowboys always win." Although it never does so in a direct or angry way (in fact the film is characterized by its gentle humor), *Smoke Signals* slyly addresses the power dynamics of historical and contemporary white culture from the perspective of its Native American characters. The film is filled with knowing allusions to Christopher Columbus, General Custer, Tom Mix, Jim Thorpe, John Wayne, *Dances With Wolves*, and TV Westerns.

Ultimately, *Smoke Signals* explores issues of memory, history, family, identity, forgiveness, and mourning. It dramatizes the day-to-day realities of contemporary life on an Indian reservation, and wryly comments on the odd mixtures of traditional Native and contemporary American cultures. The film ends with a montage of raging rivers while a narrator asks rhetorical questions about the nature of forgiveness. The audience is asked to ponder the past. How do we forgive our fathers, for what they did, or for what they *didn't* do? The film offers no easy answers to those questions, but suggests that to understand the present, we must also understand the past. That theme is also expressed in the form of the film itself. It makes extended use of flashbacks, intercutting, and framing effects that create for the spectator a unique cinematic space in which the past and present seem to commingle, forever affecting one another. Even the film's title draws

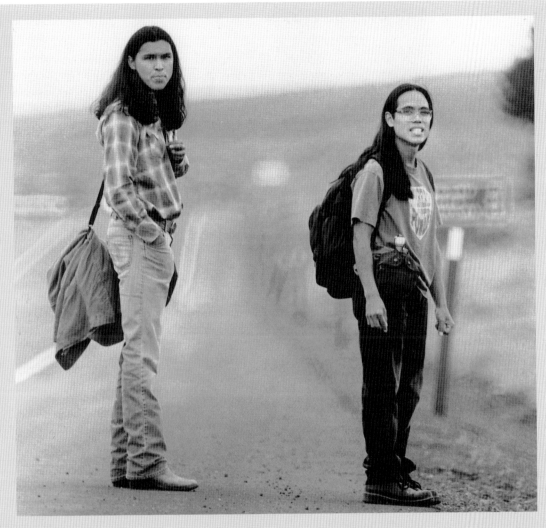

Adam Beach and Evan Adams play two young men on a journey in *Smoke Signals* (1998), the first American independent film written, directed, and produced by Native Americans.
Smoke Signals, dir. Chris Eyre, copyright © 1998, Miramax. Photo: Jill Sabella

attention to the theme. The signs and symbols of the past, the smoke signals historically used by Native Americans to communicate with one another, drift into the future, where they can still be decoded, hopefully before they disappear altogether.

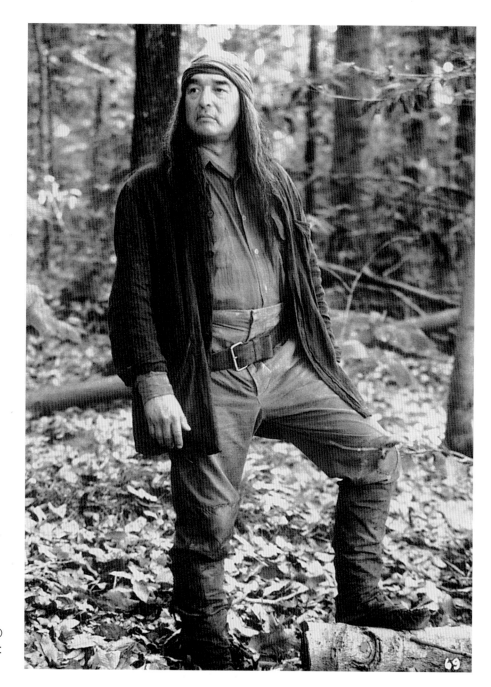

Graham Greene in *The Education of Little Tree* (1997), an independent film that centered on an 8-year-old Cherokee boy educated by his grandparents in Native American ways.
The Education of Little Tree, dir. Richard Friedenberg, copyright © 1997, Paramount. Photo: Jan Thijs

Conclusion: Twenty-First-Century Indians?

One of the most significant books to chronicle the brutal history of the Indian Wars, *Bury My Heart at Wounded Knee*, was adapted for the small screen by HBO in 2007. Recent Hollywood films, however, have tended to downplay or avoid altogether the conflicts between nineteenth-century American settlers and Native peoples (found at the core of the Hollywood Western genre), in order to focus more on the cultures of Native peoples before the arrival of the white man. For example, Mel Gibson's lush historical epic *Apocalypto* (2006) explores different aspects of ancient Mayan culture, and finds it to be at war with itself: peaceful tribes are routinely rounded up by more violent ones in order to be used as human sacrifices. In many ways, *Apocalypto* pits noble savages against blood-thirsty ones. The film has also been accused of being gratuitously violent. People are sliced and diced on screen by all sorts of primitive weapons, and decapitated heads are shown repeatedly bouncing down stone temple steps. In many ways, the film seems less like an exploration of authentic Mayan cultures than like a film designed to exploit post-9/11 fears. For example, the good guys are represented in terms of **homo-social** bonding, heterosexual procreation, and patriarchal lineage, traits that link them to contemporary Western patriarchies. On the other hand, Gibson represents the bad guys as displaced jihadists bent on destruction because of their blind allegiance to a bloodthirsty religion. Even more exploitative was the stylized action thriller *Pathfinder* (2007), a film that may also have been trying to side-step the historical racism of the traditional Western genre by creating a conflict between good Native Americans and evil Viking explorers. Yet the Native Americans' savior is himself a white man left behind by the Vikings a generation ago. While it is rarely acceptable for white actors to play Native American roles in contemporary Hollywood films, *Pathfinder* nonetheless finds a way to make a white man the savior of the Native population.

Terrence Malick's *The New World* (2005) is a more thoughtful and moody film, retelling the first contact narrative between Captain John Smith (Colin Farrell) and Indian princess Pocahontas (Q'orianka Kilcher). And while great care was taken to try to recreate the historical conditions of the initial clash between white explorers and Native peoples in Jamestown, Virginia, the film also creates an almost mythic aura about its subject matter. At first, Smith and Pocahontas are a sort of Adam and Eve in a New World garden, before they are eventually drawn apart by duties to their respective cultures. It is perhaps in the film's final third, when Pocahontas travels to England, that the film becomes most interesting. Here the "Old World" of Europe is presented as the titular *New World* for Pocahontas, one to which she has little choice but to assimilate. Malick juxtaposes the rigid contours of manicured English gardens against the free-growing ones of America, an apt visual metaphor for the ways in which both cultures structure their inhabitants' experiences. A curious film combining lush detail and a minimal, almost obscure narrative, *The New World* delighted some audiences who praised its sensual verisimilitude. Others complained about the film's artiness: its lack of **continuity editing** and incessant

Method-School mumbling. In either case, the film remains notable for reimagining this first contact narrative, attempting to explore what the cultures of both England and Native America were like before the rise of the colonies and, eventually, the Western film genre.

Questions for Discussion

1 Do children still play "Cowboys and Indians"? Where did the "rules" of such a game come from and how are they learned?

2 Many Native American terms were adopted by white settlers as place names of rivers, states, towns, and counties. What aspects of Native American cultures remain in your specific locale? What do you know about the Native cultures that once existed in your area?

3 When does a Western stop being a Western and become something else? Is a film dealing with white settlers and Native American tribes in the original 13 colonies (such as *The New World*) still a Western? Should a film that centers on a historical Native American culture before the arrival of whites (like *Apocalypto*) still be considered a Western? Why or why not?

Further Reading

Bataille, Gretchen M. and Charles L. P. Silet. *The Pretend Indians: Images of Native Americans in the Movies*. Ames: Iowa State University Press, 1980.

Churchill, Ward. *Fantasies of the Master Race: Literature, Cinema, and the Colonization of American Indians*. San Francisco: City Lights Books, 1998.

Deloria, Philip. *Playing Indian*. New Haven: Yale University Press, 1998.

Hilger, Michael. *From Savage to Nobleman: Images of Native Americans in Film*. Lanham, MD: Scarecrow Press, 1995.

Kilpatrick, Jacquelyn. *Celluloid Indians: Native Americans and Film*. Lincoln: University of Nebraska Press, 1999.

Marubbio, M. Elise. *Killing the Indian Maiden: Images of Native American Women in Film*. Lexington: University Press of Kentucky, 2006.

Rollins, Peter C. and John E. O'Connor, eds. *Hollywood's Indian: The Portrayal of the Native American in Film*. Lexington: University Press of Kentucky, 1998.

Singer, Beverly R. *Wiping the War Paint off the Lens: Native American Film and Video*. Minneapolis: University of Minnesota Press, 2001.

Weatherford, Elizabeth, ed. *Native Americans on Film and Video*. New York: Museum of the American Indian, 1981.

Further Screening

Stagecoach (1939)
Broken Arrow (1950)
The Searchers (1956)
Cheyenne Autumn (1964)
Little Big Man (1970)
A Man Called Horse (1970)

Buffalo Bill and the Indians (1976)
Powwow Highway (1989)
Dances With Wolves (1990)
The Business of Fancydancing (2002)
The New World (2005)

Chapter 6

ASIAN AMERICANS AND AMERICAN FILM

Asia is the largest continent on the planet and home to hundreds of different cultural communities. Yet, for most of the twentieth century, American film reduced the complexity of actual nations, cultures, and characters to simplified **stereotypes**. It didn't matter if the character (or actor playing a character) was from China, Japan, India, Korea, or Malaysia: he or she was marked as physically different from Caucasian characters through costume, makeup, and performance. Much as it fashioned the "reel" Indian out of a mixture of actual Native American costumes and cultures, so did Hollywood create a stock "Oriental" character. The most common Hollywood Asian was someone with shifty behavior, broken English, and above all slanting, narrow eyes that seemed to suggest a diabolical cunning. This **inscrutable Oriental** stereotype – "inscrutable" meaning "mysterious" – was a staple of classical Hollywood films, and the character type can still be found in some contemporary American films.

As with other non-white characters in Hollywood films, these stock Asian characters were usually marginalized into supporting roles. Asians frequently appeared in American films as houseboys, railroad or laundry workers, cooks, and other assorted servants. However, because they were constructed as enigmatic, Asian characters also appeared in mystery films and crime thrillers, wherein they were often villains (although sometimes detectives). Asian actors rarely got the chance to play leading roles, for, when a film called for a leading Asian *character*, classical Hollywood almost always cast a white star in the part. This "yellowface" tradition continued in Hollywood well into the 1960s and 1970s, eras when a white actor wearing **blackface** was no longer considered acceptable. Thus the Hollywood "Oriental" was usually the creation of makeup and costume artists. The character rarely had anything to do with the actual concerns or issues of Asians living in America or abroad.

In the 1970s, cultural critic Edward Said argued influentially that the West's seeming fascination with the Orient was less an interest in the actual geographic region and its cultures than a fascination with the *idea* of those places as different from white Western cultures. Said coined the term **Orientalism** to refer to the way that

Eurocentric and other white Western cultures *imagine the idea* of Asia; it does not refer to how Asian cultures actually were or are. This concept of Orientalism grows out of the theories of identity formation discussed in chapter 3, theories that suggest that for people or cultures to know themselves, they must define themselves against an **Other**. Orientalism is a theory of how Europe and Western culture defined itself by creating an image of the Orient. Thus for European nations historically, the image of the Orient became one of exotic people, seductive and sensual pleasures, and potential lawlessness – everything "civilized" Europe was supposedly not. These social constructions take on **gendered** dynamics as well: Western patriarchal cultures conceived of Eastern cultures as feminine or childlike in order to justify colonization and domination. One of the most enduring images of "the Orient" is encapsulated in the opera *Madame Butterfly*. In it, Asia is represented by the exotic, meek, and long-suffering Butterfly, a woman who will do anything for the Western man she loves, including die for him.

Today, the very word "Oriental" carries with it certain negative connotations and many Asian people find it offensive. The word "Asian" is preferred when describing the peoples or cultures derived from the Asian continent. (Sometimes one hears the quip that "Rugs are Oriental, but people are Asian.") But even terms such as "Asian" or "Asian American" are potentially reductive, as they group together different nations and cultures which, it should be remembered, have their own specificity. India, for example, is very different from Japan or Eastern Russia. Most Asian nations today are also comprised of multiple racial and ethnic groups. This chapter attempts to distinguish between some of these groups, as well as the differences between Asians and Asian *Americans*. It also surveys the way American cinema has regularly *failed* to make those distinctions, preferring to employ stock stereotypes and exotic settings that emphasize the "Oriental" over the "Asian."

Silent Film and Asian Images

Asians were relatively unknown in America until the second half of the nineteenth century, when Western expansionism allowed US citizens to come into contact with Asians – primarily Chinese men – who were crossing the Pacific Ocean to California and other Western states. Just as European immigrants came to the Eastern United States during those years, many Asians came to Western America in search of more freedoms and a higher standard of living. Asian immigrants faced a tremendous amount of discrimination and prejudice, similar to that experienced by most immigrant groups. In accordance with historical ideas about race, many Americans considered Asian people to be "not white"; in simplistic terms, white America often referred to Asians as the "yellow race." Asians were often singled out for special forms of discrimination. Many racist laws were passed that specifically disallowed Asian immigration (such as the Chinese Exclusion Act of 1882 and the Immigration Act of 1924), and there were laws passed that legislated what types of jobs Asians could and could not hold in America. This set of circumstances tended to keep Asian men in positions of menial labor, and some lingering Asian stereotypes – the Chinese laundry worker or the Asian "coolie" working on the railroad – stem from this era's discriminatory laws. In other types of immigration legislation, it became nearly impossible for Chinese men to bring their wives and families to America. In some communities, Asian American men sometimes outnumbered Asian American women by a ratio of twenty-five to one.

Some of these men gravitated toward the cities, and the urban ghettoes where they settled often became known as "Chinatowns." Excluded from the American dream of free market **capitalism** by racist work laws, some Chinese men turned toward illegal means of making money, and organized criminal gangs, or **Tongs**, in order to sell black-market goods. The so-called "Tong Wars" that occurred in various Chinatowns from about 1910 to 1930 were fought over control of illicit black-market commodities such as opium, gambling, and prostitution. White-run newspapers often capitalized on this situation to sell newspapers: Asians were now branded the "Yellow Peril" or the "Yellow Horde." Hollywood followed suit and produced many films that exploited images of Asian American criminality. Films such as *The Yellow Menace* (1916), *The Tong Man* (1919), and *Chinatown Nights* (1929) focused on underworld kingpins and secret empires. (This formula can still be found in more recent films, such as the **nostalgic Hollywood blockbusters** *Big Trouble in Little China* [1986] and *The Shadow* [1994].) These early films also often exploited the concept of **white slavery**, the idea that white women were being kidnapped by Chinese American gangs and sold into prostitution.

In fact, social fears over white/Asian **miscegenation** were at the center of many silent films. Before the Hollywood **Production Code** was written in 1930, many American films freely exploited the subject, often in highly sensationalized terms. D. W. Griffith's *Broken Blossoms* (1919) tells the tragic story of an Asian man who longs for the love of a white woman. While the Chinese man Cheng Huan (played in "yellowface" by white actor Richard Barthelmess) is a sympathetic character, the film repeatedly refers to him as "The Chink," a term now considered a racially abusive epithet but which was common parlance in the early 1900s. True to the Hollywood formula, the love between the Asian man and the white woman ends in death. The woman dies when her abusive father beats her, and Cheng Huan commits suicide over his lost love. The message of this film, and many others like it, is abundantly clear: mixed race relationships invariably end in disaster – either for the lovers themselves (as in *Broken Blossoms* or *Toll of the Sea* [1922]), or for their children (as in films like *The Forbidden City* [1918] or *East is West* [1922]).

American silent film did produce at least one Asian star, the Japanese actor **Sessue Hayakawa**. Hayakawa became a romantic leading man of his era, often playing princes or other types of exotic noblemen. On the model of the **Latin Lover** stereotype, for a brief period Hayakawa's Asian heritage made him marketable as an exotic heart-throb. One of his most infamous roles was as the businessman Tori in Cecil B. DeMille's miscegenation melodrama *The Cheat* (1915). In one of the film's more notorious scenes, Tori brands a white woman's shoulder with a hot iron, as a symbol of his sexual ownership of her. The act is meant to be cruel and diabolical, in keeping with Asian stereotypes of the era, yet many viewers also found the branding to be erotically charged. Nevertheless, Tori is still lynched at the end of the film as punishment for having desired a white woman. Sessue Hayakawa began to produce his own films when he grew weary of playing Hollywood stereotypes. He produced and starred in approximately 25 films during the late 1910s and 1920s, before leaving the United States to make films abroad. He returned to Hollywood in the late 1940s and became an occasional character actor, and is perhaps best remembered for his Oscar-nominated performance as a Japanese military officer in the World War II movie *Bridge on the River Kwai* (1957).

Asians in Classical Hollywood Cinema

Classical Hollywood cinema marginalized Asian American issues, characters, and actors by practically ignoring their existence. In the few cases where Asian American performers did find work in Hollywood films, they were usually called upon to play people *from* an Asian country, and not Asian *Americans*. Images of life in Asian countries were themselves limited. The Production Code prohibited not only scenes of sex and violence but also any frank discussion of global or national politics. During the 1930s, a civil war in China between communists and nationalists raged, but it was rarely mentioned in Hollywood films. Likewise, the arming of Japan's empire as a prelude to World War II was a forbidden topic for Hollywood movies. Furthermore, when films were made about Asian nations and peoples, Hollywood almost always cast white actors in the lead roles. For example, in *The Bitter Tea of General Yen* (1933), another Hollywood melodrama about white/Asian miscegenation, the Chinese warlord of the title is played by Swedish actor Nils Asther. In *The Good Earth* (1937), based upon Pearl S. Buck's famous novel, the noble and struggling Chinese peasants are played by Paul Muni and Luise Rainer.

More regularly, Asia and its peoples were used as exotic local color. In *Lost Horizon* (1937), for example, white people stumble into the mythic city of Shangri-la, a utopian spot located somewhere in the Himalayas. This geographical trope became quite common, and in the Universal serial *Lost City of the Jungle* (1946), the "lost city" of Pendrang is again supposedly located somewhere in the mountains of Northern India. However, in a good example of applied Orientalism, Pendrang is actually constructed out of various leftover sets from other Universal movies set in generic "exotic" places. Pendrang and Shangri-la are both presented as mysterious and mystical. They are also seen almost exclusively from the white characters' points of view, and their Asian inhabitants function mostly as extras: the films figure them as marginal even within their own cities. The few supporting Asian roles in these films are either helpful aides or villainous henchmen to the white characters, but rarely central characters themselves. Furthermore, in *Lost Horizon*, the people of Shangri-la who have speaking parts are mostly played by white actors.

Arguably, the two most pervasive images of Asians in classical Hollywood cinema were **Charlie Chan** and **Dr Fu Manchu**. Despite some major differences (Chan was a hero while Fu Manchu was a villain), both characters embody the stereotype of the inscrutable Oriental – an Asian with superior intellect who is potentially untrustworthy because of his mysterious behavior. Not surprisingly perhaps, both characters were derived from literary sources that had been written by white men in the 1920s. Both characters appeared in a slew of highly successful films and both character types were imitated in other films at other studios. Their impact has been long lasting, and films featuring the characters of Charlie Chan and Dr Fu Manchu have even been made in more recent decades.

Charlie Chan was a Chinese American detective and member of the Honolulu police force. He was created by mystery writer Earl Derr Biggers and first appeared on film in 1926. Hollywood made over 50 feature films about Charlie Chan during the next few decades. In each, the great detective is called upon to solve a murder or other criminal act, and does so through brilliant deductive reasoning, much like Sherlock Holmes. However, Charlie Chan was never played by an Asian actor. The most successful and high-budget of these films starred Swedish actor Warner Oland as Charlie Chan. When Warner Oland died, Sidney Toler took over the part, and later Roland Winters played him in a series of low-budget films. Each actor wore "yellowface" makeup in order to appear Chinese American. The few Asian actors who were cast in the films usually appeared in supporting roles as Charlie Chan's sons. Charlie Chan has been frequently criticized by many Chinese

Swedish actor Warner Oland, seen here in character makeup ("yellowface") for his role as benevolent Chinese American detective Charlie Chan.
Unidentified publicity photo, authors' personal collection

Americans not only because of his inauthentic casting, but also because he quickly became a stereotype himself. Although supposedly highly educated with a brilliant mind, Chan tended to speak in broken English and make cryptic quips that suggested both the sayings of Chinese philosopher Confucius and the silly predictions of fortune cookies. Furthermore, Charlie Chan's Chinese heritage is never really dealt with in the films, and he is never permitted much of a home life. Mrs Chan is nowhere to be seen, and his sons seem to exist merely for comic relief, frequently confounding his investigations.

Though stereotypical, Charlie Chan was arguably a "good" stereotype, in that he was an intelligent and capable hero who solved crimes that baffled even white detectives. Chan (and especially his offspring) were also Asian Americans, attempting to assimilate. Occasionally the films would even poke fun at the ignorance of white assumptions about the Chinese. The opposing "bad" stereotype was embodied by the super-criminal **Dr Fu Manchu**. Explicitly *not* interested in assimilation, Fu Manchu was an evil genius, using his "Oriental tricks" to bend the rest of the world to *his* will through conspiracy, torture, and exploitation. The character of Dr Fu Manchu was created by Englishman Sax Rohmer, and on screen, he was also played by white actors in "yellowface." Before becoming Charlie Chan, Warner Oland played Fu Manchu in a series of films. Perhaps most famously, Fu Manchu was played by horror film star Boris Karloff in *The Mask of Fu Manchu* (1932). In that **pre-Code**

British actor Boris Karloff, seen here in character makeup ("yellowface") for his role as evil criminal mastermind, Dr Fu Manchu. *The Mask of Fu Manchu*, copyright © 1932, MGM/Universal

film, Fu Manchu's cruelty is given free reign. He gleefully feeds salt water to a man dying of thirst – a man who is simultaneously having his eardrums ruptured underneath a large, tolling bell. Another victim is slowly lowered into a crocodile pit via a sand clock, while yet another is strapped into a room of gradually constricting spiked walls. Fu Manchu's daughter (played by white actress Myrna Loy) is an opium-smoking sadist who takes obvious sexual delight in seeing the white hero chained, stripped, and whipped. When MGM tried to re-release the film in the early 1970s, Asian Americans protested, and the film was eventually re-edited to tone down some of its more outlandish anti-Asian sentiments. (Current DVD copies seem to present the film in its original form.)

The characters of Fu Manchu and Charlie Chan were so popular that their character *types* were exploited by other filmmakers. For example, in *The Mysterious Mr. Wong* (1935), Bela Lugosi played an Asian mastermind obviously modeled on Fu Manchu. A thinly disguised Fu Manchu can also be seen in the "Flash Gordon" serials (1936, 1938, 1940) and in the much-later film version (1980). In those science fiction texts, the evil emperor Ming the Merciless allegedly comes from the planet Mongo, but his name, his makeup (complete with Fu Manchu moustache), and his visual décor – dragons and gongs – make him yet another Asian supercriminal stereotype. Ming was, again, played by white actors: Charles Middleton in the serials and Swedish actor Max von Sydow in the more recent film. Hollywood has also exploited the Asian detective stereotype throughout the years. Peter Lorre played a Japanese detective named "Mr. Moto" in one series of films (1937–9), while Boris Karloff played a Chinese detective named "Mr. Wong" in yet another (1938–40). The fact that two character actors of European descent, best known for playing monsters and mad scientists, were regularly cast as Asians again suggests a cultural connection between mystery, terror, and the Orient.

These two character types maintained their popularity even beyond the classical Hollywood era. Hints of Fu Manchu can be found in the first James Bond movie, *Dr. No* (1962), and in any number of more recent international thrillers. Fu Manchu himself was popular in a series of British **horror films** made in the 1960s starring Christopher Lee, and both Charlie Chan and Fu Manchu appeared in Hollywood films as late as the 1980s. In *Charlie Chan and the Curse of the Dragon Queen* (1981), British actor Peter Ustinov played the title role, while British comedian Peter Sellers starred in *The Fiendish Plot of Dr. Fu Manchu* (1980). Allegedly, contemporary Hollywood has plans to make a new Fu Manchu movie as well as a Charlie Chan film; Asian American actress Lucy Liu has been attached to the latter project. Meanwhile, contemporary mainstream Hollywood comedies continue to exploit "yellowface" stereotypes. In *Balls of Fury* (2007), Christopher Walken plays an Asian arch-fiend named Weng, complete with Oriental robes, outlandish wigs, and painted fingernails.

The most prevalent image of Asian women on screen during Hollywood's classical period was probably the stereotype of the **Dragon Lady**, a sort of female equivalent of Fu Manchu. The Dragon Lady was likely to be a spy or a criminal mastermind in her own right – but along with violence she used her sexual wiles to entrap unsuspecting white heroes. While this character type was also often played by white actresses, or Hispanic actresses such as Maria Montez, Chinese American actress **Anna May Wong** became a minor star by embodying it. Born Wong Liu Tsong, she adopted the name Anna May in order to

Anna May Wong (born Wong Liu Tsong) was a Chinese American actress who briefly achieved stardom in early Hollywood.
Unidentified publicity photo, authors' personal collection

Keye Luke was one of the most successful Chinese American actors of the classical Hollywood era, often playing Asian American supporting roles that did not require him to speak in broken English.
Unidentified publicity photo, authors' personal collection

break into the movies. She acted in films like *Toll of the Sea* and *A Trip to Chinatown* (1926), but quickly became typecast in films such as *The Devil Dancer* (1927), *Daughter of the Dragon* (1931), and *Shanghai Express* (1932). Like Sessue Hayakawa before her, Anna May Wong became frustrated at the treatment of Asian Americans in Hollywood, and she too left the United States to make films abroad.

One of the most successful Asian actors working in the classical Hollywood cinema was Chinese American **Keye Luke**, whose career lasted from the 1930s to the 1990s. Luke's roles sometimes acknowledged the existence of second-generation Asian Americans. As Charlie Chan's "Number One Son," or as Dr Lee Wong in the "Dr Gillespie" films (1942–7), Keye Luke portrayed young Asian American men successfully integrating into American society. "Number One Son" spoke slang and listened to American pop music, in contrast to his first-generation father. In *Charlie Chan at the Olympics* (1937), young Chan is even part of the US track team. However, Keye Luke was rarely given the opportunity to play anything but supporting roles. In the "Charlie Chan" films, Luke was plainly secondary to white actor Warner Oland. Similarly, Luke's Dr Wong was the assistant to white star Lionel Barrymore in the "Dr Gillespie" films. Luke was also the sidekick to the white hero in *Lost City of the Jungle*, and he performed the same function in the "Green Hornet" serials (1939–40), as Asian sidekick Kato to white hero Britt Reid. Such stereotypical roles increased as Luke moved into older character parts. In *Gremlins* (1984) and *Gremlins 2: The New Batch* (1990), for example, he plays an enigmatic Asian character from whom the title creatures originate. In Woody Allen's *Alice* (1990), his last film role, Keye Luke played Dr Yang, yet another mysterious Asian with potentially magical powers. Similarly, Korean American actor Philip Ahn played small supporting parts in over 170 different film and television projects until his death in 1978.

World War II and After: War Films, Miscegenation Melodramas, and Kung Fu

The Japanese surprise attack at Pearl Harbor on December 7, 1941, brought the United States into World War II. Hollywood worked with federal agencies to produce not only educational propaganda, but also many **war movies** meant to dramatize the international conflict and mobilize the populace to renewed fighting. In attempting to whip up support, many of these World War II war films made Japanese soldiers into bloodthirsty villains. Seemingly confirmed by the Pearl

Harbor sneak attack, the stereotype of the inscrutable Oriental was now used to represent the Japanese military in films such as *Gung Ho!* (1943), *The Purple Heart* (1944), and *Objective Burma* (1945). Such images had a material effect on Japanese Americans, who were forcibly rounded up by the thousands and sent to relocation camps during the war years. Considered to be more Japanese than American, they were thought to be untrustworthy. Much of America chose to forget or ignore those incidents for decades following the war, and it was not until the little-seen film *Come See the Paradise* (1990) that Hollywood represented that aspect of Japanese American history.

While many war films demonized the Japanese, some of them (such as *Bataan* [1943] and *Thirty Seconds Over Tokyo* [1944]) actually distinguished among different Asian nationalities, showing Chinese or Filipino characters aiding in the fight against Japan. Although these characters were shown in a positive light, they still embodied Oriental stereotypes, and were inevitably among the first to die in battle. While the menacing Fu Manchu stereotype had been reworked for the Japanese, the docile Charlie Chan stereotype had been revamped for the Chinese and other Asian nationalities. This binary was put in place again after World War II, but with the stereotypes reversed. After the Communist Revolution in China in 1949, the United States bolstered its relationship with Japan. Now, American culture increasingly regarded the Japanese as benevolent and friendly, while the Chinese were again figured as evil and diabolical. The ease with which the stereotypes were flipped indicates how much these seemingly opposite images have in common (and how little most Americans distinguished between people of different Asian nationalities).

For the next two decades, the United States would battle the possibilities of communist encroachment in Asian lands, beginning in Korea. In war movies and spy thrillers such as *The Manchurian Candidate* (1962), Chinese communists and their American agents used brainwashing and torture to advance nefarious plans for world domination. (The musical *Flower Drum Song* [1961] provides an exception to this trend, acknowledging the existence of Chinese American lives and experiences; however, the film was written, directed, and produced by white men for predominantly white audiences.) Hollywood's images of Japanese people, on the other hand, became more regularly sympathetic in films such as *Teahouse of the August Moon* (1956) and even the World War II movie *Bridge On the River Kwai*. *Bad Day at Black Rock* (1955) might even be considered a **social problem film** about small-town prejudice against Japanese Americans. In it, a war veteran (played by Spencer Tracy) comes to town to give a Japanese American man a medal that his son has won posthumously. Ten years after the war, the film points out that some Japanese Americans fought for the United States during the conflict. However, Tracy's character discovers the town's dark secret: they lynched the soldier's father in response to the attack on Pearl Harbor. Although *Bad Day at Black Rock* is a film about racial prejudice against Japanese Americans, no Japanese Americans actually appear on screen. True to the formula of the Hollywood social problem film, the film centers on a heroic white male character exposing bigotry, **hegemonically** asserting that **white patriarchal capitalist** culture is a cure for racism, and not a cause.

One cycle of 1950s films (such as *Japanese War Bride* [1952], *Sayonara* [1957], and *South Pacific* [1958]) dealt with an actual postwar phenomenon – interracial relationships and marriages between American military men and Asian women. In 1954, laws banning interracial marriage between Asians and Caucasians were struck down by US courts, and these types of relationships became even more common. To some extent, these films (and others such as *Love is a Many Splendored Thing* [1955] and *The World of Suzie Wong* [1960]) dramatized some of the prejudice and hardship faced by interracial couples of the era. Although many of the films still cast white actors into their lead Asian roles, some of them did provide excellent supporting roles for Asian American actors. (Indeed, Japanese-born Miyoshi Umeki was the first actor of Asian descent to win an Oscar – she won Best Supporting Actress for her role in *Sayonara*.) The interracial relationships shown in these films were possibly tolerable to American audiences since they usually focused on strong white men with meek and adoring Asian women, and not white women with powerful Asian men (as had many of the earlier silent films about miscegenation). One film that veers into this latter category, the adaptation of the stage musical *The King and I* (1956), cannot even fully acknowledge the attraction between the English governess and the King of Siam – not surprisingly, he dies at the end of the film before their relationship can be consummated. The property, based on the diaries of the actual English governess who lived the story, was remade yet again in 1999 as *Anna and the King*. Starring Jodie Foster as Anna and Asian actor Chow Yun-Fat as the King, the film is a typical nostalgic Hollywood blockbuster that reimagines history as romantic melodrama.

During the 1960s, the fight against communism shifted from China and Korea to the war in Vietnam, but popular American film mostly avoided the subject altogether. The lack of consensus in the nation about US involvement in Vietnam made it difficult for Hollywood to unproblematically employ its usual Oriental villain stereotypes, and so the studios opted not to discuss the situation at all. One notable exception was the film *The Green Berets* (1968), starring and co-directed by John Wayne. This was an attempt to make a pro-war Vietnam movie, and it was met with considerable scorn from many members of the 1960s counterculture, even as more conservative viewers applauded its sentiments. The film is basically a transplanted **Western** in which North Vietnamese soldiers have replaced the Indians. As such it contains many historical and cultural inaccuracies about the war and the Vietnamese people, most of whom come off as either cruelly monstrous or peripheral.

Not until after the United States had pulled out of Vietnam did mainstream American films begin to deal with the war, but only as it had impacted upon America, and not on Vietnam or Vietnamese Americans. *Coming Home* (1978) examined issues faced by some returning veterans, while *The Deer Hunter* (1978), which won an Oscar for Best Picture, followed a group of US soldiers' experiences in Vietnam and afterwards. The latter film, despite its critical and popular success, has also been called racially exploitative. The film's famous torture sequence, wherein American prisoners of war are forced to play Russian roulette by sadistic Vietnamese guards, was not historically accurate, and many Asian American groups protested against the film. Francis Ford Coppola's *Apocalypse Now* (1979), based upon Joseph Conrad's nineteenth-century novel *The Heart of Darkness*, had even less foundation in factual incident than did *The Deer Hunter*. While ostensibly critiquing the absurdity and surreality of the war, the film makes the Vietnamese people peripheral; they appear mostly as the childlike followers of a deranged US military leader played by Marlon Brando. Filmmaker Oliver Stone also explored the horrors of warfare from the American GI's point of view in his films *Platoon* (1986) and *Born On the Fourth of July* (1989). The final film in Oliver Stone's "Vietnam Trilogy," *Heaven and Earth* (1993), based upon several books of memoirs by Vietnamese author Le Ly Hayslip, remains one of the few Hollywood films that attempts to explore the war from a Vietnamese perspective.

While the Vietnam war was being mostly ignored by popular American film during the early 1970s, Asian and Asian American characters were appearing in **kung fu action movies**. Most kung fu movies were exploitation films – sensationalistic, violent, sexy, and often cheaply made abroad in Hong Kong or other parts of Asia. The popularity of these movies contributed to a martial arts craze that swept America in the 1970s. The TV show *Kung Fu* (ABC/NBC, 1974–5) quickly came under attack because of the casting of white actor David Carradine as its half-Chinese lead, Kwai Chung Caine. The most famous figure to emerge from kung fu movies was the Chinese American actor and martial arts expert **Bruce Lee**. First gaining notice as the sidekick Kato in the TV show *The Green Hornet* (ABC, 1966–7), Lee also choreographed martial arts fights and stunts for several Hollywood films. He reached international stardom producing and/or starring in several kung fu action movies, including *Fists of Fury* (1972), *Return of the Dragon* (1972), and *Enter the Dragon* (1973). Bruce Lee died of a brain hemorrhage at the height of his popularity, and that tragic early demise (he was only 32 years old) helped to establish him as an international cult figure. His son Brandon Lee also became an actor, but he too died an early death, caused by a tragic accident during the filming of the comic book action movie *The Crow* (1993).

The kung fu movie coincided with the making of **blaxploitation** films, and many of them made use of the same formulaic elements. Often in kung fu movies, white characters were constructed as villainous and racist, and audiences were encouraged to empathize with Asian heroes as they karate-chopped and kicked the (white) bad guys. As exploitation films, many kung fu movies played in inner-city theaters alongside blaxploitation films, and became popular with some African American audiences. One independent company, American International Pictures, realized that fact and began to incorporate martial arts and Asian characters into its blaxploitation films. For example, in *Cleopatra Jones* (1973), black superhero Cleopatra is aided by two African American karate experts. In *Cleopatra Jones and the Casino of Gold* (1975), Cleopatra teams with Asian crime fighter Tanny (Mi Ling) to battle a white Dragon Lady played by Stella Stevens. While these bits of reverse racial casting (white villains and non-white heroes) countered dominant Hollywood trends, it is difficult to see any of these films as making too explicit a political statement about race and social difference. Stereotypes still abound in them, and most of these films were written and directed by white men. The films were commercially calculated attempts to make money from non-white moviegoers. By the mid-1970s, the kung fu movie had waned in popularity. Yet, as part of the New Hollywood trend toward recycling and repackaging previously successful formulas, Hollywood released a kinder, gentler, martial arts movie in 1984 entitled *The Karate Kid*. The film won Japanese American actor Noriyuki "Pat" Morita an Oscar nomination for Supporting Actor, playing the role of a wise old karate expert who teaches a teenage white boy both the mental and physical aspects of the discipline. The film spawned several sequels, remakes, and even an animated TV show.

By the 1980s, media watchdog groups such as **NAATA** (the **National Asian American Telecommunications Association**) had been formed to monitor Hollywood images. Traditional Hollywood practices such as "yellowface" makeup and overt stereotyping were now forcefully challenged by consumer groups. Cambodian actor Haing S. Nor won a Best Supporting Actor Oscar for his role in *The Killing Fields* (1984), a film that explored the political violence and terror in Cambodia in the aftermath of the Vietnam war. (Dr Nor was and continued to be an outspoken human rights advocate until he was murdered in 1996, a death that some people feel was a revenge killing for his political views.) However, the economic recession of the 1980s resulted in a resurgence of anti-Asian and specifically anti-Japanese sentiment, as many American workers felt that Japanese corporations were "stealing" US markets. The gentle Hollywood comedy *Gung Ho* (1986) – and the short-lived TV series based upon it (ABC, 1986–7) – acknowledged those dynamics, centering on American and Japanese autoworkers learning how to work together. The producers of the TV show hired a Japanese American consulting firm to ensure that their representations of Asian and Asian American characters were not offensive to anyone. Still, even during this period of growing cultural awareness and sensitivity, stereotypes and stereotypical ideas persisted in formulaic Hollywood films. In action movies like *Black Rain* (1989) and *Rising Sun* (1993), Japan is represented as an exotic locale full of shifty characters and outright criminals who threaten white Americans.

Contemporary Asian American Actors and Filmmakers

Significant gains have been made for Asian American actors working in Hollywood in the last few decades, but few have reached the level of stardom regularly attained by white actors, or more recently some African American and Hispanic actors. For the most part, Asian American actors are still relegated to supporting and often stereotypical roles. For example, Gedde Watanabe, who received second billing after Michael Keaton in *Gung Ho*, continues to find himself marginalized. Watanabe's character in *Sixteen Candles* (1984) is named Long Duk Dong, a sophomoric locker-room joke, and his Japanese tourist in *Gremlins 2* seems solely defined by his stereotypical obsession with cameras. Watanabe's experience is not unique. Despite earning a Best Supporting Actor nomination for his role in *The Sand Pebbles*

(1966), Japanese American actor Mako continued to be cast in small supporting roles in Hollywood films until his death in 2006, including that of a Japanese military officer in the nostalgic Hollywood blockbuster *Pearl Harbor* (2001). Japanese American actor Noriyuki Morita similarly played "generic" Oriental roles in film and television until his death in 2005, such as the voice of the *Chinese* emperor in Disney's animated film *Mulan* (1998). Also heard in *Mulan* was James Shigeta, a Japanese American actor who has appeared in countless film and television shows since the late 1950s.

Younger Asian American actors working in Hollywood today, such as Naveen Andrews, B. D. Wong, and Russell Wong, face similar hurdles; they often find themselves most regularly cast as supporting actors in multicultural TV shows like *Lost* (2004–) and *Law & Order: SVU* (2001–7). Indian American Kal Penn and Korean-born John Cho have also appeared in many television projects; they are perhaps best known as the stars of the low-budget buddy comedies *Harold & Kumar Go to White Castle* (2004) and *Harold & Kumar Escape from Guantanamo Bay* (2008). Others actors of Asian descent, such as John Lone, who had lead roles in important independent films such as *The Last Emperor* (1987) and *M. Butterfly* (1993), tend to ignore Hollywood as best they can and seek work in Asia. In fact, Hollywood has recently

Russell Wong, the leading man of *Eat a Bowl of Tea* (1989) and the *Vanishing Son* TV series. Unidentified publicity photo, authors' personal collection

taken to hiring more actors from Asia rather than *Asian Americans*. For example, Ken Watanabe was a succesful film and television star in his native Japan before starring in films like *The Last Samurai* (2003) and *Letters from Iwo Jima* (2006). He received a Best Supporting Oscar nomination for the former role, as did Rinko Kikuchi for her work in the globe-hopping drama *Babel* (2006). Probably the best-known actor of Asian British descent is Sir Ben Kingsley; he continues to play a wide variety of roles in international cinema, but is perhaps best known for his Oscar-winning role as the Mahatma in *Gandhi* (1982).

Asian American actresses working in Hollywood today include Chinese American Lucy Liu (*Charlie's Angels* [2000], *Shanghai Noon* [2000], *Kill Bill* [2003]) and Korean American stand-up comedian Margaret Cho. The pressures placed on Cho to conform to white America's concepts of Asian American life as the star of the short-lived TV show *All American Girl* (ABC, 1994) were detailed in her one-woman show and movie entitled *I'm The One That I Want* (2000). Actress Joan Chen has the distinction of being the first Chinese-born woman to direct a Hollywood feature, the old-fashioned **woman's film** *Autumn in New York* (2000) starring Richard Gere and Winona Ryder. Ms Chen moved into directing after a brief acting career in both China and the United States. Dissatisfied with the roles she was being offered in America, she turned to directing and made the independent feature *Xiu Xiu: The Sent-Down Girl* (1998), a film that examined a young girl's life in 1970s Communist China. Like John Lone, Joan Chen often finds more substantial acting challenges in independent films like *Saving Face* (2004), or in international co-productions such as Ang Lee's *Lust, Caution* (2007).

Since the end of World War II, American moviegoers have shown an interest in films made in Asia. For example, the films of Japanese director Akira Kurosawa were art-house hits in the 1950s and 1960s. The kung fu fad of the 1970s was fueled by imported films from Hong Kong. Such interest continues to this day, as prestigious art films from all over Asia, Japanese animated films known as **anime**, and **Hong Kong action films** attract many American moviegoers. The marketability of Hong Kong's high-powered and violent action films has not been lost on Hollywood. Director **John Woo** was lured from Hong Kong to Hollywood, where he has made big-budget action films such as *Face/Off* (1997), *Mission: Impossible II* (2000), and *Paycheck* (2003). Many of the actors who first became stars in Hong Kong action films have also crossed over into Hollywood films: Jackie Chan, Jet Li, and Chow Yun-Fat have all become recognized at the American box office. Hollywood has even adapted its **black and white buddy** film formula to include Asian actors. For example, Jackie Chan co-starred with Owen Wilson in the buddy Western *Shanghai Noon* (2000), and with Chris Tucker in the formulaic *Rush Hour* films (1998, 2001, 2007). Similarly, Chow Yun-Fat co-starred with Seann William Scott in *Bulletproof Monk* (2003). In addition to Hollywood buddy films and action comedies, most of these actors still make films in Asia as well, where they get to be leading men and not just buddies or other supporting characters.

While American audiences seem somewhat interested in films about Asian cultures (as perhaps attested to by Hollywood blockbusters like *Memoirs of a Geisha* [2005]), films about Asian *American* experiences are still struggling for mainstream popularity. The careers of two directors of Asian descent, **Ang Lee** and **Wayne Wang**, exemplify many of the issues involved in this struggle. **Ang Lee** was born in Taiwan, attended the New York University (NYU) film school, and initially found acclaim writing and directing independent films. Working outside of Hollywood enabled him to tell stories about the Chinese American experience. His first three films, *Pushing Hands* (1992), *The Wedding Banquet* (1993), and *Eat Drink Man Woman* (1994), are all richly drawn celebrations of Chinese and Chinese American families. However, as Lee began to receive larger budgets and major (white) stars from Hollywood backers, his films became less and less about Chinese American culture. In the second half of the 1990s he directed a Jane Austen adaptation (*Sense and Sensibility* [1995]), a film about bored suburbanites in 1970s New England (*The Ice Storm* [1997]), and a Civil War drama (*Ride With the Devil* [1999]). While these films amply demonstrated his ability to direct more mainstream film projects, it was his direction of *Crouching Tiger, Hidden Dragon* (2000) that brought him great acclaim. The film won an Oscar for Best Foreign Language Film and earned Lee an Oscar for Best Director. *Crouching Tiger, Hidden Dragon* was a high-class, mythical Chinese revenge drama that brought the flashy style of Hong Kong action cinema to mainstream American film audiences. After his success with that action film, Lee was hired to direct the nostalgic Hollywood blockbuster *The Hulk* (2003), a film that fared poorly at the box office. Back on more familiar ground – exploring human relationships rather than special effects – Lee won an Oscar for

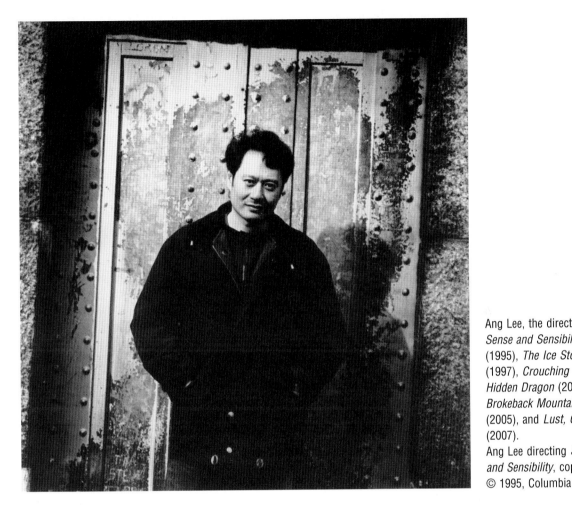

Ang Lee, the director of *Sense and Sensibility* (1995), *The Ice Storm* (1997), *Crouching Tiger, Hidden Dragon* (2000), *Brokeback Mountain* (2005), and *Lust, Caution* (2007).
Ang Lee directing *Sense and Sensibility*, copyright © 1995, Columbia

directing *Brokeback Mountain* (2005), and then made the international co-production *Lust, Caution*, a steamy spy thriller set in World War II-era Shanghai. Ang Lee's best work – whether it be *The Ice Storm*, *Crouching Tiger*, or *Brokeback Mountain* – is able to capture an almost palpable feeling of place and time, exploring the historical and cultural conditions that shape the social identities of his richly drawn characters.

Wayne Wang is another prolific Asian American filmmaker who also works in and around Hollywood today. Wayne Wang was born in Hong Kong but (like Ang Lee) educated in the United States, where he studied art, film, and television. His father, who was a big fan of American cinema, allegedly named him after John Wayne. Also like Ang Lee, Wang began his career in independent film, writing and directing *Chan is Missing* (1982). As the name implies, the film was a sort of revisionist mystery that echoed the Charlie Chan films while simultaneously exploring the diversity of the Chinese American community. His next film, *Dim Sum* (1984), also explored Chinese American cultures. Wang's first attempt to make a film centering on white characters, *Slam Dance* (1987), failed at the box office, but he did achieve considerable critical success with his film *The Joy Luck Club* (1993). Based on Amy Tan's novel about several generations of four different Chinese American families, the film was a complex and masterfully told epic. Since then, Wang has directed Hollywood-style films as well as more independent features. His Hollywood films include *Anywhere But Here* (1999), *Maid in Manhattan* (2002), *Because of Winn Dixie* (2005), and *Last Holiday* (2006), while his independent films include *Smoke* (1995), *Blue in the Face* (1995), *Chinese Box* (1997), *The Center of the World* (2001), *Princess of Nebraska* (2007), and *A Thousand Years of Good Prayers* (2007). While his independent films almost always center on matters of race, nationality, class, gender, and sexuality, even Wang's Hollywood films tend to feature multicultural casts and explore similar issues. For example, *Maid in Manhattan* centers on a poor working-class Latina (Jennifer Lopez), while *Last Holiday*, a vehicle for Queen Latifah, features an international cast including LL Cool J, Gérard Depardieu, and Ranjit Chowdhry.

Another Asian American writer-director currently making his mark on Hollywood is Taiwan-born Justin Lin. After graduating from UCLA's film school, Lin made the quirky independent feature *Shopping for Fangs* (1997). His breakthrough film was *Better Luck Tomorrow* (2002), which received favorable critical attention, a handful of accolades at independent film festivals, and wider distribution thanks to the backing of MTV and its parent company Paramount Pictures. An edgy, youthful picture – as its MTV backing would suggest – *Better Luck Tomorrow* centers on a group of Asian American high school students who are also petty thieves and criminals by night. Lin's next two films were more standardized Hollywood fare centered firmly on straight white male protagonists. *Annapolis* (2006) was a coming-of-age story set at the titular military academy, while *The Fast and Furious: Tokyo Drift* (2006) was the third installment of the popular race car franchise. Lin's most recent film, *Finishing the Game: The Search for a New Bruce Lee* (2007), earned good buzz at festivals, but little money at the box office. As a low-budget satire about the relationships between Asian Americans and the film industry, *Finishing the Game* was not considered Hollywood (or multiplex) material.

Even as the representations of Asian characters and concerns within American film have continued to improve over the course of the twentieth and early twenty-first centuries, Asian American actors and stories in contemporary Hollywood cinema continue to be somewhat marginalized. Recent independent filmmaking practice (both fictional and documentary) has allowed for much more diverse and complex representations of Asian American lives and issues. For example, the Oscar-nominated documentary film *Who Killed Vincent Chin?* (1988) is about a Chinese American man who was murdered by a white autoworker in the 1980s – not because the autoworker was angry at *Chinese American* Vincent Chin, but because he was angry at *Japan* for allegedly stealing his job. The film shows how racism allowed the murderer to generalize his hatred and then concentrate it on a single individual, and how racism was also a factor in the trial. Other recent documentaries by Asian filmmakers, including *Days of Waiting* (1990), *Maya Lin: A Strong Clear Vision* (1994), and *Breathing Lessons* (1996), have all won Oscars. Filmmaker and theorist Trinh T. Minh-ha has made important ethnographic films such as *Reassemblage* (1982) and *Surname Viet, Given Name Nam* (1989). Lee Mun Wah's *The Color of Fear* (1995) is a powerful documentary that brings together men of different races and backgrounds to discuss racism, while the films of Richard Fung and Arthur Dong tend to explore the intersections of race, nation, sexuality, and representation. Jeff Adachi's documentary *The Slanted Screen* (2006) is a fascinating look at the history of Asian American men in Hollywood cinema.

Similarly, Gregg Araki became a leading director of 1990s **New Queer Cinema**, producing provocative fictional work focused on the permeability of racial, ethnic, and sexual boundaries. Two female directors of Indian descent are also making their marks in the independent film world. Mira Nair, who first came to attention by directing the Oscar-nominated foreign language film *Salaam Bombay!* (1988), has since then directed art-house hits including *Mississippi Masala* (1991), *Monsoon Wedding* (2001), and *The Namesake* (2006). Focusing on Indian and/or Indian American cultures, Nair's films often illustrate the complex issues of **diaspora**, a term that refers to the processes of change and/or assimilation that cultural groups undergo as they move through time and geographic displacement. Similarly,

Director Mira Nair on the set of *Mississippi Masala* (1991), a popular independent film about a romance between an Indian immigrant (Sarita Choudhury) and an African American man (Denzel Washington).
Mississippi Masala, dir. Mira Nair, copyright © 1991, The Samuel Goldwyn Company

Case Study: *Eat a Bowl of Tea* (1989)

Based upon a novel of the same name by Louis Chu, *Eat a Bowl of Tea* was directed by Wayne Wang as an American Playhouse Theatrical Film. (American Playhouse was a division of PBS created to fund independent features that would air on public television. Much of their output focused on minority issues, but it was defunded by Congress in the 1990s.) *Eat a Bowl of Tea* explores issues of Chinese and Chinese American culture from within the framework of a closely knit community, recreating life in New York City's Chinatown around 1949. It deftly weaves together the historical conditions of racism, federal discrimination, and the Korean war within a warmly human family drama.

The film dramatizes in vivid terms the almost all-male composition of many 1940s Chinatowns, a situation caused by federal laws prohibiting Chinese women from entering the country. As the film opens, voice-over narration informs the viewer that it was not until after World War II that Chinese people could become citizens and, furthermore, that Chinese American war veterans could go to China and bring back a bride. This change allows two old friends, Wah Gay (Victor Wong) and Lee Gong (Siu-Ming Lau), to arrange a marriage for their children. Wah Gay's son Ben Loy (Russell Wong), a veteran of World War II, travels back to China to meet Lee Gong's daughter, Mei Oi (Cora Miao). The two fall in love and marry in China. Yet, when the two return to New York, their fathers and the entire Chinese American community put so much pressure on them to produce a grandchild that marital troubles ensue.

Within this family drama, the film explores aspects of both Chinese and Chinese American culture. When Ben returns to China to meet Mei Oi, the film shifts into subtitles as the characters there speak Mandarin (and not some sing-song version of broken English as in most classical Hollywood films). The elaborate Chinese marriage process, from the use of "mui yan" (matchmakers) and the consultation of horoscopes to the sumptuous wedding banquet, is dramatized in affectionate detail. (The traditional Chinese marriage ceremony was also one of the subjects of Ang Lee's film *The Wedding Banquet*.) Other culturally specific practices such as a Chinese funeral, theater, and the concept of "face" are dramatized within the film. "Face" refers to community standing or social pride, and when Ben Loy marries Mei Oi, father Wah Gay notes that they now both have "the big face." The Americanized Ben therefore finds himself trapped between his responsibility to his new wife and his responsibility to his father and the other men of Chinatown. The community arranges a new job for Ben Loy and everybody waits for Mei Oi to get pregnant. However, working as a restaurant manager from 8 a.m. until 3 in the morning exhausts Ben Loy, and the community's constant prying about their sex life only drives the newlyweds further apart. When a local gossip discovers a brief affair between Mei Oi and another man, the family is disgraced and forced to move away. Only after a series of both dramatic and comedic adventures do the young couple reconcile and finally find happiness in San Francisco. The Golden Gate bridge – a symbol spanning place, time, gender, generation, and both national and international cultures – dominates this final scene.

Eat a Bowl of Tea is filled with subtle pop-culture references that point out how "Orientals" were conceived of in the past. In China, as Ben Loy and Mei Oi fall in love, they are shown watching the film *Lost Horizon*. In the film clip shown, white actress Jane Wyatt plays an Asian princess who chases after the leading man, an American

Toronto-based Deepha Mehta has written and directed several international art-house hits, including *Fire* (1996), *Earth* (1998), and *Water* (2005), each of which focus on Indian cultural traditions and especially women's roles within them. Mehta's *Bollywood/Hollywood* (2002), on the other hand, is a more light-hearted romp about culture clash at a traditional Indian wedding. More recently, *Cavite* (2005), the first

Lee Gong (Siu-Ming Lau) and Wah Gay (Victor Wong) are the meddlesome fathers whose desires for grandchildren threaten their children's marriage.
Eat a Bowl of Tea, copyright © 1990, Columbia

explorer played by Ronald Colman. Wang's use of the clip reminds spectators how classical Hollywood cinema traditionally viewed Asia, and invites comparison between those images and the ones in *Eat a Bowl of Tea*. The clip also subtly points out that in *Eat a Bowl of Tea* there is an actual Chinese American actress playing a Chinese character, and not a Hollywood (white) leading lady. Later in the film, Ben and Mei Oi watch another movie – the famous Orson Welles thriller *The Lady from Shanghai* (1947) – wherein Chinatown is represented as a hotbed of criminality and vice. Even *Eat a Bowl of Tea*'s musical score comments upon the cultural clashes the film dramatizes, alternating between traditional Chinese music and American pop music of the postwar era, as when a nightclub singer croons the old standard "I'd Like to Get You on a Slow Boat to China." The film is full of such rich and subtle details that invite the spectator to see Chinese American culture in new ways – ways that have always been apparent to Chinese Americans, but perhaps far less so to other Americans weaned on nothing but classical Hollywood cinema.

film written and directed by Neill Dela Llana and Ian Gamazon, is a taut thriller set in the Philippines about the global nature of terrorism. The ongoing work of Asian and Asian American filmmakers, both in Hollywood and on independent (or international) screens, will continue to complicate and enrich the evolving story of America on film.

Questions for Discussion

1 Can you still find lingering aspects of the Fu Manchu and Charlie Chan stereotypes in contemporary popular culture? What other Asian character types now seem to be common?

2 Should Chinese American directors concentrate on making films about Chinese and Chinese American experiences, or should they "branch out" into other subjects? What might be the benefits as well as the costs of an Asian filmmaker exploring a culture not his or her own?

3 It has been noted by some cultural critics that Asian American women have an easier time becoming broadcast journalists than do Asian American men. Why do you think that might be the case, and what do those ideas tell us about dominant notions of gender?

Further Reading

Feng, Peter X. *Identities in Motion: Asian American Film and Video*. Durham, NC: Duke University Press, 2002.

Gee, Bill J. *Asian American Media Reference Guide*. New York: Asian CineVision, 1990.

Hamamoto, Darrell Y. *Monitored Peril: Asian Americans and the Politics of TV Representation*. Minneapolis: University of Minnesota Press, 1994.

Hamamoto, Darrell Y. and Sandra Liu, eds. *Countervisions: Asian American Film Criticism*. Philadelphia: Temple University Press, 2000.

Marchetti, Gina. *Romance and the "Yellow Peril": Race, Sex, and Discursive Strategies in Hollywood Fiction*. Los Angeles: University of California Press, 1993.

Ono, Kent A. *Asian American Studies After Critical Mass*. Malden, MA: Blackwell, 2005.

Said, Edward. *Orientalism*. New York: Vintage Books, 1978.

Wong, Eugene Franklin. *On Visual Media Racism: Asians in the American Motion Picture*. New York: Arno Press, 1978.

Xing, Jun. *Asian America Through the Lens: History, Representations, and Identity*. Walnut Creek: Alta Mira Press, 1998.

Further Screening

The Cheat (1915)
Broken Blossoms (1919)
Any "Charlie Chan" movie
Any "Fu Manchu" movie
Sayonara (1957)
Chan is Missing (1982)
The Karate Kid (1984)

Who Killed Vincent Chin? (1988)
Mississippi Masala (1991)
The Joy Luck Club (1993)
Eat Drink Man Woman (1994)
Better Luck Tomorrow (2002)
Cavite (2005)
The Slanted Screen (2006)

Chapter 7
LATINOS AND AMERICAN FILM

Just as the emerging culture of the United States defined its national identity by claiming to be "not Indian," the country's westward expansion also mandated another opposition: being "not Mexican." One of the methods used was the usurping of the term "American" to refer to US citizens. Theoretically, anyone from North, South, or Central America is an American, although the United States has frequently claimed the term for itself. (Admittedly, this book often replicates that use of the term, but hopefully not in a naïve way.) Marking US identity and Mexican identity as distinctly separate took on extra importance in the days of **Manifest Destiny**, when the United States aggressively wrested control from Mexico of the territories that would become Texas, Arizona, Nevada, California, and (aptly) New Mexico. (Today, some people refer to these lands as **Aztlan**, purposely denying the names given to them by the United States.) Once those lands became part of the United States, many of the individuals who lived upon them were treated as foreigners – as **Others**. Stereotypical images of how those people looked, spoke, and acted became important tools for distinguishing between white (European) Americans and people who came from Mexico. Those **stereotypes** were frequently generalized and used to describe anyone who came from any nation "south of the border." As the United States extended its dominance throughout Central America (in places such as Cuba, Puerto Rico, and Panama), the use of stereotypes – most of which represented the people of these lands as backward, lazy, and childlike – helped justify **imperialist** actions.

The two most common terms used to describe the people and cultures of Central and South America are **Hispanic** and **Latino**. **Hispanic** tends to describe people and cultures whose ancestry can be traced back to Spain, Portugal, and/or Latin America; relation to Europe and European heritage is thus an important aspect of the term. However, using it to refer to all Central and South American people ignores the fact that Spain and Portugal were not the only European powers to colonize the area: for example, Haiti was ruled by France. Furthermore, many people of these regions do not trace their heritage back to Europe. **Latino** is a term that many people prefer, and it has been used with increasing frequency since the mid-twentieth century to describe people and cultures that hail from Latin America. However, "Latin America" is itself a European designation meant to describe Mexico and all the nations of Central and South America, lands that were conquered by Europeans who spoke languages originally derived from Latin. Sometimes Latino culture is defined primarily through the use of the Spanish language; however, not all Latinos speak Spanish, and even for those who do, dialects and regional differences contribute to and underscore regional diversities. (The term "Latino" also implicitly supports a male-dominated society, since the term is **gendered** as masculine. "**Latina**" is used to refer to women and women's culture from these regions. For the sake of conciseness, this book will use "Latino" when referring to both men and women of Latin American heritage.)

As is immediately apparent, both "Hispanic" and "Latino" vastly condense and oversimplify the wide range of languages, histories, and cultures of diverse groups of people. Some Latinos trace their ancestry back to indigenous populations (such as the Incas, the Aztecs, and the Mayans) who occupied these lands before the arrival of the Europeans. For others, Latino cultures include African customs and heritages, as South and Central America were also involved in the slave trade. Still others do trace their ancestry to European colonization. Concepts of **race** thus intersect with concepts of **nationality** and **ethnicity** in complex ways. Over hundreds of years, various national, regional, and ethnic cultures have blended and intertwined across the Americas, sometimes peaceably, sometimes through violence and oppression. The conquering white Europeans maintained dominance for many years throughout Latin America, and people of color – just as in the United States – were often singled out as inferior and treated unfairly. **Racist** assumptions about the superiority of whiteness (or European heritage) still linger in many of these nations, even as the hybridity of Latino cultures would seemingly help to break apart traditional concepts of race, most specifically the idea that there is a real and socially important distinction between white and non-white people. However, racial concepts die hard. Some people even conceive of Latinos as a separate race – the so-called "brown" race – even though classical theorists of race never conceived of such a category, and (like all human beings) Latinos come in all shapes, sizes, and colors. Such attempts underline how important the concept of skin color has been to many people throughout history, and the apparent need of dominant white cultures to maintain separation and control on the basis of the concept of race.

Throughout much of US history, Americans of Latino or Hispanic descent were often cordoned off into their own neighborhoods, discriminated against in the workforce, and verbally and physically harassed. Many whose families had lived here prior to annexation were deported as aliens. Attempts to separate the United States from Latin America (and especially Mexico) continue to this day, as evidenced by the amount of energy and funds spent to police the border between Mexico and the United States. Such attitudes have been reflected over the years in films made in Hollywood, a town perhaps ironically situated relatively close to Mexico (and theoretically within the Aztlan territory). Over the past century, Hollywood films have often reinforced the sense of difference and distance between "them" (Latinos) and "us" (white Americans). Intriguingly, though, some Hollywood movies have also demonstrated a more complex cultural ambivalence toward Latinos, often based upon perceived notions of race and class. While many Latino characters in Hollywood films have been treated as racialized stereotypes, others seem to be treated as members of an ethnic group assimilating into whiteness, much like the various European immigrant groups discussed in chapter 3. As this chapter demonstrates, the dominant cultural conception of Latinos in film has been consistently negotiated and renegotiated along these lines.

The Greaser and the Latin Lover: Alternating Stereotypes

One of the earliest and most common stereotypes for representing Latinos in US cinema was the so-called **greaser**. As the name implies, the greaser was an oily, dark-skinned, and mustachioed bandit (frequently hailing from Mexico) who could be found causing mayhem in early silent cinema. In films such as *Tony the Greaser* (1911), *Broncho Billy and the Greaser* (1914), or *The Greaser's Revenge* (1914), this villainous thief was violent, cruel, and hot-tempered. A slightly milder version of this stereotype figured the greaser as shiftless and lazy – content to lie under his sombrero all day while others worked. (Compare these to the **Black Buck** and **Coon** stereotypes that dominant white culture created for African Americans.) In either case – violent or lazy – the Hollywood greaser was usually given his due by a stalwart white cowboy hero, implicitly if not explicitly a man of Northern European descent and US citizenship. The greaser stereotype has been fundamental to how Latinos have been portrayed in Hollywood cinema, and although the image has faded somewhat in more recent decades, its legacy can still be felt whenever Hollywood depicts Hispanic villainy.

As early as the 1910s, Mexico had complained to Hollywood about its ongoing practice of negatively stereotyping Mexican and Mexican American characters. Other Latin American countries began to join in the critique. By 1922, things had reached such an impasse that many countries, including Mexico and Panama, issued bans on any Hollywood films that depicted Latinos in a bad light. In order to maintain revenue from these nations, Hollywood attempted to tone down its negative images. When a greaser-type villain was needed, care was taken to create a fictionalized national context for him, so as not to offend any actual existing country. For example, in the film *The Dove* (1928), a Latino-seeming tyrant lives in the fictional nation of Costa Roja, supposedly somewhere in the Mediterranean. By this ruse, Hollywood hoped to avoid offending any one given Latin American nation, but the greaser stereotype itself remained.

During the 1920s, a second recurring image of Latinos in Hollywood cinema became enormously popular: the **Latin Lover**. According to this stereotype, men and women of Latin American descent (or, as discussed in chapter 3, of Italian descent) are figured as more sensual and sexual than their North American counterparts,

Ramon Novarro was one of the leading Latin Lovers of 1920s Hollywood cinema. Unidentified publicity photo, authors' personal collection

furthering cultural assumptions about Latinos as emotional and "hot-blooded." The effect of the stereotype was to express the image of an alluring, darker-skinned sex object whose cultural difference hinted at exotic and erotic secrets, perhaps tinged with violence or sadomasochism. During the 1910s, Latina actresses Beatriz Michelena and Myrtle Gonzalez often played variations on the female Latin Lover, but by the 1920s, the Latin Lover was exemplified by male stars like **Rudolph Valentino** and **Ramon Novarro**. Valentino was of Italian heritage, but Novarro had been born José Ramón Samaniegos in Durango, Mexico. Other Latino actors that played Latin Lovers during these years included Gilbert Roland and Antonio Moreno. The character type was so popular that some actors pretended to be Latin for the sake of their careers. For example, actor Jacob Kranz from Budapest changed his name to Ricardo Cortez and starred as a Latin Lover in many films of the era.

While also a stereotype, the Latin Lover image conceived of Latinos very differently from the greaser: whereas the greaser was an overtly racialized Other, the Latin Lover was more of an ethnic type that could potentially be assimilated into whiteness. Whereas sexual relations between a white woman and a greaser character were considered vile and taboo, Latin Lovers of the 1920s were romantic leading men who regularly succeeded in winning the hands of the white female leads. It is important to recognize that Latin Lover stars usually had much fairer complexions (that is, they appeared "whiter") than most of the Latino actors hired to play greasers. (These racialized codes of skin color were enforced and in some cases created by Hollywood makeup artists, who regularly darkened the complexions of greaser characters.) Latin Lover stars also played a wide range of ethnic roles, suggesting that Hollywood producers viewed them as generically Other. Valentino was most famous for embodying the image of an Arabian prince (*The Sheik* [1921]), while Novarro captured hearts as a Frenchman (*Scaramouche* [1923]), an Old Testament Jew (*Ben-Hur* [1925]), and an Austrian (*The Student Prince of Old Heidelberg* [1927]). Their "not-quite-whiteness" made them exotic, but acceptable and appealing, to many moviegoers.

The popularity of the Latin Lover figure dwindled after the transition to talking pictures, possibly due to heightened **xenophobia** in the wake of the Great Depression. Mexican American (and other Latino) communities faced a great deal of social and economic discrimination during this period. Racist work laws were passed and many Mexican Americans became migrant farm workers in order to survive. Some whites blamed Mexican Americans for "stealing" jobs from white workers, implying that Mexican Americans were lesser citizens. In some parts of the Southwest, Latinos – regardless of their US citizenship or national heritage – were forcibly herded onto freight trains and sent "back" to Mexico. Southern California, the home of the major film studios, was at the center of much of this discrimination. As classical Hollywood consolidated its industrial structure and aesthetic form, few opportunities existed for Latinos either behind or in front of the camera. Although a vibrant Mexican American community lived near the Hollywood studios, employment opportunities – beyond menial labor – were practically non-existent.

Most **classical Hollywood cinema** about Latino characters consisted of films either set in the distant past (as in **Westerns** such as *In Old Arizona* [1929] or **action-adventure movies** like *The Mark of Zorro* [1940]), or else centered on rich and urbane Latin American sophisticates. Rarely did classical Hollywood film acknowledge contemporary Mexican American lives. The film *Bordertown* (1935) stands as a rare example, although the leading Mexican American role was played by Paul Muni, an actor of Eastern European descent. Muni used dark pancake makeup and a slicked-back haircut, coupled with a Mexican accent, to enact the role of Johnny Ramirez, a failed Mexican American lawyer now running a casino. Ramirez, stereotypically hot-blooded and hot-tempered, becomes entangled in a series of love affairs and criminal misdeeds. When Johnny proposes marriage to an Anglo-Saxon society woman he has been dating, she rejects him because of his class and ethnicity. Johnny is more of a greaser type than he is a Latin Lover, and his desire for an Anglo woman is figured as taboo. True to Hollywood narrative formulas in stories about **miscegenation**, the white women dies while trying to escape from Johnny's romantic overtures.

While Irish Americans and Italian Americans were becoming increasingly understood as white during these years, *Bordertown* illustrates that many Mexican Americans were still considered to be racialized Others – unable to assimilate and a threat to the mythical purity of white women and white culture. Furthermore, the classical Hollywood practice of casting Anglo actors to play leading Latino roles reveals how race, class, and sexuality were interconnected in 1930s film. When white stars played upper-class Latinos, they were regarded as "nearly white," and they could form successful romantic relationships with white characters. When white stars (more infrequently) played peasants or lower-class Latinos, they appeared in darker makeup (like Muni in *Bordertown*), and their romances usually ended in tragedy. Minor supporting roles as peasants or servants were sometimes awarded to actual Latino actors during the classical Hollywood era. For example, **Leo Carrillo**, who traced his heritage back to California long before it became part of the United States, had a long career as a supporting character actor in Hollywood films, often playing comedic peasants and sidekicks. He is perhaps best known for playing Pancho, the sidekick to the Cisco Kid, in a series of low-budget Westerns and television shows.

One of the most famous Latina actresses ever to appear in classical Hollywood films was **Dolores Del Rio**. At first, Del Rio was cast in supporting roles, playing a wide variety of ethnic types and female Latin Lovers. However, by the 1930s, her star persona evolved to match the types of films Hollywood was making about urbane people from Latin American nations. In films such as *Flying Down to Rio* (1933), *Wonder Bar* (1934), *In Caliente* (1935), and *I Live for Love* (1935), Del Rio played wealthy, sophisticated, and glamorous women who hailed from Latin American cities. Rio de Janeiro, Buenos Aires, and Havana were often represented in films of this era as modern urban paradises laden with sensual pleasures like

Dolores Del Rio briefly became a leading lady in classical Hollywood cinema; in the 1940s she returned to Mexico to make films such as *Maria Candelaria* (1944).
Unidentified publicity photo, authors' personal collection

music, alcohol, and romance. Both the cities and the people who lived in them were thus tinged with aspects of the Latin Lover stereotype. Del Rio's sensual characters were upper-class and chaste (as opposed to lower-class and wanton), so they often found comfort and protection in the arms of white leading men. By the late 1930s, Del Rio grew tired of Hollywood typecasting, and in the 1940s she returned to Mexico and starred in several films of the Mexican cinema's so-called "Golden Era," including *Maria Candelaria* and *Las Abandonadas* (both 1944).

World War II and After: The Good Neighbor Policy

Onscreen images of Latin American cities and their urban sophisticates increased in the early 1940s. This marked rise was due to a governmental propaganda plan known as the **Good Neighbor Policy**, a series of federal initiatives and programs designed to recognize and celebrate US ties with Latin American nations. As the war in Europe accelerated, the United States felt the need to shore up relations with its neighboring countries, promoting the idea of hemispheric unity to make sure that Central and South American nations did not align themselves with the so-called Axis powers (Germany, Italy, and Japan). As an important part of the Good Neighbor Policy, Hollywood was enlisted to create films and images that would celebrate Latino cultures and the ideal of friendship between nations of North, Central, and South America. Having lost the profits from distributing their films in Europe due to the war, Hollywood studios were eager to court the Latin American market. As early as 1939, Warner Brothers released *Juárez*, a historical biography about one of Mexico's most famous presidents. Although President Juárez was played by Paul Muni, the film was very reverential in its treatment of Mexico, and made repeated comparisons between President Juárez and President Lincoln, as if to underscore the similarities between Mexico and the United States.

Juárez was a historical drama, but most of Hollywood's Good Neighbor Policy films enacted hemispheric unity by placing US and Latin American citizens in fiesta-themed musicals. For example, Disney's *Saludos Amigos* (1943), which translates into English as "hello friends," was a combination of live action shorts and animated sequences, all of which drew parallels between the culture of the United States and those of Central and South America. In one cartoon segment, Goofy learns that although South American cowboys wear different types of clothing and use different types of tools, they are basically the same as North American cowboys. Disney's *The Three Caballeros* (1945) was a similar compilation film. Each of the three "good guys" of the title represents a different geographic region, nation, and culture. Donald Duck hails from the United States, Panchito the Rooster is Mexican, while José Carioca is a Brazilian parrot. Throughout the film the three friends learn about each other's cultures and generally role-model friendship between North and South America. Both Disney films were released to great success at home and abroad. US citizens learned something about their neighbors, and many moviegoers in South America were flattered that Hollywood was paying attention to their customs and cultures.

20th Century-Fox also figured the Good Neighbor Policy as a non-stop fiesta, producing a cycle of Latin American musicals including *Down Argentine Way* (1940), *Weekend in Havana* (1941), and *That Night in Rio* (1941). The choice of the musical genre was an important one, for the structure and function of the musical often show people working in harmony, transforming the world through song and dance. It was thus the perfect form in which to promote the ideals of hemispheric unity. Fox's Good Neighbor Policy musicals showed talented musicians, singers, and dancers from North, Central, and South America all coming together to perform on screen, sometimes literally putting on a cooperative fund-raising musical show within the movie. With striking use of Technicolor, these musicals envisioned pan-American bonds as elaborate and excessive holiday celebrations. Following in the wake of Fox's success, every other studio in Hollywood produced Latin American musicals during the early 1940s. An entire Latin music craze took hold in the United States during these years, and people learned to dance the conga, the samba, and the rumba. Cuban American bandleaders Xavier Cugat and **Desi Arnaz** became radio and recording stars and even appeared in a few Hollywood movies.

Probably the most famous Hispanic performer in the Good Neighbor Policy musical was **Carmen Miranda**, the so-called Brazilian Bombshell. Born in Portugal and raised in Brazil, Miranda first became a singing star in Latin America, appearing in a handful of Brazilian films during the 1930s. After a spectacular run of performances in New York City nightclubs, 20th Century-Fox placed her under contract in 1940. Miranda was known for her outrageous costumes, suggestive lyrics, and comedic turns of phrase. In *The Gang's All Here* (1943), for example, Miranda sang a number entitled "The Lady in the Tutti Frutti Hat," her head piled high with bananas, pineapples, and strawberries. Audiences of the 1940s often regarded Carmen Miranda as the true star of these films, even though she was usually a supporting character and had very little to do with the story *per se*. Although she was sometimes paired with a white male actor in a (comedic) romantic way, she was never considered to be real competition to the films' blonde-haired, blue-eyed leading ladies. Carmen Miranda (who, as a Brazilian, spoke Portuguese) was indiscriminately cast into any Good Neighbor Policy musical, whether it took place in Brazil, Cuba, or Argentina.

Other Hispanic actresses who rose to prominence in the 1940s included Margo, Lina Romay, and Maria Montez (an actress from the Dominican Republic who played mostly in low-budget adventure movies made at Universal). **Lupe Velez** (born Maria

Guadalupe Villalobos Velez) also became famous during these years, often playing comedic and hot-tempered Latinas. She was even dubbed the "Mexican Spitfire" after her most successful screen role. Like Dolores Del Rio, Velez had begun her Hollywood career playing everything from Eskimos to Swedes. However, it was the title role in *Hot Pepper* (1935) that cemented her image as a comedic Latina. Just as the Good Neighbor Policy was forming, Velez's career took off as she starred in a series of films at RKO including *Mexican Spitfire Out West* (1940), *Mexican Spitfire Sees a Ghost* (1942), and *Mexican Spitfire's Elephant* (1942). However, also like Del Rio, Velez found herself typecast into these one-dimensional roles. Most of the Good Neighbor Policy films featured only happy, carefree, childlike Latinas, rather than complex dramatic characters. And so, in 1944, Velez returned to Mexico and starred in the serious drama *Nana*. Sadly, shortly thereafter, Lupe Velez committed suicide, allegedly over unhappy love affairs. She was only 36 years old.

One Hispanic actress, Margarita Cansino, found even greater stardom during this era, but she did so by softening and/or denying her Hispanic heritage – in effect, assimilating into whiteness. Cansino's early work in nightclubs and films foregrounded her ethnicity: a Latin American-influenced dancer with dark hair who sang in Spanish. However, after winning a contract at Columbia Pictures, Margarita Cansino became **Rita Hayworth**. Hollywood makeup artists and publicists went to work transforming Cansino, a minority-ethnic bit player, into a major Hollywood star. With a less ethnic-sounding name, dyed hair (oftentimes red or blonde), and a hairline raised via electrolysis, Rita Hayworth became one of Hollywood's biggest stars. Throughout the 1940s and 1950s, she starred in both musicals and dramas such as *Cover Girl* (1944), *Gilda* (1946), *Miss Sadie Thompson* (1953), *Salome* (1953), and *Pal Joey* (1957). Sadly, this felt need for actors and actresses to make over or deny their ethnic heritage – in order to be cast in something other than stereotypical supporting roles – was a common occurrence in Hollywood throughout most of the twentieth century. Even in contemporary Hollywood, celebrities undergo plastic surgery to make themselves look younger, but also to make themselves appear less ethnic. In assimilating to a white ideal of beauty, people who undergo cosmetic and plastic surgery continue to reinforce the idea that **whiteness** is the most desirable state of being.

Actors of Hispanic descent also saw their careers boosted by the Good Neighbor Policy. One of the more successful Latino actors of the era was Cesar Romero, who traced his ancestry back to Cuba. A dancer, singer, and accomplished dramatic actor, Romero played Latin Lovers in the 1930s, appeared in Good Neighbor Policy musicals in the 1940s, and by the 1960s and 1970s had become a character actor in crime thrillers, Westerns, and Disney comedies. Today he is perhaps best remembered for his continuing role as the arch-villain "The Joker" on the original *Batman* TV series (ABC-TV, 1966–8). Another Latino star to emerge during this era was Fernando Lamas, who had been an actor in Argentina before making his Hollywood debut in the musical *Rich, Young, and Pretty* (1951). Ricardo Montalban, born in Mexico City, also rose to prominence during the 1940s. MGM signed him to a contract in 1948, and he played Latin Lovers in films such as *Neptune's Daughter* (1949) and *Two Weeks with Love* (1950). Like Romero, Montalban may be best remembered

International leading man, character actor, and founder of Nosotros, Ricardo Montalban is seen here in the Mexican film *Sombra Verde* (a.k.a. *Untouched*, 1954).
Sombra Verde (a.k.a. *Untouched*), copyright © 1954, Calderon Productions

for his television work: from 1978 to 1984, he starred as Mr Roarke on the popular television series *Fantasy Island* (ABC-TV).

This summary of Good Neighbor Policy films and successful Latino actors should not obscure the fact that during and after World War II, Mexican Americans still faced a tremendous amount of prejudice and discrimination. Violence between whites and Latinos occurred in a number of cities, sometimes in response to wartime workplace integration. William Randolph Hearst's newspaper chain repeatedly suggested that Nazi powers were using Mexican American gangs to weaken America from within its own borders. Such reports incited much social violence, including the so-called **Zoot Suit Riots** of 1943. In a series of random attacks, off-duty servicemen stationed in and around Los Angeles tore through Mexican American neighborhoods, destroying property, beating innocent people, and raping women. The zoot suit, a type of fancy fashion worn by many young Mexican American men of the era, made them easily identifiable targets. In most cases, these attacks were carried out without any official repercussions, and in many instances the Los Angeles police arrested Latinos rather than the servicemen. (The terror of the Zoot Suits Riots is powerfully captured in more recent independent films such as *Zoot Suit* [1981] and *American Me* [1992].)

In other words, while the Good Neighbor Policy films reached out to Latino people in other countries, Hollywood films rarely represented Latino people *within* the United States. Hollywood's postwar cycle of **social problem films** did on a few occasions tackle discrimination against Hispanic Americans. *A Medal for Benny* (1945) begins with a Congressional Medal of Honor being posthumously awarded to Benjamin Martin, a Mexican American war hero. As the film unfolds, it explores the economic and social injustices faced by many Mexican American citizens in one California town, and draws well-rounded and sympathetic portraits of a variety of Latino people. Other social problem films that focused on Latino issues include *The Lawless* (1950), *Right Cross* (1950), and *My Man and I* (1952). The social problem cycle ended somewhat abruptly in response to the **Red Scare** in Hollywood, and the resultant **blacklist** of suspected communists in the film industry. A group of these blacklisted people went on to make *Salt of the Earth* (1953), about striking Mexican American workers at a zinc mine owned and operated by unscrupulous Anglo Americans. Unfortunately, because of the reputation of the filmmakers, most theaters refused to book the film and few people saw it.

The 1950s to the 1970s: Back to Business as Usual?

During the 1950s and 1960s, Hollywood's approach to Latino issues and Latino characters returned to patterns and practices employed in the decades before the Good Neighbor Policy. A number of actors of Hispanic descent – including Anthony Quinn, Jose Ferrer, and Mel Ferrer – gained considerable fame, but usually did so by downplaying (if not altogether ignoring) their Hispanic heritage. True to Hollywood casting practices, these actors played a variety of ethnic roles, but rarely Hispanic citizens of the United States. **Anthony Quinn**, who had been born to a Mexican mother and an Irish father, won an Oscar for his supporting role in *Viva Zapata!* (1952), playing the brother of Mexican revolutionary Emiliano Zapata. However, the lead role of the film, Zapata himself, was played by Anglo actor Marlon Brando in dark makeup. Such practices continued into the 1960s, with actors such as Paul Newman (*The Outrage* [1964]), Peter Ustinov (*Viva Max!* [1969]), and Jack Palance (*Che!* [1969]) putting on dark makeup for roles as Latino bandits and revolutionaries. Bandleader Desi Arnaz became a major television star on *I Love Lucy* (CBS, 1951–7), but only after his wife, comedian Lucille Ball, insisted that he be hired to play her husband; network executives had qualms about showing a "mixed marriage."

The resistance to showing Arnaz and Ball as a romantic couple demonstrates how many Americans of the 1950s still regarded Latinos as racially Other. Further examples can be drawn from the adaptation of the greaser stereotype into that of the violent, dirty, and sexually aggressive Latino gang member, seen in movies like *Blackboard Jungle* (1955) and *Touch of Evil* (1959). Supposedly the greaser gang members of *Touch of Evil* are balanced by a heroic Mexican police detective, but he is played (rather unconvincingly) by white actor Charlton Heston in heavy brown makeup. The film adaptation of the musical *West Side Story* (1961) also upholds this stereotype of Latinos (this time Puerto Ricans) as gang members, even as it simultaneously calls for greater understanding between people of different ethnicities. Telling the story of a young Puerto Rican immigrant and her Polish American beau, the film ends predictably on a tragic note, as the bigotry and prejudice of gang life result in the death of the male lead. *West Side Story*'s Anglo creators had good intentions, but they have been criticized for casting non-Latinos in most of the major parts, including Natalie Wood as Maria, the lead Latina, and Greek American George Chakiris as her brother Bernardo. The film did boost the career of at least one Latina actress: Rita Moreno won a Best Supporting Actress Oscar for her role as Maria's friend Anita. However, Moreno did not work in Hollywood for several years after *West Side Story*, because she repeatedly refused to appear in film projects that only wanted to cast her as a Latina gang member.

By the mid-1960s, Hollywood Westerns were returning to the classic greaser stereotype. It was almost as if "bloodthirsty redskins" were being replaced on American movie screens by "bloodthirsty Mexican banditos." Arguably, the **civil rights movement** was making the United States aware of how the Western **genre** had been used to both demonize Native Americans and rewrite historical **genocide**. Thus, as it became politically incorrect to stereotype Native Americans as violent beasts, Hollywood Westerns simply remade their villains into Mexican or Bolivian greasers. In films like *The Professionals* (1966), *The Wild Bunch* (1969), *Butch Cassidy and the Sundance Kid* (1969), and a number of Italian-made **spaghetti Westerns** starring Clint Eastwood (like *The Good, the Bad, and the Ugly* [1966]), Latinos are portrayed as corrupt, slovenly, violent, and/or inept criminals.

With such stereotypes in place even after the classical Hollywood era had ended, Latino performers still had few options. Rita Moreno turned to the stage, the recording industry, and television, becoming one of the very few Americans to win an Oscar, a Tony, a Grammy, and an Emmy award. Other Latino actors chose to downplay their ethnicity and seek work under more "white-sounding" names. Raquel Welch, born Jo Raquel Tejada and of Bolivian descent, became a major Hollywood sex symbol, but only by (in her own recent admission) staying "in the closet" as a Latina. Like Rita Hayworth before her, Raquel Welch felt she needed to overcome her ethnic heritage before she could be accepted as a major Hollywood star. Similarly, actor Ramon Estevez somewhat effaced his Latino heritage by changing his name; as Martin Sheen, he has become one of Hollywood's most prolific film and television actors. Sheen is also a dedicated political activist and father of two other Hollywood actors, Charlie Sheen and Emilio Estevez.

The prevalence of cinematic stereotypes and the felt need to efface one's ethnic heritage in order to succeed in Hollywood indicate the era's baseline level of bias against Americans perceived as Other than white. Consequently, with the rise of militant civil rights protests in the 1960s, many Mexican Americans and other Latinos became radically politicized. Mexican American activists began using the terms **Chicano** and **Chicana** (the feminine form of the word) as a source of cultural pride, and to individuate themselves from catch-all labels like "Latino" or "Hispanic". Probably the most famous figure to emerge from these civil rights struggles (sometimes referred to as **La Causa**, "The Cause") was **Cesar Chavez**, a man who founded and directed the United Farm Workers Union. Although he worked mainly to raise the standard of living for migrant farm workers (most of whom were Mexican American), Chavez became a symbolic leader for all Latinos struggling against bias and discrimination. Chicano and Latino activism also focused attention on mass media representations. Some groups pressured public broadcasting stations to air shows dedicated to La Causa. Other activists created festivals promoting Latino filmmakers, and still others worked with the media watchdog group **Nosotros**, which translates into English as "We" or "Ourselves." Created and directed by actor Ricardo Montalban in the early 1970s, Nosotros dedicated itself to improving the image of Latinos in film, television, and advertising. Throughout the 1970s, Nosotros was able to convince several companies to discontinue their use of offensive corporate logos, such as the Frito Bandito (a take-off of the greaser stereotype) and the Chiquita Banana woman (a reworking of Carmen Miranda's image).

Very few films and television programs indicated a growing awareness of the Chicano movement. In *Mr Majestyk* (1974), a Slavic-Mexican farm owner (played by Charles Bronson) battles Italian gangsters against the backdrop of "real-life" Chicano struggles, but the film borrows more from the era's **blaxploitation** action aesthetic than it does from the social problem film. The TV series *Chico and the Man* (NBC, 1974–8) was set in a Mexican American neighborhood of East Los Angeles, but it drew protests because it featured no Chicano actors – star Freddie Prinze came from a Hungarian and Puerto Rican background. (Producers responded by hiring Mexican American performers in later seasons.) The comedy team of Richard "Cheech" Marin and Tommy Chong linked Chicano culture to the **counterculture** through hippie drug humor in comedy routines and films, beginning with *Up In Smoke* (1978). In some respects, their humor was based on a rejection of the morality of the white establishment. Yet it was also easy to read "Cheech" as an updated version of the lazy greaser stereotype, a none-too-bright Latino who wants nothing more than to lie around and "mellow out" with the aid of herbal enhancement. Even in the face of growing Latino activism, the legacy of the greaser could still be felt, especially in violent and sensationalistic stories about Latino gang life such as *Badge 373* (1973), *Boulevard Nights* (1979), and *Walk Proud* (1979).

Expanding Opportunities in Recent Decades

During the 1980s and 1990s, more and more doors began to open in Hollywood for Latinos, both in front of and behind the camera. Today, Latino actors from diverse backgrounds (such as Andy Garcia, Jimmy Smits, Benicio Del Toro, Esai

Morales, Hector Elizondo, Edward James Olmos, and Antonio Banderas) can be regularly seen on television and at neighborhood multiplexes. Latina actresses (such as Elizabeth Pena, Maria Conchita Alonso, Sonia Braga, Jessica Alba, and Salma Hayek) have in most cases not reached the same level of stardom as their male peers, but they do maintain careers in show business. Probably the most famous Hispanic American actress of the era is **Jennifer Lopez**, born in New York City to Puerto Rican parents. In 1990, Lopez moved to Hollywood and became a dancer on the hit television show *In Living Color*. Today she is both a major recording artist and a Hollywood actress, starring in films such as *Selena* (1997), *Out of Sight* (1998), *The Cell* (2000), *Maid in Manhattan* (2002), and *Monster-In-Law* (2005). Her salary for *The Wedding Planner* (2001) reportedly made her the highest-paid Latina actress in Hollywood history. Most of these actors and actresses no longer feel the need to Anglicize their names or shy away from Latino roles. Being Latino in America is increasingly understood as an ethnicity similar to being Irish American or Italian American. While prejudice and bias still exist in many places – especially against Latino Americans who do not speak English – other Latinos are being absorbed into dominant notions of whiteness.

However, such developments in Hollywood and in culture-at-large have not occurred smoothly, and most media watchdog groups would agree that the struggle for balanced images and opportunities is far from over. For example, Latinos are still vastly underrepresented on network television, even as Spanish-language television networks such as Univision and Telemundo have grown tremendously since the 1980s. And for every Hispanic-produced or -themed project that gets made in Hollywood, many more never find funding. A planned Hollywood film about Cesar Chavez has been stuck in development for many years. White men still dominate the Hollywood film and television industry as network executives, film producers, directors, and writers. While major Latino film stars have emerged, old Hollywood formulas are still pressed into service. For example, the producers of *The House of the Spirits* (1993) and *The Perez Family* (1995) hired Anglo performers to play lead Latino roles. Gangster and reworked greaser stereotypes of Latinos still appear in films like *Scarface* (1983), *Colors* (1988), and *Training Day* (2001), while the appeal of the Latin Lover continues unabated. Also, in the age of the **nostalgic Hollywood blockbuster**, reworkings of old "south-of-the-border" extravaganzas have reintroduced new viewers to old character types in films like *The Cisco Kid* (1994), *The Mask of Zorro* (1998), and *The Legend of Zorro* (2005).

One of the first Latino filmmakers to break into the industry came directly from the Chicano movement of the 1960s. Mexican American playwright and activist **Luis Valdez** was the son of migrant farm workers and was greatly inspired by the work of Cesar Chavez. In the 1960s, Valdez founded a theater group called El Teatro Campesino that performed at the farms where migrant laborers worked and lived. Valdez also made a critically acclaimed short film, *I am Joaquin* (1969), using an epic poem by Rodolpho Gonzales to represent different aspects of Chicano identity. Valdez's first feature film was adapted from one of his plays, *Zoot Suit*. Shot in two weeks on a very low budget, the film retains Valdez's radical theatricality as it dramatizes both the mythical origins of Chicano culture and the real-life injustices faced by Mexican Americans during the Zoot Suit Riots. While *Zoot Suit* was not a financial success, his next film, *La Bamba* (1987), was seen as an attempt by Hollywood to reach out to Latino audiences. Tri-Star Pictures distributed this bio-pic about 1950s pop singer Ritchie Valenzuela in both English and Spanish versions. The film was a hit, but other studios did not follow on its lead in producing more Latino-themed work.

One of the lead actors in both the play and film of *Zoot Suit* was **Edward James Olmos**, a man who has since then become an important advocate for Latino-themed projects in Hollywood. Raised in east Los Angeles, Olmos began to make a name for himself in films like *Wolfen* (1981) and *Blade Runner* (1982), and on the popular television show *Miami Vice* (NBC, 1984–9). Olmos has taken advantage of his growing recognition to help get various projects made, either acting in, producing, or directing independent films like *The Ballad of Gregorio Cortez* (1982), *Stand and Deliver* (1987), and *American Me*. Like Valdez, Olmos has always been outspoken about political causes – not just Chicano causes, but also those dedicated to youth education and civil liberties generally. In 1992, for example, Olmos was on the streets of Los Angeles, broom in hand, helping to clean up the city after the riots spurred by the acquittal of the police officers accused of beating African American Rodney King. Since then, Olmos has continued to work in numerous film and television projects including *Selena*, *The Road to El Dorado* (2000), *American Family* (PBS, 2001–2), and *Battlestar Galactica* (2003–8).

As with several other groups surveyed in this book, the rise in independent film-making in recent decades has afforded new and greater opportunities for Latino filmmakers. For example, while actor Raul Julia is primarily remembered for playing Gomez Addams in the Hollywood films *The Addams Family* (1991) and *Addams Family Values* (1993), he first gained cinematic acclaim in independent films about Latinos such as *Kiss of the Spider Woman* (1985) and *Romero* (1989). Another Latino director who has found more opportunities as an independent rather than Hollywood filmmaker is **Gregory Nava**. He first attracted critical attention with *El Norte* (1983), a film about the plight of two Guatemalan teenagers who, after their parents are killed in a massacre, make their way to the United States as (illegal) immigrants. Harsh and uncompromising, the film had received some funding from PBS's American Playhouse series, and won an Oscar nomination as Best Foreign Language Film. Nava has since gone on to write and direct *My Family/Mi Familia* (1995), a bio-pic about the Latina pop star *Selena*, and *Why Do Fools Fall In Love?* (1998), another bio-pic about a pop star, Frankie Lymon. Nava also created, produced, and directed the television series *American Family*, which had been developed by CBS. When CBS declined to air it, it was picked up and shown on PBS in 2002.

Gregory Nava's most recent film, *Bordertown* (2006), is an uneven mix of politics and Hollywood formula. In trying to be both a real-life social problem film and a Hollywood conspiracy thriller, the film failed to satisfy audiences desiring either format, and it was barely seen theatrically outside of film festivals. The film is based on the real-life series of rapes, murders, and/or disappearances of estimated thousands of young women since the mid-1990s in the border town of Juárez,

Mexico. As the opening titles reveal, many of these young women were displaced rural and/or indigenous people forced to work in border-town factories in order to survive. The main story focuses on a Mexican American journalist (Jennifer Lopez) who travels to Juárez to investigate the story. Ultimately, the film alleges a conspiracy between corrupt policemen, Mexican and American businessmen, and even US politicians – all of whom profit from the economic exploitation of these young workers. Nava ties this all back to the passage of NAFTA, the North American Free Trade Agreement, a series of international agreements that has exacerbated the exploitation of cheap labor in poor nations by US and multinational corporations. The film is thus set within a "culture of murder" where young women are figured as disposable cogs in a patriarchal capitalist machine, used for both their labor and their sexuality. Unfortunately, these points often get lost amid the film's formulaic car chases, assassinations, flashbacks to childhood trauma, and undercover sting operations. *Bordertown* is a film filled with serious and important ideas about economic and sexual exploitation, political corruption, and Mexican–American relations, but its Hollywood style (which Nava had probably hoped would help it reach a wider audience) tends to mute or obscure its very worthwhile messages.

Probably the most successful Latino filmmaker of the early 2000s is Mexican American **Robert Rodriguez**. Born and raised in Texas, Rodriguez burst onto the movie scene with an independent, super-low-budget gangster film, *El Mariachi* (1991). Critics and Hollywood executives were stunned that a film with such breathtaking action sequences was allegedly shot for only $7,000. The major studios soon beckoned, and Rodriguez remade/reworked *El Mariachi* into the big-budget Hollywood feature *Desperado* (1995), starring Antonio Banderas and Salma Hayek. Successfully crossing over into other mainstream Hollywood genres, Rodriguez directed the gory vampire film *From Dusk Till Dawn* (1996), and the teen horror movie *The Faculty* (1998). *Spy Kids* (2001) – which Rodriguez wrote and directed – became a smash hit and spawned two sequels. Some critics have complained that Rodriguez's work is too narrowly defined. For example, *Once Upon a Time in Mexico* (2003) was another shoot-'em-up in the *Desperado* vein, while *The Adventures of Shark Boy and Lava Girl 3-D* (2005) was yet another technologically fantastic family film. Most recently, Rodriguez has returned to the genres of pulp fiction and horror, filming the ultra-violent *Sin City* (2005) and *Planet Terror*, part of the double-feature film *Grindhouse* (2007). Yet no matter what genres he works within, Rodriguez usually finds a way to mix action-oriented filmmaking with Chicano characters, culture, and settings. His many commercial successes have cemented his reputation as a solid, bankable director in Hollywood.

More and more the American film scene is being enriched by non-native talent. For example, three Mexican directors have recently garnered acclaim in the United States, making both independent and Hollywood films. Alejandro González Iñárritu produced and directed the international art-house hit *Babel* (2006), released through Paramount's "independent" subsidiary Paramount Vantage. Truly a global picture, *Babel* focuses on an American couple in Morocco (Brad Pitt and Cate Blanchett), their Mexican housekeeper and her nephew (Adriana Barraza

Director Robert
Rodriguez, seen here
on the set of his Mexican
American vampire movie,
From Dusk Till Dawn
(1996).
From Dusk Till Dawn,
dir. Robert Rodriguez,
copyright © 1996,
Dimension

and Gale Garcia Bernal), and an emotionally disturbed teenager in Japan (Rinko
Kikuchi). The film dramatizes the connections between these disparate individuals, as well as the forces that work to keep them apart. A very well-reviewed film,
Babel was nominated for seven Oscars, including Best Picture, Best Director, and
Best Screenplay, and two Best Supporting Actress awards (for Adriana Barraza
and Rinko Kikuchi). Another prominent Mexican director, Guillermo del Toro,
has recently made art-house hits such as *Pan's Labyrinth* (2006) as well as the

Hollywood blockbusters *Hellboy* (2004) and *Hellboy 2* (2008). Similarly, Alfonso Cuarón became a global figure with his art film *Y Tu Mama Tambien* (2001), and has since gone on to direct the English-language hits *Harry Potter and the Prisoner of Azkaban* (2004) and *Children of Men* (2006).

Just as Asian-born actors like Jet Li or Chow Yun-Fat have become familiar faces in American cinema, so have Mexican actors like Gael Garcia Bernal and Salma Hayek. Hayek makes for an especially interesting case study in race, gender, class, and sexuality in contemporary American film. Born in Mexico to a Lebanese businessman and Mexican opera singer, Hayek's mixed ethnicity and now-global career immediately challenge simplistic notions of nationality and race. Early in her career, her beauty and talent helped her land the lead role in *Teresa* (1989), a popular Mexican telenovela (a sort of finite soap opera form originating in Latin America). Yet when she arrived in Hollywood, she found herself marginalized into small (mostly television) roles that exploited her good looks and recalled age-old stereotypes of Latin Lovers. Mexican American director Robert Rodriguez helped boost her US career, casting her in his films *Desperado* and *From Dusk Till Dawn*. (However, her role as a sexy Mexican vampire in the latter film is arguably an example of racist, sexist stereotyping: the film's white male heroes must battle their ultimate Others – female monsters from south of the border.) Hayek was well received in other independent films such as *Dogma* (1999) and *Timecode* (2000), and also starred in the Hollywood blockbuster *Wild Wild West* (1999). Yet it was her dream project, *Frida* (2002), a bio-pic about the famed Mexican artist Frida Kahlo, that earned Hayek her highest accolades. Hayek produced the film herself, chose theater and film director Julie Taymor to direct, and starred in the title role (for which she was Oscar nominated). More recently, Hayek has directed and produced work for television, including *Ugly Betty* (2006–), a show about a young Latina that challenges its viewers to think about beauty and body image. Salma Hayek may have initially traded upon her good looks and lingering assumptions about Latin Lovers in order to break into show business, but she has since then become a respected and successful actor and producer in Hollywood.

Conclusion: A Backlash Against Chicanos?

According to many statistics, in the early years of the twenty-first century, Hispanic Americans became the nation's largest ethnic minority group (edging out African Americans). The ascendance of stars such as Jennifer Lopez, Jessica Alba, and Salma Hayek seems to indicate a growing assimilation of Hispanic people into dominant notions of whiteness within US society. However, in the aftermath of 9/11, many Hispanics and Hispanic Americans have come under attack, as issues of national security have inflamed passions about illegal (mostly Mexican) aliens living and working in the United States. Continued efforts to restrict and penalize such people – including housing bans, workplace raids, and the proposed construction of a border wall between the United States and Mexico – have sent a chill through many

Case Study: *My Family/Mi Familia* (1995)

Co-written and directed by Gregory Nava, and produced by Anna Thomas (the same team responsible for making *El Norte*), *My Family/Mi Familia* is an epic drama that chronicles the lives of the fictional Sanchez family. Through them, the filmmakers dramatize many of the key issues that faced Mexican Americans throughout the twentieth century. The film confronts issues of discrimination, crime, and economic hardship that have historically hindered many in the Latino community, and shows how those issues are interrelated. The Sanchez family puts human faces on those issues, and the richly drawn and acted characterizations of the family members are an important improvement on Hollywood's usual one-dimensional stereotypes. Like several other films used as case studies in this book, *My Family/Mi Familia* was partly financed by American Playhouse Theatrical Films, before Congress slashed its funding. Producer Anna Thomas found further production support for the film from Hollywood mogul Francis Ford Coppola, and the film was released on the independent art-house circuit, where it received generally positive reviews.

The film begins in the 1920s, when Jose Sanchez (Jacob Vargas) leaves his Mexican village and travels to California in search of a better life, and continues into the 1990s as his offspring deal with their own children. Narrated by Jose's oldest son, Paco (Edward James Olmos), the film interweaves multiple stories throughout the decades. Two of the main characters in the film, Chucho (Esai Morales) and Jimmy (played as an adult by Jimmy Smits), become involved in criminal activity.

While these characters may seem to uphold the gang-member stereotype, the film explains the social pressures that lead some young Chicanos to gang life. For example, Chucho delivers an angry speech about how Anglo society only respects money, and how he needs to do whatever is necessary (that is, sell drugs) in order to succeed. As the narrator, Paco describes how the frustration of limited opportunities leads Chucho and his friends to aggressive expressions of machismo. The viewer is also shown the literally deadly effects of discrimination that scar Jimmy and turn him to violence. In addition, the film uses a number of family members to balance the gangster images of Chucho and Jimmy: Paco joins the navy, one sister runs a restaurant, another becomes a nun and then a political activist, while yet another goes to UCLA and becomes a lawyer.

The film also uses the family to represent a variety of moments in the history of the Chicano community of east Los Angeles – from the character of El Californio, who had been living in Los Angeles before it became part of the United States, to the forced deportations of the Great Depression, to the conflicts of political asylum and immigration of the 1980s. Signposts of Latino culture help recreate the feel of each era. Folkloric music accompanies the early parts of the film, while mariachi and mambo music (and snippets from *I Love Lucy*) are used in the 1950s sequence. In the 1980s, telenovelas appear on Spanish-language TV, and Latino dance music is heard. The film also tells its story in a cinematic version of "magical realism," a Latin American literary style

Mexican and Mexican American communities. Nightly news reports about violence and drugs along the border, as well as films like *Traffic* (2000) and *Bordertown* that center on such issues, may also be contributing to anti-Hispanic sentiments among some Americans.

Spanglish (2004) is one of the few Hollywood films attempting to deal with the issues facing Mexican workers in the United States. The film stars Spanish actress Paz Vega as Flor, a Mexican domestic servant working for the family of a Los Angeles chef (Adam Sandler). Written and directed by Hollywood liberal James L. Brooks (*Terms of Endearment* [1983], *As Good as It Gets* [1997], *The Simpsons*), the film is a rather clunky comedy melodrama that never really delves too deeply into

Part of the extended Sanchez family in Gregory Nava's *My Family/Mi Familia* (1995).
My Family/Mi Familia, dir. Gregory Nava, copyright © 1995, New Line. Photo: Rico Torres

that borrows from the heritage of oral culture. Paco, the narrator, is constantly passing on legends and history through storytelling. Also consistently with magical realism, the history of the family includes mystical moments that mix Roman Catholicism with Mexican folk beliefs. Thus, Gregory Nava creates a rich tapestry of character and culture, held together through both Paco's narration and the use of visual metaphors, such as the bridges prominently featured throughout the film. These bridges literally represent the spatial divide between east Los Angeles (the Mexican American community) and the rest of the city. However, they also symbolize the span of cultures, nations, and eras that not just the characters but all of America encompass and traverse.

the issues it is supposedly dramatizing. On the other hand, the independent film *Fast Food Nation* (2006) – based on Eric Schlosser's best-selling exposé of industrial food production in America – presents a much more harrowing look at how major US corporations regularly use (and abuse) undocumented Mexican workers in their never-ending search for more profit. The black comedy fantasy *A Day Without a Mexican* (2004) also approaches similar issues with satiric wit. And, in a slightly different register, *The Three Burials of Melquiades Estrada* (2005), starring and directed by Tommy Lee Jones, is another thoughtful take on US–Mexico border relations, embedded within a humane and respectful story about a Texas ranch hand attempting to honor his Mexican friend's dying wish.

Spanish actress Paz Vega plays Flor, an undocumented Mexican who works as a domestic servant for a wealthy Los Angeles family in *Spanglish* (2004); Flor comes to America to find a better life for herself and her daughter (Shelbie Bruce). *Spanglish*, dir. James L. Brooks, copyright © 2004, Columbia Pictures

Even in the face of such a potential backlash, more and more Hollywood studios are taking notice of Hispanic audiences (if not their issues). For example, prints of Hollywood films with Spanish subtitles are being released more often for distribution in minority-ethnic neighborhoods. Dreamworks released Spanish-subtitled versions of all of its films, and its animated film *The Road to El Dorado* (2000) took care to solicit input from experts on Latino culture. Still, the great diversity of Latino cultures makes it difficult for Hollywood to market to a unified whole. A film about Mexican Americans might do very well at the box office in California or Texas, where the majority of Latinos are of Mexican heritage. However, the same film might flop in southern Florida, where the Latino population tends to have more ties to Cuba and Puerto Rico. The Latino community as a whole, so varied and diverse, continues to struggle for equal access to the rights and privileges of American culture. Likewise, in Hollywood, Latino filmmakers continue to struggle to be heard and have their stories told.

Questions for Discussion

1   Can you identify examples of the Latin Lover stereotype in contemporary popular culture? What does the stereotype tell us about how gender and sexuality are constructed in relation to race and/or ethnicity?

2   As with many other ethnic groups in contemporary America, assimilation is a controversial issue. What is at stake for Latinos who choose to assimilate to white ideals versus those who maintain a more pronounced ethnicity?

3   Popular music has often featured Latino artists and idioms more regularly than Hollywood movies have. Why do you think there may be more opportunities for Latino musicians than for Latino actors and filmmakers?

Further Reading

Berg, Charles Ramirez. *Latino Images in Film: Stereotypes, Subversion, and Resistance.* Austin: University of Texas Press, 2002.

Fregoso, Rosa Linda. *The Bronze Screen: Chicano and Chicana Film Culture.* Minneapolis: University of Minnesota Press, 1993.

Hadley-Garcia, George. *Hispanic Hollywood: The Latins in Motion Pictures.* New York: Carol Publishing Group (A Citadel Press Book), 1990.

King, John, Ana M. Lopez, and Manuel Alvarado, eds. *Mediating Two Worlds: Cinematic Encounters in the Americas.* London: BFI, 1993.

List, Christine. *Chicano Images: Refiguring Ethnicity in Mainstream Film.* New York: Garland Publishing, 1996.

Noriega, Chon, ed. *Chicanos and Film: Essays on Chicano Representation and Resistance.* New York: Garland Publishing, 1992.

Noriega, Chon. *Shot in America: Television, the State, and the Rise of Chicano Cinema.* Minneapolis: University of Minnesota Press, 2000.

Noriega, Chon and Ana Lopez. *The Ethnic Eye: Latino Media Arts.* Minneapolis: University of Minnesota Press, 1996.

Ranucci, Karen and Julie Feldman. *A Guide to Latin American, Caribbean, and US Latino Made Film and Video.* Lanham, MD: Scarecrow Press, 1998.

Reyes, Luis and Peter Rubie. *Hispanics in Hollywood: An Encyclopedia of Film and Television.* New York: Garland Publishing, 1994.

Woll, Allen L. *The Latin Image in American Film.* Los Angeles: Latin American Center, University of California Press, 1977.

Further Screening

Flying Down to Rio (1933)
Bordertown (1935)
Down Argentine Way (1940)
Saludos Amigos (1943)
A Medal for Benny (1945)
Salt of the Earth (1953)
West Side Story (1961)

Zoot Suit (1981)
El Norte (1983)
La Bamba (1987)
El Mariachi (1991)
Frida (2002)
Babel (2006)
Fast Food Nation (2006)

INTRODUCTION TO PART III:

What is Class?

Class is a term used to categorize people according to their economic status. It thus frequently involves a consideration of income level, type of profession, inherited wealth and family lineage, and a diffusely understood idea of "social standing." Historically, most societies have made distinctions among their members according to some kind of class division. Under such **class systems,** citizens are very aware of their class standing or social worth. Class standing can form a strong basis for a person's overall identity, much as race, ethnicity, gender, sexuality, and ability also contribute to one's sense of self. For example, people raised as members of the so-called **working class** (associated with physical labor, or industrial or blue-collar jobs) may carry aspects of that identity throughout their lives, even if they shift in income level to the professional or **middle class** (more associated with administrative, managerial, or white-collar jobs that require advanced university education). A strong class system helps keep a society's power structure in place, **hegemonically** encouraging members of each class to stay where they are in the socio-economic hierarchy.

Compared to some nations (for example, historical England or India), the United States likes to think it does not have a strongly defined class system. One of the many reasons the 13 colonies broke away from England in the first place was a revolt over the strictness of the British class system. By repudiating the concept that certain persons were endowed by God with a divine right to power and wealth, the fledgling United States of America asserted that "all men were created equal." (However, remember that the framers of the Constitution felt that only *white men* that owned land should have equal access to wealth and power.) In its formation, the United States attempted to reject England's rigid class system and replace it with a system that would purportedly allow all individuals to accumulate wealth and rise in class standing according to their ability and ambition. Citizens of the United States were not to be hampered by a mental conception of their "place." This national concept – the freedom to pursue happiness without socio-economic class barriers – has often been called the **American Dream,** and over the years this dream has come to be shared by women and people of color as well as white men. Closely tied to the American Dream is the ideology of <u>rugged individualism</u>, where in each citizen is expected to take responsibility for his or her own success. This emphasis on individualism also works against a sense of a shared class identity.

To this day, America takes a certain pride in considering itself a "classless" society, but it is wrong to think that the nation has no class issues. Class standing still matters to most Americans, whether or not they admit it. The dominant economic organization of the United States is and always has been <u>capitalism</u>, a system based on economic competition among individuals – and more recently, economic competition among corporations, a state of affairs now referred to as **corporate capitalism**. Just as the concept of **whiteness** is so endemic to American culture that it often goes unnoticed, the pervasiveness of capitalism often makes it difficult for Americans to recognize its omnipresence. Under capitalism in general, success is measured by wealth and the things it can buy, including power. Economic standing is arguably the most important gauge for assessing a person's social worth. Thus the American Dream has often been defined in terms of material wealth – owning land, one or more homes, several cars, expensive jewelry and clothing, and so forth. More modestly, the American Dream can simply be freedom from want, in addition to the numerous other freedoms (speech, assembly, religion, the pursuit of happiness) guaranteed by the Constitution and the Bill of Rights. Yet these freedoms for all citizens to do or say what they want, or live as they might desire, are usually tied to economic success: the more money one has, the more ability one has to do or say what one wants.

Put simply, in America those with the most wealth have the most privilege and the most power. Wealthy families – those of the <u>upper classes</u> – use their positions of advantage to keep or increase their economic status (and thus their power) over generations. They attend the best schools, are placed in good jobs, and can hire the best lawyers, doctors, and economic advisors. By making large contributions to political campaigns, supporting lobbying efforts, and buying media time to promote candidates who share their points of view, the wealthy are able to get advantageous tax and business laws passed. While a wealthy individual may not intentionally attempt to oppress others, such oppression can result. For example, laws that ease pollution standards or safety requirements in factories directly benefit the owners of these companies (who do not have to spend the extra money required for compliance), and such actions may have a directly adverse affect on people working in or living near the factories. Even stronger examples can be drawn from business executives who work to keep the level of the basic hourly wage at a minimum, or avoid paying health insurance for their employees. The effect of these laws and business practices works to keep lower-income groups locked into their socio-economic place, while corporations, business owners, and stock holders continue to benefit monetarily.

More broadly, capitalism and rugged individualism encourage Americans to compete rather than cooperate with one another. We are taught to assess other people by their economic status, or more simply give in to the feeling that we must "keep up with the Joneses," that is, be as materially successful as our neighbors. The success or capability of the United States itself is often measured by its corporate economic power. During the 1950s, the common political opinion that "What's good for General Motors is good for the country" directly linked national strength to corporate business strength. Similar attitudes persist to the present day, as can be seen in the importance of the stock market as an indicator of American stability and strength. When Islamic terrorists attacked the United States in the fall of 2001, various analysts advised citizens to buy stock in order to keep the market up and thus show the world that the terrorists had not succeeded in hurting the nation.

While most Americans would readily acknowledge the importance of material success in their lives, far fewer want to admit that our unwritten class system may actually work to curtail or corrupt American ideals. While basing one's core identity on a class standing *is* a **social construct**, one's class standing *does* exist and have a concrete and material effect on one's life, even if one denies it. A lack of **class consciousness** (an awareness of a class system and one's place within it) empowers the dominant **ideology** of capitalism as much as a strongly defined class system. Capitalist ideologies work to disarm, mask, or suppress any possible complaints based on class inequity. Except during periods of depression or recession, American mass culture largely ignores the existence of economic hardship. The news media rarely covers poverty, hunger, or economic disparity – except during the holidays for a "feel-good" piece on middle-class or corporate charity showing the benevolence of capitalism and the American Dream. Such benevolence cannot be relied on, though, as many individuals rebuff requests from homeless people and concertedly try to ignore their very existence. Americans can even deny their own economic oppression. Studies show that most of the population self-identifies as middle-class, even though statistically many of those individuals would be placed into lower classes on the basis of their yearly salaries. (The term "lower-class" itself ascribes to a hierarchy that American capitalism tries to efface.) Self-identifying as middle-class may help to keep people from considering themselves discriminated against or disempowered.

The propagation of the American Dream suggests that the only thing holding a person back from wealth (and thus happiness) is their own lack of drive and determination. Some Americans are quick to blame individuals for economic hardship, overlooking the role that capitalism might play in the creation and perpetuation of unemployment, poverty, and homelessness. The myth of the American Dream coincides with the traditions of the **Protestant work ethic**, which dates back to the colonial era and equates hard work and devotion to labor with goodness and devotion to God. According to the Protestant work ethic, if one works hard enough, one will be rewarded by God both in this life and in the next. Some argue that the ethic encourages the wealthy to engage in charity (thus helping support and spread the American Dream). Others, though, have often used the ethic to argue the exact opposite: poverty is God's punishment for an individual's ignorance, laziness, or sin, and thus should not be rewarded with charity. Other socio-cultural concepts examined in this book are often used as excuses for failed capitalist endeavor. For example, since American success is tied to the notion of rugged individualism, *lack* of material success is often thought to reveal insufficient masculinity (which, according to traditional standards, should be *very* rugged and *very* individual).

Seemingly in response to this implied criticism (less economically successful men are somehow inadequate), many economically struggling groups in the United States place a heavy importance on masculine strength and ability. "Machismo" is often a strong component of working-class cultures, whether white or non-white. Popular culture debates also invoke **stereotypical** ideas of race and ethnicity to avoid a potential critique of capitalism, constructing minorities as "inherently" ignorant, lazy, or corrupt. In this way, racism is used to mask capitalism's failures, when in fact racist practices can and do *create* economic disparity when non-white people are discriminated against in hiring and promotion. All of these ideological currents work to obscure and uphold the complex socio-cultural and economic dynamics of **white patriarchal capitalism.** They tend to blame individuals for social problems that may instead be caused by the ignorance, prejudice, greed, and/or economic exploitation that capitalist ideologies create and foster.

Most cultural studies of class are derived from <u>**Marxism,**</u> so named for economic theorist Karl Marx. Over 100 years ago, Marx argued that economic systems (such as capitalism) form the **base** of society, and that everything in the **superstructure** of a society (that is, those ideological institutions that arise from its economic base, such as law, culture, and media) must necessarily reflect and endorse the economic system that produced them. Thus one can see that there may be economic imperatives at the base of superstructural concepts such as racism and **sexism.** For example, the American colonial economy was strongly tied to the institution of slavery, and thus many historians have argued that racial stratification developed to justify this form of capitalist exploitation. Also, a sense of male superiority helps to justify treating women as property or goods to be traded from father to husband. Following these ideas about base and superstructure, one can understand how American films (produced as part of a capitalist economic base) must repeatedly construct superstructural representations that uphold and celebrate capitalism. The next two chapters will show how class difference in American society has been represented in American film, as well as how capitalist imperatives have affected the film industry itself.

Chapter 8

CLASSICAL HOLLYWOOD CINEMA AND CLASS

As per basic Marxism, American culture has consistently produced images that reflect its **capitalist** economic base, and its motion pictures are certainly part of this dynamic. This chapter will describe and analyze the myths of class and wealth concocted prior to and during the classical Hollywood era, as well as those historical moments when national or industrial changes posed a challenge to the stability of those myths. Broadly speaking, American popular cinema has always centered on and dramatized the middle and upper classes, mostly as a way of supporting and celebrating capitalism. The stories that Hollywood told, especially during the first half of the twentieth century, *did* admit that economic stratification existed in the United States. However, rather than critiquing aspects of class oppression inherent in capitalism, most of those films went on to show how easily such stratification could be overcome. Hollywood's ability to fabricate optimistic tales of economic success in the national marketplace extended well beyond the screen. At the same time as audiences thrilled to stories about able-bodied young men climbing the rungs of the economic ladder, they also fantasized about Hollywood itself as a land of opportunity. And although studio executives routinely exploited their employees, the film industry consistently publicized itself as a prime example of the American Dream fulfilled.

Setting the Stage: The Industrial Revolution

Almost from the nation's birth, American writers, artists, and politicians fashioned an image of America as a land exploding with economic potential. The vast resources of the American territories seemed large enough for all individuals to fulfill their dreams. Yet economic disparity existed from colonial days. Almost all Americans of African descent were enslaved and denied the chance to rise economically. Native Americans were considered less than human and also not invited to share in the nation's potential wealth. Women were, for the most part, economically dependent upon their husbands. Even white men were at times kept as **indentured servants**, *de facto* slaves created by a legal contract. The economic disparities felt by some citizens in the years immediately following the Revolution spurred a number of local uprisings, such as Shay's Rebellion (1786) and the Whiskey Rebellion (1794). Still, belief in the American Dream helped quell potential class antagonisms, and its promise spread throughout the world, eventually luring hundreds of thousands of immigrants from around the globe to a country where the streets were thought to be "paved with gold."

Throughout the nineteenth century, as the nation expanded westward, America continued to be figured as a land of endlessly renewable opportunities. If a man faced failure where he was, he could pick up his belongings and move further west to begin again. Visions of cheap land in Oklahoma or Oregon, or of gold in California or Alaska, encouraged people to migrate west in search of success. By the end of the 1800s, however, the limits of the American West had been defined and the promise of the frontier was being closed off. Farmers and other non-urban folk grew increasingly dependent on (and indebted to) urban banks for loans and mortgages, and to big city industries for processing and manufacturing their raw goods. If crops failed, and farmers were unable to make their mortgage payments, banks could and would foreclose on their homes. If Wall Street traders sensed over-production, prices on crops would fall, resulting in less money being returned to the farmers. Rural areas were also dominated by major coal or oil companies that employed the local citizenry in dangerous work for long hours and low pay.

While rural America faced these challenges, the nation was also experiencing an enormous surge in urban populations. By the early 1900s, more Americans lived in and around cities than in rural areas. A number of factors fueled this increase. First, new populations of immigrants from Europe were settling in major Eastern cities. Second, more and more African Americans were moving from Southern farms to Northern cities in hopes of better jobs and less racial oppression. Lastly, the **Industrial Revolution** greatly increased the number of jobs available in urban centers. It required a redefinition in the concept of "work" itself. Before this era, the typical mode of work was artisanal: individual workers (with apprentices perhaps) plied a skilled trade, hand-making whole items such as shirts, clocks, earthenware, etc. The shift to an industrial mode meant moving to a system in which individuals each performed a small part of the manufacturing process. For example, one worker would only sew shirt collars, another only attach buttons, and so forth. This industrial system, aided by new machines and better power sources, substantially speeded up the rate of production, but also made workers dependent on factory managers and company owners for their livelihood. Workers were increasingly treated like cogs in a machine, doing menial labor for long hours and low pay, in factories with little or no safety code. Many workers (including children) lost their hearing, their limbs, or their lives in factory accidents or fires.

The Industrial Revolution thus brought with it a widespread exploitation of workers, both in America and around the world. Various social reform groups began protesting against these developments, creating agrarian cooperatives, denouncing big business, and forming the first modern-day <u>labor unions</u>. Unions are formed when disempowered workers band together as a collective in order to seek better wages or improved working conditions. In forming a union, workers unite in a shared struggle against their economic exploitation. Unions faced (and still do face) strong opposition from the capitalist bosses whose power they would seek to mitigate. From the early twentieth century, unions have been repeatedly outlawed by federal and state legislatures, and portrayed as anti-American in the mass media. Newspapers, controlled by big businesses, consistently portrayed early union organizers as traitorous, morally bereft, or just plain stupid. Playing on **nationalist** and **ethnic** antagonisms, images in editorial cartoons pictured labor agitators as threatening foreign anarchists or as rural malcontents who were too busy looking backward to see the advantages of the modern industrial era. From its earliest days, American cinema often fell into similar modes of **representation**, replicating the images and **ideologies** of the other mass media.

Early Cinema: The Rise of the Horatio Alger Myth

The mass production created by the Industrial Revolution also mandated the growth of mass consumption, and American culture devised low-cost pleasures and entertainments that working men and women could enjoy. Arcades, amusement parks, vaudeville theaters, and dime museums flourished at this time. So did cinema. **Thomas Edison**'s first attempt at motion pictures, **kinetoscopes**, were peep-show films that were placed in storefronts at boardwalks and other urban working-class districts. Many of the earliest **nickelodeons** were also converted storefronts in the middle of immigrant or working-class neighborhoods. Although Edison and his colleagues were not from the working classes, the entertainments they produced (including films of cockfights, boxing matches, female exotic dancers, muscle men, and city street scenes) were what they *thought* the urban lower classes would enjoy.

While it is easy to read such business decisions as condescending, a number of early films were very conscious of the attitudes and outlooks of immigrant and working-class spectators. Some of these early films point out the disparity in treatment between the lower and upper classes, and how the law was rarely on the side of poor people. *The Kleptomaniac* (1905), for example, compares a wealthy woman being slapped on the wrist for attempting to steal a watch with a starving woman being thrown in jail for trying to take a loaf of bread. *One is Business, the Other Crime* (1912) draws a similar parallel: it contrasts a poor man's turn to overt thievery with a tycoon's legal machinations to take other people's money. Films such as *The Moonshiner* (1904) demonstrated sympathy for poor folks trying to survive, even when it meant working outside the law. Police were sometimes figured as enforcers of an unjust economic system, as hired guns who broke up union meetings and treated workers unfairly. Many early comedies depict policemen as inept and bumbling, a tradition that would carry into the famous Keystone Kops comedies of the 1910s and 1920s. Even some of Edison's films could inadvertently disparage police officers. A short entitled *Move On* (1903) was sold to theaters as an urban market scene with "amusing" immigrants being lorded over by a cop on the beat. Yet immigrant audiences could easily have reversed the intended power dynamics and understood the cop as the interloper into *their* community.

Many of these films and others like them drew heavily from the traditions of **muckraking journalism**, a practice that exposed in sensationalistic terms the injustices visited upon immigrants and the working class. At the same time, some films also tapped into a movement known as **Populism**, which had become a major force in American politics during the 1890s. Populism grew out of the rural population's discontent with the Industrial Revolution. It critiqued the modern, industrial society and advocated a return to agrarian values based on collective brotherhood rather than selfish money-grubbing. Based predominantly in the South and the Midwest, Populism's call for social change linked itself to issues of patriotism and Christianity, rather than a shared sense of economic struggle. One of D. W. Griffith's early films, *A Corner in Wheat* (1909), has strong ties to both rural Populism and urban muckraking journalism (specifically Upton Sinclair's literary exposé of the meatpacking industry, *The Jungle*). Griffith's film tells the story of a wealthy businessman speculating in wheat futures, whose business machinations make him rich even as they push farming families to the brink of starvation. The film uses cross-cutting (editing back and forth between two separate story strands) to contrast the tycoon's wealthy urban society with the poor farming community. In the end, the tycoon is ironically killed as he becomes trapped in a silo and buried alive in wheat. At the end of the film, even though the individual businessman has died, his rich colleagues are still feasting on a sumptuous banquet while the farmers huddle around a meager meal.

As narrative cinema developed throughout the first decades of the century, one type of story formula rose to prominence, becoming so popular it became known as the **Horatio Alger myth**. Horatio Alger was a former New England minister who wrote **dime novels** – cheap, often sensationalistic books that working men could afford. Alger's stories recounted the exploits of street urchins who rose to the top levels of society, often with the charitable aid of a kindly benefactor. Starting with little or nothing but a "get-up-and-go" attitude, Alger's heroes (always white and male) were rewarded for their gumption by gaining a successful career in industry, a valuable fortune, and the camaraderie of other businessmen. Alger's very popular novels reworked the American Dream for turn-of-the-century urban America, and helped disseminate the idea that anyone (male) could succeed in America if he simply tried hard enough. Early cinema quickly picked up this narrative formula, and films expressing the Horatio Alger myth can be found throughout American film history, from early silent films such as *The 100-to-1 Shot* (1906) and *Barney Oldfield's Race for Life* (1913) to the latest Hollywood blockbuster. In many ways, the Horatio Alger myth is the basis for **classical Hollywood narrative form**, in which white male heroes with consistent pluck and determination overcome hardship or villainy and obtain (economic) success by the end of the film.

Concurrent with the development of narrative cinema, the exhibition of movies took place in nickelodeon theaters, most of which were located in urban, working-class, and/or immigrant communities. White middle-class Americans were told that villainy, alcoholism, and drug use occurred in nickelodeons, and that women could be accosted and even kidnapped in such places. Middle-class reformers began to target nickelodeons as dens of iniquity that needed to be shut down. At one point, the New York City police department closed down all of the city's nickelodeons, while in other places they were shut down because of safety regulations. While safety was a genuine issue (the flammability of early celluloid film caused many tragic fires), many of the claims about the early movie houses were obviously exaggerated. Such claims were meant to play on white middle-class fears of immigrants and working-class people, and, in so doing, worked to keep people of different ethnic and class backgrounds from interacting socially.

With the reputation of the film industry under attack, both exhibitors and producers turned away from their working-class constituency and attempted to assuage and woo the middle class. Throughout the 1910s, this shift was accomplished by building opulent theaters (the so-called **movie palaces**) in middle-class neighborhoods and by making films that focused on middle-class characters. The films of D. W. Griffith mark the shift in American film away from a predominantly working-class audience to one of middle-class sensibilities. While his earlier films (such as *A Corner in Wheat* or *One is Business, the Other Crime*) often made explicit critiques of unchecked capitalism, his later films increasingly uphold middle-class values. While they still tend to draw comparisons between the "haves" and the "have-nots" in the modern industrial age, many of Griffith's later films suggest that chastity, temperance, and hard work are the solutions to complex socio-economic problems, and not some sort of organized working class. For example, the strike shown in *Intolerance* (1916) only leads to death and grief for the characters, whereas following the Golden Rule brings salvation. Significantly, some of Griffith's films use middle-class Christian dogma as an ideological apparatus to quell working-class dissent in the same manner he used Christianity to justify the overt racism in *The Birth of a Nation* (1915), as discussed in chapter 4.

By the end of World War I, American cinema had become a widespread, mainstream entertainment, employing the Horatio Alger myth and espousing middle-class values that celebrated the riches that could be accumulated (by some) under capitalism. Even women of the 1920s could be included in these Horatio Alger tales, and Hollywood films told stories of secretaries or shop clerks "living the American Dream" by finding and marrying a rich businessman. The myth was also apparent in any number of silent film comedies. In the films of slapstick comedians Buster Keaton and Harold Lloyd, **protagonists** overcome incredible (and often hilariously outlandish) obstacles in order to win respect and success. Through dogged determination and humorous strokes of fortune, these comic characters inevitably proved their abilities and fulfilled the American Dream. **Harold Lloyd**, in his persona as an energetic, young, American middle-class everyman, was the most popular comedian in the United States during the 1920s. His most famous film, *Safety Last* (1923), shows the hero as a junior executive at a department store who is trying to get a promotion and thus have enough money to marry his girlfriend. Although he is continually faced with setbacks, including a famous climb up the side of the

Harold Lloyd (right) was silent cinema's middle-class everyman. His predicament here is typical, but he will climb the ladder of success by the end of the film.
Unidentified publicity photo, authors' personal collection

department store building – a climb that visually echoes his climb to success – Lloyd's protagonist succeeds in all his goals and is rewarded by his boss for his efforts. Perfectly embodying the 1920s version of the Horatio Alger myth, Lloyd's films demonstrate how Hollywood filmmaking had for the most part abandoned a working-class view of urban life in favor of middle-class attitudes.

One silent film comedian stood apart from these social currents, and by and large continued to make films that espoused the viewpoint of the economically dis-possessed. In his character of "The Little Tramp," **Charlie Chaplin** created power-ful images of life outside the system. (Chaplin's attention to economic hardship was perhaps due in large part to his impoverished childhood in Great Britain, where class stratification was more manifest in the social consciousness.) In film after film (both shorts and features), Chaplin's Tramp snubs middle-class life in favor of the freedom of the open road. He often battles comically with people who symbolize

Charlie Chaplin's "Little Tramp," seen here in *The Gold Rush* (1925), acknowledged the economic inequities that most Hollywood films either ignored or suggested could be easily overcome.
The Gold Rush, copyright © 1925, United Artists

middle- or upper-class values, such as snooty butlers, wealthy dowagers, and the police force. The Tramp's ingenuity usually triumphed over the haughtiness and bullying of his antagonists, yet Chaplin's films did not ignore the realities of economic hardship. For example, in *The Gold Rush* (1925), Chaplin's starving Tramp is reduced to eating his own shoe, a powerful image of the failure of the American Dream. Films like *Easy Street* (1917), *The Immigrant* (1917), *The Kid* (1922), *City Lights* (1931), and *Modern Times* (1936) may have romanticized poverty to a degree (for comic effect), but they also communicated the desperate circumstances that still faced many Americans. And unlike the films of Harold Lloyd, Chaplin's Tramp rarely enacted the Horatio Alger success story, marking these silent comedies as an exception to the rule of popular Hollywood cinema.

The influence of the Alger myth on cinema extends well beyond actual film narratives: the Hollywood industry itself became regarded as an embodiment of the myth. While white Anglo-Saxon men (such as Thomas Edison) dominated the early years of cinema, by the end of the 1910s a number of poor immigrant entrepreneurs, mainly of Jewish descent, had become major power brokers in the business. Starting in relative obscurity, these men parlayed their economic beginnings (mostly running nickelodeons in ghetto neighborhoods) into film production companies. By the 1920s, they were the heads of major Hollywood studios. Their remarkably swift climb up the economic ladder appeared to supply evidence of the opportunities that the United States provided for impoverished but eager individuals. Similarly, movie-fan magazines gushed about the overnight success stories of movie stars. From the 1910s until the end of the classical studio age in the 1950s (and even to a degree after), issue after issue of fan magazines told avid readers how relative nobodies were picked out of nowhere to become screen idols: how Hollywood had made their lives into a Horatio Alger story. For example, Joan Crawford was a young working-class woman who happened to win a beauty contest that got her noticed by MGM executives, who transformed her into a star. Lana Turner was famously "discovered" sitting at the counter of a soda shop and whisked into a life of Hollywood glamor. Before **Rock Hudson** became one of Hollywood's leading romantic idols, he had been working as a truck driver. Such romantic versions of success or stardom enticed many aspiring men and women to abandon their less-than-promising jobs for Hollywood. They were hoping that luck might shine on them as well, but the reality behind the myth was somewhat darker than they had been led to believe.

Hollywood and Unionization

The business practices of Hollywood during its classical period were frequently harsh and exploitative, and the struggle to unionize various aspects of the film industry throughout the 1920s and 1930s proved to be difficult and fraught with strife. Throughout the first half of the twentieth century, it was common for big businesses to use their clout with state and federal governments to legislate against unionization. Union organizers were branded anarchists, communists, and foreign agitators – every term that could image them as "un-American." The film industry was no different in its outlook on unions than any other major industry of the era. Although the heads of the new studios had themselves come from lower-class backgrounds and had fought to make their own place in the industry against more established businessmen, these same individuals, once they came to power, sought to close off competition and exploit their employees. Fan magazines may have publicized Hollywood as a land where dreams came true, but the major studios worked tirelessly to keep unions from helping the average film worker achieve those dreams. Although not the only factor, one of the reasons movie moguls centered their industry in southern California was that, unlike the East Coast, unions had not yet gained significant strength there. Consequently, the studios could pay day laborers much less money and force them to work under less stringent workplace regulations (thus keeping budgets lower and profits higher). This type of exploitation extended to actors as well. Non-contract actors were often made to work 15 hours or more each day. Some companies refused to pay actors for days in which they were not actually photographed, even if they were out on location for a production.

By the end of the 1920s, unionization loomed as a greater threat to the Hollywood studios. After World War I, a number of small unions, centering on one specific craft, attempted to gain a foothold, and they began to call for strikes against the studios. **IATSE** (the **International Association of Theatrical Stage Employees**) added "and Motion Picture Machine Operators" to its union title and declared itself an industry-wide union for all behind-the-camera workers. The studios responded in a number of fashions. Employees were often fired if it was discovered that they had attended a union meeting, even if they had not become members. The studios also hired thugs to threaten or beat up union organizers. Executives played the small unions off against each other, agreeing to recognize one union over its competitors if the chosen union would accept less pay and longer hours. The **Academy of Motion Picture Arts and Sciences**, while best known for its Oscar awards, was formed by Hollywood executives in 1926 initially to function as an "in-house" union, thus preventing any outside parties from taking away control. Lastly, the studio system itself created a social and economic hierarchy among different film workers, so that certain people considered themselves middle- or upper-class artists (directors, actors, writers) and not working-class laborers (set builders, lighting technicians, custodial employees, etc.). This stratification helped to keep varied studio employees from seeing a shared cause against the executives. Artists frequently disdained the blue-collar laborers, and laborers distrusted the artists.

The year 1926 also saw the debut of the **Studio Basic Agreement** This agreement granted recognition to IATSE and some other small craft unions, but left the film industry as an **open shop** in which the studios could still hire non-union workers. While this might have seemed to be a satisfactory solution for all involved, the relationship between the studios and unions remained (and remains) divisive. The 1926 Studio Basic Agreement left many workers in the industry (including actors, writers, directors, and animators) still without a union. Furthermore, as IATSE gained power, it often collaborated with the studios to crush smaller unions, regardless of the needs of individual workers. During the 1930s, IATSE was overrun by organized crime, and the union squeezed money out of its members and gave them little support in return. Evidence suggests that the studios even paid bribes to corrupt IATSE officials in order to keep the union from striking, and in 1941, Willie Bioff and George Browne of IATSE were indicted for racketeering in the film industry. This corrupt system allowed the major studios to continue to exert inordinate control over their employees, even as it appeared that they were acquiescing to labor's demands.

The entire motion picture industry faced great economic hardship with the onset of the **Great Depression** in the early 1930s. The heady economic optimism of the 1920s came tumbling down with the stock market crash of 1929. Almost overnight, people's savings were wiped out. Thousands were suddenly unemployed, with no prospect of a new job on the horizon. Banks failed. Mortgages on farms and houses were foreclosed, creating a surge of homelessness. Many Americans began to doubt the benefits of unchecked capitalism, and the Depression was increasingly understood by many as caused by greedy businessmen and the manipulations of unscrupulous stock speculators. People began to view bankers, stock brokers, and corporate executives as the enemy. Further outrage grew out of President Hoover's decision to let American businesses themselves handle the crisis, instead of stepping in to help the victims and punish those who had caused the calamity. When jobless World War I veterans marched on Washington DC in 1932, President Hoover called out the army to quell what he thought was an insurrection. The American Dream as espoused by Horatio Alger was exposed as a myth and not reality.

At the movies, attendance slumped, and almost all the Hollywood studios found themselves deep in debt (most even had to declare a form of bankruptcy). Having just taken out major loans from banking institutions to purchase theaters and pay for the conversion to sound, the heads of the studios now were overseen by New York businessmen, who pressured for cost reduction. To stem their economic losses, the studios laid off hundreds of workers and initiated drastic pay cuts, regardless of union agreements. Such actions shocked and radicalized many film workers at all levels of production – carpenters, writers, and actors alike. In response, new labor organizations began to coalesce, much to the studios' displeasure. Some film workers (as did many Americans in general) began learning about **socialism** and **communism**, searching for a viable alternative to the seemingly failing and dishonest practices of industrial capitalism. Only the intervention of newly elected President Roosevelt's **National Industry Recovery Act** (**NIRA**) gave workers some security. The NIRA guaranteed workers a minimum wage and a maximum number of hours they could be asked to work, as well as the right to organize and bargain collectively through representatives of their own choosing. In light of this, 1933 saw the formation of the **Screen Actors Guild** and the **Writers Guild of America**. A few years later, the **Directors Guild of America** was formed. (Note the use of the term "guild" here instead of "union": this reinforced the sense that these particular workers were artists, and further divided them from laborers and labor unions.) Not surprisingly, the studios fought against such organizing, and they even benefited from parts of the NIRA. For example, while the NIRA guaranteed certain rights to organized labor, it also protected industries from anti-trust lawsuits, and thus Hollywood's **oligopoly** could not be legally challenged. By the end of the 1930s, although more and more unions had been established in Hollywood, studio executives still maintained an inordinate amount of power.

Class in the Classical Hollywood Cinema

The Depression impacted upon the representation of class issues within **classical Hollywood cinema** in myriad ways. The usual Hollywood film had been (and still is) known for its sumptuous and glossy production values, subtly yet insistently displaying the appeal of material wealth. Classical Hollywood characters frequently wore glamorous clothes, slept in lavish bedrooms, ate at swanky restaurants, and lived in beautiful mansions. For example, the classical Hollywood melodramas of Greta Garbo or the musicals of Fred Astaire and Ginger Rogers almost always center on wealthy people enjoying privileged lives. Those types of movies thus presented beautiful worlds free of economic strife that filmgoers could enter and dream about for the price of a ticket. While those types of lush, escapist films remained popular throughout the Great Depression, some moviegoers began to distrust their cheery optimism and rich glamor. In response, the studios significantly revamped the types of films that they made during the early 1930s. For the first time since the early nickelodeon days, mainstream American pictures increasingly questioned the viability of capitalism. Some films began to deal with the nation's economic crisis in more realistic terms – Warner Brothers' Depression-era musicals almost always focus on out-of-work theater people. Some of the popular comedians of this period also did not embody the American Dream. Instead, stars like the Marx Brothers, W. C. Fields, and Mae West used their anarchic wit in a declaration of comedic war on upper-class pretensions.

Hollywood films of the early 1930s sometimes turned the Horatio Alger myth on its head. *Wild Boys of the Road* (1933) followed Depression-era youths as they looked for work, but instead of success, they find dashed hopes, poverty, crime, rape, and an accidental amputation. Heroines no longer got ahead by being good girls and marrying a rich husband; now, in films such as *Red Headed Woman* (1932) and *Baby Face* (1933), they sold their bodies to the highest bidder, using their wiles to "trade up" from a mailroom clerk to the head of the company. Heroes still showed dogged determination to succeed, but some had given up trying to find success through legitimate means and were now going outside the law to do so. **Gangster films** such as *Little Caesar* (1930), *Public Enemy* (1931), and *Scarface* (1932) proliferated during this period. Still other films implied a critique of the capitalist system, depicting everyday people struggling against establishment institutions like the government and big business. Even though most of these films eventually punished those who transgressed middle-class morality or civil law, audience sympathy by and large went to those characters who were fighting against the system. Furthermore, the downfall of such larger-than-life figures as those portrayed by James Cagney, Edward G. Robinson, and Barbara Stanwyck pointed out that even these extraordinarily charismatic and driven individuals could not succeed in Depression-era America, whether playing by the rules or not.

Such pessimism and critique did not last long. The enforcement of the Hollywood **Production Code** in 1934, after sustained complaints from civil and religious groups, reinstated middle-class morality and more optimistic stories. President Roosevelt, who had been elected in 1932, also worked tirelessly to promote a sense of the system working *for* the common man and not against him. As a means to solve the economic catastrophe, Roosevelt's administration tempered American capitalism with various socialist ideas such as welfare, work programs, farm subsidies, and social security. Roosevelt's so-called "New Deal" quickly shifted the mood of the country into supporting the establishment instead of resisting it. This restoration of faith in American institutions brought to an end much of the pessimism and class antagonism of pre-Code Hollywood, and ushered in a new generation of films that upheld a belief in the United States as a land of opportunity. Warner Brothers, for example, tied its new films directly to the optimism of the Roosevelt administration, calling them a "New Deal in Entertainment!" Gangster films and **social problem films** about the Depression subsided, and a new form of comedy emerged during the second half of the decade. These **screwball comedies**, as they were termed, often told stories of the wealthy and the poor coming together and finding common ground (usually symbolized by a rambunctious romance). Social class struggle was thus reworked into a story about a working-class woman meeting her wealthy boyfriend's family (as in *Easy Living* [1937]), or about the attraction between an heiress and a butler (as in *My Man Godfrey* [1936]). The **happy endings** of most screwball comedies, wherein the couple stops sparring and realizes their romantic compatibility, suggest that antagonisms between classes (as represented by each half of the couple) can also be resolved.

Arguably the most influential purveyor of the American Dream in the 1930s was director **Frank Capra**, a man who rose to fame directing screwball comedies. He won three Oscars during this period, and made some of the biggest box office successes of the decade. Capra himself had lived the Horatio Alger myth, beginning life in a lower-class environment before becoming one of the most successful and powerful men in Hollywood. Films like *Lady for a Day* (1933), *It Happened One Night* (1934), *Mr Deeds Goes to Town* (1935), *You Can't Take It With You* (1938), *Mr Smith Goes to Washington* (1939), and *Meet John Doe* (1941) repackaged the American Dream for Depression-era audiences. Drawing on the traditions of Populism, Capra's films often featured rural or small-town fellows who stand up to ominous odds and somehow triumph, thus proving that "the American way" does indeed work. What made these films different from Hollywood's previous Horatio Alger success stories was that Capra made the obstacles facing the hero much more dire and menacing. Capra knew that a bright happy ending would be all the more powerful if the darkness before the dawn was pitch black: thus his protagonists often lack confidence in themselves (and the American Dream) before they ultimately succeed in the final reel. In Capra's classic Christmas movie, *It's a Wonderful Life* (1946), George Bailey (played by James Stewart) is so despondent over his failed economic situation that he is about to commit suicide.

The villains in Capra's films are usually corrupt power brokers – bankers, businessmen, politicians, etc. In this way, his films lightly critique but still affirm **hegemonic** capitalism. Rather than suggesting that big business itself is to blame for working-class hardships, these films instead show such problems to be caused by aberrantly villainous wealthy individuals. In Capra's films (and in Hollywood films in general), it is an individual man who is wrong, not the system itself. The **hegemonic negotiation** of capitalism in *It's a Wonderful Life* works in this manner: wealthy businessman Mr Potter (Lionel Barrymore) is presented as selfish, greedy, and evil, and that is why he is the villain. The fact that capitalism itself might cause or allow selfish, greedy, and evil things to happen is hinted at but never explicitly stated. In fact, the hero, George Bailey, is also a capitalist entrepreneur, but a "good"

The romance between Clark Gable's newspaper reporter and Claudette Colbert's heiress in the screwball comedy *It Happened One Night* (1934) suggested that all social classes could come together, a message that Depression-era audiences apparently wanted to hear.
It Happened One Night, copyright © 1934, Columbia

one, running a savings-and-loan business for his friends and neighbors. The evil millionaires that are sometimes portrayed in American films are thus not presented as endemic to the institution of capitalism. Furthermore, those wicked power brokers are sometimes depicted as foreigners (thus not how a wealthy *American* would act), living in another historical era (thus not a problem in *today's* economy), or simply one bad apple that needs to be taken out of a system that is working just fine. Occasionally a Hollywood movie will sound the idea that wealth corrupts, or that "money cannot buy happiness." Those "moral" lessons – just as surely as those implied by the Horatio Alger myth – also praise the superiority of middle-class people and values.

Case Study: *The Grapes of Wrath* (1940)

While Hollywood films by the mid-1930s had begun reasserting the power of the American Dream, other art forms maintained a more critical stance toward the country's economic problems. Theater, for example, with plays such as *Street Scene, Dead End, Golden Boy, The Cradle Will Rock*, and *Pins and Needles*, raised issues about capitalism and class struggle that American films feared to acknowledge. Some of the more popular Depression-era plays were adapted into films in the latter half of the 1930s, but this usually required extensive revision to soften their criticism of big business, the law, and capitalism itself. Such was also the case with John Steinbeck's Pulitzer prize-winning novel *The Grapes of Wrath*. The book tells the story of a typical Midwestern family forced to leave their farm due to a great drought that has turned the land into a giant dust bowl. Steinbeck did not scrimp on his depiction of the desperation, violence, and despair these itinerants faced in their search for work and a new home. The novel was adapted into a film by 20th Century-Fox in 1940. The year of production is important because, by the time the film came out, the country was significantly on the economic upswing and the socio-economic problems of the Joad family could be regarded as historical and not contemporary.

Steinbeck had used the journey of the Joads to express leftist, socialist sympathies, critiquing the way the capitalist system beat down hapless workers. In particular, he narrated the growing class consciousness of young Tom Joad as he witnesses the exploitation of his family and others by big agricultural companies and the banks. However, such a forthright attack on corporate institutions could not be made in Hollywood, particularly with Chase Manhattan Bank as the major stockholder of 20th Century-Fox. (Steinbeck was incensed to learn of this connection after he had already sold the novel to the studio.) Darryl F. Zanuck, the head of the studio, worked closely with scriptwriter Nunnally Johnson and director John Ford to keep the film as hard-hitting as possible – without actually hitting any precise targets. Throughout the film, the question of who is to blame for the suffering and degradation that the Joads face is left purposefully vague. An ill-defined "they" is responsible for spreading around thousands of handbills advertising only 800 jobs in California. "They" are also the ones who come to burn out a transient camp of migrant workers. And just when it seems that the film is indicting the police for collaborating with evil employers, a character points out that those men are just hired security men with tin badges, and not official agents of the law. When Tom Joad (played by Henry Fonda) asks a man who drove all the people off the farms, the answer given is the dust storms – not banking or corporate interests.

Where the film does remain tough and unblinking is in its depiction of the Joads' struggle. Shot in a stark and realist style of cinematography, the images of the deserted farms and the transient camps approach the look of famous Depression-era news photographs. The framing and visual design also provide silent commentary on the suffering: as one family watches a bulldozer plow down their homestead, the camera travels down to the ground to show the tire treads running over the shadows of the family. In a possible sly allusion to the comment that it is just "dust" that has caused these people's suffering, the film consistently shows the stylish cars of the bankers and bosses driving away and kicking up dust on the dispossessed workers.

The film also includes some of the socialist rhetoric of Steinbeck's novel, most famously in Tom's final speech wherein he suggests that "a fellow ain't got a soul of his own, just a little piece of a bigger soul." Yet the film redirects these sentiments into a discussion of family – a much more palatable topic for Hollywood and America than socialism. Thus, rather than being a story about young Tom's ideological awakening, the film becomes the story of a family struggling to stay together during hard times. In this way, Ma Joad (played by Jane Darwell in an Oscar-winning performance) becomes central to the picture. Throughout, she consistently talks about holding the family together, emphasizing that as the key point of the story. In depicting the hardships of the Joads and other wayfarers, the picture repeatedly focuses on families, with particular emphasis on hungry children. In this way, when Tom talks about being part of "a bigger soul"

Members of the cast of *The Grapes of Wrath* (1940), one of the few American films of the era that attempted to dramatize the harsh economic realities of the Great Depression.
The Grapes of Wrath, copyright © 1940, 20th Century-Fox

or when Ma concludes the film declaring that "we are the people," such talk is tied to notions of family bonding and not socialism. In the most direct attempt to create distance between the film's outlook and socialism, Tom actually asks a man "What is these 'reds'" he hears people talk about. The man replies, 'I ain't talkin' about that one way or the other" and quickly changes the subject.

Also, the film only uses a section of the entire novel, and reorders some events and actions to create a more optimistic ending. In the book, the Joads stop at a friendly, clean camp run by the Department of Agriculture. Steinbeck's novel follows this moment of charitable help and rest with the Joads being hired as scabs for a disreputable peach farm and being treated almost like inmates. The film switches these events so that things seem to be getting better for the family by the end of the picture. To emphasize this, once the Joads enter the government camp, the film is brightly and evenly lit, and the

soundtrack is filled with birds chirping and children laughing, instead of dogs braying and winds howling. This sequence thus represents the federal government as kind-hearted and not as part of the problem. The script also takes Ma's declaration of eventual triumph from another part of the novel to end the film on a more positive note. Nonetheless, while Hollywood inevitably tinkered with the ideas presented in Steinbeck's novel, the film still emerged as a stark and sympathetic portrayal of rural working-class families. The mere mention of "reds" in a Hollywood film that does not immediately and concisely demonize them is in itself a remarkable achievement. Although Steinbeck worried about what would happen to his novel when it was "Hollywood-ized," he went on to announce his approval of the final picture. *The Grapes of Wrath* is today considered to be one of the best classical Hollywood representations of Depression-era life and issues.

Conclusion: Recloaking Class Consciousness

The Great Depression of the 1930s was one the worst economic crises in US history, and it presented a large challenge to the dominance of American capitalism, both as an economic system and as a set of ideological assumptions and beliefs. The Great Depression affected not only how class issues were depicted in American film, but also how the industry made films, as various unions struggled to wrest some control away from studio moguls. However, by the end of the 1930s, the major Hollywood studios still retained their economic power base, and the pleasures and advantages of capitalism were for the most part once again being championed by Hollywood films. While the Depression had made many people painfully aware of class stratification, and made others question the viability of capitalism, American film's hegemonic negotiation of class issues kept the core values of capitalism firmly in place.

Questions for Discussion

1 What do you consider your own class standing to be? Do you see class represented in Hollywood movies in ways that match accurately your own experience of class?
2 The Horatio Alger myth was and is an important aspect of America's self-image as a capitalist democracy. In what ways does classical Hollywood narrative form "speak" the Horatio Alger myth? Can you give examples of the myth in other films you may have seen? Can you think of current stars whose lives seem to embody the myth?
3 The gangster film is in many ways about what one can and cannot do in America to succeed monetarily. When you watch a gangster film, who do you "root" for – the gangsters or the police? What are the implications of those identifications?

Further Reading

Bergman, Andrew. *We're in the Money: Depression America and Its Films*. New York: New York University Press, 1971.

Brownlow, Kevin. *Behind the Mask of Innocence – Sex, Violence, Prejudice, Crime: Films of Social Conscience in the Silent Era*. New York: Knopf, 1990.

Clark, Danae. *Negotiating Hollywood: The Cultural Politics of Actors' Labor*. Minneapolis: University of Minnesota Press, 1995.

Horne, Gerald. *Class Struggle in Hollywood, 1930–1950*. Austin: University of Texas Press, 2001.

Ross, Murray. *Stars and Strikes*. New York: AMS Press, 1967 (1941).

Ross, Steven J. *Working-Class Hollywood: Silent Film and the Shaping of Class in America*. Princeton: Princeton University Press, 1998.

Sklar, Robert. *Movie-Made America: A Cultural History of American Cinema*. New York: Vintage Books, 1994.

Zaniello, Tom. *Working Stiffs, Union Maids, Reds, and Riffraff: An Organized Guide to Films about Labor*. Ithaca, NY: ILR Press/Cornell University Press, 1996.

Further Screening

Intolerance (1916)
The Gold Rush (1925)
Scarface (1932)
Wild Boys of the Road (1933)
Modern Times (1936)

Easy Living (1937)
Stella Dallas (1937)
Meet John Doe (1941)
It's a Wonderful Life (1946)

Chapter 9

CINEMATIC CLASS STRUGGLE AFTER THE DEPRESSION

This chapter examines the marked swings in attitude about American **capitalism** and class issues that occurred during the second half of the twentieth century – and how those swings affected what was shown on the nation's movie screens. World War II attempted to unite the nation across class boundaries (and to a lesser extent, across racial and **gender** boundaries), but during the immediate postwar period, powerful capitalists in business and government sought to reconsolidate their interests by dividing the nation once again. They did so by exploiting the **Red Scare**, accusing labor organizers and leftist, socialist thinkers of being **communist**, and therefore, in the eyes of some people, un-American. By the 1960s, members of the **counterculture** were rebelling against the conformity and materialism of the 1950s, and voicing a strong critique of capitalist exploitation (as well as **racism**, **sexism**, and the war in Vietnam). By the 1980s, the pendulum had swung back in the other direction, and material wealth and greedy acquisitiveness were once again celebrated in **dominant ideology** and national culture. The early 1990s saw yet another backlash to American materialism due to the rise of **slackers**, young people who, like their 1960s precursors, sought to drop out of a capitalist system that they felt was corrupt and unjust. In the first years of the twenty-first century, recessions in the American economy loomed again, forcing more and more individuals to question the actual benefits of unchecked or **deregulated** capitalism. The various failures of and challenges to capitalism over the last 50 years have necessitated a strong ideological agenda to maintain capitalist supremacy, and most American movies have done their part to uphold the nation's economic base and class structure.

From World War II to the Red Scare

Although the Roosevelt administration initiated a number of **socialist**-inspired acts and programs to reverse the slide of the **Great Depression**, the biggest spur to the national condition occurred with the shift to a wartime economy. The need to speedily produce tanks, ships, planes, and other weaponry for American and Allied armed forces created an abundance of jobs. As men left their peacetime jobs and entered the war effort as soldiers and sailors, the need for industrial workers expanded so much that women were encouraged to enter the workforce in unprecedented numbers. By the early 1940s, unemployment in the United States was virtually non-existent. American unions also seemed to gather greater strength during these war years. Major unions, including **IATSE**, agreed to hold off strikes while the war was being waged, and since workers were in such demand, many unions were able to garner better pay and safer working conditions for their members. Yet, while the war years seemed to signal an end to worries about the viability of capitalism – especially with so much war propaganda promoting the triumph of "the American way" – some signs that there were doubts about the system still appeared. **Wildcat strikes** (not sanctioned by national unions) occurred regularly during the war, and some industrialists were accused of war profiteering, that is, overcharging the government for materials in this time of need.

By the end of the war, a growing number of pulp novels (roughly equivalent to **dime novels** of the early 1900s) and films were painting a picture of American life as grubby, dark, and filled with greed and selfishness. Sometimes grouped together as "hard-boiled" literature, the detective novels of Raymond Chandler and the bleak tales of James M. Cain and Cornell Woolrich focused on characters who were willing to do anything for wealth and power – seduction, blackmail, even murder. While these written works had gained in popularity throughout the Depression, many of them first made it to the screen around the end of World War II, initiating an important cycle of films that French critics termed **film noir**, because of the films' gritty night-time settings and even darker subject matter. Films like *Double Indemnity* (1944), *The Postman Always Rings Twice* (1946), and *Out of the Past* (1947) seemed to express doubts about what exactly American soldiers had been fighting to protect. The main characters in film noir can often be found leading lives of quiet desperation, feeling trapped in their economic situation, having failed to attain their version of the American Dream. The plots then revolve around the illegal and immoral schemes these characters make in order to achieve their dreams. However, true to the **Production Code**'s mandates, their actions lead not to freedom and wealth, but to an even greater sense of entrapment, paranoia, guilt, or death.

As might be suspected from that brief description, film noir is unrelentingly pessimistic about American culture and the American way of life. Some of these films provide a fairly explicit critique of capitalism, and this makes them similar to the **social problem film** that was also a trend in postwar Hollywood filmmaking (although there were few of these that dared treat capitalism itself as a social problem). Indeed, certain writers and directors specifically used film noir in order to communicate such a critique. Screenwriter Carl Foreman's script for *Champion* (1949) uses an aggressive boxer (played by Kirk Douglas) as a metaphor for the cannibalistic competitiveness of capitalism, a competitiveness that leads to the boxer's doom just as he wins the national title. In another example, screenwriter/

director Abraham Polonsky's *Force of Evil* (1948) follows a man (John Garfield) so caught up in trying to get ahead in a money-driven society that he betrays his friends and family, acts that lead to tragedy.

Such cinematic critiques of the system began appearing after the war just as the major studios began a concerted effort to rein in the power of the unions. Although 1946 was one of the most profitable years in Hollywood's history, movie attendance began to plummet in the following years. Americans began moving to the suburbs and away from urban theaters, and television began to grow in popularity as a rival to film. Hollywood was also confronted with anti-trust rulings (the so-called **Paramount Consent Decrees** first issued in 1948) that caused more economic hardship for the studios. In response, Hollywood executives again began slashing payrolls and canceling contracts. More and more film workers began to be treated as independent contractors and not studio employees. They lost the security of ongoing employment, and had no guarantee of maximum hours or benefits. In response to these developments, a number of major strikes erupted during these years, strikes that sometimes escalated into pitched battles outside studio gates, complete with overturned cars, lead pipes, tear gas, and fire hoses.

The response by the studios (and big business in general) to such strikes was to accuse labor organizers of being communists. With the **Cold War** against the Soviet Union just beginning, the Red Scare – paranoia about communist infiltration – was growing to a fever pitch. Accusing dissatisfied American workers of communist sympathies had the effect of branding them as dangerous, international traitors who were trying to destroy America from within. At this time, the Congressional committee called **HUAC (House Un-American Activities Committee)** began to hold hearings to investigate whether communists were running rampant throughout the nation's industries, including Hollywood. Certain studio executives (such as Walt Disney and Louis B. Mayer) used the opportunity to name and defame union organizers who had challenged them. In 1947, when HUAC called 10 suspected screenwriters and directors to testify before them (including Polonsky, director of *Force of Evil*), many of them invoked their Constitutional rights and refused to answer the committee's questions about their political beliefs. Rather than respecting these rights, however, the committee indicted and imprisoned most of these men, who collectively became known as the **Hollywood Ten**.

Such actions threw Hollywood into a panic. Some actors and directors attempted to band together in support of the Hollywood Ten, but to little avail. Public sentiment against alleged communist infiltration had been whipped up so strongly that most Americans were willing to let essential American freedoms such as speech, thought, and assembly be curtailed. Individuals who had joined leftist, socialist, or communist groups during the years of the Great Depression were now considered traitors, rather than part of the American give-and-take, free-speech debate, political process. As noted in chapter 3, Jewish film workers and executives were especially worried, since a common **anti-Semitic** ideology of the era already equated communism with Jews. In order to distance themselves from possible accusations, Hollywood moguls met together and agreed not to hire anyone who was under even the slightest suspicion of being a communist. Under this system born of fear and hysteria, even an unsubstantiated rumor was enough to bar someone from employment.

The **blacklist** of those barred included thousands of film workers (actors, writers, directors, etc.) and destroyed the careers of many talented people. Many never worked in films again, some died from stress and humiliation, and some committed suicide. A few writers, such as *Champion*'s Carl Foreman, were able to continue writing under false names (or **fronts**), while actors and directors were forced to move into theater or leave the profession altogether. The blacklist in Hollywood (and television) lasted into the 1960s, when the changing tenor of the times finally acknowledged the abuses of civil, human, and Constitutional rights caused by the Red Scare. But throughout the 1950s, the blacklist helped to keep Hollywood moguls powerful and local unions in check – anyone who attempted to organize or call a strike could be easily accused of communist sympathies. The major national unions were of no help, since they were just as fearful of losing their power base. Consequently, both the studios and IATSE fully cooperated with HUAC investigations and the formation and enforcement of various blacklists.

The fear of being branded a communist substantially affected the subject matter of film noir and effectively ended the social problem film altogether. Now, film noir detectives began searching for Soviet spies instead of tracking greedy murderers and blackmailers. And any film that tried to examine social conditions in the country was viewed as chancy and dangerous, unless it was understood to support the status quo of the blacklist era. For example, **Elia Kazan** was one of the foremost directors of social problem films in the late 1940s (including *Gentlemen's Agreement* [1947] and *Pinky* [1949]), before he cooperated with HUAC and named suspected communists. A few years later Kazan won an Oscar for directing *On the Waterfront* (1954), a film in which mobsters, trying to control a union of dock workers, are defeated by a single hero who testifies about them before a congressional committee. Many people understood the film to be a thinly veiled valorization of Kazan's own actions before HUAC, and even by the 1990s, many Hollywood insiders had not yet forgiven him. (When he received a special honorary Oscar in 1998, many in the audience refused to stand or even applaud.) More regularly, Hollywood films of the era ignored politics altogether, and went about celebrating materialism and the glories of capitalist excess.

One **independent film** of the era, *Salt of the Earth* (1953), actually dared to confront the problems of capitalist exploitation in a direct manner. Made by blacklisted filmmakers, and based on actual events, the film was financed by the Mine, Mill, and Smelters Union, which itself was kicked out of the national CIO labor union for supposed communist ties. The film follows a group of Mexican American workers who strike against a racist and exploitative mining company. Not only does the film champion the rights of the working *man*, it also addresses issues of gender. For example, when the men are imprisoned for striking, the women take to the picket lines, even over the objections of their men. In this way, the film dramatizes how sexism is a social concept that can be used to divide rather than unite the working class. The movie was outspokenly socialist in its sympathies. Right-wing vigilantes continually disrupted its filming and, when it was finally completed, distributors and exhibitors refused to handle it. In such conservative times, a movie critical of the capitalist system was tantamount to a treasonous betrayal of the United States itself.

From Opulence to Counterculture

The dissenting voice of *Salt of the Earth* was a lone cry in the wilderness. Throughout the 1950s, Hollywood more regularly produced escapist entertainment: historical epics, opulent musicals, and lush comedies. The content of most of these films unabashedly celebrates materialism and conspicuous consumption. Homes were bigger, cars were faster, and everything was newer and brighter. Also, the films themselves were sold as lavish and expensive productions, with the implication being that their bigger budgets made them better films. (The fact that many Hollywood epics of the era were produced overseas in order to exploit cheaper labor was not widely publicized.) Comedies and musicals like *How to Marry a Millionaire* (1953), *Sabrina* (1954), and *Funny Face* (1957) showcase an abundance of fashion, furniture, cars, and new consumer goods for audiences to appreciate, envy, and eventually purchase. The musical *Silk Stockings* (1957) makes an explicit comparison between American consumer capitalism (represented by Fred Astaire as a Hollywood producer) and the joyless, drab Soviet world (embodied by Cyd Charisse as a Russian agent). In the end, the Russian agent realizes she too wants what American capitalism has to offer – namely a husband (Astaire) who will buy her expensive evening gowns and the titular silk stockings.

Any criticism of American capitalism happened between the lines, in subtle and obscure ways. *Will Success Spoil Rock Hunter?* (1957) could disparage 1950s corporate lifestyles because the film was presented as a gaudy sex comedy. Director Douglas Sirk also provided a critique of upper- and middle-class repression in melodramas such as *Magnificent Obsession* (1954), *All that Heaven Allows* (1955), and *Written on the Wind* (1956). Many other melodramas, including *Rebel Without a Cause* (1955), *Picnic* (1955), and *The Apartment* (1960), also offered subtle critiques of class and/or the corporate lifestyle. These critiques reflected what was occurring in culture-at-large. American life in general was becoming increasingly conformist, with both blue-collar and white-collar men feeling trapped in their work routines. Wives and mothers, surrounded by new "time-saving" gadgets in the home, often felt bored and trapped in their suburban tract homes. People of color were tired of being stuck in low-paying jobs and renewed their fight against the racism that was keeping them from realizing their American Dreams. The younger generation in particular seemed to rebel against the confining structures of 1950s life. Not remembering the economic hardships of the Great Depression, teenagers and college students increasingly refused to ignore the unhappiness that lay beneath the veneer of their supposedly happy suburban lifestyle.

The growth of the **Beat movement** during this era signaled a dissatisfaction with the status quo. The Beats were writers and avant-garde filmmakers like Jack Kerouac,

Allen Ginsberg, Alfred Leslie, and Robert Frank, who, in their work, vocally disdained the crass materialism of 1950s America. They espoused the philosophy and practice of hitting the open road – traveling the nation almost like gypsies – in order to escape the conformity and phoniness of middle-class suburban lifestyles. The Beats' critique evolved and throughout the 1960s they were joined by other voices of dissent, including those of women, racial and ethnic minorities, and homosexuals. These large, loose social movements of people were often referred to collectively as the counterculture, because they all countered the dominant middle-class culture. Importantly, the counterculture also included people who protested against US involvement in the Vietnam war. Demonstrators pointed out the economic links between the Vietnam war and the national economy: maintaining involvement in warfare – whether it was World War II, the Cold War, or the Vietnam war – helped to keep the US economy flourishing. Ties between military and corporate interests, the so-called military-industrial complex, were seen as driving national economic policy, exploiting poor people both at home and abroad. The lives of both Vietnamese peasants and poor Americans (who, due to lack of options, made up a large portion of the armed forces) were understood as fodder for the machinations of the military-industrial complex, which was, in effect, turning human lives into economic gain. In response to such critiques, a large portion of the younger generation (and many others who agreed with these viewpoints) attempted to reject American capitalism and find new ways of living. Many openly espoused communist ideals, "dropping out" of the capitalist system and experimenting with new ways of organizing social structures, such as communal living and/or a return to agrarian lifestyles.

Hollywood did a poor job of responding to the concerns of the counterculture, if and when it acknowledged them at all. Hollywood studios (as they always had) promoted capitalism and the status quo, and countercultural audiences had little interest in seeing multimillion-dollar blockbusters like *Doctor Dolittle* (1967) or *The Happiest Millionaire* (1967). Many members of the counterculture turned to independent and **avant-garde films** for more enlightened and enlightening cinema. The so-called New American Cinema of the late 1950s and early 1960s had grown out of Beat filmmaking and new advances in 16 mm film production. Filmmakers like Lionel Rogosin (*On the Bowery* [1956]) and Shirley Clarke (*The Cool World* [1963]) made intimate documentaries that explored social issues in America. John Cassavetes explored working-class lives and issues in hand-made fictional films such as *Shadows* (1957), *Faces* (1968), and *A Woman under the Influence* (1974). An occasional actor and director in Hollywood, Cassavetes always returned to low-budget independent filmmaking to make the kinds of films he wanted to make – those that explored issues that Hollywood films would not touch.

Countercultural audiences also turned to collective documentary filmmaking groups such as Newsreel for information about topics that corporate-owned news organizations failed to cover. For entertainment, the urban counterculture turned increasingly to foreign cinema and **underground film**. Underground film was a loosely defined avant-garde movement that often rejected (or made fun of) conventional Hollywood subject matter and style. And just like the filmmakers of the

New American Cinema, these avant-garde filmmakers often worked in collective, communal, and improvisational ways. The films of pop artist Andy Warhol, made in collaboration with his friends and acquaintances, specifically lampooned the Hollywood myth that anyone could become a star. By literally taking dispossessed people off the street (including hustlers, drug addicts, and drag queens) and putting them into films as "superstars," Warhol's group satirized Hollywood's version of the Horatio Alger myth. Director John Waters, who made outrageous fictional features in the tradition of underground film, also cast a variety of marginalized people to star in his gleeful satires of middle-class pretension and competitiveness (*Pink Flamingos* [1972]), *Female Trouble* [1975], *Desperate Living* [1977]). Furthermore, in trying to counteract the prevailing concept of cinema as a business (one controlled solely by capitalist interests), both the New American Cinema and underground filmmakers explored new methods of distribution and exhibition. Rather than battling to be shown in mainstream theaters, their films were typically exhibited at film festivals, midnight screenings, or even big parties and concerts.

With younger people turning away from Hollywood films in droves, and older audiences opting to stay home and watch television, the major studios faced a heavy recession toward the end of the 1960s. Throughout the decade, many of them were bought out by large corporate conglomerates that continually hired and fired studio executives in the hope of finding someone who could hit upon a winning box office formula. Younger filmmakers – many of whom considered themselves to be part of the counterculture – suddenly found they were in positions of power in Hollywood, and some films of the era did begin to address countercultural issues, albeit in highly **mediated** forms. *Bonnie and Clyde* (1967) and *The Graduate* (1967), for example, sided with young outsiders battling against conformity and the established order of capitalist America. Both films also used stylistic techniques that were experimental by Hollywood standards (such as jump cuts, handheld cameras, and zoom lenses). In 1969, one low-budget independent film wedded the Beat philosophy of hitting the road to a countercultural critique of America. *Easy Rider* (1969) tells the story of two young men on the fringes of society (played by Peter Fonda and Dennis Hopper) who go on the road "in search of America." Their motorcycle journey brings them into contact with a cross-section of late 1960s America: hippy communes, farmers, the police, drug dealers, small town Americans, prostitutes, and rednecks. In the end, having failed to find any real truth or meaning in their search for America, they are brutally shot to death by two men in a pick-up truck, men who see the youthful travelers as un-American and ultimately less than human. While the film was obviously very different from typical Hollywood fare, Columbia decided to distribute it, and it became one of the year's biggest box office successes.

As its ending implies, *Easy Rider* is a pessimistic film, and its critique of American culture extends to the youth movement as well as to the nation's more established institutions. For a brief moment, the film's success ushered in some films that examined American culture in serious and/or satiric ways. Films such as *Five Easy Pieces* (1970, directed by Bob Rafelson), *Harold and Maude* (1972, directed by Hal Ashby), and *Mean Streets* (1973, directed by Martin Scorsese) all attempted

Easy Rider (1969) was a pessimistic account of the American Dream gone sour.
Easy Rider, copyright © 1969, Columbia

to show both the emptiness of American capitalism and the tragic consequences facing lower-class people who still chased after the American Dream of material success. Having knowledge of film history, some of these filmmakers used old Hollywood genres and styles to express their sentiments. For example, Robert Altman reworked the Western in *McCabe and Mrs Miller* (1971), showing how American corporate greed was the true villain of the old West, and not "bloodthirsty redskins." Similarly, Peter Bogdanovich's *The Last Picture Show* (1971) employed stylistic techniques associated with Western director **John Ford** in order to depict the gradual economic death of a small Texas town. Roman Polanski's *Chinatown* (1974) used film noir conventions to explore the social and sexual corruption of the wealthy and powerful. Martin Scorsese's *Alice Doesn't Live Here Anymore* (1974) reworked the domestic melodrama to tell the story of a widowed working-class mother trying to survive. And Robert Altman's *Nashville* (1975) is a revisionist musical that exposes – among other things – the desperation of working-class people trying to "make it big" in the country music industry.

Five Easy Pieces (1970) starred Jack Nicholson as a man plagued by the emptiness of American capitalist culture. *Five Easy Pieces*, copyright © 1970, BBS/Columbia

Many of these sophisticated and self-conscious films about American culture (and the relation of Hollywood to that same culture) were made by filmmakers who collectively became known as the **Film School Brats.** They were the first generation of American filmmakers who had gone to film school, where they were exposed to ideas about how Hollywood film relates to American culture-at-large. At first, some of these young filmmakers were interested not only in making more leftist, politically engaged films, but also in trying to change how Hollywood itself was structured. For example, producer Bert Schneider left his job at Columbia to help form the independent company **BBS**, and proceeded to aid the careers of various countercultural and politically radical artists. BBS produced *Easy Rider* and Schneider himself helped finance the making of *Hearts and Minds* (1974), a documentary that condemned US involvement in Vietnam. Francis Ford Coppola, one of the first Film School Brats to get directorial work at the major studios, decided to break away from the Hollywood system by starting **American Zoetrope** in 1969. Putting its headquarters in San Francisco instead of Los Angeles, American Zoetrope was initially envisioned as a filmmaking commune – with people contributing to a film in a variety of capacities rather than according to the traditional Hollywood division of labor. BBS, Zoetrope, and other independent companies at the time hoped for a restructuring of how American cinema was made – one that would foster creativity and no longer be beholden to market interests. However, such hopes would be mostly unfulfilled.

Box: Class on Television

Arguably, American television has historically presented more images of working-class Americans than has Hollywood film. From TV's earliest days, with series such as *The Goldbergs* (1949–56), *The Life of Riley* (1953–8), and perhaps most famously *The Honeymooners* (1955–6), network television consistently showed what life was like for struggling working-class people. In the early 1950s, television often aired original theatrical productions that dealt with working-class lives. One of these, *Marty* (1953), was so critically and popularly acclaimed that it was remade as a theatrical film which won the Oscar for Best Picture of 1955. The proliferation of these working-class images may have had something to do with preconceptions of who was watching TV during those early years. Series producers, network executives, and corporate sponsors often thought of their audiences as from the lower classes (much as early American filmmakers did). They assumed that people with higher incomes went to the theater, the museums, or the movies, while working-class people watched television because it was more affordable. After the initial monetary outlay for the set, television was to all intents and purposes free entertainment. Consequently, programming that reflected working-class lives would theoretically win more viewers for the sponsors' advertisements.

However, as the 1950s progressed, network television provided more and more images of middle-class life. The famous situation comedies of the era (such as *Father Knows Best* [1954–60], *Leave it to Beaver* [1957–63], and *The Donna Reed Show* [1958–66]) helped to construct an image of America comprised of white suburban families, and consequently those shows captured that type of audience for advertisers as well. By the mid-1960s, the most popular shows on TV were rural sitcoms such

as *The Andy Griffith Show* (1960–8), *The Beverly Hillbillies* (1962–71), *Gomer Pyle USMC* (1964–9), and *Green Acres* (1965–71). However, the people watching those shows were soon deemed by networks the "wrong kind" of audience, since advertising studies decided that they had less disposable income than more educated, urban audiences. Sponsors thus turned to shows that appealed to higher-income viewers, even if that meant a smaller overall audience, since those viewers had more spending money. By the early 1970s, almost all of the rural sitcoms had been cancelled.

That did not mean a total end to representations of working-class characters, as the new relevance of "quality television" allowed for a number of dramatic and comedy series (like *All in the Family* [1971–9]) that reflected more realistic social issues. For example, *The Waltons* (1972–81) was a nostalgic family drama set during the Great Depression. Other shows followed the exploits of poor black families (*Good Times* [1974–9], *Sanford and Son* [1972–7]), or – in keeping with the American Dream – upwardly mobile black families (*The Jeffersons* [1975–85]). Shows about the lower classes almost disappeared during the Reagan era, though, in favor of shows about wealthy families. Dramas like *Dallas* (1978–91), *Dynasty* (1981–9), and *Falcon Crest* (1981–90) were matched by sitcoms such as *Family Ties* (1982–9), *The Cosby Show* (1984–92), and *Growing Pains* (1985–92). Yet, by the end of the 1980s, a number of shows seemed to signal a backlash against these high-income family programs. *Married with Children* (1987–97) was initially entitled *Not the Cosby Show*, and its working-class characters consistently lampooned middle-class taste. *Roseanne* (1988–97), about a working-class family struggling to make ends meet, was one of the most popular

The Honeymooners was a very popular 1950s television sitcom that centered on a working-class bus driver (Jackie Gleason, center), his wife Alice (Audrey Meadows), and his friend Norton (Art Carney).
The Honeymooners, copyright © 1952–1957, CBS-TV

shows of the 1990s. Even *The Simpsons* (1989–) presents a less-than-upwardly-mobile family and the forces that work against them, specifically the corrupt nuclear power plant owner, Mr Burns. As cable, home video, and the Internet continue to siphon away higher-income audiences, broadcast networks may continue this trend of once again appealing to a working-class constituency.

New Hollywood and the Resurrection of the Horatio Alger Myth

By the mid-1970s, many of the dreams and aspirations of the counterculture had either been assimilated into a more mainstream, middle-class consciousness, or faded away altogether. Some people felt that the work of the 1960s had been accomplished – the United States did get out of Vietnam in 1975 and there was a growing acceptance of racial and ethnic diversity. Other people grew disillusioned and cynical – President Richard Nixon resigned in disgrace in 1974 after his role in the Watergate scandal came to light, and the economy began to slump once again. People became more insular and isolated as the communal counterculture dissolved. The younger generation got older and was drawn into the realities of the work world, whether it was blue-collar or white-collar. People were slightly more aware of economic disparity in America, but any hopes for a revolution (or even serious reform) that would overturn or regulate capitalism had been effectively dashed. And as the 1970s became the 1980s, what little bit of interest in working-class issues there was began to evaporate. The popular culture of the 1980s celebrated personal success measured via acquired wealth. The new **yuppies** (young urban professionals) of the decade were a symbol of upward mobility – they flaunted their homes, cars, clothing, and jewelry as old-fashioned capitalist status symbols. Films in America went from being subtly critical of the dominant ideology to gung-ho celebrations of **white patriarchal capitalism**, often expressed through the era's most successful filmmaking formula, the **nostalgic Hollywood blockbuster**.

The shift from countercultural tendencies to support of the dominant ideology can easily be seen in the continuing careers of the Film School Brats. Many of these filmmakers quickly fell into patterns comparable to the classical Hollywood **studio system**. While American Zoetrope was conceived as a communal effort, for example, Coppola soon took over as the reigning mogul. Also, unlike those working in underground or avant-garde cinemas, independent fictional filmmakers were still interested in making money. Indeed, while independent filmmakers often try to do things differently from the major studios, they still work within the general industrial system. Warner Brothers, for example, had originally financed the founding of American Zoetrope, making the supposedly revolutionary group dependent on Hollywood money from the outset. Zoetrope would close and reopen repeatedly over the next decades as various studios gave or withdrew support. In consequence, most of this new generation of filmmakers increasingly abandoned radical experimentation in subject matter and technique and tried to make commercial hits.

The huge success of many of these films (such as *The Godfather* [1972], *Jaws* [1975], and *Star Wars* [1977]) signaled a resurrection of escapist moviegoing and pulled Hollywood out of its financial slump. The structure of this **New Hollywood** – whose most visible figures were creative producer-directors such as Steven Spielberg, George Lucas, and Francis Ford Coppola – allowed most of the Hollywood studios to maintain their power within the industry via **distribution** and marketing. The success of these first few nostalgic Hollywood blockbusters encouraged filmmakers to make more movies like them. Thus they gave rise to myriad sequels and copy-cat films, all of which purported to be "good old-fashioned entertainment." Such a return to conventional genres and formulas quickly eliminated any criticism of capitalism or economic disparity. Instead, in the mid-1970s, as part of the nostalgic impetus, the Horatio Alger myth was dusted off and repackaged. Films like *Rocky* (1976) and *Saturday Night Fever* (1977) used vaguely realist styles to retell stories of the American Dream. In both films (and many others like them), a working-class man makes a better life for himself through sheer determination and hard work, with little-to-no discussion of the institutionalized factors that, in the real world, work to inhibit such mobility.

Interestingly, both *Rocky* and *Saturday Night Fever* center on Italian American protagonists. By linking their class status to their national/ethnic identity, the films affirm that the Horatio Alger myth can and does work for all Americans, regardless of race or ethnicity. In this way, American popular culture promotes free market capitalism as the answer to racial inequality (and not as a cause or byproduct of it). It is now not unusual for Hollywood to tell Horatio Alger stories about people of color, in films like *Trading Places* (1983) or *The Pursuit of Happyness* (2006). However, such films also tend to disguise class issues as racial/ethnic ones. This is a noticeable trend in films made since the mid-1970s, as Hollywood films repeatedly construct stereotypical images of American poverty as endemic to racial/ethnic communities. While certainly racism has contributed to poverty in those communities, what is often missing from Hollywood films is consistent representation of poor *white* characters. The effects of this are multiple. On the one hand, it allows racists the chance to rationalize poverty as being the fault of those affected by it, and not the result of racism institutionalized in capitalist practice. On the other, it keeps a consideration of class hidden beneath racial and racist imagery. For example, a few years before *Rocky* and *Saturday Night Fever*, **blaxploitation** films had regularly pointed out economic discrimination faced by African Americans. *Superfly* (1972), for example, pivots on the fact that money is needed to escape ghetto life. However, rather than being understood as a movie about class (as it might have been if the story focused on white characters), the film was instead mostly understood as being about race. Interestingly, the gangster film formula used in *Superfly* almost always focuses on a non-white protagonist. Thus, the discourse on capitalism occurring in these films is obscured because the discourse on race or ethnicity is so much easier to recognize.

When Hollywood does use white characters to discuss class issues in America, the films tend to focus on poor *rural* whites, people who are often dismissed with the epithet **white trash**. This can been seen occurring in late 1970s comedies and dramas about the New South. The **New South** was a term used to describe the results of the economic resurgence that occurred during this era in the Southern half of the nation. This resurgence took place primarily because Northern businesses were moving there in search of less state regulation and fewer organized unions, developments which created a new working class of poor white Southerners. Low comedies such as *Smokey and the Bandit* (1977), *Convoy* (1978), *Every Which Way But Loose* (1978), and *Take This Job and Shove It* (1981) showed white working-class men of the New South battling the establishment (represented by bosses, politicians, and the police) in order to maintain their livelihood and masculine dignity. As usual in Hollywood films, though, it is not the system itself that is to blame for the hardships these men encounter, but rather a few corrupt individuals who abuse it for personal gain.

Probably the most serious and well-regarded film of this New South trend was *Norma Rae* (1979). Based on a true story, this film tells the story of a young Southern woman (played by Sally Field, who won an Oscar in the part) who works in a textile factory. Norma Rae becomes politicized when a union tries to organize the local workers. Filmed on location, *Norma Rae* uses a strongly realist style in order to expose the harshness of factory working conditions and the low standard of living the workers must endure. Like *Salt of the Earth*, *Norma Rae* also dramatizes how fear and distrust among different social minorities can and does keep the working class divided. For example, the white Baptist workers must learn to overcome their distrust of the Jewish union organizer, and the film shows that both black and white workers are needed to make the union strong. The film especially emphasizes that labor struggles involve women as well as men, and that traditional notions of "a woman's place" can weaken collective working-class strength. Sometimes such racial/ethnic/gender strife is encouraged by those in power. In *Norma Rae*, the executives at the cotton mill try to derail unionizing efforts by spreading rumors that a union would take jobs away from white laborers and give them to black workers. (This is still a common ploy of racist politicians who frighten poor white Americans into voting for them by convincing them that they will protect their jobs from being "stolen" by undeserving non-white people.) The movie thus emphasizes how racism and other social "isms" can be and have been exploited to keep citizens of the lower classes from finding a common cause.

Norma Rae, along with a handful of other films (*The China Syndrome* [1979], *Silkwood* [1983]), proved to be the last gasp of a more socially concerned, class-conscious era of Hollywood cinema. Instead, nostalgic Hollywood blockbusters, including films that revived the Horatio Alger myth, proved to be the most popular films of the 1980s and 1990s. *Raiders of the Lost Ark* (1981) and a myriad other adventure films focused on the chase for valuable treasures. Ostentatious wealth and "good" greed were on display once again in films like *Arthur* (1981), *Class* (1981), and *Risky Business* (1983). *Flashdance* (1983) and *Working Girl* (1988) were typical Horatio Alger narratives, this time about working-class women finding romance with their bosses while making their career dreams come true. The popular film *Footloose* (1984) took place in an economically depressed working-class town, yet the film seems to blame one conservative preacher for the town's problems. Furthermore, the solution to the town's economic woes seems to be consumerism – the teenage hero encourages people to buy records, clothes, and other things in defiance of the preacher's dictates. However, where these people find money in their budgets to acquire these things is left purposely vague.

These films and many others of the era reflected a shift toward conspicuous materialism in the nation's culture, a shift that was also reflected by the election of President Ronald Reagan in 1980. An actor during the classical Hollywood era,

Based on a true story, *Norma Rae* (1979) starred Sally Field as a working woman who fought for unionization at a Southern textiles plant.
Norma Rae, copyright © 1979, 20th Century-Fox

Reagan promoted the American Dream relentlessly, and implied that anyone who found problems in American society was being unpatriotic. The Reagan presidency began during a severe recession, and the White House's economic strategy to cope with the recession was quickly dubbed **Reaganomics.** This plan basically revolved around the idea that spending lots of money would stimulate the economy, as in *Footloose*. Federally, the national debt soared as the government practiced heavy deficit spending. The deficit also grew due to increased tax cuts, which went mainly to the wealthy and to big corporations, under the theory that financial health for the richest would eventually "trickle down" to the middle and lower classes. Big businesses and corporations were also deregulated through a series of new laws and initiatives that removed federal guidelines on trade, pollution, and corporate mergers. Across culture-at-large, Reaganomics encouraged individuals to indulge in conspicuous consumption, and contributed to the rise of the yuppie. A number of common catch phrases of the era, such as "greed is good" or "the person who dies with the most toys wins," revalued ostentatious materialism. Throughout the decade, the gap between the richest and poorest Americans continued to grow.

Just as the 1930s had Frank Capra as its predominant cinematic proponent of the American Dream, the 1980s had writer-director **John Hughes**. Aiming mainly at younger audiences (whom the studios had calculated were the viewers with the most "disposable income"), Hughes created hip, wisecracking comedy/dramas that upheld notions of <u>rugged individualism</u> and class mobility for a new generation. Films like *The Breakfast Club* (1985), *Pretty in Pink* (1986), and *Some Kind of Wonderful* (1987) showed working-class teenagers lifting themselves out of their situation and finding acceptance and happiness. While sometimes mentioning that being rich and having lots of nice things did not necessarily make someone happy, or characterizing upper-class teens as snobs, Hughes's films celebrated the pleasures of consumerism. Molly Ringwald's character in *Pretty in Pink* may learn that the poor boy who has a crush on her has some inner worth – but she still chooses the rich boy at the end of the film. The rich best friend in *Ferris Bueller's Day Off* (1986) may have issues with his father, but the film also invites viewers to desire his father's Ferrari.

In contrast to John Hughes's output are the films of writer-director **John Sayles**. Unlike most of the Film School Brats, who started with independent ideals and gradually succumbed to the demands of the box office, Sayles began writing low-budget horror films and used his minor successes (and production experience) to move into more personal and socially conscious independent filmmaking. His first directorial effort, *The Return of the Secaucus Seven* (1980), examined how a group of former 1960s leftists maintained (or did not maintain) their radical ideals. (This film predates the bigger-budgeted, less-politicized Hollywood version of the same story, *The Big Chill* [1981].) Other Sayles films, such as *The Brother from Another Planet* (1984), *Matewan* (1987), *Eight Men Out* (1988), *City of Hope* (1991), *Lone Star* (1996), *Limbo* (1999), *Sunshine State* (2002), and *Honeydripper* (2007), continued to focus on class (as well as race, gender, and sexuality). Interestingly, Sayles's scripts are often structured around multiple protagonists, giving equal weight to many characters' viewpoints and desires. This structure runs counter to both the conventional individual hero of **classical Hollywood narrative form** and the capitalist promulgation of rugged individualism. His films depict a complex world in which the social categories of race, class, gender, and sexuality interact and interrelate. As such, they are a more accurate description of America on film than are most formulaic Hollywood movies.

Although the country's growing deficit threatened a new recession at the end of the 1980s, capitalism was further promoted as "winning" major ideological victories. Chiefly, Reagan's strategy of spending more on weapons than the Soviet Union did seemed to hasten its collapse, and capitalism was touted as having "beaten" communism. Nevertheless, the deficit was making some people worry that the latest generation would spend their lives paying off the debts incurred by their parents' generation. Images of "downwardly mobile" young adults or slackers became prevalent during the early 1990s in films like *Singles* (1992), *Reality Bites* (1994), and, appropriately, *Slacker* (1991). Disillusioned with the rampant materialism of the 1980s, slackers showed their abandonment of the American Dream by holding

Titanic (1997) is a film filled with class issues that are swept aside in favor of an epic love story and computer-generated special effects.
Titanic, dir. James Cameron, copyright © 1997, 20th Century-Fox and Paramount

non-demanding jobs instead of pursuing careers, listening to grunge music instead of pre-packaged pop songs, and wearing used clothing instead of the latest expensive fashions. However, by the mid-1990s, computers and the Internet were fueling another burst of economic growth. Slackers who had "goofed around" with computers were suddenly "dot-com millionaires." By the end of the Clinton presidency, the federal government was working with a budget surplus rather than a deficit. And as the millennium approached, the few cinematic representations of class struggle that made it to the screen seemed to take place, as usual, in other countries and/or in other eras. *Titanic* (1997), the most economically successful film of all time (as of this writing), places class division safely in the 1910s – and even then downplays any potential exploration of the topic in favor of epic Hollywood romance and special effects disaster scenes. Indeed, the story itself is even framed by a search for a valuable diamond necklace, a narrative device that seems to imply that acquiring wealth is the only reason why anyone today would even care about the sinking of the *Titanic* in the first place.

Case Study: *Bulworth* (1998)

Bulworth presents one of the most outspoken critiques of American capitalism that has ever been made in a Hollywood feature film. The movie was a personal project of Hollywood film legend Warren Beatty, who conceived the story, co-wrote the screenplay, co-produced the film, and directed it himself. Beatty's status in Hollywood helped him to get the film made, and he was even able to get 20th Century-Fox to distribute it fairly widely. Beatty had become a star in the 1960s, and he should be considered part of the Hollywood counterculture that briefly tried to change mainstream filmmaking in that era. He starred in *Bonnie and Clyde* and *McCabe and Mrs Miller*, and later directed and starred in *Reds* (1981), a film about American socialist John Reed. Beatty's film *Bulworth* uses dark humor and satire to expose the socio-political and cultural links between class and race, and demonstrates how racism is often used to mask or mute class issues. The film also voices a forceful critique of contemporary American corporate capitalism (including the media), specifically underlining how its influence has corrupted the democratic process itself.

Beatty stars in the film as Senator Jay Bulworth, a cynical politician battling to win a Democratic primary in California. The film quickly reveals that Bulworth has lost an enormous amount of money in a bad stock market decision, and in order to provide for his daughter, he takes out a ten million dollar life insurance policy – and then hires an assassin to kill him. Thinking that nothing matters any more, the Senator begins to say whatever he feels like saying, instead of the carefully planned speeches and comments prepared by his re-election staff. The story shifts when Bulworth starts to enjoy voicing his honest opinions, and the rest of the film shows him trying to put a stop on the hit while pursuing his new and shockingly forthright outlook. In various interviews and debates, the Senator points out how corporate interests contribute to political campaigns in order to get politicians to take their side on issues such as welfare, the environment, and free trade. The film focuses most directly on health-care reform, and the attempts by large insurance companies to keep the federal government from nationalizing health care, a development that would effectively reduce the profits earned by various health-related industries. The Senator himself, before his transformation, had been guilty of accepting favors from the insurance companies in return for votes against nationalized health care.

However, *Bulworth* is not an experimental or underground film, and so various elements are used to soften its critique. While it criticizes "big insurance," no specific company is named in the film, and although the insurance companies are implicated in the tragic finale of the picture, the actual extent of their involvement is also not directly shown. The tone of the film is comedic, which possibly blunts some of the political barbs. Beatty portrays the Senator as a bumbling fool, trying to talk with food in his mouth, or falling into a fountain. Beatty also makes Bulworth look ridiculous when he starts to adopt black urban culture as his personal style. Furthermore, Bulworth's actions, and his political statements, are supposedly tied to his nervous breakdown, which again might allow some viewers to merely dismiss his remarks as nonsense. Lastly (and importantly), although the film strongly criticizes the privilege and power of white male wealth and privilege, the picture itself revolves around yet another white heterosexual upper-middle-class able-bodied male as a potential leader and visionary – with the oppressed to follow as disciples. This is most strongly felt in the presence of Beatty's co-star Halle Berry, playing a lower-class inner-city African American female who starts as Bulworth's antagonist but becomes his willing follower.

Nonetheless, even with these structural drawbacks, *Bulworth* consistently attempts to stay true to its political commitment. Even the film's final credit listing eradicates

Conclusion: Corporate Hollywood and Labor Today

Although the film industry today has changed a great deal from the classical Hollywood studio system, the differences are mostly in degree and not in kind. Just as Hollywood was dependent on major banking institutions during the 1930s,

These shots of *Bulworth* (1998) show star Warren Beatty as a wealthy senator in crisis and a champion for the urban ghetto population.
Bulworth, dir. Warren Beatty, copyright © 1998, 20th Century-Fox. Photos: Sidney Baldwin

"class divisions" between stars and bit players by listing every speaking actor in alphabetical order. In the final scene of the film, a black street philosopher, played by socialist theorist Amiri Baraka, turns his gaze to the camera and says to the audience, "You got to be the spirit, not just a ghost." Ending the film this way exhorts the viewer to take responsibility, become conscious of the issues that corporate capitalism would rather obscure, and enact some form of resistance. However, almost exemplifying Senator Bulworth's contention that the corporate-owned telecommunications industry attempts to squelch honest and hard-hitting discussions of political issues, *Bulworth* was released by 20th Century-Fox with very little fanfare. Studio representatives claimed that the film was hard to sell. This was no doubt true, since the film is specifically criticizing Hollywood's practice of turning issues into easily packaged products. Distributed in the summer of 1998, *Bulworth* garnered many positive critical reviews, but was quickly lost amid the onslaught of the major nostalgic Hollywood blockbusters of the season, films such as *Godzilla*, *Armageddon*, and *Doctor Dolittle*.

so today it is dependent upon its corporate conglomerate ownership. Practices of **vertical integration**, **saturation booking** and **advertising**, **synergy**, and cross-promotion all help keep the Hollywood industry stabilized and dominant. The development of new distribution technologies has also increased Hollywood's control over American film. With the rise of cable TV, home video, and most recently the Internet, Hollywood executives are finding and controlling new exhibition outlets for their products. And while the studios and producers make more and more money through these new outlets, little-to-no compensation is being offered to the myriad other people who worked on these films. The Writers Guild of America and the Screen Actors Guild have had to strike or threaten strikes in order to get their share of these new profit revenues. Other, less powerful workers' groups are still mostly excluded from these ongoing royalties. New technologies have also affected film labor through the increased reliance on **computer generated imagery** (**CGI**). While CGI has created a number of new jobs in optical effects, it also eliminates the need to hire numerous extras, set builders, and costume makers. Today, any given Hollywood action blockbuster (such as *Titanic*, *The Mummy* [2000], or *The Lord of the Rings* [2001]) can computer generate armies of extras that can be used and reused without having to be paid.

The major Hollywood corporations still reign over the industry through their domination of distribution. While some independent production companies do attempt to champion quirky or offbeat films, the filmmakers that want to make the most money know they must distribute through Hollywood channels – which means they must fashion their films according to the typical Hollywood formulas. Furthermore, independent film companies are increasingly being absorbed into the Hollywood majors, and it is often hard to tell an independent film from a Hollywood one. Technically, George Lucas is an independent filmmaker, but his Lucasfilm Company functions much like Paramount or Disney, making commercial motion pictures, with George Lucas himself unquestionably in charge as the studio mogul. This type of independent production also creates problems for organized labor. No longer tied to individual studios, film workers now function as free agents, signing new contracts from project to project. Independent producers are expected to agree to union demands for set wages and work hours, but in fact, many productions purposely avoid hiring unionized employees in order to cut costs. Another major strategy for cutting costs has been to shoot films outside Hollywood in areas where unions have less strength. The ascendance of such <u>runaway productions</u> since the 1950s has exploited film workers abroad, people who get paid less for more hours and are expected to do more hazardous labor. For example, while *Titanic* vaguely addresses issues of class division, the climactic sinking of the ship was shot in waters off the coast of Mexico, where local extras were forced to stay in water for hours in the middle of the night, and a number were injured.

The **hegemonic negotiation** of capitalism in America continues to respond to and ameliorate disturbances in our national economy. For example, the "dot-com" boom of the 1990s failed to live up to its hype, and major corporations failed or were downsized. Many people found themselves unemployed. Mismanagement and greed, which flourished under federal policies of deregulation, in many cases contributed to these corporate failures. The September 11, 2001, terrorist attacks on America also slowed the economy, as many Americans scaled back their spending habits. The administration of George W. Bush responded much as the Reagan administration had: with tax cuts for corporations and the wealthy, as well as an increase in deficit spending. Although some Americans expressed anger at the revelations of shady dealings of corrupt corporations such as Enron, a potentially larger protest of national economic policy was supplanted by a wave of patriotism after 9/11.

Certain films did attempt to address some of the era's economic issues. *The Insider* (1999), about the powerful tobacco industry, and *Erin Brockovich* (2000), about a corrupt public utilities corporation, were based on true stories and won multiple Oscars. *North Country* (2005) and *Michael Clayton* (2007) continued this trend, making heroes out of characters fighting corporate corruption. Several recent documentaries have also tackled the effects of deregulated multinational corporations on the average American worker and consumer. *Enron: The Smartest Guys in the Room* (2005) explores the behind-the-scenes hubris and villainy that led to that company's collapse. Michael Moore's *Sicko* (2007) is about the health-care industry and how it often fails the people it is allegedly designed to serve. *Who Killed the Electric Car?* (2006) is an eye-opening film that suggests that backroom dealings between the oil industry, the automobile industry, and the politicians they control have kept America from innovating safer, cheaper, and less-polluting forms of transportation. More generally, *The Corporation* (2004) examines the legal and social history of the corporation itself as a business model, revealing that corporations often have the same rights as (or even greater ones than) do actual human beings.

Yet, for the most part, American popular culture has continued its obsession with wealth and materialism. Rather than discussing lack of access to health care, the loss of worker pension programs, or the still-sizeable unemployment figures, American citizens have increasingly focused on the comings and goings of ultra-rich celebrities. While some figures (such as Paris Hilton) came from long-wealthy families, others (such as Britney Spears) were newly rich, and thus provided a new generation of Horatio Alger figures. Many Americans not only followed the daily exploits of these celebrities, but also strove to follow in their footsteps by chasing after immediate economic success and fame through lotteries, gambling, and/or reality TV series such as *American Idol* (2002–) or *Deal or No Deal* (2005–). Such dreams not only revive the Horatio Alger myth but rework the notion of rugged individualism – with less emphasis on the hard work one has to do to succeed, but still emphasizing individual gain rather than a shared struggle against systemic economic disparity.

Hollywood films have also responded to this growing trend. Reflecting the connections between gender and class in this era, a number of **chick flicks** focus on a Cinderella-figure entering the urban high life. While films like *The Princess Diaries* (2001), *The Prince and Me* (2004), and *The Devil Wears Prada* (2006), and TV shows like *Ugly Betty* (2006–), often assert that one's inner integrity is more important than material wealth, the films are also marketed to audiences as a chance to see what living the lush life is like. Chick flicks, though, are not the only indicators of this new "quick-fix" Horatio Alger era, as the Adam Sandler remake of *Mr Deeds* (2002) and the aptly named *Cinderella Man* (2005) attest. Major Hollywood blockbusters continue to revolve around literal treasure hunts, as in the *Pirates of the Caribbean* franchise (2003, 2006, 2007), or the *National Treasure* films (2004, 2007).

Although President Bush claimed the post-9/11 recession had ended by 2004, many parts of the American economy did not bounce back. The strongest sector was the housing market, as real estate values soared and new mortgage practices allowed more people the opportunity to buy a home. But by the end of the Bush presidency, the housing market bubble was collapsing, taking with it a number of banks that had approved of risky loans, and new fears of recession loomed. As of this writing, it is too soon to tell what impact these developments will have on American filmmaking. However, the nation has survived depressions and recessions, cycles of boom and bust, and will probably do so in the future. The related myths, formulas, and formations of capitalist ideology, which Hollywood and other aspects of pop culture have promulgated throughout the last century, will undoubtedly continue to be pressed into service. Hollywood will continue to validate the American Dream.

Questions for Discussion

1 Can you think of any recent Hollywood films that make a hero or heroine out of a very rich or a very poor person? If so, do the films celebrate the upper or lower classes, or do they espouse the superiority of being middle-class?

2 Name some other films where class intersects with race, ethnicity, gender, and/or ability. Do the films actually deal with class issues, or are economic issues "hidden" by ideas or concerns about race, ethnicity, gender, and/or ability?

3 How truly "free" is our nation if all of its media artifacts are produced and/or regulated by a handful of business conglomerates? What does "free speech" mean in our contemporary culture? Do some people have more "free speech" than others?

Further Reading

Biskind, Peter. *Easy Riders, Raging Bulls: How the Sex-Drugs-and-Rock'n'Roll Generation Saved Hollywood.* New York: Simon and Schuster, 1998.

Ceplair, Larry and Steven Englund. *The Inquisition in Hollywood.* Los Angeles: University of California Press, 1983.

Grainge, Paul. *Brand Hollywood: Selling Entertainment in a Global Media Age.* London and New York: Routledge, 2008.

Holmlund, Chris and Justin Wyatt. *Contemporary American Independent Film: From the Margins to the Mainstream.* London and New York: Routledge, 2005.

James, David E. *Allegories of Cinema: American Film in the Sixties.* Princeton: University of Princeton Press, 1989.

Lewis, Jon, ed. *The New American Cinema.* Durham, NC, and London: Duke University Press, 1998.

Neale, Steve and Murray Smith, eds. *Contemporary Hollywood Cinema.* London and New York: Routledge, 1998.

Quart, Leonard and Albert Auster. *American Film and Society Since 1945.* Westport, CT, and London: Praeger, 1991.

Ryan, Michael and Douglas Kellner. *Camera Politica: The Politics and Ideology of Contemporary Hollywood Film.* Bloomington: Indiana University Press, 1988.

Wasko, Janet. *Hollywood in the Information Age.* Austin: University of Texas Press, 1994.

Further Screening

Force of Evil (1948)
Salt of the Earth (1953)
On the Waterfront (1954)
Silk Stockings (1957)
Easy Rider (1969)
A Woman under the Influence (1974)
Rocky (1976)

Norma Rae (1979)
Silkwood (1983)
Matewan (1987)
Sunshine State (2002)
8 Mile (2002)
North Country (2005)

Part IV
GENDER
AND AMERICAN FILM

INTRODUCTION TO PART IV:

What is Gender?

Preceding chapters of this book have examined how Hollywood films have represented issues of race and class, and how those images have changed over the years in relation to broader social and industrial events. In the next several chapters, we turn to an examination of how American film represents (and has represented) sexual difference – how it depicts what it means to be a man or a woman. As it is a fundamental ideological tenet of **patriarchy** that men and masculinity are privileged over women and femininity, it should come as no surprise that Hollywood film has always privileged men and male roles over women and female roles. Partly this is due to the perseverance of **classical Hollywood narrative form**, which has always worked to privilege men as the active and powerful heroes of Hollywood film, while relegating women to the role of love interest waiting to be rescued. The other formal axes of film, including cinematography, editing, and sound design, and especially visual design (costume, makeup, hair, and lighting), construct images of how women and men are supposed to *be*. Indeed, most of the elements employed by Hollywood films to demarcate sex roles are also broad cultural ones, as men and women in our society routinely make themselves up and select costumes for daily life, much as actors and actresses do for the parts they play. Thus, for over 100 years, movies have frequently defined what is beautiful, what is sexy, what is manly, and how men and women should "properly" react in any given situation.

As with other social groups examined in this book, there have been tremendous gains since the early twentieth century for the idea of equality between men and women. Historically, however, there has been a great deal of discrimination based upon sex roles in America, both within the Hollywood industry and in culture-at-large. A division of labor between the sexes was a cultural "norm" of American business life until very recently: women rarely had a chance to advance beyond supporting secretarial jobs, as powerful men promoted other men into more advanced positions. Today, some American women would probably say they feel they have equal rights and privileges. Thanks to the activism of previous generations, women today can go to college and enter most careers if they choose to do so. There are women executives in Hollywood and most other industries, female politicians, and seemingly no limits on what women can hope to achieve. Yet an actual survey of the country in terms of sex roles still shows great disparities between women's percentage of the population (approximately 51 percent) and their representation in Hollywood film and in other social institutions. According to some recent surveys, there are still twice as many men on Hollywood screens as there are women. A quick look into the boardrooms and legislative bodies of the United States reveals that women comprise nowhere near half their memberships. Why are women still frequently underrepresented in both the workplace and popular culture?

Part of the answer to that complex question lies in the nature of **hegemonic patriarchy** itself. While women gained the right to vote (in 1920) and have more and more opportunities in all aspects of society, there is still a strong cultural expectation that women should prefer a domestic life – that women should want to stay at home and raise children. In reality, many women in today's economy choose to work outside the home while others need to work to support themselves and/or their families. Today's women are thus often expected to have careers *and* to be full-time homemakers, a dual demand that has rarely been placed on men (although more and more single-parent men of our era are finding themselves in that situation). Also, because sex roles and the social expectations that go along with them are such an intimate part of our everyday lives, discrimination based on sex may be subtler and harder to "see" than discrimination based on race or class. Such bias is often called **sexism**, the belief that one sex is inherently superior to the other. Sexism is pervasive in our society, and usually is expressed as the patriarchal assumption that men are more capable or "better" human beings than are women. Sexism, like **racism**, may also work in reverse – there are some women who feel that being a woman is essentially better than being a man. Still, those beliefs are usually formed in response to historical and ongoing discrimination against women and do little to challenge patriarchal assumptions and institutions.

To understand these concepts more clearly, we need to introduce the difference between the terms **sex** and **gender**. The word **sex** can refer to sexual acts (as in "having sex"), but it is also used to describe the biological or chromosomal make-up of human beings. Science tells us that people of the male sex are male because they have an XY chromosome. People of the female sex carry an XX chromosome. (Indeed, every human embryo starts out as female until the Y chromosome "turns on" and helps shape some fetuses into males.) The word **gender**, on the other hand, refers to the social, historical, and cultural roles that we think of as being associated with either the male or female sex. While sex may be defined by the terms "male" or "female," gender is best defined by the terms **masculinity** and **femininity** – how the male and female sexes are characterized culturally. **Femininity** (as defined by patriarchy) is usually associated with being small, quiet, passive, emotional, nurturing, non-aggressive, dependent, and weak. **Masculinity** (as defined by patriarchy) is usually associated with being large, loud, and active, with non-emotional aggression and strong leadership abilities.

For a great part of the twentieth century, most people (including medical professionals) confused sex and gender, assuming that all social differences between men and women were the result of biological hardwiring. Patriarchal discourse still tries to claim that being of the male sex automatically means being of masculine gender, and that being of the female sex automatically means being of feminine gender. By equating being female with being feminine (dependent and weak), patriarchal culture is able to discourage women from gaining power of their own. When people believe that gender roles are biologically determined and not **socially constructed**, they are less likely to challenge the status quo, and thus patriarchal interests remain uncontested. While most scholars today believe that there is a biological basis for some differences between the sexes, they also acknowledge that most of the lived, everyday differences between men and women are due to culturally constructed gender roles. In other words, a person's sex is formed by genetics, while a person's gender is *learned*.

Sex	Gender
Male	Masculinity
Female	Femininity

The first column lists two sex identities, based on biological factors. The second column lists two gender identities, based on social factors.

Developmental studies with children have shown that by the age of six or so, most human beings have developed an inner sense of themselves as either male or female. This is termed our **gender identity**. We get ideas about what it means to be a boy or a girl from **ideological** institutions such as the family, the schools, other children, and the media. This happens both consciously and unconsciously, and it may begin in the first minutes of life if we are wrapped in either a pink or a blue blanket. From that moment on, girls are expected to like pink, be quiet, and prefer to play with dolls. Boys are taught that "real" boys choose blue colors, engage in rough-and-tumble activities, and play with toy trucks. Of course, not all girls like to play with Barbies and not all boys like to play with Tonkas. Children who do not confirm to expected gender roles may be teased by classmates and shunned by families. Men who are physically weak or emotional have been the butt of jokes, while strong women have often been demonized for being unfeminine. In this way, patriarchal culture insures the continuation of traditional gender roles, and of the sexist hierarchy inherent in them. A good illustration of this hierarchy can be found by comparing sensitive boys and tough girls. While both groups pose problems for patriarchal ideology, a sensitive boy will usually be teased and harassed much more than a girl who likes sports. A girl being masculine is a "step up" in the gender hierarchy, whereas a boy being sensitive is a "step down" to the level of the feminine, and must therefore be more harshly condemned.

Such shaping continues beyond childhood. Popular culture continually reinforces differences between men and women. Same-sex or **homosocial groups** like sports teams, fraternities and sororities, and even some classrooms, work to divide human beings into two camps on the basis of sex and gender expectations. Frequently such groups are overtly based on the assumption that male groups are better than female ones. Some people even go so far as to suggest there is a war between men and women: the common phrase "battle of the sexes" is indicative of that idea. The popular self-help craze of the 1990s, summed up in the title of the book *Men are From Mars, Women are From Venus*, even suggested that men and women were best understood as alien species from separate planets. Partly this binary opposition between our ideas of masculinity and femininity is necessary because socially and psychologically we tend to define one against the other. Just as we might define whiteness as not being black, or Asian, or Native American, we define masculinity as that which is not feminine. If being masculine is thought to be tough, then being feminine is thought to be tender. If masculinity is active, then femininity must be defined as passive. These binary oppositions that we use to define traditional gender can sometimes be **internalized** and lock us into very narrow roles that may not be good for us. For example, men who are afraid to admit their emotional feelings may silently suffer from depression because they feel they cannot talk about it. Women who want a career may accept being housewives because they feel that is what is expected of them.

Thus, gender is a concept deeply ingrained into our everyday lives and culture. It functions, like most ideologies, in both conscious and unconscious ways. Even the very words we use to communicate carry subtle gender biases. Some languages (such as French or Spanish) have "gendered" nouns, a situation that suggests a large network of meaning about what is masculine and/or feminine for a given culture. In English, we have separate pronouns for male and female (his, her) and a whole slew of words such as mail*man*, milk*man*, *man*hole, and *man*kind that obviously carry a sexist bias. Other aspects of gendered language are more subtle. Referring to men as "men" and women as "girls" (or "honey," or "baby," etc.) is another way that language itself can convey ideas about appropriate gender behaviors and the respect afforded to each. In yet another example, ships and cars are often spoken of as female, despite the fact that they are inanimate objects. Is this because they can be possessed by men and add to a man's prestige, the way some older men use younger women as "trophy" dates or wives? Perhaps you have heard the slogan "real men don't eat quiche." As a tiny, singular bit of popular culture, the saying works to define gender in powerful ways. It tells us that in the late twentieth century, quiche was considered a feminine food (perhaps because of its French connotations, or its constituent elements of milk and eggs), and that in order to be thought of as masculine, "real" men had better avoid it. (A big steak, on the other hand, is a meal for a "real" man.) Gender roles and expectations permeate our culture, language, and media in ways both subtle and obvious.

Chapter 10

WOMEN IN CLASSICAL HOLLYWOOD FILMMAKING

As a **capitalist** industry working within **hegemonic patriarchy**, it should not be surprising that the classical Hollywood **studio system** afforded special privileges to men, both in front of the camera as actors, and behind it as production personnel. **Classical Hollywood narrative form** dictated active and central roles for male characters, while most of the decisions made behind the cameras were also controlled by men. Men were the financial backers of the industry, the heads of studios and studio departments, and almost always the directors and producers of individual films. Before and during Hollywood's classical era (roughly the 1930s–50s), filmmakers often felt that women – *by their very nature* – were unsuited for these types of professional positions. Hollywood was not unique in this division of labor between the sexes; the rest of corporate America also believed that women were better suited to jobs as secretaries and receptionists rather than managers or division heads. Consequently, women who wanted to work in film production were often relegated to "**feminine**" jobs as secretaries, minor assistants, and "script girls." (A script girl's job was to aid the film director by overseeing and maintaining continuity between shots.)

However, a close examination of the history of American cinema before and during its classical era reveals that these **gendered** expectations were not absolute. A few women did become motion picture directors and producers, and there were also women who had successful careers as screenwriters. Of course, female movie stars and actresses were more numerous and better known than those few women working behind the camera. Through the characterizations of those stars and actresses, one can examine the evolving types and meanings of femininity throughout the first half of the twentieth century. For example, what was considered appropriate feminine behavior was often different in one era from that in another: what it meant to be a woman varied from decade to decade (as it still does). These changes, both behind the camera and in front of it, provide ample evidence of how **hegemonic** notions of gender were negotiated and reinforced in American cinema from its inception until the 1950s.

Images of Women in Early Cinema

The images of women in early American cinema were mostly drawn from the gender roles and representational codes of the Victorian era (so named for England's Queen Victoria, who ruled from 1837 to 1901). The "good" or socially approved Victorian middle-class woman was a paragon of virtue. As a young woman, she was childlike, and frequently associated with innocence, purity, and the need to be protected. She was often "put on a pedestal" and worshipped by the men in her life, namely her father and her brothers. When she got to be a certain age, she would be married off to a suitable young man; in many cases, this marriage would be an arranged one between families and not necessarily take into consideration the feelings of either husband or wife. This young woman would then become a wife and mother – her devotion and loyalty would be transferred from her father to her husband. The middle-class Victorian woman's life was tightly controlled by these men. It was expected that she would not work outside the home, and indeed in middle-to-upper-class homes she was expected to have servants who would do the housework for her. Her most important task was to produce and raise children, yet a virtuous Victorian woman's **sexuality** would never be displayed in provocative clothing or words. She would be assumed to be a virgin when she married, and it was taboo even to suggest that she might have sexual interests or desires. Sex for procreation was her duty, not her pleasure. Her lord and master was her husband, and she had little chance of removing herself from that situation should it turn violent or abusive.

If one examines female roles in the earliest American films, one can see that "good" women are – like their Victorian models – usually virginal daughters who, if they work at all, do "women's work" such as sewing and cooking. They are rarely active participants in the narrative, except as victims or prizes. They sit and wait patiently for their husbands to return home to them. Frequently, they are associated with childlike behavior and small animals such as birds and squirrels, an editing trope that seems to suggest that women are naturally cute and defenseless. They need fathers and husbands to protect them from the sexual advances of other men. (If a man does manage to seduce a good woman, she often chooses her own death over such a disgrace.) Actresses such as **Lillian Gish** and **Mary Pickford** frequently embodied this type of Victorian heroine. Lillian Gish's fluttery mannerisms and batting eyelashes suggested she was a delicate flower, constantly in danger and needing the protection of a good man. Similarly, Mary Pickford's screen persona was of a small child-woman. Although many of Mary Pickford's girl-women were scrappy fighters, Hollywood set designers would construct oversize props and chairs for her to sit in to reinforce the idea she was childlike and innocent.

Victorian culture and early cinema also promulgated images of "bad" women, usually defined as such because they were (unlike "good" women) explicitly sexualized. Hundreds of plays, magazine stories, and early films routinely presented "loose" or "fallen" women (who had perhaps had a child out of wedlock) as immoral and tragic. Within these narratives, such women were thrown into the street and ostracized

Mary Pickford, affectionately know by her fans as Little Mary, often embodied concepts of Victorian femininity in early Hollywood movies. Unidentified publicity photo, authors' personal collection

from society. These texts taught severe **ideological** lessons to young women of the era: to be sexual outside of marriage most often led to ruin. In judging women according to their sexual propriety (or its lack), Victorian culture and early film simplistically divided women into two groups. This cultural construct defining women on the basis of their sexuality has been dubbed the **virgin–whore complex,** and it still exists to various extents in today's contemporary culture. Many men feel that "good" girls should be virginal and that men should not marry a woman too free with her sexuality. Yet American men have also clearly desired the freely sexualized woman and taken advantage of her situation for both sexual pleasure and capitalist profit. The virgin–whore dichotomy of the Victorian era is represented in many early American films and continues to linger within the representational codes of classical and even contemporary Hollywood cinema.

The Industrial Revolution was also having profound effects on women both in real life and on movie screens. As more and more of the nation's population resided in and around big cities, many younger, unmarried women entered the workforce. With electrified machines now doing much of the physical labor, women were increasingly considered capable of performing certain jobs. Women found employment not only as secretaries and store clerks, but also as factory workers. With these new jobs, they ostensibly earned their own income. Often, however, this money was handed over to the head of the household (that is, the father) to help support the entire family. Yet many young women did have more and more discretionary income to go to amusement parks, restaurants, and the movies – sometimes even without a male escort! Many people were bothered by this small surge in women's independence, fearing that it would upset the "natural" balance of female dependence on men. Even more shocking were the people of this era who called for equal rights for women, advancing the cause of **feminism**. One of these activists, Rebecca West, wrote as early as 1913, "I myself have never been able to find out precisely what feminism is: I only know that people call me a feminist whenever I express sentiments that differentiate me from a doormat." Mainstream American society worked to demonize this **first wave** of feminism in many ways, branding some of these pioneering women criminal radicals or madwomen. Some were deported from the country, while others were imprisoned in institutions or silenced in other ways.

The era's moral reformers castigated not only feminist activists but also the less radical working girls who were having fun on their own in the big city. A number of people argued that these women were destroying the foundations of civilization by abandoning traditional gendered behaviors in order to pursue new pleasures. They also warned that these women were placing themselves in physical danger from pimps, kidnappers, and drug pushers – criminals who supposedly thrived in such disreputable places as amusement parks and movie houses. The early **nickelodeons** and movie theaters, as mentioned previously (see chapters 2 and 8), were considered disreputable and unsavory – and thus not a place in which any respectable woman might be found. As if to reinforce those ideas, a number of early feature-length films such as *Traffic in Souls* (1913) and *Inside the White Slave Traffic* (1914) warned female moviegoers that their newfound urban independence could easily lead to kidnapping and forced prostitution. The fact that this possible situation was dubbed **white slavery** by the popular culture of the era underscores certain racial and capitalist ideologies: white women (being the "best" type of woman) were allegedly more desirable and thus more valuable as commodities or as victims. Furthermore, the image of a white woman being enslaved to a non-white man (which is what this rhetoric implied) was especially inflammatory, projecting generic male desire onto a non-white (and therefore more bestial) racial group.

White slave films were not the only racially inflected cinematic image used to negotiate women's "proper place" place during the 1910s. For example, the stereotype of the **vamp** was also very common. The vamp was a dark and exotic woman who used her potent sexuality to control white men, often leading them to their doom. ("Good" girls were more likely to be represented as blonde and blue-eyed.) Vamp was short for vampire, a monster that drains the life blood out of his or her victims. Thus the vamp – a sexually active woman often of another **race, ethnic-**

Theda Bara, whose studio-given name was allegedly devised by mixing up the letters in the phrase "Arab Death," was early Hollywood's most famous vamp. Unidentified publicity photo, authors' personal collection

ity, or **nationality** – was figured as a predatory monster who drained men of their money and morals. In *The Birth of a Nation* (1915), the mulatto character Lydia is figured as evil not only because of her mixed racial status, but because she is intelligent and conniving and can wield sexual power over men. Early Hollywood's most famous vamp was **Theda Bara**, a dark-haired actress born in Ohio under the name Theodosia Goodman. Studio executives allegedly devised her movie name by reversing and scrambling the letters in the phrase "Arab Death," and she was promoted as a dark, exotic, and alluring beauty from another culture. As such, Theda Bara represented white patriarchal America projecting its sexual fantasies and desires upon a non-white or foreign figure, a trope that we have already seen at work in representations of Arab, African American, Asian, and Hispanic women (see chapters 3, 4, 6, and 7).

In 1920, the fight to gain equal rights for women scored a major success when their Constitutional right to vote, granted in 1918, finally came into force. Among the other successes of first wave feminism was yet another new type of woman – a young, urban, career-oriented woman who quickly became a cultural stereotype known as the **flapper**. The flapper rejected Victorian notions of what a woman was, and developed her own style. She wore shorter bobbed hair, with strands of pearls over plain, shorter dresses that deaccentuated her curves; she smoked and danced in public; and she even had sex outside of wedlock. While this initially seems a radical overthrow of the Victorian image of women, the flapper represents a **hegemonic negotiation** that allows new ideas to come into play but reaffirms concepts basic to keeping patriarchal capitalism in place. For example, a flapper's independence was chiefly defined by her freedom to buy things in order to reconfigure her personal style, and not by any kind of radical political critique: in most novels and films in which she appeared, the flapper was still out to find a husband. (Contemporary capitalism still works in similar ways, taking advantage of feminist sentiment by advertising that women can become liberated by purchasing certain products such as Virginia Slims cigarettes or Nike sports equipment.)

The flapper and the new openness about sexuality that she represented were depicted in many films of the era. Sex comedies such as Cecil B. DeMille's *Male and Female* (1919) and *Don't Change Your Husband* (1919) and Erich von Stroheim's *Foolish Wives* (1922) often implied that this new sexual morality would only lead to tragedy and death, but the flapper was an instant hit in films because of her vivacious and sexy attitude. Probably the most famous film flapper of the era was **Clara Bow**. In the film *It* (1927), based on a popular book of the same name, she cemented her image as the high-spirited, free-wheeling flapper and even became known as "The IT Girl." ("IT" was a euphemism for the flapper's magnetic energy and sexually free spirit.) However, Clara Bow's career was short-lived. As nasty rumors about her private life began to tarnish her public image, she suffered a series of mental and physical breakdowns. Acknowledging how the Hollywood studio system could actually destroy the lives of those it created and valorized, Bow once remarked that "being a sex symbol is a heavy load to carry, especially when one is tired, hurt, and bewildered." As for many Hollywood stars before and after her, the demands of playing a bigger-than-life construction of ideal femininity became a difficult chore for Clara Bow. Those demands and expectations, combined with the public's ever-more conservative leanings during the years of the **Great Depression**, eventually forced "The IT Girl" off the screen at the age of 28.

Early Female Filmmakers

As noted above, most American business concerns throughout the first half of the twentieth century were dominated and controlled by white men. Men were in control of the American film industry practically from its outset, as **Thomas Edison** and his cohorts worked to monopolize the new technology. Women at this time rarely had the economic power to bankroll a film company or indeed produce a single film project, unlike any number of male businessmen who invested in the new medium of motion pictures. Furthermore, traveling the country (or the

Clara Bow embodied the image of the 1920s flapper, a young woman who was much more sexually liberated than her Victorian predecessors. Unidentified publicity photo, authors' personal collection

world) with a camera and a projector, filming events and setting up screenings in new cities and towns, would have been impossible for most women of the era even to attempt. As cinema became a massive industry in the 1910s and 1920s, its potential for wealth and power led to a consolidation of male dominance under the classical Hollywood studio system. Yet, because filmmaking was such a new industry, during its first few decades what constituted a "**masculine**" job versus a "feminine" one was not always immediately apparent. Consequently, although it was still plainly a male-dominated environment, the slapdash organization of early filmmaking did afford some opportunities for some women to become filmmakers. Most of the women who did so were white, and in many cases they came from middle-to-upper-class backgrounds, a social position that facilitated their move into motion pictures. Historical evidence indicates that during these years it was much easier for a white woman to move into and excel within institutionalized film-making than it was for a man of color.

Film historians credit **Alice Guy-Blache** as the first to tell a fictional narrative on film, when, as a secretary at the French film studio Pathé, she was given a chance to use one of the cameras. Remarkably, she was also experimenting with sound film technology as early as 1903. Guy-Blache's success as writer, director, and cinema-tographer made her one of the most important filmmakers of early international cinema; she eventually moved to the United States and ran her own studio, Solax Pictures, during the 1910s. A number of female stars of that decade (including Mary Pickford and Lillian Gish) also gained enough power to organize their own production companies, and as early as 1912, at least 20 **independent film** companies were being run by women. These pioneering women in the early film industry worked to make film direction a socially acceptable position for women. They countered the idea that directing a film was necessarily a masculine job (one that needed a powerful leader commanding a mostly male crew) by arguing that a woman's femininity gave her the taste and artistry to create good films. Furthermore, they argued, a woman's motherly instincts made her ideal for getting a cast and crew to work together in harmony. Emphasizing both the all-round talent of these women and the less-regimented structure of early filmmaking, many female filmmakers fulfilled multiple roles in these productions. For example, Helen Gardner, a pro-minent screen star of the 1910s, produced, directed, wrote, and even designed the costumes for her films. Nell Shipman worked as a writer for Universal, and then produced, directed, and starred in her own independent films.

Lois Weber was probably the most successful and well-known female director of the silent era. Her films frequently dealt with issues of importance to women of the era, such as birth control, which was an important part of the fight for women's sexual and reproductive freedom. Some of Weber's films, such as *Where Are My Children?* (1916), tackled these issues in a straightforward way, arguing for the neces-sity of the availability of birth control information. Even making these films was a brave gesture, for at that time, any mention or discussion of birth control was con-sidered obscene in most areas of the United States. People were arrested and sent to prison for distributing literature on the subject. Within a few years, as the Hollywood industry consolidated itself under male control, such issues would be deemed inappropriate and banned from movie screens altogether. Lois Weber also helped the careers of other aspiring female filmmakers, hiring other women to write or perform other jobs within her productions. Throughout the next decade, female filmmakers in Hollywood formed a network of professional friendships that helped them navigate through an increasingly male-dominated domain.

Yet, as the industry streamlined itself into the studio system of production, oppor-tunities began to dwindle for female directors. Women working in film production were increasingly blocked from leadership positions and compartmentalized into traditionally feminine jobs such as secretaries and seamstresses. While makeup and costume design might be considered feminine jobs, the Hollywood makeup and costume departments were run by men. (It was not until the 1950s and 1960s that a woman, Edith Head, would gain fame as a Hollywood costume designer.) Women *were* able to maintain a presence as film editors, mainly because editing was initially not seen as creative work (but merely cutting and pasting) – although it could also be due to the perception that stitching shots together was similar to sewing. Mostly though, women remained in high demand as screenwriters. As part of the film industry's attempt to gain respectability, a number of studios hired female directors and screenwriters because they were thought to convey higher moral values. Many researchers now estimate that about half of all the films made in the United States during the 1910s and 1920s were written by women. **Anita Loos** is often considered the model of silent film scripting, famous for initiating a romantic yet slang-oriented style referred to as the "rosy-fingered dawn" school (after one of the era's typical title card clichés). Other major female screenwriters of the period include June Mathis, Bess Meredyth, and **Frances Marion**, who became the first person to win two Academy Awards in any field, and the highest-paid screenwriter in Hollywood during the 1930s. Contrary to later suppositions that female writers were only adept at crafting romance films or family melodramas, these women wrote for all **genres**: Westerns, historical epics, swashbucklers, and prison films. Screenwriting had become such a common position for women that a career guide for American women published in the 1920s included a chapter on writing for the cinema.

However, when a revised edition of this career guide was published at the end of the decade, that chapter had been eliminated. The coming of sound technology and the Great Depression was forcing Hollywood studios into economic partnerships with large and powerful banking and communication companies, and filmmaking became less and less an artisanal practice and much more of a corporate business enterprise rooted firmly in patriarchal capitalist ideals. The achievements of women in the industry became more limited. Previously successful women retired or were forced out of the business. Lois Weber was so destitute at the end of her life that her friend Frances Marion had to pay for her funeral. Furthermore, reissues and credit listings of the films of many female directors (such as those by Weber and Shipman) sometimes credited their husbands as director – further erasing these women's accomplishments. Frances Marion herself was dropped from her screenwriting contract at MGM in the mid-1930s, not because her work was of poor quality, but because she had become vice-president of the newly formed Writers Guild. The Guild sought better pay and working conditions for all writers, both female and male, and the capitalist studio bosses tried to crush it.

Probably the most famous female filmmaker of the classical Hollywood era was **Dorothy Arzner**, a woman who made 16 films in 15 years for various major studios. Arzner negotiated the all-male world of **classical Hollywood cinema** production by positioning herself as "one of the boys." She frequently wore tailored suit-dresses, talked tough, and even smoked cigars, in order to gain the respect of the men she worked among (and who worked for her). Arzner's career spanned both silent and sound cinema and she worked in a number of different genres, although she was eventually pegged as a director of the "woman's film" (see below). Arzner had been born into an upper-middle-class family in San Francisco, worked as an ambulance driver during World War I, and entered filmmaking as a typist and then a script

Film director Dorothy Arzner made many films in classical Hollywood; in order to be accepted by her male co-workers, she often dressed and behaved in a masculine manner.
Unidentified publicity photo, authors' personal collection

girl. Within a few years, she had become an editor, a screenwriter, and then a second unit director (directing minor shots such as crowd scenes, inserts, and special effects). In 1926 she was offered a job directing *Fashions for Women* (1927), and the success of that film earned Arzner a contract with Paramount Pictures. There she directed Clara Bow in one of her "flapper" pictures, *The Wild Party* (1929).

Arzner is best known for several sound films she made after she left Paramount and became a freelance director in and around Hollywood. *Christopher Strong* (1933) starred a young Katharine Hepburn as a strong-willed flying ace who meets and falls in love with a married man. The subject matter itself (a relationship with a married man) and the strong career-oriented woman played by Hepburn distinguish the film as a rare Hollywood attempt to expand roles for women on screen as well as question patriarchal assumptions. In *Craig's Wife* (1936), Arzner directed a tale about a woman who marries for material wealth rather than love, gently critiquing both capitalism and patriarchy. *Dance, Girl, Dance* (1940) was a melodrama about dancers and show girls. The film celebrates **homosocial bonding** between women and critiques the patriarchal practice of showcasing scantily clad chorus girls. After a making a movie about a female spy, *First Comes Courage* (1943), Arzner retired from feature filmmaking, although she remained active making training films for the Women's Army Corps (WAC), directing theater productions, and working in both radio and television. In her later years she taught at the University of Southern California's film school, where she inspired a new generation of filmmakers and film historians who were just beginning to unearth the sketchy history of women in Hollywood.

The only other female filmmaker during Hollywood's classical era to have any success comparable to Dorothy Arzner's was **Ida Lupino**. Lupino, who in 1949 started her own production company, had worked her way into the director's chair by first becoming an accomplished and popular actress. In the first few years of the 1950s, Lupino made low-budget **social problem films** that often tackled subjects such as rape, bigamy, and unmarried motherhood. In the 1960s she directed mostly television shows, but she did direct the popular comedy *The Trouble with Angels* (1966). Like Arzner, Lupino needed to overcome **sexist** bias on her sets. Rather than make herself into one of the boys, as Arzner had done, Lupino encouraged the use of the nickname "Mom" by her coworkers. In a way reminiscent of arguments made by early female filmmakers, she thus tapped into the respect that most men of the era felt for their mothers (if not for women in general), and used that respect in order to accomplish her vision of a film. While both Lupino and Arzner managed to maneuver through what had become an overwhelmingly male-dominated industry, their accomplishments did not open many doors for other women during this period. Ultimately, the fact that there were only two women film directors of note in Hollywood during its classical period (while there were hundreds if not thousands of men) demonstrates how completely the American film industry was dominated by men.

Images of Women in 1930s Classical Hollywood

Recall that during the first few years of the Great Depression, Hollywood's form and style codified into what is now known as the **classical Hollywood style**. Some of the most famous female movie stars of the twentieth century are associated with this era: Greta Garbo, Mae West, Barbara Stanwyck, Marlene Dietrich, Bette Davis, Joan Crawford, and Katharine Hepburn, just to name a few. Most of these women were considered glamorous beauty queens, which meant that both onscreen and in real life they dressed in designer gowns, wore impeccable hair and makeup, and could be seen frequenting the best and most beautiful homes and nightclubs in America. Because of their popularity with the public, some of these stars were able to maintain a degree of control over their own projects. Katharine Hepburn often battled studio bosses over roles that she felt were demeaning, and Greta Garbo had input in choosing her leading men and cinematographers. Mae West was known for writing all of her own dialog (she had been a playwright and vaudeville star before coming to Hollywood). Like many of the characters these and other actresses played in the early 1930s, West's onscreen persona was gutsy and sexy: she was best known for her racy double entendre jokes that suggested she was a sexual free spirit who was untethered to any one man, be it father or husband. Marlene Dietrich and Greta Garbo also appeared as strong female characters who frequently challenged the patriarchal status quo. In *Morocco* (1930) for example, Dietrich wears a tuxedo and seduces both men and women. In *Queen Christina* (1933), Garbo's character professes that she would rather "die a bachelor" than marry, and she ends the film alone.

Also recall that Hollywood had adopted its **Production Code** in 1930 (see chapter 2) as an attempt to quell calls for censorship but, until it was enforced in 1934, Hollywood movies actually got a bit racier as failing companies tried to woo Depression-era audiences back into their theaters. The appearance of strong, forward, and sexualized heroines in the early 1930s was thus the result of those economic and industrial factors, as well as of the increasing liberalization of sex roles that had occurred throughout the 1920s. However, there were other people in the country who objected to the sort of forthright sexuality that was the hallmark of many of these **pre-Code films**. They argued that the Great Depression had been brought about by wild, godless licentiousness, including the "scandalous" behavior of independent women and flappers. Demands for federal censorship of the movies by activist groups such as the Catholic **Legion of Decency** eventually forced the industry to censor itself via the **Seal of Approval** provision (put into effect in 1934). Suddenly, many of the strong female roles that actresses such as Greta Garbo and Marlene Dietrich had specialized in were curtailed. While most actresses were able to shift into roles thought by the censors to be more appropriate, others suffered

Mae West was one of Pre-Code Hollywood's most notorious leading ladies; she wrote most of her provocative dialog herself.
Unidentified publicity photo, authors' personal collection

badly. Mae West, whose career depended on her racy sexual innuendo, was hobbled by the new Hollywood censors. Her film work after the Production Code was put into effect was sparse and tepid compared to her pre-Code work. Adding insult to injury, during the same period of time the conservative newspaper magnate William Randolph Hearst used his newspapers to carry on a "smear campaign" against many of these same actresses. Hearst's newspapers dubbed them "box office poison" and suggested to filmgoers and filmmakers alike that their careers were (or should be) finished.

This is not to say simplistically that pre-Code films had great roles for women and those after 1934 did not. The differences are perhaps rather minor from a twenty-first-century perspective. Hollywood films had always tended to be about men, and to punish sexually active "bad" women while rewarding "good" women with romance and marriage. Most Hollywood genre films of the 1930s, both pre- and post-Code, were still centered on men and tended to simplify female characters into basic types drawn from the virgin–whore dichotomy. The gangster film, for example, focused on guys with guns (on both sides of the law), with women figured either as the gangster's moll (the sexualized whore figure) or as the G-man's wife (the virgin–mother). The Western also dealt predominantly with male adventure, and women's roles usually were reduced to either the saloon girl (itself a Hollywood euphemism for prostitute) or the good daughter of a rancher (or perhaps a virginal schoolteacher). In the **horror film** or **action-adventure movie**, women were primarily helpless victims waiting to be carried off by monsters or marauding madmen, so that they might be saved by patriarchal heroes. The musical and the romantic comedy initially seem to offer more equity to men and women, as these genres focused on heterosexual courtship, thus giving men and women fairly equal screen time. Yet, even within that format, the gender codes of the day regarding clothing, makeup, courtship, and marriage all work to reinforce traditional gender roles. In Western patriarchal culture, it is the man who asks the woman to dance, pays for dinner, and proposes marriage. Women do not have the option of reversing those gender roles in most 1930s Hollywood films. Also, the musical genre frequently features scantily clad chorus girls, allegedly as a visual treat for men in the audience. (The dynamics of such processes of **objectification** will be explored more fully in the next chapter.)

The one Hollywood genre devoted to women and allegedly to women's issues was comprised of melodramas known as **woman's films**. These films are also sometimes referred to as "soap operas," "weepies," "tearjerkers," and/or "chick flicks." The films in this genre were made (written, directed, produced) largely by men,

The woman's film *Imitation of Life* (1934) was remade by Douglas Sirk in 1959. In this first version, Louise Beavers helps Claudette Colbert succeed in business, but she is still treated as a second-class citizen because of her race. *Imitation of Life*, copyright © 1934, Universal

creating stories that *they* thought would attract a female audience. (One should also note the lack of a matching "man's film" genre – because most of the rest of Hollywood cinema *is* "man's film.") Consequently, the woman's film usually presents conventional, patriarchal ideas about what it supposedly means to be a woman. Centered on the lead female character's romantic and/or domestic trials and tribulations, woman's films present the family and home environment as the proper sphere for women. Also, as terms like "tearjerker" indicate, these films appeal directly to viewers' emotions, on the assumption that women are more emotional than men. Thus, while the woman's film genre presents a special niche where female characters were front and center, patriarchal notions of gender were continually reinforced.

The types of stories that proliferated in the genre attempted to teach women lessons about their proper function under patriarchy. Women were constantly forced to realize their place as traditional mothers or housewives, and punished in a variety of ways if they ever stepped outside of those sanctioned boundaries. The 1970s feminist film critic Molly Haskell identified four basic themes in these films. The first theme is sacrifice, in which a woman learns to give up her own life and/or personal happiness for someone else's. In *Stella Dallas* (1937), for example, a lower-class mother chooses to absent herself from her daughter's life so that the daughter may marry a wealthy man. The second thematic variation in the woman's film is affliction, a film formula in which a woman contracts a terrible disease, leaving her only a short time to find happiness (that is, a man). In *Dark Victory* (1939), a strong-willed and independent heiress is humbled by a fatal brain tumor, but finds brief happiness submitting herself to the medical and romantic care of her male doctor. A third narrative variation involves a woman having to make a choice, either between her career and a man, or between which man she wants to marry. In the former, she finds happiness in choosing conventional romance, or loneliness and despair in choosing her career. (In comparison, how often are male characters forced to choose a career or romance – as if one cannot have both?) In the latter formulation of the choice narrative, the man who exhibits most strongly the ability to take care of the woman usually wins the day. And finally, some women's films focus on competition between women – again, usually over a man.

As should be apparent, these films might be called "woman's films," but they still almost invariably stress the primacy of male figures and patriarchal structures in women's lives. Even a comedy like *The Women* (1939), written by Clare Booth Luce and starring an all-female cast, does little to foster women's rights or freedoms. Instead, the women fight and claw over men, reinforcing the idea that women must compete and not cooperate, and that finding that right man is the ultimate source of female happiness. All four narrative patterns that Haskell identifies taught women the lessons that patriarchal culture wanted them to learn: how to be submissive to a man, how to be "beautiful" in order to attract a man, and what the terrible cost of not finding a man and raising a family would be. Indeed, women who do not marry in Hollywood films are routinely depicted as neurotic spinsters or bitter, hardened, and unhappy women. One of the more explicit examples of this overt sermonizing occurs in *Lady in the Dark* (1944). In this woman's film with musical numbers, Ginger Rogers plays a magazine publisher who seeks psychotherapy because she is unhappy with her life. She is eventually told by her psychiatrist that she needs a man to "dominate" her. The "**happy ending**" of the film finds her handing over her successful business to her new husband so that she can settle into her "proper" role as submissive wife. While the moral of *Lady in the Dark* seems absurd to twenty-first-century audiences, it should be remembered that the ideologies it encodes were common, everyday beliefs. And the fact that they were ratified by "medical science" (in this case psychiatry) lent further credence to the notion that biological sex and patriarchal gender constructs were one and the same.

Almost all of the actresses of the early 1930s who had gained stardom playing strong and independent women were playing in women's films by the end of the decade, learning what price had to be paid for such independence. Yet recent feminist film critics have explored how the genre might actually critique patriarchy because it exposes the biases, hardships, and unhappiness that it can create. While ostensibly teaching women how to be good housewives and mothers, the large amount of suffering that goes on in these films also lays bare the enormous burdens women have had to deal with in male-dominated societies. Women who went to these movies for "a good cry" may have been using the genre as an emotional release from their day-to-day pressures under patriarchy. Some of these films might also be potentially subversive of dominant patriarchal ideas, because, like today's television soap opera, they sometimes explored the problems of traditional marital relations. Rather than the usual Hollywood film that ended with heterosexual coupling and a "happily ever after" assumption, many melodramas and women's films focus on what happens when a marriage goes sour, and as such, open up a space for a potential critique of the institutions and ideologies oppressive to women.

World War II and After

The day-to-day experience of Americans during World War II exemplifies how gender roles are formed via processes of social construction rather than a biological inevitability. When America entered the war, a great shift in the nation's conception of femininity was purposely engineered. With men being drafted into the armed services to serve as soldiers, sailors, and marines, the ranks of American factory workers quickly became depleted. In order to fill empty spots on assembly lines, keep production high, and support the overall war effort, American women were increasingly recruited to enter the workforce. This shift from homemaker to bombmaker required a redefinition of gender roles in America, and the federal government specifically set out to promote the idea of a tough, new, working woman. This image of the new woman was best exemplified by **Rosie the Riveter**, a composite propaganda figure that was used in print and media campaigns to promote the idea that women should leave their homes and enter the workforce. As her name and image implied, Rosie was a strong woman who could tie back her hair, roll up her sleeves, and do a "man's job," such as working a rivet gun. Whereas men continued to be valued for their strength, intelligence, and courage, now it was expected that women could and should also exhibit those qualities. The pre-war idea of femininity (soft, passive, weak) had to yield to a new definition of what a woman was and what she could accomplish. Many thousands of women joined the newly formed WAC or WAVES (Women Accepted for Volunteer Emergency Service), while unprecedented numbers of others entered the workforce in order to build the necessary machinery of warfare.

Hollywood did its part to promote this new image as well. A number of female stars encouraged women to join the workforce by being photographed "on the job" in factories and on assembly lines. A number of films also showed women working at defense plants, and as nurses, WAVES, and WACs. (Granted, while pictured as capable and responsible, Hollywood heroines continued to be glamorous and alluring rather than strong and sweaty.) Hollywood realized that with men at war, women and children comprised the bulk of the domestic audience, and arguably more women's films got made during this period than any other. Subtle differences in filmmaking formulas and genres can occasionally be found in World War II era films. For example, in the horror movie *Return of the Vampire* (1943), the vampire hunter is not a little old man named Professor Van Helsing, but rather a strong female scientist who defeats the monster when he threatens her family. Even some combat films showed women fighting for victory, such as *So Proudly We Hail* (1943) and *Cry Havoc* (1943).

When the war ended and American men returned from overseas, many women in factory jobs were unceremoniously fired so that returning veterans could be hired in their place. In the place of Rosie the Riveter, there was an attempt to shift the American image of women back to where it had been before the war. Women were bombarded by images in the mass media that told them happiness and fulfillment could be found as a housewife and mother. Magazine ads, radio programs, newspaper columns, and (of course) movies presented new suburban homes as a woman's paradise, complete with automatic clothes washers and dryers, dishwashers, refrigerators, and garbage disposals. Such a rapid shift in gender roles did not happen smoothly, however, and behind these smiling, shiny images of domestic bliss lay no small degree of tension between the sexes. In Hollywood, a type of filmmaking which became known as **film noir** arose in the late 1940s and seemed to reflect directly on these tensions. In film noir, women were not simple-minded heroines waiting to be saved by the hero. Instead they were deadly **femme fatales** – or **black widows** – women who lured men into their sphere of influence and would just as easily murder a man as marry him. In a way, the femme fatale of film noir was an updated version of the vamp. Pictured as the center of the web of evil in these films precisely for pursuing her own desires (sexual and otherwise) instead of passively supporting the male lead, the femme fatale had to be punished severely, usually by death. Being a strong, self-sufficient woman had gone from admirable to reprehensible in a very short time. (Film noir will be dealt with more fully in chapter 12.)

The sexual aggressiveness of the femme fatale mirrored an America that was becoming more open about its sexuality in the postwar years. During the war years, sexual mores became a bit freer – both men and women engaged in pre- and extra-marital sex more often, perhaps because of the impending threat of death that hung over the country at that time. In the late 1940s and early 1950s, scientific surveys about American sexual habits were published by the Kinsey Institute, which painted a far different picture of American sexual behavior than did Hollywood movies. Throughout the 1950s, audiences showed a growing interest in foreign films such as *And God Created Woman* (1957) – films that often dealt much more frankly with sex than did Hollywood films. The burgeoning of a burlesque/nudist exploitation cinema further demonstrated to Hollywood that there was a demand for sexually suggestive and revealing films, and the Production Code was weakened (though not overturned) during the 1950s. First, a Supreme Court ruling (*The Miracle* Decision, 1952) said that movies did indeed have the First Amendment right to free speech of any kind. Second, a series of financially successful independent films were released without the Production Code's Seal of Approval. The most famous of these is *The Moon is Blue* (1953), a sophisticated sex comedy which dared to use the word "virgin." Its success, even without the Seal of Approval, demonstrated that American audiences were ready for a more adult approach to matters of sex and sexuality.

While the 1950s showed a greater acknowledgment of sexual matters, mainstream Hollywood cinema repackaged the highly sexualized female role to great popularity. The threatening sexuality of the femme fatale was replaced by the luscious naïveté of the so-called **blonde bombshell** – embodied in many films by actresses such as Marilyn Monroe, Jayne Mansfield, and Mamie Van Doren. Curvaceous and alluring, the blonde bombshell was never very bright, but she had the ability to stop men cold in their tracks because of her sex appeal. Interestingly, the term itself seems to acknowledge the blonde bombshell's destructive capacity. Yet, unlike the femme fatale, the bombshell never quite understood just how sexy she was: many men in the films and in the audience lustily desired her, but she remained oblivious to their advances. Consequently, while the femme fatale appeared in lurid crime thrillers, the blonde bombshell appeared in comedies, with much of the humor arising over her simple-minded sexual antics.

As blonde bombshells (and their brunette and/or raven-haired counterparts, such as Elizabeth Taylor and Sophia Loren) provided one image of the 1950s woman, a number of actresses also represented the sweet, dependent image of the suburban housewife (or sweet young girl dreaming of such a life). Stars such as Doris Day, Debbie Reynolds, and Sandra Dee were fresh-scrubbed, wholesome girls-next-door. In the increasingly sexualized atmosphere, the virginal characters these actresses played often had to fend off advances from men, but they managed to hold out until the wedding night and the promise of living "happily ever after" in a prefabricated home, vacuuming while wearing high heels and pearls. The endorsement of this domestic lifestyle for women could be found in both comedies and dramas – even blonde bombshells were shown longing for a split-level home with a modern kitchen and a junior executive husband to clean up after.

Woman's films (and other domestic melodramas that were not marketed exclusively to women) continued to illustrate ideas about gender, but the issues raised in these films grew increasingly problematic during the 1950s. While attempting to reinforce traditional ideas about a woman's correct behavior and social sphere, the increased interest in adult themes and treatments complicated the usual moral stances of the genre. The stage works and original screenplays of **Tennessee Williams** and **William Inge** were adapted into many steamy melodramas during the 1950s and early 1960s. Williams's *A Streetcar Named Desire* (1951), *Baby Doll* (1956), *Cat on a Hot Tin Roof* (1958), and *The Roman Spring of Mrs. Stone* (1961) featured lust, madness, sexual repression, child brides, and male gigolos. William Inge properties such as *Come Back Little Sheba* (1952), *Picnic* (1955), *Bus Stop* (1956), and *Splendor in the Grass* (1961) also examined sex and sexual repression in more frank and forthright ways. Even less prestigious melodramas seemed to have a hard time in presenting a convincing picture of women finding fulfillment through clean countertops and a whiter wash. Films like *Peyton Place* (1957), *The Best of Everything* (1959), and *A Summer Place* (1959) often exposed the pressures and resentments that were building up in the collective unconscious of American women – before clamping the lid back down on the pot and claiming that everything was fine.

Thus, it might be argued that the film melodramas of the 1950s present a patchwork critique of the era's gender relations. Many of them acknowledge that "something is wrong" with gender relations while trying desperately to maintain traditional values. Even as the decade saw increasing numbers of women enter the workforce, the dictates of postwar American culture still taught that a woman's place was in the home. Many 1950s melodramas expose this paradox and give voice to the frustration many women felt in trying to be a "happy housewife" when they might have preferred something more free and independent. Told repeatedly by

Case Study: *All that Heaven Allows* (1955)

Film critics and historians often cite the films directed by Douglas Sirk as among the most interesting melodramas of the era. Working at Universal, Sirk made films that were very popular at the time, winning Academy Awards and making money at the box office. Some of the films he made were remakes of popular woman's films of the 1930s: *Magnificent Obsession* (1954) was originally made in 1935 and *Imitation of Life* (1959) was first filmed in 1934. Redoing these old films would seem merely to repackage and update old ideas and lessons about a woman's proper place in American society. At first glance, and possibly to a majority of the audiences who saw these films in the 1950s, such an assessment might make sense. Hollywood films (and television shows) *were* mirroring the widespread effort in American society to erase or reduce the gender equity approached during World War II, by placing women back into the home. *All that Heaven Allows* (1955), while not a remake of a 1930s woman's film, seems to illustrate many of these same issues. The film is focused on home life, with most scenes occurring in living rooms, kitchens, and bedrooms. The plot centers on romance and family. Also, the lead female character suffers emotionally through most of the film's running time, mainly for seeming to step outside patriarchal propriety. Yet Sirk's films often contain elements that work against the upholding of the old-fashioned attitudes common to the woman's film genre. While the stories themselves seem to be arguing for traditional ideas about gender, *how* the stories are told seems actively to critique this idea.

All that Heaven Allows stars Jane Wyman as Carrie, a suburban widow with college-age children, and Rock Hudson as Ron, the gardener with whom she falls in love. The dramatic conflict arises when the rest of the town reacts badly to their relationship: everyone in Carrie's country-club community is scandalized that the upstanding widow of a respected businessman is "consorting" with someone "beneath her station" (that is, a working-class laborer). They also whisper about Ron being younger than Carrie. Both the age disparity and the class disparity imply that Carrie is the dominant one in the relationship, which is inappropriate in a male-dominated society. Her children are distraught that she is disgracing their father's name, and vaguely shocked to realize their mother may have her own sexual desires. The entire population pressures Carrie to end her relationship with Ron and go back to what they want her to be – a quiet, unassuming widow and mother, keeping her home and her reputation spotless.

The film's visual design works to emphasize how the pressure for Carrie to conform makes her feel as if she is trapped in a cage. Her house is cluttered with furniture and knick-knacks that are reminders of her previous marriage, giving her little room to move. Carrie is often photographed within frames (windows, mirrors, doorways, even a reflection on a TV screen) to emphasize her isolation. Shadows and window frames create a sense of bars, as if Carrie is literally imprisoned in her upper-middle-class home. The color scheme of the house is all black and white, which creates a sense of sterility and lack of life. This stands in contrast to the home that Ron builds for her, refurbishing a deserted mill. The main room is uncluttered and open, with a high beamed ceiling. The colors are warm earth tones (browns, oranges, yellows), and the large picture window he installs creates a sense of openness and freedom, blurring together indoor and outdoor worlds.

In many ways, the film critiques small-town and suburban pettiness, and champions the free-spirited, Thoreau-inspired lifestyle of Ron and his friends. Carrie must learn not to care about social propriety and follow her own heart. In this way, the film makes some sharp observances about how stressful life could be in the 1950s. Yet, in terms of gender politics, the film reinforces many traditional notions. Carrie is being asked to give up structuring her life around one man (her first husband) in order to start structuring her life around another. When Ron asks Carrie to be strong and stand up to her

American culture that being a suburban wife should be the ultimate happiness for them, many women could not understand why they were still so unhappy. Many women considered themselves sick for feeling this way, and psychiatric therapy and prescriptions for tranquilizers and anti-depressants (sometimes nicknamed

In *All that Heaven Allows* (1955), Jane Wyman as Carrie is surrounded by the artifacts of her former life; here her children confront her for not behaving in a socially acceptable manner.
All that Heaven Allows, copyright © 1955, Universal

back-stabbing friends, she responds that he wants her to "be a man." He laughs and answers, "Only in this one way." As the film goes on, Ron begins to pressure Carrie almost as much as her children and her friends do. She asks him to wait until the children have become adults before they get married, and he refuses. He fears that if he gives in this one time, he will give in to any number of things, including living in "her" house – implying that he must maintain his masculine power in the relation- ship. By the end of the film, Carrie does give up every- thing and returns to his bedside (in *his* home) to care for him after a hunting accident.

Such an ending sends conflicting messages. To some viewers, the reunion of Carrie and Ron provides the tearful happy ending to a conventional woman's film.

Others, though, may wonder just how "free" Carrie has become by rejecting the country-club set for Ron. While the converted mill is arguably warmer and more open than Carrie's home in town, the visuals often imply that it is not as heavenly as the narrative would have one believe. A number of arguments between Ron and Carrie occur in the mill, and the color scheme invariably turns bluish at these points, suggesting coldness instead of warmth. Also, while the big picture window seems much more expansive than the windows of Carrie's house, the window is still noticeably latticed. In the final shot of the film, the camera pans from Carrie at Ron's side to the picture window, where a deer romps around outside. Just because the bars are wider here does not mean that Carrie is not still in a cage. According to later interviews

"mother's little helpers") gained popularity during the 1950s and 1960s. By the 1960s, however, American society could no longer keep a lid on the bubbling pot of women's discontent, and a new hegemonic negotiation of gender would have to begin.

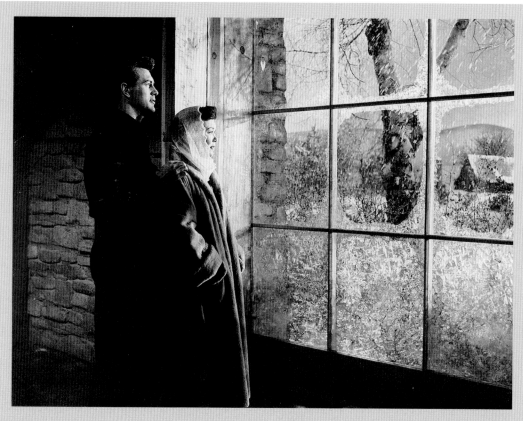

In *All that Heaven Allows* (1955), Carrie and Ron (Rock Hudson) stand before the window of the home he builds for her. The window suggests both the expansiveness and the limits of their relationship.
All that Heaven Allows, copyright © 1955, Universal

given by director Douglas Sirk, these sorts of critical elements were deliberately placed – created subtly through the visual design (props, color, lighting) rather than through explicit dialog. Thus, while it is possible to read this film as a perfect embodiment of the conservative lessons espoused by the Hollywood woman's film, it is also possible to read it as a sly critique of the genre and its ideological imperatives.

Questions for Discussion

1   Think about how gender is constructed in your life. What do you do that makes you masculine or feminine? Have you ever been accused (or accused others) of not being "properly" masculine or feminine? What is at stake in these distinctions?

2   The woman's film is still a relatively popular genre in Hollywood. Do these more recent examples follow the classical pattern of the genre? Do they still uphold patriarchy or do they ever make a case for female independence?

3   Does the virgin–whore complex still exist in American culture? Can you find examples from your own experience? From more recent films or TV programs?

Further Reading

Carson, Diane, Linda Dittmar, and Janice R. Welsch, eds. *Multiple Voices in Feminist Film Criticism*. Minneapolis: University of Minnesota Press, 1994.

Cook, Pam and Philip Dodd, eds. *Women and Film: A Sight and Sound Reader*. Philadelphia: Temple University Press, 1993.

Gledhill, Christine, ed. *Home Is Where the Heart Is: Studies in Melodrama and the Woman's Film*. London: BFI, 1987.

Haskell, Molly. *From Reverence to Rape*. New York: Holt, Rinehart, and Winston, 1974.

Kaplan, E. Ann, ed. *Women in Film Noir*. London: BFI, 1998.

Kuhn, Annette. *Women's Pictures: Feminism and Cinema*. New York: Verso, 1994.

Kuhn, Annette, ed. *Queen of the B's: Ida Lupino Behind the Camera*. Westport, CT: Greenwood Press, 1995.

Landy, Marcia. *Imitations of Life: A Reader on Film and Television Melodrama*. Detroit: Wayne State University Press, 1991.

Lang, Robert. *American Film Melodrama*. Princeton: Princeton University Press, 1989.

Mayne, Judith. *Directed by Dorothy Arzner*. Bloomington: Indiana University Press, 1994.

Rosen, Marjorie. *Popcorn Venus: Women, Movies, and the American Dream*. New York: Coward, McCann, and Geoghegan, 1973.

Stamp, Shelley. *Movie-Struck Girls*. Princeton: Princeton University Press, 2000.

Further Screening

It (1927)
The Wild Party (1929)
Morocco (1930)
Christopher Strong (1933)
I'm No Angel (1933)

Stella Dallas (1937)
The Old Maid (1939)
The Women (1939)
Magnificent Obsession (1954)
Peyton Place (1957)

Chapter 11

EXPLORING THE VISUAL PARAMETERS OF WOMEN IN FILM

The previous chapter explored the role of women in early American filmmaking, and surveyed the types of roles and storylines that were available to women during Hollywood's classical period. That chapter focused primarily on issues of **literary design**, but it also touched upon other formal axes (such as lighting, setting, and props) that contribute to the overall cinematic **representation** of women in Hollywood film. This chapter continues to examine issues of **film form** and focuses more directly on how women were specifically filmed and edited in Hollywood movies – how their bodies were presented to the camera and thus to the spectator. In so doing, this chapter will address the differences in the ways mainstream Hollywood films have photographed women and men. Furthermore, many of these basic issues regarding the cinematic representation of **gender** can be modified and adapted into tools with which we might also investigate the cinematic representation of race and **sexuality**. The theoretical models and concepts discussed below have thus had enormous impact on how issues of social difference are understood within film studies. What follows is an introduction to (and to some degree a necessary simplification of) some of those concepts, as well as a consideration of how those same theories may be inadequate or in need of more complex formulations.

Ways of Seeing

Throughout the 1960s, a growing number of people (both women and men) began to question, critique, and rebel against the traditional concepts of womanhood that had pervaded American society in previous decades. By the end of the 1960s, women's liberation had joined the crowd of political movements aimed at overturning the white heterosexual male power structure. **Feminist** concepts began to affect various academic disciplines. For example, historians began to research for the first time in any consistent way the role of women in history and how concepts of **femininity** have changed over the years. Feminist researchers in the humanities began to reclaim female authors and artists, while feminist scientists criticized and explored **sexist** concepts within their disciplines. Feminism also profoundly affected the fledgling academic area of film studies. Building upon concepts of cinema as a product and conduit of **ideology**, film scholars began to examine how films replicated and disseminated **patriarchal** concepts, helping to maintain a sexist status quo. (As should be obvious, this book continues in this critical tradition.)

Two very important works were published in the early 1970s that shifted the focus of feminist film analysis away from **content** – what women could and did do within classical Hollywood stories – to the ways and means that Hollywood **form** represents women regardless of their storylines. These two works differ in their specific subject matter, but contain strong parallels that help reinforce each other's arguments. The first to appear was John Berger's *Ways of Seeing*, a survey of visual culture that attempted to map out the ways that Western society literally teaches individuals "how to look" at the world. Berger does this by examining billboards, magazine ads, photographs, and paintings. His book explores how visual culture keeps **capitalism** stabilized, and how it can promote national pride. In a highly influential section, Berger also analyzed the history of female portraiture in Western painting. Complete with numerous reproductions of actual paintings, *Ways of Seeing* points out a tradition of representing women as properties that belong to men. In earlier periods, of course, women *were* considered men's property – often handed over from father to husband-to-be as part of a business transaction. These paintings thus often pictured women as part of the "goods" that belonged to a wealthy male, and the paintings themselves were usually commissioned by men as symbols of their material wealth.

Hence, Berger concludes that these paintings do not portray women realistically, as complex and individualistic human beings. Rather, the paintings transform actual women into objects, devoid of individual will or subjectivity. This process, whether it occurs in portraiture, advertising, or the cinema, is called **objectification**. A strong support for this argument can be found in the tradition of painting nude female subjects with their eyes turned away from the painter. By not looking back directly, the women in the paintings deny their own agency and grant all the "power of the gaze" to the male painter and the man who commissioned the painting. The females represented on the canvas have no control; rather they are on display for the male's enjoyment. Importantly, Berger implicates the style of Western painting in this discussion. During the European Renaissance, painters developed the **quattrocento style**, which created a sense of perspective and three-dimensionality. The use of quattrocento style constructs a viewing position for whoever gazes at the painting, organizing the world represented on the canvas for that one viewpoint. In other words, the viewer becomes the implied center of the world constructed in the painting. When portraits of women are painted in the quattrocento style, then, the implied male viewer (whether it is the man who actually commissioned the painting or any other man who looks at it) is structured as its center, as the dominant and empowered figure, and thus reinforces patriarchal **hegemony**.

Berger's work points out that such objectification of women has had a long history. The fundamental concepts that governed female portraiture in earlier centuries can be found in various areas of the mass media today. Because patriarchal capitalism is still the dominant ideology of the Western world, conceiving of women as objects that can be bought and sold (or used to help sell other products) has become a standardized practice within the advertising industries. Television commercials and magazine advertisements frequently use beautiful women to entice presumably heterosexual male customers, and in so doing, they often make an implicit comparison between the woman's body and the product being sold. Just what is being sold by a bikini-clad woman in a beer ad? The beer itself, or the promise of further sexual excitement that purchasing the product will allegedly provide? This specific formulation of female objectification has also been given a racialized twist in more recent years, as in the advertisements for Kahlua & Cream that implicitly compare the café-au-lait-colored liquor to a sexy model of mixed racial heritage. The ads want to capitalize on the exotic and erotic lure of the model in order to sell Kahlua as likewise exotic and erotic. In so doing, they reduce the image of the woman to an object that can be consumed for pleasure by the male spectator.

Although Western culture has changed a great deal over the past two centuries, because of these "ways of seeing" many contemporary American women still develop a sense of self-worth based primarily on how they look, rather than how talented or intelligent they are – or what they may have accomplished in their lives. As in Hollywood narrative form, men in Western culture are taught that it is their birthright to *do* things (run, jump, desire, look) while women remain relatively immobile in order to be the object of the **male gaze**. The fashion industries, the makeup and cosmetic industries, and even the health and fitness industries constantly bombard women with the message that they are not complete or perfect unless they have the right hairstyle, the right bone structure, the right makeup, the right clothes, the right body, ad infinitum. Advertisements constantly treat women's bodies as objects that can be sculpted and remade into some supposed ideal form. In order to change their bodies, women are encouraged to buy their femininity – through fashion, makeup, diet pills, liposuction, or various forms of plastic surgery. (Of course, the concept of "ideal beauty" is itself ideologically determined, since it has historically been racially constructed in the West as fair-haired whiteness. Although our concepts of beauty are changing in the twenty-first century, some non-white women are still undergoing skin bleaching and plastic surgery in order to attain a Western ideal.) Women are thus encouraged to be complicit in their own objectification. Once they have internalized the ideology that their self-worth is based upon their public image, some women believe that achieving total objectified desirability is the only thing that will give them happiness and fulfillment. Obviously, women's pursuit of this mythical ideal keeps patriarchal domination in place and supports the ideology and practices of consumer capitalism.

Berger's observations about painting and advertising can be applied to film without much trouble, as cinema is yet another arm of the mass media that creates

Marilyn Monroe epitomized the blonde bombshell in 1950s Hollywood movies. Here her body is made into a spectacular display in *How to Marry a Millionaire* (1953).
How to Marry a Millionaire, copyright © 1953, 20th Century-Fox

idealized visual images of women. Film is also an industry that encourages people to buy and consume products. Hence, it is unsurprising to find that women are consistently objectified in mainstream Hollywood movies. The technology of cinema recreates on the film strip the quattrocento perspective, and the Hollywood star system strongly supports the packaging and selling of women's images. Even after her death, for example, Marilyn Monroe's image continues to attract attention. From silent filmmaker Mack Sennett's Bathing Beauties to **Jennifer Lopez**'s revealing awards-show fashion choices at the turn of the millennium, women have consistently been placed on display for the pleasure of a male-dominated society.

"Visual Pleasure and Narrative Cinema"

At about the same time as John Berger wrote *Ways of Seeing*, feminist film scholar Laura Mulvey wrote a highly influential essay entitled "Visual Pleasure and Narrative Cinema." Mulvey's arguments shared much with Berger's, yet she also drew upon existing psychoanalytic frameworks to examine the specific ways that **classical Hollywood cinema** manufactures its images of women. As the title of the article makes clear, Mulvey was interested in understanding how mainstream narrative cinema creates pleasure for viewers. She explored how the psychoanalytic concepts of **narcissism** and **voyeurism** can be used to explain how visual pleasure is generated. **Narcissism**, a pleasure of the self, is created when narrative cinema encourages spectators to identify with characters in the film. With such identification, viewers are able to feel as if they themselves are experiencing great adventures and accomplishing extraordinary deeds. On the other hand, **voyeurism** is a visual pleasure that arises from looking at others in a sexualized way. A common term to describe someone who enjoys voyeuristic pleasure is a "Peeping Tom." Part of the pleasure derived from voyeurism comes from watching people who are not aware they are being watched (thus giving the watcher a sense of power or control). Since film is fundamentally based on watching, cinema falls easily into the realm of voyeurism. Hollywood narrative cinema, in particular, creates entertainment by presenting to spectators people who do not seem to know their lives are being watched. The convention of actors not "breaking the fourth wall," that is, not acknowledging the camera, therefore helps maintain a voyeuristic framework for Hollywood filmmaking.

Because classical Hollywood cinema operates within a patriarchal society, Mulvey contends that these two modes of visual pleasure created by narrative cinema must contain male biases. In most Hollywood films, the narcissistic pleasure of identification usually involves identifying with the male characters, the ones who are active and aggressive. On the other hand, the voyeuristic pleasures created by cinema primarily involve looking at the female characters onscreen. Thus, classical Hollywood cinema aims most of its films at a presumed male heterosexual audience member, forcing individuals outside this group to adapt to a male point of view – the so-called "male gaze" that objectifies women – or else risk finding the film unpleasurable. Mulvey supports her contentions by analyzing one of the most basic formal elements of Hollywood narrative cinema: the use of **editing** techniques to create relationships between subjective and objective points of view. An **objective shot** is one that is not tied to a character's point of view, but rather a shot that most clearly conveys the action of the scene. In Hollywood films, almost all of the shots are objective and omniscient – they show the spectator, from the best possible angle, what he or she needs to see in order to follow the story. The rarer **subjective shot**, however, is tied to a specific character's point of view – a shot that literally shows the spectator exactly what a character is seeing. Imagine a shot of a prison cell where a single prisoner goes to the window and looks out. That shot is an objective one, as we see the prisoner from the camera's perspective alone (there are no other prisoners in the cell to whom the view can be attributed). The very

Objective shot – not tied to a character's point of view

Subjective shot – tied to a character's point of view

In classical Hollywood films, objective shots of the male protagonist are often followed by subjective shots of what he is looking at, a formal pattern that directly ties the spectator to the protagonist's point of view.

next shot, however, is likely to be a subjective one, as we cut from the objective shot of the prisoner looking out the window to a subjective shot of what he is seeing outside the window. The audience member is thus tied into that character's point of view: spectators are literally placed inside the head of that character and are able to see through his eyes. This sequence of shots thus strongly activates both narcissistic and voyeuristic pleasures. The shared experience of the subjective shot (shared by both character and audience member) allows the spectator to imagine himself as being the character on the screen (narcissistic pleasure), while what that character is looking at activates voyeuristic pleasures.

Linking shots of people looking and shots of what they are looking at is one of the basic building blocks of classical Hollywood storytelling. Mulvey observes that this simple formal trope of Hollywood editing itself carries and encodes powerful gender dynamics. Chiefly in Hollywood films, male characters are the ones doing the looking (subjective shots are assigned to them) while female characters are usually the ones that are being looked at (objectified from the male character's point of view). This configuration also recreates the effect of quattrocento perspective: by cutting from someone looking to what they are looking at, the film places the viewer inside the character's viewpoint, constructing the viewer's place as the center of the world created by the film. Examples of these objective/subjective shot configurations are so numerous that they are impossible to list. From the very first silent story films to present-day Hollywood blockbusters, examples abound. One of the earliest films to play with this formal trope, *As Seen through the Telescope* (1903), objectively depicts an elderly gentleman peering through a telescope, followed by a subjective shot of what he is looking at: a female bicyclist's exposed ankle (which was pretty sexy back in 1903). D. W. Griffith, a key figure in the standardization of Hollywood storytelling form, consistently used the type of editing patterns that Mulvey describes. In *The Birth of a Nation* (1915), Griffith continually cuts from Ben Cameron gazing romantically or Silas Lynch gazing threateningly to shots of

Elsie Stoneman (who demurely does not return the gaze, as was considered proper etiquette). Even when the objectivity and subjectivity of individual shots are not so clearly demarcated, Hollywood cinema repeatedly thematizes men looking at women: Clark Gable stares lustily at Jean Harlow in *Red Dust* (1932), Humphrey Bogart tells Ingrid Bergman that he is "looking at you, kid" in *Casablanca* (1943), and every male in sight gawks at the voluptuous Jayne Mansfield in *The Girl Can't Help It* (1956). In the blockbuster hit *Titanic* (1997), Jack (Leonardo Di Caprio) asks Rose (Kate Winslet) to pose for him so that he (and the audience) might enjoy the sight of her nearly naked body. Throughout mainstream narrative cinema, men are positioned as the ones in control of the gaze while women are positioned as the objects of that controlling gaze.

Mulvey goes on to point out the multiple ways in which women are placed as the objects of the male gaze. All of the above examples show male *characters* within the film gazing at women. But on another level, the Hollywood film industry itself has been (and continues to be to a large extent) male-dominated. Hence, male directors, producers, writers, and cinematographers all use the camera as an instrument to look at women. From this vantage point, the controlling aspects of the male gaze become even more apparent, as the men behind the camera instruct the woman in front of the camera what to do. The French New Wave filmmaker Jean-Luc Godard, who was a big fan of Hollywood filmmaking, once quipped that "film history was the history of boys photographing girls." Thus, in Mulvey's formulation, the three gazes that comprise cinema in the first place (the gaze of the camera, the gaze of the characters at each other, and the gaze of the spectator toward the screen) are all inherently male, *even when the actual spectator is a woman*. When objective and subjective shots are arranged in the manner described above, each of those three gazes becomes the same thing. Thus, a male character's gaze at an objectified woman is also the gaze of the camera *and* the gaze of the implied male viewer who paid money to see female bodies displayed in this manner. Women in the audience are forced either to identify with the objectified female or else inhabit the male character's point of view. In either scenario, "real" women remain marginalized while the "image" of women remains objectified.

These gendered gaze dynamics are played out within popular film narratives as well as within specific shot configurations. One of the stories replayed over and over again in popular cinema is the "Cinderella" story, in which the mousy young girl is transformed into a beautiful woman so that she may win the man of her dreams. Probably without exception, every version of this tale includes an example of these editing patterns, as the "Prince Charming" lays eyes on the newly transformed heroine. Among the more recent reworkings of this story are *Pretty Woman* (1990), wherein Richard Gere becomes speechless as he sees Julia Roberts turn from a prostitute into a high-class beauty. In the teen comedy *She's All That* (1999), Freddie Prinze, Jr, watches with amazement as his ugly duckling date reveals that she has become a swan. These dynamics can even be found in Hollywood films directed by women. In *The Mirror Has Two Faces* (1996), directed by Barbra Streisand, Jeff Bridges is stunned as Streisand herself is made over from frumpy housewife into a desirable sex kitten.

These last few examples also draw attention to another of Mulvey's points: within Hollywood cinema, women are usually carefully prepared to maximize their ability to attract sexualized attention from the heterosexual male spectator. Even when a woman is the hero of the film (as in *Alien* [1979] or *Tomb Raider* [2001]), her sexualized body is still on full display. Filmmakers often find (sometimes very contrived) ways to get female characters out of their work clothes and into bikinis, underwear, or sheer negligees. Hence, every aspect of an actress's bodily appearance receives the utmost attention. Actresses usually spend hours having their hair and makeup prepared before they step onto a movie set. Their costumes are intricately designed to maximize what are considered their most sexually appealing aspects, and downplay their "problem areas." Various techniques with the camera have also been used to enhance an actress's visual appeal. For example, filters and gels can be used on camera lenses to hide wrinkles, and special lenses can minimize facial features such as a nose deemed too large. Actresses such as Barbra Streisand and Claudette Colbert often preferred a specific side of their face for profile shots, and studio publicists were quick to comply.

Historically, women in Hollywood film have also been carefully lit to make them seem all the more alluring and stellar. By the 1920s, the Hollywood industry had developed a lighting style known as **three-point lighting**, which made stars seem luminescent. This style involved, as the term indicates, three separate light sources. The **key light** was the brightest light, and was usually aimed at the front of the star from above and slightly to the side. The **fill light** was less bright than the key light, and was aimed from above the star on the opposite side to the key light. The fill light helped lighten any shadows possibly caused by the key light (for example, a dark nose shadow across the side of a star's face). The **back light** was of lesser intensity, and placed behind (and usually slightly above) the star, to create a "halo effect" – a glowing outline around the star's hair and body, as if the light was radiating directly out of them. Such elaborate lighting helped separate the stars from the set, and focus audience attention on them – but also worked to make female stars all the more radiant and attractive to the male gaze. Many of these techniques of lighting, costume, and makeup are also applied to male characters and actors in Hollywood films, though rarely to the same extent and for the same purpose of arousing the viewer. These considerations will be discussed more fully below.

With female characters structured into mainstream narrative cinema as "things to be looked at," Mulvey also notes the distinction between what men are allowed to do in films and what women are allowed to do. Limited to "looking pretty," women must remain relatively passive and somewhat outside the action of the story. In contrast, the men drive the story forward: they chase the bad guys, accomplish great feats, and in the process romance and "win" the girl. In some ways, women are presented as an impediment to the action narrative

Back

Key
Fill

Three-point lighting was and is the Hollywood standard; it focuses attention on the star and creates a glamorous look. For an example of the effect, see the photo of Rita Hayworth on p. 250.

245

– a problem that the men must deal with as part of the resolution of the conflict. Sometimes this involves female characters specifically as antagonists, but even "good girls" can cause problems for heroes. For example, it has become a cliché that the sweet young ingénue always tends to trip and fall while the hero is trying to make good their escape. Beyond this, however, Mulvey contends that female characters, simply in their "to-be-looked-at-ness," often tend to bring the narrative to a halt. For example, imagine a scene in which two male characters are having an argument that is central to the conflict that is driving the movie. In the middle of the argument, a beautiful woman walks by. The two men stop talking for a moment, because they have to look at this beautiful creature – and so does the audience. Then, after she has left the room, the argument can recommence and the story can pick up where it left off. Variations on this idea can be found in countless Hollywood movies – in some comedies, massive fistfights come to a halt while some starlet wanders through the beer hall. Musicals often function in this manner: the story proceeds until everything stops for a musical number that showcases lots of chorus girls in skimpy outfits. One can even find examples in cartoons: Bugs Bunny always knows how to distract Elmer Fudd from his goal of "hunting wabbits" – by dressing up as a beautiful female. In Disney's *Aladdin* (1992), Princess Jasmine distracts the villain by putting herself on display, and when she kisses him, all the characters stop to gape at her action.

Thus, in Hollywood films, a woman's power is associated with her ability to use her sexual allure to arrest the narrative action. While unable to be active in the way that the male characters are, a woman's ability to draw the male gaze gives her the ability to bring the narrative to a halt. As limited as this power obviously seems to be, Mulvey concludes that even this poses a threat to patriarchal domination, and that Hollywood cinema attempts to contain that threat in one of two ways. The first is a method of **investigation and punishment**. In many films the male characters (and hence the male viewers as well) are able to diminish, if not totally negate, the female's power by uncovering and unveiling her mysterious allure. Mulvey uses some of director Alfred Hitchcock's films to show how this process works. In *Vertigo* (1958), for example, Scottie (James Stewart) is fascinated by the ghostly and sensual Madeline (Kim Novak). The film is filled with subjective shots of him staring uncomprehendingly and longingly at her (and her not looking back, just as in the portraits analyzed by John Berger). As a detective, Scottie spends the film trying to solve the mystery of Madeline, and it is only at the end of the film, as Madeline is murdered, that Scottie realizes how he has been manipulated by a con job. The entire film might thus be understood as being about the investigation and punishment of Madeline's power over Scottie.

Such attempts to "figure out" and thus control the dangerously beautiful woman have structured many Hollywood movies. This process of investigation often entails and encourages a more intense employment of the male gaze. Men stare harder at these mysterious women in the hope that the power of the male gaze will penetrate the female's beautiful armor. At times, once her shell is cracked by the male gaze, the woman can then be reclaimed by the hero. For example, Humphrey Bogart's character in *The Big Sleep* (1946) spends most of the film trying to determine whether Lauren Bacall's character is trustworthy or not. Once he learns all her secrets, though, she turns into the typical "good girl," supporting his authority rather than potentially challenging it. At other times, however, the female character's power is not sufficiently quelled after the mystery has been solved. Consequently, re-establishing male dominance involves physically punishing the female – either with imprisonment (as happens to Mary Astor's character in the Humphrey Bogart film *The Maltese Falcon* [1941]) or with death (as happens to Lizabeth Scott's character in *Dead Reckoning* [1947]).

According to Mulvey, the other method that Hollywood uses to contain women's onscreen sexual power is **fetishization**. Fetishization in general involves excess emotional or sexual investment in a particular object. For example, most people have heard of the idea of a "foot fetish," in which a person focuses their sexual desires on a specific part of the body, the foot, instead of the entire individual. Psychoanalyst Sigmund Freud tied fetishization specifically to male fears of lack of control. He asserted that the male psyche, in attempting to reassert a sense of control and power, might sometimes focus obsessively on one object that *can* be controlled. Tied to the way women are figured under the male gaze, fetishization works further to objectify women in order to make them less of a threat. If they are regarded as objects and not fully capable human beings, then women can be kept in a subordinate position. Throughout the years, American culture has singled out and fetishized certain areas of the female body as the center of male heterosexual attraction. During the 1940s, there was an emphasis on women's legs. Betty Grable, America's top box office movie star during World War II, had her legs insured by Lloyd's of London. By the 1950s, there was a shift to fetishizing women's breasts. Other aspects of American culture fetishize the female posterior. Music videos and Howard Stern's radio and television shows come quickly to mind as pop culture venues in which the fetishization of women's body parts is not just practiced but actively celebrated.

In Hollywood films, fetishization can occur when the female body is broken by the camera and editing patterns into a collection of smaller objectified parts: hands, feet, legs, hair, breasts, etc. Close-ups of women's body parts appear repeatedly in Hollywood films. Objective and subjective shot configurations function in tandem with this process of fetishization. Shots of various female body parts are often preceded by or followed by shots of men looking at those parts. Many times, women are introduced in movies by only showing a part of their body. Lauren Bacall's character in *Written on the Wind*

This famous World War II publicity photograph of Betty Grable is a good example of the way that female bodies are objectified – put on display for the male gaze.
Unidentified publicity photo, authors' personal collection

(1956) is introduced behind a bulletin board, so that all the audience sees is her legs. The first shot of *Pillow Talk* (1959) (after the credits) is of female legs putting on pantyhose, before the camera pulls back to reveal that they belong to Doris Day. A more recent example would be the introduction of Julia Roberts's character in *Pretty Woman*: a series of individual shots of her legs putting on hose and boots, her midriff as she puts on a halter top, her rear as she adjusts her leather miniskirt, and the back of her head as she straightens her blonde wig, before the film finally shows a full shot of her entire body. By breaking the female body down into individual parts, and valuing certain parts more than the whole, patriarchal culture subtly refuses to recognize women as whole and entire human beings. Women are instead figured as composites of fetishized body parts that are thought to appeal directly to the sexual desires of men.

Good examples of cinematic objectification and fetishization can be found in the musical numbers choreographed and directed by **Busby Berkeley**. Considered one of the greatest geniuses of the Hollywood musical, Berkeley created elaborate numbers that reveled in putting women's bodies on display, invoking the theatrical tradition of **tableaux**. Tableau numbers began on the stage, as producers like Florenz Ziegfeld showcased women in various elaborate headdresses and revealing gowns. In a tableau number, chorus girls do nothing more than take a stately walk across the stage or down a staircase. Audience enjoyment thus derives from the mere act of gazing at these women and not from their singing or dancing abilities. Busby Berkeley's "By a Waterfall" number in *Footlight Parade* (1933) is famous for its inventive parading of chorus girls in various states of undress. After star Dick Powell sings a chorus of the song at some shady glen, he falls asleep and girlfriend Ruby Keeler takes the opportunity to join dozens of chorus girls in a nearly nude bathing sequence. While the women are wearing bathing suits, they are made of skin-toned material, with plastic bathing-cap/wig headgear artfully draped to cover their nipples. The objectification of the chorus girls is also exemplified by their blending into the scenery – they are often photographed as if they were part of the décor. For example, at one point, the chorus girls stand astride various levels of a column which spouts streams of water, creating a "human fountain" (as the preview trailer for the film advertised at the time). All the chorus girls (except for star Keeler) are costumed in the same manner, making it further difficult to distinguish or individualize any of the women. Berkeley presents them as mass-produced items, not individuals.

Throughout the nine-minute extravaganza, chorus girls are photographed in a variety of erotic and fetishistic ways. One underwater shot looking up at their splayed legs serves an as excellent example of fetishization: the women are represented by rows and rows of individual body parts. Berkeley was also famous for his overhead camera shots of chorus girls creating kaleidoscopic designs. When the women form the "human fountain" described above, Berkeley cuts to an overhead shot as they sit on the fountain and stick their legs out. Within the overhead shot, it appears as if the viewer is watching dozens of disembodied legs performing tricks. The overhead shots in general make it hard to distinguish among women, and indeed to regard them as women at all. Rather, these geometric patterns can make the

The "human fountain" of chorus girls from *Footlight Parade* (1933), a spectacular Busby Berkeley musical number in which women are positioned as interchangeable and objectified building blocks of a male fantasy. *Footlight Parade*, copyright © 1933, Warner Bros.

women seem to be mere cogs in a machine. Intriguingly, these kaleidoscopic patterns often have a sensual quality of their own. Usually organized in some circular shape, the patterns shift and reconfigure themselves as the chorus girls move in and out of the center, or move their arms and legs up and down. The sense of pulsation and vibrancy in these circular shapes creates a symbolic representation of the ultimate disembodied fetish – a vagina without a body – and the way Berkeley has the camera move forward and pull back from these overhead patterns does seem to create a veiled sense of sexual intercourse. While such a reading of the number

Case Study: *Gilda* (1946)

Gilda stands as a powerful example of how women have been represented in classical Hollywood cinema, and exemplifies many of the concepts discussed in this chapter. The film stars **Rita Hayworth**, one of the biggest "pin-up" girls of the World War II era. As was discussed in chapter 7, Columbia Pictures visually refashioned Hayworth's image to diminish her **Latina** heritage. This included dying her hair, and raising her hairline through electrolysis. Hayworth thus personifies how both women and racial minorities were often objectified and even recreated by the white patriarchal media industries of the era. *Gilda* remains one of Hayworth's best-remembered films, and it capitalizes on the beautiful persona created for the actress by the studio. In the film, she is repeatedly placed on display both for the male characters in the film and for the viewer. She is introduced as her new husband calls out to her and asks, "Are you decent?" The film cuts to inside her bedroom, and Gilda comes up from the bottom of the screen, flipping her long hair back, until she is framed in a close-up and answers slyly, "Who, me?" In this shot, although Gilda is ostensibly still getting ready to go out for the evening, Hayworth's makeup and hairstyling are both impeccable. Although she flips into the shot, once she comes to rest to say her line, the shot provides a good example of three-point lighting, including the "halo effect" around her hair. The film is marked throughout by such lushly arranged close-ups, in which no hair is out of place, and a back light is perfectly placed on Gilda no matter where she may be.

Gilda's close-ups are almost always intercut between shots of a man, or a group of men, looking at her. The storyline involves Gilda in a romantic triangle in which she must choose between two men: she marries a rich casino owner, but then finds that a man from her past has become her husband's assistant. Both men gaze at Gilda longingly, although the old flame Johnny (Glenn Ford) both desires and distrusts her – a position eventually

Rita Hayworth as the overtly sexualized *Gilda* (1946). The narrative will see to it that she is investigated and punished for her sexualized transgressions against the male protagonist.
Gilda, copyright © 1946, Columbia

may seem scandalous to some readers, the sexual drive of the overall number is consistent with Berkeley's usual style. Indeed, one of his more outrageous musical numbers (from *The Gang's All Here* [1943]) features chorus girls poking giant bananas in and out of a strawberry-strewn female kaleidoscope. While the sexual symbolism of the number was overlooked by many American viewers, the number adopted by the husband as well. The reactions of both men serve as a good example of both the fascination and fear created in classical Hollywood cinema by the representation of such a beautiful woman. *Gilda* is thus also a story of men trying to penetrate and solve the mystery of the dangerously alluring woman. Seemingly aware of the position in which she has been placed by the male characters, Gilda decides not to fight against her objectification but to revel in it. She consistently performs throughout the film: playing the guitar, singing tunes, doing a variety of nightclub acts. As one might expect, the audience for all these performances is shown to be predominantly, if not exclusively, male.

The most famous moment in the film occurs when Gilda performs "Put the Blame on Mame" at the casino's nightclub. At this point in the story, her husband seems to have died in a plane crash. Johnny has decided to punish Gilda by marrying her, but only to control her and keep her caged. In a secondary plot, the local police are investigating illegal doings at the casino. As the police inspector interrogates Johnny about these dealings, he paces nervously – but he is nervous about Gilda, not the police investigation. The "problem" that she represents as a beautiful, alluring woman is more disturbing to Johnny than his potential arrest. The inspector tells Johnny that he can see that something seems to be bothering him. Johnny tries to laugh it off and says that he will look in a mirror to see if that is actually true. However, before he can do so, music starts to filter in from outside the office and Johnny rushes to the window to look down at the nightclub floor. There, Gilda struts on stage to begin her musical number. This lengthy description points out how the activities of the plot (the intrigue between Johnny and the inspector) are interrupted by the "to-be-looked-at-ness" of Gilda. The conversation also foregrounds Johnny's need to look, and Gilda's number is framed by his gaze out the window at her.

While singing the song, Hayworth as Gilda is carefully manufactured to heighten her allure. Although she repeatedly tosses her head, whenever the film cuts to a new camera angle, her hair is miraculously back in perfect shape. She ostensibly has only a spotlight on her during her nightclub performance, but the filmmakers consistently use a back light for every fetishized close-up of her, no matter where she is on the floor. Her costume also works to accentuate her to-be-looked-at-ness. The tight-fitting, strapless black sheath seems to hide nothing of Hayworth's body from view. (Hayworth was actually pregnant when she filmed this sequence, and a carefully placed bow on the bodice of her dress works to shift attention away from the early signs of that pregnancy.) Gilda's number is also a striptease, and she rolls off her gloves and a necklace and throws them to the eager male audience. When the song finishes, the film cuts to men shouting for more. She replies that she would love to, but she has never been good with zippers. Men in the audience (the active lookers and doers, according to Mulvey's model) rush out to undo the zipper on her gown and she (the passive, looked-at object) simply stands there, not even looking at the men who are pawing at her. Indeed, throughout the number, there are shots of Johnny, the inspector, and other men staring directly at her, but Gilda is never shown directly returning a look at anyone; she is merely there to be adored. Yet that is her power – and Gilda was performing this striptease number precisely to shame Johnny. (Even the song itself describes a woman's allure as destructive power. "Put the Blame on Mame" tells how Mame's sensuality allegedly started the great Chicago fire.)

Johnny responds by having the casino bouncer yank her off the stage, where Johnny then slaps her across the face in an attempt to reassert his dominance. By the end of the film, he discovers that Gilda had never actually betrayed him in their earlier relationship, that she was acting like a loose woman in retaliation for the hurt that *he* had caused *her*. Her mystery solved, Johnny's masculine privilege is restored and their relationship can end happily.

was understood as a smutty joke by British film censors, who cut it from the film altogether.

Berkeley also had a reputation for working his chorus girls relentlessly, forcing them to submit perfectly to his designs. The "By a Waterfall" number itself also eventually foregrounds that these women are all under the control of one man.

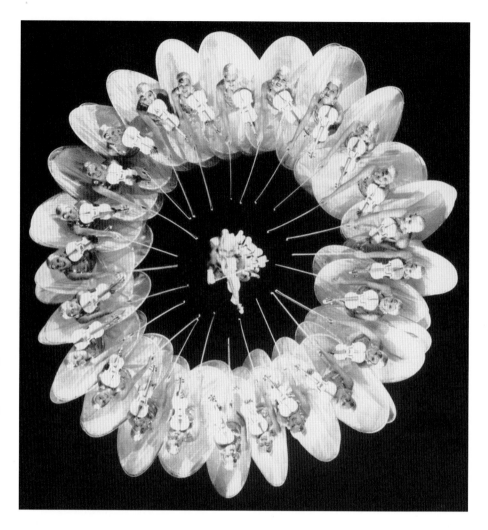

This typical kaleidoscopic shot from Busby Berkeley's *Gold Diggers of 1933* positions women as abstract cogs in a machine, or petals on a flower.
Gold Diggers of 1933, copyright © 1933, Warner Bros.

While some could argue that the number shows women enjoying a private space of their own while the male character sleeps, their presentation for the camera is definitely fetishized and for the sexual pleasure of the male gaze. Furthermore, the number ends when it is revealed that it has all been the dream of star Dick Powell. (In all sorts of ways, this musical number gives new meaning to the phrase "wet dream.") Consequently, the male character (and filmmaker, and spectator) have been authoring and directing what has transpired, fetishizing the female body in order to maintain control and power over it. While Berkeley stands as an important historical figure in the fetishization of women in Hollywood cinema, this process remains typical to the present day. Anyone who has ever watched a music video has seen examples of such objectification and fetishization of the female body. Usually, once people have been introduced to how fetishization works in Hollywood cinema, they can easily find examples of it the very next time they go out to the movies or turn on the television set.

Conclusion: Complicating Mulvey's Arguments

Gilda does seem to exhibit its star Rita Hayworth in perfect concordance with Laura Mulvey's contentions in "Visual Pleasure and Narrative Cinema." Yet the movie also points out issues not addressed by Mulvey's initial article: namely, that representing gender (and analyzing those representations) encompasses more than just women. Representations of men and masculinity are just as **socially constructed** as are those of women, and need to be explored in a similar manner. For example, *Gilda* begins with Johnny as a down-and-out grifter who is literally seduced by the casino owner into becoming his employee. At the casino owner's urging, Johnny gets new clothes and a new haircut and generally cleans himself up, as he rises in rank at the casino to become the owner's personal assistant. Consequently, Johnny's looks and his body are put on display here for the approving gaze of the casino owner, as well as the spectator. Exactly what happens when a male character is objectified in this manner? How does objectifying men in Hollywood film differ from objectifying women?

It is true that most of classical Hollywood's glamor industry and cinematographic conventions worked to represent women in the ways described above, but male stars in Hollywood were also being carefully costumed, made up, and photographed in objectifying ways. From silent film stars such as **Rudolph Valentino** and Douglas Fairbanks, to Clark Gable and **Rock Hudson**, to Tom Cruise and Brad Pitt, male stars in Hollywood have also been carefully packaged and represented for the voyeuristic pleasure of the viewer. Indeed, this trend has only increased in recent decades as Hollywood has come to recognize that women (and gay men) in the audience might enjoy the spectacle of a man's objectified body. However, in our culture, the very act of placing the male body on display is often seen as feminizing, precisely because such a procedure is so closely tied to female bodies. Sometimes a highly objectified male star can be the victim of a public backlash: many men of the 1920s considered Rudolph Valentino unmasculine even as their wives and girlfriends were swooning for him. What the opening section of *Gilda* inadvertently shows is that although the onscreen objectification of men is ostensibly for the voyeuristic pleasure of female spectators, a male–male homoerotic effect is created, since *Gilda* and films like it were still directed and photographed by men. In other words, men behind the camera were objectifying men in front of the camera, and men in the audience were being asked to gaze at other men in a voyeuristic way. This situation, which places a male spectator in the position of gazing erotically at another man, can cause discomfort for men for whom **homosexuality** is disturbing. That discomfort may then be another reason why men are far less frequently objectified in classical Hollywood cinema than are women. (The traditional Hollywood objectification of women certainly allows for lesbian gazes between women in the audience and onscreen female characters, but those homoerotic aspects were rarely acknowledged either by the men behind the camera or by those in the audience.)

There are other differences in the way male bodies and female bodies are represented on Hollywood screens. For starters, consider how makeup is used for men versus women. Everyone in the movies wears makeup, but female characters (as in real life) wear makeup that transforms their everyday looks into something man-made. Male characters in Hollywood films wear makeup that makes it seem as though they are *not* wearing make-up at all. Next, consider the context in which male and female bodies are displayed. As Mulvey and others have noted, women get undressed and stand passively before the camera's gaze with the slightest narrative excuse, and in so doing often bring the story to a halt. When men disrobe in Hollywood film, it is frequently part of an action sequence. In other words, when the male body is on display, it is as an active, powerful, and dangerous (as well as sexy) weapon wielded against other men. One can frequently find this type of objectification of the male body in action movies and Westerns, and it has become something of a cliché that the hero's shirt will be torn open during a particularly rough fight with an opponent. The male body is also sometimes displayed in Hollywood films during or after torture scenes; here the point is again to show how the male hero's body can take brutal punishment but still defeat the bad guys. Action stars from the 1980s and 1990s such as Arnold Schwarzenegger, Sylvester Stallone, and Jean-Claude Van Damme often showcased their large, muscled bodies in their films, but almost always while running, fighting, shooting, and generally "kicking ass." Sometimes these active male bodies are framed from a female character's point of view, again creating a male–male homoerotic feel for male spectators. Another way to sum up these differences would be to examine the phenomenon of the chorus boy in the Hollywood musical. While the chorus boy can be found in some Hollywood films (especially in **pre-Code** musicals), he is nowhere near as endemic to the genre as is the chorus girl. Busby Berkeley never shot a number objectifying the bodies of 100 chorus boys.

The arguments and ideas discussed in this chapter are not without their detractors. Many fault the **essentialist** aspects of Mulvey's contentions – that *all* Hollywood films must *always* objectify women. Her ultimate contentions have provoked outcries because they imply that any female viewer who enjoys mainstream narrative cinema is agreeing to her own oppression. Mulvey also ignores the presence of gay and lesbian spectators for whom the two pleasures of narcissism and voyeurism potentially collapse into one. Her ideas, based as they were on essentialist psychoanalytic models, also fail take into consideration the historical changes that have occurred in the film industry since Hollywood's classical age. For example, switching the genders of the gazer and the object can be and is done in contemporary Hollywood films, although it is still a relatively rare occurrence. *Thelma and Louise* (1991) is a good example of a more recent film that flips the genders of the active doers (women) and passive sex objects (men). In one scene, director Ridley Scott inverts the usual Hollywood form and allows Geena Davis's character to erotically objectify Brad Pitt's. Between objective shots of her lustful gazing, the film offers the audience her subjective shot of Pitt's glistening torso. While the scene was probably pleasurable for women and gay men in the audience, it may be another reason why many men hated the film, even to the point of decrying its supposed "man-hating" politics on the op-ed pages of many American newspapers. While the scene may have provoked unwelcome homoerotic tensions for some male viewers, the controversy it (and the entire film) sparked is illustrative of the gendered currents of American film spectatorship. Men who hated the film probably were not identifying with Thelma and Louise, despite the fact that the film's narrative, cinematography, and editing all work to encourage such identification. Many male filmgoers refuse even to attend movies about women and women's issues, and thus never experience female characters' "ways of seeing." Conversely, most female filmgoers have been trained to be quite adept at seeing filmic worlds from a male point of view.

An example such as this also problematizes the very concept of cinematic identification in the first place. Do subjective shots really create an absolute link of identification between the character and the spectator? Certainly some spectators resist those identifications. Other spectators may identify with different characters during different parts of the movie. Perhaps a spectator identifies with the sensibility of the director behind the camera and with no onscreen character at all. Most likely spectatorship is a far more free-floating and complex process than Mulvey first theorized. Since her influential article was published, many other film scholars have presented counter-theories arguing for a more complex relationship between women and mainstream cinema. However, Mulvey's basic arguments have maintained their strength, and they continue to have a lasting impact on how gender is discussed in film scholarship. Finally, they point out in important ways how the very form of Hollywood cinema (and not just its content) has objectified and continues to objectify bodies – sometimes male bodies, but usually female.

Questions for Discussion

1 Think about your own relationship to voyeurism and narcissism. Do you make it a habit of seeing movies that star your favorite sexy actor or actress? Is pretending to be a movie character and vicariously sharing his or her adventures part of your pleasure in moviegoing?

2 List some other examples of how women's bodies are objectified in popular culture – advertisements, music videos, film, and TV. How do women relate to those images, and how do men relate to them?

3 What happens to the gendered dynamics of spectatorship when the male body is put on display? Are women in our culture more likely to "accept" sexual objectification than are men?

Further Reading

Berger, John. *Ways of Seeing*. London: BBC/Penguin, 1972.

Carson, Diane, Linda Dittmar, and Janice R. Welsch, eds. *Multiple Voices in Feminist Film Criticism*. Minneapolis: University of Minnesota Press, 1994.

Fischer, Lucy. "The Image of Woman as Image: The Optical Politics of *Dames*." In *Sexual Stratagems: The World of Women in Film*, ed. Patricia Erens. New York: Horizon, 1979.

Kaplan, E. Ann. *Women and Film: Both Sides of the Camera*. New York: Methuen, 1983.

Lehman, Peter. *Running Scared: Masculinity and the Representation of the Male Body*. Philadelphia: Temple University Press, 1993.

Mizejewski, Linda. *Ziegfeld Girl: Image and Icon in Culture and Cinema*. Durham, NC: Duke University Press, 1999.

Mulvey, Laura. *Visual and Other Pleasures*. Bloomington: Indiana University Press, 1989.

Thornham, Sue. *Feminist Film Theory: A Reader*. New York: New York University Press, 1999.

Further Screening

Footlight Parade (1933)
The Maltese Falcon (1941)
The Girl Can't Help It (1956)
Barbarella (1968)

Pretty Woman (1990)
Thelma and Louise (1991)
Tomb Raider (2001)
300 (2006)

Chapter 12
MASCULINITY IN CLASSICAL HOLLYWOOD FILMMAKING

The previous two chapters attest to the fact that most of the critical work on **gender** issues in media (and in society generally) has been devoted to analyzing images of women. Living within **patriarchal** cultures, women have traditionally been less empowered and accorded fewer rights and opportunities than men. Thus, discussion of gender often centers on the ways that women have been discriminated against in the media (and in society generally). This gives women's history and experiences a renewed attention, attention that a male-dominated society has often dismissed or overlooked. Yet discussing gender solely in terms of women's issues may inadvertently make the **social construction** of gender seem to be an idea of importance only to women. Such work may accidentally create a sense that, because "the male" functions as a central or default category in patriarchal society, its "female Other" is the only socially constructed gender category. To rectify that possible misconception, many scholars now recognize the importance of studying not only how **femininity** is constructed within patriarchal cultures, but how **masculinity** is constructed as well. In this way, these broader **gender studies** (as opposed to only women's studies) attempt to denaturalize the **hegemonic** superiority of males, and show that masculinity and femininity are not absolute terms, but are in fact dependent on one another. (Recall that masculinity is often defined as not feminine, and vice versa.) Males are conditioned by **ideology** and cultural standards just as much as females are, and typed into socially learned gender roles. American society teaches and fosters certain types of behaviors in men – the ones commonly thought of as masculine (aggression, strength, leadership, lack of emotion) – in order to maintain and reinforce patriarchal privilege.

Privilege is a key point: while many women struggle against the limitations placed on them by their gender role, men tend to be rewarded for taking on a traditionally masculine gender role. Patriarchal privilege is so endemic that most men are not even aware of the comparative ease with which they move through life (much as "white" individuals are often oblivious to the opportunities they have in comparison to those considered "non-white"). Some men, however, will admit to an unease similar to what women feel about their gender role: the ideals of traditional masculinity are perhaps as hard to actually embody as are those of traditional femininity. For example, from a very early age, boys are taught what is appropriate for their gender and what is not. They are taught to suppress their emotions ("boys don't cry") and endure hardship without complaint ("take it like a man"). Patriarchal cultures deem these good traits for men to acquire, but are they really? Some men become so conditioned by those ideals that they are unable to develop intimate relationships. Other men ignore signs of illness and suffer silently, leading to increased mortality rates for men over women. Some men feel tremendous pressure to be "good providers" for wives and families, and they may develop serious doubts about their own self-worth if they are not as wealthy or famous as the next man. Thus men are confined in their own way within American patriarchal culture. They are expected to live up to certain standards of masculine behavior, to constantly prove to themselves and to others that they are indeed "real men," that is to say, not like women.

Patriarchal culture provides a variety of ways for men to encounter, negotiate, and manage their relationships to these masculine ideals. Primarily, boys are expected to emulate their fathers, and other father figures. Boys and men are encouraged to learn masculine behavior through belonging to and participating in **homosocial groups** – all-male spaces or activities such as clubs, athletic teams, fraternities, lodges, and the armed forces (all-male until the latter part of the twentieth century). In these realms, men learn how to embody traditional images of masculinity, through both conscious and unconscious study and imitation (whether of how to sink a three-point shot in basketball or how to dismantle a rifle). These homosocial spaces work not only to instill a sense of masculinity (by quite literally excluding the feminine), but also as spaces for men to grapple with their own doubts about their abilities to succeed as men. The individuals who form an all-male group (team, pledge class, platoon, etc.) often form close bonds based on all of them helping each other "be all that they can be." However, that bonding is usually heavily negotiated through competition and aggression, since the masculine ideal contradicts the "feminine" emotions of love and nurturing that such close relationships might invoke.

Mass media and other organized entertainments also provide the ways and means of acquiring masculinity within American culture. For example, spectator sports have proliferated during the last century as a demonstration of male athletic superiority – most of them endorse a vision of masculinity that the men watching are encouraged to imitate or at least measure themselves by. Advertisements (in print, on billboards, and on television) also present images of masculinity, and usually tell the men watching them that consuming certain products (trucks, beer, razors, cologne) will help the male spectator become like that image. Similarly, television shows and motion pictures present examples of the masculine ideal for boys and men to admire and idolize. However, as the conclusion to the previous chapter pointed out, placing masculinity on display for the **male gaze** is markedly similar to the sexual **objectification** of women in American visual culture. Consequently, mass media representations of men consistently work to represent "real men" as powerful active agents sexually desired by women, and to eradicate or denigrate any possible homoerotic or feminized aspects of masculinity.

Almost from its outset, American film granted primacy to men in the stories that it told. Narrative is driven by action, and if patriarchal ideology asserts that men are the doers (while women are the "done-unto"), then narrative films are inevitably going to focus on men. While women were accorded a special **genre**, the **woman's film**, men had no need for such a ghetto. Everything else that Hollywood produced was automatically a man's film. Regardless of the genre, images of the masculine ideal remained central. The **Western** revolves around the lone cowboy riding the range, bringing justice and civilization to the frontier with a maximum of male heroics. The **gangster film** focuses on men attempting to gain success and prove their mettle through violent criminal action. The **action-adventure movie** similarly centers on male **protagonists** becoming mythic masculine heroes through amazing journeys or quests. The **war movie** also quite consciously rehearses how to be the right kind of man under the hardships of battle. The centrality of the male in American cinema (and Western culture in general) is implicated in the term most people use to designate the main character of any story: the hero, not the heroine, or the gender-neutral term "protagonist."

As was discussed in chapter 10, the motion picture industry in the United States was dominated by men from its very beginnings, even as the newness and relative decentralization of the medium did enable a few women to become filmmakers. Men founded and controlled the film industry as it became standardized through-out the 1910s and 1920s, and in general, the classical Hollywood **studio system** replicated the patriarchal business practices endemic to its era. Accompanying and justifying this rule by men were assertions that men were, by their very nature, better than women. Producers and directors, so the argument went, needed to be leaders and exhibit a strong powerful will in order to command the cast and crew. People working in various technical areas (cinematographers, set builders, electricians, etc.) needed to have mechanical know-how. Traditional masculine ideals implied that men were better suited for these roles, while traditional feminine ideals excluded women from those roles regardless of their skills. Furthermore, as the classical Hollywood studio system increasingly limited filmmakers to certain specialized fields (a director or a cinematographer, but not both), people moved into those fields through apprenticeships and guilds. Such a system created another all-male space, in which older men taught younger men how to do their job – by and large excluding women (as well as racial and **ethnic** minorities) from their ranks. While unions gained a foothold in the industry to protect the rights of the working class, union organization worked to further entrench male domination in various fields by regularly refusing to grant women membership.

Patriarchal ideology works to naturalize male dominance and superiority so that people often do not even think of gender issues when discussing men. Just as audiences tend to think that stories are about race only when those stories deal with racial minorities, some spectators might only consider a film to be about gender if it deals with women's issues. However, every film ever made is arguably about both masculinity and femininity in some way – because gender permeates our understanding of being human, and because both terms are defined as opposites and not overlapping concepts. When patriarchal ideology is functioning smoothly, most people do not notice how gender is being rehearsed and reinforced in culture. However, when ideological standards of gender are in flux, the construction of gender becomes more apparent. Different images of men and women collide with each other, battling for social legitimacy and acceptance. Just as the previous chapters have shown how cinematic images of women helped both to reveal and to form their era's social construction of female gender roles, this chapter aims to examine how popular moviemaking attempts to naturalize male gender roles. Although patriarchal dominance has been maintained throughout the history of American cinema, the masculine ideal has shifted over time. What constitutes a "real man" has varied throughout film history, as hegemonic standards of gender have evolved and been renegotiated.

Masculinity and Early Cinema

At the time that cinema was invented, American masculinity was undergoing just such a shift. The nation's transformation from a more rural to urban environment was increasingly forcing people to change their means of support from one of independent production (such as running a farm or a trade) to wage labor in urban factories. Whereas early citizens often built their own log cabins, raised their own livestock and produce, and made their own clothes, by the end of the 1800s more and more Americans were performing jobs for wages that they then used to *buy* homes, food, and clothing. This shift had enormous impact on the social understanding of masculinity. Men, who had been previously seen as the sole creator and owner of the home and its goods, were now beholden to other men (factory bosses and owners) in order to survive. In this way, the necessity of factory wage labor diminished a man's capacity to live up to the masculine ideal of previous generations. Furthermore, as discussed in chapter 10, women were also becoming more prominent in the urban workforce at this time, further blurring the lines between male and female labor, social roles, and activities.

As this brief description indicates, this particular shift in masculinity was tied specifically to economic concerns – strongly linking issues of patriarchy to issues of **capitalist** control. As if to acknowledge (or perhaps mask) the fact that capitalism was forcing traditional masculinity to adapt to less masculine positions, dominant culture began to champion a new and more virile vision of masculinity. President Theodore Roosevelt (a "rough rider" who urged men to "speak softly and carry a big stick") promoted a veritable cult of outdoor male athleticism, asserting that those who were truly manly were closer to nature. However, this resurgent masculinity was also associated with pure brute strength and heavy manual labor, and it therefore was able to reassure many working-class men that they too were part of the masculine ideal, thus keeping them from potentially challenging capitalist ideology. (A similar process has often occurred in the cultures of American racial/

ethnic minorities. Masculinity is sometimes overemphasized in minority cultures in an effort to diffuse the sense of disempowerment that results from racial or ethnic discrimination.)

Film became a popular entertainment among the urban population of this era, and the cult of masculinity found its way into the subject matter of even the earliest motion pictures. A number of the first films made by **Thomas Edison** and his associates were short scenes that celebrated male homosocial spaces: barber shops, cockfights, and card games. Since the earliest films were mainly "photographs come to life," little more was done in these pictures than present the all-male space and the men themselves. Boxing matches became another popular subject for early cinema, especially since some states had banned live fights, but had no laws against showing *films* of fights. One of the more famous male bodies on display in Edison's early films was the sideshow strongman Sandow, who posed and flexed for the camera. The Sandow film presents an insistent performance of vibrant masculinity, but also places the man on sexual display, which may have had unintended effects. Similarly, Edison's filmic recreations of male-exclusive spaces also become problematic for patriarchal culture: is his film of two men dancing meant to be homosocial or **homosexual**?

The shift to narrative filmmaking helped solve this dilemma: by placing masculine figures in stories instead of simply on display, it encouraged individuals to identify with the male characters instead of admire them as objects. Two of the most famous early story films made in the United States function in this manner. Edwin S. Porter's *Life of an American Fireman* (1902) shows heroic, action-oriented men taking charge and rescuing a helpless woman and child. Fireman films were quite popular in the early 1900s, illustrating the perils of urban life (when housing and fire codes were substandard or haphazard) as well as a new urban profession that upheld the cult of masculinity. Porter went on to even greater success the following year directing *The Great Train Robbery* (1903). Rather than celebrating modern urban masculinity, this film copied the Western flavor and heroic mythmaking of the dime novel and Wild West show. Although the film has many elements common to the crime and chase film genres, it is considered by many historians to be the first film Western. One of the most prolific of American film genres, the Western promotes a masculine ideal of a strong, unemotional, aggressive hero closely tied to nature and hard manual labor. In this way, urban males who had little contact with the type of outdoor active masculinity championed by Theodore Roosevelt could at least sit in a **nickelodeon** and fantasize that they were a rugged cowboy hero. For

The star image of John Wayne, seen here as a cowboy hero in a publicity shot, represented the epitome of American masculinity for decades. Unidentified publicity photo, authors' personal collection

261

the next few decades, Western cowboy heroes such as William S. Hart and Tom Mix taught men and boys important lessons about masculinity. In the 1930s, **John Wayne** rose to prominence as the quintessential cowboy hero in a number of Hollywood Westerns, and in the early years of the twenty-first century, his cowboy image is still considered by many to be the epitome of American masculinity.

Masculinity and the Male Movie Star

Just as early narrative filmmaking developed certain genres, so too did it develop recurring character types: the fireman, the cowboy, the sweet young maiden. Certain actors and actresses quickly became associated with these types, and avid moviegoers soon were able to distinguish them from other actors – even though early films did not generally list who the actors were. As the classical Hollywood studio system began to codify, studio executives realized that actors who had a loyal following could help sell product. Thus, the **movie star** was formed not only out of the narrative style of classical Hollywood, but also out of its business structure. Studios groomed promising actors, molding them into popular figures of desire that would then draw audiences to films. Stars functioned then as they do today: as mythic (but manufactured) icons that epitomize for audiences certain aspects of gender, beauty, **sexuality**, and class. As part of the mythmaking, effeminate male actors were taught to swagger and fight, while more masculine actresses were feminized via etiquette lessons and classes in fashion and makeup. Perhaps unsurprisingly, many of the first movie stars were women – thus equating the "to-be-looked-at-ness" of movie stars with the type of gendered objectification discussed in the previous chapter. Yet movie stars such as **Mary Pickford** and **Theda Bara** were soon matched by various leading men. Hollywood had to negotiate how to encourage a bond between the male viewer and the male star without also creating a sense of sexual attraction; in other words, Hollywood needed to create male stars without implicitly turning them into feminized objects of an erotic gaze.

Such concerns preoccupied Hollywood studios and American society in general as female fans of male stars became a major topic of discussion. Recall that by the 1920s, women were seen as being increasingly independent, with aspirations and sexual desires of their own. The visible growth of women's culture worried many cultural commentators and further threatened traditional notions about masculinity. Those issues came to a crisis point within the career of **Rudolph Valentino**, an actor of Italian descent famous for his portrayals of sensual **Latin Lovers**. In his films, Valentino's body was often placed on erotic display for the assumed female spectator. Garbed in exotic or period costumes, Valentino's star image was thus associated with sensuality rather than rugged adventuring. While multitudes of female fans actively worshipped him, some male moviegoers grew antagonistic toward him, partly because he was competition for their women's attention, but also because Valentino's objectified star image was uncomfortably close to the objectified star images of female bodies. He was deemed too pretty. Men weren't supposed to

Rudolph Valentino, seen here as *The Son of the Sheik* (1922), was the embodiment of the 1920s Latin Lover. He was thought too pretty by some (male) commentators. *The Son of the Sheik*, copyright © 1922, Paramount

pose like that! Male newspaper columnists began to smear Valentino's masculinity by suggesting he was effeminate. They cited his enormous female fandom as an example of how "out of hand" modern women had become. When Valentino died suddenly in 1926, thousands of women mobbed his funeral, inducing what reporters described as a general hysteria. The event marks a rising cultural awareness of women's active (and public) sexual desire – and many men's discomfort with that same development. Although Valentino stands as the most famous example of these conflicting gender currents surrounding that era's male stars, many other actors of the period (including John Barrymore, John Gilbert, and Ronald Colman) faced similar hurdles.

In general, male actors since the early twentieth century have constantly had to deal with aspersions on their manhood, since acting has traditionally been looked down upon in American society as a less-than-manly profession. Different actors have created different strategies for managing their relation to masculinity. For example, while Douglas Fairbanks's star image placed his body on display in elaborate costumes similar to Valentino's (as Zorro, Robin Hood, or the Thief of Baghdad), his image also stressed energy, athleticism, and agility. Fairbanks's body could safely be presented as spectacle as long as it was constantly in motion – in sword fights, bounding up walls, running, leaping, and springing from adventure to adventure. Similarly, the era's cowboy stars were usually represented riding, roping, and fighting, not seductively lounging by the campfire. Displaying the male body through a narrative performance of masculine virility has become a common trope in Hollywood filmmaking, one that helps negotiate the effeminizing effect created by objectifying men onscreen.

The performance of virility (or its lack) was central to a number of major comic male stars during the silent period. Slapstick comedians such as **Charlie Chaplin**, **Harold Lloyd**, Buster Keaton, and Harry Langdon created personalities that seemed to mock the masculine ideal. Chaplin and Keaton were small, scrawny figures who seemed overpowered by everyone around them. Harold Lloyd centered his comic persona on his thick, black-rimmed eye-glasses, creating a sweet but weak every-man. Harry Langdon went even further, presenting himself as a pudgy innocent, half-adult, half-baby. While all four of these actors used their lack of masculine attributes for comedic effect, the climaxes of their films usually show them triumphing over the odds and becoming "real men" through heroic feats. In *The General* (1926), for example, Keaton's character is regarded as a coward, but manages to save his beloved and defeat the enemy during the Civil War. In *The Freshman* (1927), Lloyd's puny undergraduate goes on to score the winning points in the biggest football game of the season. In *The Strong Man* (1926), Langdon's soft, childlike character somehow subdues a much larger and aggressive bully who has harassed him throughout the film. Most of these comedians were also exceptionally gifted physical artists, and their films often feature situations in which they can exhibit their acrobatic skills. Thus, while many of the great silent film comedies begin with a problematic image of masculinity, their biggest laughs and pleasures result from the stories they tell: stories of weaklings who rise to the occasion and ultimately affirm their masculinity.

The **Great Depression** created a new crisis in masculinity. With the economic downturn, thousands of men were put out of work, disabling them from their role as family providers. Such figurative emasculation seemed to necessitate an even stronger image of masculine prowess on American movie screens. Films from the era often eschewed the refined leading man image of many 1920s male stars in favor of actors who displayed a rougher, tougher sensibility. (John Gilbert, for example, was allegedly drummed out of the business because his voice was not sufficiently masculine for 1930s audiences.) New sound movie stars like Clark Gable and **James Cagney** spoke gruffly and tersely, and seemed to be always spoiling for a fight. Cagney became a star in the gangster film *Public Enemy* (1931), in which he not only shot it out with other urban mugs but showed he could handle a woman by shoving a grapefruit in her face. Gable first came to attention in *A Free Soul* (1932), in which he showed who was boss by giving co-star Norma Shearer some rough treatment. The increased representation of men's violence toward women at this time seems to indicate an insecurity about male dominance – an insecurity that could only be quelled through excessively violent means. Gable and Cagney were accompanied by other similarly rough-hewn male stars, including John Wayne, Gary Cooper, and Humphrey Bogart. Male filmgoers looked to these male stars to learn how to talk, to walk, to handle women, to handle other men – in other words, to learn how to perform masculinity successfully in their own daily lives.

Certain film genres of the classical era made the performance of masculine virility more of a challenge, and the male stars linked to those genres had to create

In *Public Enemy* (1931), James Cagney played a guy so tough he thought nothing of abusing a woman by shoving a grapefruit in her face. *Public Enemy*, copyright © 1931, Warner Bros.

strategies for upholding their masculinity. For example, while the musical genre presents plenty of opportunities for male viewers to witness chorus girls in various stages of undress, the genre has often been considered to be more appealing to women than to men. Part of this perception may be due to the emphasis on song, dance, and romance, which not only enlarges the importance of the lead female character, but also stresses emotionality – a trait that "real men" were not supposed to show. Two of the biggest male stars of the Hollywood musical used different methods for surmounting these problems. Fred Astaire never projected a sense of rugged masculinity – his first screen test famously judged him as having no star potential because of his thin body and unconventional looks. However, his star image was one of wealth and class, and he rose to prominence as the debonair musical partner of ultra-feminine Ginger Rogers. Furthermore, Astaire's films were often filled with male supporting characters who were even less conventionally masculine than he was. In comparison to them, Astaire looked more virile. The other famous male dancer of classical Hollywood cinema, Gene Kelly, worked tirelessly throughout his career to assert that his dancing was hard work – that the athletic skills required to perform it were hard-won masculine accomplishments. Even his 1958 television special was entitled *Dancing: A Man's Game*.

Another genre of the classical era that figured male stars in interesting ways was the so-called **screwball comedy**, a sort of combination of slapstick and romantic comedy that worked to negotiate social and sexual tensions between men and women. Screwball comedies deal quite literally with the battle between the sexes, with male and female characters both verbally and physically sparring. For example, in *Nothing Sacred* (1937), Frederic March knocks Carole Lombard unconscious with a punch; however, she later knocks him out as well. The emphasis on competition and combative courtship often meant that women got to win a few rounds of the fight, even though by the end of the films the men have usually reasserted their dominance. Interestingly, the rise of the genre occurred simultaneously with the enforcement of the **Production Code** (adopted in 1930, enforced in 1934), and many film historians today understand the screwball comedy to be a rechanneling of the era's open sexuality (now forbidden by the Code) into a less overt form: a comedic battle between lovers. In this way, censorship efforts may have helped to construct a public notion of sexuality tinged with violence and brutality.

Many of the male stars of screwball comedies were similar to those softer, more romantic, and good-looking stars of the 1920s. Cary Grant, for example, rose to fame in screwball comedies such as *Bringing Up Baby* (1938), *His Girl Friday* (1940), and *The Philadelphia Story* (1940). In them, Grant's suave characters are challenged by strong women who want to do things their own way. Grant uses comedy to negotiate this struggle and to maintain his masculinity, that is, his dominance over women. Intriguingly though, such dominance is often tenuous. While Grant has thoroughly tamed Katharine Hepburn by the end of *The Philadelphia Story*, in *Bringing Up Baby* her character seems only to allow him to *think* that he has won the upper hand. In *His Girl Friday*, Grant's character successfully wins back his wife (Rosalind Russell), but does so in order to keep her working as a reporter for his newspaper and not as a small-town housewife. The film thus appears to give "permission" for a woman to hold what was traditionally a male job, even as it is clear that she will be taking orders from Cary Grant both at home and at work. Just as the male stars of the silent slapstick comedy found humor in negotiating hegemonic masculinity, so did the male stars of screwball comedy. What marks these films as different is that the silent comedies almost always reaffirmed masculinity in their final reels, while screwball comedies often barely returned to patriarchal norms.

A late screwball comedy starring Cary Grant, *I Was a Male War Bride* (1949), pushes the reversal of gender roles just about to the breaking point. Directed by Howard Hawks (who had also made *Bringing Up Baby* and *His Girl Friday*), *I Was a Male War Bride* focuses on a French officer (Grant) who is forced by military bureaucracy to take on a female role when he marries a member of the US armed forces. The climax of the film even has Cary Grant dressed in a skirt and wig, passing himself off as a woman. Although the film ends with all the gender-bending complications settled, the resolution happens in the final seconds, leaving little time for the viewer to feel reassured that traditional masculinity has indeed triumphed. While the screwball comedy and the male stars who performed in them usually managed to uphold male dominance in the end, the often equivocal sense of that dominance acknowledged that masculinity was still frequently in flux. It was being challenged by the ever-changing shifts in women's roles in American society of the era.

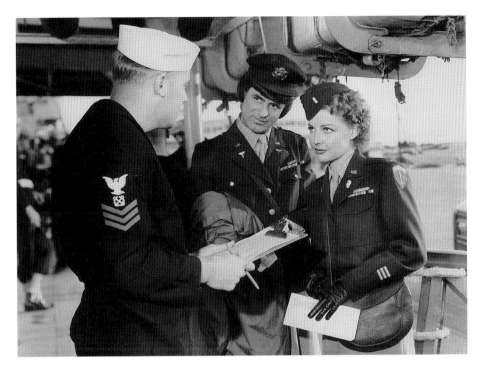

In the screwball comedy, gender roles are often inverted; in *I Was a Male War Bride* (1949), Cary Grant ends up in a wig and a skirt.
I Was a Male War Bride, copyright © 1949, 20th Century-Fox

World War II and Film Noir

Arguably, World War II altered gender relations in the United States more than any other event of the twentieth century. As discussed in chapter 10, the wartime economy encouraged a new image of a stronger, more capable American woman. It also necessarily promoted the strength, courage, and power of American men – ideological conditioning that helped to assure everyone that we were indeed "tough enough" to win the war. Thus, while American culture reconceived femininity as stronger and more capable (that is, more "masculine"), it also worked overtime to instill traditional ideals of masculinity in men themselves. Military training drilled into enlisted men the value of aggressive action, suppressed emotion, and leadership under duress. As with most all-male spaces, men helped each other deal with the pressures caused by those expectations, acting as support and encouragement in an arena where the performance of virile masculinity literally meant life or death.

Cinema reinforced the triumphant masculinity of the American male soldier throughout the war. In numerous **war movies**, GIs rose to the occasion and performed their duty with stoic bravery. Many war films told stories of new recruits having to learn how to function in the armed services as part of a team and not as individuals. Consequently, these films (and the military itself) did renegotiate certain aspects of masculinity: men were no longer expected to be strong loners (as

While enacting masculine bravado and heroism, John Agar and John Wayne in *Sands of Iwo Jima* (1949) also typify the strong homosocial bonds formed during the war (and in war movies). *Sands of Iwo Jima*, copyright © 1949, Republic

in the Western) but were instead expected to become effective members of a unit. For example, James Cagney in *The Fighting 69th* (1940) and John Garfield in *Air Force* (1943) start each film playing within their star personas as cocky, street-wise, and aggressive individuals. The story of each film, however, goes on to show that success in wartime requires working together as a group, suppressing masculine individuality under a chain of male command. Hollywood films of the 1940s also glorified the male bonding of GI buddies in order to further this redirected image of masculinity. Male duos became routine on film screens during the war, and the comedy team of Bud Abbott and Lou Costello shot to the top of the box office in a series of military-related comedies. Bob Hope and Bing Crosby also paired off in a series of buddy/road comedies including *Road to Singapore* (1940) and *Road to Morocco* (1942). Even the classic wartime romance *Casablanca* (1943) ends not with a male–female clinch, but with two men marching off to join the fight. As Humphrey Bogart remarks to Claude Rains in the film's famous last line, "This looks like the beginning of a beautiful friendship."

While wartime propaganda attempted to paint a picture of robust American manhood, the actual fighting of the war had strong effects on men and masculinity. Many strong and able-bodied men died in the war; their masculinity could not overcome mortar shells and bullets. Others suffered from injuries or horrible wartime experiences that left them permanently disabled in body or mind. Combat creates enormous mental stress, and many men returned from the war with nightmares, flashbacks, crippling anxiety, and/or depression, a constellation of psychological symptoms now known as post-traumatic stress disorder. However, having been conditioned to be stoic and suppress complaints, many American men of the era lived silently with such symptoms. Many felt that no one wanted to know what they had endured. In fact, a documentary made by Hollywood director John Huston, entitled *Let There Be Light* (1945), was suppressed by the military precisely because it presented too vivid a picture of how badly the war had scarred some soldiers mentally. Even those soldiers who did not require major medical attention experienced difficulties readjusting to regular home life, where people had not experienced the horror of war and had no comprehension of what they had been through.

Some of the **social problem films** that were produced during the postwar years attempted to address the difficulties of readjustment that many returning veterans faced. Some of these films dealt with disabled veterans and their attempts to feel like whole men again. *Pride of the Marines* (1945) showed John Garfield's character dealing with returning home blind. *The Men* (1950) focused on wheelchair-bound Marlon Brando coming to grips with his injuries. Other films, such as *Till the End of Time* (1946), attempted to account for the more general sense of dislocation felt by returning veterans. Possibly the most famous social problem film of postwar readjustment was *The Best Years of Our Lives* (1946). The film centered on a trio of returning soldiers, each grappling with different problems that compromised their sense of masculine identity. One character (played by Fredric March) returns to an ostensibly happy home and good job, but feels somehow separated from it all and seeks solace in alcohol. Another (played by Dana Andrews) returns a war hero, but comes back to limited working-class options and a social environment that has no use for yesterday's heroes. The third (played by real-life amputee Harold Russell) comes back from the war without his lower arms, and is worried about how his long-time girlfriend will react to his altered body. By the end of the film, all three men find a method of reawakening their confidence and feeling integrated back into society. The film seemed to say much to American society; in dramatizing concerns about postwar masculinity, it became a major box office hit and won multiple Oscars, including Best Picture of the Year.

Men returning from the war faced another, often more personal complication to their sense of masculinity: stronger, independent women. For some men, it seemed as if women had taken over – in jobs, in communities, and even in the home. As if to restore proper patriarchal order, American culture attempted to deny or denigrate the stronger women that wartime conditions had created. Women were unceremoniously fired from their jobs in order to create employment opportunities for returning men. Veterans were granted federal loans to help them obtain higher education, train for better-paying careers, or buy homes – loans that were for the most part unavailable to women. As discussed in chapter 10, postwar representations of women in film and on radio attempted to place women back in the home, refiguring them as happy wives and mothers, not workers in the public sphere. Yet most cultural historians note that many American men still felt vaguely threatened by women. Many women fought to maintain their jobs and their independence. While birth rates did soar after the war, so did divorce rates. Many couples who married quickly during the war discovered they had no substantial relationships when they were reunited. Men and women had had very different experiences of the war, and the two often did not easily mesh.

In *Double Indemnity* (1944), Fred MacMurray's character is seduced and then betrayed by a femme fatale played by Barbara Stanwyck, seen here lurking in the shadows behind a door.
Double Indemnity, copyright © 1944, Paramount

Nowhere are the worries about postwar gender relations more overtly expressed than in a spate of films that would became known as **film noir**, so named because of their dark stories and even darker settings ("noir" is French for black). In these films of nightmarish urban angst, male characters experience a heightened state of masculinity in crisis. Rather than presenting strong, assertive, and confidently victorious heroes, noir films center on men who feel trapped by their social or economic situations. Male characters in films like *Double Indemnity* (1944), *Detour* (1945), *The Postman Always Rings Twice* (1946), or *The Lady from Shanghai* (1946) are everyday working stiffs, locked into a humdrum life, whose one attempt to escape that confinement inevitably pulls them into a world of crime, murder, and paranoia. The visual look of film noir itself expresses this sense of entrapment. Most of the stories take place at night, as shadows close in around the characters. A variety of objects (horizontal blinds, staircases, ceiling fans, etc.) create more shadows, as if the figures are trapped behind bars or caught in giant spiderwebs. In noir films, the camera often frames the action at out-of-kilter angles, creating a feeling that the world is out of balance and uncontrollable.

The pervasiveness of film noir style infiltrated almost every genre during the postwar period (Westerns, musicals, comedies, the woman's film), but was most connected to the mystery-thriller genre. With stories often drawn from the hard-boiled detective fiction of Raymond Chandler and Dashiell Hammett, the mystery genre meshed neatly with the complex visual style of film noir. Detective plots keep the hero (and the audience) figuratively in the dark, lacking confidence about who to trust and what is actually happening. The hero wanders through a narrative maze that may or may not completely resolve itself. Spectator identification

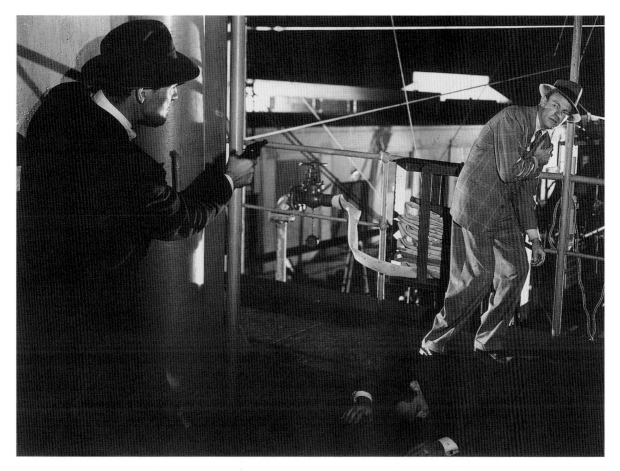

This shot from *T-Men* (1947) exemplifies the dark, twisted, and out-of-kilter mise-en-scène of film noir.
T-Men, copyright © 1947, Eagle-Lion

with the beleaguered male hero is heightened through formal devices such as flashbacks and voice-over narration, all of which tie the spectator to the protagonists' subjective point of view. The viewer thus experiences the story through the sometimes quite confused mind of the film noir hero, and not from some objective, omniscient point of view. The plots of film noir thrillers also often include multiple double-crosses, in which characters switch sides as various aspects of the mystery are revealed. Good and evil are thus blurred together, and even the hero's morality frequently comes under question. Noir films do not always end happily, either. Sometimes the hero dies in his quest to take control of his life.

One constant method for performing masculinity in these films was (in an accurate use of the word) the manhandling of women. Film noir protagonists treat women roughly – through either dismissive one-liners or actual physical abuse. Such aggression toward women was central to film noir because the key to the intrigue and mystery usually involved a woman. The film noir **femme fatale** encapsulated the threat that women in postwar society seemed to represent to men. In these films,

Case Study: *Dead Reckoning* (1947)

Humphrey Bogart starred in many films noir, and in *Dead Reckoning* he embodies his usual persona of a weary, disillusioned tough guy determined to solve a dangerous puzzle laid before him. *Dead Reckoning* ties film noir directly to postwar anxieties by casting Bogart as Captain "Rip" Murdock, a soldier returning home with his war buddy, Sergeant Johnny Drake. During a ceremony meant to honor their accomplishments, Johnny mysteriously disappears, and Murdock becomes determined to find his pal. He finds Johnny's charred body in a morgue in Gulf City, and the rest of the film details Murdock's attempt to do right by his friend and bring the murderer to justice. Gulf City, like most film noir environments, is presented as an asphalt jungle, filled with danger, secrets, and double-crosses. Much of the action takes place at night, and scenes taking place indoors are often shot with low-key lighting, creating distorted shadows. The film is also partially told in flashback, beginning as Murdock tracks down a Catholic priest in Gulf City (importantly, a priest who was in the trenches with the enlisted men during the war) in order to recount his story. With the flashback comes Murdock's voice-over narration, explaining his deductive reasoning, as well as his emotional attitude toward various events and people. Hence, in a stylized fashion, the film evokes several issues of postwar readjustment for veterans, while Murdock's quest is itself linked to the strong emotional bonds forged between men during the war.

The main person that Murdock investigates is a night-club singer named Coral (Lizabeth Scott), who was connected with Johnny via a prior murder case. In keeping with the shifting nature of character in film noir, it is revealed that Johnny was a suspect in a murder before escaping the police, changing his name, and enlisting in the army. Coral, as the femme fatale, is introduced by the film much as Rita Hayworth was in *Gilda* (1946; see chapter 11), as a stunning and objectified beauty, but one that cannot be trusted. A carefully coifed and made-up blonde in a slinky black dress, Coral is beautifully packaged, but Murdock suspects that she may be lying about Johnny. Although Murdock investigates other suspicious figures throughout the film, he primarily tries to ascertain whether or not Coral can be trusted.

Murdock's uncertainty toward Coral is mirrored by the film's presentation of her. In certain scenes, she is lit and framed as if she was a predatory menace – shadows partially covering her face (and intentions), and shot from distorted angles. In other scenes, she is presented as a sweet young thing needing Murdock's protection – now shot in plain daylight in a regular medium shot. The shifting nature of her identity is also thematized by the number of names given to her throughout the film. Although her given name is Coral, she also goes by the nickname Dusty, and Murdock gives her another nickname, Mike. Each of the names corresponds to various possible identities. Dusty is used by Murdock when he begins to distrust her (note how the name has unclean connotations), but when he warms to her, he calls her Mike. This use of a male name seems to associate Murdock's possible love of Coral/Dusty/Mike with the intense homosocial bonds he and Johnny shared.

Whatever name he gives her, it is clear that Murdock is attempting to control the femme fatale. Even his act of renaming her is an assertion of his dominance. And throughout the film he tests her, questions her, and tells her what to do, in order to assure himself that he is in charge and that she is not making a fool of him. During one of their ostensibly more relaxed moments (when he thinks she can be trusted), Murdock describes his perfect

women know secrets that men do not. Women tend to act helpless and needy at the beginning of these films, but they are in fact only performing that pose to hide their ruthless ambitions. They lure humble working men into crime and murder by promising sex, happiness, and escape. And although other men may endanger the hero during the course the film, it is the femme fatale who sits at the center of the web: she is the ultimate threat. Her intended emasculation of the man must

In *Dead Reckoning* (1947), noir protagonist "Rip" Murdock (Humphrey Bogart) is beaten and battered by thugs. The murder trial inevitably leads back to a deceitful woman, played by Lizabeth Scott.
Dead Reckoning, copyright © 1947, Columbia

woman as pocket-sized – one that he can keep in his coat pocket and take out to admire, but too small to cause too much trouble, and susceptible to being put back in the pocket if she starts to act bossy. When Coral/Dusty/Mike tries to object to such blatant **sexism**, Murdock cuts her off with "Get back in my pocket," and she smiles and shuts up. While the manifest sexism of this speech surprises many viewers today, the film attempts to justify such ideas by ultimately revealing that Coral is indeed untrustworthy. She has not only committed the original murder, but also killed Johnny. During the climactic road trip, she tries to kill Murdock, but he manages to crash the car, killing her but receiving only slight injuries himself. Murdock gets justice for his dead buddy and thwarts the evil machinations of another femme fatale. Masculinity emerges battered, but triumphant.

therefore be repudiated through an excessive use of force. The film noir hero physically wrestles the gun from the femme fatale's hand, slaps her, turns her over to the police, or even kills her himself. Perhaps unsurprisingly, film noir usually resolves its gender tensions in favor of its male protagonists, but the films themselves seem to indicate just how threatened and unsure **hegemonic patriarchy** was during the postwar years.

Masculinity in 1950s American Film

Men continued to be traditionally masculine in many films of the 1950s, although other films began to represent a newer, softer type of masculinity. Still others seemed to suggest that living up to the masculine ideal was a difficult, if not impossible, task. The lingering effects of World War II and the new corporate economics of the 1950s were changing the social understanding of masculinity. Even some stars' personas began to change. For example, Jimmy Stewart had risen to popularity in the 1930s and 1940s playing shy, idealistic young men who epitomized the ideal average American "Joe." In the 1950s, however, Stewart increasingly played men with psychological scars, men who were trying a little too hard to pretend that everything was fine and that they were still in control of their lives. In several films directed by Alfred Hitchcock (including *Rear Window* [1954], *The Man Who Knew Too Much* [1956], and *Vertigo* [1958]), Stewart's all-American guy was twisted into an obsessed neurotic. In Westerns directed by Anthony Mann (including *Winchester '73* [1950], *The Naked Spur* [1954], and *The Man from Laramie* [1955]), Stewart's cowboy heroes verged on psychosis in their quest for control and vengeance. Another traditionally heroic Western star, Gary Cooper, acknowledged the strain of performing stoic masculinity in *High Noon* (1952), playing a sheriff who is plainly frightened by an impending gunfight. Even the iconic image of John Wayne was challenged. In the Western *The Searchers* (1956), it is suggested that Wayne's patriarchal character might be misguided, obsessive, and pathologically racist – a disturbing shading to his usual strong and silent hero role.

These older stars were not the only ones displaying cracks in masculine confidence. A new generation of actors hit the screens in the 1950s, and they were often cast as young men straining under the pressures of being a man. Actors like Marlon Brando, James Dean, Montgomery Clift, and Paul Newman created characters that were introspective, tied in emotional knots, and yearning for a sense of release from the stress of conforming to a set of expectations about traditional masculinity. In their films, these men cried, had emotional outbursts and mental breakdowns. This was a far different image of men than had been promulgated during the previous 30 years of Hollywood cinema. Part of this new image was a result of the **Method School** of acting, in which many of these actors were trained. The Method encouraged actors (both men and women) to create their roles from within, to become the character in the way they thought and felt, rather than mold the part to their own view of the world or pre-existing star persona. For male actors, this often led to getting in touch with the characters' emotions – hence, the Method encouraged less emotional restraint in male performances, and subsequently in the cultural representation of masculinity.

Yet the rise of this new conflicted image of masculinity (whether from young or older actors) was not simply a by-product of a new acting style. Men in American society continued to feel pressure to conform to expected notions of gender, especially as life in the 1950s became increasingly corporate and conformist for many men. While the war had attempted to promote men working as a group, many men felt emasculated by the era's corporate culture – leaving on commuter trains in identical gray-flannel suits, going to interchangeable junior executive white-collar jobs, sitting in rows of desks or similar small offices, but not actually doing any hands-on physical labor. Indeed, a popular novel and film of the era was titled just that: *The Man in the Gray Flannel Suit* (1957). In the film, the "man" (played by Gregory Peck) struggles to find meaning in his cookie-cutter lifestyle. Gregory Peck's star image worked to resolve male tensions in many 1950s films. In films like *The Big Country* (1958) and *Man in the Gray Flannel Suit*, he has to learn that masculinity comes from within, that it does not need to be constantly exhibited. Quiet, dignified masculinity was also at the core of **Sidney Poitier**'s star persona, where it helped negotiate potential racial tensions. Poitier became the nation's first black movie star by embodying a soft-spoken, honorable, and self-assured masculinity.

While a number of Hollywood films acknowledged the strains that some men were feeling, almost all of these films (like most Hollywood movies) nonetheless prop up and support patriarchal ideals by the end of the film. *Rebel Without a Cause* (1955), starring James Dean, is a good example of such **hegemonic negotiation** around issues of masculinity. In the film, Dean's troubled teenager desperately searches for a male role model. The film suggests Dean is troubled precisely because his father (Jim Backus) is not traditionally masculine enough. Although his father is a successful businessman with wife and family, he is depicted as hen-pecked and weak – never more so than when his son finds him picking up a spilled tray of food in a frilly woman's apron. The implication is that American men were becoming tragically soft – effeminized – in the postwar years. In fact, a specific 1950s ideology of "Momism," which accused the nation's mothers of turning virile American men

In the 1950s, James Dean came to represent a new kind of masculinity – more introspective and more emotional. Unidentified publicity photo, authors' personal collection

275

Rock Hudson became a major Hollywood star in the 1950s by embodying traditional masculinity; the fact that he was gay was hidden by his Hollywood bosses.
Rock Hudson from *Send Me No Flowers*, copyright © 1964, Universal

into sissies, could be read about in newspaper and magazine columns. By the end of *Rebel Without a Cause*, Dean's teenager has constructed his own family, becoming the responsible, courageous father figure that he himself has not had. The film thus acknowledged changing ideas of masculinity in the 1950s, blamed them on women and weak men, but then restored a newer, arguably more sensitive version of patriarchal dominance.

These last few paragraphs may give the impression that masculinity in the 1950s was characterized primarily by neurosis and hysteria. While a sense of "masculinity in crisis" did pervade many films of the era, many others (especially Westerns and action-adventure movies) went about reinscribing traditional masculine ideals. For example, Howard Hawks told people he made *Rio Bravo* (1959) precisely because of his disgust with the compromised masculinity of *High Noon*. Other films presented their male characters as almost cardboard cutouts of male sturdiness and strength, and some new stars were groomed to embody the traditional image of male power. **Rock Hudson**'s name itself was concocted by the actor's studio to evince a sense of determination and confidence, and Hudson's image through the decade was as a strong, dedicated, and loyal male figure. Hudson was matched at this time by the granite-willed heroics of Charlton Heston in a number of elaborate historic epics such as *The Ten Commandments* (1956), *Ben-Hur* (1959), and *El Cid* (1961). Standing tall and proud, neither Hudson nor Heston seemed worried or insecure about their ability to fulfill their patriarchal responsibilities.

William Holden and Kirk Douglas emerged as major stars in the 1950s as well, and they also seemed to fit into the same general category as Hudson and Heston – broad-shouldered, uncomplicated "man's men." Yet these two stars often bridged the gap between an almost decaying traditional male image and a newer, conflicted, more sensitive one. Both actors frequently played characters who attempted to convince themselves and the people around them of their confidence and bravado, but beneath their solid virile appearances there was often weariness and a lurking insecurity. William Holden (in *Sunset Boulevard* [1950], *Stalag 17* [1953], *Picnic* [1955], and *The Bridge on the River Kwai* [1957]) and Kirk Douglas (in *Champion* [1949], *Detective Story* [1951], and *The Bad and the Beautiful* [1952]) enacted macho men who seemed vaguely aware that their assertions of patriarchal power and privilege were all a sham.

American society in the 1950s worked tirelessly to pretend that the old gender roles were still in force, regarded as natural and inevitable. Yet tensions were beginning to reach a breaking point as the decade ended. Societal mandates had not convincingly induced all women back into the home to be solely wives and mothers. Men were increasingly complaining about the stresses and pressures of trying to live up to traditionally gendered expectations. These dissatisfactions over traditional gender ideals, coupled with other social concerns about Vietnam and civil rights, would fuel the **countercultural** movement of the 1960s. As hard as Hollywood films and the rest of American culture at that time tried to resolve these problems, the tensions increased, heralding a larger crisis that would necessitate yet another hegemonic renegotiation of gender roles.

Questions for Discussion

1 What are some of the most prevalent ways that masculinity is constructed in popular culture? Is it always constructed in opposition to femininity? What are some of the various traits that make a man a "real" man?
2 Masculinity, like femininity, has changed over the decades. Can you think of differences in how your own grandfathers, fathers, and male siblings have experienced and continue to experience "being male"?

3 Many people today argue that there is a crisis in masculinity – that most violent crime is committed by men and that our culture teaches boys that violence is part of being a man. Do you agree or disagree? What role does popular culture – movies, TV, comic books, video games – play in the construction of violent masculinity?

Further Reading

Cohan, Steven. *Masked Men: Masculinity and the Movies in the Fifties*. Bloomington: Indiana University Press, 1997.

Cohan, Steven and Ina Rae Hark. *Screening the Male: Exploring Masculinities in Hollywood Cinema*. London and New York: Routledge, 1993.

Copjec, Joan, ed. *Shades of Noir: A Reader*. New York: Verso, 1993.

Edwards, Tim. *Cultures of Masculinity*. New York: Routledge, 2006.

Kirkham, Pat and Janet Thumim, eds. *You Tarzan: Masculinity, Movies and Men*. New York: St Martin's Press, 1993.

Krutnick, Frank. *In a Lonely Street: Film Noir, Genre, Masculinity*. London and New York: Routledge, 1991.

Lehman, Peter, ed. *Masculinity: Bodies, Movies, Culture*. New York: Routledge, 2001.

Naremore, James. *More than Night: Film Noir and its Contexts*. Los Angeles: University of California Press, 1998.

Penley, Constance and Sharon Willis, eds. *Male Trouble*. Minneapolis: University of Minnesota Press, 1993.

Studlar, Gaylen. *This Mad Masquerade: Stardom and Masculinity in the Jazz Age*. New York: Columbia University Press, 1996.

Further Screening

The Sheik (1921)
The General (1926)
Public Enemy (1931)
Detour (1945)
I Was a Male War Bride (1949)

The Men (1950)
Sunset Boulevard (1950)
Rebel Without a Cause (1955)
The Man in the Gray Flannel Suit (1957)

Chapter 13

GENDER IN AMERICAN FILM SINCE THE 1960S

This chapter discusses how Hollywood film has adapted (or not) to the great cultural changes brought by the **feminist** movement of the 1960s and 1970s. It traces the images of women and men in American film from that period to the present day. While many assumptions and expectations about **gender** roles in America have been challenged in recent years, many things about gender and media culture have also stayed relatively constant. Many simple **genre** formulas of the past have been reinscribed and remade into huge box office hits, the so-called **nostalgic Hollywood blockbusters**. Only rarely have those genre formulas been updated to match the changing times in which we now live. Most Hollywood films still center on men – their problems and their adventures – and still tend to **objectify** the image of women as sexualized spectacles. Even though more women produce and direct films in today's Hollywood than ever before, only rarely do their films challenge Hollywood **form** or critique **patriarchal** structures. **Masculinity** and **femininity** are still constructed by the movies in specific ways that promote the separate and unequal status of men and women in America.

Second Wave Feminism and Hollywood

Much of how we think about gender today is due to the feminist movement that began to affect mainstream American culture during the 1960s. This wave of feminist writing, consciousness raising, and activism is sometimes referred to as **second wave feminism**. (Recall that **first wave feminism** had occurred earlier in the century around issues such as contraception and women's suffrage [see chapter 10]. The early feminist movement is sometimes divided into first and second "waves" because between the 1920s and the 1960s there was very little organized political activism around women's issues.) Second wave feminism began in response to the pressures placed on American women after World War II to return to the home to be housewives and mothers. One of the first and most influential books that addressed the status of American women in the 1950s was Betty Friedan's *The Feminine Mystique*, published in 1963. Friedan defined her concept of the "Feminine Mystique" as the culturally constructed image of passive, homebound, uneducated, eroticized, and cosmeticized femininity (as promoted in Hollywood films and network television). Friedan's book explored the fact that many American women were not happy being trapped into these very limited roles – they yearned for more freedoms and choices in their lives. As a solution to the problem, Friedan encouraged her readers to become educated, to become independent both financially and emotionally, and to fight for equal opportunity in all aspects of their lives. Friedan's book and others, such as Simone de Beauvoir's *The Second Sex*, helped to jump-start the feminist movement of the 1960s.

The feminism of the 1960s was also tied to the other major social trends of the era, including the **civil rights movement** and opposition to the Vietnam war. It was primarily women – mothers and wives in many cases – who helped spur the anti-war movement in the first place. Women were instrumental in many other **countercultural** and civil rights groups as well, but they often still found themselves making the coffee and doing the dishes while the men discussed politics. Many women began to realize that in many civil rights groups fighting for equality and freedom, the focus was solely on equality and freedom *for men*. For example, one African American civil rights leader of the period infamously quipped that the only position for women within his civil rights collective was "prone," a **sexist** joke meaning that women were needed only as sex partners for men within the movement. Statements such as that one outraged women working for equal rights, and as the 1960s progressed, many of them decided to break off from protest groups focused on racial issues or the war and start their own women's rights groups.

The largest and best known of these feminist groups was the **National Organization for Women** (**NOW**), which was founded by author Betty Friedan in 1966. NOW has been the mainstream, moderate voice of middle-class American feminism since its inception. But, just as other civil rights groups of the late 1960s became increasingly strident and violent, some feminist groups formed to pursue radical agendas that called for violence against men and the entire patriarchal system of US culture. Radical feminist Valerie Solanas published her *SCUM Manifesto* in 1968. (SCUM stood for the Society for Cutting Up Men.) The *SCUM Manifesto* was a scatological howl of protest meant to shock and scandalize the nation, and prove that women could be as angry and violent as could men. Valerie Solanas later shot pop artist Andy Warhol, whom she saw as a sexist oppressor because of his use of women's images in his work. Warhol survived the attack and Solanas went to jail, but in more recent years there has been a renewed interest in her writings and her story. The **independent film** *I Shot Andy Warhol* (1996), directed by Mary Harron, depicts aspects of Solanas's life and some of the feminist issues of the 1960s.

Most feminist groups of the era did not advocate violence of any kind. Violence was understood as stemming from *male* aggression and women's feminist organizing more often took the form of grassroots **consciousness-raising groups**. The slogan "the personal is the political" became a hallmark of the 1960s women's movement. The phrase acknowledged that women's oppression occurred internally through the **ideological state apparatuses** of family life, notions of domesticity and femininity, and the media. The idea of traditional marriage, wherein a woman owed her livelihood and allegiance to her husband, was itself forcefully critiqued. If both husband and wife worked outside the home, why was the woman still expected to prepare dinner every night? Why were women expected to obey their husbands, even if they turned abusive? Why was access to birth control only available through men? Women's issues of the 1960s crossed all aspects of life, from the tiniest personal details of private relationships to the role of women in the federal government. Feminism therefore quickly became a variety of *feminisms*, with radical, moderate, and conservative feminist groups arguing about the proper way to advance women's equality. Women's lives and issues had become a thriving arena for civil rights struggle.

Hollywood made very little response to 1960s feminism. The industry did little to open its ranks to women filmmakers. As with other political issues of the 1960s (the war in Vietnam, civil rights more generally, etc.), Hollywood was not anxious to court controversy, and there was barely any interest in producing films that might be understood as forthrightly feminist. Instead, Hollywood continued to turn out standardized genre films, few of which featured particularly strong roles for women or acknowledged that any new social movements were underway. Film musicals and comedies such as *Mary Poppins* (1964), *The Unsinkable Molly Brown* (1964), *The Great Race* (1965), and *Thoroughly Modern Millie* (1968) did gently explore issues of female independence. Yet the films are all set in the early part of the twentieth century and deal with issues more common to first wave feminism than to second wave feminism. Similarly, Barbra Streisand starred as a strong working woman in the musicals *Funny Girl* (1968) and *Hello Dolly* (1969), but those films were safely set in the 1910s and the 1890s, respectively.

More regularly, the new Hollywood woman was figured as a more overtly sexualized version of the 1950s sex kitten or **blonde bombshell**. Just as Hollywood's reaction to first wave feminism emphasized the sexuality of the **flapper**, so studio films in the 1960s primarily pictured women's liberation as *sexual* liberation. The birth-control pill for women had become available at the start of the decade, and that development allowed many women a more self-controlled sex life. Women could now have the same kind of carefree sexual exploits that men had always enjoyed. A film like *Sex and the Single Girl* (1964), its title drawn from a contemporary sociological study by Helen Gurley Brown, promised to titillate audiences with its updated flapper character (played by Natalie Wood). However, with the **Production Code** still in place, many of those Hollywood films could not deliver on their sexual promises.

As such, an entire independent **sexploitation cinema** arose. Similar to the 1950s burlesque and nudist camp films from which they evolved, 1960s sexploitation cinema offered (mostly) female nudity and simulated sexual encounters for a (mostly) male audience. (Intriguingly, a filmmaker named **Doris Wishman** directed approximately 30 films in the sexploitation genre, making her one of the most prolific female filmmakers ever – at least in terms of the number of films that she completed.)

Most sexploitation films played in rundown urban theaters, and their popularity helped to weaken local and state censorship laws. Those legal developments, along with the debut of the **MPAA Ratings System** in 1968, allowed for the creation and circulation of hardcore pornographic X-rated films. For a short time in the early 1970s, attending pornographic movies was even a chic fad, and films like *Deep Throat* (1973) were listed by Hollywood trade papers as being among the top money-making films of those years. Wanting to cash in on some of the profits, Hollywood began incorporating sexploitation tactics and appeal into many of its movies. A famous sexploitation filmmaker, Russ Meyer, was even put under contract (albeit briefly) at 20th Century-Fox.

Many of the most popular films of the late 1960s and early 1970s were male–male **buddy films** such as *The Odd Couple* (1968), *Butch Cassidy and the Sundance Kid* (1969), *Easy Rider* (1969), *Midnight Cowboy* (1969), and *The Sting* (1973). Unlike the buddy films of the World War II era, however, these new pictures were far from joyous affairs. They often wistfully recreated earlier eras where "men were real men" and/or pessimistically suggested that American culture was coming undone because American masculinity itself was in decline. The fact that the heroes of many of these films often die in the final reel is one indication of this pessimism. Women were usually peripheral to these films, and some critics referred to them as platonic love stories between men, because most of them do posit male **homosocial bonds** as stronger and more important than any other type of relationship, including **heterosexual** coupling. When women do appear in the films they are often there as love (or more regularly sex) objects, a narrative function which serves to let the audience know that despite their love and longing for one another, the buddies are indeed heterosexual. This narrative "use" of women continues to this day in films and cultural institutions that celebrate homosocial bonds between heterosexual men.

The felt threat to masculinity caused by the rise of feminism resulted not only in the revival of the buddy film but also in increased images of aggression and violence against women. The new Ratings System allowed not only greater amounts of gratuitous sex but greater amounts of gratuitous violence to be seen on movie screens. Now it was regular Hollywood practice to show machine guns, knives, and other weapons ripping through flesh in gory detail. Disturbingly, some films of the era feature very graphic visualizations of sexualized violence, including rape. Stanley Kubrick's *A Clockwork Orange* (1971) features several scenes in which women are brutally assaulted by the film's charismatic hero; many viewers were outraged because this ironic and complex film eventually turns its rapist into a victim of the state and seemingly ignores or even celebrates his sexual crimes. Sam Peckinpah's *Straw Dogs* (1971) and Alfred Hitchcock's *Frenzy* (1972) also featured extended rape sequences. While most of these scenes were allegedly meant to call attention to the horrific nature of violence (and violence against women), sometimes they were understood by viewers as endorsing such acts. *Klute* (1971) more forthrightly presented the horrific nature of sexual violence but, somewhat problematically, the film explored women's issues by focusing on a prostitute (Jane Fonda, in an Oscar-winning performance). Furthermore, in *Klute* and other films

The Sting (1973) was a popular buddy film starring Robert Redford and Paul Newman, the actors who had also starred in *Butch Cassidy and the Sundance Kid* (1969).
The Sting, copyright © 1973, Universal

of this era, there is a sense that women are being punished for asserting their independence.

Along with *Klute*, Hollywood films of the late 1960s and 1970s did slowly begin to deal with contemporary issues facing women. *Rachel, Rachel* (1968) starred Joanne Woodward as a small-town school teacher facing severely limited options in both her professional and personal life. Other **woman's films** of the period include *Diary of a Mad Housewife* (1970), *Alice Doesn't Live Here Anymore* (1974), *Mahogany* (1975), *Julia* (1977), *The Turning Point* (1977), and *An Unmarried Woman* (1978). One of the most popular Hollywood films of the period to address feminist issues was the slapstick comedy *Nine to Five* (1980). In it, three working women (played by Lily Tomlin, Dolly Parton, and Jane Fonda) avenge themselves upon their sexist boss. It also should be noted that all of these films were produced and directed by men, although women did have input into many of the films' stories or screenplays. However, just as in the classical Hollywood period, these woman's films were controlled by male interests. The films are "updated" to the extent that they tentatively celebrate women's independence and touch on other feminist issues, yet most of them still fall back into old melodramatic formulas wherein women are forced to choose between careers and families.

By the late 1970s, Hollywood's tentative feminism had also extended to a new version of masculinity. The **sensitive man** – one who was in touch with his feelings and was nurturing to others – was briefly on display in many of the just-mentioned woman's films and in a small cycle of films that explored male parenting. In *The Champ* (1978), *Kramer vs. Kramer* (1979), *Ordinary People* (1980), *Author, Author* (1982), and *Table for Five* (1983), men learned how to become the primary caretakers (the conventional role of mothers) for their children, as opposed to distant bread-winners. However, many of these films celebrate the new man by demonizing the new woman. For example, *Kramer vs. Kramer* begins with a wife abandoning her husband and son, while in *Ordinary People*, a cold and harsh mother is seemingly to blame for a son's attempted suicide and a family's dissolution. The "sensitive man" drama was a brief cycle, and as the 1980s progressed, Hollywood stories of men getting in touch with their feminine sides were more likely to be presented as outright comedies. This trend continued in films such as *Tootsie* (1982), *Mr. Mom* (1983), *Three Men and a Baby* (1987), *Mrs. Doubtfire* (1993), *Big Momma's House* (2000), and *What Women Want* (2000). The image of the sensitive man is a good example of how **hegemonic patriarchy** is negotiated in Hollywood films. Whether drama or comedy, these films demonstrate that men can surpass women as parents (and even as *women*). They reinforce traditional gender roles by asking audiences to laugh at the idea of men "acting" like women. Although the traditional image of masculinity is slightly altered within these films, they still assert patriarchal centrality and importance by being about men in the first place.

Into the 1980s: A Backlash against Women?

The 1980s have been frequently theorized as an era in which the ideals of second wave feminism experienced a sort of cultural **backlash** – a strong adverse reaction in political and cultural spheres to feminist gains and goals. Much of this backlash to women's growing independence coincided with the presidency of Ronald Reagan (elected twice, in 1980 and 1984). Reagan had aligned himself with fundamentalist Christian groups such as the **Moral Majority** as well as fiscally conservative Republicans, and together they formed a powerful voting bloc that sought to curtail programs and policies (such as child-care programs and school loans) that had

Box: Women and American Television

In many ways, women's roles on American television have mirrored those in mainstream American film, and both have reflected the changing sociocultural constructions of gender throughout the decades. Early television programming of the late 1940s and 1950s also inherited ideas (and sometimes whole shows) from radio. For example, most network executives and advertisers assumed women made up the largest audience, since TV (like radio) was in the home – and most women were supposedly housewives. So cooking shows and soap operas were created and aimed at them, especially during the daytime hours. Such programs often reinforced the idea that a woman's place was in the home. Yet a number of women had important creative positions on these programs (such as soap opera writers Irna Phillips and Agnes Nixon), jobs rarely available to women in the film industry at that time.

Many early prime-time shows also featured housewives, perhaps the most famous being *I Love Lucy* (1951–7), which itself was an adaptation of a radio program called *My Favorite Husband*. The premise of the show was that Lucy (Lucille Ball) would concoct all sorts of madcap schemes (many centered on getting into her husband Ricky's nightclub show) that would then lead to comedic situations. While on one level Lucy is a dim-bulb housewife, her comic antics routinely upset Ricky's patriarchal authority, and she was clearly the star of the show. Lucille Ball was also a shrewd businesswoman, having formed the TV production company Desilu with real-life husband Desi Arnaz (who also played her TV husband Ricky).

As early TV was only capable of broadcasting to large urban areas, most programs took place in big cities. Because of that, early TV did feature a somewhat diverse range of female figures, including Jewish and African American women (*The Goldbergs* [1949–55], *Beulah* [1950–3]) and single working women (*Our Miss Brooks* [1952–6], *My Friend Irma* [1952–4], *Private Secretary* [1953–7]). As TV became more available to the rest of the country, though – and as many people moved into newly constructed suburban communities – programming became more homogenized. TV shows like *The Adventures of Ozzie and Harriet* (1952–66), *Father Knows Best* (1954–60), *Leave it to Beaver* (1957–63), and *The Donna Reed Show* (1958–66) presented an idealized white life in affluent middle-class suburbs, where Dad worked in a white-collar job, Mom baked cookies, and the kids were always well mannered. Women on TV were now almost exclusively white housewives who seemed inordinately content in this role.

By the mid-1960s, some programs began to – at least obliquely – hint that not all women found ultimate bliss vacuuming the living room wearing high heels and pearls. A spate of series debuted about young women chasing their own desires, much to the dismay of their fathers; these included *The Patty Duke Show* (1963–6), *Gidget* (1965–6), and *That Girl* (1966–71). A few domestic sitcoms even showed *adult* women negotiating social expectations of meek femininity with their own sense of power. Samantha on *Bewitched* (1964–72) and Jeannie on *I Dream of Jeannie* (1965–70) both had magical powers, but they were also housewives contained within patriarchal marriages, or, in the case of the genie Jeannie, within a magic lamp/bottle owned by her "Master." (Jeannie was also forced to wear skimpy pseudo-Arabian garments for most of the show.) Yet, like Lucy's before them, their magical antics always threatened to upset the patriarchal status quo.

A few shows in the latter half of the 1960s did attempt to integrate women into more action-centered narrative formulas. Dramatic series such as *Honey West* (1965–6), *The Girl from U.N.C.L.E.* (1966–7), *The Mod Squad* (1968–73), and the British import *The Avengers* (1966–9) showed women as private detectives and secret agents. *Star Trek* (1966–9) had a slew of "space bimbos" for Captain Kirk to woo and bed, but it also had several female officers (even if they too were clad in mini-skirts and go-go boots). Interestingly, in the original pilot for *Star Trek*, the spaceship *Enterprise* had a high-ranking officer named Number One, played by series creator Gene Roddenberry's soon-to-be wife, Majel Barrett. Number One was apparently so threatening to network executives that they insisted she be dropped from the cast when the show went into production. Still, Gene Roddenberry was deeply committed to both racial and gender equality, and his shows and movies (especially the later incarnations of *Star Trek*) have always tried to feature diverse casts; *Star Trek: Voyager* (1995–2001) eventually featured a female spaceship captain played by Kate Mulgrew.

Things changed a great deal for women on TV in the 1970s. Trying to reach upscale audiences (that is, those with more disposable income), CBS programmed a number of more urban, socially relevant shows. *The Mary Tyler Moore Show* (1970–7) dealt with a single woman more focused on her career than on romance. Produced by its star's own production company (MTM Enterprises), it gave rise to several other single-female-centered hits including *Rhoda* (1974–8) and *Phyllis* (1975–7). *Maude* (1972–8) was a spin off from Norman Lear's groundbreaking *All in the Family*, and centered on an outspoken feminist played by Bea Arthur. Yet the 1970s was not all emancipated women – ABC rose to the top of the ratings game with its "jiggle formula," exemplified by shows like *Charlie's Angels* (1976–81) and *Three's Company* (1977–84). Charlie's Angels were three private detectives, but they were always subservient to their male boss, and the series writers contrived ways to get them into revealing outfits week after week. (This formula for female action heroes has not changed all that much in recent years, either on TV or in Hollywood.) To its credit, during these years ABC also aired the popular female buddy sitcom *Laverne and Shirley* (1976–83).

The 1980s saw the rise of more female buddy sitcoms (*Kate & Allie* [1984–9], *The Golden Girls* [1985–92], *Designing Women* [1986–93]), and even a female buddy police detective show, *Cagney & Lacey* (1982–8). TV in the 1980s was also overrun with prime-time soap operas like *Dallas* (1978–91), *Dynasty* (1981–9), and *Falcon Crest* (1981–90), most of which represented women as conniving matriarchs, glamorous scolds, or sexpots. Reflecting the era's return to conservative values, the 1980s also saw the revival of the family sitcom. On shows like *Family Ties* (1982–9), *The Cosby Show* (1984–92), and *Growing Pains* (1985–92), women had careers outside of the home, but were rarely shown *at work* – they were more often depicted taking care of their husbands and children. *Murphy Brown* (1988–98) countered this trend. Created by Diane English and starring Candice Bergen, the show focused on Murphy's career as a TV journalist; the show became the center of an intriguing "real-life" controversy when Vice President Dan Quayle claimed that Murphy was a bad role model for wanting to be a single mother. The protagonist of *Roseanne* (1988–97) was not a career woman *per se*, but as a lower-middle-class mother of three, she often worked outside the home (as well as inside it). Roseanne has also been championed by some feminist critics for the way in which her body image – big, loud, and unruly – directly opposes the usual patriarchal definitions of quiet, subservient femininity.

The rise of narrowcasting and subscription channels in the 1990s and 2000s provided venues for new images of women on television. The cable channels Oxygen and We are purportedly aimed at women, but mostly feature re-runs of old TV movies and woman's films. HBO had a hit with *Sex and the City* (1998–2004), a popular comedy set in New York City about four working women and the men in their lives. While some decried the show for its seeming endorsement of premarital sex, others complained that although the women were in charge of their own work and sexuality,

Roseanne Barr, creator and star of *Roseanne* (1988–97), a popular television show about a working-class family in middle America.
Roseanne, copyright © 1988–97, Carsey-Werner Company/ABC-TV

their interests in high-priced fashion and designer shoes represented yet another way that women were trapped within the larger structures of patriarchal capitalism. Most recently, Showtime has offered *The L Word* (2004–), a show about lesbian friends liv-

ing in Los Angeles; the show was initially advertised as a sort of replacement for *Sex and the City*, complete with the promise of sex, fashion, and melodramatic intrigue.

In addition to favoring white characters in general, TV has also maintained a sexist segregation over the decades. Both advertisers and TV executives still aim day-time and night-time soap operas at women, while more action oriented shows, news, and sports broadcasts continue to be aimed at men. (Recent studies suggest that men may be leaving fictional TV altogether, as they increasingly tune in to all-sports channels such as ESPN.) Despite women's considerable successes as (day-time) talk-show hosts, news anchors, production executives, and all sorts of fictional doctors, lawyers, and politicians (and even vampire slayers!), according to some sources men still outnumber women on TV by as much as four to one. This statistic, of course, needs to be further complicated by other factors that this brief overview has only hinted at: scheduling, types of roles, overall screen time, production personnel, race, class, sexuality, etc. Just as in Hollywood filmmaking, women have made tremendous gains both behind the television camera and in front of it, but full equality between the sexes has yet to be reached.

benefited American women and children. Ironically, a cornerstone idea of those conservative preachers and politicians was **family values**, a catch phrase that sounded benign but which attempted to define a "real" or "true" family as one wherein a patriarchal father has ultimate authority over a submissive wife and children. Like many of the policies of the Reagan administration (such as reigniting the Cold War), the "family values" platform was **reactionary** – it sought to return the country to the ideas and **ideologies** of an earlier era, in this case the supposedly "better" era and attitudes of the 1950s. Perhaps the most significant blow dealt to the women's movement during the 1980s was the death of the **Equal Rights Amendment** (**ERA**) in 1982. This Constitutional Amendment would have made it a federal crime to discriminate on the basis of sex.

As part of these campaigns to return to traditional family values, many of the ideas and ideals of feminism were mocked by fundamentalist preachers and conservative commentators. Jerry Falwell, the founder of the Moral Majority and a powerful televangelist, referred to the National Organization of Women as the National Organization of *Witches*. Falwell's use of the term was meant to invoke all of its negative connotations and quite literally demonize the goals of feminism as Satanic. Popular conservative radio pundit Rush Limbaugh railed against what he called *Femi-Nazis*, effectively turning the word "feminism" into an epithet associated with fascism. (Indeed, many people even today still fear the word "feminism." When asked, most Americans support the idea of equal rights and opportunities for men and women but far fewer will admit to being themselves "feminist.") As part of this socio-cultural attack on feminism, masculinity itself also needed to be redefined. There was a newly felt pressure for American men both onscreen and in real life to prove how tough they were. Minor media circuses surrounded politicians who had to prove to the American public that they were not "wimps" or "sissies." President Reagan himself, who entered politics after a career in the movies, often capitalized on his tough-talking cowboy persona to maintain his popularity with voters.

Hollywood film reflected these trends in a variety of ways. The most financially successful type of film made during this era was the nostalgic Hollywood blockbuster, films like *Jaws* (1975), *Rocky* (1976), *Star Wars* (1977), and *Raiders of the Lost Ark* (1981) that updated old-time movie formulas and classical Hollywood genres. In most of these films, men are strong action heroes and women are princesses and/or passive love interests. Nowhere is this more apparent than in the era's highly popular **action-adventure movies**. Films like *Rambo* (1985), *Commando* (1985), and *Predator* (1987) gave rise to myriad sequels and imitators, and in many ways they define the anxieties and issues surrounding gender in the 1980s. Just as politicians were proving they weren't wimps in the real world, movie stars like Arnold Schwarzenegger, Jean-Claude Van Damme, and Sylvester Stallone were demonstrating that hypermasculine men could withstand any attack and still save the day, often single-handedly. Even male characters that were not as overtly muscled displayed their full-blooded machismo in action films such as *Sudden Impact* (1983), *Lethal Weapon* (1987), and *Die Hard* (1988). Most of these films reinscribed traditional concepts of masculinity and femininity – concepts that second wave feminism had been critiquing in the previous decades. Still, while they ostensibly celebrate traditional masculinity, the exponential outpouring of testosterone in these films seems to suggest cultural anxieties about those gender roles in the first place.

Anxieties about new gender roles were also on display in the few Hollywood films of the era that dealt with women in the workplace. Several films of this type, such as *Baby Boom* (1987), suggested the extreme difficulty if not impossibility of women managing both a career and family. (In fact, more and more women are being called on to do exactly that in today's economy, but Hollywood films rarely address that issue.) *Working Girl* (1988) is another film supposedly about female independence, but that nonetheless reinforces patriarchal ideals in several ways. The film shows that today's career woman (played by Melanie Griffith) *can* work her way up the ladder, although she does so with a little help from a corporate Prince

Sylvester Stallone, seen here in *Rambo* (1985), was one of several popular hypermasculine Hollywood stars in 1980s action-adventure films.
Rambo, copyright © 1985, Tri-Star

Charming (played by Harrison Ford). Even more problematically, while *Working Girl*'s heroine comes off as a dewy-eyed ingénue looking for her romantic hero, the film's villain is a conniving female executive (played by Sigourney Weaver). By placing these two female images in opposition to each other, the film encourages the viewer to choose one over the other, and also places the blame for the heroine's hardships in the workplace not on the institutionalized sexism of the corporate workplace, but on *other women*. Similarly, in the film *Disclosure* (1994), Hollywood reworked and actually inverted another serious woman's issue – sexual harassment in the workplace – into a story of a man (Michael Douglas) who is harassed by his female boss (Demi Moore). Women can and do harass men in the workplace, but in tiny proportion compared to the number of women harassed by men. But by devoting its first film about the subject to a situation in which a woman harasses a man, Hollywood again downplayed the significance of male domination and institutionalized sexism. The cultural backlash against feminism now posited that *men* were the victims of women who had overstepped their bounds and needed to be put back in their place.

The growing backlash against feminism (and the sexual revolution) was also strongly evident in one of the most profitable and disturbing genres of the 1980s: the **slasher film**. A low-budget subgenre of the **horror film**, the slasher film usually features a knife-wielding maniac killing women and teenagers in various gruesome ways. Among the most famous slasher films are *Halloween* (1978), *Friday the Thirteenth* (1980), *Dressed to Kill* (1980), and *A Nightmare on Elm Street* (1984), films that gave rise to multiple sequels and imitators. While both men and women are victims in these films, men are usually killed quickly offscreen or in shadows, while women are killed in full view, often in extended sequences of suspense and torture. The murder weapons in these films are obvious phallic symbols (such as knives, chainsaws, spear guns, electric drills, and jack-hammers), usually thought to represent male sexuality and aggression. Slasher films also repeatedly make use of subjective camera shots that put the spectator in the killer's place, as if the viewer is seeing through the killer's eyes as he murders and tortures.

Arguably, Alfred Hitchcock's *Psycho* (1960) might be considered the prototype of the slasher film subgenre but, although there were sporadic instances of the genre throughout the 1960s and 1970s, it did not become highly successful until the period of feminist backlash. Critics and filmgoers alike theorized that these cinematic attacks upon women were indicative of male frustration and rage over feminist gains. Roger Ebert of the *Chicago Sun-Times* was one of the first critics to note the trend and he repeatedly decried the rampant sexism and **misogyny** (hatred of women) that these films seemed to invoke and/or exploit. More recent feminist film scholars have attempted to demonstrate that slasher films are more complicated than simply misogynist, partly because they often feature a strong "Final Girl" hero who is often able to defeat the killer. Yet the "Final Girl" is usually a sweet, virginal character – one who represents an old-fashioned model of proper womanhood – while her sexually independent female friends wind up dead, in yet another reworking of Western patriarchy's **virgin–whore complex**.

A slightly more artsy version of the slasher films' narrative imperative to punish or demonize independent or sexually active women can be found in the era's resurgence of **film noir**. Just as Hollywood was nostalgically recycling and repackaging previous decades' science fiction and action films for 1980s audiences, it also revived film noir. Recall that this genre or style frequently explores or exploits psychosexual tensions between men and women (see chapter 12). It was first popular in the post-World War II era when men were returning from war and had to adjust themselves to the newly independent women they had left behind. Film noir blurred into conspiracy thrillers for a brief period in the early 1970s, but in the nostalgic **neo-noir** of the 1980s and 1990s, just as in classical film noir, suspicion and distrust among men and women lead to murder and mayhem. More often than not, women are figured as **black widow** spiders and conniving cheats. The neo-noir revival began in the early 1980s with a color remake of the Hollywood classic *The Postman Always Rings Twice* (1981). Also released that year was *Body Heat* (1981), in which Kathleen Turner played a very fatal **femme fatale**. Throughout the 1980s and into the 1990s, films such as *Against All Odds* (1984), *Black Widow* (1986), *Sea of Love* (1989), *Basic Instinct* (1992), and *Body of Evidence* (1993) suggested that

Jamie Lee Curtis as the "Final Girl" in *Halloween* (1978), one of the era's most successful slasher films.
Halloween, copyright © 1978, Falcon/Anchor Bay Entertainment

women could not be trusted. Once they had lured a man into their bed, these women might just as easily murder him with an ice pick as make love to him. One of the most popular films of the era about a murderous female was *Fatal Attraction* (1987). In that film, a man (Michael Douglas) cheats on his wife with a woman named Alex (Glenn Close), who eventually becomes quite unhinged. Alex harasses the man's family, boils their pet rabbit, and eventually attempts to murder the wife before she is herself shot down. In its representation of a crazy career woman out to destroy the nuclear family, the film is a perfect example of the era's conservative backlash against independent women.

A New Generation of Female Filmmakers

Male domination and institutionalized sexism still permeate the film industry as much as other workplaces in the country. Yet, in the last twenty years or so, more and more women in Hollywood have made their way into the director's chair. Just as increasing numbers of African American, Latino, and Asian American men have been able to break into directing Hollywood films, so have women. Most of these women are white, but a few women of color now also direct films released by Hollywood companies. The number of women in other aspects of film production has also continued to rise. Part of this increase is due to the changing times in which we live: women are now understood by most people as being as capable as men in most endeavors. This trend toward gender equity in the film business has also been helped by **affirmative action programs** that helped place women (as well as racial minorities) in film schools and training programs. A handful of women are now powerful Hollywood figures who have the ability to produce and direct their own projects. Dawn Steel and Sherry Lansing have even had opportunities to run major Hollywood studios. However, even though more and more women are now writing, directing, and producing Hollywood films, this does not necessarily mean that those films are feminist, or that they promote new ideas or understandings about gender. In fact, women filmmakers in Hollywood, if they want to be successful in the mass marketplace, are obliged to work within the same narrative structures and formal codings as are male filmmakers.

One can also see a bias in which women get to make films. Historically, it has been easier for women to enter the director's chair by first succeeding in some other aspect of the entertainment industry. For example, **Penny Marshall** first made a name for herself starring in the television sitcom *Laverne and Shirley*, a show that had been co-created by her brother, television producer Garry Marshall. In more recent years Penny Marshall has gone on to direct the Hollywood films *Big* (1988), *Awakenings* (1990), *A League of their Own* (1992), *Renaissance Man* (1994), *The Preacher's Wife* (1996), and *Riding in Cars with Boys* (2001). Barbra Streisand, who directed and starred in *Yentl* (1983), *Prince of Tides* (1991), and *The Mirror Has Two Faces* (1996), turned her considerable success as an actress and singer into the opportunity to direct those major motion pictures. Similarly, Oscar-winning actresses Jodie Foster and Diane Keaton have also directed films while maintaining their acting careers. Foster directed *Little Man Tate* (1991) and *Home for the Holidays* (1995), while Keaton has directed *Hanging Up* (2000) as well as the quirky independent films *Heaven* (1987) and *Unstrung Heroes* (1995). More and more actresses, including Goldie Hawn and Demi Moore, are entering film production

Penny Marshall began her show business career as an actress and has since become a successful director of Hollywood films.
Unidentified publicity photo, authors' personal collection

(though not necessarily film direction). Hawn has produced several of her own features while Moore was a producer on the popular "Austin Powers" movies (1997, 1999, 2002).

The most recent female filmmaker to win considerable acclaim is **Sophia Coppola**, daughter of the prolific **Film School Brat** Francis Ford Coppola. Sophia Coppola became the first American woman to earn a Best Director Oscar nomination, for her direction of the quirky *Lost in Translation* (2003), starring Bill Murray and Scarlet Johansson. (Her original screenplay for the film was awarded an Oscar.) Coppola followed that success with the historical drama *Marie Antoinette* (2006). Both films show young women trying to make sense of a confusing world around them, and the (possibly mistaken) choices they make attempting to gain some control over their lives. Such issues are also at work in her first film, *The Virgin Suicides* (1999), based on a novel by Jeffrey Eugenides. A period film set in the 1970s, *The Virgin Suicides* explores the lives of a strict Catholic family thrown into turmoil when one of its five beautiful daughters commits suicide. Repression – both sexual and emotional – is the major theme of the film, and Coppola's deft direction underscores the plight of the family's remaining daughters; for as much as their parents try to protect them, the girls' isolation eventually leads to tragedy. *The Virgin Suicides* is a complex film, exploring family, religion, gender, and sexuality in thoughtful and moving ways.

Increasingly, women are entering the film director's profession from the medium of television. Betty Thomas (who began as an actress) honed her craft directing for TV shows such as *Midnight Caller* (1988–91) and *Dream On* (1990–6). She has had since then success in Hollywood directing films such as *The Brady Bunch Movie*

Writer-director Sophia Coppola was the first American woman to be nominated for a Best Director Oscar, for *Lost in Translation* (2003). *Lost in Translation*, dir. Sophia Coppola, copyright © 2003, Focus Features/Universal

(1995), *Private Parts* (1997), *Doctor Dolittle* (1998), *28 Days* (2000), and *John Tucker Must Die* (2006). Similarly, Mimi Leder directed for the television series *ER* (1994–), *Midnight Caller*, and *L.A. Law* (1986–94) before directing the Hollywood blockbusters *The Peacemaker* (1997), *Deep Impact* (1998), and *Pay it Forward* (2000). Other women filmmakers have entered Hollywood's ranks after making commercially successful independent films. Penelope Spheeris first made a name for herself directing the highly acclaimed rock and roll documentary *The Decline of Western Civilization* (1981). Since then, she has had Hollywood hits with films such as *Wayne's World* (1992), *The Beverly Hillbillies* (1993), *The Little Rascals* (1994), and *Black Sheep* (1996). Likewise, Amy Heckerling began her Hollywood career with the low-budget teen comedy *Fast Times at Ridgemont High* (1982) and has since then directed popular Hollywood hits including *European Vacation* (1985), *Look Who's Talking* (1989), *Look Who's Talking Too* (1990), and *Clueless* (1995).

One thing that might be noted about the films just mentioned is that most of them tend to play by Hollywood's rules and formulas. Films such as *Big, Awakenings, Renaissance Man, Little Man Tate, Private Parts, Doctor Dolittle, Wayne's World*, and *Black Sheep* all focus on men and do little to challenge or address patriarchal form and content. (Indeed, the juvenile sexism of Howard Stern that is seemingly celebrated in *Private Parts* might be considered actively anti-feminist.) On the other hand, a few films such as *Yentl* and *A League of their Own* do attempt to address feminist issues. *Yentl* is about a young Jewish girl who must dress as a man in order to get an education, and *A League of their Own* follows the adventures of a female baseball team in the 1940s. *Clueless* is seemingly about young women in charge of their own lives, but the characters are made clownish and obsessed with consumerism and their own objectification. Women writing and directing films for Hollywood know that they must be cautious in making any sustained or serious critique of American patriarchal institutions and practices, both because film texts reinscribing dominant ideology usually sell more tickets than those critiquing it, and because the industry itself is still mostly controlled by (white) men. Thus, if women want to make films in Hollywood, they often find themselves forced to abide by Hollywood's ideological formulas. The structure of **classical Hollywood narrative form** (male heroes, female victims and sex objects, etc.) still often overwhelms any attempt to change it.

Those demands mean that women filmmakers wanting to address feminist concerns (or simply non-Hollywood issues) are usually forced to work in more independent modes. This is not to assert that there was and is no gender bias in the **avant-garde** and independent filmmaking worlds, but rather to acknowledge that historically those types of film practice have been more welcoming of minority filmmakers and subject matters than has Hollywood. For example, **Maya Deren** made a series of avant-garde films in the 1940s and 1950s that have been hailed as proto-feminist classics. Deren was a film theorist as well as a filmmaker, and she is perhaps the best-known figure of the so-called Poetic Cinema movement of the 1940s. Deren usually wrote, directed, edited, and starred in her own films. Her most famous film, *Meshes of the Afternoon* (1943), is still frequently shown in film classes and retrospectives. **Shirley Clarke** was another important figure in American independent film. From the 1950s through the 1980s, Clarke directed films and videos that focused on the harsh realities of inner-city life. Her film *The Connection* (1961) is about drug addiction, and *Portrait of Jason* (1967) is about an isolated black homosexual. Harsh and uncompromising, Clarke's best work explored topics that the Hollywood industry considered taboo. Sadly, much of her work remains very difficult to see today. Better known is the documentary filmmaker **Barbara Kopple**, who won considerable acclaim and two Oscars for her films *Harlan County, U.S.A.* (1976) and *American Dream* (1990). Although those two films focus on issues of class and unionization rather than on gender *per se*, Kopple also makes films that center on feminist issues, such as *Defending Our Daughters: The Rights of Women in the World* (1998) and *Bearing Witness* (2005). Kopple also directed *Shut Up & Sing* (2006), a film that documented the fallout and backlash that occurred when country music superstars the Dixie Chicks publicly criticized President George W. Bush. Barbara Kopple continues to be a highly regarded figure in American documentary filmmaking.

Avant-garde cinema in America and Europe became charged with feminist thought around the time of Laura Mulvey's groundbreaking critique of Hollywood, "Visual Pleasure and Narrative Cinema" (see chapter 11). Films such as *Dora* (1979, dir. McCall, Pajaczkowska, Tyndall, and Weinstock), *Thriller* (1979, dir. Sally Potter), *Riddles of the Sphinx* (1976, dir. Laura Mulvey and Peter Wollen), and *Daughter Rite* (1978, dir. Michelle Citron) attempted to question cinematic form and create a counter-cinema free of patriarchal assumptions. These difficult films alienated many audience members, including women, because of their radical style and engagement with film theory. More narrative and therefore audience-friendly independent films of the era included *Girlfriends* (1977, dir. Claudia Weill) and *Born in Flames* (1983, dir. Lizzie Borden). Also produced were the lesbian-feminist films of Barbara Hammer. In films such as *Superdyke* (1975) and *Synch Touch* (1981), Hammer playfully and politically celebrated the lesbian-feminist communities of 1970s America. Her more recent films (*Nitrate Kisses* [1992], *Tender Fictions* [1995], *The Female Closet* [1998], and *History Lessons* [2000]) examine the nature of history itself and how different media have represented women throughout the ages. Hammer's work, along with the independent and avant-garde film and video work of filmmakers like Su Friedrich, Sadie Benning, Jan Oxenberg, Andrea Weiss, and Greta Schiller, forms an important link to 1990s **New Queer Cinema** (discussed more fully in chapter 15).

Sadly, there is no real organized movement of independent feminist filmmaking in America at this time, although various industry support groups like **Women in Film** and **CineWomen** attempt to nurture and support talented new filmmakers. Every year more and more women enter the film-directing profession, and many of them produce important work that may or may not draw the attention of Hollywood. Directors like Mary Harron, Allison Anders, Tamara Jenkins, Nancy Savoca, Susan Seidelman, Martha Coolidge, Julie Dash, Maggie Greenwald, Julie Taymor, and Kasi Lemmons continue to make films that win considerable critical acclaim, if not always box office success. Most women filmmakers today work wherever they can: in television, in independent film, in music video, in commer-

Martha Coolidge has directed Hollywood films, TV shows, and cable TV movies, including *Introducing Dorothy Dandridge* (1999) and *If These Walls Could Talk 2* (2000).
Martha Coolidge directing *Real Genius*, copyright © 1985, Tri-Star

cials, and occasionally in Hollywood films, although, as this section has stressed, Hollywood films themselves are rarely able to address gender issues in significant ways. However, cable television shows and movies like *Sex and the City*, *If These Walls Could Talk* (1996), and *Introducing Dorothy Dandridge* (1999) are increasingly providing more opportunities for female filmmakers to address feminist (and other non-Hollywood) issues. The entertainment industry remains highly competitive for everyone in it, and especially so for women and people of color, who often have to overcome institutionalized sexism and racism.

Case Study: *The Ballad of Little Jo* (1993)

Like much of American film practice in the last decades of the twentieth century, *The Ballad of Little Jo* is a reworking of previous Hollywood conventions, in this case the genre of the Western. But unlike the usual mainstream nostalgic Hollywood blockbuster that unthinkingly reinscribes old genre forms and ideologies for contemporary audiences, *The Ballad of Little Jo* sets out to invert and upend the Western, to redress the biases of the classical form and provide a more realist take on the "old West." In so doing, it not only addresses the place of women within the genre and the mythology of the old West, it also tackles the racism inherent in the formula. Beautifully shot and acted, the film was written and directed by Maggie Greenwald, an independent American filmmaker who has since that time had a small **art-house** hit with her film *Songcatcher* (1999). Although *The Ballad of Little Jo* is a smart and entertaining film that encompasses thoughtful considerations of important topics, it remains little known because of its initial marginalization as an independent/art-house release.

The Ballad of Little Jo is based on an actual historical figure – a young nineteenth-century woman named Josephine Monaghan who went West and lived her life masquerading as a man simply in order to survive. The film dramatizes the limited choices women of that era had in their lives, and how they were continually at the mercy of patriarchal propriety and/or male brutality. Josephine is first driven from her East coast home and family when an out-of-wedlock affair produces a son, who is taken away from her. As Josephine heads West she is nearly raped and sold into sexual slavery by a man she thought was befriending her; after that, she decides it would be safer to travel as a man for her own protection. She dresses in male clothes – the film points out how even this simple act was against the law in those years – and cuts her face with a razor to make herself appear

more masculine. (Our culture celebrates scars on men as signifiers of their tough masculinity, while scars on women are understood as a tragic sign of lost "beauty.") Much of the following film details how Jo more than capably settles her own corner of the Wild West – herding sheep, building houses, and generally doing everything only men were thought to be able to do.

As part of the film's revisiting of the old Western myth, director Greenwald invokes a gritty realism when dealing with the nascent civilization of the Western outback. Gone are Hollywood's usual clean streets and white-clad cowboy heroes, happy school teachers and "saloon girls" with hearts of gold. Instead, Greenwald offers us a more realistic representation of dirt, rain, ill-fed people, and brutal, animalistic behaviors. In one of the most harrowing sequences in the film, a mute prostitute is brought to town by her pimp and put to work. The film does not shy away from the degradations and violence she is made to endure, and the spectator is forced to realize that this was a likely fate of many American women in the old West – a fate that classical Hollywood cinema has ignored or downplayed for almost a century.

Along with gender issues, the film also addresses the historical racism of nineteenth-century America (and by implication the Western film genre itself). The villains in *The Ballad of Little Jo* are not savage "redskins" but East coast capitalists who coldly murder people as part of their economic agenda to control the wealth of the West. Also remarkable is the character of "Tin Man" Wong, an Asian migrant worker whom Jo saves from a lynching. The "good" townsfolk were about to murder him merely for being an Asian immigrant who could potentially "steal" a job from a white man. Jo is forced to take Tin Man to her ranch as her employee in order to save his life, and the two grudgingly set up life together. It is here the film opens up and explores various parameters and

Conclusion: Gender in the Early Twenty-First Century

Over the last century, there have been tremendous gains for gender equality in many spheres of American life, but probably very few commentators would say that the playing field is now level – either in culture-at-large or at the movies. While recent

In *The Ballad of Little Jo* (1993), Suzy Amis plays a woman named Josephine who passes as a man in order to survive in the old West.
The Ballad of Little Jo, copyright © 1993, JoCo/Fine Line. Photo: Bill Foley

relations of racial and gender equity. Little Jo, a woman, "acts like a man" and runs the ranch, while Tin Man, as a non-white man, is treated like a woman and is expected to do the cooking and cleaning. Inverting the classical filmic paradigm of female objectification, Greenwald even creates a sequence in which Little Jo stares at Tin Man's objectified body as he bathes in the stream. Eventually Tin Man discovers that Jo is indeed a woman and the two begin a romance in which aspects of masculinity and femininity freely intermingle. The film thus models for the audience a relationship based on love and trust, one in which the inherent social hierarchies of race and gender have been overcome. However, Jo and Tin Man also know the townspeople would kill them if their various secrets ever became public: Jo for usurping male power and privilege, and Tin Man for daring to love a white woman. *The Ballad of Little Jo* forcefully dramatizes how respect, will, and compassion can overcome the limitations and hierarchies of race and gender roles that the townspeople – and by extension American culture-at-large – creates and enforces. The film may be a revisionist Western set in the nineteenth century, but its messages are still meaningful for American culture in the twenty-first century.

independent filmmaking has enabled some women (and men) to make interesting and important films that address issues of gender and gender inequity, mainstream Hollywood entertainment still negotiates gender in ways that uphold and maintain patriarchal privilege. The nostalgic Hollywood blockbuster formula, with its stalwart male heroes, continues to drive the industry. As was noted by many critics, the *Lord of the Rings* trilogy (2001, 2002, 2003) hardly had any female characters at all! *Gladiator*

297

(2000), *Troy* (2004), and *300* (2006) all rework old sword-and-sandal movies; as they exploit sexy male bodies in action, they are often simultaneously homoerotic and homophobic. Blockbusters adapted from comic books either present male heroes and female damsels (*Superman Returns* [2006], the *Spider-Man* films [2002, 2004, 2007]) or else allow for a few female superheroes as part of a male-run crime-fighting collective, as in the *X-Men* films (2000, 2003, 2006), and the *Fantastic Four* franchise (2005, 2007). Hermione in the *Harry Potter* franchise (2001, 2002, 2004, 2005, 2007) acts as a sort of token female wizard in a mostly male-dominated mythos as well. Similarly, the *Pirates of the Caribbean* franchise (2003, 2006, 2007) allowed Keira Knightly some occasional swordplay, but also reinscribed decades-old stereotypes about race and gender, as did *The Matrix* trilogy (1999, 2003, 2003) and the most recent *Star Wars* trilogy (1999, 2002, 2005). Even popular animated films tend to feature male protagonists and female love interests (the *Shrek* films [2001, 2004, 2007], *Shark Tale* [2004], *Ratatouille* [2007]), although they often seek to overturn some of the gendered clichés of the fairy tale genres on which they are based.

Intriguingly, over the past few decades, various male-dominated Hollywood genres have been adapted for female leads. The buddy film, which usually focuses on two men and their adventures, has been adapted into a film like *Thelma and Louise* (1991). The Hollywood sports film was adapted to be about women in *A League of their Own* and *Million Dollar Baby* (2004), and even the Western has been updated with female gunslingers in movies like *Bad Girls* (1994) and *The Quick and the Dead* (1995). The science fiction action-adventure film has also produced some strong female leads, played most notably by Sigourney Weaver in the *Alien* films (1979, 1986, 1992, 1997) and Linda Hamilton in the *Terminator* films (1984, 1991). More recently, the highly acclaimed martial arts film *Crouching Tiger, Hidden Dragon* (2000) featured women as sword-wielding warriors, while the *Tomb Raider* films (2001, 2003) featured a gun-toting, kick-boxing, death-defying female pro-tagonist whose adventures rival those of James Bond or Indiana Jones. Yet the female-centered action movie rarely enjoys the box office success that male action movies do, despite the presence of high-powered Hollywood stars, including Uma Thurman in the *Kill Bill* films (2003, 2004), Halle Berry in *Cat Woman* (2004), Charlize Theron in *Aeon Flux* (2005), and Milla Jovovich in *Ultraviolet* (2006). Arguably, Jovovich's Alice, in the *Resident Evil* film franchise (2002, 2004, 2007), has become the most financially successful female action character of the era.

While the presence of women as action-adventure heroes in Hollywood films has been seen as a step forward in Hollywood gender relations by many critics, others question the ways in which these films actually go about "equalizing" male and female roles. As noted in chapter 11, the majority of these films still try to appeal to heterosexual male spectators by objectifying their female performers. Note how the filmmakers maneuver Ripley (Sigourney Weaver) into her underwear for the climax of *Alien*, or how Lara Croft's body is constantly fetishized in tight clothes and even tighter close-ups. This formula might be traced back to the 1970s tele-vision show *Charlie's Angels*, one of the first successful mainstream entertainment products to exploit the formula of female action-adventure heroes with objectified

Thelma and Louise (1991), a feminist reworking of the Hollywood buddy genre, was a major box office hit, even as some male critics accused it of "male bashing."
Thelma and Louise, copyright © 1991, MGM-Pathé

sex appeal. That formula has been copied repeatedly in other films and television shows, and *Charlie's Angels* itself was turned into a nostalgic Hollywood blockbuster in 2000. Note also how many of these female action heroes either work for a male boss or in some way pay allegiance to the memory of lost fathers and/or husbands. Another criticism of these films is that the process of gender equalization that they seemingly undertake is a one-way avenue: women become equal with men by behaving like them. In other words, the films represent women's equality as the opportunity to be just as physically violent and brutal as men are allowed to be. Even though the films feature female leads, they arguably do so by endorsing patriarchal attitudes about masculine prowess and violent privilege.

The last two decades have also seen the rise of what critics and audiences increasingly called **chick flicks**. Films like *Pretty Woman* (1990), *Sense and Sensibility* (1995), *You've Got Mail* (1998), *Bridget Jones's Diary* (2001), *Legally Blonde* (2001), *Kate and Leopold* (2001), *The Lake House* (2006), *The Devil Wears Prada* (2006), *P.S. I*

Angelina Jolie as Lara Croft in *Tomb Raider* (2001) is an action hero, but she also appears throughout most of the film in skimpy and fetishistic clothing.
Lara Croft: Tomb Raider, dir. Simon West, copyright © 2001, Paramount

Love You (2007), and *Sex and the City* (2008) exemplify this trend. While some chick flicks are unabashed tearjerkers like classical Hollywood woman's films, others are more comedic and contemporary. The female characters in these films usually have careers and are more outspoken than their counterparts from previous eras. Also, chick flicks often stress female friendship as a support system in the face of adversity. Yet chick flicks often overtly celebrate of other aspects of traditional femininity – particularly shopping and beauty makeovers. Such celebrations of femininity reflect what some have referred to as a **post-feminist** sensibility, a fuzzy term that suggests a move beyond the goals and philosophies of second wave feminism. Post-feminism is sometimes seen as rejecting the idea that women's equality means women behaving like men. Post-feminism rests in an uneasy relationship to **third wave feminism**, the theoretical approach to gender that suggests there is no such thing as essential masculinity or femininity, that all gender roles are equally constructed by culture (and not genetics). Post-feminism supposedly "allows" women the right to choose to be conventionally feminine or not. While the issues that third wave feminism and/or post-feminism raise are provocative, patriarchal conceptions of gender are still reinforced by celebrating a woman for her beauty or her emotionality (whether or not she actively "chooses" to emphasize those facets of herself). And while chick flicks sometimes depict career women with sassy girl-friends, the main component of most chick flicks is still heterosexual romance – finding Mr Right.

At the same time as chick flicks became a more visible trend, there was a parallel rise of what some critics are calling **dumb white guy comedies**, movies about young men who fail to live up to patriarchal ideals. *Dumb & Dumber* (1994), written and directed by the Farrelly Brothers, is perhaps the prototype of this new genre. "Dumb white guys" are also at the center of popular teen sex comedies like the *American Pie* films (1999, 2001, 2003), and recent Will Ferrell and John C. Reilly comedies like *Talladega Nights* (2006), *Blades of Glory* (2007), and *Walk Hard* (2007). Although often dismissed by critics, these films arguably represent a new negotiation in **hegemonic** masculinity. On one level, they undermine and satirize masculine prowess as exemplified by films like *Troy* or *300*, showing that few "normal" men can truly live up to such lofty ideals of gender and sexuality. (Johnny Depp's bumbling Captain Jack Sparrow in the *Pirates of the Caribbean* films functions in similar ways.) Yet the films also ask audiences to laugh at their nerdish characters' failed masculinity, a process that still upholds those same ideals as natural and desirable. (In a way, these new comedies are similar to those made by silent film comedians like Buster Keaton and Harold Lloyd.) *Talladega Nights* is exemplary in this respect: some audiences can read the film as a satire of dumb white guy Ricky Bobby and his NASCAR (National Association for Stock Car Auto Racing) culture, while others may identify with him as he battles his nemesis, the stereotypical French gay race car driver Jean Girard (Sacha Baron Cohen). In many of these films, traditional masculinity is both mocked and upheld, an excellent example of the **hegemonic negotiation** of contemporary masculinity.

Interestingly, at the end of the 1990s, the chick flick and the dumb white guy comedy merged into a potential "date movie" that had something to appeal to both men and women. The enormous success of *There's Something About Mary* (1998), which combined both "sick humor" (for the guys) and sweet heterosexual romance (for the gals), led to a number of similar projects such as *Wedding Crashers* (2005), *Knocked Up* (2007), and *What Happens in Vegas* (2008). The successful merging of these two seemingly opposite types of films indicates how much they actually have in common. Both, in their own ways, update but ultimately endorse traditional conceptions of masculinity and femininity.

Contemporary Hollywood filmmaking, by drawing on certain representational patterns and formulas left over from previous decades, continues to marginalize women and women's issues while both subtly and forthrightly privileging men and masculinity. Men still dominate the Hollywood industry, both behind the camera and in front of it. America still pays millions of dollars every year to see nostalgic Hollywood blockbusters that represent men as strong active heroes and women as peripheral princesses. Contemporary Hollywood woman's films and romantic comedies still encourage women to see themselves as incomplete without a man. Also, the sexual objectification of female bodies that increasingly surrounds all Americans is rarely critiqued (or even noticed) outside of film and media classes. Nonetheless, as media consumers and media producers become more educated and aware of these issues, things will continue to change. More and more women and people of color are entering the Hollywood industry every year, and as the social understanding of gender in America continues to evolve, film in America will be part of that process.

Questions for Discussion

1 Some post-feminists argue that feminism has accomplished its goals and that women and men are now treated equally in American culture. Do your own personal experiences support that assertion or not?

2 Should women working within Hollywood make a more concerted effort to change the formulas and male biases of Hollywood film form? How can the moviegoing public be persuaded to accept such changes? What do you think is the best strategy for creating gender equity on Hollywood movie screens?

3 Do Hollywood images of women of color follow the same patterns of representation as do those of white women? Can remnants of older stereotypes – the Latina Lover, the exotic vamp, the Dragon Lady – still be discerned in Hollywood films?

Further Reading

Bell, Elizabeth with Lynda Haas and Laura Sells, eds. *From Mouse to Mermaid: The Politics of Film, Gender, and Culture.* Bloomington: Indiana University Press, 1995.

Carson, Diane, Linda Dittmar, and Janice R. Welsch, eds. *Multiple Voices in Feminist Film Criticism.* Minneapolis: University of Minnesota Press, 1994.

Faludi, Susan. *Backlash: The Undeclared War Against American Women*. New York: Doubleday, 1991.

Jeffords, Susan. *Hard Bodies: Hollywood Masculinity in the Reagan Era*. New Brunswick, NJ: Rutgers University Press, 1994.

Kaplan, E. Ann. *Women and Film: Both Sides of the Camera*. New York: Methuen, 1983.

Kuhn, Annette. *Women's Pictures: Feminism and Cinema*. Second edition. New York: Verso, 1994.

Mayne, Judith. *The Woman at the Keyhole: Feminism and Women's Cinema*. Bloomington: Indiana University Press, 1990.

Negra, Diane. *What a Girl Wants? Fantasizing the Reclamation of Self in Postfeminism*. New York and London: Routledge, 2008.

Pomerance, Murray, ed. *Ladies and Gentlemen, Boys and Girls: Gender in Film at the End of the Twentieth Century*. Albany: State University of New York Press, 2001.

Rich, B. Ruby. *Chick Flicks: Theories and Memories of the Feminist Film Movement*. Durham, NC: Duke University Press, 1998.

Tasker, Yvonne. *Working Girls: Gender and Sexuality in Popular Cinema*. New York: Routledge, 1998.

Tasker, Yvonne and Diane Negra, eds. *Interrogating Postfeminism: Gender and the Politics of Popular Culture*. Durham, NC: Duke University Press, 2007.

Thornham, Sue. *Feminist Film Theory: A Reader*. New York: New York University Press, 1999.

Further Screening

Alice Doesn't Live Here Anymore (1974)
Nine to Five (1980)
Ordinary People (1980)
Tootsie (1982)
Yentl (1983)
Fatal Attraction (1987)
Working Girl (1988)
Thelma and Louise (1991)

The Virgin Suicides (1999)
Crouching Tiger, Hidden Dragon (2000)
Songcatcher (2000)
Riding in Cars with Boys (2001)
300 (2006)
Knocked Up (2007)
Sex and the City (2008)

SEXUALITY
AND AMERICAN FILM

INTRODUCTION TO PART V:
What is Sexuality?

In its broadest sense, the word **sexuality** refers to sexual behavior – the conditions of being sexual. Sexuality is closely tied to biological urges that seem to impel human beings (and other animals) to mate. Sexuality is thus frequently connected to aspects of **sex** and **gender**; therefore, there are many **socially constructed** concepts that influence our understanding of it. For some, the only "proper" sexuality is **heterosexual monogamy** – genital intercourse exclusively between a legally married man and woman in order to produce children. Hollywood under the **Production Code** upheld the idea that heterosexual monogamy was the only proper sexual behavior (although this was always only implied because it could not be directly discussed), and many churches and civic groups today still endorse this traditional ideal. However, since the so-called **sexual revolution** of the 1960s, both men and women have begun to feel freer to explore and experiment with other types of sexual relationships. American cinema has reflected these trends, and just as in the real world, it is now not unusual onscreen to see people having a variety of types of sexual relations.

Commonly, "sexuality" is also used to describe **sexual orientation**, the deep-seated direction of one's erotic attractions and desires. Theoretically, there are an infinite number of ways that individuals might organize their sexual desires. However, Western culture has regularly reduced the plurality of those possible attractions/desires into either **heterosexuality** (wherein men are attracted to women and vice versa) or **homosexuality** (in which people of the same sex are attracted to one another). This binary oversimplifies and denies the variety of sexual desires and identities that human beings experience. For example, many people exhibit attraction to both men and women, and this is referred to as **bisexuality**. Still other people have little or no sexual attraction to anyone or anything, and this is called **asexuality**.

Many terms describing sexuality, such as "homosexuality" and "heterosexuality," are fairly recent inventions, having been coined at the end of the nineteenth century by early medical researchers. This is not to say that all sorts of sexual behaviors (including homosexuality and heterosexuality) had not existed before that time, but rather that with that act of naming, Western science now proclaimed homosexuals and heterosexuals as definite (and potentially opposing) *types of people*. With heterosexuals considered the norm, homosexuals were consequently identified as the **Other**, and because of that, twentieth-century lesbians and gay men experienced a great deal of persecution at the hands of the legal and medical establishments, various religious groups, and all sorts of social bodies and individuals. (Conversely, it has also been possible for gay men and lesbians to fight for rights and recognition on the basis of those same identity labels.) Psychologists, sociologists, and medical doctors argued back and forth for decades about what "causes" sexual orientation, and some still do. In so doing, most researchers assumed that heterosexuality was "what nature intended," and that homosexuality was a disease that could be cured. It was not until the 1970s that homosexuality was officially declassified as a pathology by the medical establishment. However, **heterosexism**, the assumption that heterosexuality is the only normal sexual orientation, and that it should be celebrated and privileged above all others, is still pervasive and usually unremarked upon in our culture.

Understanding sexuality also means understanding the differences between biological sex, gender, and sexual behavior. Some nineteenth-century sexologists, believing that everyone must be heterosexual in some **essentialized** way, theorized that homosexual men were actually female souls trapped within a male body, and that lesbians were therefore male souls trapped within a female body. This **gender inversion model** of homosexuality has been discounted since the early twentieth century. Today we separate concepts of **gender identity** (do you feel like a man or a woman?) from concepts of sexuality (to whom/what are you sexually attracted?). For example, some people feel as though they have been born into a body of the wrong sex, that is, that their internal gender identity does not match their outward biological sex. Medical science has labeled those individuals **transsexuals** (although many of them prefer to use the term **transgendered**). Some transgendered people undergo surgical procedures in order to bring their physical bodies more closely in line with their internal feelings, while others do not. Transsexuals should be differentiated from **transvestites** or **cross-dressers**, people who enjoy wearing the clothing of the opposite gender. Most cross-dressers are heterosexual, and they are rarely interested in changing their biological sex characteristics through surgery. Complicating matters even further, some people are born **intersexed**, which means that they biologically exhibit sex organs and/or sexual characteristics of both the male and female.

American society tends to understand human sexuality today in terms of sexual orientation or **sexual object choice** (to whom or what are you sexually attracted?). The phrase "sexual orientation" is preferred over the phrase "sexual preference," as most people feel that their sexuality is not something they can freely pick and choose on any given day. There are two main models of sexual identity formation that have held sway since the early twentieth century. The first is that sexuality is genetically determined. This model is known as the essentialist or **biological** model of sexuality – that one's sexuality is hardwired from birth, like left-handedness or having blue eyes. The fact that all types of sexual behaviors occur in other species lends credence to this theory. The other major model of sexual identity formation is known as the **social constructionist model**, which argues that people are born without a hardwired sexual orientation and are subsequently shaped into heterosexuals, homosexuals, or other sexualities via various social and cultural conditions. While many people over the past century have used versions of this model to argue that certain socially disfavored sexualities can be unlearned (through highly questionable medical practices such as lobotomies, castration, hormone treatments, and electroshock therapy), the model has also been used to destabilize the "normality" of heterosexuality. This model proposes that no sexuality is more healthy or natural than any other – all are equally constructed by social and cultural forces.

These two models (biological essentialism and social constructionism) are not necessarily contradictory. Many researchers now argue that while some potential for sexuality probably is hardwired into the human species, what an individual's sexuality will be and how it will express itself is also determined by the social factors and conditions that individuals experience during their lifetime. Today, while most people who study sexuality agree that sexual orientation is culturally constructed in many ways, it is nonetheless deep-seated and intricately structured into a person's overall sense of identity, and highly unlikely to be changed (or "cured"). In fact, in the 1990s, the American Medical Association formally declared that "reparative" therapies, designed to turn homosexual people into heterosexuals, were the equivalent of consumer fraud.

Since psychological research has moved away from trying to figure out what causes different sexualities, it has begun to explore why some people exhibit such passionate bigotry toward non-heterosexuals, and particularly homosexuals. This extreme fear and hatred is often termed **homophobia**. Psychoanalyst Sigmund Freud and some of his early followers theorized that homophobia is a defense mechanism against one's own homosexual tendencies. This theory is dependent upon the assumption that everyone's sexuality is potentially undefined before social forces shape us into either heterosexuals or homosexuals, and that unconscious homosexual feelings in consciously heterosexual people may become disconcerting: this is called **ego-dystonic homosexuality**. Thus, the compulsive hatred toward homosexuals that these individuals display is a vivid example of **Othering**: an attempt to displace and deny their own internal homosexual feelings. Such individuals try to eradicate homosexuality from society as a way of attempting to quell it within themselves, all the while proving to everyone around them how "not gay" they really are. Recent behaviorist researchers claim to have proven this theory by putting it to the test. They divided men into highly homophobic or non-homophobic groups on the basis of interviews and questionnaires, and then exposed each group to homosexual erotica and measured their sexual responses. The highly homophobic group showed more sexual response to the homosexual erotica than did the non-homophobic group, leading the researchers to conclude that Freud was right – homophobic people themselves have homoerotic impulses, but their conscious minds are unable to deal with it.

Our society is still so heterosexist and homophobic that it is often very difficult for individuals to come forward and identify themselves as not being heterosexual (this is called **coming out of the closet**). Homophobia and heterosexism are also deeply connected to the **patriarchal** culture in which we live, and frequently homophobia and heterosexism function as ways to enforce traditional gender roles. For example, if a boy exhibits sensitivity he may be called names such as "faggot," and a girl who doesn't want to wear makeup might be called a "dyke." In this way, the related social practices of homophobia and heterosexism work to enforce the binary opposition of traditional gender roles. Homosexuality, bisexuality, and transgendered sexualities all seem to imply the equivalence and interchangeability of male and female roles. To that extent, prejudice against gay and lesbian people (and all others who are not heterosexual) is perhaps an attempt to silence the idea of that equivalence – to maintain a sexist status quo wherein men are constructed as superior and women are denigrated as inferior.

As is evident from this brief overview, human sexuality (like race, class, gender, or ability) is a complex and highly individualistic thing. And as with other social groups, the words and symbols used to identify and describe sexuality have evolved throughout the years. The words "homosexual," "heterosexual," "bisexual," etc. were and still are used most regularly within the disciplines of medicine and psychology; the terms "gay," "lesbian," "straight," etc. are often used in more everyday language. In the 1990s, some sexual activists and academic theorists began using the term **queer** to refer collectively to all of the various non-procreative sexual identities that have just been introduced. Although a more recent term, "queer" is perhaps a more historically accurate one, as it is meant to describe sexualities that encompass but also exist outside of the simple straight–gay binary that most Western popular culture, including Hollywood film, usually configures. In so doing, Hollywood film ignores the sexualities of the millions of people who are in multifarious ways "not straight," that is, queer, and continues to contribute to the marginalization of and prejudice against those people within culture-at-large.

Chapter 14

HETEROSEXUALITY, HOMOSEXUALITY, AND CLASSICAL HOLLYWOOD

Just as socio-cultural ideas about race, class, and gender have evolved over the past century and affected the ways that those aspects of identity are represented on screen, so have depictions of **sexuality** evolved throughout the years. While this part of the book focuses primarily on how representations of **homosexuality** were manufactured before, during, and after the classical Hollywood studio era, these chapters will also recognize how images of **heterosexuality** have been constructed by film texts. Like whiteness or masculinity, heterosexuality has often been hard to "see" because it has been naturalized by patriarchal ideologies as being the "normal" state of affairs. (In fact, the study of heterosexuality – and how it relates to other social issues such as race, class, gender, and ability – is just now beginning to be undertaken within the humanities.) This chapter first reviews the heterosexual biases of Hollywood film form, then examines how homosexuality was represented in early Hollywood film. It concludes by discussing how some sexual minorities responded to classical Hollywood's representations of sexuality, and considers a few of the alternative images produced within the avant-garde cinema of the 1960s.

(Hetero)Sexuality on Screen

Heterosexuality has been present in American film since its inception. One of the first films made at **Thomas Edison**'s studio featured an actor and actress kissing and, as was discussed in chapter 2, by the 1920s almost every Hollywood film contained a romantic plot or subplot. Regardless of the genre or the specific goals of the protagonist, **classical Hollywood cinema** almost always includes the struggle to unite a male–female couple. In these films, not only is heterosexuality considered better than other **sexual orientations**, it is presented as the *only* sexual orientation. Such an assumption – that heterosexuality is the only (or only normal) sexual orientation – is a powerful aspect of Hollywood's **heterosexism**. Audiences watching these films experienced worlds wherein sexual identity was never questioned – everyone was straight, and heterosexual desire was understood as "natural" because there were no other choices.

Even as Hollywood films have more recently begun to acknowledge that the American population encompasses a variety of sexual identities, heterosexuality remains the privileged position, the center around which all others revolve, the norm against which all others are compared. For example, while heterosexual behavior is considered ordinary and unexceptional in mainstream cinema, the few non-straight people that do appear in Hollywood films tend to be conspicuously different. Straight characters are defined by their profession, their income bracket, or a variety of aspects other than their sexuality, but non-straight characters are usually defined primarily (if not solely) by their sexuality. (As we shall see, this trend often presents non-heterosexual figures as odd and eccentric, or even scary, threatening, and evil.) Furthermore, under heterosexist presumptions, only films that have homosexual characters in them are considered to be *about* issues of sexuality, much as people often think that a film is about race or ethnicity only when a racial or ethnic minority appears in it. The point to recognize is that Hollywood films always construct images of heterosexuality, just as they also (if more rarely) construct images of homosexuality. Thus, American film works **ideologically** to shape the way that both individuals and the nation as a whole make sense of sexuality in general.

Another issue that arises in studying the cinematic **representations** of sexuality (hetero or otherwise) is that sexual orientation does not always manifest itself as a highly visible social marker. There are few definitive indications that code a person as either straight or gay. For example, in Thomas Edison's early short film *The Gay Brothers* (1895), two men dance to the music of a gramophone: are we to understand that they are meant to be homosexual? They might simply be two heterosexual workers in Edison's factory performing for the newly invented camera, although the word "gay" in the title seems to imply that they are meant to be encoded as homosexual. (However, "gay" was only then evolving its contemporary meaning; throughout the first two-thirds of the twentieth century, most heterosexual people only understood the word to mean "happy.") As this example illustrates, in order to construct "visible" sexuality, characters must "perform" sexuality: they must be physically intimate with each other or indicate their desire to be so. As in real life, heterosexuals in the movies commonly make public displays of affection or desire, as when a man comments on a woman's beauty, or when a woman places a picture of her husband on her desk at work. Even more regularly, visual media texts employ **patriarchal** codes of **gender** – including hair, makeup, costume, and performance – to signal their characters' sexualities. "Real men" – that is to say, heterosexual men – are tough, bold, and assertive, and wear short hair and pants. "Real" or heterosexual women are expected to be meek, quiet, and subservient, and to wear long hair and skirts. Conversely, images of effeminate men or mannish women became the main method of representing homosexuality in early American cinema (and in some cases these conventions continue to this day).

Throughout the late nineteenth and early twentieth centuries, sexual relations between men and women were considered a delicate and frequently unspoken-of subject. Social historians point out that many of the earliest settlers of the English colonies were Protestant Puritans, who held very strict codes of behavior and considered any sex outside of procreative marital intercourse to be sinful. Interestingly, when the term "heterosexuality" was first coined by nineteenth-century medical researchers, it was used to describe a condition of disease (as was homosexuality). A heterosexual was someone who had sexual relations with someone of the opposite sex *outside the bonds of marriage*. During that era, monogamous, religiously sanctioned, and solely procreative sex between men and women was considered the only "normal" sexuality by both religious and medical figures. As we have seen in earlier chapters of this book, wanton and reckless heterosexuality was regularly used to demonize racial/ethnic minorities and members of the lower classes. More regularly, classical Hollywood narratives focus on the protagonist (either male or female) deciding between alternative types of heterosexual behavior (sex within or outside of marriage? with this partner or that one?) – with the advertising (posters, trailers) often enticing audiences with the possibilities. While indicating that there *are* multiple ways to be heterosexual, eventually one type of heterosexuality is indicated as "better": monogamous procreative marriage. Yet different ideas of what is considered "proper" heterosexuality have developed over the past century. Today, for example, sex outside of marriage and non-procreative sex have become common behaviors among heterosexuals, both in film and in real life.

Yet those changes in the cultural meanings of heterosexuality have not been without opponents. Throughout the twentieth century, various groups sought to control and censor sex and sexualized images (as still happens today in many places). Even Edison's film of a brief heterosexual kiss, mentioned above, was considered shocking, and people of that era called for its censorship. Hollywood has often been swept into these battles over censorship, as various films (as well as film stars) have caused scandals for violating what certain groups considered to be appropriate heterosexual behavior. (For example, when actress Ingrid Bergman left her husband in the late 1940s and had a child by another man, she was demonized in the press and didn't work in Hollywood for several years.) In truth, Hollywood finds itself in a paradox when it comes to sexuality. In trying to attract audiences, Hollywood films regularly include some sort of sexual titillation, but at the same time, they must appease moralists who object to such displays. Throughout Hollywood's classical period, consumer groups, the **Production Code**, and state and federal obscenity laws sought to police and regulate onscreen heterosexuality. In most cases, those same forces attempted to eradicate onscreen homosexuality altogether.

(Homo)Sexuality in Early Film

Just as images and concepts of heterosexuality have evolved over the past century, so have images and concepts of homosexuality. However, while heterosexual imagery was pervasively present, homosexuality was rarely acknowledged in early American cinema. Filmmakers shied away from obvious homosexual characters, and almost never depicted homosexual embraces or kisses. Instead, early Hollywood films used visual gender codes to construct male homosexuals as effeminate (and thus "failed") men, a stereotype that became known as the **pansy** character. Several early comic **Westerns** exploited this practice. *Algie, the Miner* (1912) and *The Soilers* (1923) include less-than-manly fellows prancing around (and in contrast with) more conventional he-men. *Wanderer of the West* (1927) introduces a shop clerk with the title card, "One of Nature's mistakes, in a land where men were men." Effeminacy in men was considered so innately odd and humorous that many silent film comedians, such as Fatty Arbuckle, Wallace Beery, and Charlie Chaplin, repeatedly cross-dressed in their films for comic effect. Even without sound dialog to explain it, films like these communicated to mainstream American society an image of what homosexuals supposedly looked and acted like: they were men that acted like women.

While pansy figures were the dominant image of homosexuality on silent American movie screens, a vibrant early example of this **gender inversion model** being applied to women can be found in *A Florida Enchantment* (1914). In this film, a woman and her African American maid (a white actress in **blackface**) swallow seeds that alter their sexual identity. Suddenly, the women are demonstrably attracted to other women, breaking off with their boyfriends in order to seduce young maidens. Conceiving that the seeds must have turned them into men, they abandon their bustles and petticoats for suits and ties. Toward the end of the film, one of the boyfriends also swallows a seed – resulting in his flirting with another man, and then donning a dress (considering himself transformed into a woman). Played for comedy, the characters (and by implication those involved in **encoding** and **decoding** the film) firmly linked same-sex attraction to the idea of gender inversion.

With such a heavy emphasis on homosexuals as people who deviated from traditional gender roles, individuals who *did* maintain traditional gender expectations were allowed a wide range of physical contact with others of the same sex during this period. For example, in many silent films the male characters hug and even kiss each other with fondness and sincerity. When two men embrace in *Flesh and the Devil* (1926), or when one man weeps and kisses his dying comrade in *Wings* (1927), most audiences at the time probably did not decode these characters as gay (the way that contemporary spectators might). Rather they were understood as heterosexual buddies – **homosocial** comrades and not homosexual lovers. Such demonstrations were allowed and considered heterosexual both in film and in culture because the men involved exhibited typically **masculine** (or in the case of two women, typically **feminine**) traits. The men in *Flesh and the Devil* are military officers, and the best friends in *Wings* are World War I pilots. No one minces, sashays, or bats their eyelashes in an effeminate way. As long as such characters upheld traditional patriarchal gender roles, most audiences probably never even countenanced the possibility of homosexual relations between them.

Early European cinema, unlike American, often had a more sophisticated take on human sexuality. When and if these films played American theaters, though, they were often so badly censored or re-edited that they lost most of their homosexual meaning. The same thing happened to the American silent film *Salome* (1923), produced by the famous lesbian actress Alla Nazimova. Based upon the play by Oscar Wilde (the famous English poet and playwright who had been imprisoned less than three decades earlier because of his homosexuality), the film featured an allegedly all-homosexual cast. It was heavily censored across the United States and for years existed as mere fragments of a feature. While Hollywood filmmakers and American audiences were happy to exploit the comedic stereotype of the pansy, they were reluctant to explore other, more complex aspects of homosexual art or homosexual lives.

By the 1920s, the American film industry was growing at an amazing pace, and its dizzying success created a slightly more open atmosphere for people to experiment with all sorts of untraditional behaviors. In Hollywood, a number of people felt freer to experiment sexually and/or express their same-sex desires more openly. A number of leading male actors, including **Ramon Novarro** and **William Haines**, led relatively open gay or bisexual lives. Rumors surrounded certain actresses as well, such as Janet Gaynor and Greta Garbo. Large numbers of gay, lesbian, and bisexual people also worked behind the cameras. In fact, it is often noted or claimed that the entertainment industries attract a disproportionately large number of homosexuals. One of the cultural reasons supporting this idea has been that theater, dance, and the related arts are considered by many to be less-than-masculine professions. Thus, the gender inversion model of homosexuality would lead people to think that any man who wanted to be an actor, a set designer, or a costume designer would have to be homosexual. Also, so the argument goes, most homosexuals of earlier decades had to remain in the **closet** and "play straight" in order to survive in heterosexual society – and because of this they became used to acting and inventing creative stories. Ultimately, the pervasive attitude that there are lots of gay people in show business may be a self-fulfilling prophecy, as homosexuals may enter the industry in the hope of finding others like themselves.

Related to this concept has been a historically consistent worry by some people that homosexuals in the entertainment industry have used their power to undermine the primacy of heterosexuality. Such worries of a "Pink Mafia" seem unfounded when looking at the history of Hollywood. While many lesbian and gay people were working in Hollywood in the 1920s, films that represent non-straight individuals in anything but a degrading comic light are extremely rare. Although some homosexual filmmakers lived slightly more open lives in the seclusion of the Hollywood hills, the majority of them still kept their sexuality a secret. Furthermore, filmmakers knew that in order to find success at the box office they had to make pictures that reaffirmed heterosexuality. The actor William Haines may not have hid from his friends and co-workers the fact that he was in a long-term relationship with another man, but onscreen he always played a heterosexual guy chasing a girl.

Actor William Haines was a top box office star in the late 1920s and early 1930s; when he refused to keep his homosexuality in the closet, he was fired from his studio contract at MGM. Unidentified publicity photo, authors' personal collection

Censoring Sexuality during the Classical Hollywood Era

The heady success of the Hollywood film studios during the 1920s had its effect on heterosexuals as well as homosexuals. Tales of torrid love affairs, quick Mexican divorces, and wild orgies filled the pages of movie fan magazines, presenting a hedonistic vision of Hollywood heterosexuality. Much of this held an appeal for American audiences in the 1920s, particularly the younger generation who were forsaking their parents' Victorian attitudes in favor of a new "Jazz Age" morality. Hollywood films also capitalized on this shift in values. A number of risqué sex comedies, made by directors such as Cecil B. DeMille and Erich von Stroheim, were released during these years. These films, such as *Old Wives for New* (1918) and *Blind Husbands* (1919), usually ended with a reassertion of traditional values: straying spouses saw the error of their ways, seducers were punished, and good, old-fashioned, patriarchal **heterosexual monogamy** triumphed – but only after the film had already titillated audiences with various sorts of sexual transgression.

Hollywood's reputation for sexual excess began to catch up with it during the 1920s, however, as a number of sex scandals rocked the industry. The most notorious of these involved star comedian Fatty Arbuckle, who was tried for manslaughter over the death of a young woman that occurred during an all-weekend party in 1921. Newspapers insinuated that the heavy-set comedian had accidentally killed the woman while forcing his sexual attentions on her. While Arbuckle was eventually cleared of all charges, the media stories effectively destroyed his career. This and other scandals also resulted in industry worries that the federal government might step in to regulate and censor American films. To keep that from happening, the studios came together to establish their own censorship board, headed by former postmaster general **Will Hays**.

When the Hays Office adopted the Hollywood **Production Code** in 1930, it forbade the depiction of any forms of explicit heterosexual display, as well as any implication of what it called "sex perversion," that is, homosexuality. (This in itself tells us something about how homosexuality was thought of at the time – as an abnormal medical condition that was inappropriate for representation in popular culture.) However, as we have seen, until the Code was enforced in 1934 – via the **Seal of Approval** provision – Hollywood films actually became *more* violent and sexual, in order to woo customers back into theaters during the darkest years of the Great Depression (see chapter 10). Husbands and wives were shown having affairs, and unmarried characters seemed to be having as much sex as were married ones. Biblical epics, such as DeMille's *The Sign of the Cross* (1932), continued to entice audiences with scenes of Roman orgies, even as the films themselves allegedly denounced such excesses.

Under such circumstances, images of homosexuals in Hollywood films were not too difficult to find. The **pansy craze**, a pop cultural phenomenon of the 1920s and early 1930s, had erupted in countless movies, plays, and nightclub acts of the era. Just as straight white New Yorkers traveled uptown to visit black nightclubs in Harlem, so they would also travel downtown to partake of the urban gay culture's

Marlene Dietrich, seen here dressed in a man's tuxedo in *Morocco* (1930), often played sexually adventurous women in pre-Code Hollywood films. *Morocco*, copyright © 1930, Paramount

drag shows and gay bars. Moviegoers were ushered into a pansy nightclub for a musical number in *Call Me Savage* (1932) and they discovered two men dancing together in *Wonder Bar* (1934). Lesbian chic was also a facet of the period. In *Morocco* (1930), a tuxedo-wearing Marlene Dietrich vamped both men and women.

In 1934, with the debut of the Seal of Approval provision, the Production Code Administration became a much more severe censor. The Administration pored over scripts and sent stacks of memos to studios, pointing out any character, situation, costume, or line of dialog that seemed to indicate anything less than strict **heterosexual, monogamous** propriety. (As discussed in chapter 10, this propriety also included strictures against sexual independence for women.) Married straight couples in Hollywood movies were expected to sleep in separate beds. Kissing had to be done with closed, dry mouths and last for only a few seconds. If it took place on a sofa or bed, the Code authorities mandated that at least one person's foot must be touching the ground! Of course, the enforcement of the Production Code did not mean that sex completely disappeared from Hollywood movies. Rather, it now had to be suggested obliquely and implied in more subtle ways. For example, when a romantic couple fell into each other's arms in front of a burning fireplace, the scene might fade to black and cut to the lovers the following morning, now wearing different clothes and smoking cigarettes. American film audiences soon learned to fill in the gaps. Other visual devices, such as dissolving from an embrace to waves crashing on the shore, or fireworks going off, or a train entering a tunnel, even more clearly suggested what the filmmakers could not depict forthrightly.

While representations of heterosexual desire had to be muted, and actual sex acts somewhat coded, heterosexual romance remained a building block of **classical Hollywood narrative form**. On the other hand, explicit representations of homosexuality were banned after 1934. Yet, just as various filmmakers discovered coded ways to suggest heterosexual coupling, homosexuality (or perhaps more accurately **queer** moments) also managed to find subtle ways onto the screen. The post-Code film *Sylvia Scarlett* (1935) is a good case in point. Much like one of Shakespeare's comedies in which men impersonate women and vice versa, *Sylvia Scarlett* created and exploited for laughs all sorts of queer situations based upon mistaken gender roles. In the film, both men and women find themselves attracted to what they think is a man, played by Katharine Hepburn. But because the film never explicitly acknowledged homosexuality itself, it managed to get past the Hollywood censors.

Connotative homosexuality became the usual way that classical Hollywood cinema represented gay and lesbian characters for the next thirty years. **Connotation** means implying or suggesting something rather than stating it outright. Thus, subtle signs that suggested gender inversion were added to characters in order to imply that they were not heterosexual. The fastidious apartment manager with his tiny mustache and clipped speech was understood by sophisticated audiences to be homosexual, just as the mannish prison matron was understood to be lesbian. Musicals and comedies still regularly featured the pansy **stereotype**, often as a supporting character in roles such as dress designers and choreographers (again connecting show business with homosexuality). Although the Production Code had forbidden filmmakers to **denotate** (or explicitly state) that these characters were homosexual, through subtle formal codes and stereotypical markers, audiences nevertheless understood them to be so.

Queer gender-bending touches were also used in Hollywood films to demarcate people who were villainous or criminal. Alfred Hitchcock was one of hundreds of directors whose films regularly employed this connotative strategy. For example, a Nazi spy in *Saboteur* (1942) speaks of having long blond hair just like a girl when he was a child: this deviance from traditional gender roles suggests a linkage between his connotated homosexuality and Nazism. Hitchcock's male killers in *Rope* (1948) and *Strangers on a Train* (1951) display a multitude of stereotypically effeminate traits, and both of those films subtly work to conflate deviance from traditional norms of gender and sexuality with murderous and psychotic criminality.

Hitchcock's *Psycho* (1960) is perhaps the best example of all: psycho-killer Norman Bates is a slightly effeminate young man who dresses in women's clothes and murders naked women. Is Norman meant to be a homosexual? A heterosexual **transvestite**? A **transsexual**? One ideological message of these films, and the thousands like them, is that people who exhibit traditional patriarchal gender identities are heterosexual heroes and heroines, whereas queer men and women are likely to be villainous or crazy.

This type of connotative coding flourished within most Hollywood genres, but especially within the **horror film**. In consistently telling tales about monstrous threats to "normality," most classical Hollywood horror films posit white heterosexual couples and institutions as normal, and everything else (non-white, non-straight, non-male-dominant) as frightening. *Dracula* (1931) and his vampiric cohorts, for example, are perhaps the most overtly sexualized of movie monsters: their attacks on both men and women are frequently represented as a form of seduction or rape. There is even an entire subgenre of the horror film known as the **lesbian vampire film**, and until the rise of gay and lesbian **independent filmmaking** in the mid-1980s, the image of the lesbian vampire was arguably the most common representation of lesbians on American movie screens. Mad scientists like *Frankenstein* (1931) and their closely bonded male assistants are always trying to create life without the benefit of heterosexual union, a queer subtext that the later cult film *The Rocky Horror Picture Show* (1975) satirically exploded. In it, Dr Frank N. Furter, a "sweet transvestite from transsexual Transylvania," constructs and brings to life a blond muscle-man for his own sexual pleasure. Overall, throughout its history the horror film has linked homosexuality with bestiality, necrophilia, devil-worship, murder, sadomasochism, and incest. Even today, some people who are prejudiced against homosexuality can only see it as a monstrous act linked with bestiality and Satanism, and not as a type of loving human relationship.

The director of *Frankenstein*, and several other classical Hollywood horror movies, was the openly gay **James Whale**. For an attuned spectator, it is easy to see Whale's homosexual sensibility at work in his films, most spectacularly in *The Old Dark House* (1932) and *Bride of Frankenstein* (1935). For both films Whale cast his old friend, female impersonator Ernest Thesiger, as a decidedly odd fellow who (in the latter film) steals Henry Frankenstein away from his bridal chamber so that the two men may continue their secret experiments in the queer creation of life. Whale was something of a rarity in Hollywood of the 1930s – an openly gay man who refused to "play straight" for his peers or for the public. (The Oscar-winning independent film *Gods and Monsters* [1998] is based on his life.) In the 1930s, most gay and lesbian people in America were forced to lead double lives, keeping their sexuality a secret. With no organized homosexual rights movement, they could be (and were) regularly fired from jobs, thrown out of social groups and leases, arrested and harassed, beaten and murdered.

In Hollywood itself, the relative sexual freedoms of the 1920s evaporated after the Code was enforced in 1934. Increasingly, "morals clauses" were inserted into employee contracts, allowing the studios to immediately dismiss workers for any behavior deemed unsavory, whether heterosexual or homosexual. Faced with the

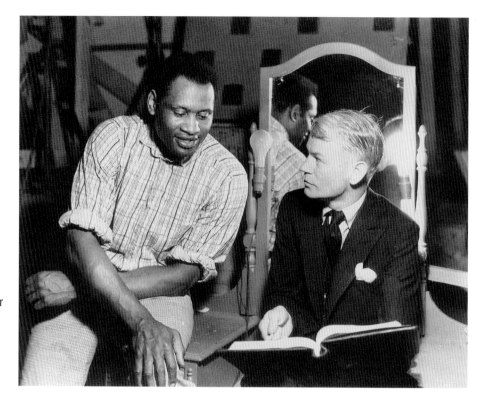

Director James Whale, who infused a gay sensibility into many classical Hollywood horror films, is seen here on the set of *Showboat* (1936) with star Paul Robeson. *Showboat*, copyright © 1936, Universal

possibility of being fired, many homosexual actors and actresses chose to hide their sexuality, aided by powerful studio publicity departments that arranged heterosexual dates or even fake weddings, known as **marriages of convenience**. Some of the famous actors and actresses from Hollywood's classical period who have been alleged to be either homosexual or bisexual include Charles Laughton, Danny Kaye, Cary Grant, Marjorie Main, Judith Anderson, Laurence Olivier, Agnes Moorehead, Marlene Dietrich, Randolph Scott, Cesar Romero, and Barbara Stanwyck. Many of these individuals went to their graves without confirming or denying their sexuality.

Directors, designers, musicians, and producers, because they were not in the spotlight as much as actors, usually did not take such drastic steps as arranged heterosexual marriages in order to remain employable. One of the most successful directors of the classical Hollywood era was **George Cukor**, a man most of Hollywood knew to be gay, but who was discreet about it. Perhaps because of his homosexuality, Cukor was pegged by the industry as a "woman's director," and he was allegedly fired from *Gone With the Wind* (1939) because leading man Clark Gable did not want to work with a homosexual director. In more recent years it has been suggested that Cukor knew of Gable's past homosexual experiences and that is why Gable had him fired. Nonetheless, George Cukor directed many classic American films during a career that spanned six decades, including *Camille* (1936), *The Women* (1939), *The Philadelphia Story* (1940), *Pat and Mike* (1952), *A Star is*

Gay Hollywood director George Cukor was discreet about his sexuality; he is seen here with Katharine Hepburn on the set of *The Philadelphia Story* (1940). *The Philadelphia Story*, copyright © 1940, MGM

Born (1954), *My Fair Lady* (1964), and *Rich and Famous* (1981). Another homosexual filmmaker who worked within the Hollywood system during the classical period was **Dorothy Arzner** (discussed at greater length in chapter 10). Arzner too was discreet about her sexuality. The pictures she directed were mostly melodramas and **woman's films**, a few of which have been reclaimed as important by both **feminist** and queer film theorists. Thus, while it was possible to be queer and have a career in Hollywood during the 1930s, one's life and livelihood were hampered to greater or lesser degrees by the constraints of the closet.

Postwar Sexualities and the Weakening of the Production Code

During World War II, many Americans became more familiar with concepts related to human sexuality. During the 1930s, a few books on sex education were tentatively published for the public (before that, they could only be sold to medical professionals), but by the 1940s sex was a topic that was being increasingly discussed in various venues. The tense and dangerous atmosphere of the war years meant that sex, or the lack of it, was often on people's minds. Some women considered it their patriotic duty to have sex with young soldiers who were shipping out and might never return. Similarly, "cheesecake" photos of female starlets were distributed to soldiers to remind them what they were fighting for, and soldiers were also shown frank instructional films about sexually transmitted diseases. Although homosexuality was certainly not encouraged by the government, under the conditions of war the American populace was predominantly segregated by gender, and strong emotional bonds were often formed between women working on the swing shift or between men at the front. Many gay and lesbian people met others like themselves for the first time during World War II. Realizing they were not alone, they began to form groups and subcultures, even within the armed services. (The history of homosexuality during World War II has been explored in the book and documentary film *Coming Out Under Fire* [1994].)

During the 1940s, psychiatric and psychoanalytic concepts were also being absorbed into mainstream culture. This meant that people now had a "scientific" vocabulary with which to discuss sex and sexuality. About halfway through the war, the armed services began using psychiatrists to identify and weed out homosexuals from the military, because it was felt that homosexual men were effeminate and would weaken the fighting caliber of their units. (A traditionally masculine man who engaged in same-sex relations was less likely to be considered a "true" homosexual and more likely to be retained.) The military's infamous "Blue Discharge" for homosexual men and women was based upon understanding homosexuality as a mental illness. Many of these dishonorable discharges chose to remain in the cities where they disembarked, rather than return to their small-town homes to face a potentially hostile reception from friends and family. It was chiefly in those cities (Los Angeles, San Francisco, and New York City) that gay and lesbian people began to congregate and set up new lives.

Homosexual rights groups such as the **Mattachine Society** (based in Los Angeles) and the **Daughters of Bilitis** (based in the San Francisco Bay area) began to organize in the postwar years; their members usually met in secret and used aliases, fearing for their safety and livelihood should they be discovered. The US government repeatedly tried to prosecute many of these groups' journals under obscenity laws, despite the fact they were social and political and not erotic in content. Reviewing these early journals from a current perspective, one can see that many of the people writing and reading them thought of themselves as mentally ill. They had so **internalized** the dominant medical construction of homosexuality that they used it as a basis for suggesting civil rights protections. Homosexuals should not be persecuted, so the argument went, but rather cured or helped to adjust to heterosexist society.

The rise of slightly more visible homosexual communities and changing scientific ideas regarding homosexuality precipitated a shift in the homosexual's social status in the postwar period. Most famously, Dr Alfred Kinsey's *Sexual Behavior in the Human Male*, published in 1948, revealed a much higher incidence of homosexual behavior among white American males than anyone had ever suspected. According to Kinsey's report, 37 percent of men surveyed had had homosexual sex. (Current statistics suggest that about 5 percent of the population self-identifies as not straight.) Kinsey also suggested that human sexuality was a fluid concept based upon social conditions and that the binary opposition homosexual–heterosexual should be replaced with a sliding scale that acknowledged that fact. Tied to this, the report helped usher in a new image of the homosexual not based on gender inversion. While the pansy stereotype did not completely disappear, American society now acknowledged that there had to be "straight-acting" homosexuals, as clearly 37 percent of American men were not pansies. Such statistics also forced a reconception of heterosexuality – now being straight meant not only "gender normal" but also not showing physical affection to members of the same sex. Heterosexual men began to fear being labeled homosexual for hugging another male friend (or sitting next to him in a movie theater). Since the 1950s, Hollywood films that depict homosocial male bonding have abandoned the embraces and kisses of silent films in favor of playful violence and (often homophobic) putdowns.

These new conceptions precipitated mass paranoia about homosexuality during the 1950s. Homosexuals were now thought to be secretly passing as straight in order to infiltrate and corrupt America. In fact, homosexuals were considered second only to communist sympathizers as the largest threat to national security during the first years of the **Cold War**. Homosexual workers were witch-hunted out of government jobs, and thousands more would be banned not only from the military, but even from private-sector jobs. (As of 2008, there is still no federal law completely prohibiting such discriminatory actions.) The linking of homosexuality to **communism** worked to drive homosexuals in the film industry further into the closet. For example, the rising career of **Rock Hudson** was insured by a constant studio-run effort to erase evidence of his homosexuality from the public eye. Hudson played brawny and masculine romantic leads, and he also married his female press agent in order to stamp out any potential rumors about his sexual orientation. On the other hand, when actor Tommy Kirk was discovered with another young man, he was quickly and quietly dropped from his contract at the Walt Disney studio.

Recall that while the dominant **Red Scare** culture of 1950s America was stressing conformity (see chapter 2), Hollywood found itself in economic difficulties because of the **Paramount Consent Decrees** and competition from television. Foreign films and American-made independent exploitation films were also cutting into Hollywood's profits. These films promised (but rarely delivered) more sex and sexuality than could be found in the usual Hollywood fare, and so they often made a great deal of money. For example, the French import *And God Created Woman* (1957) was a huge hit, primarily because it focused on the uninhibited sexuality of a **blonde bombshell** played by Brigitte Bardot. Enterprising independent filmmakers transferred theatrical striptease and burlesque acts to film, and programs of these short films also attracted heterosexual male spectators eager to see women displayed as erotic objects. Hollywood filmmakers quickly realized there was an audience for more "adult" subjects, and they too began to make sex comedies and steamy melodramas, often adapted from Broadway plays by writers like **William Inge** and **Tennessee Williams**. Many of these movies dramatized dysfunctional heterosexual relationships and dealt with issues such as lust, desire, impotency, rape, and sexual repression (albeit in still heavily coded ways).

These new adult Hollywood films encountered repeated problems with the Production Code Administration. In one famous example, the Code Administration wanted to censor the word "virgin" from the screenplay of *The Moon is Blue* (1953), but its director refused, and he released the film without the Code's Seal of Approval. When the film became a big box office hit even without the Seal, it proved to Hollywood that the Code was perhaps outmoded, and that sex was a topic that sold tickets. Many more films of the 1950s (both foreign and American) that dealt frankly with heterosexual relations contributed to the ongoing revision and weakening of the Production Code. Homosexuality, however, was still a taboo subject in Hollywood movies, and homosexual plot points in the film versions of Tennessee Williams's *A Streetcar Named Desire* (1951) and *Cat on a Hot Tin Roof* (1958) were either removed or (as usual) obliquely connotated. Perhaps most remarkably, Hollywood adapted and released a version of Williams's *Suddenly, Last Summer* (1959), in which Elizabeth Taylor plays a character who has been used by her homosexual cousin Sebastian to lure men into his circle of influence. The homosexual cousin never appears fully on screen, and in the end, he is ripped apart and devoured by a mob of men and boys upon whom he has preyed. Lurid and gothic, and full of the era's negative connotations of homosexuality (that is, that homosexuality is predatory, pedophilic, decadent, and monstrous), the film was a box office hit even as it was condemned by moral watchdog groups such as the Catholic **Legion of Decency**.

Tea and Sympathy (1956) was another film adapted from a Broadway play that challenged the Production Code with implied homosexuality. Eventually, Hollywood filmed a watered-down version of the play that shifted the issue from sexuality to gender. For example, while Sherwood Anderson's play points out that its young male protagonist Tom is taunted by his classmates for being homosexual, in the film version the classmates taunt him for simply being "unmanly." Interestingly, while Tom is singled out because of his "feminine" traits, the gruff housemaster seems to be vaguely uncertain about his own sexual orientation. Conventionally masculine (as shown in scenes of his boisterous homosocial roughhousing with his male charges), the housemaster is shown to have intimacy problems with his wife, who wonders aloud why her husband is so overtly antagonistic to the young man. Thus, buried within innuendo and connotation, *Tea and Sympathy* suggests that the husband may be dealing with repressed homosexual feelings himself, and that those are what fuels his discomfort with Tom in the first place. Drawing upon the heterosexist myth that a good woman can "cure" a gay man with her sexual charms, the play ends with the wife offering herself to the boy in order to ease him into heterosexuality. While the play ends without stating whether this provocative offer succeeds or not, the film adds a final scene, years later, informing the audience that the boy is now married – that his conversion therapy has worked. (The woman, on the other hand, having had sex outside of her marriage, has come to a tragic end.) Obviously problematic in its use of stereotypes, and full of erroneous ideas about the nature of human sexuality, the film does raise many interesting issues related to gender and sexuality in 1950s America.

In *Tea and Sympathy* (1956), a young man (John Kerr) is harassed by his classmates for being effeminate; in this publicity shot he is comforted by a house-mother (Deborah Kerr). *Tea and Sympathy*, copyright © 1956, MGM

In 1961, the Production Code was amended to allow for the depiction and discussion of homosexuality, as long as it was done with "care, discretion, and restraint." Hollywood's first few films to deal with the topic, however, fell back onto previous formulas and melodramatic clichés. In *The Children's Hour* (1962), based on a Lillian Hellman play from the 1930s, a school teacher hangs herself after her lesbianism is exposed. In *Advise and Consent* (1962), a promising young politician takes a razor to his throat when a past homosexual relationship threatens to come to light. The message in these films was clear: homosexuality was understood as a tragic flaw linked to violence, crime, shame, and, more often than not, suicide. At best, these films called for pity and sympathy for people who could not help suffering from the "illness" of homosexuality.

Not all homosexuals of the era considered themselves pitiful creatures, though, and as various other social groups began to organize and increasingly protest throughout the 1960s, many lesbians and gay men joined the struggle for civil rights. Gay and lesbian activists contributed to the vibrant American **countercul- ture** that opposed the status quo of racism, sexism, and the war in Vietnam. Perhaps unsurprisingly, the counterculture had little interest in mainstream Hollywood filmmaking, as it tended to uphold the dominance of **white patriarchal capitalism**. For inspiration, entertainment, and political meaning, the counterculture turned instead to foreign films, independent American cinema, and even more radical **avant-garde films**. It was in those American avant-garde films of the 1960s that some homosexual spectators found not only overt representations of themselves, but also a critique of Hollywood's representation of sexuality itself.

Camp and the Underground Cinema

Despite their denotative absence from American movie screens during the era of classical Hollywood cinema, many gay and lesbian people loved the movies and attended regularly. Hollywood movies offer an often-beautiful lie to spectators, and a chance to avoid reality for at least a few hours. Thus, it should not be surprising that members of any socially disenfranchised group, however defined, would be drawn to Hollywood's brand of escapism. Homosexuals were no exception, and during Hollywood's classical era many urban gay men developed a highly stylized approach to decoding Hollywood film that became known as **camp**. Camp is thus a textual reading strategy tied (originally but no longer) to a specific **subculture**. Camp is both an appreciation of Hollywood style and artifice and at the same time a critique of it. Camp reception is always a "double reading" in which the **form** and **content** of Hollywood film are both passionately embraced and simultaneously mocked. It is political in that it draws attention to issues of gender and sexuality and in so doing opens up spaces in which those roles may be analyzed and/or deconstructed.

Camp is often associated with gay men's idolization of certain Hollywood stars: Mae West, Judy Garland, Bette Davis, Joan Crawford, and Lana Turner, to name just a few. Camp is critical (often using disparaging humor as its weapon), but the idolization of these female stars by urban gay men suggests a genuine love and appreciation of them as well. Many of these female performers exuded a "bigger-than-life" quality both onscreen and off, a sense of always performing and never letting themselves be "real." This phoniness is important to camp taste, as evidenced by the fact that many camp icons were "bad" actresses or minor stars (such as Maria Montez), valued by gay spectators precisely because of their limited acting ability. It has been theorized that gay men and lesbians were drawn to these stars precisely because they mirrored the "heterosexual role-playing" necessarily practiced by most closeted homosexuals. Camp appreciation of such "bad" acting extended to certain male stars as well, such as muscle-man Steve Reeves, whose lesser acting talents pointed out that masculinity was just as much a performance as femininity. Furthermore, many of these stars, such as Judy Garland, faced other hardships in their personal lives (drug abuse, failed relationships), but were perceived as fighters as they gamely struggled through life. Gay men were attracted to both the exaggerated and performative gender of these stars (which in their extremes seem to suggest almost a parody of masculinity and femininity) as well as their determination to survive by way of that same performativity.

Camp thus became a subcultural way of simultaneously appreciating and potentially deconstructing mainstream Hollywood texts. It also formed the basis for a number of short films made by homosexual filmmakers such as Kenneth Anger, Jack Smith, and Andy Warhol. These films were part of the movement of **underground film**, American avant-garde filmmaking practice localized in and around New York City and Los Angeles in the late 1950s and 1960s. In many cases, underground films were taboo-breaking and highly controversial. Many of the movement's films, filmmakers, and exhibitors were repeatedly brought into court on obscenity charges. Underground film practice thus also helped to contribute to the demise of the Production Code, as court rulings slowly permitted more and more formerly taboo subjects to be depicted onscreen. These films were not pornographic, but they did contain some very raw and sexualized images and ideas for their era.

Many of the more famous underground films employ and engage with concepts of camp style and performance. Jack Smith's *Flaming Creatures* (1962) features characters (slave girls, vampires, Roman guards, etc.) and overly dramatic music drawn from exotic Hollywood melodramas. The cast participates in what might be called an anti-orgy: listless blank faces and body parts are wiggled at the camera in a parody of the Hollywood bacchanalia. Andy Warhol's early films also parodied Hollywood style and conventions: his actors (many of whom were drag queens) called themselves "superstars" and behaved as if they were Hollywood royalty. Warhol's radical minimalist style (long static takes of singular actions, as in the films *Eat* [1963], *Sleep* [1963], or *Couch* [1964]) further distanced spectators and by implication critiqued the lush opulence of Hollywood film. Perhaps the most famous underground film is Kenneth Anger's *Scorpio Rising* (1963), a film that combines found footage, contemporary pop songs, and a host of other cultural artifacts to examine the homoerotic cult of the motorcyclist. Incorporating footage of actual bikers and an old Hollywood movie on the life of Christ, the film compares religious cultism to the worship of the biker, and suggests that hero worship can lead to fascism.

Underground films were a short-lived and highly specialized filmmaking practice, and they provided an important social function as community-gathering events. Shown often at or after midnight in urban nightclubs and community centers, they allowed members of fledgling gay communities to meet and organize. Their status as "art" helped to legitimate camp and other aspects of homosexual culture within some mainstream circles. For example, in "Notes on Camp," published in 1964, cultural theorist Susan Sontag explored how camp as a form of urban, gay male reception practice was being assimilated into mainstream culture. She also distinguished between **naïve camp**, the camp of failed seriousness, and **deliberate camp**, the intentional construction of a film (or other cultural artifact) in such a way as to elicit a camp reaction. Naïve camp is thus a function of reception or

Case Study: *The Celluloid Closet* (1995)

Before it was a documentary film, *The Celluloid Closet* was a book by gay film critic Vito Russo (first published in 1981 and revised and updated in 1987). Both the book and the film survey the onscreen representation of homosexuality throughout the history of cinema. There had been a few other books about homosexuality in the movies (most notably Parker Tyler's 1972 book *Screening the Sexes*), but Russo's *The Celluloid Closet* quickly became a seminal text in gay and lesbian media studies. In the 1990s, award-winning filmmakers Rob Epstein and Jeffrey Freidman adapted the book into a feature-length documentary that was exhibited at independent art-house theaters, on pay TV, and via home video. In many ways, the decision to turn a book about the movies back into a film about the movies was an excellent one, because many of the characters and examples that Russo wrote about could now be collected and shown together within a single film text. Produced in conjunction with HBO Motion Pictures, the film is narrated by Lily Tomlin and features a variety of Hollywood stars, media scholars, writers, and directors introducing and commenting on film clips that illustrate the changing representations of homosexuality on American movie screens.

Like the book, the film *The Celluloid Closet* takes a roughly historical approach to its topic. It shows examples of how early Hollywood used gender inversion as a marker of homosexuality, and how it used the "pansy" stereotype as the butt of jokes. The film then explores how the Hollywood Production Code attempted to outlaw the representation of homosexuality, but also how clever

filmmakers could work around that proscription via connotation and implication. For example, a clip from *The Maltese Falcon* (1941), explained by media scholar Richard Dyer, illustrates in simple terms how costume, hair design, and music were manipulated by the filmmakers to encode a certain character as a homosexual. Audaciously, the filmmakers even had this character fondle a cane and bring it to his lips in a subtle phallic joke – one that was missed altogether by the Hollywood censors. The film also explores facets of spectatorship common to gay and lesbian audiences, and how in more recent years the figure of the homosexual moved from mere buffoon to outright threat. Hollywood stars such as Shirley MacLaine, Tom Hanks, and Susan Sarandon comment upon the gay and lesbian characters they have played, and screenwriters such as Barry Sandler (*Making Love* [1982]) and Gore Vidal (*Suddenly Last Summer* and *Ben-Hur* [1959]) talk about their experiences in confronting Hollywood heterosexism. Vidal's onscreen assertion that he put a homoerotic subtext into *Ben-Hur* actually sparked a flurry of protest in the pages of the *Los Angeles Times* when Charlton Heston, the actor who played Ben-Hur, wrote in to denounce Vidal's statements.

The Celluloid Closet is an expansive documentary made up of "talking-head" interviews and a wide variety of film clips that most Hollywood studios were convinced to let the filmmakers excerpt without paying royalties. It is an entire history of homosexuality in American film from its inception to the early 1990s, all told within a running time of 102 minutes. However, that necessary condensa-

decoding – finding something funny that was meant to be taken seriously. However, by the end of the 1960s, camp reading had become so prevalent and popular that Hollywood was itself releasing deliberately campy films such as *Candy* (1968), *Barbarella* (1968), and *Beyond the Valley of the Dolls* (1970). On television, shows such as *Lost in Space* (CBS, 1965–8) and *Batman* (ABC, 1966–8) were also produced as deliberate camp artifacts, and they briefly became pop culture sensations.

Yet, as with any subcultural artifact or practice that it is drawn back within the **hegemonic** mainstream, certain aspects of camp's specific political charge became watered down or neutralized. Artifacts of **pop camp**, such as the *Batman* television show, rarely question the dynamics of gender and sexuality (unless you start to

Peter Lorre as Joel Cairo (left) in *The Maltese Falcon* (1941). His hair, costume, hat and gloves, and cane suggest obliquely that he is homosexual – as do the expressions on the other characters' faces. *The Maltese Falcon*, copyright © 1941, Warner Bros.

tion sometimes forces the film to gloss over more finely nuanced arguments or theoretical concepts. The film also attempts to provide a **happy ending** by suggesting Hollywood's representations of gay and lesbian people are now somehow "accurate," when indeed there is still a long way to go before homosexuals are allowed equal time and equal treatment on Hollywood screens (as the next chapter will show). Nonetheless, the film remains an excellent introduction to the history of homosexuality in American film.

speculate about Batman and Robin themselves). Artifacts of **queer camp**, however, always seek to call into question the hierarchical constructions of gender and sexuality. The early work of independent gay director John Waters (including *Multiple Maniacs* [1970], *Pink Flamingos* [1972], and *Female Trouble* [1975]) are good examples of deliberate queer camp. These films star the transvestite actor Divine and consciously set out to satirize Hollywood conventions and middle-class mores. Even Hollywood produced a few deliberate queer camp texts during this era (such as *Myra Breckinridge* [1970] and *The Rocky Horror Picture Show*), but the trend was very short-lived. Even so, many of these films have since developed cult followings, and they are frequently revived in midnight shows reminiscent of the original underground film screenings.

Questions for Discussion

1 How do you "know" what you know about human sexuality? Sexuality is a topic that is often exploited to sell movie tickets and other consumer goods, but how much open discussion of it is actually permitted in our culture? In what ways is sexuality still considered a taboo topic?

2 Stereotypes linger throughout the decades. Can you identify examples of the "pansy" stereotype or the "mannish woman" stereotype in today's popular culture? Do homosexuals still meet "tragic" fates in film and television narratives?

3 What films seem campy to you, and why? What different types of camp do those films embody – naïve, deliberate, pop, or queer? Do these different types of camp overlap in some instances? How and why?

Further Reading

Benshoff, Harry. *Monsters in the Closet: Homosexuality and the Horror Film*. Manchester: Manchester University Press, 1997.

Doty, Alexander. *Flaming Classics: Queering the Film Canon*. New York: Routledge, 2000.

Dyer, Richard. *Now You See It: Studies on Lesbian and Gay Film*. New York: Routledge, 1990.

Farmer, Brett. *Spectacular Passions: Cinema Fantasy, Gay Male Spectatorships*. Durham, NC: Duke University Press, 2000.

Griffin, Sean. *Tinker Belles and Evil Queens: The Walt Disney Co. from the Inside Out*. New York: New York University Press, 2000.

Mann, William J. *Behind the Screen: How Gays and Lesbians Shaped Hollywood 1910–1969*. New York: Penguin, 2001.

Meyer, Moe. *The Politics and Poetics of Camp*. New York: Routledge, 1994.

Russo, Vito. *The Celluloid Closet: Homosexuality in the Movies*. New York: Harper and Row, 1987.

Tyler, Parker. *Screening the Sexes: Homosexuality in the Movies*. New York: DaCapo Press, 1972.

Weiss, Andrea. *Vampires and Violets: Lesbians in Film*. New York: Penguin, 1992.

White, Patricia. *unInvited: Classical Hollywood Cinema and Lesbian Representation*. Bloomington: Indiana University Press, 1999.

Further Screening

Sylvia Scarlett (1935)
Bride of Frankenstein (1935)
Rope (1948)
Tea and Sympathy (1956)
Suddenly, Last Summer (1959)

The Children's Hour (1962)
Scorpio Rising (1963)
The Rocky Horror Picture Show (1975)
Gods and Monsters (1998)

Chapter 15

SEXUALITIES ON FILM SINCE THE SEXUAL REVOLUTION

This chapter explores how **sexuality** has been represented in American film from roughly the 1960s to the present day. During the 1960s, many social and industrial changes began to dramatically alter the ways sexuality was depicted onscreen. Sexuality – especially heterosexual sex outside of marriage – was increasingly seen as both a personal right and a political tool to combat the repressive doctrines of previous decades. **Homosexuality** also began to take on a new visibility in popular culture, and, perhaps most importantly, became framed as a civil rights issue, and not a medical or criminal one. The decrease of censorship statutes, and the replacement of the **Production Code** with the **Ratings System** in 1968, allowed all sorts of sexually explicit images to reach the screen, and for a brief era, Hollywood itself even released some X-rated films. By the mid-1970s, however, Hollywood returned to moviemaking formulas that had worked in previous decades. During the 1980s, the AIDS crisis impacted in complex ways on American sexual mores, and partly in response to that state of affairs, new modes of thinking about human sexuality began to be formulated in both academic circles and independent filmmaking. In the early twenty-first century, Hollywood is slowly becoming more inclusive of America's diverse sexual cultures; however, Hollywood filmmaking almost always still upholds the hegemonic dominance of white patriarchal heterosexuality, or **heteronormativity**.

Hollywood and the Sexual Revolution

The term **sexual revolution** is sometimes used to describe the great social and cultural changes regarding sex, gender, and sexuality that took place throughout Western culture during the 1960s and 1970s. As such, the sexual revolution is closely intertwined with the rise of the **counterculture**, for sex and sexuality were integral to many of the social causes for which the counterculture was fighting. Young people and hippies rejected middle-class values and the sexual hypocrisy of earlier generations. They recommended to the nation that "if it feels good, do it." Similarly, women's rights activists knew that female sexual autonomy was a key to equality with men, and they worked hard for access to birth control and legalized abortion. Some civil rights workers recognized how **white patriarchal** control of sex and sexuality kept the races separate and unequal, while anti-war protestors exhorted the nation to "make love, not war." In some cases, sex and sexuality (or "free love" as it was sometimes called) were seen as the answer to all of America's political problems, most of which the counterculture blamed on repression, greed, and hypocrisy. If everyone felt free to make love however and whenever they saw fit, so the argument went, the world could be transformed from a hate-filled violent sphere into a loving, utopian space.

Other cultural, scientific, and industrial developments aided and abetted the sexual revolution throughout the 1960s. The birth-control pill for women became increasingly popular throughout the decade, and allowed women greater opportunities for sexual encounters without the risk of pregnancy. *Playboy* magazine (and its many, many imitators) became sexual primers of a newly liberated sexual lifestyle; the *Playboy* ethos promised that happiness and upscale success went hand in hand with casual sex. In state and federal courts, ongoing legal decisions struck down laws prohibiting sexually explicit books, magazines, and movies. The striptease and burlesque movies of the 1950s gave way to full-scale **sexploitation** films – feature films that showcased female nudity and simulated sex. By the start of the 1970s, after the fall of the Production Code, sexploitation films had evolved into **adult** or **pornographic films**, films that showed full male and female nudity and an array of actual sexual acts. For a few years in the early 1970s, pornographic films played alongside Hollywood films at malls and drive-ins, and the adult film *Deep Throat* became one of the top-grossing films of 1973. (The recent documentary *Inside Deep Throat* [2005] explores the impact that film had on 1970s American culture.)

Hollywood initially had a hard time coping with the sexual revolution (as it did with the counterculture in general). Slowly, Hollywood films of the 1960s began to feature heterosexual **protagonists** and **love interests** who went to bed together even though they weren't married. The popularity of the James Bond films in that era is due partly to 007's sexual magnetism and ability to bed a series of beautiful women. In many ways, James Bond was the epitome of the *Playboy* male. The Bond films were British imports, however, and just as in the 1950s, American moviegoers were turning to **foreign films** and/or **underground films** for more adult entertainment. Forced to compete, Hollywood began to address many formerly taboo subjects, and incorporate into Hollywood filmmaking the sexually explicit styles of foreign and **avant-garde** films. For a brief moment in the late 1960s and early 1970s, the various categories of art film, exploitation film, pornography, and Hollywood film blurred together to an unprecedented degree. One X-rated Hollywood film, *Midnight Cowboy* (1969), about a male hustler in New York City, even won an Oscar for Best Picture.

However, many critics decried the newly sexualized Hollywood, and there was a public **backlash** to theaters that screened X-rated films. With the rise of the **Film School Brats** in the early and mid-1970s, Hollywood fell back into its previously successful formulas. These new blockbusters were usually sexier and more violent than those of earlier decades, but the **genre** formulas and **ideological** meanings of the films remained about the same. Straight male protagonists continued to defeat the villain and "get the girl" by the final reel. This aspect of **Hollywood narrative form** has changed very little over the last few decades. Occasionally, the heterosexual romance is between people of different races or ethnicities, but **heterosexual monogamy** is almost always the implied endpoint of those cinematic relationships. **Woman's films** also continue to be made in Hollywood, but they too almost always revolve around "the search for Mr Right." Heterosexual relations are so much a part of the Hollywood formula that they are rarely even noticed to be a constructed aspect of Hollywood narrative form.

Film and Gay Culture from Stonewall to AIDS

Although sporadic protests and civil rights demonstrations in favor of gay rights occurred throughout the 1960s, the "birth" of the modern gay and lesbian civil rights movement is often associated with the **Stonewall Riots**. On June 26, 1969, police raided the Stonewall Inn, a small New York City bar frequented by all kinds of gay and lesbian people, **transgendered** people, and **queers** of color. It was business as usual for the police officers, but on that particular night the patrons fought back. (Movie star and gay icon Judy Garland's funeral had been the night before, and some historians point to that loss as inciting the patrons' simultaneous rage and courage.) Angry lesbians and drag queens of color led the way in the fight, leading to three nights of riots, demonstrations, and discussions of civil rights for homosexual Americans. Within months, many national newspapers and news magazines were announcing the birth of a new liberation movement similar to those being created by women, African Americans, Native Americans, and Latinos. Suddenly, a new minority group demanding fair and equal treatment came into mainstream America's view.

In the next few years, all sorts of lesbian and gay groups – both political and social – began forming. Political action groups such as the Gay Activists Alliance and the Gay Liberation Front were formed. Various lesbian groups also were established within and without the larger feminist movement of the 1970s. (Many lesbians felt more comfortable associating with straight women's groups than with gay male groups.) Gay pride festivals and parades began to be held in major urban areas every year in June, commemorating the anniversary of the Stonewall Riots. A major victory of the early gay and lesbian **civil rights movement** occurred when the American Psychiatric Association removed homosexuality from its list of mental disorders in 1974. On a more personal level, gay and lesbian rights activists (then and now) stressed the importance of **coming out of the closet**, the announcement of one's sexuality to family, friends, co-workers, etc. Coming out demonstrates that homosexual people are indeed everywhere – not just in the professions that Hollywood films had turned into clichéd stereotypes.

When the lesbian and gay civil rights movement burst forth at the end of the 1960s, the number of **representations** of gay and lesbian people in mainstream cinema was on the rise. Sporadic attempts to provide more realistic images of gay life were interspersed with the typical negative **stereotypes**. Right around the demise of the Production Code, even before the Stonewall Riots, movies such as *Reflections in a Golden Eye* (1967), *The Sergeant* (1968), *The Fox* (1968), and *The Detective* (1968) attempted to explore homosexuality (and its repression) with some degree of complexity. However, in most of these films the homosexual characters still face tragic endings – murder, disgrace, violence, and so forth. In films like *Staircase* (1969) and *The Gay Deceivers* (1969), swishy homosexual stereotypes continued to be used as the butt of jokes.

Two of the most famous (and least offensive) films released during this era were *The Killing of Sister George* (1968, about lesbians in the British television industry) and *The Boys in the Band* (1970, about a group of gay friends in New York City). Both of these films had been based on successful stage plays and might be said to represent more realistically what gay and lesbian lives were like in the late 1960s. Both films explore issues of romance, the closet, the possibility of blackmail and job loss, internalized homophobia, and the burgeoning (but still mostly underground) gay and lesbian culture of many cities. While these films may seem overly melodramatic or stereotypical by today's standards, they did capture a certain slice of reality for many urban homosexuals of their era. In part, these films got made and/or released by major Hollywood companies because the financially precarious

In this scene from *The Killing of Sister George* (1968), Childie (Susannah York) and George (Beryl Reid) attend a costume party dressed as classical Hollywood comedy team Laurel and Hardy. *The Killing of Sister George*, copyright © 1968, Palomar Pictures/ Cinerama Releasing

studios were willing to try anything in order to reconnect with their missing audience. (Remember this is also the period when Hollywood began to reach out to black urban audiences through the production of **blaxploitation** films; see chapter 2.) A very few other films, such as *Cabaret* (1972), handled queer sexualities with straightforward nonchalance, in so doing suggesting that homosexuality was just another facet of a character, and not a tragic or comedic flaw around which an entire moral lesson could be framed.

As we have seen with race and gender issues, Hollywood's new-found freedom of representation did not necessarily translate to "better" images of gays and lesbians. Rather, Hollywood throughout the 1970s tended to use its new license to **denote** more clearly the same homosexual stereotypes that it had employed **connotatively** in the past. Men in dresses or with pink poodles were still used as jokes in cop movies and action films, when they weren't child molesters or assassins. Lesbians were still figured as tough prison matrons or as outright monsters, as in a series of European **lesbian vampire films** (released widely in the United States) such as *Daughters of Darkness* (1971), *The Vampire Lovers* (1971), and *Lust for a Vampire* (1972). Another campy British **horror film**, *Dr Jekyll and Sister Hyde* (1972), reworked the "Dr Jekyll and Mr Hyde" story so that the monster was now a murderous transsexual. When Hollywood itself released a movie about a *heroic*

Based on a successful play, *Boys in the Band* (1970) explored issues faced by urban gay men in the late 1960s. *Boys in the Band*, copyright © 1970, Leo/Cinema Center transsexual avenger, *Myra Breckinridge* (1970), there was such public and industrial outcry over the film (and specifically its metaphoric rape of a cowboy actor) that Hollywood generally has shied away from representing transgendered people ever since, except as queer psycho-killers. In fact, the **cross-dressing** psycho-killer popularized in Alfred Hitchcock's *Psycho* (1960) has become such an overused stereotype, it is now something of a cliché.

Hollywood films also continued to whitewash the queer sexuality out of both historically queer characters and gay cultural innovations such as the urban discotheque. *Saturday Night Fever* (1977), which became one of the highest-grossing films of the decade, told a story set in Brooklyn's disco nightclubs without acknowledging that the musical idiom had been innovated by urban black and gay subcultures. By the time a more gaily tinged disco film was released in 1980 (*Can't Stop the Music*, starring the Village People and directed by Nancy Walker), America had realized disco's gay and black connections, and disco's popularity was suffering a severe cultural backlash. Now millions of white teenagers were encouraged to believe that "disco sucks."

Indeed, the prevalence of "killer fags" and "vampire lesbians" reflected growing fears in some quarters of American society about the new gay activism. By the late 1970s, many right-wing conservative Christian groups began to frame the growing gay rights issue as a moral one, and were openly attacking the idea of gay and lesbian visibility and basic civil rights protection. Former pop singer Anita Bryant's highly public crusades against gay people in Florida, and the Briggs Initiative campaign in California, were just two attempts of the era to deny homosexuals equal protection under the law. This opposition to gay rights became even more intense with the election to the American presidency in 1980 of Ronald Reagan, a man who had aligned himself with conservative religious groups such as the **Moral Majority**, the forerunner of the **Christian Coalition**. Many of those groups based their political platforms on the buzz phrase **family values**, which was basically an anti-feminist, anti-gay program to keep straight white men in control of the nuclear family and at the top of the socio-cultural hierarchy.

Hollywood mirrored this shift to conservatism right around the time of Reagan's election by releasing a series of queer psycho-killer horror movies: *Dressed to Kill* (1980), *Deadly Blessing* (1981), *Windows* (1980), *The Fan* (1981), and perhaps most (in)famously *Cruising* (1980). What was different now was that many of these films were met with organized protests from gay and lesbian civil rights organizations. The controversy over the film *Cruising*, which drew a link between New York City's urban gay scene and knife-wielding psychopaths, was an especially interesting case. Some critics found the film to be horribly homophobic (it seems to equate gay sex with murder on several occasions), while other gay critics (most notably Robin Wood) thought the film examined the murderous effects that can arise from the *repression* of homosexuality. Nonetheless, *Cruising* was thoroughly denounced by most gay and lesbian media watchdog groups at the time of its release. The protests may have only drawn more attention to an otherwise generic and sordid thriller, but they also demonstrated to the film industry that gay and lesbian audiences were now willing to challenge the Hollywood status quo.

Making Love (1982) was a rare Hollywood film that centered on homosexuality. In it, a married doctor (played by Michael Ontkean, left) comes to terms with his homosexuality.
Making Love, copyright © 1982, 20th Century-Fox. Photo: Wynn Hammer

Perhaps to atone for such images, Hollywood also released a handful of films in the early 1980s that seemed to go out of their way to create sympathetic gay and lesbian characters, and to examine issues of gender and sexuality in a serious dramatic light. *The World According to Garp* (1982) featured a supporting transgendered character, while *Personal Best* (1982) dramatized a lesbian relationship and issues of bisexuality. 20th Century-Fox released *Making Love* (1982), a melodrama about a married couple coming to terms with the husband's latent homosexuality. The public's differing responses to the same-sex love scenes in these films is illustrative of America's relative discomfort in seeing two men in sexual situations as opposed to two women. As explored in chapter 11, visual culture in America often "expects" women to be **objectified** for the pleasure of a male gaze. As such, the "girl–girl" photo-spread or video scene has been a staple of straight men's pornography for decades. Usually these girl–girl scenes can be distinguished from actual lesbian ones: made as they are by straight men for consumption by straight men, the women in these texts invariably enact traditional patriarchal constructions of femininity and play to the objectifying male gaze.

In contrast, the image of two men together on screen leaves a straight male spectator with no one to identify with except a gay man, and this situation can cause an acute discomfort in some male spectators. This discomfort is akin to **homosexual panic**, a term that refers to someone becoming highly agitated when confronted with his or her own potential homosexual feelings. Perhaps you have attended a screening of a movie in which two men kiss on screen and heard an audience member make derogatory comments or other disruptive noises. It seems as if the degree of identification evoked by the spectator–text relationship is disturbing enough to cause some people to assert, affirm, and vocally perform their own heterosexuality

– letting others around them know that they are not aroused by the gay images. In psychoanalytic terms, this need to deny or rebuke homosexuality is possibly indicative of a repressed conflict with it in the first place.

Far more popular with early 1980s American audiences were the frothy Hollywood comedies *Victor/Victoria* and *Tootsie* (both 1982). The former was a lush, old-fashioned musical farce, which slyly explored questions of sexuality and gender. Based on a German film from 1933, *Victor/Victoria* starred Julie Andrews as a destitute female opera singer in 1930s Paris who masquerades as a male drag queen in order to find work. When an American gangster (played by rugged actor James Garner) falls for "him," the film begins to explore the nature of sexual attraction. Victor/Victoria's best friend, Toddy, is openly gay and played with considerable wit and charm by Robert Preston. Although Victoria eventually reveals her female sex to the gangster, so that the two may share a traditional Hollywood **happy ending**, Toddy is also allowed to find romantic happiness with the gangster's tough-as-nails bodyguard (played by ex-football star Alex Karras).

Tootsie also explored gender and sexuality in a similar gentle, humorous manner, using the premise of a male actor (played by Dustin Hoffman) who pretends to be a woman to land a job on a television soap opera. Although *Tootsie* shied away from sexuality *per se* (there are no substantial gay or lesbian characters in the film), it did raise questions about gender roles in contemporary society, asking its audience to think about what it meant to be a man or woman in America in 1982. Popular music and fashion were also exploring similar issues at this time: gender-bending bands such as the Eurythmics and Culture Club were popular on the new televisual medium of MTV, and it seemed as though the country was ripe for an open discussion of sexuality and gender. But it was not to happen in a reasoned manner, because the hysteria of the early years of the AIDS crisis created a new knee-jerk demonization of gay and lesbian people, as well as a substantial backlash against the idea of gay and lesbian civil rights.

The AIDS Crisis

In 1981, the *New York Times* ran its first story about a newly identified disease that appeared to be afflicting gay men in urban areas. AIDS (acquired immunodeficiency syndrome), which had first been named GRID (gay-related immunodeficiency), was eventually shown to be caused by a virus that impairs the body's ability to fight off other diseases. The AIDS virus (also called HIV, or human immunodeficiency virus) therefore does not kill its host, but rather reduces the host body's ability to protect itself from a variety of other infectious diseases. Until 1985, when the highly publicized death of movie star **Rock Hudson** from AIDS-related diseases made mainstream America confront the epidemic, the government and much of American society had remained unconcerned about the disease. Perhaps this lack of concern was caused by the perception that only "social undesirables" such as homosexuals and intravenous drug users were contracting the syndrome. For others, panic and hysteria overwhelmed the discourse surrounding AIDS until it was discovered that the virus could only be transmitted through sexual intercourse or through the sharing of contaminated blood products. Even then, Congress repeatedly blocked attempts to fund either scientific research or educational campaigns about AIDS.

Sadly, many right-wing politicians and religious leaders (especially television evangelists) used the AIDS epidemic as "proof" of God's vengeance against homosexuals. (The fact that lesbians rarely got the disease seems to have escaped their notice, but it did lead some people at the time to quip that lesbians must then be God's chosen people!) Hemophiliacs who contracted AIDS were constructed by the media as the innocent victims of a plague allegedly caused by promiscuous gay men. This new wave of demonization initially had the expected effect on gay actors: driving them deeper into the closet, especially if they *were* HIV positive and in danger of unemployment. (Bisexual actor Brad Davis, who died of complications due to AIDS, left an angry letter to be published posthumously that condemned the way the film industry was dealing with actors who had the virus.) President Reagan, aligned with conservative Christian groups, was reluctant even to speak about AIDS during his terms in office. The perceived neglect of federal and state governments in the face of the crisis enraged many Americans and led to the formation of more activist political groups, such as **ACT-UP (AIDS Coalition to Unleash Power)** and the **Lesbian Avengers**. These groups often used then-developing home video technology to document their protests, capture police abuses on tape, and preserve a historical record of protests and demonstrations that were regularly ignored by national and local news programming. The work of these video coalitions was often shown in gay and lesbian community centers and helped to educate and energize a new generation of activists in the fight against AIDS.

As with other controversial issues in American culture, television did an arguably better job in responding to AIDS than did the Hollywood film industry. In 1985, the Emmy-winning television drama *An Early Frost* became the first widely seen movie to dramatize a gay man's struggle with AIDS. By contrast, Hollywood would not release a similar film about AIDS until eight years later, when Tom Hanks starred in *Philadelphia* (1993). It should be noted that both of these movies follow the usual Hollywood **social problem film** format, downplaying politics in favor of melodrama. They both also feature white men as their central protagonists, despite the fact that men of color were and are disproportionately more likely to be diagnosed with AIDS. Many men of color may not have been exposed to safer sex campaigns produced by and for gay men in urban communities, because gay men of color are sometimes less likely to be wholly out of the closet and/or welcomed into predominantly white gay communities. And as the government was stalling on its educational campaigns – or sabotaging them by refusing to allow a discussion of gay sex within them – many people, including teenagers and people in rural communities, remained ignorant of the ways in which they could protect themselves.

While the president, Congress, and Hollywood was busy ignoring AIDS as a social reality, the ongoing popularity of the **slasher film** during the 1980s worked to instill the idea that sexually active people would die a particularly horrible death.

Within these films, a psychosexual maniac kills women and teenagers in horrible phallic ways: knives, chainsaws, arrows, spears, drills, etc. are all pressed into service as teens have sex and are then murdered. As was discussed in chapter 13, those films and their depictions of brutalized women can be understood as part of a backlash to the **feminist** gains of the 1970s. However, just as 1950s science fiction films reflected America's fears and paranoia about communism, the 1980s slasher film also seems to demonstrate in metaphoric ways our nation's fear and hysteria over sex and sexuality during the first decade of the AIDS crisis. Other horror films about killer viruses and infected ghouls passing on their monstrous fluids were also quite popular during the decade.

More realist representations of the AIDS crisis and contemporary gay and lesbian lives could be found within the burgeoning independent and foreign film markets. Gay American independent films such as *Buddies* (1985), *Parting Glances* (1986), and *Longtime Companion* (1990) all dealt with the impact of the AIDS crisis on gay men in New York City. *Desert Hearts* (1985) was about a lesbian college teacher who "comes out" during the pre-Stonewall era. The British import *My Beautiful Laundrette* (1986) explored the connections between race, class, gender, and sexuality in contemporary London, focusing on an upper-class Pakistani man (Gordon Warnecke) and a lower-class, white punk rocker (Daniel Day-Lewis) who fall in love and start a business together. Another very popular independent film, *Kiss of the Spider Woman* (1985), starred William Hurt (who won an Oscar for the role) as an effeminate gay man imprisoned in a South American jail. Into his cell is placed a macho revolutionary played by Raul Julia, and together the men learn to live together and develop a bond of love. The film, based upon Manuel Puig's novel of the same name, explores the connections between political and sexual oppression, differing constructions of **masculinity**, and the role that popular cinema has had in creating life-sustaining fantasies, as well as politically dangerous illusions.

Gay and lesbian documentary filmmaking also thrived during these years. Following in the footsteps of *Word is Out* (1977), an independent documentary made by a collective of gay and lesbian filmmakers, gay and lesbian documentaries continued to bring to light stories and issues that the mainstream media ignored. Some of these films, such as *Before Stonewall* (1985) and *Silent Pioneers* (1985), documented forgotten aspects of gay and lesbian history. The Oscar-winning *The Times of Harvey Milk* (1984) chronicled the rise to power of our nation's first openly gay city councilor, as well as his eventual assassination by an unhinged right-wing politician. Other documentaries focused on AIDS. *Common Threads: Stories from the Quilt* (1989) created profiles of people who had died from AIDS and were subsequently commemorated with banners in the AIDS Memorial Quilt. *Silverlake Life* (1993) was a gut-wrenching personal video diary made by two lovers as they expired from the disease. Marlon Riggs's personal video documentary, *Tongues Untied* (1989), remains the era's definitive statement on what it was like to be a queer black man in the 1980s. Although *Tongues Untied* was aired on many PBS stations, many other public television stations refused to carry the documentary because of its "controversial" content, and it was even denounced in the US Senate because it had received some federal funds.

The ongoing radical activism generated by the AIDS crisis spread to other issues related to sexual discrimination – breast cancer, homophobia, and the role of the media. When *Silence of the Lambs* (1991) revealed that its gruesome serial killer was some kind of a transsexual/transvestite, and when *Basic Instinct* (1992) told its tale of a murderous bisexual woman, gay rights groups took to the streets in protest. Activists attempted to block the filming of *Basic Instinct* and threatened to disrupt the 1992 Academy Awards. The media watch group **GLAAD (Gay and Lesbian Alliance Against Defamation,** founded in 1985) insured that such protests would not go away quickly. In response to the increased and ongoing pressure from the publicity generated by these actions, various studio heads in Hollywood convened and announced the formation of **Hollywood Supports**, an organization devoted to dealing with both AIDS discrimination and homophobia within the entertainment industry. By 1994, over 800 "AIDS in the Workplace" seminars had been held, and by the end of the decade, every studio had added **sexual orientation** to its non-discrimination policy, and was offering domestic partner benefits to gay and lesbian employees.

Queer Theory and New Queer Cinema

During the years of civil disobedience that arose from the AIDS crisis, Western popular culture, including Hollywood film, increasingly began to acknowledge (however problematically) that homosexuality existed. Yet sexuality itself was still mostly understood as an either/or binary, reducing the diversity of human sexuality to simplified concepts of "gay" and/or "straight." In so doing, the sexualities of the millions of people who are in multifarious ways neither gay nor straight are ignored, shunted aside, and discriminated against. Activists began to use the word **queer**, as in the group name **Queer Nation**, to designate a "community of difference" inclusive of a broad variety of sexual *identities* and *behaviors*. Queer was not only meant to acknowledge that there are many different ways to be gay or lesbian, but also to encompass and define other sexually defined minorities for whom the labels "homosexual" and/or "heterosexual" are less than adequate: bisexuals, cross-dressers, transgendered people, interracial couples whether homosexual or heterosexual, disabled sexualities, sadomasochistic sexualities whether homosexual or heterosexual, etc. Even heterosexuals can be queer – the so-called **straight queer** – because queer as a theoretical concept encompasses all human sexual practices while rejecting the opposing binary hierarchies of sexuality and gender that currently govern our understanding of them.

The term "queer" gathers together multiple marginalized groups into a shared political struggle, as well as flings back at mainstream American an epithet that had been used to oppress non-straight people for decades. In the same way that many African American civil rights workers in the late 1960s felt increasing rage, queer activists were tired of a "go-slow" response to AIDS. People were dying because of it. Queer people were angry and they demanded to be recognized as part of American

Box: Queer TV

As with classical Hollywood filmmaking, early network television had its own censorship mechanisms that forbade the open acknowledgement or representation of homosexuality, or any other form of queer sexuality. Yet, as in classical Hollywood cinema, queer traces could still be found in early TV shows and stars, as in the recurrence of drag comedy on Milton Berle's variety shows, the gay auras of performers like Jack Benny and/or Liberace, or the butch tomboy persona of *Annie Oakley* (1952–6). Also, as pop art influenced mainstream American culture in the 1960s, a number of intentionally campy TV series such as *The Wild, Wild West* (1965–9), *Batman* (1966–8), *Bewitched* (1964–72), and *Lost in Space* (1965–8) exploited queer subtexts in more-or-less subtle ways. Although today the official taboos against depicting gay and lesbian characters on TV have been more or less abandoned, queer subtexting has endured across the decades. For example, the more recent syndicated hit *Xena: Warrior Princess* (1995–2001) had a huge lesbian fan following despite the fact that Xena and her gal-pal Gabrielle were never made explicitly homosexual.

In the 1970s, as homosexuals began to become more visible in the real world, TV did begin to acknowledge their presence. Mary Richards on *The Mary Tyler Moore Show* (1970–7) learned that her close friend Phyllis had a gay brother, and in one notable *All in the Family* (1971–9) episode, Archie Bunker was forced to re-examine his prejudices when he learned that his macho bar-buddy was gay. In a later series of episodes, Archie also befriended a female impersonator, who in her final episode was murdered by gay-bashers, much to the horror of the Bunker family. Starting in the 1970s, a number of made-for-TV movies (including *That Certain Summer* [1972], *A Question of Love* [1978], *Sergeant Matlovich vs. the U.S. Air Force* [1978], and *An Early Frost*) also focused on gay and lesbian characters and issues. The most popular queer show of the 1980s was the campy prime-time serial *Dynasty* (1981–9); supporting character Steven Carrington was gay in some seasons and straight in others. Still, the show was so popular that gay bars hosted *Dynasty* theme nights at which female impersonators appeared as bigger-than-life divas Krystal (Linda Evans) and Alexis (Joan Collins).

In the wake of the "Gay Nineties," network and cable television began to feature openly queer characters more and more frequently, either as recurring or as one-shot characters. But the breakthrough TV event of the 1990s occurred when Ellen DeGeneres and her sitcom character *Ellen* came out of the closet in 1997. This much-anticipated event (queer audiences had been reading the show as lesbian for years before it "officially" became so) became a media circus. It was denounced by homophobes and praised by liberals. Emotions ran high enough that bomb-sniffing dogs were used to secure the *Ellen* studios on the day that the coming out episode was filmed. And although some sponsors withdrew from the program and a few television stations refused to air the hour-long episode, it became one of the most watched and talked about TV events of the decade.

However, the openly gay *Ellen* was quickly cancelled by ABC (it had run from 1994 to 1998). That same year, *Will & Grace* (1998–2006) began to air on NBC, and its formula was arguably more successful with mainstream audiences. Lawyer Will and designer Grace are a good example of Hollywood's gay male/straight female buddy formula, and their heterosocial relationship comprised the central structure of the show. Although the show was popular with many different audiences, it rarely mentioned issues vital to contemporary gay men (such as AIDS or institutionalized heterosexism), and Will's gay friend Jack was criticized by some for being yet another version of the age-old **pansy** stereotype. *Will & Grace*'s success led to several copycat sitcoms (such as *Normal, Ohio* [2000] and *It's All Relative* [2003–4]), but none of them was on the air for long.

The cast of *Will & Grace* (1998–2006), a popular TV show that brought likable queer lead characters into American living rooms.
Will & Grace, copyright © 1998–2006, NBC-TV

Free of network regulation and the demands of sponsorship, subscription TV channels like HBO and Showtime have been able to produce and air more complex images of queer people and queer issues. Such programs have included made-for-TV movies (*If These Walls Could Talk 2* [2000], *The Laramie Project* [2002], *Normal* [2003]), mini-series (*More Tales of the City* [1998], *Angels in America* [2003]), and series (*Six Feet Under* [2001–5], *Queer as Folk* [2000–5], and *The L Word* [2004–]). Queer TV has also expanded into "narrowcast" pay and cable networks with the pay-per-view channel Here! TV (launched in 2003), and Logo (launched in 2005). Logo was created from within the corporate giant Viacom, and as part of the MTV Networks, it is aimed at younger, more multicultural audiences. As an advertiser-supported, basic or expanded cable channel, Logo cannot feature the kinds of explicit content Here! TV can, and it tends to edit the R-rated films it airs. Logo's original programming has included *Noah's Arc* (2005–7), about African American gay men, and *Rick & Steve: The Happiest Gay Couple in All the World* (2007–), an animated show that pulls few punches as it satirizes contemporary queer culture. The rise of queer TV has been important in bringing queer lives and queer issues to mainstream America, especially to people who would never go out to see a Hollywood film about queers (let alone an independent one).

culture and to have their concerns addressed. As one famous queer activist protest chant of the era proclaimed, "We're here, we're queer, get used to it!" This new use of the term signaled yet another shift in the public's understanding of sexuality.

While queer activists were demonstrating in the streets, universities across the nation and in Canada and Europe began to discuss what was soon labeled **queer theory**. In acknowledging the vast array of sexual desire that lies beyond the neat categories of heterosexual and homosexual, queer thinkers began to theorize on the fluid and **socially constructed** nature of sexuality. Following the work of scientists as different as biologist Alfred Kinsey and psychoanalyst Sigmund Freud, queer theorists argue that human sexualities – or races or genders for that matter – are not either/or propositions, but fluctuating, socially determined positions. Drawing upon **camp** notions of role-playing, queer theorists have analyzed all gender and sexuality as performative acts, not essential identities. For example, in order to iden- tify as a heterosexual, one has consistently to enact that identity – by voicing one's desires out loud, hanging up posters of ideal members of the opposite sex, or pos- sibly harassing someone who does *not* identify as heterosexual. Gay bashings, verbal or physical, thus become another way of asserting or performing heterosexuality. Queer theory, then, examines the social construction not only of homosexuality but of heterosexuality as well, in order to examine the ways and means by which **hegemonic patriarchy** constructs and maintains the idea that only one form of sexuality (married-straight-white-man-on-top-of-woman-sex-for-procreation-only) is normal and desirable. In fact, heterosexuality is itself a multiple and varied thing, sharing similar acts, behaviors, and desires with other types of sexual orientations (and movies and TV programs often revolve around the lead characters deciding which type of heterosexual behavior to follow).

These moves toward understanding sexuality in the terms defined by queer activism and queer theory are not without their opponents. Queer theory plays into the fears of social conservatives and the religious right, in that it does present a challenge to patriarchal concepts of gender and sexuality. Some gay men and lesbians hate the term "queer" because of the pain and anger associated with the word as an epithet. Some people prefer the strict categorization of either homo- sexual or heterosexual, refusing to believe that bisexuality is a possible orientation. Still other queers don't like the idea of straight queers, who are seen by some opponents as potentially diluting or reappropriating the struggle of "true" queers. And despite queer theory's focus on diversity, white males still tend to be the most seen and heard of queer spokespeople. Nonetheless, there are among most queer theorists, activists, and cultural producers the desire for and discussion of various forms of social diversity.

Queer theory has had an impact on many disciplines within academia, most notably within the humanities. In film and literature studies, people began to exam- ine the queerness of texts. A text might be considered queer if it was made by queers. This led to new research into contemporary and historically queer figures, and to explorations of how sexuality influences textual production. A text might also be considered queer if it is decoded by queers. Queer texts could also be ones that fea- ture queer content, either with overtly queer characters or with more broadly defined queer aspects. For example, it has been suggested that some literary and cinematic *forms* are themselves best understood as queer – film genres like the horror film, the musical, and the animated film, for example, construct unreal worlds in which queer forces can and do run amok. In its most general usage, queer theory tries to show how *all* sexualities are unique and complex socially constructed aspects of identity – that the full range of human sexualities cannot be contained within simplistic and hierarchical labels.

In the early 1990s, a cinematic movement, quickly dubbed the **New Queer Cinema**, arose from within gay and lesbian independent filmmaking. Its films used queer theory as structuring principles and were more overtly political than what had come before. New Queer Cinema openly challenged notions of taste, form, and ideology, as well as race, class, gender, and sexuality. Some of the important films of this movement were *Poison* (1991), *Swoon* (1991), *Paris is Burning* (1991), *The Living End* (1991), *My Own Private Idaho* (1991), *Zero Patience* (1993), *Go Fish* (1995), and *Watermelon Woman* (1995). New Queer Cinema has also been called "Homo Pomo" because the movement's films partake of postmodern ("pomo") styles and ideas, as does queer theory itself. Both **postmodernism** and queer theory focus on permeable boundaries, the blurring of styles and genres, and more generalized border crossings – whether those borders be sexual, regional, national, ethnic, or racial.

New Queer Cinema questions models of **essentialist** identity formation, and frequently challenges supposedly objective social constructs such as history itself. For example, films like *Swoon* and *Watermelon Woman* show how concepts of sexuality (as well as the historical record) have been constructed by those in power. New Queer Cinema simultaneously draws on minimalism and excess, appropriation and pastiche, the mixing of Hollywood and avant-garde styles, and even the mix of fictional and documentary style. For example, *Poison* is made up of three interwoven stories told in different cinematic styles. *The Living End* reappropriates the Hollywood road movie for HIV-positive queers, while *Zero Patience* is a ghost-story musical about AIDS. As might be expected from this brief overview, New Queer films tended to be activist and energetic. They were meant to be thoughtful, unruly, demanding, and sometimes shocking.

Although most New Queer films attempted to focus on the social construction of race, gender, class, and sexuality, many of them still carried a white male bias. Under **white patriarchal capitalism**, queer white men were still more readily able to obtain funding for projects than were women and people of color. Cheryl Dunye's *Watermelon Woman* was the first American film directed by an open lesbian of color, and that didn't happen until 1995. Jennie Livingston, who made the queer art-house hit *Paris is Burning* in 1991, has been unable to raise funding for another feature-length motion picture. On the other hand, at least one of New Queer Cinema's white male directors, Gus Van Sant, has also worked in mainstream Hollywood, directing films such as *Good Will Hunting* (1997) and *Finding Forrester* (2000). Unlike his earlier New Queer Cinema work and his more recent independent films (*Elephant* [2003], *Last Days* [2005]), Gus Van Sant's Hollywood films reflect more usual Hollywood **form** and **content** – realist storytelling that generally ignores or represses the topics of sexuality and gender.

Gus Van Sant was one of the leading directors of New Queer Cinema; he has since gone on to direct successful Hollywood films like *Good Will Hunting* (1997). Gus Van Sant directing *To Die For*, copyright © 1995, Columbia. Photo: Kerry Hayes

New Queer Cinema was also accused of recirculating old stereotypes such as the queer psycho-killer. A surprising number of New Queer films dealt with queers who commit murder. While many of the films attempted to show how and why social forces and/or sexual repression can cause individual characters to become violent, some viewers understood these films as simply reconfirming negative stereotypes. New Queer Cinema was also charged with snobbery or elitism, since it frequently engaged with issues of queer and postmodern theory – concepts of which many filmgoers had little to no knowledge. New Queer Cinema was thus sometimes less "audience pleasing" because it was challenging to audiences weaned on Hollywood style. In fact, in many cases the films deliberately critiqued or questioned Hollywood style, as did the feminist avant-garde films of the 1970s.

Nonetheless, the relative success of New Queer Cinema opened up new opportunities for all sorts of independent queer filmmaking (as did new distribution outlets such as subscription TV channels and direct-to-home DVD sales). Audiences desiring "feel-good" Hollywood-style narrative movies with happy endings can now find them in films like *The Incredibly True Adventure of Two Girls in Love* (1995), *Edge of Seventeen* (1998), *Billy's Hollywood Screen Kiss* (1998), *Better than Chocolate* (1999), *But I'm a Cheerleader* (1999), *D.E.B.S.* (2004), and *Dorian Blues* (2004). Most of these small films draw upon the conventions of Hollywood narrative form and the genre of the romantic comedy, but insert lesbian and gay lovers into previously heterosexual roles. A subgenre of films centering on groups of gay friends also attempts to provide easy-to-enjoy entertainment for queer audiences. Films such as *Love! Valour! Compassion!* (1997) and *The Broken Hearts Club* (2000) mix humor

The Incredibly True Adventure of Two Girls in Love (1995) is an old-fashioned romantic comedy about two young women from different backgrounds – one is upper-middle-class and African American while the other is working-class and white.
The Incredibly True Adventure of Two Girls in Love, dir. Maria Maggenti, copyright © 1995, Smash Pictures/Fine Line. Photo: Alyson Levy/Fine Line

with a few tear-jerking moments, but represent predominantly upper-middle-class white male characters. Still, even queers of color and transgendered people have become the subjects of independent features such as *Latin Boys Go to Hell* (1997), *The Adventures of Sebastian Cole* (1998), and *Punks* (2001).

Hoping both to entertain and educate, documentary features about queer people also continue to be produced in unprecedented numbers. Some, like *Paris Was a Woman* (1995), *Paragraph 175* (1999), and *When Ocean Meets Sky* (2004), examine forgotten aspects of gay and lesbian history. Others, like Arthur Dong's *Licensed to Kill* (1997) and the PBS "Frontline" documentary *Assault on Gay America* (2000), explore the psychosexual motivations behind gay-bashings, drawing upon research that suggests that many homophobic people are themselves conflicted about their own sexuality. (These ideas are also thematized in the fictional features *American Beauty* and *The Talented Mr Ripley* [both 1999].) Other documentaries take up specific queer concerns, such as the idiosyncratic sexualities that arise from the conflation of race, gender, and region. For example, *Southern Comfort* (2001) centers on transgendered people living in the deep

Love! Valour! Compassion! (1997), based on a Broadway play by Terrance McNally, centers on a group of gay friends who vacation together in the country.
Love! Valour! Compassion!, dir. Joe Mantello, copyright © 1997, Fine Line. Photo: Attila Dory

South, while *Venus Boyz* (2002) explores female-to-male gender-benders in New York and London. Still other documentaries, such as *One Nation Under God* (1993), *Trembling Before G-d* (2001), *Family Fundamentals* (2002), and *For the Bible Tells Me So* (2007), focus on the conflicts between queer sexualities and fundamentalist religions. Yet another batch of recent documentaries is beginning to address the growing phenomenon of lesbian and gay people getting married and raising children; these films include *Daddy & Papa* (2002), *Making Grace* (2004), *We are Dad* (2005), and *All Aboard! Rosie's Family Cruise* (2006).

Critics have debated whether New Queer Cinema was but a brief moment in film history (the early 1990s) or a more ongoing style (or even genre) of filmmaking. For example, although many independent queer films of the late 1990s and 2000s tend to be more conventional in style and content, other films of the period (including some of the documentaries just mentioned) seem to be made according to "New Queer" aesthetics. *Hedwig and the Angry Inch* (2001), for instance, is a very unconventional faux-documentary musical bio-pic about a transgendered

Case Study: *Go Fish* (1995)

Directed by Rose Troche and written by Guin Turner (who also stars), the New Queer Cinema hit *Go Fish* began its life as a Chicago-based short film project entitled *Max and Ely*. Along the way it caught the attention of producer **Christine Vachon**, an independent filmmaker sometimes referred to as "the godmother of New Queer Cinema." Vachon has produced many important films of the movement, including *Swoon, Poison, Stonewall* (1995), *Velvet Goldmine* (1998), *Hedwig and the Angry Inch*, and *A Home at the End of the World* (2004). Vachon guided *Go Fish* through its production process and it was sold to Goldwyn, an art-house film distributor, after premiering at the Sundance Film Festival. The film became an instant art-house hit in cities across America.

Go Fish is a good example of New Queer Cinema because it combines standard Hollywood narrative elements (a romantic comedy plot that features two women meeting and slowly falling into a relationship) with more avant-garde touches and musings on queer politics. Stylistically, the film often punctuates its realist narrative sections with experimental sequences. One such sequence explores the nature of marriage via multiple and overlapping audio and visual tracks. As different women in the film put on and take off wedding gowns, voice-overs comment upon the privileges and pressures of marriage as a patriarchal institution. Another sequence begins as an apparent gay-bashing, but it is a lesbian who is attacked by other lesbians, who forcibly question their "victim" on how she can "really" be a lesbian if she has occasional casual sex with her male friend. Further exploding the realist space of conventional narrative cinema, the film employs a Greek chorus of characters (or are they the actors playing the characters?) that comments upon the developing romance. At another point characters discuss what responsibility queer filmmakers have to show positive images – and what exactly a positive or negative image might be. The film is thus acknowledging its own status as a queerly produced film with a diverse array of images. And although the central relationship is between two white women, their friends are of mixed races, ethnic backgrounds, class statuses, and professional abilities. Combining both traditional aspects of Hollywood form (realist narrative, the conventions of romantic comedy) with more playful and political avant-garde touches, *Go Fish* emerges as a unique and fresh film, in terms of both its content and its style.

rock star. *Tarnation* (2003) is a personal expressionist documentary about growing up gay with a mentally disturbed mother. Barbara Hammer's *History Lessons* (2000) deals with questions of queer history and its erasure, as does *Brother to Brother* (2004). New Queer Cinema's interest in historicizing queer sexualities and interrogating media forms can also be found in a recent crop of highly acclaimed award-winning films (discussed below) including *Boys Don't Cry* (1999), *Far From Heaven* (2002), *The Hours* (2002), and *Brokeback Mountain* (2005).

Hollywood Responds to New Queer Cinema

The rise of New Queer Cinema did not go unnoticed by Hollywood, which briefly tried (unsuccessfully) to market a few films that explored more open parameters of sexuality, such as *Three of Hearts* (1993) and *Threesome* (1994). Would Hollywood ever find a marketable gay or lesbian hero? They (arguably) did so in *Philadelphia*, and in *To Wong Foo, Thanks for Everything, Julie Newmar* (1997), a film that was a thinly veiled Hollywood version of the independent Australian film hit *The Adventures of Priscilla, Queen of the Desert* (1994). Both *To Wong Foo* and *The Adventures of Priscilla* are comedies that focus on a trio of drag queens traveling cross-country, meeting and eventually overcoming hardship and prejudice. *To Wong Foo* even had a racially mixed cast: Patrick Swayze, Wesley Snipes, and John Leguizamo. Still, as with African Americans on television, Hollywood seems more comfortable with gay characters if they are comedic, whether in supporting roles (Harvey Fierstein's character in *Mrs. Doubtfire* [1993]) or as leads, as in *The Birdcage* (1996) – itself another Hollywood remake of a foreign film hit, *La Cage aux Folles* (1978).

By the end of the 1990s, a new Hollywood formula for depicting male homosexuality was evident. This reworked the Hollywood buddy formula so that it comprised a straight female lead and her gay male best friend. Hollywood films such as *My Best Friend's Wedding* (1997), *The Object of My Affection* (1998), *The Next Best Thing* (2000), and *De-Lovely* (2004) explored the close bonds of friendship that often exist between gay men and straight women. Traditionally, such women have been called "fag hags," a term indicative of patriarchal bias that simultaneously denigrates both women and gay men. While no one dies tragically in these new age buddy films, and some of them were moderate box office successes, they still tended to chafe at Hollywood's demand for happy heterosexual closure. Some, like *The Next Best Thing*, conservatively imply that the bonds between gay men and straight women can only lead to heartbreak and ugly courtroom drama. Needless to say, all of these films feature white protagonists of both sexes, and to date no lesbian version of the formula has been attempted by Hollywood filmmakers.

Probably the most interesting thing to happen to queer cinema in recent years has been its mainstreaming via success at independent film festivals and award ceremonies. While *The Times of Harvey Milk* and *Common Threads: Stories from the Quilt* had both won Oscars for Best Documentary Feature, by the late 1990s queer films were winning an unprecedented number of accolades. For example, all of the following films with queer content have been recent Oscar contenders and/or winners (in various categories): *Gods and Monsters* (1998), *American Beauty, The Talented Mr. Ripley, Being John Malkovich* (1999), *Boys Don't Cry, Before Night Falls* (2000), *Mulholland Drive* (2001), *Far From Heaven, The Hours, Frida* (2002), *Monster* (2003), *Kinsey* (2004), *Capote* (2005), *Transamerica* (2005), and *Brokeback Mountain*. Many of these award-winning films are direct descendents of New Queer Cinema: most are queer in form as well as content and some were even made by filmmakers who helped to define the original movement.

Importantly, most of these films were produced and/or distributed by major Hollywood studios via their special art-house divisions. Recall that during the 1990s, almost all of the major Hollywood studios acquired various independent companies (Miramax was bought by Disney, Fine Line was purchased by Time/Warner), or else they established their own vaguely separate "independent" distribution outlets such as Sony Pictures Classics, Fox Searchlight, or Focus Features (a division of Universal). While this development further blurs the borders between independent and mainstream film production, it has also arguably allowed more serious and thoughtful queer-themed films to be produced and more widely distributed than ever before. Conceived of and advertised as prestige pictures that just happen to have queer content – rather than queer films *per se* – these films are made by famous directors and feature well-known movie stars. Unlike the more truly independent films discussed in the previous section, these Hollywood-independent hybrids can and do break out of the art-house ghetto and play at multiplexes across America.

Boys Don't Cry was one such film, and undoubtedly helped to spread understanding about transgendered people to middle America. Based on actual events, the film tells the story of a female-to-male pre-operative transsexual named Brandon Teena who, when his secret was discovered, was brutally raped and later murdered by the same people who had previously befriended him. Directed by Kimberly Peirce and produced by New Queer alumnus Christine Vachon, *Boys Don't Cry* might have gone the route of most queer independent films, had not the film won an Academy award (for Hilary Swank's portrayal of Brandon) and then been more widely distributed by Fox Searchlight Pictures. Like most New Queer films, *Boys Don't Cry* complicates issues of gender and sexuality and acknowledges how other realms of social difference – in this case class and region – affect identity. Everyone in *Boys Don't Cry* is seemingly living at or below the poverty line: they are trapped, limited, and uneducated. The Nebraska they inhabit is a world of trailer parks, drug and alcohol abuse, and dead-end jobs. Brandon lies about his gender and says he is in the process of having a sex change operation, but it is clear that he will never have the money to pay for one, and so he remains a target of queerphobic violence.

Far From Heaven is another good example of a recent queer film that garnered critical acclaim and wider distribution. Written, directed, and produced by New Queer filmmakers Todd Haynes and Christine Vachon, *Far From Heaven* earned four Oscar nominations (Original Screenplay, Cinematography, Original Score, and Lead Actress Julianne Moore) and was distributed by Universal's "independent" subsidiary Focus Features. As with the best of Todd Haynes's films, *Far From Heaven* is a comment on cinematic style as much as it is a queer exploration of race, class, gender, and sexuality. Stylistically, the film is a meticulous recreation of a 1950s Hollywood melodrama that pointedly deals with issues a 1950s melodrama could never acknowledge under the dictates of the Production Code: interracial heterosexual romance and repressed male homosexuality. By foregrounding the formal conventions of the classical Hollywood **woman's film**, *Far From Heaven* asks its viewers to think about how past and current film genres shape our ways of thinking about race, class, gender, and sexuality. Similarly, *The Hours* was another queer take on the melodrama that was honored with nine Oscar nominations (and one win, for Nicole Kidman's Best Actress turn as Virginia Woolf). A Miramax-Paramount co-production, and based on Michael Cunningham's Pulitzer prize-winning novel of the same name, *The Hours* is structured a bit like Todd Haynes's seminal New Queer film *Poison*: it intercuts three different but thematically related

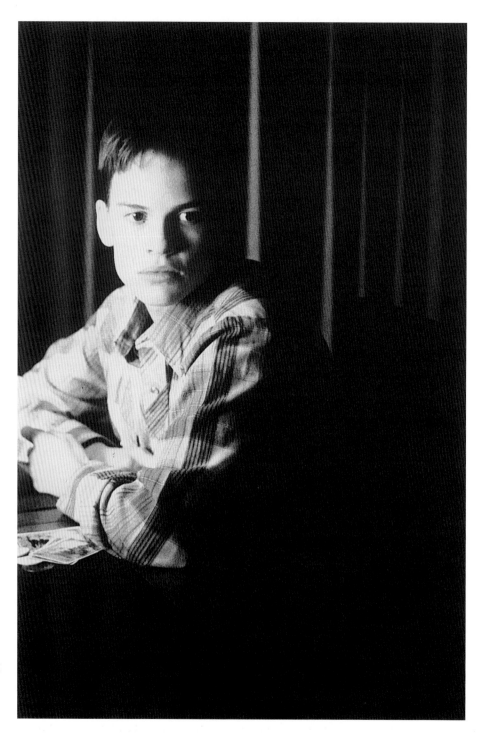

Hilary Swank won an Oscar for her role as Brandon Teena in *Boys Don't Cry* (2000), a film based on a real-life hate crime.
Boys Don't Cry, dir. Kimberly Pierce, copyright © 2000, Killer Films/Fox Searchlight. Photo: Bill Matlock

Dennis Quaid and Julianne Moore in Todd Haynes's highly acclaimed *Far From Heaven* (2002), a film that recreates 1950s film style but explores topics that that era's films could not: a homosexual husband and an interracial romance. *Far From Heaven*, dir. Todd Haynes, copyright © 2002, Focus Features/Universal

stories, each focusing on a single day in the life of three different women living in different times and places. What emerges is a historicized look at the possible lives and relationships that white middle-class women across 100 years of Western history have had available to them.

The Oscar ceremony for 2005 was labeled the "queerest ever" by many pundits, with major nominations and awards going to Hollywood–independent hybrids *Brokeback Mountain*, *Capote*, and *Transamerica*. Yet such a showing has not heralded a sea change in the ways that Hollywood deals with queer characters or queer actors: there has been no flood of queer films at the multiplex, and being openly gay or lesbian remains difficult for most actors. Many queer actors (and/or their agents and advisors) still fear that the public will not accept them in a heterosexual role. However, performers like Ellen DeGeneres, Wilson Cruz, B. D. Wong, Alan Cumming, Chad Allen, Rupert Everett, Rosie O'Donnell, Nathan Lane, Neil Patrick Harris, and Sir Ian McKellen are leading the way in being openly gay or lesbian in Hollywood. (One might note, however, that many of these individuals come from or continue to work in theater or television, arguably two realms that are more queer-friendly than is Hollywood narrative filmmaking.) Still, the vast majority of queer Hollywood stars remains in the closet, a fact that reinforces the notion that there is something wrong or shameful about being gay or lesbian. Behind the camera, though, more and more Hollywood queers are finding the space and acceptance to be who they are, producing, directing, and writing films and television shows in unprecedented numbers. Yet the content of mainstream Hollywood film, still beholden to aging formulas and box office demands, remains resolutely **heterosexist**. In so being, Hollywood continues to marginalize queer people and queer issues, much in the same way as it continues to construct marginalized and stereotypical images of women, the lower classes, people of color, and the disabled.

(Hetero)Sexualities in Contemporary American Cinema

As is hopefully obvious, just as cinematic images of homosexuality have changed over the years, so too have images of heterosexuality. The chaste kisses and careful embraces that represented heterosexual desire during Hollywood's classical period have given way to a wide variety of more explicit heterosexualities in both Hollywood and independent film. The traditions of heterosexual dating, mating, marriage, and child-rearing have all undergone shifts in recent decades. Pre-marital sex between men and women is no longer the taboo topic that it once was, either in films or in the real world. Today's films about engaged couples almost always depict them as sexual intimates, and comedies about young men trying to lose their virginity have become so popular they arguably now form their own genre. In yet another shift in heterosexual relations, some sociologists have declared the death of dating in favor of "hooking up," casual short-term sexual relationships rather than more long-term heterosexual romances. The recent independent film hit *Juno* (2007) follows a teen who becomes pregnant after one such encounter. But rather than exploit (or moralize about) her unwed teen pregnancy, Juno, her family, and the film itself are relatively blasé about what is becoming a fairly common occurrence in contemporary American culture.

Heterosexuality – like homosexuality – is also raced, classed, gendered, as well as shaped by notions of (dis)ability. In other words, people may experience heterosexuality differently according to their racial backgrounds, class status, gender, or level of physical ability. For example, many people from Asian cultures are reticent about flaunting heterosexual desire, and images of Asian and Asian American heterosexuality that appear in the movies may be somewhat tentative and cautious. (That said, they can also be exceedingly passionate, as in the independent film *Lust, Caution* [2007].) On the other hand, generations of cultural attitudes about African Americans as overly sexualized have led to movies and television programs full of images of black heterosexual desire that are obvious and flagrant. Similarly, class affects one's understanding and experience of heterosexuality. Traditional heterosexual relationships and marriage may be more important to lower-income or working-class people because they hope to consolidate relationships that are both romantic and economic. On the other hand, wealth creates more options for individuals, and can allow for more experimental forms of heterosexuality. (The market-created **metrosexual**, for example, is a heterosexual man who allegedly has a "gay sensibility" about fashion, food, and hair care products.) Images of disabled heterosexualities are only rarely depicted in mainstream films, perhaps because they seem to run counter to the usual Hollywood fantasy of strong, athletic men making love to nubile young women. And of course, it is mostly a given that many women and men experience heterosexuality differently. Movies and TV (and especially music videos) often promote a "player" image for men and a more romantic or emotional one for women.

It is a rare film that actually acknowledges (hetero)sexuality as a complex topic, and not just an unquestioned structuring principle. For example, the independent cult film *Secretary* (2002) works as both a depiction of a sadomasochistic heterosexual affair and a sly critique of the power dynamics inherent in traditional heterosexuality. *Palindromes* (2004) uses audacious black humor (and multiple actors playing a single protagonist) to investigate the abortion debate and teenage sexuality. *Short Bus* (2006) explores a variety of sexualities, effectively obliterating any line between "normal" sexualities and "abnormal" ones: heterosexual relations in the film are just as queer as the homosexual ones. *Short Bus* is also part of a recent trend by some independent filmmakers to include explicit hard core sexual images in their films. For example, the British film *Nine Songs* (2004) focuses on a heterosexual affair, partly by focusing in great detail on the actual sex involved in it. Yet these films are often met with cries of impropriety and calls for censorship, and because of the structure of the Hollywood industry, more of these films are being made abroad than within the United States. The recent documentary *This Film is Not Yet Rated* (2006) provides a fascinating look at the ways the **MPAA Ratings System** works to shape and contain American sexualities on screen.

With the increasing awareness and acceptance of homosexuality in America, though, conceptions of heterosexuality have also had to be reconsidered. The issue of gay marriage has challenged the meaning(s) of straight marriage. This might explain the recent increase in movies, TV, and other areas of popular culture that seem fixated on weddings. **Chick flicks** such as *The Wedding Planner* (2001), *My Big Fat Greek Wedding* (2002), *27 Dresses* (2008), and *Sex and the City* (2008) all focus on the ritual and celebration so central to **heteronormativity**. Their narratives may expose tensions or ruptures in patriarchal heterosexual monogamy, but in the end, most all of them resolve with a full and heartwarming embrace of traditional heterosexual marriage. **Dumb white guy comedies** also depict a form of male "heterosexual panic," with the leading male characters continuously scrambling to prove that they are heterosexual *enough*. Ben Stiller has appeared in a number of such films, including *There's Something About Mary* (1998), *Meet the Parents* (2001), and *Along Came Polly* (2004). In these films, Stiller's characters are insecure, and many jokes arise when he says or does things that raise suspicions about his sexual orientation. Yet, by the end of the film, his heterosexual identity has been reaffirmed and he gets the girl. And as some films began to hybridize the chick flick and dumb white guy comedy, they too began to emphasize weddings. *Meet the Fockers* (2004) and *Wedding Crashers* (2005) merge male "heterosexual panic" humor with climactic nuptial events.

The Adam Sandler comedy *I Now Pronounce You Chuck & Larry* (2007) highlights a number of these issues. It, too, is a dumb white guy comedy that focuses on marriage – and, in this case, gay marriage. In it, two straight firefighters pretend to be gay so they can get domestic partner benefits from the city. The rest of the film becomes a comedy of sexual panic: Chuck and Larry have to convince everyone that they are gay, while simultaneously maintaining their heterosexuality. The film ultimately suggests that being gay is not all that different from being straight, especially if being gay means you are still macho and desirous of a wedding. More outré queer sexualities (ironically embodied by the promiscuous and group-sex-loving Chuck) must ultimately be contained within heteronormative, monogamous, and implicitly procreative unions. While the film was felt by many audiences to be offensive – for its racism, its sexism, its very premise that pokes fun at a real civil rights issue – it nonetheless makes available to its viewers a liberal critique of heterosexism. Of course, *I Now Pronounce You Chuck & Larry* is a sophomoric multiplex comedy and not a thoughtful independent film about serious issues. Yet its very existence speaks volumes about the current state of sexualities on screen in America. As various sexual identities fight for attention and acceptance in the real world, American film will continue to negotiate the issues at hand.

Questions for Discussion

1   Some popular musical groups of the last two decades have also adopted queer styles and images. Can you name some? Why might it be easier for popular musicians to be more queer than movie stars or Hollywood film characters?
2   What do politicians and some religious figures have to gain by demonizing gay and lesbian people? What do the media and advertising industries have to gain by reaching out to gay and lesbian people?
3   How does queer theory relate to the social construction of other concepts discussed throughout this book? In what ways might today's understandings of race, ethnicity, class, gender, and ability be considered queer?

Further Reading

Becker, Ron. *Gay TV and Straight America*. New Brunswick, NJ: Rutgers University Press, 2006.

Benshoff, Harry M. and Sean Griffin. *Queer Images: A History of Gay and Lesbian Film in America*. New York: Rowman and Littlefield, 2006.

Capsuto, Steven. *Alternate Channels: The Uncensored Story of Gay and Lesbian Images on Radio and Television*. New York: Ballantine Books, 2000.

Doty, Alex. *Making Things Perfectly Queer*. Minneapolis: University of Minnesota Press, 1993.

Doty, Alex and Corey Creekmur, eds. *Out in Culture*. Durham, NC: Duke University Press, 1995.

Dyer, Richard. *Now You See It: Studies on Lesbian and Gay Film*. New York: Routledge, 1990.

Dyer, Richard. *The Culture of Queers*. New York: Routledge, 2002.

Ehrenstein, David. *Open Secret: Gay Hollywood 1928–1998*. New York: William Morrow, 1998.

Fuss, Diana, ed. *Inside/Out: Lesbian Theories/Gay Theories*. New York: Routledge, 1991.

Gever, Martha, John Greyson, and Pratibha Parmar, eds. *Queer Looks*. New York: Routledge, 1993.

Hanson, Ellis, ed. *Out Takes: Essays on Queer Theory and Film*. Durham, NC: Duke University Press, 1999.

Keller, James R. *Queer (Un)Friendly Film and Television*. Jefferson, NC: McFarland, 2002.

Pullen, Christopher. *Documenting Gay Men: Identity and Performance in Reality Television and Documentary Film*. Jefferson, NC: McFarland, 2007.

Tropiano, Stephen. *The Prime Time Closet: A History of Gays and Lesbians on TV*. New York City: Applause Theater and Cinema Books, 2002.

Walters, Suzanna Danuta. *All the Rage: The Story of Gay Visibility in America*. Chicago: University of Chicago Press, 2001.

Further Screening

The Killing of Sister George (1968)
Boys in the Band (1970)
The Times of Harvey Milk (1984)
Desert Hearts (1985)
Longtime Companion (1990)
My Own Private Idaho (1991)
The Incredibly True Adventure of Two Girls in Love (1995)

But I'm a Cheerleader (1999)
Hedwig and the Angry Inch (2001)
Far From Heaven (2002)
The Hours (2002)
Brokeback Mountain (2005)
Transamerica (2005)

ABILITY
AND AMERICAN FILM

INTRODUCTION TO PART VI:
What is Ability?

Many dictionaries define **ability** as the power or capacity to do things, to act according to one's skills or talents. Like being white, middle-class, male, and heterosexual, a certain baseline level of ability is usually assumed to be the unremarked-upon norm in Western societies. We tend instead to recognize and speak more regularly of departures from that norm, either in terms of abilities that seem to surpass the baseline (as in the idolization of certain sports stars), or in terms of abilities that are judged to be below the baseline, conditions to which the term **disability** is commonly applied. Yet note the immediate hierarchy constructed by this line of thinking – some people are "above normal" while others are "below," terms that tend to suggest class standing, social worth, and cultural desirability. The very prefix "dis-" attached to "ability" suggests a state of negation or reversal. Indeed, like many of the other labels used to categorize groups of people within our culture, the simple label "disabled" is reductive and often carries misleading connotations. It is reductive because there are an infinite numbers of ways that individuals might be differently abled – through inherited conditions, via something that affects fetal development, through disease or accidents, acts of war or aggression, and even the "normal" process of aging. One disability may have very little similarity to any other type of disability, and some people that might be labeled that way by others do not apply the label to themselves. Many deaf people reject the term disability altogether.

Nonetheless, Western culture tends to use disability as an umbrella term that can refer to a great variety of mental, physical, emotional, and/or developmental conditions. The (current) legal definition of disability, set forth in the **Americans with Disabilities Act (ADA)** of 1990, does not distinguish between type, severity, or duration of the disability. It broadly states that a disability is "a physical or mental impairment that substantially limits one or more of the major life activities" such as walking, dressing, bathing, eating, etc. Perhaps most commonly, disability refers to some degree of impairment in one's seeing, hearing, and/or motor or mental activity. But even within that more specific definition, individuals can be more-or-less sighted, or more-or-less hearing. Some people with impaired motility use wheelchairs while others may walk with braces or prosthetic limbs. Still, ability and disability are words that English-speaking people have been conditioned to use for decades, if not centuries. Like many of the other binaries explored within this book (white–black, male–female, straight–gay), the binary abled–disabled is a false dichotomy, wherein abled is defined by and privileged over disabled. Just as masculinity is often defined as the opposite of femininity (despite so many overlapping *human* traits shared by men and women), the abled–disabled binary works to separate people into two distinct groups, and in the process suggests the superiority of one group over another.

For centuries, Western cultures actively discriminated against people they considered to be disabled. In the past, some forms of disability were even equated with frightful monstrosity, criminality, and/or some other form of moral deviance. Greek myths detail misshapen monsters opposed by stalwart heroes of perfect musculature. Passages in the Bible prohibit "the blind" or "the lame" from approaching God, and when Jesus cured disabled people, it was often implied that they were disabled precisely because they were sinners. For centuries, left-handed people were considered by many to be in league with the Devil. Shakespeare's Richard III is an excellent example of how disability has often been conflated with criminality in Western culture. Richard has a humpback, limp, and palsied arm, and these physical markers are meant to correlate with his nefarious criminal deeds. In yet other examples, for centuries people believed that birth defects and/or other congenital conditions were caused by sinful mothers (or more rarely sinful fathers). Other conditions such as epilepsy were thought to be caused by demonic possession. Because of these attitudes, people with all sorts of physical and mental impairments were shunned, ostracized, or locked away in attics or asylums.

Such attitudes were slowly changed with the ascendancy in the nineteenth century of the **medical model of disability**. Rather than regarding physical differences as signs of evil, the medical model sees them as genetic or biological conditions that objectively could affect anyone. Instead of shunning such people, the medical model seeks to understand the causes of disabilities and to bring disabled people into the realm of everyday life. With the development of the medical model over the course of the nineteenth and twentieth centuries, people with disabilities began to be treated in more humane ways. Special schools were created, like the Columbia Institution for the Deaf, now known as Gallaudet University. Medical procedures continued to advance, and some causes of disability (like polio) have been virtually eradicated. Today, new technologies allow for the detection *in utero* of numerous inherited and congenital conditions. However, while the medical model of disability is obviously a much more positive outlook on physical difference than what had come before it, an increasing number of people have grown ambivalent about it as well. In particular, the medical model regards physical and mental differences as diseases or negative states that must be cured, or failing that, cared for or treated in various ways. At times, the medical model has been used to evoke pity for these individuals' alleged lack of "normality," and to try as much as possible to make them "normal" (through surgeries, prosthetic limbs, learning how to lip-read, etc.). Over the past decades, though, many individuals whom society might label as disabled have refused to regard themselves as such. Rather, many have begun to challenge exactly who gets to decide what is considered "normal."

Such developments have led to what theorists call the **social model of disability**, a way of thinking that understands disability as a function of the interaction between an individual and society. Whereas the medical model of disability tends to focus on individuals' impairments, the social model of disability focuses on the culturally disabling attitudes and institutions that limit people with different abilities. The social model of disability theorizes disability not as a static condition but instead as a social construction that is always open to modification and redefinition. Who gets to decide who is "disabled"? When does poor eyesight become a disability? When does normal human variation in body length or weight become a medical condition or a process of disease? If a deaf person functions as well as a hearing person, who is to say that he or she is disabled? Unlike the medical model of disability, the social model asks broader questions about cultural attitudes. Among other things, the social model of disability allows us to examine the ways in which our youth- and beauty-obsessed culture defines what is ugly or unhealthy. It points out how both science and other aspects of culture have been drawing lines between normal and abnormal for centuries, if not millennia.

The social model of disability has also alerted us to how the language we use to discuss disabilities shapes the cultural understanding of those conditions. These labels have varied over the years, and many now carry negative connotations and are no longer used to describe people with disabilities. Words like "crippled," "dumb," "idiot," "Mongoloid," and "invalid" tend to frame people with disabilities as less than human. Similarly, the terms "midget" and "dwarf" are now rarely used in polite conversations; the preferred term is "little people." Some deaf people hate the term "hearing impaired," as it signifies a lack of something they are happy to do without. Still other people prefer the term "differently abled" instead of disabled, since that wording stresses that one is still able to do things for oneself, albeit sometimes in a different way. In summation, many people with disabilities resent language that reduces them solely to their impairment. Thus even "disabled person" does not mean the same thing as "person with a disability." The former seems to imply that the person's whole identity is disabled, whereas the latter term suggests a condition that is but one part of an individual's overall identity. Ultimately, the social model of disability insists that people with disabilities are unique individuals and not just medical conditions. And analogously to how we use the terms racism and sexism, the term **ableism** is sometimes used to describe ways of thinking and speaking about disabilities that are biased, reductive, or outright negative and oppressive. (Similarly, some in the deaf community use the term **audism** to refer to attitudes and practices that privilege the hearing over the deaf.)

Many debates continue to rage about the best way to deal with various disabilities, even within and between groups of people with similar abilities. For example, the American Council of the Blind sued the US Department of the Treasury, claiming that its paper currency discriminated against blind people; yet the National Federation for the Blind protested *against* such a lawsuit. Within deaf culture, there has been an ongoing debate between oralism (deaf people learning to speak aloud) and the use of sign language. Also, a sizable portion of the deaf community is adamantly against the use of cochlear implants (which may restore some degree of hearing to some deaf people). Just as with the other groups studied within this book, there are wide ranges of opinions, attitudes, actions, and beliefs shared among groups as diverse as the deaf, the blind, or the differently abled. And just as the cinematic images of disability have changed over the years, so will our real-life understanding of such conditions continue to evolve.

Chapter 16

CINEMATIC IMAGES OF (DIS)ABILITY

For centuries before the creation of cinema, people with congenital impairments and/or other physical anomalies were sometimes exhibited as curiosities in traveling circus "side shows" or "freak shows," where "normal" people were invited to laugh, jeer, pity, or otherwise be entertained by such "atrocities." Deaf and blind people were routinely segregated from the world, locked away in special schools or other types of institutions. Early American cinema, which was born in the era of the freak show, sometimes mirrored the freak show's allure and appeal, using human oddities and freakish-looking characters to frighten or titillate audiences. (On the other hand, the age of silent cinema allowed deaf audiences to share largely the same sense of moviegoing as hearing audiences.) However, just as with the other groups of people examined in this book, things have changed a great deal since then. By the mid-twentieth century, most "freak shows" had been disbanded, and more reasoned and compassionate attitudes began to prevail.

However, as film historians like Martin F. Norden have pointed out, many stereo-typical images of disability continue to linger, especially in relation to Hollywood film genres. For example, physical anomalies continue to be staples of mystery and **horror films,** while acquired disability is a foundational element of many **war movies.** Disability has also been associated with class, specifically with the idea that poverty somehow causes disability, or conversely that disability results in poverty. Disability in American film is also heavily gendered. As this chapter explores, women with disabilities (especially deafness or blindness) tend to be used cinematically to evoke sympathy and/or victimization, whereas men with disabilities are more often linked to anger, violence, sagacity, and/or tragedy. Nonetheless, the developing contemporary trend is toward representing people with disabilities as living and breathing human beings, complete with all the joys and sorrows of so-called "normal" or able-bodied people. This chapter focuses primarily on the intertwining historical evolution of cinematic images of the deaf, the blind, and those with physical anomalies either congenital or acquired.

Disabled People in Early American Film:
Curiosities and Freaks

The earliest movies (**actualities**) were often little more than short slices of life, focusing on visually interesting subject matter, whether athlete, dancer, or event. Some of them focused on disability, primarily because disabilities presented or allowed for unique or startling images. As silent films, early movies were also drawn to the representation of sign language: *Deaf Mute Girl Reciting "Star Spangled Banner"* (1902) was one such film. Short films that taught and revealed the intricacies of sign language were made into the 1910s. Other early films used disabilities to create comedic situations. *The Near-Sighted Cyclist* (1907) and *Near-Sighted Mary* (1909) used poor vision to spark laughs, much as the popular cartoon character *Mr Magoo* would do decades later. Wooden legs were unexpectedly removed and used as clubs or other comedic props in countless slapstick comedies. Still other early films exploited the idea of the false cripple or con man. For example, in Edison's short film *Fake Beggar* (1898), the "joke" is that a blind man really can see – he is merely pretending to be blind in order to play on people's sympathies. *Fake Beggar* was followed by many imitators, including *Fraudulent Beggars* (1898), *The Beggar's Deceit* (1900), *The Fake Blind Man* (1905), and *Two Ladies and a Beggar* (1909). Such character types can be found in literature as well as film: Victor Hugo's famous novel *The Hunchback of Notre Dame* (as well as its many filmic incarnations) contains a subplot about a group of unscrupulous beggars and thieves who only pretend to be disabled.

Such representations carried on the generations-old tradition of regarding disabled people with suspicion or fear. While the **medical model of disability** was already spreading by the advent of motion pictures, the older monstrous freak image remained somewhat prevalent. As American motion pictures shifted from actualities into longer fictional narratives, the genres of crime and horror became common places to find images of disability. One of the most famous silent movie stars, Lon Chaney, specialized in criminal or horrific roles that usually featured some form of physical disability. Intriguingly, Chaney had been born to deaf parents, and film historians often suggest this is why he became a great silent film actor – because he had to learn at an early age how to communicate through gesture and facial expression. By the 1920s, Chaney was known as "The Man of a Thousand Faces" for his extreme characterizations, and for the physical contortions he actually endured to bring them to the screen. For example, in *The Penalty* (1920) he played a gangster without legs, an effect Chaney achieved by strapping his lower legs to his upper legs and walking on his knees. Chaney's Quasimodo, *The Hunchback of Notre Dame* (1923), was more of a sympathetic figure but was nonetheless associated with horrific misdeeds.

In *The Unknown* (1927), a bizarre Freudian melodrama, Chaney plays a circus performer named "Alonzo the Armless" who throws knives with his feet. But Alonzo's disability is a sham – he straps his arms tightly to his body to avoid being identified as a thief (and later a murderer). Then, when he falls in love with a woman

(Joan Crawford) who says she cannot stand to be touched by men, Alonzo black-mails a doctor into surgically removing his arms for real. By the end of the film, Alonzo has devised a plot to have his rival's limbs torn off by a team of horses; instead he is trampled to death himself. Assisting Alonzo in his nefarious deeds is a "little person" named Cojo (John George), linking yet another form of physical difference with villainy.

Alonzo the Armless exemplifies one particular (and particularly nasty) stereo-type of people with disabilities: the **Obsessive Avenger**. This monstrous character type frequently appears in mystery and horror films. He (and he is almost always male) is a man so embittered by his disability or disfigurement that he expresses his fury through a revenge plot, usually taken out upon the able-bodied people he feels have wronged him. A quick glance at Lon Chaney's career reveals that he portrayed this character repeatedly, perhaps most famously in the first cinematic version of *The Phantom of the Opera* (1925). Although attitudes about disabilities have changed over the years, this stereotype is at the core of every *Phantom of the Opera* remake, including the more politically correct and sympathetic Andrew Lloyd Webber musical version (2003). The Obsessive Avenger can also be discerned in the disfigured monsters of *Mystery of the Wax Museum* (1933), *House of Wax* (1953), *The Abominable Dr Phibes* (1971), and even more recent slasher film series like those derived from *Friday the 13th* (1980) and *A Nightmare on Elm Street* (1984). Like the stereotype of the fake cripple, the Obsessive Avenger also has had a long liter-ary tradition, including Shakespeare's Richard III, Captain Ahab from *Moby-Dick*, and Captain Hook from *Peter Pan*.

Horror star Bela Lugosi as Ygor, the hunchbacked assistant to the mad doctor in *Son of Frankenstein* (1939). Ygor is evil because of his deformity as well as his close relationship to the Monster (Boris Karloff). He is also out for revenge.
Son of Frankenstein, copyright © 1939, Universal

365

Even when not obsessive avengers, hunchbacked dwarfs, disfigured monsters, armless policemen, and "deaf-mute" servants with bulging eyes regularly populate the gothic world of both classical and contemporary horror films. And while most of these monsters are created by professional makeup artists to frighten "normal" moviegoers with the spectacle of physical deviance, occasionally horror movies feature actors with real-life disabilities. For example, Rondo Hatton was a B-movie actor who suffered from acromegaly, a medical condition which slowly caused his facial bones to grow in misshapen ways. In response, Hollywood cast him as a scary creature named The Creeper in films such as *House of Horror* (1946) and *The Brute Man* (1946). Similarly, in the 1970s, people with missing limbs were used to portray half-human snake-men in the film *Sssssss* (1973).

The most notorious example of casting people with disabilities in a horror film is Tod Browning's *Freaks* (1932), a film that was contracted by the prestigious MGM studio, and then quickly disowned by them when they saw the finished product. (The film was banned in Great Britain for decades and it circulated in America for years on the exploitation film circuit before being restored and critically rehabilitated.) For *Freaks*, director Tod Browning – who had worked with Lon Chaney on many of his films – cast real-life side show performers in a macabre tale of illicit love and revenge. The plot centers on a "normal-sized" trapeze artist named Cleopatra (Olga Baclanova) who marries little person Hans (Harry Earles), and then begins to poison him so that she may inherit his money. The rest of the side show denizens discover the plot, and in a horrific climax, chase Cleopatra through a muddy rainstorm and descend upon her with knives. In a final sequence, it is revealed that the "freaks" have cut off Cleopatra's legs and scarred her face – she now too has become a monstrous "chicken woman" trapped within the side show. In more recent years, *Freaks* has been both condemned and celebrated in relation to its depiction of people with disabilities. While clearly the film exploits its disabled performers as Obsessive Avengers, the film also presents them as fairly well-developed human beings with their own feelings and desires, as opposed to simply repellant monsters. And in addition to Harry Earles as Hans, *Freaks* also gave film work to many other people with disabilities, including little person Daisy Earles, and Daisy and Violet Hilton, real-life conjoined twins. The Hilton Sisters later starred in *Chained for Life* (1951), a low-budget exploitation film about their lives.

Classical Hollywood often made use of little people as actors, though almost always as supporting characters and rarely in roles that explored what life might have actually been like for them. Probably the most famous example of such casting was for *The Wizard of Oz* (1939), for which MGM allegedly scoured every side show in the nation to find enough little people to play the Munchkins. And while the Munchkins are far from monstrous, they are childlike and ultimately little more than local color in the bizarre land of Oz. A lesser-known film from the same era, *The Terror of Tiny Town* (1938), featured an "all midget" cast. The film was an independently produced B Western, featuring songs amid the usual Western trappings. Basically a one-shot genre variation, it is interesting to compare *The Terror of Tiny Town* to the era's black-cast Westerns; the formula was so popular and well known that it was easily adapted for different minority film productions. Casting

This scene from *The Wizard of Oz* (1939) exemplifies the classical Hollywood approach to using little people in film: as fantastic supporting characters who are almost part of the décor, not as human characters.
The Wizard of Oz, copyright © 1939, MGM

African Americans or little people in a Western perhaps suggests their equivalency to the white, full-sized actors who usually appeared in such films, but at the same time the Western formula obscures any real-life issues that such minorities may have been facing in those years. Plus it should be noted once again that films like *The Terror of Tiny Town* or *The Bronze Buckaroo* (1939) were not mainstream Hollywood productions, and thus were cheaply made and sparsely distributed.

Little people were more regularly used in classical Hollywood cinema to stunt-double children and babies, play sidekicks to mad doctors and villains, and – increasingly in more recent Hollywood cinema – enact fantasy or science fiction characters from inside elaborate costumes. **Billy Barty** was one such performer. As a child he played babies in films like *Gold Diggers of 1933* (1933) and in series of shorts starring Mickey Rooney. By the 1950s and 1960s, Barty was working on television as a character actor. Some of his most beloved characters were performed from inside elaborate full-body costumes for Sid and Marty Krofft Productions, a company that produced memorable children's shows like *Pufnstuf* (1970) and *Sigmund and the Sea Monsters* (1973). And as the science fiction/fantasy boom of the late 1970s continued to flourish throughout the 1980s, Barty had memorable supporting roles in *Masters of the Universe* (1987) and *Willow* (1988). Always a staunch supporter of human rights, Barty founded the Little People of America in 1957, and the Billy Barty Foundation in 1975. He died in 2000, after a career that spanned an amazing 70 years.

One of the best-known "little people" actors in Hollywood, Billy Barty is seen here in the fantasy film *Willow* (1988). His career spanned seven decades.
Willow, dir. Ron Howard, copyright © 1988, MGM

Other little people who acted in classical Hollywood films include Angelo Rossito and Michael Dunn. Rossito, like John George from *The Unknown*, often played sidekicks to mad doctors and villains in B horror movies like *Spooks Run Wild* (1941), *The Corpse Vanishes* (1942), *Mesa of Lost Women* (1953), and *Dracula Versus Frankenstein* (1971). He too worked for Sid and Marty Krofft and appeared in several fantasy films throughout his career. Michael Dunn was the first little person to be nominated for an Oscar, for his role in *Ship of Fools* (1965), a *Grand Hotel*-type melodrama set aboard an ocean liner. Yet despite his acting talents, Michael Dunn also played villains and sidekicks. One of his most enduring characterizations was the memorable arch-fiend Dr. Miguelito Loveless on the television show *The Wild Wild West* (1965–8).

Romanticizing Disability in Classical Hollywood Melodramas

While older attitudes toward disabled individuals as freaks still held sway in much early twentieth-century American cinema, the medical model of disability also began to have its affect on motion pictures. Rather than being regarded as horrifying mistakes of nature, a number of disabled characters were presented in sympathetic terms. While definitely an improvement, such images contained their own problems, and created a new stereotype: the disabled person as the **Sweet Innocent**. In regarding disability as a disease or genetic condition, Sweet Innocents were characters constructed as undeserving of such hardship, inviting the audience to feel pity for their plight, and to hope for a cure to their condition. Often, Sweet Innocent characters were also incredibly poor – and were offered up as evidence of the horrid conditions that the poor and working classes faced during the Industrial Revolution. (The lack of safety regulations in factories did often lead to the loss of limbs, eyesight, or hearing during this period.) Although they called attention to such class oppression, such characters were made into almost saint-like creatures (practically the polar opposite of the Obsessive Avenger stereotype), so that middle-class audiences could shed an easy tear over them rather than feel accosted and/or uncomfortable. Rather than express anger over their conditions, Sweet Innocents were almost implausibly humble, gentle, and perpetually cheerful despite having a disability. At times, due to the charity of a kindly person, an operation could be paid for to cure them, invoking more tears from the audience – but this time of joy.

Sweet Innocent characters often came in the form of children, and one of the best-known is the young boy Tiny Tim in Charles Dickens's *A Christmas Carol* (which has been adapted for film and television numerous times). Yet the most typical version of the Sweet Innocent stereotype in American films of the era is the young adult female. The era's social understanding of **femininity** regarded women as passive, weak, and in need of rescue, which blended more easily into the Sweet Innocent image than did aggressive **masculinity**. (Indeed, it is quite easy to see how the ideology of **patriarchy** positions being female/feminine as a form of disability in and of itself.) Thus, the Sweet Innocent woman was shown needing the help of a good (and physically robust) man – either in protecting her from some oppressor who wants to exploit her, or in getting her medical treatment to "cure" her.

Most commonly, Sweet Innocent women were represented as blind. In films like D. W. Griffith's *The Cricket on the Hearth* (1909) and *Orphans of the Storm* (1921), and in **Charlie Chaplin**'s *City Lights* (1931), blind young women are literally unable to see the evil that surrounds and threatens them. At other times, their blindness makes them innocent of prevailing social prejudices. In *City Lights*, for example, the sweet young blind girl who peddles flowers falls in love with the sighted man who takes care of her, unaware that he is Chaplin's poor Tramp character. A much later example of this device occurs in *A Patch of Blue* (1965), when blind waif Selina (Elizabeth Hartman) falls in love with her benefactor (Sidney Poitier), not recognizing that he is African American. While these young women cannot see the men in their lives, there is often an emphasis on the men looking at them. The men often comment that these young blind women are somehow even more beautiful (in their innocence) than are other women. In this way, the Sweet Innocent type elicits a striking version of female **objectification**, with various men gazing upon a woman who literally has no power to look back – even at herself.

Of course, in real life, men were just as likely as women to be blind or otherwise differently abled. Yet images of blind men varied a great deal from images of blind women, and arguably still do to the present day, seemingly in order to support a sense of traditional masculine power. Thus, while blind women were figured as Sweet Innocents, blind (or more rarely deaf) men were often figured as **Saintly Sages**. This character type, because of his disability, has supposedly developed his other senses to extraordinary degrees. This stereotype bleeds into the social perception that blind people are gifted "seers" in some other way – and in films they sometimes appear as wise "all knowing" characters who dispense knowledge and wisdom to the protagonists. A good example of this occurs in the film *Bride of Frankenstein* (1935), when the monster stumbles into the hut of a blind hermit. Since he cannot see the monster and thus pre-judge him, the hermit welcomes the creature into his home, feeding him and befriending him. The film's visual style makes the hermit almost saint-like – his long robe, white beard, and kindly demeanor set him apart from the film's sighted characters, who are all too ready to persecute the sympathetic monster.

As *Bride of Frankenstein* indicates, such sentimental, romanticized, and gendered images of disability persisted into the Great Depression. In a period when many men already felt emasculated due to rampant unemployment, images of disabled men (other than as menacing villains) were relatively rare. Significantly, President Franklin D. Roosevelt, who was unable to walk due to polio, was never photographed in his wheelchair for fear of making him (and by extension, the United States) appear weak. The era's **woman's films**, on the other hand, regularly centered on women and disability. (Recall from chapter 10 that "affliction" and "sacrifice" are two of the four defining themes of the classical Hollywood woman's film.) For example, in *Sarah and Son* (1931), Ruth Chatterton plays a woman searching for her lost son, and she is terrified to think that he may be "deaf and dumb"; she is greatly relieved when it turns out that this particular child is *not* her son. *Magnificent Obsession* (1935, 1954) and *Dark Victory* (1939) are more famous melodramas that show how strong women – going blind – have to become dependent on men for love, care, and/or a possible cure. In *A Woman's Face* (1941), Joan Crawford plays a woman embittered by a facial scar that is regarded as a disability, because it destroys her feminine beauty. (Whereas scars on men add to a man's rugged appeal, a woman with a scar is ruined for life.)

Disability in War Movies and Social Problem Films

The technological advances of the Industrial Revolution helped create both modern forms of warfare (aircraft, tanks, rapid-firing guns, chemical weapons) and advances in medical science that were used to treat the men wounded by these. In previous centuries, soldiers injured in war usually died of their wounds – even minor ones – but by the twentieth century, more and more soldiers could and did survive their wounds, often with some form of disability. Film historians have noted that images of disabled people did seem to increase following World War I (though, as previously discussed, often more in crime and horror films than actual war films). One of the era's few popular stories depicting a wounded soldier adapting to civilian life is the repeatedly filmed male melodrama *The Light That Failed* (1916, 1923, 1939). Based on a Rudyard Kipling story, it tells of a painter who learns that a war injury is slowly robbing him of his eyesight. Yet, rather than coming to terms with his condition, the narrative focuses on his attempt to complete what he feels will be his last masterpiece before he goes completely blind. The narrative creates the unspoken sense that his life will be over once his sight is gone. In fact, after the painter does become completely blind, he somehow manages to re-enlist in order to find a manly death on the battlefield rather than live a seemingly disempowered existence.

Disabled veterans became more frequent onscreen characters during and after World War II, due to the increase in actual war movies and **social problem films**. (Recall that Hollywood's postwar social problem films also tackled issues such as racism and anti-Semitism.) Disabled veterans in World War II-era films tended to embody one of two stereotypes: the **Noble Warrior** or the **Tragic Victim**. The Noble Warrior presents the injured man as heroic and proud, thus valorizing the brave and selfless sacrifices made by members of the armed services. Conversely, the Tragic Victim presents an innocent young man cut down in the prime of life. Perhaps unsurprisingly, the Noble Warrior image dominated films made during the war, showing that America's injured vets were still strong and committed to victory. Both *Thirty Seconds Over Tokyo* (1944) and *Since You Went Away* (1944) partake of this trope. The first film features Van Johnson as a soldier who loses a leg but still goes on fighting the fight; the latter film is a sprawling tapestry of wartime America that features a subplot about injured veterans. The Tragic Victim image began to be used more in the postwar years, and can also be found in more recent anti-war movies that figure disability as the tragic consequence of unchecked militarism.

Once the war ended, Hollywood social problem films proliferated, and many of them dealt with issues facing disabled veterans. *Pride of the Marines* (1945) featured John Garfield as a soldier blinded and embittered by a grenade blast. In typical Hollywood fashion, he begins to recover his eyesight by the end of the film. *Till the End of Time* (1946) centers on three returning vets, one of whom has lost both legs. Probably the most important of these films was the Oscar-winning *The Best Years of Our Lives* (1946). Directed by William Wyler (who had himself lost some of his hearing during his service in the war), the film centers on the problems of adjustment faced by several returning veterans, including a double amputee played by Harold Russell. Russell was an actual veteran who had lost his hands in a train-ing-related accident. Although some Hollywood insiders felt it was in "poor taste" to feature an actual amputee in the film, most critics hailed the film and Russell's performance in it. Russell was awarded an Oscar for Best Supporting Actor as well as a special Oscar for "bringing hope and courage to his fellow veterans."

While most of the films just mentioned featured disability subplots, the topic was the central issue of *The Men* (1950), produced by well-known social problem filmmaker Stanley Kramer. In it, Marlon Brando plays a Tragic Victim veteran who cannot adjust to being paralyzed from the waist down. The filmmakers took pains to present an authentic story. They based their film on the experiences of actual wheelchair-using veterans, shot in a real-life VA hospital, and hired 45 disabled veterans to act in the film. Again, films about disabled veterans bring to light how disability can and often does relate to issues of gender. To be masculine in Western culture is to be in control: to be dominant, forceful, useful, and productive. Thus the crises in many of these postwar social problem films center on how disabled men can still be men – that is, how they can still earn a living, make love to a woman, and provide for a family. Freudian psychoanalysis suggests that losing a limb, or becoming blinded, is a form of symbolic castration – that it will make a man feel like less of a man. Thus many of these dramas foreground dependency as a form of hell suffered by such men.

A few social problem films of the era made interesting connections between people with disabilities and other forms of discrimination. For example, in *Home of the Brave* (1949), James Edwards plays a young African American soldier suffering from post-traumatic psychological paralysis caused by his war experiences *and* the era's baseline racism. The film ends with the black soldier cured and befriended by another soldier who has lost his arm. James Edwards also appeared in *Bright Victory* (1951), about a group of blind veterans. Here blindness functions as metaphoric racial blindness; one character doesn't realize that Joe is black. In this film, blindness becomes the impetus for a critique of racism and a broader understanding of humanity.

In most postwar social problem films, disability was no longer regarded as frightening (though perhaps still as pitiable). Rather, it was regarded as something that needed to be addressed by the population at large. Thus, while still working within the medical model of disability, the films did try to recognize actual options available to people with disabilities, rather than overly romanticized notions of either miraculous cures or tragic ends. As Hollywood movies, most of these films ultimately suggest that recovery and reintegration for their troubled veterans are possible; this is how their **happy endings** are configured. And although the Tragic Victim stereotype often touches on aspects of the Sweet Innocent stereotype, Tragic Victims in the era's social problem films are presented as complex personalities and not one-dimensional Innocents. For example, the injured veterans shown are at times angry, frustrated, and/or depressed. And in tandem with traditional notions of masculinity, they are also shown coming to realize that they are ultimately responsible for making new lives for themselves, rather than meekly depending on others. The films also start to acknowledge the existence of disabled communities and cultures, which help teach the characters how to be self-reliant.

While these new attitudes toward disabled veterans helped make representations of disabled males more acceptable (and complex), one can also see this shift occurring in a film like *Johnny Belinda* (1948). A beautifully shot melodrama, *Johnny Belinda* does invoke the Sweet Innocent stereotype in its story of Belinda, a young deaf woman (played by Jane Wyman in an Oscar-winning performance) who is heavily dependent on a kindly doctor (Lew Ayres) who reaches out to her in her silence. However, the film quickly complicates the Sweet Innocent stereotype by showing Belinda's pluck and intelligence. We are meant to feel injustice for her when she is referred to by her family and the other villagers as a "Dummy." Another dramatic conflict is set in motion when Belinda is sexually assaulted by a man from the village who feels her deafness will hide his crime. As the film goes on, Belinda becomes increasingly capable of taking care of herself, as well as the son she gives birth to as a result of the attack. At the climax of the film, Belinda shoots her attacker when he bursts into her home trying to take the child away from her. *Johnny Belinda* was also one of the first major studio pictures to depict sign language, something that endeared the film to many members of the deaf community. The deaf community had spent decades trying to convince mainstream society that sign language was a legitimate language, and Belinda's use of it was a further indication of a specific culture arising from a disability as well as its members' growing self-reliance.

A little over a decade later, *The Miracle Worker* (1962), which originated as a live television drama and then a Broadway play, continued these trends toward the depiction of self-reliant disabled people, cultures, and communities. The story centers on Irish American Annie Sullivan (Anne Bancroft) learning how to teach her deaf and blind pupil Helen Keller (Patty Duke); both actresses won Oscars for their work. Although the film begins in a rather gothic way – amid twisted angles and spooky shadows, baby Helen's parents discover that she has become deaf and blind via a childhood illness – it soon moves from frightening to enlightening. Annie herself has limited sight and comes to Helen after having been horribly abused in various asylums until rescued by a school for the blind. Annie uses what she has herself learned to reach out to Helen, most particularly the use of a sign language that Helen can feel. The climax of the film occurs when Annie's teaching finally breaks through to Helen, opening up a whole new world of possibilities. As with *Johnny Belinda*, *The Miracle Worker* emphasizes Helen's (and Annie's) vitality and intelligence. Even though Helen's family regards her as a Tragic Victim, treating her more like a pet or wild animal than a human being, repeated scenes show her as intuitive and cunning, knowing how to strategize in order to get what she wants. Annie quickly realizes this, and the film endorses her refusal to pity Helen or treat her any differently than any other person. A major set piece of the play and film occurs when Annie demands that Helen behave properly at the dinner table. In a lengthy and highly physical skirmish, they engage in a battle of wills and wits that shows both women as strong, determined individuals rather than Sweet Innocents or Tragic Victims.

Representations of disabled individuals as intelligent, capable people deserving of understanding continued to develop throughout the postwar years. For example, the one-armed war veteran played by Spencer Tracy in *Bad Day at Black Rock* (1955) is not only the hero of the film, but is shown effectively defending himself in various fistfights. In *A Patch of Blue*, Gordon (Sidney Poitier) helps the blind girl

Patty Duke and Anne Bancroft both won Oscars for their performances in *The Miracle Worker* (1962), a film that challenged many stereotypes about deaf and blind people. *The Miracle Worker*, copyright © 1962, United Artists/MGM

Selina, but by teaching her to rely on herself rather than be dependent on others. Like *Johnny Belinda* or the World War II-era disabled veteran films, however, these and other movies of the period often drew upon older stereotypes even as they attempted to counter and move beyond them. Thus, the protagonist of *Bad Day at Black Rock* can be viewed as a version of a Saintly Sage, and while *A Patch of Blue* takes place in modern times, Selina is very similar to the Sweet Innocent in *City Lights*. Possibly the best example of this "both-and" quality is blind Susy Hendrix (Audrey Hepburn) in the thriller *Wait Until Dark* (1967). Susy shows her ability to thwart a group of violent criminals who invade her apartment, especially during a climactic scene where she douses all the lights to put her, the villains, and the audience all at an equal level of sightlessness. Still, the film encourages audiences to regard Susy as a version of a Sweet Innocent threatened by evil around her. Furthermore, all of these portrayals are by non-disabled performers enacting their idea of a person with a disability, much as white actors of preceding decades put on makeup in order to play racial minorities, a trend that would be increasingly challenged (though not done away with) in more recent decades.

Disability and the Counterculture

From the 1950s through to the 1970s, when people were influenced by **counter-cultural** ideals that espoused love, understanding, and equality for all Americans, the cinematic images of people with disabilities began to change, often reflecting these new attitudes. Yet such changes were often incremental, and the stereotypes of preceding decades continued to linger. Although the 1980s would see the rise of more enlightened films about the disabled (as well as the first deaf movie star), physical disabilities continued to be linked with (male) Obsessive Avengers in films like *Moby Dick* (1956), *Dr Strangelove* (1964), and many, many mystery and horror films. The real killer in the popular TV show *The Fugitive* (1963–7) was a one-armed man (as he was when the film was turned into a **nostalgic Hollywood blockbuster** in 1993). Blind and/or deaf women appeared as victims in more thrillers like *The Tingler* (1959) and *See No Evil* (1971). The baroque horror melodrama *What Ever Happened to Baby Jane?* (1962), about a former actress (Joan Crawford) with paralysis and her mentally deranged sister (Bette Davis), played on the same disabled-woman-as-victim trope; but which sister was the monster and which was the victim? Several horror films of the 1970s – including *It's Alive* (1974), *Eraserhead* (1977), and *The Brood* (1979) – centered on monstrously deformed newborns, a trend some film historians relate to the tragedies caused by thalidomide in the 1960s. (Thalidomide was an anti-nausea drug prescribed for pregnant women that was later discovered to cause severe birth defects.)

The James Bond series, which began with *Dr No* in 1962, has repeatedly used physical difference (along with race, nationality, and queer sexualities) to make its master criminals and/or henchmen into freaks. For example, Dr No, besides being half Chinese, has prosthetic hands. The arch villain in *Thunderball* (1965) wears an eye patch, while Blofeld in *You Only Live Twice* (1967) has a scarred face. The "**blaxploitation** Bond" film *Live and Let Die* (1973) has a full cast of African American villains, including Tee-Hee, a large black man with a mechanical claw, and Whisper, an obese villain who apparently cannot speak above a whisper. Francisco Scaramanga, *The Man with the Golden Gun* (1974), has a third nipple, and is aided and abetted by his little person henchman Nick Nack (Hervé Villechaize, who would also be featured as a less-threatening sidekick in the *Fantasy Island* TV show [1978–84]). In both *The Spy Who Loved Me* (1977) and *Moonraker* (1979), Richard Kiel plays a giant-like character named Jaws, complete with a mouthful of gleaming steel teeth. Even more recent Bond films employ the same tropes: Le Chiffre in *Casino Royale* (2006) has a physical abnormality that causes him to leak blood from one eye. Like the old *Richard III* trope, these villains' physical abnormalities are used to signify their moral corruption, as well as underscore the heroic status of James Bond as the epitome of able-bodied white heterosexual masculinity.

Other films of the 1960s and 1970s continued to romanticize disability, often by literally dramatizing a romance between someone with a disability and an able-bodied partner. These films tend to be love stories in which the able-bodied partner helps the disabled person overcome his or her limitations, finding love and/or redemption in the process. For example, in *Butterflies are Free* (1972), Goldie Hawn plays a woman who helps a blind man (Edward Albert) escape his over-protective mother and become a more fully functioning person. *Ice Castles* (1978) is about a blind figure skater and her supportive boyfriend. *Voices* (1979) is a love story about a deaf teacher (Amy Irving) and a hearing musician (Michael Ontkean). *The Other Side of the Mountain* (1975), based on a true story, is about a champion skier who becomes paralyzed, and the man who helps her regain her life; the film was so popular it spawned a sequel three years later. In focusing on how these individuals "triumph" over the "adversity" of their disability, these melodramas rarely acknowledge another adversity: societal discrimination, whether intentional or through ignorance. These films show how disabled heroes or heroines must adapt to the world around them, but rarely suggest that perhaps the world itself might need to adapt its attitudes as well.

While all of the usual older stereotypes of people with disabilities could be found in films of the era, another form of representation began to emerge that seemed strongly tied to the growth of the counterculture, and its questioning of traditional American values. Increasingly, disabled characters were used in films in symbolic ways. This was most obvious in the few films made during this era about the Vietnam war. The Noble Warrior image was virtually supplanted by the Tragic Victim stereotype, and rehabilitation was depicted as more difficult than in pervious eras. In these anti-war films, disability is a caustic metaphor for the failures of national policy that many felt created, caused, or exacerbated the Vietnam war. One of the most disturbing of these films was (formerly blacklisted writer) Dalton Trumbo's *Johnny Got his Gun* (1971). A fiercely anti-war parable, the film centers on a quadruple amputee who has also lost his eyes, ears, mouth, and nose. Trumbo had originally written the story in 1939, using World War I as the historical backdrop, but it could not be made until the end of the studio era. While a more realistic treatment of disability appeared in *Coming Home* (1978), with Jon Voight in an Oscar-winning performance as a wheelchair-using Vietnam veteran, the film also associated his compromised masculinity with the compromised moral standing of the nation. John Savage's amputee character in *The Deer Hunter* (1978) works similarly, to symbolize loss as well as the nation's inability to achieve some form of victorious closure on the Vietnam war. And although based on the real life of disabled Vietnam veteran Ron Kovic, *Born On the Fourth of July* (1989) verges on symbolism as well, presenting Kovic (as played by Tom Cruise) as an embodiment of the country's eventual disillusionment with its government's handling of the war.

Disability as countercultural metaphor was not just restricted to anti-Vietnam war films. The quirky Otto Preminger film *Tell Me That You Love Me, Junie Moon* (1970) is a character study about three people who are "misfits" in mainstream society. Liza Minnelli plays a woman with a facial scar, Robert Moore plays a homosexual in a wheelchair, and Ken Howard plays a man with epilepsy. The three of them bond over their shared status as outsiders, but the film also promotes the usual ideological messages about gender and disability. Thus, Minnelli's character is "disabled" precisely because her "to-be-looked-at-ness" has been compromised. Similarly, the men's masculinity is compromised by their motor disabilities (and the gay character's sexuality). Surely the film of the era that uses disability most metaphorically is Ken Russell's film of the Who's rock opera *Tommy* (1975). Its title character (Roger Daltry) spends the first half of the film as a "deaf, dumb, and blind kid" before becoming a "pinball wizard" and a pop culture messiah. A psychedelic mish-mash decrying bad parenting, celebrity worship, and religious cultism, *Tommy* is not really a film about disability *per se*, even though it takes satirical aim at the idea that religious faith is enough to bring "eyesight to the blind."

Thus, while the 1970s romantic melodramas focused almost exclusively on the individual disabled person rather than the larger social system, these "countercultural metaphor" films focused on the failings of the dominant culture, but with minimized connection to the material lives of individuals with disabilities. Yet the rise of the counterculture and its various civil rights movements did contribute to people in disabled communities conceptualizing themselves as minority groups that had been treated in prejudicial ways. Disabled people started demanding equal access and opportunity, much as people of color, women, and homosexuals were also doing. The 1970s saw a new age in attempts to create awareness and acceptance of people with different abilities. Various protests and actions led to the inclusion of Braille on public surfaces such as elevator panels, the provision of sign language translators at public events, and increasing wheelchair access to and within municipal buildings. Members of the deaf community banded together to protest films like *Voices*, especially because it did not hire a deaf actor to play a deaf character, and laud the TV movie *And Your Name is Jonah* (1979), especially because it had. Following in the footsteps of the blaxploitation horror film *Blacula* (1972), deaf filmmaker Peter Wolf made *Deafula* (1974), a vampire story "spoken" in American Sign Language. And although *Deafula* was very hard to see outside of deaf communities, millions of Americans could tune in weekly to see wheelchair-using detective *Ironside* (1967–75) solving crimes on television. Robert T. Ironside was played by able-bodied actor Raymond Burr, but the show nonetheless emphasized that his disability was not something to be pitied, and that it in no way hampered his success. Millions of people also watched Louise Fletcher use sign language in her Oscar acceptance speech (as Best Actress for *One Flew Over the Cuckoo's Nest* [1975]) to thank her deaf parents.

This era of activism also saw the rise of the **social model of disability**, shifting attention away from the ideologies of disease and disorder and onto the ideologies that construct definitions of ability and disability. Increasingly, films began to include more complex and rounded disabled characters, and/or indict the cruelty of those who would exploit and ostracize them. David Lynch's *The Elephant Man* (1980) is one such film, rewriting the history of the side show freak and challenging many previous stereotypes about disability. Based on a true story of the Industrial Revolution (and a popular Broadway play), *The Elephant Man* was the cruel epithet used to name John Merrick, a man whose physical body was so badly deformed he was exhibited for years as a living monstrosity. Through the use of black and white film, canted angles, and expressionistic lighting, director Lynch at first also invites the viewer to see Merrick (John Hurt) as a monster, even as he is also the Tragic Victim of his "owner," a cruel carnival barker named Bytes (Freddie Jones). Paralleling the development of the medical model of disability, Merrick is rescued by surgeon Frederick Treves (Anthony Hopkins), who initially wants to study and possibly cure him. However, Treves and his circle of friends and colleagues eventually realize that Merrick is a human being and not a test case. (At one memorable moment Merrick turns upon those who would harm him, asserting that "I am not an animal! I am a human being! I am a man!") *The Elephant Man* thus encourages viewers to consider who is the real monster: John Merrick, or the people around him (and the viewer himself or herself is implicated in that question). Popular with audiences and critics alike, *The Elephant Man* garnered eight Oscar nominations, including one for John Hurt as John Merrick.

A few years later, the film *Mask* (1985) dealt with similar issues, but in a modern setting. Also based upon a true story, *Mask* tells the story of Rocky Dennis (Eric Stoltz), a young man with a cranial malformation, and his rebellious mother (Cher), who wants the best for him. Like *The Elephant Man*, *Mask* is more about the cruelties inflicted upon Rocky and his family by ignorant and uncaring townspeople than it is about pity or fear. Both films ask so-called "normal" Americans to challenge their own presumptions and prejudices about people who look differently than they do, and to realize the common humanity that all of us share. One year later, another major Hollywood film would address similar issues, this time in relation to the deaf community. And unlike its usual practice of hiring hearing actors to play deaf parts, this time Hollywood cast many deaf actors in central and supporting roles. As the following case study demonstrates, *Children of a Lesser God* (1986) became a popular and critical hit, partly because it dealt with many of the issues facing deaf people in America in complex, compassionate, humane, and artful ways.

Case Study: *Children of a Lesser God* (1986)

One of the best-known films to center on issues related to deaf people, *Children of a Lesser God* began life as a Broadway play by Mark Medoff. Set at a New England school for deaf children and teenagers, the story centers on the blossoming relationship between James Leeds (William Hurt), a speech and language teacher, and Sarah Norman (**Marlee Matlin**), a former pupil of the school who now works there as a custodian. As they fall in love, the film dramatizes issues related to such a hearing/non-hearing relationship, explores Sarah's lingering bitterness toward her mother, and challenges common misconceptions about deaf people. A major studio release, *Children of a Lesser God* was nominated for five Oscars including Best Picture and Best Screenplay. Marlee Matlin, in her film debut, won the award for Best Actress, and has since then gone on to become the most prominent and successful deaf actress in Hollywood. Ultimately,

although the film tells a specific story about a deaf woman and a hearing man, its themes open onto larger issues of gender and (hetero)sexuality, specifically the need for communication between men and women, or indeed, between anyone and everyone else.

Director Randa Haines employs several visual metaphors for the developing relationship between James and Sarah, one of the most prominent being water. As the film opens, Sarah is sleeping through a violent thunderstorm while James takes a ferry to Kittridge Island, where the school is located. The ferry is an obvious motif – a something that shuttles people back and forth across a dividing space – and it comes to signify the connection and communication that slowly develop between James and Sarah. When James first confesses his love for Sarah, she is swimming in the school's pool, and James's falling into the pool with her is symbolic of

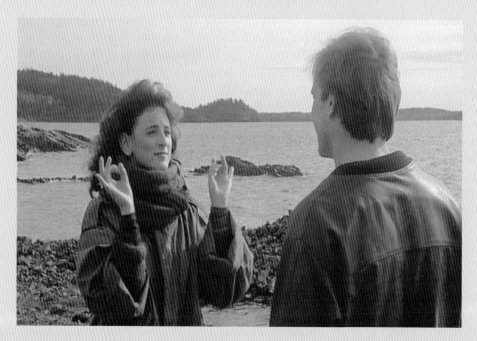

Deaf actress Marlee Matlin won an Oscar for her leading role in *Children of a Lesser God* (1986); she and co-star William Hurt are shown here by water, a running motif in the film.
Children of a Lesser God, dir. Randa Haines, copyright © 1986, Paramount

his falling in love. At this point, Haines frames the now-kissing couple in a haunting underwater slow-motion shot that seems to suggest an otherworldly quality. Their sexual relationship separates them from the world around them, paralleling the way Sarah has allowed her deafness to isolate her from the speaking world. Another shot of Sarah sitting alone on a rocky promontory surrounded by lapping waves conveys a similar idea about her isolation; pointedly, this set-up is resolved when she comes down from the rocks, joins James on the beach, and agrees to go out to dinner with him. Finally, when the couple reunites for the film's happy ending, they do so on the ocean shore.

Music is another important motif the film uses to dramatize its issues. James's teaching uses music to help his students learn to speak, a technique the school's director (Philip Bosco) initially criticizes but later comes to accept, especially after James's students impress everyone at a school assembly by performing a musical number. At another point, James's love of Bach becomes an issue in his relationship with Sarah; he tells her he can no longer enjoy his favorite composer because he knows that she cannot share in his appreciation. Sarah asks him to "show me the music," but James is too awkward and embarrassed to move his body. Sarah, on the other hand, had previously danced very expressively to the song "I'll Take You There" on her first date with James. Her dance and song seem to suggest how music can (like the ferry) connect people across a divide. His reluctance to dance, perhaps related to his ideas about traditional masculinity, is another potential roadblock in their relationship. Fortunately, the two find they can communicate quite effectively without words (or music or dancing) through making love.

Yet before falling for James, Sarah has been highly suspicious of him (and all men). In her teenage years, she found she could relate to boys sexually; however, she was treated by them as nothing but a sex object. They used her body but never learned to communicate with her as a person. Sarah is also initially leery of James because she prefers to use sign language exclusively while James wants to teach both her and his students to lip-read and speak aloud. For Sarah, use of sign language is a mark of pride and difference from the hearing world; as the film goes on it also suggests that Sarah is unwilling to speak because she thinks she will look and sound (as her mother puts it) "awful." As Sarah tells James at one

point, "I don't do anything I can't do well." When he finally backs her against a brick wall and forces her to speak, she releases an anguished wail and runs away from him. This contest between Sarah's signing and James's speaking is clearly gendered as well; she resents the fact that James literally has to speak for her. At one point he even seems rather chauvinistic, forthrightly telling (rather than asking) her to quit her job and move in with him. Although she eventually does do that, by the end of the film she is also asserting her own desires, pursuing a new job and making plans for college.

Throughout the film, Sarah slowly reveals more reasons for her anger and resentment. She is bitter that many hearing people think that deaf people are mentally retarded; she herself was misdiagnosed as such until the age of seven. There is also an uncomfortable scene at a poker party, where the hearing guests speak about her, rather than to her. At that same party, the school director also crudely implies that all deaf people cheat at cards, because they have secret visual signals that they alone can detect. Toward the end of the film, Sarah finally confronts her mother, who sent her away to boarding school at the age of five. Yet Sarah's mother (Piper Laurie, also nominated for an Oscar) harbors her own resentments. She reveals that in the past she blamed Sarah for destroying her marriage: her husband left them both because he felt a deaf child reflected poorly on his masculinity. Eventually mother and daughter reconcile, and Sarah and James find their way back to one another.

As many critics have noted, although the film follows the narrative arc of the play, the play was much more invested in deaf activism than is the film. In a major Hollywood release, the filmmakers may have felt it necessary to eliminate or tone down the play's activist stance. Also true to Hollywood form, heterosexual romance occupies center stage, and is part and parcel of the film's happy ending, possibly suggesting that a (deaf) woman needs a (hearing) man. (Recall that many of the 1970s melodramas about romancing a person with disabilities implied similar things.) Yet, despite these critical observations, *Children of a Lesser God* was a cinematic milestone in the representation of deaf people, deaf communities, and deaf issues. Simultaneously specific and general in its meanings, the film stresses the importance of love and communication for all people, across whatever barriers may oppose them.

A More Enlightened Age?

After the success of *Children of a Lesser God*, Marlee Matlin became the most recognized deaf actor in Hollywood. However, Hollywood's generic formula blockbusters (centered on able-bodied masculinity) have trouble accommodating deaf or disabled actors. Since her Oscar win, Matlin is seen more on TV than at the multiplex: she has created memorable characters for shows like *Reasonable Doubts* (1991–3), *The West Wing* (1999–2006), and *The L Word* (2007–). Little people actors like Warwick Davis and Kenny Baker continue to find roles in fantasy films such as the *Star Wars* films (1977, 1980, 1983, 1999, 2002, 2005) and the *Harry Potter* films (2001–7), even though they are often covered in makeup or hidden inside full-body costumes. (Kenny Baker played R2-D2 in the *Star Wars* films.) However, a few recent films have cast little people as a truly human and complex characters. For example, the independent film *The Station Agent* (2003) centers on Peter Dinklage as a little person obsessed with trains; he reluctantly befriends a Cuban hot dog vendor and a middle-aged divorcee. Peter Dinklage also had an amusing turn as the gay lover of the deceased in the dark comedy *Death at a Funeral* (2007), but he too has played magical fantasy figures in films like *The Chronicles of Narnia: Prince Caspian* (2008).

Most Hollywood films, however, continue to cast able-bodied actors in disabled roles. In fact, throughout the last two decades, able-bodied actors playing characters with intellectual or physical disabilities have repeatedly become Oscar winners (much as they had in earlier decades). For example, Al Pacino won the Oscar for playing a blind man in *Scent of a Woman* (1992), while Tom Hanks won an Oscar as the mentally challenged *Forrest Gump* (1994). Other Oscar winners playing

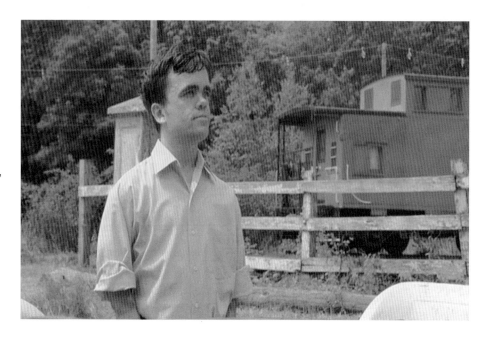

Peter Dinklage starred in *The Station Agent* (2003), a poignant character study of a man whose identity is not wholly defined by his status as a little person. *The Station Agent*, dir. Thomas McCarthy, copyright © 2003, Miramax

disabled include Dustin Hoffman in *Rain Man* (1988), Daniel Day-Lewis in *My Left Foot* (1989), Geoffrey Rush in *Shine* (1996), and Jamie Foxx as *Ray* (2004). This trend is interesting to compare to the similar one of heterosexual actors winning Oscars for playing gay in films like *Kiss of the Spider Woman* (1985), *Philadelphia* (1993), and *Capote* (2005). And although this trend is less pronounced for women, it is curious to note that Hillary Swank's two Oscar wins have been for playing transgendered in *Boys Don't Cry* (1999) and disabled in *Million Dollar Baby* (2004). Some cynics now suggest that a heterosexual, able-bodied actor playing queer or disabled is almost sure to garner an Oscar nomination.

Several of these films have been quite controversial, as they raise questions about the ethics of assisted suicide for severely disabled people, usually those with quadriplegia (paralysis affecting all four limbs, often caused by an injury to the spinal cord at the level of the neck). This was the subject of the earlier play and film *Whose Life is it Anyway?* (1981), and it is also a central focus of both *Million Dollar Baby* and the Spanish film *The Sea Inside* (2004), an Oscar-winner for Best Foreign Film. (All three films have been critiqued as **ableist**, since they seem to suggest that suicide is preferable to quadriplegia.) The life and death of actor Christopher Reeve are notable in relation to these films. A well-known stage and screen actor (*Superman* [1978], *Somewhere in Time* [1980]), Reeve was paralyzed from the neck down after a horseback riding incident in 1995. Yet rather than give up, he became a highly visible figure, writing an autobiography and continuing to act, produce, and direct both film and television projects. He also made numerous public appearances, lending his fame and "can-do" persona to disability causes. He died in 2004.

Other contemporary films continue to use disability in metaphoric terms. For example, Rinku Kikuchi plays a young deaf Japanese woman in *Babel* (2006), but her deafness is as much a metaphor for the film's theme of global miscommunication as it is a defining trait of her character. Tim Burton's *Big Fish* (2003) features a giant man and conjoined twins who again serve as metaphoric figures within a larger narrative context about community and belonging. Similarly, the independent film *Brothers of the Head* (2005) is about conjoined twins who become rock and roll stars; it is more a commentary on the exploitative aspects of the music business than it is a film about the issues facing real-life conjoined twins. At the multiplex, comic book action films like the *X-Men* franchise (2000, 2003, 2006) are also intriguing in terms of disability metaphors. Professor Xavier (Patrick Stewart) uses a wheelchair, but he also has superhero powers, as do the rest of his crime fighting X-Men (and X-Women). Perhaps reflecting more modern sensibilities about dis/ability, today's superhero comics and movies often suggest (albeit in mostly displaced ways) that being differently abled is a good thing.

Perhaps the most important recent trend in Hollywood films that feature disabled characters is that some of the films are not explicitly about their characters' disabilities. These films show people with disabilities as having more to their lives than just being disabled. For example, the Stephen King adaptation *Silver Bullet* (1985) is about a boy in a wheelchair who has to battle a werewolf. *The Bone Collector* (1999) stars Denzel Washington as a quadriplegic homicide detective tracking down a serial killer. In *Alien: Resurrection* (1997), French actor Dominique Pinon plays a disabled space trader who still gets to battle aliens and even survive the film. Arguably, the work of the Farrelly brothers (Peter and Bobby) exemplifies this trend. The writer-directors behind popular comedies like *Dumb & Dumber* (1994), *Kingpin* (1996), and *There's Something About Mary* (1998), the Farrelly brothers often make films about a particular disorder or condition. *Kingpin* is about a one-handed bowling champion (Woody Harrelson), while *Stuck on You* (2003) is about conjoined twins played by Matt Damon and Greg Kinnear. While some have accused the brothers of exploiting or trivializing disability (specifically multiple personality disorder in *Me, Myself & Irene* [2000] and obesity in *Shallow Hal* [2001]), others see their films as attempts to normalize such conditions.

The Farrelly brothers also make it a point to hire actors with intellectual or physical disabilities to play supporting roles in most of their films (even as the demands of the Hollywood system force them to use able-bodied actors as the leads). One recent film the brothers produced, *The Ringer* (2005), is about a man (Johnny Knoxville) who poses as intellectually disabled in order to rig the Special Olympics. The filmmakers worked closely with Special Olympics officials and eventually received their endorsement; the film features many disabled performers including Edward Barbanell, an actor with Down's syndrome. Yet it is sometimes hard to tell if films like these are encouraging audiences to laugh at the situations surrounding people with disabilities, or instead at disabled people themselves. In today's ironic media culture, films are often constructed to have multiple appeals, allowing some audience members to laugh at a certain character's naïve prejudices, while other audience members may be laughing at that same character's politically incorrect jokes. (Compare this tactic to that used by many **dumb white guy comedies** as discussed in chapter 15.)

A concerned deaf father in the documentary *Sound and Fury* (2000), a film that explores the moral and ethical issues of cochlear implants. *Sound and Fury*, dir. Josh Aronson, copyright © 2000, Aronsonfilm/ Artistic License

Some of the quadriplegic rugby players featured in the popular documentary *Murderball* (2005); although they ae limited in their movements, their masculinity is far from compromised. *Murderball*, dirs. Henry Alex Rubin and Dana Adam Shapiro, copyright © 2005, MTV Films/ Paramount

As with most of the other groups discussed throughout this book, documentary filmmaking continues to explore the varied issues relating to people with disabilities in much more complex ways than does Hollywood. The PBS film *Through Deaf Eyes* (2007) is a concise history of deaf Americans from the early 1800s onward. It explores the historical controversies over sign language versus speech and lip-reading ("oralism"), and the rise of the deaf community as a vocal civil rights block. It also features short excerpts from the work of several deaf filmmakers. (In fact, recent years have seen the rise of deaf films festivals in places like California, Illinois, and Maine.) Another issue touched upon in *Through Deaf Eyes* – cochlear implants – is the central subject of the Oscar-nominated film *Sound and Fury* (2000). Cochlear implants (which were developed in the 1980s) are hearing-assist devices that bypass the ear altogether: they consist of an external microphone receiver that transmits electrical impulses directly to the auditory nerve. *Sound and Fury* documents the pros and cons of cochlear implants, a debate that threatens to tear apart three generations of the Artinian family. Another recent festival and art-house hit was the documentary *Murderball* (2005), about quadriplegic men who play brutal rugby matches in high-tech wheelchairs. The popular appeal of *Murderball* arguably rests on its celebration of traditional notions of heterosexual masculinity: its wheelchair-using protagonists are still "real" men, as exemplified by their wives, girlfriends, and the rough-and-tumble wheelchair rugby they play.

As technology continues to advance, the relationships between disabled people and the cinema continues to change. Today, closed captioning regularly allows deaf people access to Hollywood films, and new technologies that create alternative, descriptive soundtracks have made films more accessible to the blind. Although still marginalized for the most part, deaf actors and actors in wheelchairs continue to lobby Hollywood for more and better parts – parts that still regularly go to hearing and able-bodied actors. One such advocacy group, Abilities United Productions, works to promote actors with disabilities as well as commercial screenplays about characters with disabilities. Media watchdog groups also now proliferate, and make themselves heard within the Hollywood industry. The live action film *Mr Magoo* (1997), based upon the old cartoons about a near-sighted man, was protested by various advocacy groups for the blind. Similarly, *The Da Vinci Code* (2006) was met with protests from NOAH (the National Organization for Albinism and Hypopigmentation), precisely because of its Obsessive Avenger stereotype of a villainous albino monk. In the twenty-first century, such stereotypes continue to find their way onto American movie screens, but they are increasingly challenged by advocacy groups and concerned citizens. As with the other minority groups studied within this book, attitudes about (and images of) people with disabilities have evolved across the history of American cinema, but the journey is far from over.

Questions for Discussion

1 According to some accounts, there have been over 50 villainous albinos in American film and television in the last 50 years. Can you name some of them? What other films can you name that still use physical disability to suggest a character is criminal and/or monstrous?

2 As discussed throughout this chapter, issues of ability are tied to issues of gender and sexuality in complex ways. Can you think of images of disabled people who are also people of color? How does race/ethnicity impact on the portrayal of those characters (if it does)?

3 During the Industrial Revolution, disability was often associated with the poor or working-class. Do films today still link disability to economic hardship? How does class affect the portrayal of those with disabilities (if it does)?

Further Reading

Enns, Anthony and Christopher R. Smit. *Screening Disability: Essays on Cinema and Disability*. Lanham, MD: University Press of America, 2001.

Friedman, Lester D., ed. *Cultural Sutures: Medicine and Media*. Durham, NC: Duke University Press, 2004.

Klobas, Lauri E. *Disability Drama in Television and Film*. Jefferson, NC: McFarland, 1988.

Longmore, Paul. "Screening Stereotypes: Images of Disabled People," *Social Policy* 16:1 (1985) 31–7.

McRuer, Robert. *Crip Theory: Cultural Signs of Queerness and Disability*. New York: New York University Press, 2006.

Norden, Martin F. *A Cinema of Isolation: A History of Physical Disability in the Movies*. New Brunswick, NJ: Rutgers University Press, 1994.

Pointon, Ann with Chris Davis, eds. *Framed: Interrogating Disability in the Media*. London: BFI, 1997.

Schuchman, John S. *Hollywood Speaks: Deafness and the Film Entertainment Industry*. Urbana: University of Illinois Press, 1988.

Snyder, Sharon L. and David T. Mitchell. *Cultural Locations of Disability*. Chicago: University of Chicago Press, 2006.

Further Screening

Freaks (1932)
The Best Years of Our Lives (1946)
The Men (1950)
Coming Home (1978)
Children of a Lesser God (1986)
Born on the Fourth of July (1989)

The Bone Collector (1999)
Big Fish (2003)
The Station Agent (2003)
Murderball (2005)
Through Deaf Eyes (2007)

Chapter 17

MAKING CONNECTIONS

In an effort to present the history of race, class, gender, sexuality, and ability in American film in a concise and organized manner, this book has been structured according to separate sections concerned with specific types of identity. Yet, as the very first chapter of this book pointed out, issues of identity are not clear-cut or simple. Individuals self-identify along a number of categories. No one is *only* their race or *just* their gender. Furthermore, these categories of identity intersect and affect each other. Throughout this book, connections between various identities have been stressed. How do attitudes about race interrelate with concepts of class, or with gender and/or sexuality? How are gender and sexuality themselves intertwined? How do issues of ability connect to all of the above? In other words, discourses of race/ethnicity, class, gender, sexuality, and ability are all woven together in complex ways to form the structures of America's **dominant ideologies**.

This chapter contains further case studies that emphasize how the concerns raised in the rest of this book overlap and influence each other. Many of the films discussed in this chapter were made somewhat recently, and so show how these issues are still alive and interrelated in the present-day United States. This is not to say, however, that such interconnections are new developments. Some examples from the classical Hollywood period have been included as a reminder that concepts of race, class, gender, sexuality, and ability have always affected each other. (Case studies of older films in previous chapters also highlight this.) Just as stylistic formal choices in literary design, visual design, cinematography, editing, and sound design combine in a film to impart a message or idea, so too do the various identity categories discussed in this book build on each other in complex ways. Some films acknowledge shared oppression across different forms of identity, while other films employ stereotypes from multiple categories of identity. Intriguingly, some films challenge dominant ideology in one area, but uphold it in another. As such, each film can be understood as being in **hegemonic negotiation** with the dominant ideologies of American culture. These additional case studies are offered as further examples of the types of critical thinking about movies that can tell us much about America's history, present-day culture, and perhaps even the future of America on film.

Case Study 1: *Queen Christina* (1933)

Queen Christina is often cited as a prime example of an attempt to represent a queer character in a Hollywood film during the classical studio era. The film is purported to be a biography of a Renaissance Swedish monarch that historians now generally regard as lesbian (although, it is important to note, the modern usage of the term "lesbian" did not exist during Christina's lifetime). Furthermore, key people involved in the making of the film were also lesbian or bisexual. For example, although star actress Greta Garbo enacted many of classical Hollywood's greatest heterosexual romantic figures (such as *Mata Hari* [1931], *Anna Karenina* [1935], and *Camille* [1936]), offscreen Garbo had various sexual relationships with women, including Salka Viertel, one of *Queen Christina*'s screenwriters.

The film itself was made just before the institution of the **Production Code**'s Seal of Approval provision (1934), and thus is perhaps a bit more forward in its representation of sexuality than would be possible only a short time later. That said, the depiction of Christina as possibly queer is dealt with solely through implication rather than directly asserting that she could be lesbian. In fact, the main narrative specifically involves her romance with a male ambassador from Spain (John Gilbert). Thus, the film is a good example of the type of picture that features a **connotative** queer, one who might be decoded in different ways by different audiences. Some viewers might focus on the opening sections of the film, where Garbo as Christina struts around in breeches and actively resists efforts by members of her court to get her married. (In the 1930s, women wearing pants was still considered unusual and unfeminine.) When warned that she could die "an old maid," she proudly asserts that, on the contrary, she would instead die "a bachelor!" In possibly the most forthright moment of the film, Christina greets her lady-in-waiting by tenderly clasping the young woman's face and giving her a full kiss on the mouth.

As these moments suggest, much of the lesbian connotation associated with Christina is tied to gender expectations: in the 1930s, women with masculine appearances or behaviors could be assumed to be lesbian. *Queen Christina* emphasizes this link when, after finally falling in love with a man, Christina sheds her masculine garb for more conventional gowns and jewelry. The film seems to be saying that once Christina engages in heterosexual passion, she will invariably become softened and passive – that is to say, more traditionally feminine. Yet, this focus on unraveling traditional gender expectations also suggests another reading of Christina's sexual identity. She could (in the parlance of today's sexologists) also be a female-to-male **transgendered** person. Throughout the film, Christina's behaviors (both personally and in her public life as queen) tend to construct her as a heterosexual male. After all, she does run a country, wear pants, kiss women, and regard herself as a potential bachelor. One cannot really know for certain whether Christina is "actually" lesbian, bisexual, heterosexual, or transgendered; however, she is spectacularly queer to the extent that one simplistic label cannot begin to adequately describe her.

Thus, even as the film progresses and its narrative starts to focus more directly on Christina's heterosexual romance, an unproblematic heteronormativity is never completely attained. For example, when Antonio, the Spanish ambassador, first meets Christina, he mistakes her for a boy. This makes the scene where they decide to share a bedroom (and a bed) fraught with male–male homoerotic desire, among all the other queer desires floating about. Antonio definitely seems to be aroused by this person, and is somewhat confused and unnerved by these feelings until Christina disrobes and is revealed to be biologically a woman. Later, after their (mostly?) heterosexual liaison becomes public, Christina's own court disapproves of it as an unsanctioned form of

Greta Garbo and John Gilbert in *Queen Christina* (1933), a film about the strong-willed monarch of Sweden who dressed and ruled like a man.
Queen Christina, copyright © 1933, MGM

sexuality: one does not tryst – even heterosexually – with a foreigner. Furthermore, when defending her relationship with Antonio, Christina is figured as the dominant half of the couple. Antonio stays quietly in the background as would the traditional "little woman." His associations with Spanish art and leisure link him to the conventionally feminine as well.

The film ends with Christina giving up the throne for Antonio, only to discover that her lover has been killed in a duel. As she and his dead body sail away, Christina walks to the prow of the ship to face whatever lies ahead.

In the most famous moment of the film, the camera moves into an extreme close-up of Garbo's celebrated face. Directed to show no emotion whatsoever, Garbo in her final appearance as Christina allows audiences to project their own emotions and desires onto her. Is she exhibiting sadness at the loss of her heterosexual lover? Hope for a new life unfettered by her royal court? The ambiguity of Christina's emotions (or lack thereof – yet another sign of traditional masculinity that Christina exhibits) mirrors the ambiguity of her gender and sexuality.

Case Study 2: *The Old Maid* (1939)

The Old Maid is a typical example of the classical Hollywood **woman's film**, one containing complex and at times contradictory messages about class, gender, and (hetero)sexuality. It announces its focus immediately after the opening credits, by showing a newspaper headline heralding the impending Civil War, but then scanning down the page to a close-up of "Wedding Announcements." The film then dissolves to a bride, Delia (Miriam Hopkins), being attended to by her cousin Charlotte (Bette Davis). In these few shots, the opening sequence establishes a sense that women's lives are centered on men and marriage rather than national politics. And while it unfolds during the Civil War and its aftermath, most of *The Old Maid* takes place in the parlors and bedrooms of its main female characters, making it quite literally a domestic, home-bound melodrama. In fact, the entire film is organized around weddings – three ceremonies and one interrupted one occur over the course of the movie.

True to the dictates of nineteenth-century white patriarchal capitalism, getting married is presented as the normal "career" for women. Rather than training for some profession, women are shown preparing themselves to attract the best possible (that is, wealthiest) mate. Thus, in the opening scenes, Delia marries someone other than Clem (George Brent) precisely because Clem does not have enough money. As its title suggests, the film dramatizes the "horrors" of not getting properly married. Soon after Delia dumps Clem, Charlotte (who will become the old maid of the title) has a one-night fling with him; he promptly heads off to war and dies, leaving her an unwed mother. Then, in order to protect her new daughter Tina from the scandal of illegitimacy, Charlotte suffers throughout the film by denying that the child is hers. The sacrifice goes so far as letting Delia adopt the child, and making Tina come to despise Charlotte as a harping old maid aunt. In countless ways, Charlotte (and the audience) are taught the horrible fate that awaits women who do not enter into proper heterosexual relations.

The idea that a woman might marry *and* have a career is also regarded as scandalous. Charlotte is constantly pressured by everyone around her to get married and give up a career she obviously enjoys: running a foundling home (which initially helps her keep Tina near her without arousing suspicion). Marriageable women must come from good backgrounds (that is, be wealthy) but they cannot be the ones to make the money. This is dramatized during the final portion of the movie when the lack of public knowledge about Tina's social background threatens to derail her marriage to the boy she loves. It is only when Delia (from a respectable and prominent family) legally adopts her that the wedding is allowed to proceed.

Along with sacrifice and choice, *The Old Maid* involves another one of the classical Hollywood woman's film's central themes: competition between Delia and Charlotte – first over Clem, and then over Tina. The two regularly fight each other rather than share a sense of oppression under patriarchal capitalism that might perhaps allow them to work together to resist it. The voice of **heteronormative patriarchal capitalism** is embodied in the film by character actor Donald Crisp as the family doctor. He is presented throughout the film as the ultimate authority figure, all knowing (he even knows Charlotte's secret) and constantly dispensing advice to the women.

Yet, while the women feel the pressure to obey men and devote their lives to them, those same men tend to be pushed to the margins of the film's narrative. Clem is only onscreen during the first 10 minutes of the film, and the man Delia eventually marries also dies by the mid-point of the film. Thus, as a melodrama centered on women, the film represents Charlotte, Delia, and Tina as strong-willed characters with their own desires and determinations (albeit only within the domestic sphere). Furthermore, the women are shown sometimes resisting the demands made by the men. Delia rejects Clem's claim on her, and later expertly manipulates another man who plans to marry Charlotte into stopping their wedding. Charlotte argues with the doctor when he tries to give her advice on how to run the foundling home, and Delia's elderly grandmother is shown early in the film also angrily refusing the doctor's orders (even using her cane to try and smash up the room in resistance). Also, while ostensibly teaching an object lesson about sex outside marriage, the film (particularly through the use of "tear-jerking" music) invites us to feel sorry for Charlotte rather than that she has been justly punished.

In *The Old Maid* (1939), Miriam Hopkins and Bette Davis pursue two very different versions of femininity. Hopkins is glamorous, posed in fur and fancy dress next to crystal ware, while Davis is matronly, posed with apron and tea kettle next to the kitchen sink.
The Old Maid, copyright © 1939, Warner Bros.

Under the pressures placed upon them, Delia and Charlotte react by consciously taking on certain gender roles, almost like costumes. To get her way, Delia presents herself as extremely feminine – always with her hair done up in magnificent blonde curls, and wearing a number of glamorous period fashions with lots of adornments (fringe, lace, jewels). Such feminine trappings hide her sharp mind, which reveals itself fully only when she and Charlotte are alone. Charlotte, on the other hand, carefully creates the persona of the spinster aunt, wearing dowdy clothes and her hair in a tight bun. The film even shows her practicing ways of speaking in order to get the proper "old maid" inflection. In this aspect, the film underlines the fact that gender is not biological or natural, rather it is something consciously learned and performed.

The film also presents Charlotte and Delia's **homosocial** relationship as ultimately stronger than any of their bonds with men. Toward the end of the film, after the various men in their lives have died or gone away, the two women move in together to raise Tina jointly. From a contemporary perspective, Charlotte, Delia, and Tina almost role-model a lesbian family. And instead of a traditional heterosexual embrace, the film ends with Delia and Charlotte reconciling their final differences as "their daughter" is wed: the two link arms, smile at each other, and walk back into their home to live the rest of their lives together. (While it may seem that such a reading is a bit of a stretch, it should be noted that Zoe Akins, who wrote the original play on which *The Old Maid* was based, was a lesbian, and that Edmund Goulding, who directed the film, was gay.) But whether homosocial or homosexual, or something queerly in between, the story of Charlotte and Delia dramatizes the limited options that women had under nineteenth-century patriarchal capitalism, and at least a few ways that women were able to form meaningful bonds within it.

Case Study 3: *The Gang's All Here* (1943)

The Gang's All Here is a splashy Technicolor musical with Latin rhythms made in the midst of World War II (thus an example of a **Good Neighbor Policy** film). The film extolled the strength and determination of the United States (both the armed forces and the home front) in winning the fight, and simultaneously provided wartime audiences with lavish escapism from the tensions caused by the war. The story deals with a nightclub entertainer (Alice Faye) who falls in love with a soldier on leave (James Ellison), only to discover when he returns from battle that he is technically engaged to another woman (Sheila Ryan). By the end of the film, all the romantic problems have been resolved. The "other woman" is more interested in pursuing a career in show business than in getting married, something that is "acceptable" to wartime ideology since entertainers were seen as an important part of the war effort. Yet the stylized sexuality of *The Gang's All Here* has also made it a much-loved **camp** artifact, a film that both celebrates and pokes fun at the notions of heterosexual romance.

The plotline of *The Gang's All Here* is almost negligible – it is definitely overshadowed by the spectacle of the sexualized musical numbers concocted by director/choreographer **Busby Berkeley** (see chapter 11). True to Berkeley's **auteur** style, his musical numbers revel in the cinematic **objectification** of the female body. Chorus girls are shown in revealing garments lying around the set in "come-hither" poses while the camera whirls around them in **voyeuristic** fascination. Later, in the "Polka Dot Polka" finale, young women wearing form-fitting leotards are positioned for the camera to once again sail up and around them. In most of Berkeley's musical numbers, the chorus girls are not asked to dance much, but simply to move their hands and feet in almost mechanical patterns. For example, in the "Polka Dot Polka," the women stand around while slowly moving electrified neon hula hoops and giant polka dots. The sexual nature of these sequences is probably most

Carmen Miranda was the star of many Good Neighbor Policy musicals made at 20th Century-Fox, including *The Gang's All Here* (1943).
Unidentified publicity photo, authors' personal collection

obvious in "The Lady in the Tutti Frutti Hat" number, wherein the women stand around manipulating giant bananas.

"The Lady in the Tutti Frutti Hat" is sung by **Carmen Miranda**, the Brazilian performer who became a major icon of the Good Neighbor Policy (see chapter 7). The number is an outrageous celebration of Miranda's typical "fruit basket" headwear (a stylized version of the folk fashion of Bahian natives in Brazil). While perhaps showing interest in and acceptance of Latin culture, the number is extremely cartoon-like (including Miranda's squeaky voice), and presents Latin America almost like a theme park for US tourists to revel in, without any real sense of the region's economics, politics, or culture. In fact, giant bananas, ripe strawberries, and nubile chorus girls create an environment overflowing with abundance just waiting to be sampled by the North American (presumably male) spectator. The song itself (as does Miranda's opening number where she is hauled into New York City in a cargo net overflowing with consumer goods) equates Miranda with the edible bounty of South America. And all of this is meant implicitly for a male consumer: Miranda sings that she only takes her hat off – making herself available for "kissing" and more – for "Johnny Smith," the generic American GI.

Such aspects may make it seem as if *The Gang's All Here* is a very sexist and racist text – and it is definitely possible to read it as such. Yet the film focuses strongly on the female characters rather than the male ones, and invites viewers to identify with the women's point of view. The two biggest stars in the film are Alice Faye and Carmen Miranda. The male lead, James Ellison, was a minor player, and he is offscreen for large sections of the film. Significantly, because he could not sing or dance, he is excluded from the female-centered musical numbers. Furthermore, the film evokes the feeling that it is disinterested in its standardized boy-meets-girl plot, most obviously when it does not even feature a final romantic clinch between Faye and Ellison. (Instead the almost psychedelic "Polka Dot Polka" number ends the film.) The romantic scenes that *are* included are performed in a very stylized manner, with Faye and Ellison often facing more toward the camera than to each other as if to emphasize the artificiality of the romance. Some of the dialog also acknowledges the clichéd nature of musical comedy, as when Faye and Ellison notice that the studio orchestra has begun to play soft music, an obvious trope of Hollywood romance. In this way, the typical Hollywood heterosexual romance is made to seem as obviously fake as the giant bananas and neon hula hoops featured in the musical numbers.

The mannered artificiality of *The Gang's All Here* made it a strong favorite for **camp** readings by gay men of previous generations. In minimizing the importance of the heterosexual love plot in favor of the crazy production numbers, and in making heterosexuality seem almost unnatural, the film perhaps unwittingly spoke to queer audiences in multiple ways. Furthermore, because the film places men at the periphery of the musical numbers, it is possible to read those sequences as female homosocial or even lesbian utopias. Carmen Miranda herself became a camp icon very quickly in the 1940s – she was almost immediately imitated by a slew of Hollywood stars in drag from Mickey Rooney to Bugs Bunny. Miranda's flamboyant persona was often a staple of the male drag acts that flourished during the war years, both at home on Broadway and in shows put on by GIs for each other. Gay fans of Miranda would attach special meaning to the moment when, in "The Lady in the Tutti Frutti Hat," she sings that "every day I feel so gay, and when I'm gay I dress this way – something wrong with that? No!"

Carmen Miranda's fabulously stylized star image also complicates accusations that her persona reflected ethnocentric (or even racist) stereotypes. While some audiences may have assumed Latin Americans really looked and acted like Carmen Miranda, many other audiences certainly enjoyed her as a wild exaggeration that could even be said to be not just a stereotype but perhaps a parody of the stereotype itself. (This is certainly the way Miranda's roles and publicity interviews presented her, as a deft comedienne winking at rather than embodying the character she performed.) Hence, the film's emphasis on artificiality not only denaturalizes heterosexual romance and traditional gender roles, it also potentially destabilizes racial stereotyping. While *The Gang's All Here* initially seems like a piece of incredibly fluffy escapism, it is precisely the feel of the film that allows it to give off such complex messages about race, gender, and sexuality.

Case Study 4: *A Patch of Blue* (1965)

This prestigious Hollywood **social problem** film was written and directed by Guy Green, a British director who first made a name for himself as the Oscar-winning cinematographer of David Lean's *Great Expectations* (1946). *A Patch of Blue* tells the story of Selina D'Arcy (Elizabeth Hartman), a young white blind woman. Selina shares a dingy run-down apartment with her prostitute mother Rose-Ann (Shelley Winters in an Oscar-winning supporting role) and Rose-Ann's father "Ole Pa" (Wallace Ford), both of whom use, abuse, and berate Selina on a daily basis. Selina contributes to the family's meager income by stringing beads for the kindly Mr Faber, a man who occasionally takes Selina to the local park, a treat that seems to be Selina's only luxury in life. One day in the park, Selina meets African American accountant Gordon Ralfe (Sidney Poitier). As he comes to know her, Gordon realizes how Selina has been mistreated throughout her young life: she has never attended school or been taught to read Braille, she has barely any self-confidence, and she was once raped by one of her mother's clients.

Despite his brother Mark's warnings about getting involved with a white woman from a dubious background, Gordon befriends Selina, and the two become very close. At the end of the film, Gordon helps Selina start a new phase of her life by getting her away from Rose-Ann and enrolling her in a special school for the blind.

A Patch of Blue suggests many interesting things about how race, class, gender, sexuality, and disability were understood in the mid-1960s. It tries to draw subtle analogies between the ways that racial minorities and people with disabilities were treated during the era. It suggests the growing civil rights consciousness of the **counterculture**, especially when Selina reacts badly to a man who tells her she has "no right" to be out on the street alone. In a rage, Selina realizes she has "no rights at all," and then she slowly begins to fight for them (with the aid of Gordon). However, while the film tries to suggest that disability may be a civil rights issue, it tends to overlook or soft-pedal other civil rights struggles of the era, most prominently those of African Americans and

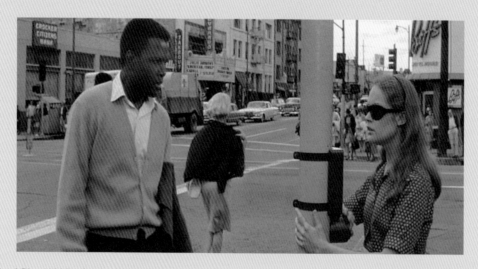

In *A Patch of Blue* (1965), Gordon Ralfe (Sidney Poitier) helps the blind Selina D'Arcy (Elizabeth Hartman) become more independent and aware of her civil rights.
A Patch of Blue, copyright © 1965, MGM

those of women. For example, the film almost ignores the era's institutionalized racism altogether. Although two old women scowl at Gordon and Selina in the park, perhaps thinking they are a miscegenated couple, most of the era's baseline racism is displaced onto the character of Rose-Ann, Selina's mother. As a shrewish whore character, Rose-Ann is thoroughly demonized, while Selina herself falls back into the sexist stereotype of the weak, defenseless, objectified woman dependent on a male savior. In an ironic reversal of the usual dynamics of the male gaze and the cliché of eyeglasses making women appear unattractive, it is only *after* Selina puts on sunglasses (to hide her scarred eyes) that Gordon tells her "Now you're a very pretty girl."

In fact, Selina is very much written and played like the usual Hollywood stereotype of the **Sweet Innocent** blind woman. Her youthfulness, naïvety, and limited vocabulary figure her as almost childlike, and at one point Gordon does refer to her as a "baby." (In a fantasy sequence early in the film we see a sighted Selina running through the park in slow motion as if she were a young girl or a forest sprite; in a way, she has never grown beyond the age of five, when she was blinded.) However, while it was often suggested that the disabilities of the Sweet Innocent stereotypes of earlier decades were caused or exacerbated by the excesses of industrial capitalism, Selina's lower-class mother Rose-Ann is portrayed as the villain in this tale. In a flashback sequence, Rose-Ann's improper sexuality is shown to be directly responsible for Selina's blindness: Rose-Ann was sleeping with another man when Selina's father came home from the war, and in the ensuing fight, Rose-Ann tossed a bottle of acid toward Selina's father, but hit Selina's face instead, leaving her blind and slightly scarred. In the present-day parts of the film, Rose-Ann is conniving, cruel, uncouth, and unapologetically racist; it is revealed that she drove away nine-year-old Selina's only friend because she was black. Toward the end of the film, Rose-Ann and her equally trashy friend Sadie decide to move in together in order to open a brothel, and it is suggested that Selina may even be forced into prostitution by her own mother.

In contrast to Rose-Ann, Gordon is presented as rising into the middle class, having gotten an education (he listens to classical music and sings lullabies in French) and a white-collar job. (His brother Mark, a doctor, is likewise moving up the class ladder.) The film suggests that **rugged individualism** has aided Gordon and Mark in overcoming racial oppression – and that Selina should follow their example. Thus, while helping her, Gordon also teaches Selina to take care of herself – educating her on how to walk across a street by herself, or how to use a pay telephone. Plainly, escaping from the oppression of lower-class life to a "respectable" middle-class school for the blind will continue this process for her.

Sidney Poitier's role in *A Patch of Blue* is another one of those characterizations that earned him the somewhat ironic nickname of "Saint Sidney." As with his Oscar-winning role in *Lilies of the Field* (1963), Poitier's Gordon is a man who seems to spend most of his time helping white women in need. Side-stepping the era's still-controversial issues of interracial dating and sex, Gordon is willing to walk away from his relationship with Selina at the moment that it verges on consummation. Instead, he tells Selina that "there are many kinds of love," suggesting that their love may be platonic. Although the ending of the film is rather open – Gordon and Selina may get together at some future time – the film carefully negotiates its interracial romance. Although there are two kisses from Gordon upon Selina's forehead, and one rather passionate embrace when Selina kisses him, the film still cannot imagine a happy (that is, romantically coupled) ending for them.

As is typical with Hollywood films in general, in *A Patch of Blue* the social and cultural moorings of racism, sexism, and ableism are distilled into personalized character traits. However, this also allows to the film to explore the devastating effects of internalized, **ego-destructive** discrimination. Gordon helps Selina discover her potential, but Selina also perhaps encourages Gordon's own sense of self-worth. Toward the end of the film, she tells him that "I think you're beautiful," a statement rarely made about a man and even more rarely about a black man in the 1960s. Gordon wistfully replies, "Most people would say the opposite." Although the film partakes of many stereotypes and problematic representations, it nonetheless uses its central conceit – that of (racial) blindness – to make a statement about the potential beauty and worth of each and every human being.

Case Study 5: *Erin Brockovich* (2000)

Erin Brockovich is an interesting hybrid of the Hollywood **social problem film** and the contemporary **woman's film**. Based on a true story, the film follows a crusading (self-taught) paralegal assistant as she helps her boss win an unprecedented settlement from a corrupt public utilities corporation, Pacific Gas & Electric. Yet the film is also something of a woman's film, dramatizing how Erin (Julia Roberts) must find a way to balance the demands of her job against those of her three children and the man with whom she is romantically involved. While the film models some fairly unconventional ideas about gender roles – Erin's boyfriend George (Aaron Eckhart) is mostly content being a "house-husband" while she goes off to work – it also dramatizes how Erin's job does indeed have adverse effects upon George and her children. (At one point George does leave her, and Erin's son resents

his mother's prolonged absences.) Similarly, while the film takes aim at the corruption of corporations that will do anything to increase profit, it also celebrates its own brand of **capitalism**: as part of the film's happy ending, Erin and her boss Ed Masry (Albert Finney) are rewarded for their "humanitarian" crusade with considerable monetary success.

As the film begins, Erin is unsuccessfully job-searching, and director Steven Soderbergh employs a ragged jump-cut **montage** sequence to underline the considerable effort and fruitless repetition of Erin's quest. A former beauty queen and stay-at-home mom, Erin realizes that she has few marketable skills aside from her drive and intelligence. When a car driven by an emergency room doctor runs a red light and plows into Erin's car, she comes into contact with lawyer Ed Masry, who tries

Julia Roberts as the protagonist of *Erin Brockovich* (2000), seen here with her boss Ed Masry (Albert Finney). Erin is allowed to be passionate about her family, her romance, and her career as a crusading paralegal.
Erin Brockovich, dir. Steven Soderbergh, copyright © 2000, Jersey Films/Columbia TriStar

to win some damages for the injured Erin. Yet, in the courtroom, the opposing team of lawyers uses Erin's gender and class status against her – they subtly suggest she is an unfit mother because she has had two husbands (and no current one), and that as a poor woman, her words are not as trustworthy as those of the male doctor. When Erin bursts into profane language in the courtroom, her fate is sealed, and she loses her case. Angry with Ed, she works her way onto his staff, telling him that she doesn't need pity, she needs a paycheck.

Erin's forthright manner, salty tongue, and somewhat tawdry wardrobe are meant to signify her proud **working-class** status; the film shows how they also make her a target of discrimination, not only in the courtroom, but also on a daily basis in Ed Masry's law office. The other "girls" who work there initially shun her precisely for those same attributes. As Erin gets more involved in a toxic tort case – residents of the small town of Hinkley have been plagued by cancers and other medical disorders because PG&E has not properly disposed of its chemical waste – she seems to do so out of genuine compassion for the suffering townspeople. She also realizes that her pursuit of truth and justice in this case is more than just a job, and she refuses to quit it even when George asks her to so that she can spend more time with the family. The more traditional, reversed-gender situation, where a father/husband works away from home for days at a time, is hardly ever commented upon in Western patriarchies. Such men are good providers, not bad fathers. But because Erin is female, she is expected to put her children before her job. (Apparently, some viewers of the film could never get past this aspect of Erin's rough-hewn persona – comments condemning her as a poor role model for women or a bad mother can still be found on Internet bulletin boards discussing the film.)

Erin's down-to-earth demeanor, however, allows her to connect with the residents of Hinkley in ways that no legal professional could. The "smoking gun" that eventually seals the fate of PG&E comes from a former plant worker who will only speak to her. Erin's full figure also allows her access to the county water records; she uses her sex appeal to manipulate a naïve clerk (Jamie Harrold) into granting her access. While women in Hollywood films have traditionally used their sexuality to lure men into doing their bidding, here the twist is that Erin is using her sexuality for a more humanitarian cause. When asked by her boss how she is able to get access to such information, she quips "They're called boobs, Ed." Another moment in the film expresses a similar theme about the nature of women's sexuality under patriarchy. When Hinkley resident Donna Jensen (Marg Helgenberger) is diagnosed with malignant tumors, she wonders aloud if she will still be a "woman" because her diagnosis means she will soon have "no uterus and no breasts."

As Erin discovers that PG&E has allowed poisonous hexavalent chromium to seep into the ground water surrounding Hinkley, the film underlines how greedy corporations can take advantage of unsuspecting citizens. It also points out how most of us take clean water for granted. Multiple shots of iced tea glasses, coffee cups, children in swimming pools, and water hoses used to wash cattle – all potentially contaminated – underline the pervasiveness of the chemical threat. At another point, Erin exposes the hypocrisy of PG&E's high-powered law team, offering them water that she tells them has been brought in especially from Hinkley for them to drink. (They refuse it.) After it is revealed that PG&E has lied to the residents of Hinkley for decades about the dangers to life and limb it has knowingly caused, the residents are awarded a $333 million settlement. Erin's children eventually realize the good of the cause that their mother has worked for, although the film leaves George's fate open to question. In the final shot of the film, Erin returns to work on another case.

Popular with mainstream audiences as well as critics, *Erin Brockovich* was nominated for five Academy Awards including Best Picture; Julia Roberts won the Oscar for Best Actress. Although it follows many Hollywood conventions about underdog heroes and humanitarian crusades, *Erin Brockovich* presents a strong modern woman finding a sense of purpose in her life, one that includes but also goes beyond being a mother and a wife. Such a character is all too rare in contemporary Hollywood filmmaking.

Case Study 6: *8 Mile* (2002)

8 Mile marked the feature film debut of rap musician Eminem, and as such was carefully tailored to reinforce his pre-existing persona as a successful recording star. Specifically, the film borrows various autobiographical aspects from Eminem's life, such as being raised in a **working-class** community of Detroit (south of 8 Mile Road), and using his talent as a rapper to rise up from those meager conditions. As such, the film focuses on issues central to the urban poor and working classes. At the same time, however, the film explores how economic status intersects with issues of gender, sexuality, and, most prominently in this case, race. In particular, the film is careful to negotiate the potential problem of focusing on a white male protagonist who practices a musical idiom that arose primarily from within urban African American cultures. The film also addresses the sexism, homophobia, and tendency to glorify violence that many have critiqued as endemic within much rap music. Ultimately, although the film exposes the harsh realities of poor and working-class lives, it is somewhat ambiguous about the solution to those inequities. Ironically, while it critiques certain "rags to riches" clichés, Eminem did become rich and famous through his rapping. The film also attempts to critique various aspects of **white patriarchal capitalism**, but just as often seems to validate hegemonically the same dominant ideologies.

The first moments of the film exemplify how class issues are often obscured by racial concerns. We are introduced to Jimmy (Eminem), or B-Rabbit (as his friends call him), getting himself ready to compete in a rap battle at a local underground club. The scene is constructed in such a way as to recall a parallel moment in *The Jazz Singer* (1927), another film that deals with the intersections of music, race, and masculinity. Thus, the first time Jimmy is shown on screen, he is reflected in a mirror dressed almost in a sort of blackface costume (including a black knit cap), and practicing poses associated with black rap culture. Throughout the film, Jimmy has to defend being a white guy "trying to be black." In this opening rap battle (which he loses), his opponent scornfully calls him "a tourist." Later, Jimmy is dismissively referred to as "Elvis" and as "Vanilla Ice," two other white men who became pop stars by taking up – some might say "stealing" – African American musical styles. When discussing the possibilities of "making it" in the music industry, one African American character baldly asserts that "it's always easier for a white man to succeed in a black man's medium." (The film also references the history of such cross-cultural issues when it shows another character watching *Imitation of Life* [1959], a famous Hollywood woman's film about a black maid and her light-skinned daughter who passes for white.)

The attacks on Jimmy's **whiteness** are also related to his compromised **masculinity**. His "choking" during the opening rap battle is regarded as a sign of cowardice and ineptitude by everyone in the club. His masculinity is also challenged on the streets by rival gangs. Jimmy is smaller than most of the other men in the film, and is unable to defend himself when a group of guys decide to beat him up. His boss disparages his work ethic, and even at home his mother (Kim Basinger) and her new lover (who is only slightly older than Jimmy) make him feel emasculated. Jimmy has also broken up with his girlfriend upon learning that she is pregnant – another sign of his inability to live up to social expectations as a good provider. Alex (Brittany Murphy), the new girl in Jimmy's life, even-

In a shot that recalls a similar one from the classic film *The Jazz Singer* (1927), rap star Eminem prepares himself for a musical performance in the film *8 Mile* (2002). *8 Mile*, dir. Curtis Hanson, copyright © 2002, Imagine Entertainment/ Universal tually dumps him for Wink (Eugene Byrd), because he seems more likely to succeed in the music business than does Jimmy.

The film ties all of Jimmy's hardships to his economic status. After leaving his first girlfriend, Jimmy is literally living on the streets without a car. He eventually is forced to move back in with his mother, who herself lives in a dingy trailer home. Jimmy does have a job – but a low-wage one in an automobile factory that barely covers his needs. He is not seen as an exception, though. Everyone around him faces similar hardships. The meager environment is emphasized by repeated shots of abandoned buildings and barren winter landscapes, as well as in the drab and dark colors that pervade the film. Unsurprisingly, perhaps, Jimmy and his friends express their frustrations and/or try to better their situation by living on the outskirts of the law. However, the film is careful not to portray them as hardened criminals. For example, although they are shown doing "drive-by shootings" for fun, it is with a paint pellet gun. Although they do get involved in a gang fight, no one is killed. And when the gang consciously commits arson, it is done for a higher moral purpose: they torch an abandoned house because it has been the site of numerous assaults on women, assaults that the police and the city politicians have failed to curb.

Such illegal activities express the characters' despair of finding success within the system. Instead, Jimmy and many of the other characters hold onto hopes of "making it big" through chance or talent. Jimmy's rhymes are both an outlet for his frustrations, and his potential ticket out of the slums. (The man who gives Jimmy the most encouragement to pursue a music career is aptly named Future [Mekhi Phifer].) Alex aspires to leave Detroit and become a model. Even Jimmy's mom has dreams of a more lucrative future: she hopes to win big by playing bingo. All of these dreams, however, seem both incredibly clichéd (the performer waiting to be discovered has been used in musicals for decades), and unlikely to come true. Jimmy's friend Sol George (Omar Benson Miller), the most politicized member of the group, points out that corporations are bulldozing the projects and putting up casinos designed to take money from people rather than help them make their dreams come true. While Future continually encourages Jimmy to get his rhymes out to the public, Jimmy's strongest connection to the music industry is Wink, who is eventually revealed as a low-level shark willing to use Jimmy rather than help him (and steal his girl in the process).

Jimmy reaches a turning point in his life when he starts to use his talent as a rapper to help others rather than for his own self-aggrandizement. His first victory in a rap battle happens during an impromptu exchange outside the auto plant. The scene begins with an African American female (Miz-Korona) finishing her rhymes, followed by an African American man (Xzibit) who spends much of his performance degrading her as a "bitch," and calling an effeminate African American male employee a "faggot." Forgetting his usual nervousness about rhyming in public, Jimmy jumps in and expertly shreds his opponent's sense of dominance. Jimmy bonds with the others in this scene instead of looking out only for himself. His victory also may be seen as an attempt to counter rap music's sexist and homophobic reputation, even if his rap "Paul's gay; *you're* a faggot!" is not exactly queer-positive. Ironically, however, this encounter still upholds traditional concepts of white masculinity, since Jimmy is still figured as taking care of people "weaker" than himself. Also somewhat problematically, his new-found assertiveness is immediately rewarded by Alex with sex in a corner of the factory. Similarly, although the film shows female rappers (including one woman chanting "If we don't respect our sisters, who will?"), it **objectifies** Alex's body throughout its running time. And even though Jimmy calls his lunch truck opponent out on his sexist remarks, he is not above cutting down subsequent opponents as "pussies" and "bitches."

Now having confidence in himself, Jimmy wins round after round in the film's final climactic rap battle. When his African American competitors call him out for being white, Jimmy is no longer rattled. Rather than hiding behind layers of dark clothes and a black knit cap (as he did at the start of the film), Jimmy now wears a sleeveless gray shirt and drops his pants defiantly to show his white butt. In his final rap, he flips the tables to argue that class identity is more important than race by exposing his black opponent Papa Doc (Anthony Mackie) as middle-class: "I am white, I'm a fuckin' bum! You went to Grandbrook – that's a private school" and "He's not a gangsta! His real name is Clarence! I *am* white trash!" The crowd goes wild and Jimmy is victorious. Yet, unlike Eminem in real life, Jimmy does not become rich and famous through rapping. Winning the rap battle gives him a better sense of his own self-worth, but afterwards he heads back to work at the auto plant. Such an ending runs counter to Hollywood's usual **Horatio Alger**-style happy ending, but it is truer perhaps to the economic experiences of most Americans. Jimmy acknowledges the realities of his situation, and what he needs to do to make a better life for himself: not to chase after impossible dreams but to step up and be a man. Ultimately then, while empathizing with the working class, *8 Mile* continues to endorse rugged individualism and the **Protestant work ethic** over organized protest for systemic change. Combined with its focus on white heterosexual masculinity, the film does not "rage against the machine" anywhere near as much as it seems to do.

Case Study 7: *Better Luck Tomorrow* (2002)

Better Luck Tomorrow is a good example of how contemporary young multicultural filmmakers can use the independent film scene to break into the Hollywood industry. Written and directed by Asian American Justin Lin, the film was shot on an extremely low budget, but was noticed at film festivals and picked up for distribution by Paramount through its MTV Pictures arm. Paramount/MTV was probably attracted to *Better Luck Tomorrow* because of its high school protagonists, even though they are all Asian American. Their plight is a cross-cultural one, however: they live in suburban Southern California and feel an overall contempt for their bland **middle-class** existence. Yet the film's tone is ambivalent,

and it seems to reinscribe as many stereotypes as it seeks to dispel.

Director Lin emphasizes the stultifying sameness of the youth's suburban neighborhoods through static, unmoving shots. This sense of emptiness is further underscored by the total lack of parents in the film: they supposedly exist, but they are never seen and only occasionally mentioned. Attempting to break out of their suburban angst, the young men start committing petty crimes, and then partaking in increasingly dangerous and violent thrills. While this may sound like they are becoming counter-cultural rebels, their actions are still centered around material gain (money, expensive toys, parties) – and they

Director Justin Lin's *Better Luck Tomorrow* (2002) focuses on four Asian American high school students by day who are also petty criminals by night.
Better Luck Tomorrow, dir. Justin Lin, copyright © 2002, MTV Films/Paramount

still hold onto the typical **American Dream** of getting into good colleges so they can have successful careers. Consequently, *Better Luck Tomorrow* seems ambivalent about its subject matter. The film criticizes the suburban middle-class, but seems to endorse typical middle-class desires. Its young characters are caught in a **hegemonic negotiation** with the ideals of **patriarchal capitalism**.

While all of the above matches the pattern of many Hollywood teen films since the 1980s, *Better Luck Tomorrow* differs by focusing on the lives of Asian American students instead of Anglo Americans. In particular, the narrative revolves around a circle of characters that might seem initially to play into one of the more recent stereotypes associated with Asian Americans: the brainy overachiever. For example, the opening sequences of the film show the variety of ways Ben (Parry Shen) and his friends organize their lives around getting into the best universities possible – through constant studying, excessive extra-curricular activities, and inordinate public service programs.

Yet the film works to complicate this stereotype in a number of ways. First, because the film makes Ben the protagonist rather than a supporting or bit player, the audience is able to learn more about him, to see him as a multi-faceted person, and perhaps to identify with him. Also, while the plot revolves around his interactions with similar overachievers, they are also distinguished as unique individuals with their own personalities. The film thus represents a diversity of Asian American characters rather than presenting them as identical examples of the same stereotype. Furthermore, the film stresses the huge amount of pressure Ben and his friends face on a daily basis in trying to live up to expectations – stresses that result in extreme and dire consequences by the end of the picture.

The narrative also transposes the usual place that the Asian American overachiever student has in these high school films: rather than being the nerdy outsiders, Ben and his cohorts become the hip, popular kids that wield social and economic power. They do so by using their intellects to run scams, create a black market for tests and papers, and eventually sell drugs and pull heists. In the most obvious example of flipped roles, when a group of white athletes make fun of the young men at a party, Virgil (Jason J. Tobin) points a gun at the main antagonist; the rest of the gang proceeds to pummel and kick the athlete into submission.

As this description indicates, the attempt to flip the overachiever stereotype takes a violent turn, and suggests yet another cultural stereotype – that of the Asian gang (or **Tong**) member. Similar to the film's ambivalence over middle-class values, *Better Luck Tomorrow*'s use of violence can be read as a critique of domination, but it could also be decoded as glamorizing it. Although the film gets darker and more ominous as its characters fall deeper into criminal behavior, Lin also uses a number of techniques to make Ben and his gang seem cool and enviable. There are repeated slow-motion shots of the gang walking in unison with their eyes hidden behind sunglasses, and fast-cut montage sequences of them enjoying the alcohol, drugs, and sex that are the capitalist rewards of their new criminal lives.

Thus, in many respects, the film's attempt to provide less degrading images of Asian American men falls back onto conventional images of violent masculinity and capitalist gain. Ben and his buddies are cool as long as they can beat up people, shoot guns, and have lots of women around them. And although there is also a top Asian American female student in the film (who has ambitions to be a police officer), she functions in the plot simply as a potential prize for which three of the guys are competing. (At another moment, Ben and Virgil discuss the rumor that she has acted in a porn video, reinforcing another common female Asian stereotype – the exotic sex worker.) Virgil, who is constantly mocked as a virgin and a wimp, is the one most prone to violent outbursts through which he attempts to show that he is a man. Although one reading of the film might suggest that its characters are unwittingly trapped within the structures of **white patriarchal capitalism**, another suggests just the opposite – that the way for young Asian men to become successful in America is to follow the lead of traditional white masculinity and capitalist gain, no matter what the cost.

Case Study 8: *Saving Face* (2004)

The debut film of writer-director Alice Wu, *Saving Face* is a warm human comedy/drama about a family of Chinese Americans living in and around New York City. Granddaughter Wil (Michelle Krusiec) is a promising surgical resident at a major metropolitan hospital. Her 48-year-old widowed mother Ma (Joan Chen) lives with her own parents in the suburb of Flushing, where they are part of a tightly knit group of other Chinese Americans. Wil's Grandpa and Grandma, who left mainland China decades ago during the communist revolution, are staunch supporters of Chinese cultural traditions, and Grandpa is especially protective of his family's honor ("face"). Thus when it is revealed that that Ma is pregnant, Grandpa throws her out of his house and she moves into the city to stay with her daughter. But Wil has her own secrets, and as she falls in love with a beautiful dancer named Vivian (Lynn Chen), she and her family must confront the fact of her sexuality.

Much of the drama (and comedy) of *Saving Face* arises from culture clash: the clash of generations, of genders, and of old traditions versus new ones. Staunch patriarch Grandpa has firm beliefs about the proper rules and behaviors for women; he sets off to find his daughter a suitable husband to marry, regardless of how Ma may feel about him. Ma is herself rather ethnocentric, making snide and racist jokes about Wil's African American neighbor Jay, and later cutting Wil out of her life when Wil refuses to keep her homosexuality closeted. Americanized Wil, who prefers simple and functional clothing to fancy feminine ware, has a hard time dealing with Ma, especially after Ma moves in with her and starts to redecorate her apartment. Even Vivian is torn between family duty and her own desires. Although Vivian's divorced mother knows about her sexuality and supports her, her father (who is a top surgeon at Wil's hospital) pressures Vivian to pursue classical ballet dancing,

In the recent independent film *Saving Face* (2004), Joan Chen plays a single woman who finds herself pregnant at the age of 48; her daughter (played by Michelle Krusiec) faces similar scorn from friends and family when she falls in love with another woman.
Saving Face, dir. Alice Wu, copyright © 2004, Sony Pictures Classics

even though she prefers more expressive modernist dance forms. Each of the film's three central characters – Wil, Ma, and Viv – eventually learns to follow their own true desires rather than allow themselves to be corralled into what their parents (and by extension their local Chinese American social group) think is appropriate for them.

Saving Face is also about communication, or the lack thereof. Like many other Asian cultures, the Chinese American culture depicted in *Saving Face* is a stoic, terse, and almost unspeaking one. As one of the characters remarks, chiding a moody Ma, "only Americans freak out about menopause." Emotions are not to be expressed or explored, and personal desires are to be suppressed in favor of what tradition dictates. (Compare these attributes to those associated with traditional Western **masculinities**.) Thus, Ma refuses to name her baby's father out of fear of what others might think. Even Wil is generally rather **closeted** about her relationship with Viv, and is too shy to kiss Vivian in public. Viv chides Wil for treating her like an "illicit affair," and in one humorous moment, a small girl watching them together in a park suggests they should just kiss, already. Furthermore, Ma already knows all about her daughter's sexuality (having walked in on Wil with a date years before), yet they have never spoken of it. Thus Ma continues to try to set up Wil with eligible Chinese American men, because that is what tradition dictates. Ironically, despite all this lack of communication between family members, the film's peripheral characters (who inhabit the Chinese social club) gossip constantly – they speak of and about their friends and acquaintances but only behind their backs. It is these whispers that comprise the social pressure to conform to norms, and to hide one's true desires.

Ultimately, the actual father of Ma's baby is revealed by Wil as Ma is about to marry Mr Cho, a man her father has picked out for her but whom she does not love. (Comically, this burst of truth amidst all the secrecy works like a virus or a bomb, and several members of the wedding audience spontaneously confess their own secrets.) Wil urges her mother to marry the man she does love – and the one who truly loves her – and both mother and daughter run from the room to the airport where Wil catches up with Viv. Viv, who has grown tired of Wil's reticence about their relationship, is about to board a plane to join the Paris Opera Ballet, following her father's wishes. Although Wil is still unable to kiss Viv in public, she does confess her love for her. Not satisfied, Viv boards the plane alone. However, a happy ending is in store "three months later," when all the principal characters run into one another at the Chinese social club. Wil and Viv dance together in the center of the floor, an open declaration of their love for all to see, a move that scandalizes some members of the club, while others accept them happily. Grandpa grumbles, as usual, but he has learned (however begrudgingly) to accept his family for who they are.

If all of this sounds rather over-the-top and melodramatic, filmmaker Alice Wu is acutely aware of that fact, and playfully comments on it throughout the film. Ma is addicted to Chinese soap operas and watches them constantly, even as her own real-life situation becomes equally convoluted. *Saving Face* acknowledges both the appeal of melodrama (by the end of the film even Wil and next-door neighbor Jay are anxiously tuned in to Ma's soap operas), as well as its potential political ramifications. While melodramas and/or soap operas have often been dismissed as "**chick flicks**" or "weepies" – pointless entertainment for silly women – *Saving Face* asserts the feminist axiom that "the personal is the political." In other words, while oppression based on gender and sexuality may vary from culture to culture, it often takes place in the home and within the nuclear family – the very structures that are supposed to nurture and unconditionally love their members. *Saving Face* reminds us of what families should and should not be, and the importance of being true to oneself. It may be about Chinese Americans in New York City, but the life lessons it dramatizes are quite possibly universal to families everywhere.

Case Study 9: *Crash* (2004)

Crash is a well-intentioned **social problem film** about the racism and sexism of everyday life. Written and directed by Paul Haggis as a small-budget independent film, *Crash* earned much critical acclaim, was released widely in 2005, and went on to win that year's Best Picture Oscar. A mosaic film made in the style of Robert Altman or Paul Thomas Anderson, *Crash* cuts back and forth between some twenty-plus major characters interacting in contemporary Los Angeles. At the start of the film, a white district attorney (Brendan Fraser) and his wealthy spoiled wife (Sandra Bullock) are car-jacked by two black thugs (Larenz Tate and Chris "Ludacris" Bridges). An African American TV director (Terrence Howard) and his mixed race wife (Thandie Newton) are stopped by a racist and sexist cop (Matt Dillon) who humiliates them and sexually abuses the wife. His white rookie cop partner (Ryan Phillippe) asks to be reassigned after witnessing this act, but encounters his own difficulties with his black chief. Meanwhile, an African American police detective (Don Cheadle) investigates a possible case of police corruption that is also tinged with racist implications, all the while caring for his drug-addicted mother. A Hispanic locksmith (Michael Peña), who has moved his family away from a gun-riddled neighborhood, comforts his traumatized daughter and deals with racism on the job. Ultimately, a lack of communication between the locksmith and a Persian American shopkeeper (Shaun Toub) leads to the shop being broken into and vandalized,

This iconic image from *Crash* (2004) depicts Matt Dillon as a racist and sexist police officer who nonetheless rescues an African American woman from a burning car. Does the film make him into yet another great white savior?
Crash, dir. Paul Haggis, copyright © 2004, Lions Gate Films

sending the angry shopkeeper – armed with a gun – after the locksmith.

As this brief (and incomplete) synopsis suggests, *Crash* is a film full of racially and sexually charged situations that seem to bring out both the best and the worst in its multiple protagonists. In fact, that seems to be one of the overarching messages of the film: that all human beings are capable of both good and evil, especially in stressful situations. Similarly, good intentions may produce bad outcomes, and vice versa. For example, Matt Dillon's cop rescues from a burning car the same woman he had sexually abused the night before. His rookie partner, who tries to do the right thing in reporting the abuse, ends up shooting and killing a black hitchhiker and then trying to hide the body. Similarly, the car-jackers are likable, smart, and funny, and at the end of the film the one played by Ludacris rescues a van-load of Asian immigrants from being sold into modern-day slavery. Even the shopkeeper – who thinks he has accidentally shot the locksmith's daughter – is transformed and redeemed by the act because unknown to him his gun was filled with blanks, thus preventing him from committing a terrible crime.

The seeming lack of meaningful and compassionate human connections in the modern world (often underscored by the film's use of harsh lighting) is another of the film's themes. That is why humans are reduced to crashing into one another – like cars – because they have built up steel and glass walls to separate themselves from one another. (A very different film also named *Crash*, made by David Cronenberg in 1996, explores a similar theme in more disturbing psychosexual ways.) In this later *Crash*, even friends and lovers treat one another poorly. For example, Jean, the district attorney's wife, confides to her friend that she is always angry, but does not know why. Her "friend" coolly ignores this invitation to talk, and later refuses to help Jean get to the hospital after a

bad fall because she is too busy getting a massage. In more overt ways, the film is full of people shouting hateful and racist invective at one another. Ironically, writer-director Paul Haggis has set his film during the Christmas season, implicitly asking viewers to think about just how far these characters have fallen from some sort of "love thy neighbor" Christian ideal. A climactic image of a St Christopher statuette buried in the dirt seems to suggest the same idea: the modern world has abandoned Judeo-Christian ideals of love and compassion.

Yet, for all of its interesting characters and situations, the film has also been accused of being overly simplistic in presenting racism simply as the result of anger and lack of communication, when in fact there are much larger historical and economic contexts to it, including slavery and imperialism. (One moment in the film – when Jean confesses to her Hispanic maid that she thinks of her as her best friend – opens onto a potential critique of class and capitalism: do we really live in a world where friendship and love have to be paid for?) Similarly, while the film does dramatize how racism is institutionalized in the legal profession and the police force, it also offers almost an apology for it, via the Ryan Phillippe character who must learn that the job itself will most likely turn him into a racist and a killer. Furthermore, his experiences with his commander in chief suggest that racism or sexism cannot really be effectively challenged – instead they must be endured. Perhaps most obviously, the white male policeman played by Matt Dillon is made so heroic and sympathetic (especially as he cares for his sick and dying father) that one may tend to forgive or overlook his racist and sexist words and actions. Nonetheless, *Crash* raises many important questions for discussion, even as it perhaps fails to delve too deeply into the various causes of them, and rather pessimistically refuses to suggest any possible solutions to them – other than perhaps the continuing need to "love thy neighbor."

Case Study 10: *The Prize Winner of Defiance, Ohio* (2005)

Based on a childhood memoir by author Terry Ryan, *The Prize Winner of Defiance, Ohio* centers on a large, working-class, Irish American, Catholic family struggling to survive in postwar America (roughly the 1950s and 1960s). It is a somewhat revisionist account of that era, in that the Ryan family is far from the usual image of 1950s middle-class wealth and happiness (as had been promulgated by TV shows like *Leave it to Beaver* [1957–63] and *Father Knows Best* [1954–60]). In fact, the Ryans can barely afford to pay the milk delivery man. Gentle, warm, and intimate in scope, the film paints a vivid picture of what life was like for many **white working-class** families in postwar America. It also subtly dramatizes how the era's ideological assumptions about **gender** and **sexuality** tended to exacerbate the family's economic woes.

The film focuses primarily on the clan's indomitably cheerful mother, Evelyn Ryan (Julianne Moore), who also narrates the film in clever computer-generated superimpositions that suggest her character's multiple aspects. Evelyn is a housewife who is constantly cooking for, cleaning for, and comforting her 10 children, as well her husband Kelly (Woody Harrelson), a man who works in a machine shop but whose wages can barely cover his family's expenses. However, Evelyn (in between her domestic duties) also supplements the family's income by writing prize-winning jingles for contests sponsored by Madison Avenue advertising firms. As she herself tells the camera in a playful moment of direct address, entering contests "was a lucrative way for overworked housewives to use their underused wits." However, Evelyn's success

Computer-generated effects allow Julianne Moore as *The Prize Winner of Defiance, Ohio* (2005) to narrate her own story. In another scene composed with careful framing, father Kelly (Woody Harrelson) is represented as isolated from his wife and children because of his stubborn masculine pride.
The Prize Winner of Defiance, Ohio, dir. Jane Anderson, copyright © 2005, Dreamworks SKG

with words only frustrates and alienates Kelly, whose buddies at the machine shop tease him about his wife being the real breadwinner of the family. To assuage his threatened masculinity, Kelly takes solace in radio sports broadcasts and hard drink.

As the film progresses, Kelly's drinking develops into what today we would most likely consider alcoholism, but for the Catholic Ryans it is just another cross they must bear with stoicism. Those who could offer the family help fail to do so: the policemen called to the house after one of Kelly's drunken rampages merely drink coffee and chat with him about baseball. The family's priest subtly suggests that Evelyn is to blame for her husband's drinking, implying that she does not try hard enough to make her husband a proper home. (The film presents ample evidence to the contrary!) Meanwhile the children – who witness most of these events – are terrified that their father is going to hurt their mother (or one of them). Neither religion nor the legal system is able to see Kelly's violent alcoholism as a problem, let alone challenge his unspoken authority within the home.

The Prize Winner of Defiance, Ohio also shows that these attitudes about gender and heterosexual relations arise not just from the characters themselves, but also from the world which they inhabit. When Kelly and Evelyn put a down payment on a new home (with money that Evelyn has won), the bank manager is condescending toward her and only addresses Kelly – money is the man's domain. The film also uses the Ryans' television set to show how attitudes about gender and class permeate the media. Somewhat ironically, the family watches *Queen for a Day* (1956–64), a popular TV game show that awarded a lavish consumerist fantasy to the woman who told the best "sob story." At another point the TV shows a beauty pageant contestant saying she would not vote for a female president of the United States because "women are very high strung and emotional people." Such moments invite the film viewer to compare the era's dominant ideological assumptions about gender with the reality of the Ryan household: it is father Kelly who is emotional and unstable while mother Evelyn is a pillar of calm and compassion. For example, after one struggle with Kelly, Evelyn falls to the ground shattering 12 bottles of milk and badly cutting her wrists. As her children and husband react with hysteria, Evelyn calmly tells them what they need to do: get a towel for the blood, retrieve her purse, and call a neighbor to take her to the hospital. Later Evelyn writes short rhymes that playfully question the old adage "No use crying over spilt milk," and those together with several lingering shots of the bloody milk suggest the pain and violence that can be found at the very heart of traditional maternal domesticity.

The Prize Winner of Defiance, Ohio sounds a harsh critique of class and gender relations in postwar America, yet the film remains warm and optimistic, much like Evelyn herself. She possesses a Zen-like attitude about making the most out of any moment – good or bad – and takes special care to instill in her daughter Terry the notion that she can make her life anything she wants it to be. The film ends with actual footage of the Ryan children, now middle-aged adults, including Terry who we learn moved to San Francisco and wrote the book on which the film was based. And although the film does not make it obvious (the younger Terry is represented as a tomboy nicknamed "Tuff"), Terry was a lesbian who later married her long-time partner in San Francisco when it was briefly legal to do so. The film's lesbian-feminist perspective is also enhanced through the contributions of filmmaker Jane Anderson, best known for writing and directing the TV movies *Normal* (2003) and *If These Walls Could Talk 2* (2000), both of which focused on queer characters in small-town America. Thus, in its content and creation, *The Prize Winner of Defiance, Ohio* maps a decades-long journey of struggle and social change – from the limited and limiting ideologies of postwar gender and sexuality to a new millennium where women of all sorts are freer to be who they want to be, and do the kinds of work they want to do.

Case Study 11: *Brokeback Mountain* (2005)

The release of *Brokeback Mountain*, possibly one of the most important American films of recent years, was an unprecedented cultural event. Never before had such a widely released American film represented a decades-long love affair between two men, let alone had them played by handsome Hollywood heart-throbs like Heath Ledger and Jake Gyllenhaal. *Brokeback Mountain* was far more culturally groundbreaking than the occasional Hollywood drag-queen farce (such as *The Birdcage* [1996] or *To Wong Foo, Thanks for Everything, Julie Newmar* [1997]) precisely because it queers traditional concepts of American **masculinity** and the film genre most closely tied to its representation, the **Western**. The film powerfully dramatizes the processes and effects of both social and **internalized homophobia**, and continually blurs the borders between straight and gay, homosocial and homosexual. It uses the tools of **queer theory** to examine a specific time and place (the American Midwest from the 1960s through the 1980s) in order to reveal the multiple social discourses and institutions that frame and delimit all human sexualities, including heterosexuality. Above all, *Brokeback Mountain* is a film about a notoriously difficult-to-dramatize concept: the homosexual **closet**.

Brokeback Mountain was directed by Taiwanese American filmmaker **Ang Lee** (discussed in chapter 6), whose breakthrough film *The Wedding Banquet* (1993) also focused on issues of race, class, gender, sexuality, and nationality/regionality. For *Brokeback Mountain*, Lee employed his usual careful attention to framing and detail, creating a precise cinematic world full of complex characters (of various sexual orientations) whose identities are limited by the ideological apparatuses and institutions in which they find themselves enmeshed. Cowboys Jack Twist (Jake Gyllenhaal) and Ennis Del

Heath Ledger and Jake Gyllenhaal played rugged, traditionally masculine ranch hands who fall in love in the independent cross-over hit *Brokeback Mountain* (2005).
Brokeback Mountain, dir. Ang Lee, copyright © 2005, Focus Features/Universal

Mar (Heath Ledger) are who they are because of their gender and sexualities, but also because of their regional and economic circumstances. Both have followed careers in ranching because their educational and career choices have been so limited. They drift into their traditionally masculine jobs much as they drift into their marriages to Lureen (Anne Hathaway) and Alma (Michelle Williams): not so much out of desire or love for their spouses, but because it is what is expected of them. This social expectation of **heteronormative** behavior is also figured as a pressure on the women: while the husbands are expected to be good providers and protectors, the women are expected to silently stand by them no matter what. Everyone is trapped.

Thus when Jack and Ennis suddenly find themselves in a sexual and romantic relationship, they have very little knowledge of how to deal with it. Ennis is terrified that their secret will be revealed; he recounts a story from his youth in which he was made to witness the end results of a violent gay-bashing. As he grows older he becomes more and more paranoid, and still cannot imagine or even countenance the possibility of a life with Jack. Ennis's stoicism – a conditioned part of his traditional masculinity – works to confine him within his limited and nearly loveless existence, even though on some level he realizes it is destroying him. As he ruefully tells Jack, "If you can't fix it . . . you gotta stand it." In a way that is also true to traditional concepts of masculinity, Ennis is prone to violent outbursts that serve to express what he will not or cannot say with words. For example, when Alma finally confronts Ennis about the nature of his relationship with "Jack Nasty," Ennis brutally twists her arm and threatens to punch her. Realizing he cannot hit a woman, he heads into the streets, where his anger and frustration are quickly displaced onto an attack on a random motorist. By the end of the film, Ennis has become almost a complete emotional zombie – his love for Jack never fully expressed, and his relationships with everyone else tenuous, at best.

Jack's character is a bit more knowing about the possibilities open to rural Midwestern queer men in the 1960s, although he hides these knowledges from everyone, including Ennis. Thus both Jack and Ennis maintain heterosexual identities within their public lives (and even to some extent within their private homosexual lives). And this is perhaps what many filmgoers found so troubling about the film: Jack and Ennis – although homosexual lovers – look just like ordinary heterosexual men, or ranch hands, or cowboys. They are not identifiable (and thus knowable) as, for example, "Queer Eye" fashion designers from New York City. In fact, Jack and Ennis both explicitly state to each other that they do not consider themselves gay. In this way, the film destabilizes **patriarchal heteronormativity**, queerly teasing out the interrelated connections between homosexuality, heterosexuality, and male homosociality. In this respect, the scene between Jack and the ranch foreman outside the Childress social club is highly significant, as it encapsulates much of the film's subversive effect. In it, a ranch foreman invites Jack to a "cabin down on a lake" to "drink a little whiskey, fish some, get away, ya know?" The uncertain meanings of this brief exchange are highly disruptive of patriarchal heteronormative discourses and knowledges: is the invitation strictly homosocial, or is it a not-so-thinly-veiled homosexual proposition? Of course, different audiences can read this scene in different ways, just as they did the film as a whole. Yet this one moment, as does the entire film, suggests the intimate proximity of male homosocial and male homosexual desire. After all, what "normal" straight guy doesn't long to get away from his wife and kids and spend a few days camping in the woods with his best buddy?

Pundits of every shape and size weighed in on the many meanings of *Brokeback Mountain*: was it a specifically gay cowboy story (as it had been simplistically dubbed by the mainstream press) or a tragic, universal romance about star-crossed lovers à la *Romeo and Juliet*? Would the film's release herald a new era in the representation of gay and lesbian people in Hollywood films? (As of this writing, it seems it has not.) How "faithful" was the film to the actual experiences of rural queer men of recent decades? Apparently it was very faithful: as *Brokeback Mountain* won countless awards and garnered critical acclaim, entire websites were created by its fans to share their own stories about coming out, falling in love, and being queer in rural America. Although the film lost that year's Best Picture Oscar (to *Crash*), it remains highly significant for the ways in which it queers the myth of the American West and its most iconic figure, the overtly macho cowboy or rancher.

Case Study 12: *Quinceañera* (2006)

This multiple-award-winning independent film from writer-directors Richard Glatzer and Wash Westmoreland centers on Magdalena, a 14-year-old Mexican American girl played by Emily Rios. Magdalena finds herself pregnant a few months before her quinceañera, a special party held within many Latino cultures to celebrate a girl's fifteenth birthday. Immediately disowned by her religious father, Magdalena finds refuge in the home of her older and loving relative Tio Tomas (Chalo Gonzales), a man who is also sheltering her cousin Carlos (Jesse Garcia), a tough-acting teenager who has been similarly tossed out of his home for being gay. Deftly weaving together issues of race, class, gender, region, religion, and sexuality, *Quinceañera* is a warm human drama set against the complex social institutions that define and challenge human identities and relations.

Shot on location, *Quinceañera* is steeped in the local traditions of Echo Park, a historically Mexican American neighborhood slightly north of downtown Los Angeles. Culturally specific foods such as *champurrado* (a warm thick chocolate drink), as well as traditions such as *padrino* (sponsorship or gift-giving) and *Cinco de Mayo* (a Mexican heritage and pride celebration held each year on the fifth of May), figure prominently in the film's plot, and the film begins and ends with colorful quinceañera celebrations. Yet the film shows how this one culturally specific tradition means many different things to different people. To Magdalena's father, it is a milestone in a girl's spiritual life, the day on which she becomes a woman eligible for marriage. To Magdalena and her friends, it is a chance to have a formal, almost wedding-like party, complete with Hummer limousines, tuxedos, and expensive ball gowns. To others, it is a chance to show off one's wealth (by spending a lot of money for an opulent party), and to still others, it is a chance to celebrate community with one's friends and family. (Although

Herman (J. R. Cruz) and Magdalena (Emily Rios) are young Mexican American lovers in the independent film hit *Quinceañera* (2006). Meanwhile, Magdalena's cousin Carlos (Jesse Garcia) is facing his own issues related to sexuality, class, and ethnicity.
Quinceañera, dir. Richard Glatzer and Wash Westmoreland, copyright © 2006, Sony Pictures Classics

ironically that community warmth is shown to have its limits: at the start of the film Carlos is forcibly ejected from his own sister's quinceañera.) Furthermore, the filmmakers show how the quinceañera is an important social institution that shapes the identities of young Latina women – how they are expected to epitomize traditionally patriarchal definitions of delicate and passive femininity. Two video clips within the film – one from the TV show *America's Next Top Model* (2003–) and the other a kitschy and overly produced home video of an "actual" quinceañera – also suggest a comparison of the different ways the social meanings of gender are negotiated and performed.

Class and sexuality also permeate the film and delineate its characters' lives. Most obviously, Magdalena and Carlos are both disowned for what their families perceive to be improper sexualities. Then, their safety with Tio Tomas is threatened when he receives an eviction notice from his new landlords – two white bourgeois gay men who have bought the property on which he has lived for 28 years. In fact, gentrification – the buying up of property and subsequent displacing of the urban poor by more affluent people – is a major theme in *Quinceañera*. Gary and James, the gay landlords, are not presented in very flattering terms. They continually **objectify** young Latino men, even as they begin a three-way sexual relationship with Carlos. In this way, the film suggests links between sexual and economic exploitation. Although Carlos and Gary eventually begin to develop deeper feelings for one another, ultimately even the sexual relationship that first brought them together cannot overcome the barriers of class and ethnicity. They both agree somewhat wistfully that they come from wholly other worlds. Although sex and sexuality may be powerful forces that can possibly transgress the barriers of race and class, ultimately the film suggests the difficulty of maintaining such relationships in a world so heavily determined by

them. Like the chain link fence the film uses as a visual motif, the social discourses of race, class, gender, and sexuality may allow for certain connections between people while also keeping them isolated in other ways.

Magdalena's dilemma is ultimately resolved when a clinic doctor convinces her family that she is still technically a virgin, despite her pregnancy. It is revealed that Magdalena and her boyfriend Herman (J. R. Cruz) have in fact not had sexual intercourse, but that he had ejaculated on her thigh during a session of heavy petting. Though a very rare occurrence, pregnancy without penetration is a phenomenon documented within the medical literature. (In an amusing aside that demonstrates his macho sensibilities, when Herman learns of this situation he boasts that his sperm must be strong swimmers!) Magdalena's father Ernesto (Jesus Castanos), who runs his own tiny store-front ministry, accepts the fact his daughter's pregnancy is indeed a miracle, much like the Virgin Birth of Jesus Christ. (The Christian allegory is obviously signaled by Magdalena's name as well as Herman's quip that they should name their baby Jesus.) Carlos's story is left more open-ended, although he delivers a moving speech at the funeral of Tio Tomas, calling his beloved uncle a saint, and noting how Tomas "loved everyone and judged no one," a Christian ideal that permeates the structure and content of the film itself.

Filmmakers Richard Glatzer and Wash Westmoreland based *Quinceañera* on their own experiences living in Los Angeles, watching the gentrification of Echo Park by guppies (gay urban professionals) like themselves. Both had made small independent gay feature films before (including *Grief* [1993] and *The Fluffer* [2001]), but *Quinceañera* represents a maturation of their skills. Dealing with richly nuanced characters and social situations in complex and caring ways, *Quinceañera* was a film festival favorite (winning major awards at Sundance) and it remains a thoughtful and audience-pleasing film.

GLOSSARY

ability: power or capacity to do things, to act according to one's skills or talents.

ableism: ideologies and institutions that favor the able-bodied over people with disabilities; similar to racism or sexism.

Academy of Motion Picture Arts and Sciences (AMPAS): originally founded as a trade guild for film artists, and best known today for awarding Academy Awards (Oscars).

Ch7 **action-adventure movie:** film genre, usually focused on a hero's quest, with a lot of explosions, chases, and thrilling sequences.

Ch5 **actualities:** the very first films; short "slices of life" that were recorded by the camera.

ACT-UP (AIDS Coalition to Unleash Power): gay activist group formed in response to the 1980s AIDS crisis.

ADA: *see* Americans with Disabilities Act.

ADC (American-Arab Anti-Discrimination Committee): well-known advocacy group for Arab Americans; has increasingly protested Hollywood's stereotypical images of Arabs and Arab Americans.

adult films: X-rated films that depict sexual intercourse.

Ch5 **adult Western:** more sophisticated Westerns of the 1950s that began to question some of the genre's underlying assumptions.

affirmative action programs: federal and state programs designed to help women and minorities gain access to higher education and other training programs.

AIDS Coalition to Unleash Power: *see* ACT-UP.

Ch5 **AIM:** *see* American Indian Movement.

American-Arab Anti-Discrimination Committee: *see* ADC.

American Dream: expression that encapsulates national myths about equality and the free pursuit of wealth and happiness.

Ch5 **American Indian Movement (AIM):** civil rights group devoted to Native American issues; founded in the 1960s by Russell Means.

Ch3 **American melting pot:** metaphor that expresses how various immigrant cultures and traditions are supposed to be forged together into an overall sense of American identity.

American Zoetrope: independent film production company founded by Francis Ford Coppola.

Americans with Disabilities Act (ADA): federal statute that prohibits discrimination against people with disabilities.

AMPAS: *see* Academy of Motion Picture Arts and Sciences.

anarchist: someone who believes in toppling all forms of social control and/or government.

Ch6 **anime:** Japanese animation, often science fiction in nature and aimed at adult audiences.

antagonist: villain or other force opposing the protagonist in classical Hollywood narrative form.

Ch4 **antebellum:** literally, "pre-war"; usually refers to the era before the Civil War.

Ch3 **anti-Semitism:** prejudice against or hatred of Jews.

Arnaz, Desi: Cuban bandleader who became a 1950s television star on *I Love Lucy*.

art-house theaters: theaters that show independent or foreign films.

Arzner, Dorothy: one of the only women to direct films during the classical Hollywood era.

asexuality: state of having no sexual desire or interest.

Ch3 **assimilation:** blending into the ideals and assumptions of white patriarchal capitalist culture.

audism: the privileging of hearing people and concerns over deaf ones; similar to racism or sexism.

auteur studies: examining the work of a particular film artist (usually the director). According to auteur theory, a director often encodes consistent stylistic and thematic meanings into all of his or her films.

avant-garde film: type of independent and artisanal film practice that uses cinema to create a mood, tone, or concept rather than tell a story.

Ch7 **Aztlan:** Chicano name for the southwestern United States that used to be part of Mexico.

back light: part of three-point lighting; can create a halo effect around an actor's head.

backlash: opposing response to a cultural trend. The rise of feminism in the 1970s was met with opposition or backlash during the 1980s.

Bara, Theda: silent film actress most famous for playing the dark and exotic vamp character.

Barty, Billy: one of the most prolific little people actors in Hollywood. His career lasted from the 1930s to the 1990s.

base: in Marxist theory, the economic system upon which an entire culture "rests." The base determines the nature of the superstructure.

BBS: independent production company of the late 1960s that inserted some countercultural values into its films.

Beat movement: movement of 1950s writers and filmmakers who critiqued American consumerism and suburban conformity.

Berkeley, Busby: director and choreographer during the classical Hollywood era, best known for his kaleidoscopic arrangements of chorus girls.

Big 5: the major Hollywood studios during the classical era: Paramount, Metro-Goldwyn-Mayer (MGM), Warner Brothers, RKO, and 20th Century-Fox.

biological essentialism: model of identity that suggests that people are the way they are because of their genetic makeup. This model ignores or de-emphasizes the role that society and culture have in shaping identity.

bisexuality: state of being sexually attracted to both men and women.

black and white buddy: formula for a Hollywood comedy or action-adventure film, or a TV show, that pairs an African American star with a white star in order to attract both white and black audiences.

Black Buck: stereotype of a hypersexual and hypermasculine African American man.

black widow: conniving female character who will often lead a man to his death. *See also* femme fatale.

blackface: popular theatrical tradition of the 1800s that featured white performers darkening their faces with makeup in order to perform comedic stereotypes of African Americans.

blacklist: list of suspected communists who were not to be employed by Hollywood studios during the Red Scare.

blaxploitation films: cheaply made films of the early 1970s that featured strong, aggressive African American leads, sometimes battling racist white characters and institutions.

blonde bombshell: highly sexualized woman in 1950s culture.

bloodthirsty savage: stereotype of an aggressive, violent Native American always ready to attack white settlers.

Bow, Clara: actress best known for embodying the flapper character type of the 1920s.

Brown v. Board of Education: landmark 1954 Supreme Court decision that declared "separate but equal" Jim Crow Laws unconstitutional.

buddy film: film genre that usually centers on two men as they travel the nation or engage in other action-adventures.

Cagney, James: Irish American classical Hollywood film star best known for playing gangsters as well as patriotic characters.

camp: specific type of negotiated reading that simultaneously mocks and revels in a text's artificiality or manneredness. Originated in gay male culture in order to "denaturalize" societal norms of gender and sexuality.

Cantor, Eddie: popular Jewish stage and early film star who often sang in blackface makeup.

capitalism: economic system that promotes competition between businesses without governmental regulation. Under capitalist ideology, success and worth are measured by one's material wealth. It is the dominant economic system of the United States.

Capra, Frank: classical Hollywood director whose films often championed American middle-class ideals and the Horatio Alger myth.

Carrillo, Leo: Latino character actor in classical Hollywood films and later television.

Caucasoid/Caucasian: historically, people of the "white race" (people descended from European heritage).

Causa, La: Chicano term for the Latino civil rights struggle.

CGI: *see* computer generated imagery.

Chan, Charlie: famous Asian American detective character in literature and film.

Chaplin, Charlie: the first global cinematic superstar. His comedic "Little Tramp" character became known around the world during the late 1910s and 1920s.

Chavez, Cesar: man who led the United Farm Workers Union; fought for civil rights for Mexican Americans and other Latinos.

Chicano/a: gendered terms used to refer to Mexican Americans. Chicano is masculine, Chicana feminine.

chick flick: contemporary term for films aimed at women.

Christian Coalition: group designed to increase the influence of conservative Christian theology on local, state, and federal politics.

cinematography/cinematographic design: one of the five formal axes of cinema, encompassing aspects of film stock, lens choice, camera speed, framing, and camera movement.

CineWomen: Hollywood support group that promotes women in the industry.

civil rights movement: broad social and political movement of the 1950s and 1960s that promoted equal rights for people of color, women, and other minorities.

Clarke, Shirley: independent film and video artist who first rose to prominence as part of the New American Cinema movement of the early 1960s.

class: social categorization based upon economic status.

class consciousness: awareness of class and issues related to it.

class system: social structure that assigns people to specific groups based upon wealth, social standing, and/or heredity.

classical Hollywood cinema: films produced within the studio system of the classical Hollywood era (roughly 1930s to 1950s).

classical Hollywood narrative form: the way Hollywood films structure their stories. Components include single characters (protagonist, antagonist, love interest) with individualized goals and desires, simplified versions of good and evil, linear narrative, and closure.

classical Hollywood style: overall form and structure of most Hollywood films in the 1930s and 1940s.

classical Westerns: Westerns associated with Hollywood's classical era; Westerns thought to be the best exemplars of the form.

climax: most dramatic or exciting part of the film, when the protagonist meets and defeats the antagonist.

closet: metaphoric term for the state of secrecy many queer people were (and still are) expected to maintain about their sexuality. *See also* coming out of the closet.

closure: resolution of a Hollywood film; usually a "happy ending" where the antagonist is defeated and any remaining loose ends are neatly resolved.

Cold War: antagonism between the United States (and its allies) and the Soviet Union (and its allies) from the late 1940s to the late 1980s. It never erupted into full-scale battle, but espionage, sabotage, and nuclear buildup were common factors.

Colleen: common stereotype of Irish American women during the 1920s. The Colleen sought to assimilate by being bright-eyed and good-natured.

colonialism: control of a region and its people by outside nations. For hundreds of years, European nations colonized much of the rest of the world.

coming out of the closet: declaring one's queer sexual identity to family, friends, and co-workers. A tactic of the modern gay rights movement, coming out allows non-straight people to be honest about their lives with those they encounter.

commodification: process under capitalism whereby an idea or a thing is turned into a marketable good.

communism: economic system in which the government controls and distributes material wealth equitably among all of society's members.

computer generated imagery (CGI): filmmaking innovation that can create special effects and even entire characters via the use of sophisticated digital animation techniques.

connotation: practice of implying something rather than stating it directly.

connotative homosexuality: the way classical Hollywood style suggested certain characters might be gay or lesbian without directly asserting as much.

consciousness-raising groups: small, informal groups designed to allow people to share personal experiences about some issue; very influential in spreading feminism in the 1960s.

Ch2 **content:** what a work of art or cultural artifact is about. That content is then expressed through form and style.

Ch5 **continuity editing:** system of rules in Hollywood filmmaking that govern how shots are to be made and put together in order to preserve screen space and time and "spoon feed" important information to the spectator in an understandable way.

Coon: stereotype of an African American male as a lazy, shuffling, and ignorant fool.

Coppola, Sophia: Oscar-winning writer and director of *Lost in Translation* (2003) and daughter of Film School Brat Francis Ford Coppola.

corporate capitalism: type of capitalism dominated by large multinational businesses.

corporate conglomerate: large, often multinational and economically intertwined group of companies that work together to maximize profit and undermine competition.

Ch7 **counterculture:** loose coalition of 1960s groups who all opposed the dominant culture; hippies, civil rights workers, women, people of color, young people, etc.

cross-dresser: someone who wears the clothing of the opposite sex; transvestite.

Crusades: series of wars during the Middle Ages in which Christian European armies sought to occupy the Holy Lands and other areas of the Middle East.

Cukor, George: famous Hollywood director who was discreet about his homosexuality. He worked from the 1930s into the 1980s.

cultural artifact: any text produced and then decoded by a reader (spectator). Movies, books, songs, ads, speeches, fashion, and food are all cultural artifacts.

cultural imperialism: promotion of one nation's cultural artifacts around the globe, especially to the extent that another nation's artifacts are excluded.

cultural studies: broad area of research and theory that attempts to explain how culture works in relation to history, economics, diversity, etc.

culture: characteristic features, behaviors, and artifacts of a group of people.

Daughters of Bilitis: group founded in the 1950s that sought to organize lesbians around social and political issues.

decoding: process by which a reader (spectator) makes sense of a text; dependent upon the reader's own social and historical positioning as well as on how the text has been encoded by its producers.

Del Rio, Dolores: Mexican American actress who briefly became a star in classical Hollywood, often playing upper-class women from Latin America.

deliberate camp: intentionally making a text so over-the-top or "bad" that a spectator is encouraged not to take it seriously.

denotation: practice of stating something directly (as opposed to implication or connotation).

deregulation: removal of laws and codes that monitor and oversee big business practices.

Deren, Maya: American avant-garde filmmaker of the 1940s and 1950s.

diaspora: dispersion abroad of a specific culture.

dime novels: cheap, sensational nineteenth-century books that often told Western adventure stories.

Directors Guild of America: union of film directors founded in the 1930s.

disability: condition that substantially limits one or more major life activities; broadly used to describe limitations in hearing, seeing, motor activity, and/or mental functioning.

displacement: psychological defense mechanism in which a person or group projects their own negative traits onto another person or group.

distribution: aspect of the film business; the shipment of film prints to places of retail (theaters or video stores).

documentary: type of non-fiction film practice that uses real life as its basis. Instead of using scripts, sets, and actors, documentary films focus on real-life people and events.

dominant ideology: pervasive and often unremarked-upon set of assumptions and beliefs that structure any given group or culture. The dominant ideology of Western culture is white patriarchal heterosexual capitalism.

dominant reading: the decoding of a text – as it was intended (by its producers) to be decoded.

Dragon Lady: stereotype of an Asian woman as cunning, deceitful, and sexually manipulative.

dumb white guy comedies: Hollywood farces of the 1990s and 2000s that negotiate masculinity by focusing on male characters whose traditional masculinity is compromised in some way.

Edison, Thomas: man credited with inventing cinema in the United States in the 1890s.

editing: one of the five formal axes of film form; the cutting and pasting together of individual shots in order to create a feeling or idea, or tell a story.

ego-destructive: type of discrimination wherein individuals internalize negative self-concepts from culture and judge themselves less worthy than other members of society.

ego-dystonic homosexuality: state of having same-sex attractions but being disturbed by those feelings because of internalized homophobia.

Ch1 w1 **encoding:** process by which the producers of a cultural artifact place both conscious and unconscious meanings into a text.

Equal Rights Amendment (ERA): proposed Constitutional Amendment designed to outlaw discrimination based on gender. The ERA was defeated in the 1980s.

ERA: *see* Equal Rights Amendment.

essentialist: type of belief held to be naturally true or biologically supported; person who holds such a belief. These beliefs are often unwavering and absolute.

ethnic group: group of people sharing certain cultural customs.

Ch3 **ethnicity:** social grouping based upon shared culture and custom.

Ch3 **ethnocentrism:** regarding one's ethnic group as better than another.

Ch5 **ethnographic film:** type of documentary that records a culture or a way of life.

Ch5 **Eurocentrism:** practice of understanding the world and its various cultures from a European perspective.

exhibition: retail aspect of the film business, wherein films are screened before a paying public.

experimental film: another term for avant-garde film.

Ch5 **experimental Westerns:** films with some Western imagery or ideas but made before the category "Western film" was established. Most genres pass through an experimental stage before they become recognized as a genre by both filmmakers and audiences.

exploitation films: cheaply made and sensational movies that promise to show moviegoers more sex and violence than can be found in usual Hollywood fare.

family values: buzz phrase often associated with the rise of the religious right in the 1980s; meant to describe and endorse a patriarchal heterosexual family as the ideal.

femininity: cultural expression of female gender. Femininity is associated with passivity, nurturing, emotionalism, etc.

feminism: movement promoting equal rights regardless of gender.

femme fatale: woman who leads a male character to his death; common character type in film noir.

fetishization: over-investing something with erotic value; according to feminist theory, one of the ways that women's bodies are displayed in film.

fill light: one of the three sources of three-point lighting; used to "fill in" shadows cast by the key light.

Ch2 **film form:** structure or shape of the cinematic medium; encompasses aspects of literary design, visual design, cinematography, editing, and sound.

film noir: genre or style characteristic of 1940s postwar films, in which obsessed and greedy individuals double-cross one another amidst shadowy sets and distorted camera angles.

Film School Brats: Steven Spielberg, George Lucas, Martin Scorsese, et al.; a generation of filmmakers who rose to prominence in the 1970s after having studied film at universities.

first wave feminism: movement of feminism that happened roughly at the beginning of the twentieth century, centered on issues such as women's suffrage and birth control.

flapper: common female character type of the 1920s. She expressed liberation in shorter hair and higher hemlines, as well as by smoking, drinking, and being more free with her sexuality.

Ford, John: prolific Irish American director of Hollywood Westerns and war films.

foreign films: films produced outside the United States; usually exhibited in America in urban independent theaters or on video (if at all).

form: how the content of a work is expressed, the shape that it takes.

front: person (or name) used to mask the identity of another. Blacklisted writers often continued to work in Hollywood by writing under an assumed name or front.

Fu Manchu, Dr: diabolical Asian super-criminal found in film and literature.

gangster film: film genre that focuses on the rise and fall of a violent mobster figure.

Gay and Lesbian Alliance Against Defamation: *see* GLAAD.

gender: social role assigned to males or females in any given historical culture.

gender identity: one's sense of one's own gender.

gender inversion model: historical model of homosexuality that theorized that gay men were actually women's souls trapped in a male body and that lesbians were really male souls trapped in female bodies.

gender studies: study of how any given historical culture defines concepts of masculinity and femininity.

genocide: destruction of an entire race, ethnicity, or other cultural group.

genre: type of fictional film produced within an industrial context. Common Hollywood genres include the war film, the musical, the gangster film, etc.

Gish, Lillian: famous silent film actress who often embodied Victorian ideals of femininity.

GLAAD (Gay and Lesbian Alliance Against Defamation): media watchdog group monitoring film and television images of homosexuals.

glass ceiling: metaphoric term meant to express the unspoken limit to which a non-white, non-male person can hope to rise within a company or field of endeavor.

Good Neighbor Policy: federal propaganda programs, enacted during World War II, designed to promote good will between North, Central, and South America.

greaser: derogatory stereotype of Latinos, and especially Mexican Americans, as slovenly, violent bandits.

Great Depression: severe economic crisis that affected the United States from the stock market crash of 1929 until the start of World War II.

Guy-Blache, Alice: French filmmaker who was one of the first women to make fictional films.

Haines, William: popular Hollywood actor of the 1920s who was fired from MGM when he refused to keep his homosexuality a secret.

happy ending: type of narrative closure usually found in Hollywood cinema as the protagonist defeats the antagonist and "gets the girl."

Harlem Renaissance: flowering of African American art, literature, theater, and culture centered in Northern American cities, 1920s to 1930s.

Hayakawa, Sessue: Japanese American actor who played both leading romantic and character parts.

Hays, Will: former postmaster general of the United States whom Hollywood hired to head the Production Code Administration.

Hayworth, Rita: actress of Hispanic descent who became a major Hollywood star of the 1940s and 1950s.

hegemonic negotiation: theory of how culture changes as opposing ideas are encountered by the dominant ideology. The critical charge of an opposing idea is often softened or negated as it is incorporated within the dominant ideology.

hegemonic patriarchy: fluctuating state of patriarchal dominance.

hegemony: fluctuating state of dominant ideology; also, the ongoing struggle to gain the consent of the people to a system that would govern them. *See also* hegemonic negotiation.

heteronormativity: the structures and ideologies that privilege heterosexuality as natural or given within Western societies; similar to heterosexism.

heterosexism: assumption that heterosexuality is the best or only sexual orientation.

heterosexual monogamy: type of relationship held up as the ideal by some Western cultures, wherein one man and one woman marry and maintain sexual fidelity to each other.

heterosexuality: sexual attraction to members of the opposite sex.

high art: aspects of culture that are thought to be tasteful and edifying. Examples include ballet, opera, and classical music.

high concept: idea for a film that can be explained in a few words; often used to describe contemporary Hollywood film projects.

Hispanic: people whose ancestry can be traced back to Spain, Portugal, and/or Latin America; culture derived from the same roots.

Hollywood film: motion pictures made and/or distributed widely by the major Hollywood companies.

Hollywood Indian: image of the Native American as conceived of by Hollywood filmmakers.

Hollywood narrative form: *see* classical Hollywood narrative form.

Hollywood Supports: support group founded in the 1990s to deal with AIDS in the Hollywood workplace.

Hollywood Ten: group of directors and screenwriters in the late 1940s who refused to answer questions before HUAC and were sentenced to jail.

homophobia: extreme fear or hatred of homosexuals. A person who is homophobic may have conflicts about his or her own sexuality.

homosexual panic: controversial term used to describe the feeling of anxiety that may occur when someone discovers his or her own homosexual feelings.

homosexuality: sexual attraction to members of the same sex.

homosocial bonds: ties of love and loyalty that bind together homosocial groups.

homosocial groups: non-sexual same-sex groups based on friendship, loyalty, love, or shared interests. Examples include fraternities and sororities, sports teams, sex-segregated military units, etc.

Hong Kong action films: stylishly violent action-adventure films made in Hong Kong since the 1970s, which have attracted a cult following in the United States.

Horatio Alger myth: the idea that anyone in America can rise to economic success through hard work and the aid of friendly benefactors; so named after the pulp novels written by Horatio Alger that repeatedly asserted such themes.

horizontal integration: when a corporation controls various related product lines. Contemporary Hollywood companies are horizontally integrated because they are part of giant media companies that also produce newspapers, books, TV, music, theme parks, etc. This makes it easy to sell products in synergy.

horror film: film genre that uses monsters and madmen to create fear in an audience.

House Un-American Activities Committee: *see* HUAC.

HUAC (House Un-American Activities Committee): Congressional committee that investigated communism in the United States in the 1940s and 1950s.

Hudson, Rock: rugged Hollywood actor who rose to prominence in the 1950s. His homosexuality was not publicly acknowledged until his death from AIDS-related causes in 1985.

Hughes, John: popular filmmaker of the 1980s whose works often focused on white, middle-class teenagers.

IATSE (International Association of Theatrical Stage Employees): industry-wide union for individuals working behind the camera.

iconography: signs and symbols that identify a film genre; the settings, costumes, props, and characters usually associated with a specific film genre.

ideological state apparatuses (ISAs): social institutions (such as the family, the government, religion, school, and media) that support an ideology through education and example rather than through overt coercion.

ideology: systematic body of concepts that expresses values and beliefs, especially about human lives and cultures. Ideology is conveyed through speech, sound, image, and all cultural texts.

image studies: aspect of cultural studies; research that explores the ways and means people and things are represented in media systems.

imperialism: practice of gaining control over other nations and territories through repressive, violent means.

incorporation: absorption or assimilation of a subcultural style or artifact into the dominant culture. *See also* commodification.

indentured servants: individuals legally contracted to work for others for a set period of time.

independent film: films made and exhibited without the financing or distribution arms of the major Hollywood companies. The term may also include foreign films, documentaries, and avant-garde films.

Indian: collective term used to describe Native American people and cultures. *See also* Hollywood Indian.

Indian Story: genre (or subgenre of the Western) in early film that focused on Native American lives without the Western's usual violent conflict between Indians and settlers.

Indian Wars: series of battles fought between the United States and various Native American tribes; roughly 1850 to 1900.

Industrial Revolution: historical era (roughly 1840–1910) in which multiple new mechanical and electrical inventions were developed; when individual artisanal production was replaced with factory-based mass production of consumer goods.

Inge, William: famous playwright of the twentieth century whose sexually provocative stories were made into Hollywood films in the 1950s and 1960s.

inscrutable Oriental: stereotype of cunning and mysterious Asians or Asian Americans.

institutionalized discrimination: when bias is embedded in social structures such as schools, government, business, or the media.

internalized discrimination: when negative concepts about a race, gender, class, or sexuality are felt by members of those groups to be true. Such a process may be ego-destructive, that is, damaging to one's sense of self.

internalizing ideology: making ideas and beliefs about things that circulate in culture and society one's own ideas and beliefs.

International Association of Theatrical Stage Employees: *see* IATSE.

intersexed: people who are born with both male and female sexual characteristics.

investigation and punishment: according to feminist film theory, one of the ways male characters and male spectators control their fear of women.

invisible style: film style that doesn't call attention to itself as being a style. Classical Hollywood style is often considered invisible.

ISAs: *see* ideological state apparatuses.

Italian Neorealism: Italian film movement of the 1940s that regularly represented Italians as poor, working-class people.

Jim Crow Laws: racist laws that until the mid-twentieth century segregated white people from black people in housing, jobs, and public accommodations.

jingoism: believing that one's national grouping is superior to all others.

Jolson, Al: famous Jewish vaudeville and early film star best known for singing jazz in blackface makeup.

Kazan, Elia: Hollywood filmmaker who often made social problem films and cooperated with HUAC during the Red Scare.

key light: brightest light of three-point lighting, positioned above and to the side of the subject to illuminate one side of a person's face.

kinetoscope: early peep-show device that exhibited short movies, patented by Thomas Edison.

Kopple, Barbara: Oscar-winning American documentary filmmaker whose work usually focuses on class.

kung fu action movie: popular 1970s genre of cheaply made martial arts films.

labor unions: groups of workers who band together to bargain collectively for better wages and benefits.

Latin Lover: handsome and exotic, sexually alluring leading man of Italian or Hispanic heritage; a prominent character type in Hollywood film.

Latino/a: gendered terms used to refer to people or cultures that originate from Latin America. Latino is masculine, Latina feminine.

Lee, Ang: successful Chinese-born director of mainstream Hollywood films as well as independent films focusing on Chinese American culture.

Lee, Bruce: Chinese American martial arts expert who rose to fame in 1970s kung fu action movies.

Legion of Decency: Catholic group founded in the 1930s to protest against sex and violence in Hollywood films. For many years the Legion issued its own film ratings.

Lesbian Avengers: activist group of the 1990s centered on civil rights for homosexuals.

lesbian vampire film: subgenre of the horror film that forthrightly conflates homosexuality and monstrosity.

linear narrative: way of telling a story in chronological order, with a beginning, middle, and end. Most Hollywood films employ linear narrative.

literary design: one of the five formal axes of film; encompasses all aspects of a production that have been scripted including character, setting, dialog, theme, and title.

Little 3: the three classical Hollywood companies (Universal, Columbia, and United Artists) that were not as powerful as the Big 5, but more lucrative than the Poverty Row studios.

Lloyd, Harold: famous silent film comedian who often played "everyman" figures.

Loos, Anita: famous playwright and screenwriter of the early twentieth century.

Lopez, Jennifer: highly successful Latina singer and actress of the 1990s and 2000s.

love interest: in classical Hollywood narrative form, the (usually female) character designed to provide romance or sex appeal as a sideline to the (usually male-centered) plot.

low art: cultural artifacts generally thought to be trashy or a bad influence on people. Examples include comic books, pornography, rock music, and most television.

Luke, Keye: Chinese American character actor in Hollywood, 1930s to 1990s.

Lumière Brothers: French brothers who in 1895 were the first to project cinematic images onto a big screen for an audience.

Lupino, Ida: one of the few women to direct films in Hollywood during its classical period. Lupino moved into directing and producing after being an actress.

lynching: mob torture and murder of an individual, often by hanging; historically used by white people to terrorize non-white communities.

Mafia: organized crime "family" of Italian or Italian American descent.

Magical Negro: Hollywood stereotype that figures African Americans as subservient characters who use their "mystical powers" to help white people in distress.

major studios: historically, the Big 5 studios in classical Hollywood. Today the term might be used to describe a company that releases Hollywood films.

male gaze: concept of feminist film theory that argues that all the looks associated with classical Hollywood cinema – the look of the camera, of the characters at one another, and of the spectators at the screen – are either male or assumed to be. As such, women can only be "looked at" and objectified by the male gaze.

Mammy: stereotype of an African American woman as an overweight caretaker of white people.

Ch5 **Manifest Destiny:** ideological program of nineteenth- and twentieth-century America used to justify US expansion into foreign lands and territories.

Marion, Frances: successful female screenwriter in classical Hollywood cinema.

marriages of convenience: arranged heterosexual weddings used to disguise the homosexuality of either bride or groom (or both) in order to maintain their status within heterosexist society.

Marshall, Penny: one of the more prolific female directors working in contemporary Hollywood.

Marxism: system of economic thought based upon the writings of Karl Marx.

masculinity: roles and behaviors associated with being male in any given culture. In contemporary Western culture, masculinity is thought to include strength, leadership ability, and the restraint of emotional expression.

Matlin, Marlee: Oscar-winning deaf actress who continues to have a successful career in contemporary Hollywood film and television.

Mattachine Society: early homosexual rights group, 1950s to 1960s.

Means, Russell: Native American actor and activist who founded AIM (American Indian Movement) in the 1960s.

mediated: how "reality" is changed or distorted (in ways both subtle and obvious) as it passes through communication systems such as (but not limited to) film or television.

medical model of disability: set of ideas and assumptions that understands disability in terms of disease and/or cure.

melanin: human skin pigment that gives all human beings their skin color.

Method School: type of acting that influenced Hollywood from the 1950s onward.

metrosexual: heterosexual man who cares about his appearance, and who adopts some of the lifestyle choices often associated with urban gay men (fashion, fine dining, etc.).

Micheaux, Oscar: the most prolific African American director of race movies.

Mick: derogatory term for and stereotype of a loud, violent, drunken Irish American.

middle class: category of people whose economic status is neither upper- nor lower-class. Middle-class people often work at managerial or professional jobs.

military-industrial complex: term widely used by the counterculture to describe the economic connections between American corporations and the armed services; the linkage of civilian industry to the business of war.

minority groups: groups who may be underprivileged and marginal to dominant culture because they are perceived as being fewer in number or less in power.

minor studios: another term for the Little 3.

Ch4 **minstrel show:** popular nineteenth-century theatrical format in which white entertainers donned blackface makeup and performed as stereotypical African Americans.

Miranda, Carmen: Latina singer from Brazil who appeared in 1940s Hollywood musicals.

Ch4 **miscegenation:** outmoded term used to describe sexual or romantic relations between people of different races.

mise-en-scène: formal axes of film having to do with visual design and framing.

misogyny: hatred of women.

Mongoloid: historically, people of the "yellow race" (people with Asian and/or Native American roots).

monopoly: when one company controls an entire industry and can then minimize or eradicate competition.

montage: editing.

Moral Majority: religious and political group of the 1980s that sought to return the nation to patriarchal ideals.

movie palaces: opulent movie theaters built during the 1910s and 1920s.

movie star: actor who becomes popular and widely recognized.

movie studios: film production factories, often with multiple sound stages and back lots.

Ch2 **MPAA Ratings System:** begun in 1968, the Ratings System serves as a consumer guide to the movies, and assigns each film a rating (G, PG, R, etc.) based on its perceived appropriateness for different audiences.

muckraking journalism: the practice of exaggerating or fabricating news in order to drum up fear and sell more newspapers (or get people to watch more TV).

mulatto: outmoded term for someone of mixed racial heritage.

Muslim Terrorist: the most common current Hollywood stereotype of Arabs or Arab Americans.

NAACP (National Association for the Advancement of Colored People): powerful twentieth-century civil rights group devoted to African American issues.

NAATA (National Asian American Telecommunications Association): media watchdog group designed to monitor images of Asian Americans in the media.

naïve camp: the camp of failed seriousness; when an artifact is produced without camp intent but is ironically decoded as silly or humorous.

narcissism: according to psychoanalytic film theory, one of the visual pleasures associated with cinema; the pleasure of identifying with characters onscreen.

National Asian American Telecommunications Association: *see* NAATA.

National Association for the Advancement of Colored People: *see* NAACP.

National Industrial Recovery Act (NIRA): set of federal initiatives issued during the Great Depression that aimed to revamp American business practices and invigorate the nation's economy.

National Organization for Women (NOW): feminist civil rights group established in 1966.

Ch3 **nationalism:** believing that one's national grouping is superior to all others.

Ch3 **nationality:** social grouping based upon geographical and/or political boundaries.

Ch3 **Nativism:** nineteenth-century ideology that stressed that "America should be for Americans" and not for foreigners.

Nava, Gregory: Latino director of independent films since the 1980s.

Ch1 W1 **negotiated reading:** when a reader (spectator) decodes a text partly according to the ways that it was encoded and partly in ways that it was not.

Negroid: historically, people of the "black race" (people descended from African heritage).

Ch4 **neo-blaxploitation:** frequently violent genre films of the 1990s that centered on African American characters.

neo-noir: nostalgic revival of film noir in the 1980s and 1990s.

New Hollywood: Hollywood in the 1970s (and after) when it once again became economically successful via blockbuster filmmaking, saturation booking, and saturation advertising.

New Queer Cinema: movement of independent filmmaking that arose in the 1990s that makes use of concepts drawn from queer activism and queer theory.

New South: economic boom in the Southern US in the latter half of the twentieth century that occurred when Northern industries moved there in search of cheaper labor and fewer unions.

nickelodeons: the first theaters devoted solely to movies, roughly 1905–12. The term means "nickel theater."

NIRA: *see* National Industrial Recovery Act.

Ch5 **noble savage:** stereotype of Native Americans as childlike and primitive, but imbued with purer and more "natural" instincts.

Noble Warrior: stereotype of a wounded veteran who takes his (or more rarely her) disability in their stride; often found in pro-war movies.

Ch1 **Nosotros:** media watchdog group formed by actor Ricardo Montalban in the 1970s to promote better images of Latinos.

Ch2 **nostalgic Hollywood blockbuster:** big-budget Hollywood film that refashions storylines and genre formulas from previous eras for contemporary audiences.

Novarro, Ramon: Mexican American actor famous for playing Latin Lover types in silent films.

NOW: *see* National Organization for Women.

objectification: turning a person into a sexualized object. In Hollywood film, the male gaze is said to objectify women.

objective shot: shot not tied to a character's point of view. Most shots in Hollywood film are objective shots.

Obsessive Avenger: stereotype of a disabled or disfigured man who exacts revenge on "normal" society; often found in crime and horror films.

Ch2 **oligopoly:** control over an industry by several companies that work together to stifle competition.

Olmos, Edward James: prolific contemporary Latino actor and civil rights advocate.

open market economy: state of business affairs in which companies are free to compete without governmental regulation or interference.

open shop: place of business that employs both union and non-union workers.

oppositional reading: process by which a reader (spectator) decodes a text in ways not intended by those who encoded it.

Orientalism: theoretical concept suggesting that the West has defined the Orient as its Other; theory of how the West assumes the East to be exotic, sensual, lawless, etc.

Other: person or cultural group against which one defines one's own self or culture.

Othering: process by which one culture defines itself against another, often by ascribing undesirable traits (shared by all humans) to a specific cultural group.

pansy: common classical Hollywood stereotype of an effeminate male homosexual.

pansy craze: period in the 1920s and early 1930s when effeminate male homosexuals were popular entertainers.

Paramount Consent Decrees: series of court decisions starting in 1948 that ruled that the Hollywood studios did have illegal control over the industry. Most vertically integrated studios were forced to sell off their theaters throughout the next decade.

passing: process wherein light-skinned people of color deny their racial or ethnic backgrounds in order to be accepted as white. Gay and lesbian people also may pass for straight.

patriarchy: literally, rule by the father; a culture in which men and masculinity are valued above women and femininity.

persona: image or facade associated with a star and his or her roles; may or may not encompass aspects of the star's actual personality.

Pickford, Mary: silent movie actress of Irish descent famous for playing childlike heroines.

Poitier, Sidney: the first African American leading male star in Hollywood films, roughly 1950s and 1960s.

pop camp: type of mainstream camp artifact; often without a critique of gender or sexuality.

Populism: rural ideology of the late nineteenth century that critiqued industrialization.

pornographic films: X-rated films that depict sexual intercourse.

post-feminist: broadly used term meant to signify the era after second wave feminism.

postmodernism: broad set of ideas describing the economic and cultural milieu of corporate conglomerate capitalism. Postmodern theories and/or aesthetics are often marked by fragmentation, semiotic excess, and the blurring of boundaries.

Poverty Row studios: small studios such as Republic, Monogram, or Producers Releasing Corporation that made low-budget features, roughly 1930s to 1940s.

pre-Code films: Hollywood films made between 1930 and 1934, in the years before the Production Code was enforced with the Seal of Approval provision.

pre-sold: when a cinematic property is adapted from another medium wherein it has already gained public recognition.

producer: person or persons who make texts; those who encode meaning into cultural artifacts.

production: phase of financing, writing, designing, directing, and editing a film before it is distributed to theaters.

Ch2 **Production Code:** self-censoring set of rules and regulations that Hollywood adopted in 1930 and imposed upon itself from 1934 until the Code was replaced by the Ratings System in the late 1960s.

Ch1wl **propaganda:** cultural artifact that overtly attempts to sway opinion; may distort or ignore reality as it makes an emotional appeal to spectators.

protagonist: central character of a Hollywood film, commonly referred to as the hero.

Protestant work ethic: belief that hard work will lead to earthly success and heavenly favor.

quattrocento style: European painting style that emphasized three-dimensionality and perspective.

queer: people and artifacts commonly found outside compulsory heterosexist ideologies.

queer camp: type of camp that voices a critique of gender and/or sexuality.

Queer Nation: activist group of the 1990s that attempted to use queer theory to invoke a broad coalition of support.

queer theory: collection of ideas and suppositions that seeks to understand sexuality as a fluctuating, socially constructed aspect of all human beings, rather than as a set of rigid essentialist identities.

Quinn, Anthony: Oscar-winning actor of Irish and Mexican heritage. He played a variety of ethnicities throughout his long career.

Ch3 **race:** category of human beings based upon external features such as skin color and hair texture. Historically three races were classified – Caucasoid, Negroid, and Mongoloid.

Ch4 **race movies:** independently made films (1910s to the early 1950s) that featured all-black casts and were exhibited exclusively in black neighborhood theaters.

Ch3 **racism:** belief that human beings can be designated as superior or inferior on the basis of their racial characteristics.

Ratings System: *see* MPAA Ratings System.

reactionary: political position of extreme conservatism, marked by the desire to reinstate an outmoded form of social control.

readers: subjects who decode a text. Film readers are often called spectators.

Reaganomics: President Reagan's economic strategy for the nation, characterized by deficit spending, corporate deregulation, and tax cuts for the wealthy.

Ch **Red Scare:** paranoia about communism common in 1950s America.

Ch5 **representation:** process of presenting an image of something in order to communicate ideas or tell a story.

representational systems: mediated systems we use to communicate with one another, such as language, art, literature, movies, TV, and the Internet.

repressive state apparatuses (RSAs): social forces such as armies, wars, police forces, and terrorism that exert social control through violence and/or the threat of violence.

Rodriguez, Robert: contemporary Latino director of mainstream Hollywood films.

Rosie the Riveter: propaganda figure of World War II that promoted women as strong and capable of working in a factory.

RSAs: *see* repressive state apparatuses.

rugged individualism: popular phrase in American culture that champions the lone citizen taking responsibility for his or her own success.

runaway production: US film production made outside the country in order to exploit cheap labor.

Saintly Sage: stereotype of a wise blind man who has insight and knowledge that others may lack.

saturation advertising: contemporary Hollywood practice of blanketing the nation with ads for a film about to open.

saturation booking: contemporary Hollywood practice of releasing a film to thousands of theaters at once.

Sayles, John: contemporary independent American filmmaker whose films feature large, diverse casts and focus on issues of race and class.

Screen Actors Guild: union of film actors founded in 1933.

screwball comedy: classical Hollywood film genre that focuses on a sometimes violent battle of the sexes.

Seal of Approval: begun in 1934, this was a way of "enforcing" the Hollywood Production Code by specifically labeling films that had been passed by the board of censors.

second wave feminism: feminist movements of the 1960s and 1970s, centering on issues such as reproductive rights and economic equality with men.

sensitive man: version of masculinity briefly popular in the 1970s and early 1980s. He was in touch with his feelings and was capable of nurturing others.

sex: biological aspects of being male or female (such as chromosomes or physical characteristics), as opposed to gender, the social roles assigned to male or female beings.

sexism: ideology that promotes one sex as inherently better than another. More commonly, sexism is used to refer to the belief that men are superior to women.

sexploitation cinema: soft-core sex films of the 1960s made and distributed outside mainstream Hollywood channels.

sexual object choice: current theory used to understand sexual attraction. Heterosexual desire involves a differently sexed object as its choice, whereas homosexual desire involves a same-sex object.

sexual orientation: direction or aim of one's sexuality. Commonly perceived sexual orientations include homosexual, heterosexual, and bisexual.

sexual revolution: psycho-sexual and social changes of the 1960s, when men and women felt freer than in previous decades to explore their sexuality.

sexuality: state of being sexual; commonly used to describe sexual orientation.

Sharif, Omar: Egyptian-born actor who became one of the first Arab stars in Hollywood films of the 1960s.

shot: basic building block of cinema; one uninterrupted run of film through the camera. Shots are then combined via editing to create meaning or tell a story.

slackers: slang term for young people in the 1990s who chose not to pursue high-paying careers.

slasher film: popular 1980s subgenre of the horror film, centering on a knife-wielding maniac.

Ch3 **social construct:** idea or identity defined and determined by history and culture. Its meaning may fluctuate in relation to the time and place of its use.

social constructionism: explanation of identities as being the result of cultural conditioning rather than biology. Under social constructionist models, identity is shown to fluctuate according to history and culture, not be a fixed or essentialized thing.

social model of disability: approach to disability issues that examines the relationship between society and individuals with disabilities.

Ch7 **social problem film:** Hollywood film genre that explores topical issues such as racism or homophobia (but usually from a white patriarchal capitalist perspective).

socialism: economic and ideological system which balances governmental regulation of industry, equitable distribution of basic human resources, and free market enterprise.

socially constructed: *see* social constructionism.

sound design: one of the five formal axes of cinema, encompassing all auditory stimuli that accompany the visual part of a film.

Ch5 **spaghetti Westerns:** violent and cynical Westerns of the 1960s that were made in Italy.

Ch1 w1 **stereotypes:** oversimplified images of a person or group.

Stonewall Riots: street-fighting in New York City in 1969 that is said to have sparked the modern gay rights movement.

straight queer: person who self-identifies as heterosexual but who embraces queer theory as a social or political philosophy.

Studio Basic Agreement: 1926 contract between Hollywood bosses and workers that created an open shop while also granting recognition to some unions.

Ch2 **studio system:** assembly-line-like process used by classical Hollywood to produce movies.

style: how a given film, director, genre, or movement organizes cinema's formal elements into a coherent and consistent system.

Ch1 W1 **subculture:** culture of a marginalized or minoritized group. The texts and practices of a subculture are always in hegemonic negotiation with the dominant culture.

subgenre: subdivision of a genre identifiable to audiences and filmmakers. For example, the slasher film is a subgenre of the horror film.

subjective shot: shot meant to represent a character's point of view; allows the spectator to "see through the eyes" of the character.

superstructure: in Marxist theory, all the elements of culture and ideology that are determined by a given society's economic base.

428

Sweet Innocent: stereotype of a disabled woman or child as a saintly, uncomplaining figure meant to be pitied.

synergy: simultaneous marketing of related product lines. When a Hollywood blockbuster is released, the film, its soundtrack CD, a novelization, toys, games, comic books, and other products are often sold concurrently. Each product advertises the others and increases revenue.

tableaux: theatrical tradition of presenting a living, but static image to the audience; often associated with putting the female body on display, but also used for emphasis in early films.

text: any cultural artifact that can be decoded by a reader.

thematic myth: deep structure or ideological significance of a genre.

third wave feminism: anti-essentialist approach to gender that understands all concepts of masculinity and femininity to be socially constructed.

three-point lighting: system of Hollywood glamor lighting comprised of a key light, a fill light, and a back light.

token: single character (or person) used to deflate charges of bias within a film or institution; for example, the hiring of one black actor in an otherwise all-white film or institution.

tokenism: making only a minimal effort to be truly multicultural; in film, the creation of a minority role to deflate a potential charge of racism, sexism, homophobia, etc.

Tongs: criminal gangs found in US Chinatowns, roughly 1910s to 1930s.

Tonto: character name of the Lone Ranger's Native American sidekick.

Tragic Mulatto: stereotype of an African American woman of mixed race heritage who usually finds only death or disgrace.

Tragic Victim: stereotype of an embittered disabled person, often associated with anti-war movies in which disabled veterans are used to dramatize the high cost of war.

transgendered: preferred term for describing a transsexual person.

transsexual: medical term describing a person whose psychological gender identity does not match their physical sex characteristics.

transvestite: cross-dresser; commonly, a man who wears women's clothing.

Uncle Tom: stereotype of an African American male as a devoted servant to his white master.

underground film: movement of American avant-garde filmmaking of the 1960s that often explored sexual subcultures.

upper class: category used to describe people and families of great wealth (often inherited) and social standing.

Vachon, Christine: prolific independent producer of New Queer Cinema.

Valdez, Luis: Mexican American independent theater and film director, tied to the Chicano civil rights movement.

Valentino, Rudolph: actor of Italian descent who became the most famous Latin Lover of the 1920s.

vamp: image of a dark-skinned and exotic woman who might lead a white man to his downfall, common in 1910s and 1920s cinema.

Velez, Lupe: Latina actress known for a series of low-budget films in which she played the "Mexican Spitfire."

Ch2 **vertical integration:** when one company owns or controls the production, distribution, and retail aspects of an industry. The Big 5 companies in classical Hollywood were vertically integrated because they all made and distributed their own films to their own theaters.

virgin–whore complex: ideological approach to women found in Western culture; defines women in simplistic sexual terms as either "good" (the virgin) or "bad" (the whore).

visual design: one of the five formal axes of cinema, encompassing aspects of sets and props, costume, makeup, lighting, blocking, and color.

voyeurism: sexual pleasure that comes from looking at another person; one of the basic visual pleasures of cinema, according to psychoanalytic film theory.

Wang, Wayne: independent filmmaker whose work often focuses on Chinese American culture.

Ch6 **war movie:** Hollywood genre that dramatizes men coming together to fight a battle.

Ch3 **WASP:** common abbreviation for "White Anglo-Saxon Protestant," historically the dominant population group in the United States.

Wayne, John: famous classical Hollywood actor who came to epitomize traditional American masculinity in both Westerns and war movies.

Weber, Lois: female filmmaker during the silent years who often addressed feminist issues.

Ch5 **Western:** genre that centers on a cowboy hero as he attempts to tame the wilderness, including its Native American inhabitants.

Whale, James: openly gay director of many classical Hollywood horror films.

white: term used to describe the alleged skin color of people categorized as Caucasian.

Ch1 w1 **white patriarchal capitalism:** dominant ideology of the Western world; suggests that heterosexual Caucasian males and gaining wealth are the most important things in the world.

white slave films: genre of films from the 1910s and 1920s that suggested that white women were at great risk of being kidnapped by non-white criminals.

Ch6 **white slavery:** practice of kidnapping white women and forcing them into prostitution; a common racialized fear of early twentieth-century American culture.

white trash: pejorative term used to describe poor people of Caucasian descent.

Ch3 **whiteness:** characteristics that identify an individual or a group as belonging to the Caucasian race.

Ch5 **Wild West show:** popular nineteenth-century theatrical entertainment that featured acts related to the old West, including fictional vignettes about cowboys and Indians.

wildcat strikes: work stoppages unsanctioned by official union leaders.

Williams, Spencer: African American filmmaker who wrote and directed race movies and later starred on television in *Amos 'n' Andy*.

Williams, Tennessee: famous playwright of the mid-twentieth century whose sexually frank and provocative works were made into Hollywood films.

Wishman, Doris: rare female sexploitation filmmaker of the 1960s and 1970s.

woman's film: genre that focuses on alleged "women's issues" such as romance, courtship, and parenthood.

Women in Film: Hollywood support group designed to promote women in the film industry.

Wong, Anna May: Chinese American actress in classical Hollywood, who often played Dragon Lady roles.

Woo, John: director of Hong Kong action films and more recent Hollywood block-busters.

working class: category of people, usually employed to do manual labor or factory work, whose hourly wages barely meet their economic needs.

Writers Guild of America: union of screenwriters formed in 1933.

xenophobia: irrational fear and/or hatred of foreigners.

Yiddish-language films: small-budget films made by and for the Jewish community in the 1920s and 1930s.

Young Deer, James: Native American filmmaker of the 1900s and 1910s.

yuppies (young urban professionals): 1980s term used to describe economically acquisitive and career-oriented people.

Zoot Suit Riots: series of attacks on Mexican Americans in and around Los Angeles during 1943, perpetrated by white servicemen on leave.

INDEX